Historical Dictionaries of Literature and the Arts
Jon Woronoff, Series Editor

Historical Dictionary of Latin American Literature and Theater

Richard Young
Odile Cisneros

*Historical Dictionaries of
Literature and the Arts, No. 45*

The Scarecrow Press, Inc.
Lanham • Toronto • Plymouth, UK
2011

Published by Scarecrow Press, Inc.
A wholly owned subsidary of The Rowman & Littlefield Publishing Group, Inc.
4501 Forbes Boulevard, Suite 200, Lanham, Maryland 20706
http://www.scarecrowpress.com

Estover Road, Plymouth PL6 7PY, United Kingdom

British Library Cataloguing in Publication Information Available

Library of Congress Cataloging-in-Publication Data

Young, Richard A., Ph. D.
  Historical dictionary of Latin American literature and theater / Richard Young,
Odile Cisneros.
      p. cm. — (Historical dictionaries of literature and the arts ; no. 45)
  Includes bibliographical references.
  ISBN 978-0-8108-5099-6 (cloth : alk. paper) — ISBN 978-0-8108-7498-5
(ebook)
  1. Latin American literature—Dictionaries. 2. Latin American literature—
Bio-bibliography—Dictionaries. 3. Authors, Latin American—Biography—
Dictionaries. 4. Theater—Latin America—Dictionaries. I. Cisneros, Odile. II.
Title.
  PQ7081.Y68 2011
  860.9'0003—dc22
                                                                    2010020531

Printed in the United States of America

Contents

Editor's Foreword

Latin America was discovered by Europeans five centuries ago, but alas, its literature was only "discovered" a few decades ago, and initially only from a few authors and a few remarkable novels. But what a treasure it has turned out to be! There are literally thousands of authors, working in every possible genre—poetry, novels, short stories, other fictional forms, and theater. And they have been writing very intriguing, and sometimes breathtaking, works that are of interest not only to their fellow nationals or Latin Americans in general but also to the global reading public. We have seen this with Mario Vargas Llosa, Gabriel García Márquez, and Isabel Allende most recently, but they are following in the footsteps of countless others whose names are becoming more familiar. Of course, Latin America once looked like a literary backwater, and maybe it was, latching on to every trend in Europe and then the United States and making noble efforts. But this is no longer the case, because it has generated some of its own styles, perhaps most significantly magic realism, but also specific Latin American genres like indianismo, indigenismo, gaucho literature, and concrete poetry. Meanwhile, Latin American authors have been producing best sellers and winning the top literary prizes.

It is therefore fortunate to have a guide to this still largely unknown but plentiful source of world literature. The *Historical Dictionary of Latin American Literature and Theater* is a big book, and it has to be merely to chart its impressive dimensions. The chronology, going back to the 16th century and stretching on into the 21st, shows just how long the tradition actually is. The introduction reminds us that Latin America is not only an impressively vast but an amazingly varied continent, with numerous countries (and these having different regions); several languages in addition to Spanish and Portuguese; and different historical, political, and social contexts. But it takes the dictionary section to sort much of this out, with about a thousand entries on specific authors as well as a broad entry on each country and the main literary trends and genres. Admittedly, even then this can only be a starting point, so the bibliography points toward further reading on each of the countries and major authors. This further reading, by the way, may take the reader back to the historical dictionary to better understand the overall situation or find leads to yet other books and authors.

This volume was written by Richard Young and Odile Cisneros. Dr. Young, who received his PhD from the University of Alberta in Canada, taught in what is now its Department of Modern Languages and Cultural Studies for about four decades. This has given him ample experience in enlightening students about the wealth of Latin American literature and more generally society and culture. And he has also turned toward his fellow academics and the broader public with a number of books, articles, and translations, in English and Spanish. Dr. Cisneros has joined more recently, with a doctorate from New York University and specializations in Mexican and Brazilian literatures, more specifically modern and contemporary poetry, among other things. She has published articles and reviews on these topics and is also a very active literary translator. Between them, they have left very few stones unturned, and what they have found will benefit students, professors, and especially readers who were not aware just how rich this vein is.

Jon Woronoff
Series Editor

Acknowledgments

The authors wish to acknowledge the help of three graduate students from the Department of Modern Languages and Cultural Studies and the Program in Comparative Literature at the University of Alberta for their invaluable assistance in this project. Thanks to Volha Isakava and Pablo Markin for their work in the preliminary compilation of Brazilian entries, and to Sabujkoli Bandopadhyay for her help with the Spanish American chronologies.

Reader's Note

The entries in the dictionary refer to the literature and theater of the Spanish- and Portuguese-speaking countries of continental Latin America and do not include countries in the Caribbean. In each author entry the name is followed by the country of birth and the principal literary activities of the author. Further information on the country can be found in its respective entry.

Dictionary entries are in alphabetical order and follow current practices in library cataloging. Last names in Spanish and Portuguese customarily have more than one part and include the last names of both parents. Some authors, whether in Spanish or Portuguese, such as Pablo Neruda, Elena Poniatowska, and Jorge Amado, are known by a single first and last name, and are listed in this way in the dictionary (i.e., "Neruda, Pablo," "Poniatowska, Elena," or "Amado, Jorge"). Many others use more than one last name. In Spanish, the last name inherited from the father appears first and is used for alphabetical listing. Thus, the entries for Gabriel García Márquez and Mario Vargas Llosa are located under "García Márquez, Gabriel" and "Vargas Llosa, Mario" respectively. In Portuguese, the most common modern practice for alphabetizing names is also to list by the name inherited from the father, which is the format preferred in this dictionary. However, in contrast to Spanish, the father's name in Portuguese customarily appears at the end. Thus, the entries for Joaquim Maria Machado de Assis and João Guimarães Rosa are listed under "Assis, Joaquim Maria Machado de" and "Rosa, João Guimarães" respectively. A few names do not follow this format because common usage has determined otherwise and produced different practices for some names, which are adopted in both our dictionary and modern library catalogs. For further clarification of the different forms used to catalog names in Portuguese, readers should consult the entries for individual authors in the online catalog of a major

North American library, such as the New York Public Library (www .nypl.org) or the Library of Congress (www.loc.gov).

The titles of works of literature and theater are given first in Spanish or Portuguese. These are followed by parentheses that include the date of publication and the title in English. English titles in *italics* refer to published translations. Those without italics are our translations of the titles.

To facilitate the rapid and efficient location of information and make the dictionary as useful a reference tool as possible, extensive cross-references have been provided. Within individual dictionary entries, terms that have their own entries are in boldface the first time they appear. Further cross-referencing is indicated by *See* and *See also*.

Chronology

1492   Latin America: Christopher Columbus arrives in the New World. The diary of his voyage and encounter with the land and its people marks the beginning of Latin American literature.

1500   Brazil: Pedro Álvares Cabral reaches the coast of Bahia on 23 April. His secretary, Pero Vaz de Caminha, writes *Carta do Descobrimento do Brasil* to the king of Portugal.

1521   Mexico: Fall of the Aztec capital, Tenochtitlán, to Hernán Cortés.

1538   Bolivia: Incorporation of the territory into the Viceroyalty of Peru as "Upper Peru."

1541   Chile: The city of Santiago is founded by Pedro de Valdivia.

1556   Brazil: Manuel da Nóbrega pens his *Diálogo Sobre a Conversão do Gentio.*

1563   Brazil: José de Anchieta writes his 4,000-verse Latin poem *De Beata Virgine Dei Matre Maria* on the beach of Iperoig.

1569   Chile: Publication in Spain of the first part of *La Araucana*, Alonso de Ercilla's epic poem of conquest and resistance. **Mexico:** Bernardino de Sahagún completes his *Historia general de las cosas de Nueva España.*

1570   Brazil: Pero de Magalhães Gândavo writes *Tratado da Terra do Brasil* and publishes his *História da Província de Santa Cruz a que Vulgarmente Chamamos Brasil* in 1576.

1587   Brazil: Gabriel Soares de Sousa pens his *Tratado Descritivo do Brasil em 1587.*

1589   Colombia: Juan de Castellanos publishes *Elegías de varones ilustres de Indias.*

1604   Mexico: Publication of *Grandeza mexicana*, Bernardo de Balbuena's lyric evocation of Mexico City.

1609   Peru: Publication of the first part of *Comentarios reales de los Incas*, the Inca Garcilaso de la Vega's account of pre-Columbian and postconquest Peru.

1611   Mexico: Diego de Hojeda publishes *La Christiada*, Spanish America's first religious epic.

1628   Mexico: Publication in Spain of the first volume of plays by the dramatist Juan Ruiz de Alarcón. A second volume appears in 1634.

1632   Mexico: Publication of Bernal Díaz del Castillo's *Historia verdadera de la conquista de la Nueva España*, written over 50 years earlier.

1636   Colombia: Juan Rodríguez Freyle begins work on *El carnero*, his chronicle of the history of Colombia and life in Bogotá in the early colonial period, eventually published in 1859.

1654   Brazil: Antônio Vieira preaches his sermon *Santo Antônio aos peixes*; the first volume of his *Sermões* appears in 1679.

1690   Mexico: Publication of Carlos de Sigüenza y Góngora's *Infortunios de Alonso Ramírez.*

1691   Mexico: Sor Juana Inés de la Cruz writes her *Respuesta a Sor Filotea de la Cruz.*

1695   Brazil: Zumbi dos Palmares, leader of the runaway slave community of Palmares and later a national hero, is captured and killed.

1700   Brazil: Portuguese language and culture are imposed; efforts to replace Indian languages are stepped up in 1750.

1703   Guatemala: By about this date Francisco Ximénez had begun his transcription of the *Popol Vuh.*

1732   Peru: Pedro de Peralta y Barnuevo publishes *Lima fundada, o conquista del Perú*, his epic poem on Peru and the founding of its capital.

1750 Brazil: The Treaty of Madrid recognizes Portuguese claims to all areas effectively occupied.

1768 Brazil: Aracadian poet Cláudio Manuel da Costa publishes his *Obras* in Lisbon.

1769 Brazil: Publication of Basílio da Gama's epic poem *O Uraguai*.

1775 Spain: Alonso Carrió de la Vandera, a visiting colonial official, writes *El lazarillo de ciegos caminantes*, an account of a journey from Buenos Aires to Lima.

1779 Brazil: José de Santa Rita Durão publishes his epic poem *Caramuru*.

1788–1789 Brazil: First serious anti-Portuguese plot, known as the Inconfidência Mineira, appears in Minas Gerais.

1792 Brazil: Tomás Antônio Gonzaga publishes *Marília de Dirceu* and is deported to Mozambique.

1807 Brazil: The court of the Portuguese Prince Dom João VI sails from Lisbon and settles in Rio de Janeiro after Napoleon's invasion of the Iberian Peninsula.

1810 Argentina, Mexico: Declaration of Independence (25 May in Argentina, 16 September in Mexico).

1815 Brazil: The Portuguese prince regent raises the Estado do Brasil to the status of Portugal's equal partner in a newly created "United Kingdom." **Venezuela:** Simón Bolívar completes his celebrated reflections on American independence in his *Carta de Jamaica*.

1816 Mexico: Publication of *El periquillo sarniento* by José Joaquín Fernández de Lizardi, considered the first truly Spanish American novel.

1818 Chile: Independence is proclaimed (12 February).

1820 Uruguay: *Cielitos*, a collection of verses by Bartolomé Hidalgo, is published and establishes an interest in the literary potential of the life and customs of the gaucho.

1822   Brazil: Independence is proclaimed (7 September), followed by the coronation of the Emperor Pedro I and an invitation to José Bonifácio de Andrade e Silva to form the first ministry (1 December).

1823   Costa Rica, El Salvador, Guatemala, Honduras, Nicaragua: Formation of the United Provinces of Central America, which lasted until 1840, by which time the five nations involved had declared their sovereignty. **Venezuela:** Andrés Bello publishes *Alocución a la poesía*, his call for consideration of the poetic quality of the Americas.

1824   Peru: Independence from Spain is won.

1825   Bolivia: Becomes an independent country with Simón Bolívar as its first president. **Brazil:** War with Buenos Aires over the attempt of Cisalpine Province (modern Uruguay) to secede and join Argentina. Portugal recognizes Brazilian independence. **Ecuador:** José Joaquín Olmedo publishes his celebrated poem, *La victoria de Junín, canto a Bolívar*, in honor of independence and the liberator Simón Bolívar.

1826   Mexico: Publication of *Xicoténcatl*, an anonymous historical novel and the first important novel to appear after independence.

1828   Brazil, Uruguay: Modern boundaries between Brazil and Spanish America are established when Great Britain forces recognition of an independent Uruguay, which wins full autonomy after a process begun in 1811.

1829   Argentina: Juan Manuel Rosas becomes governor of Buenos Aires Province and rules with dictatorial power almost without interruption until 1852. **Chile:** Andrés Bello accepts an invitation to serve in the government and takes up permanent residence.

1830   Brazil: Coffee emerges as the major export and fuels the economy for the next 140 years. **Ecuador, Colombia, Venezuela, Panama:** Breakup of Gran Colombia, formed in 1819, creates the autonomous republics of Ecuador, Colombia, and Venezuela, with Panama remaining part of Colombia until seceding in 1903 after entering an agreement with the United States about construction and control of the Panama Canal.

1831   Brazil: Emperor Pedro I abdicates in favor of his son, Pedro II.

1832   Argentina: Esteban Echeverría publishes *Elvira, o la novia del Plata*, one of Latin America's earliest works of romanticism.

1836   Brazil: Publication of *Suspiros Poéticos e Saudades* by Domingos José Gonçalves de Magalhães inaugurates the national romantic movement.

1839   Argentina: Esteban Echeverría writes his celebrated short story "El matadero," an allegory of violence under the rule of Juan Manuel Rosas.

1845   Argentina: Publication of *Facundo* by Domingo Faustino Sarmiento.

1846   Brazil: The romantic poet Gonçalves Dias publishes *Primeiros Cantos.*

1850   Brazil: The slave trade ends, bringing about the end of the largest slave economy in the world, which had more slaves than free persons.

1851   Argentina: Publication of *Amalia*, José Mármol's anti-Rosas novel, one of Latin America's most popular works of romanticism.

1857   Brazil: José de Alencar publishes the indianist novel *O Guarani.*

1864   Argentina, Brazil, Paraguay, Uruguay: Outbreak of the six-year War of the Triple Alliance between Paraguay and its neighbors, with disastrous consequences for Paraguay.

1865   Brazil: José de Alencar publishes the novel *Iracema.*

1867   Colombia: Publication of Jorge Isaacs's *María*, Latin America's most widely read 19th-century novel. **Mexico:** Execution of the Emperor Maximillian after restoration of the republic under President Benito Juárez following the failure of French intervention (begun in 1862).

1868   Brazil: Antônio Castro Alves publishes his abolitionist poem *O Navio Negreiro.*

1870   Brazil: Antônio Castro Alves publishes *Espumas Flutuantes.*

1872   Argentina: Publication of the first part of *Martín Fierro* by José Hernández, the most prominent work of gaucho literature. **Peru:**

Ricardo Palma begins the publication of his first series of *Tradiciones peruanas*.

1875 Brazil: Bernardo de Guimarães publishes the antislavery, regionalist novel *A Escrava Isaura*.

1879 Bolivia, Chile, Peru: Outbreak of the War of the Pacific, ending in 1884 with disastrous consequences for Bolivia and Peru. **Ecuador:** Publication of *Cumandá, o un drama entre salvajes* by Juan León Mera, the country's most significant romantic and indianist novel.

1881 Brazil: Machado de Assis publishes *Memórias Póstumas de Brás Cubas*. Aluísio Azevedo publishes *O Mulato*, the first novel to deal with interracial same-sex relations.

1884 Argentina, Uruguay: The dramatization of Eduardo Gutiérrez's *Juan Moreira* introduces the figure of the gaucho to the stage.

1888 Brazil: Parliament approves total and immediate abolition of slavery without compensation (13 May). Olavo Bilac publishes his parnassian volume *Poesias*. **Nicaragua:** Rubén Darío publishes *Azul*, a collection of poems often taken to mark the beginning of Spanish American *modernismo*. **Uruguay:** Publication of Juan Zorrilla de San Martín's *Tabaré*, one of the founding texts of the national literature.

1889 Brazil: The Republic is proclaimed. **Mexico:** Ignacio Manuel Altamirano completes *El Zarco*, his romantic historical novel set during the French intervention. **Peru:** *Aves sin nido*, one of the first novels of Peruvian indigenismo, is published by Clorinda Matto de Turner.

1890 Brazil: Aluísio Azevedo publishes his naturalist novel *O Cortiço*.

1893 Brazil: João Cruz e Sousa publishes two volumes of symbolist poetry, *Missal* and *Broquéis*.

1899 Brazil: Machado de Assis publishes *Dom Casmurro*.

1900 Uruguay: *Ariel*, José Enrique Rodó's groundbreaking discussion of Latin American culture, is published.

1902 Brazil: Euclides da Cunha publishes his naturalist account of the Canudos War, *Os Sertões*. **Uruguay:** The staging of *Canillitas* by Florencio Sánchez, a play about a newspaper vendor, gives the dramatist his breakthrough in Buenos Aires.

1903 Mexico: Publication of Federico Gamboa's *Santa*, a popular naturalist novel and the source of the country's first sound movie.

1908 Argentina: Publication of *La gloria de don Ramiro* by Enrique Larreta, a significant example of Latin American prose *modernismo*.

1909 Argentina: Publication of *Lunario sentimental*, a collection of poems by Leopoldo Lugones, one of the major works of Latin American *modernismo*.

1910 Mexico: Beginning of the Mexican Revolution.

1912 Brazil: Augusto dos Anjos publishes his only but highly successful volume of poetry, *Eu*.

1915 Brazil: Afonso Henriques de Lima Barreto publishes *Triste Fim de Policarpo Quaresma*. **Mexico:** Publication of *Los de abajo* by Mariano Azuela initiates the novel of the Mexican Revolution. Ramón López Velarde, considered one of his country's national poets, publishes *La sangre devota*, his first collection of verse.

1916 Argentina: Alfonsina Storni publishes her first collection of verse, *La inquietud del rosal*.

1917 Uruguay: Publication of *Cuentos de amor, de locura y de muerte*, one of the best known collections of the widely influential short story writer Horacio Quiroga.

1918 Peru: *Los heraldos negros*, César Vallejo's collection of avant-garde poetry, is published.

1919 Bolivia: Publication of *Raza de bronce* by Alcides Arguedas.

1922 Brazil: The "Week of Modern Art" in São Paulo inaugurates Brazilian modernism (February). The Brazilian Communist Party is founded. **Argentina:** *Historia de arrabal*, a novel representative of Spanish American naturalism, is published by Manuel Gálvez.

1923 Argentina: Jorge Luis Borges returns to Buenos Aires from Europe, the same year he publishes *Fervor de Buenos Aires*.

1925 Brazil: Oswald de Andrade publishes his avant-garde poetry volume *Pau Brasil*. **Mexico:** Publication of *La raza cósmica* by José Vasconcelos, one of the major contributions to discussions of national identity after the revolution.

1926 Argentina: Ricardo Güiraldes publishes *Don Segundo Sombra*, a classic Latin American novel of the land and exploration of the figure of the gaucho in the national psyche. **Colombia:** Publication of *La vorágine*, José Eustasio Rivera's classic novel of the jungle.

1928 Brazil: Mário de Andrade publishes his rhapsodic novel *Macunaíma, O Herói sem Nenhum Caráter*. Oswald de Andrade publishes "Manifesto Antropófago" in *Revista de Antropofagia*. **Mexico:** Introduction of the avant-garde through the formation of the group Los Contemporáneos; publication of *El águila y la serpiente* by Juan Luis Guzmán, a novel of the revolution that follows the campaigns of Pancho Villa. **Peru:** Publication of José Carlos Mariátegui's highly influential book *Siete ensayos de interpretación de la realidad peruana*.

1929 Argentina: Roberto Arlt publishes *Los siete locos*, his novel of crime and anarchy in early 20th-century Buenos Aires. **Brazil:** Plínio Salgado, Menotti del Picchia, and Cassiano Ricardo publish the nationalist "Manifesto do Verdeamarelismo ou da Escola da Anta." **Panama:** Rogelio Sinán's book of poetry, *Onda*, introduces the avant-garde to his country. **Venezuela:** Rómulo Gallegos publishes *Doña Bárbara*, his classic novel of the land.

1930 Argentina: The first of a series of 20th-century military governments seizes power in a coup. **Brazil:** A bloodless military coup installs Getúlio Vargas as dictator. Manuel Bandeira publishes *Libertinagem* and Raquel de Queirós publishes *O Quinze*. **Ecuador:** Members of the Grupo Gayaquil publish their signature collection of short stories of social realism, *Los que se van*.

1931 Argentina: Victoria Ocampo founds the literary review *Sur*. **Brazil:** Jorge Amado publishes his regionalist novel *O País do Carnaval*. **Chile:** Vicente Huidobro publishes *Altazor*, one of Latin America's major works of avant-garde poetry.

1932 Bolivia, Paraguay: Outbreak of the Chaco War (ends in 1935). **El Salvador:** Suppression of a peasant uprising with such brutality it was called *La Matanza* and became the point of reference for future revolts.

1934   Brazil: Graciliano Ramos publishes *São Bernardo*. **Ecuador:** Jorge Icaza publishes *Huasipiungo*, an indigenista novel that becomes one of the classics of the genre.

1937   Brazil: The Estado Novo is initiated under the dictatorship of Getúlio Vargas. Publication of several important works: *Vidas Secas* by Graciliano Ramos, *Olhai os Lírios do Campo* by Érico Veríssimo, and *Viagem* by Cecília Meireles. **Mexico:** Rodolofo Usigli's most successful early drama, *El gesticulador*, a satire on political corruption, is staged.

1940   Argentina: Adolfo Bioy Casares publishes *La invención de Morel*, a classic novel combining elements of science fiction and the fantastic.

1941   Peru: Publication of *El mundo es ancho y ajeno*, Ciro Alegría's landmark novel of South American indigenismo.

1943   Brazil: José Lins do Rego publishes *Fogo Morto*.

1944   Argentina: Jorge Luis Borges publishes *Ficciones*, one of his most widely read collections of short stories. **Brazil:** Clarice Lispector publishes *Perto do Coração Selvagem*.

1945   Brazil: The army persuades Vargas to leave power, restoring democracy and free elections; publication of *A Rosa do Povo* by Carlos Drummond de Andrade.

1946   Argentina: Juan Domingo Perón is elected president. **Chile:** Gabriela Mistral becomes Latin America's first recipient of the Nobel Prize for Literature.

1947   Mexico: Publication of the novel *Al filo del agua* by Agustín Yáñez, marking a change in direction for the novel of the Mexican Revolution.

1948   Argentina: Leopoldo Marechal publishes *Adán Buenosayres*, a seminal Argentinean novel. Ernesto Sábato publishes his first novel, *El túnel*. **Colombia:** Assassination of liberal presidential candidate Jorge

Eliécer Gaitán sparks the *bogotazo* and the 17 years of conflict that followed, known as *la violencia.*

1949 Guatemala: Publication of *Hombres de maíz* by Nobel Prize winner Miguel Ángel Asturias, one of the major novels of Spanish American indigenismo. **Mexico:** Juan José Arreola publishes *Varia invención*, one of his early collections of short stories.

1950 Chile: Publication of Pablo Neruda's major work, *Canto general*, an epic collection of poems on the human and natural history of Latin America. **Mexico:** Publication of *El laberinto de la soledad* by Octavio Paz. **Uruguay:** Juan Carlos Onetti publishes *La vida breve*, the novel that introduces his fictional town of Santa María.

1951 Brazil: Publication of *Romanceiro da Inconfidência* by Cecília Meireles.

1952 Argentina: Death of Eva Duarte de Perón (26 July).

1954 Argentina: In *En la más médula*, Oliverio Girondo's avant-garde poetry experiments with language reach their highest point. **Brazil:** Publication of *Itinerário de Pasárgada* by Manuel Bandeira and *Fazendeiro do Ar* by Carlos Drummond de Andrade. **Chile:** Nicanor Parra publishes *Poemas y antipoemas*, seeking a simple form of poetic expression.

1956 Brazil: Publication of João Guimarães Rosa's masterpiece *Grande Sertão: Veredas*, João Cabral de Melo Neto's *Morte e Vida Severina*, and Fernando Sabino's *O Encontro Marcado.*

1957 Mexico: Rosario Castellanos publishes *Balún-canán*, one of the novels marking the emergence of neo-indigenismo in Spanish America. **Nicaragua:** Pablo Antonio Cuadra's classic play *Por los caminos van los campesinos* about revolution and foreign intervention is staged.

1958 Brazil: Haroldo de Campos, Augusto de Campos, and Décio Pignatari launch concrete poetry with "Plano Piloto Para Poesia Concreta." **Peru:** Publication of *Los ríos profundios* by José María Arguedas, a novel that marked a transition in indigenista literature.

1959 Brazil: Lúcio Cardoso publishes *Crônica da Casa Assassinada.*

1960 Brazil: Clarice Lispector publishes her landmark short story collection, *Laços de Família*.

1962 Mexico: Publication of *La muerte de Artemio Cruz* by Carlos Fuentes.

1963 Colombia: Foundation of the Teatro Experimental de Cali under the direction of Enrique Buenaventura.

1964 Brazil: With inflation in excess of 100 percent, the army seizes power (31 March–1 April). Publication of *A Paixão segundo G.H.* by Clarice Lispector. **Mexico:** Publication of *La tumba* by José Agustín, the first novel of *La Onda* and the representation of contemporary youth culture in fiction.

1966 Argentina: Publication of Julio Cortázar's boom novel *Rayuela*. **Brazil:** João Cabral de Melo Neto publishes *Educação Pela Pedra*, and Jorge Amado publishes *Dona Flor e Seus Dois Maridos*. **Colombia:** Foundation of La Candelaria theater collective under the direction of Santiago García. **Peru:** Mario Vargas Llosa publishes *La casa verde*, another celebrated boom novel.

1967 Argentina: *El campo*, Griselda Gambaro's dramatization of authoritarianism and oppression, is staged. **Bolivia:** Capture and death of Ernesto "Che" Guevara (8 October) after his failure to promote a popular revolution in South America. **Brazil:** Antonio Callado publishes *Quarup*. **Colombia:** Publication of *Cien años de soledad*, Gabriel García Márquez's landmark novel of the boom and magic realism, and Latin America's most widely read novel of the 20th century. **Guatemala:** The novelist Miguel Ángel Asturias is awarded the Nobel Prize for Literature.

1968 Mexico: The killing of students by government forces during a student demonstration, known as the Tlatelolco Massacre (2 October).

1969 Mexico: Publication by Elena Poniatowska of the first of her testimonial novels, *Hasta no verte, Jesús mío*. **Uruguay:** Cristina Peri Rossi publishes her first novel, *El libro de mis primos*, exposing the malaise afflicting Uruguayan society. **Venezuela:** César Rengifo's drama *Las torres y el viento* is staged.

1970 Ecuador: Publication of *Siete lunas y siete serpientes* by Demetrio Aguilera Malta, a major contribution to magic realism and the indigenista novel in Spanish America. **Peru:** Alfredo Bryce Echenique publishes his breakthrough novel *Un mundo para Julius*.

1971 Chile: The poet Pablo Neruda is awarded the Nobel Prize for Literature. **Uruguay:** Publication of Eduardo Galeano's important collection of essays on economic exploitation, *Las venas abiertas de América Latina*, and of Mario Benedetti's verse novel *El cumpleaños de Juan Ángel*, about the life of a revolutionary.

1972 El Salvador: Roque Dalton publishes *Miguel Mármol y los sucesos de 1932 en El Salvador*, a testimonio of a revolutionary life.

1973 Brazil: Osman Lins publishes his novel *Avalovara*. **Chile:** Overthrow of the constitutionally elected president Salvador Allende in a military coup headed by Augusto Pinochet.

1974 Guatemala: Hugo Carrillo stages his dramatization of Miguel Ángel Asturias's novel *El señor presidente*. **Paraguay:** Publication of Augusto Roa Bastos's *Yo el supremo*, one of Latin America's major political novels.

1975 Brazil: Inácio de Loyola Brandão publishes his novel *Zero*. **Nicaragua:** Publication of Ernesto Cardenal's *El evangelio de Solentiname*, a key work in the author's spiritual journey and the movement of Liberation Theology.

1976 Argentina: A military junta, headed by General Jorge Videla, takes over the government in a coup (24 March). Manuel Puig publishes his best known novel, *El beso de la mujer araña*. **Brazil:** Darcy Ribeiro publishes his novel *Maíra*, and Ferreira Gullar publishes his 2,000-verse *Poema Sujo*. **Ecuador:** Publication of *Entre Marx y una mujer desnuda*, by Jorge Enrique Adoum, one of Latin America's notable examples of the new novel.

1978 Chile: *Casa de campo*, José Donoso's allegorical novel of the rise and fall of Salvador Allende, is published.

1979 Nicaragua: Fall of the government of Anastasio Somoza as the Sandinista Liberation Army takes control.

1980   Argentina: Publication of *Respiración artificial*, Ricardo Piglia's novel written during the dictatorship.

1981   Argentina: Foundation of Teatro Abierto to revitalize the theater and challenge abuses of power.

1982   Chile: Publication of Isabel Allende's international best seller *La casa de los espíritus*, one of Latin America's best known works of magic realism. **Colombia:** The novelist Gabriel García Márquez is awarded the Nobel Prize for Literature. **Guatemala:** Publication of the testimonio *Me llamo Rigoberta Menchú y así me nació la conciencia*. **Nicaragua:** Omar Cabezas publishes his memoir of the Sandinista revolution, *La montaña es algo más que una inmensa estepa verde*. **Uruguay:** Publication of *Primavera con una esquina rota*, Mario Benendetti's novel of imprisonment and exile.

1983   Argentina: Failure of the military junta to capture the Malvinas/Falkland Islands from Great Britain leads to the fall of the junta and free elections. Juan José Saer's best known work, the new historical novel *El entenado*, is published. **Brazil:** Rubem Fonseca publishes his novel *A Grande Arte*. **El Salvador:** Publication of Claribel Alegría's account of a woman revolutionary, *No me agarran viva: la mujer salvadoreña en lucha*. **Nicaragua:** Sergio Ramírez's novel *¿Te dio miedo la sangre?*, set in the regime of Anastasio Somoza, is published.

1984   Brazil: Publication of João Ubaldo Ribeiro's *Viva o Povo Brasileiro*, Nélida Piñon's *A República dos Sonhos*, and Haroldo de Campos's *Galáxias*.

1985   Brazil: Redemocratization with restoration of direct election of the president. **Chile:** Antonio Skármeta publishes *Ardiente paciencia*, the first version of what would eventually be known as *Neruda's Postman*.

1986   Colombia: *La nieve del almirante*, the first of the Maqroll el Gaviero novels by Álvaro Mutis, is published.

1988   Nicaragua: Publication of Gioconda Belli's best-selling novel *La mujer habitada*.

1989   Brazil: Milton Hatoum publishes *Relato de um Certo Oriente*. **Mexico:** Publication of Laura Esquivel's best-selling novel *Como agua para chocolate*.

1990   Chile: First performance of Ariel Dorfman's original stage version of *Death and the Maiden*, on imprisonment and torture under dictatorship. **Mexico:** The poet and essayist Octavio Paz is awarded the Nobel Prize for Literature.

1993   Brazil: Manoel de Barros publishes his poetry book *O Livro das Ignorãças*.

1994   Brazil: Fernando Bonassi publishes *Subúrbio*.

1995   Mexico: Carlos Monsiváis publishes a collection of his chronicles of life and culture in Mexico City in *Los rituales del caos*.

1997   Brazil: Paulo Lins publishes *Cidade de Deus*, his story of drug dealing in a district of Rio, which became the basis of a successful film.

1998   Chile: Publication of *Los detectives salvajes* by Roberto Bolaños.

2001   Argentina: Luisa Valenzuela publishes *La travesía*, a novel of exile and return.

2002   Brazil: Bernardo Carvalho publishes *Nove Noites*. **Colombia:** Gabriel García Márquez publishes *Vivir para contarla*, the first volume of his memoirs.

2003   Brazil: Chico Buarque publishes *Budapeste*.

2004   Brazil: Nélida Piñon publishes *Vozes do Deserto*. **Chile:** Pedro Lemebel publishes *Adios, Mariquita linda*, a collection of chronicles of queer Santiago.

2005   Brazil: Milton Hatoum publishes his prize-winning novel *Cinzas do Norte*. **Chile:** Publication of *Zorro*, a novel by Isabel Allende about the legendary comic-book hero. **Nicaragua:** Gioconda Belli publishes her novel *El pergamino de la seducción*. New poems by Ernesto Cardenal appear in *Versos del pluriverso*.

2006   Chile: Publication of *Inés del alma mía* by Isabel Allende, a novel based on the life of Sor Juana Inés de la Cruz. **Mexico:** Carlos Fuentes publishes a volume of short stories, *Todas las familias felices*.

2007 **Argentina:** César Aira publishes *Las curas milagrosas del doctor Aira*. **Brazil:** Bernardo Carvalho publishes the novel *O Sol Se Põe Em São Paulo*. **Chile:** Publication of *Jamás el fuego nunca* by Diamela Eltit. **Mexico:** Publication of the novel *El Velázquez de París* by Carmen Boullosa.

2008 **Chile:** Publication of *La casa de Dostoievsky*, a novel by Jorge Edwards. **Colombia**: Publication of William Ospina's historical novel *El país de la canela* and of Germán Castro Caycedo's *El palacio sin máscara*, an account of a 1985 guerrilla assault on the Palace of Justice in Bogotá. **Nicaragua:** Sergio Ramírez publishes his crime novel *El cielo llora por mí*.

2009 **Brazil:** Luís Fernando Veríssimo publishes his novel *Os Espiões*, Chico Buarque publishes his novel *Leite Derramado*, and Rubem Fonseca publishes *O Seminarista*.

2010 **Peru:** The novelist Mario Vargas Llosh is awarded the Nobel Prize for Literature.

Introduction

Latin American literature is today recognized internationally for its originality, diversity, and capacity to interpret the singularities of Latin America to the reader. Whether in poetry, the novel and short story, nonfiction, or theater, there is an abundance of talented writers, including several in each genre with strong international reputations whose works have earned them prestigious prizes and have been translated and distributed or performed throughout the world. It was not always so, however. With a history of more than five centuries and cultural roots that reach into the traditions of Europe, Africa, and the Americas, contemporary Latin American literature and theater have a long and complex pedigree. Yet for much of that period, literary expression in the region was highly derivative, founded on genres and trends fashioned in the Old World and brought to the New by travelers and immigrants. Even as the colonies gained political independence at the beginning of the 19th century, they did not immediately become free of external cultural influences. During the 19th century and the first decades of the 20th, Latin American literature remained a marginal phenomenon, largely unknown beyond its borders. It was only as the new republics matured and became more conscious of their individuality as nations, as their societies grew and became more complex and diverse, that literature acquired a greater presence. Indeed, literature itself played a significant role in the process of self-awareness by representing and interpreting Latin Americans to themselves and therefore contributing, in due course, to images of the region conveyed to the world at large.

The role of literature in the formation of the national imagination has its origin in some of the early chronicles of the conquest and colonization, such as the *Comentarios reales* of El Inca Garcilaso de la Vega for Peru or the epic account of the conquest of Chile by Alonso de Ercilla, in which the stories of preconquest civilizations are narrated at the same time as the first European impressions of the Americas are recorded. This process of familiarization with the new continent, begun for the Europeans with their arrival, was re-energized during the first century of independence under the influence of 19th-century romanticism, as the peoples of the new nations began to take further stock of themselves and their environment. The likes of José de Alencar in Brazil, Jorge Isaacs in Colombia, and José Mármol in Argentina examined society and identified its characteristics through fiction. A few decades later, in the early 20th century, Eustasio Rivera in Colombia, Rómulo Gallegos in Venezuela, and Ricardo Güiraldes in Argentina were among another generation of writers, whose "novels of the land" described unique ways of life that had taken shape in the Americas, principally in rural areas. The works that they and some of their predecessors produced have become classics of Latin American literature, not just because they evoke times gone by, but also because their narratives continue to strike a chord in the national psyches of Latin Americans and have contributed to the formation of social identities.

Of course, in addition to showing readers to themselves, as if holding a mirror up to their lives, literature has other functions. It often serves as the nation's conscience, thereby giving the writer the task of monitoring the national moral compass, a role that has had significant implications for Latin America. Writers in Latin America have traditionally been held in high regard as representatives and spokespersons of their national culture. Many have aspired to or held high political office or have held significant appointments in their countries' diplomatic service, and a good number have been career diplomats. Among luminaries who belong in these groups are Domingo Faustino Sarmiento (Argentina), Rómulo Gallegos (Venezuela), Pablo Neruda (Chile), Miguel Ángel Asturias (Guatemala), João Guimarães Rosa (Brazil), João Cabral de Melo Neto (Brazil), Rosario Castellanos (Mexico), and Octavio Paz (Mexico). Thus, major writers have a prominent cultural status, and the most prominent among them, such as Jorge Luis Borges (Argentina), Pablo Neruda, and Gabriel García Márquez (Colombia), are thought of as cultural icons, writers whose lives and work embody something of the spirit of the nation.

Given the role and social status of writers in Latin America, it is hardly surprising that their navigation through the turbulent political waters of the continent since independence has often placed them in jeopardy. Some, such as the Argentinean Rodolfo Walsh, have paid for their activism and writing with their lives. Many others, among them the Uruguayan Juan Carlos Onetti, the Argentinean Jacobo Timerman, and the Salvadoran Roque Dalton, have spent time in prison. Many more have spent years abroad, unable to return to their own countries. Indeed, Latin American literature is often characterized as a literature of exile. For some writers, drawn to Paris, Madrid, or other cultural capitals of the world, exile is voluntary. For a great number, however, exile was forced upon them, and in some cases, they were fortunate to escape with their lives. This condition, common enough already in the 19th century, was especially prevalent in the 20th. The list of writers of recent generations who, for any number of reasons, have lived for extended periods outside their own countries includes some of the most recognizable names: the Mexican Carlos Fuentes, the Uruguayan Mario Benedetti, the Argentineans Julio Cortázar and Luisa Valenzuela, the Peruvian Mario Vargas Llosa, the Brazilian Murilo Mendes, and the Chilean José Donoso. At the same time, of course, those who remained at home in conflicted times had to find creative ways to defeat censorship and, faced with the difficulties of publication or performance, genres such as theater found their very existence threatened.

In view of the political and social history of Latin America and the extent to which they are reflected in the literature of the region, perceptions of the past are often shaped by literary representations, especially when these have coalesced in a literary genre or subgenre. The theme of revolution, for example, enters many works and is especially strong in the literature of countries that have endured protracted periods of revolutionary conflict and civil war. Such conflicts are represented in the early part of the 20th century in the novel of the Mexican Revolution, which was initiated by Mariano Azuela in 1915 and has resonated across the century even in the work of later Mexican writers such as Elena Poniatowska, Ángeles Mastretta, and Laura Esquivel, who not only narrate historical events, but analyze the consequences of the revolution in the decades that followed it. In a similar vein, the civil strife that afflicted the countries of Central America in the second half of the 20th century is expressed through the prose, poetry, and theater of the region, such as in the work of the Salvadorans Manlio Argueta and Claribel Alegría and the Nicaraguans Gioconda Belli, Ernesto Cardenal, and Pablo Antonio Cuadra.

Revolutions in Latin America, as exemplified by those in Mexico and Central America, originated in resistance to dictatorial regimes and the desire to replace them with a more humane social order. Indeed, the tyrannical regimes and the tyrants that have punctuated the history of most Latin American countries underlie literary phenomena such as the dictator novel, which, from its beginings in the 19th century with writers such as Esteban Echeverría and Domingo Faustino Sarmiento, has served to portray both historical and contemporary political figures. Its 20th-century contributors include the Paraguayan Augusto Roa Bastos, the Chilean Enrique Lafourcade, the Guatemalan Miguel Ángel Asturias and the Ecuadorian Demetrio Aguilera Malta. The desire for a more egalitarian society that fuels the dictator novels also fostered literary *indigenismo*, part of a broader social movement that began to make headway in the early decades of the 20th century, especially in the Andean countries of Ecuador, Bolivia, and Peru, in favor of recognition of the human and civil rights of indigenous peoples. *Indigenismo* has a counterpart in the literary representation of Latin Americans of African descent and advocacy in favor of the same range of political and social rights and freedoms, a movement that has grown in importance throughout Latin America and is especially significant in countries with large minorities of neo-Africans, such as Brazil, Colombia, and Ecuador.

The commitment of writers to a just society, as expressed in these movements, continues today in Latin America. It has made writing by and about women, gays, and lesbians a very visible element of the contemporary literary landscape, part of the quest for the equitable social treatment of all citizens and their honest representation in literature. At the same time, with a knowledge of history, it has made writers, often at a cost to themselves, wary of the personal ambitions of their leaders and vigilant with respect to the stability of social and political institutions under pressure from both local and global forces. Yet, it should not be concluded on this basis that Latin American literature is to be seen exclusively for its political or social commitment and content. Like all literatures, it is also a highly creative phenomenon in which the social and natural worlds are represented and analyzed in terms that aesthetically engage the reader's imagination, a characteristic no better represented than in the products of Spanish American *modernismo*, in the various forms of avant-garde expression of the first half of the 20th century, notably Brazilian modernism, or in the capacity of magic realism to tap the atavistic and the mythological in versions of storytelling that draw extensively on oral traditions of narrative. In all these respects, Latin American literature serves the very basic role, common to all literatures, of representing the social worlds and inner lives of its writers and readers.

DEFINING LATIN AMERICA

Although it may be possible to characterize Latin American literature by referring to some of the most salient characteristics that associate it with the part of the world to which it belongs, there still remains the question of exactly which countries it encompasses. The term "Latin America" originated in Second Empire France under Napoleon III (1851–1870) when, at the time of the French intervention in Mexico and the installation of Maximilian as emperor (1864–1867), it served politically to assert a cultural connection between the Americas and the romance-language-speaking countries of Europe. For better or worse, given the varied cultural and geographical connotations the term has subsequently acquired, it has remained in use ever since. Most commonly it embraces the Spanish- and Portuguese-speaking countries of the continental Americas, from Mexico in the North to Tierra del Fuego in the far South and the Spanish-speaking islands of the Caribbean. For some it may also include the French Caribbean and even the English- and Dutch-speaking islands of the region, although the term "Latin America and the Caribbean" is often used to designate this broader area. More recently, the modified "Latin/o America" has emerged in critical writing as a term used to embrace an even wider territory, not only the regions traditionally designated, but also the Latin American diaspora in North America. In this *Historical Dictionary of Latin American Literature and Theater*, the definition of Latin America is more restricted, and the territory covered is limited to Brazil and the 16 Spanish-speaking republics of the continental mainland: Argentina, Bolivia, Chile, Colombia, Costa Rica, Ecuador, El Salvador, Guatemala, Honduras, Mexico, Nicaragua, Panama, Paraguay, Peru, Uruguay, and Venezuela.

As a designator of culture, "Latin America" evokes the conquest by Spain and Portugal and the imposition, not just of their languages, but of their culture in all its forms during a colonial regime that lasted for more than three centuries. Such a view, however, offers an essentially Eurocentric perspective. It excludes the cultures of Native Americans who even today are a majority in the populations of countries such as Peru, Ecuador, and Bolivia and overlooks the cultural hybridity that evolved from miscegenation between the old and new inhabitants of the continent. It does not include the millions of Africans brought to the Americas as slaves and whose culture has spread widely throughout the region, particularly in countries initially dependent on the plantation economies that exploited their labor. Finally, it does not allow for the flood of migrants of different ethnicities and nationalities, from regions as diverse as Europe, Asia, and the Middle East, who have arrived since the mid-19th century and have contributed significantly to population growth and cultural diversification.

Thus, although "Latin America" remains in use, it now designates a region of extraordinary cultural diversity within which are also contained the differences created by the existence of distinct nations. Latin America is linguistically varied, not just on account of the continued use of native American languages and the presence of Portuguese and Spanish, but as a result of the different registers that have evolved in the Spanish-speaking countries and the regional particularities of language that have emerged in every country of the continent. Moreover, as the countries of Latin America approach the bicentennial of their national independence, they can look back across their own history and the formation of communities, social traditions, and lifestyles that differ from those of their neighbors. Literature in Latin America represents and expresses all this variety. Although it is possible to detect certain commonalities in their development from colonial times to the present, as outlined in the following paragraphs, and therefore to speak of a Latin American literature, each of the national literatures embraced by this regional designation is also a product of the particular historical idiosyncrasy of the social environment in which it was formed. Latin American literature is therefore not just one literature, but a combination of many, whose writers collectively embody the diversity mentioned above.

LATIN AMERICAN LITERATURE AND THEATER

The Colonial Period

The indigenous peoples of Latin America were devastated by the arrival of the Europeans. Their populations were decimated, not just by the trauma of conquest but also by contact with diseases against which they had no immunity. Although indigenous cultures were by no means eradicated or assimilated, their social evolution and the development of their forms of expression were constrained and subordinated to the colonial regime. Much has remained through oral transmission, and a material legacy of the myths and history of the past is preserved in documents such as the Mexican codices and archaeological sites across the continent. The superiority of the conquerors, however, was not only in their weaponry and technology. These speakers of Spanish and Portuguese, already in possession of a sophisticated literary system, also had more potent languages through which to lay claim to the newly found lands they had subdued.

Latin American literature has its beginning in the writings of Europeans produced in the immediate glow of their encounter with the new continent and its inhabitants. Among the earliest were the diary of Christopher Colombus's first voyage, addressed to the Catholic Kings Ferdinand and Isabella of Spain in 1492, and Pero Vaz de Caminha's description of the newly found territory of Brazil in a letter written to Manuel I of Portugal in 1500. A plethora of diaries, letters, memoirs, narratives, histories, and treatises followed, a body of documents belonging mainly to the 16th century, that would come to be known collectively as the chronicles of the conquest and colonization of America. Some, like the letters to the Spanish crown from Hernán Cortés in Mexico (1520–1526) and from Pedro de Valdivia in Chile (1552), were written by the commanders of military campaigns. Others, such as Bernal Díaz del Castillo's memoir of the conquest of Mexico, penned (1555?–1584) long after the events he experienced, were the work of former soldiers. Many, including the multivolume histories of the Spanish Indies by Bartolomé de Las Casas and Gonzalo Fernández de Oviedo, are invaluable documents of the period, and much of what was written, such as Pedro de Cieza de León's account of the colonization and history of early Peru, carries the stamp of officialdom, whether because it was written under royal commission or addressed to the crown.

The chronicles were not just narratives of events that told the story of the military campaigns. Many examined the moral and ethical consequences of the discovery and conquest of a new world and the colonization of its people. A significant number of the chroniclers, men like the Franciscans Toribio de Benavente (also known as Motolinía) and Diego de Landa, were members of religious orders whose accounts documented the Christianization of the Americas. The Portuguese-born Pero de Magalhães Gândavo and his compatriot Gabriel Soares de Sousa, like many of their contemporaries in Brazil and elsewhere in colonial America, were interested in the natural history of the territories and in promoting immigration to the new lands. The interests of the chroniclers also encompassed the history and culture of indigenous peoples, although there were those who wrote about it mainly to condemn it as idolatry as well as those who strove to describe and understand it. Among the latter were Bernardino de Sahagún, whose celebrated *Florentine Codex* is one of the richest sources of information about life in Aztec Mexico.

In this veritable flood of documents that represented the European view of the conquest and the newly acquired territories, the indigenous perspective was not entirely overwhelmed. The transcription of texts such as Nahuatl poetry in Mexico and the Quiché creation myths told in the *Popol Vuh* from Guatemala would eventually permit some pre-Columbian voices to be heard. At the same time, acquisition of the language of their masters by native and mestizo populations ensured, through the likes of Huaman Poma de Ayala and El Inca Garcilaso de la Vega in Peru, and Hernando Alvarado Tezozomoc in Mexico, that the view from the other side of the conquest also circulated in the new linguistic environment. But the chronicles of the conquest and colonization were predominantly Eurocentric, a record of the incorporation of the Americas into the European worldview. As such, they were also a body of foundational texts, providing a basis for thought and perception that would endure during the colonial period and against which the independent countries of Latin America would eventually write their own histories.

With cultural life in the colonies centered on the viceregal courts, literature evolved under the influence of Spain and Portugal and followed the fashions of Europe. From the very beginnings, however, the New World realities sowed tensions among Old World practices. The Americas introduced a new content to literature, new languages and mythologies, and in the process put established literary genres to new uses. Historians of the conquest left traces of the popular 16th-century novel of chivalry in their writings, while epic poets found new subjects to extol worthy of their genre. The first part of Alonso de Ercilla's heroic account of the conquest of Chile appeared in 1569. It inspired continuations and imitators and was one of Latin America's earliest epic poems in a tradition that includes poems by Bernardo de Balbuena and Diego de Hojeda in the 17th century and Basílio da Gama and José de Santa Rita Durão in the 18th. The 17th-century baroque produced the Mexican Sor Juana Inés de la Cruz, the foremost lyric poet of her time, and the satirists Juan del Valle y Caviedes and Gregório de Matos e Guerra, who took aim at the foibles of colonial society in Peru and Brazil, respectively. By contrast, the Arcadian poets of the Minas Gerais school, influenced by elements of the 18th-century Enlightenment and neoclassicism, sought to reflect the clear rationalism of their age.

When the theater came to Latin America from Europe, it found a role in two of the main spheres of activity of the colonial world. Religious theater, in the form of biblical tales, miracle plays, and allegories, was adopted by the missionary priests and friars in the campaign to Christianize local populations and was well established by the 16th century, with repertoires that included plays written for local audiences. At the same time, a secular theater began to establish roots, especially in association with the viceregal courts, where a dramatic performance often marked an important civic occasion or served simply to entertain. Although there were some local dramatists, such as Fernán González de Eslava in Mexico and Pedro de Peralta y Barnuevo in Peru, secular theater in the colonial period mainly imitated its European sources or was characterized by plays written by European dramatists. An independent public theater would not emerge for many years.

Writing in prose began, of course, with the chronicles of the conquest and colonization, but spread to other domains as more towns and cities were established and grew and as social institutions acquired roots and stability. Local history, religion, morality, and medicine figure prominently among the subjects of books written in the colonial period. Prose fiction, as an established genre, still belonged to the future where Latin America was concerned, but there were some significant stirrings in the colonial period. Juan Rodríguez Freyle's chronicle of New Granada, written between 1636 and 1638, acquires the character of narratives of everyday life. Francisco Núñez de Pineda y Bascuñán's 1673 account of his capitivity among the Mapuche in Chile foreshadows 19th-century captive narratives. Carlos de Sigüenza y Góngora's 1690 story of the life of Alonso Ramírez, sometimes considered Latin America's first novel, has many of the elements of an adventure novel, and Alonso Carrió de la Vandera's travelogue, of 1775 or 1776, of a journey between Buenos Aires and Lima not only has a direct connection with the Spanish picaresque tradition, but frequently appears to engage in narrative for its own sake.

The 19th Century

The change from colony to nation was completed in Latin America before the end of the first quarter of the 19th century. With the exception of Brazil, which declared itself an independent monarchy in 1822 and became a republic in 1889, the transition was not a quiet one. There have also been many tempestuous periods since then in a history punctuated by internal civil strife, revolutions, invasions, and wars between nations. For the most part, whether in exile or at home, and in spite of periods of suppression and censorship, literature has grown and thrived. In the 19th century it already benefited from greater overall freedom of expression, wider access to influences from Europe and North America, and the spread of printing, which was still very restricted even in the late colonial period.

The spirit of criticism of late colonial society is well reflected in the journalism and fiction of the Mexican José Joaquín Fernández de Lizardi. The triumph of the revolution was captured in neoclassical verses by the Ecuadorian José Joaquín de Olmedo, and aspirations for the future of the continent were voiced by the Venezuelan-born Andrés Bello. His optimism must have seemed short lived, however, as the newly liberated nations struggled to preserve their freedoms against authoritarianism and the reinstatement, albeit in different guises, of the old regime. The struggles that ensued in Argentina, for example, are amply described in Domingo Faustino Sarmiento's *Facundo* (1845) against the motif of a conflict between civilization and barbarism, a theme that would reverberate in various countries of Latin America for a number of decades to come.

In the midst of all the changes, the dominant literary movement of the 19th century was romanticism. It entailed a literary revolution, which, for Latin American writers, came about through their encounter with European authors, especially from France, beyond the hitherto customary Spanish and Portuguese canon. It also heralded a wave of liberalism that would have a profound impact on social and political life in Latin America at the same time that it caused conflict with more conservative-minded sectors of society that resisted change. Romanticism developed in the climate of revolution in late 18th-century Europe, but arrived late in Latin America, its passage hindered by the Napoleonic Wars in Europe and the Wars of Independence in the Americas. *Elvira, o la novia de la Plata* (1832; Elvira, or The Bride of the River Plate), by the Argentinean Esteban Echeverría, was one of its earliest manifestations in Spanish America; the work of the noted Brazilian romantic poets Domingos José Gonçalves de Magalhães and Antônio Gonçalves Dias did not begin to appear until the 1830s and 1840s, respectively.

In contrast to the ordered control of the 18th century, romanticism fostered a spirit of rebellion in both the content and form of literature. It emphasized individualism, a sympathy with nature, an interest in the past, and above all, the supremacy of love and the emotions. With respect to the past, the pre-Columbian era and the conquest and colonial periods provided subjects for two genres: the historical novel, following the model launched by Sir Walter Scott (1771–1832), and the *tradición*, initiated by the Peruvian Ricardo Palma. Both retained their popularity throughout the 19th century and beyond. Sentimental novels, by authors such as José de Alencar, Ignacio Altamirano, Jorge Isaacs, José Mármol, and Juan León Mera, invoked many of romanticism's most hallowed devices. Their stories of star-crossed lovers, however, were more than mere indulgence in some of the literary commonplaces of the age. Like historical fiction, they were also vehicles used to examine some of the pressing issues emerging in the newly formed nations, problems in existing social and political structures, racial separation and mixing, urban life, and relations with the natural environment. Among such foundational texts should also be included several narrative poems. José Hernández's *Martín Fierro* (1872) and Juan Zorilla de San Martín's *Tabaré* (1888), for example, both belong in this category. Hernández's work, in particular, is one of the core pieces of Argentinean gaucho literature around which formulations of national identity would take shape well into the 20th century. There are, then, strong connections among romanticism, nationalism, and the emergence of models of identity, some of them drawing on how coexistence with indigenous people and African slaves was perceived by populations that originated in Europe.

Long after the force of romanticism as a literary movement had declined, romantic sensibility persisted, and it would regain much of its vigor in the popular music and film melodramas of the 1930s and 1940s. In the 19th century, however, as the pendulum of literary taste swung away from romanticism, it moved toward a greater preoccupation with everyday life and social reality. This trend, represented in fiction through the tendencies of *costumbrismo*, realism, and naturalism, gave rise to work by some remarkable writers: the *costumbristas* Jotabeche (José Joaquín Vallejo) from Chile and Fray Mocho (José Álvarez) from Argentina; the realists Alberto Blest Gana (Chile) and Emilio Rabasa (Mexico); and the naturalists Aluísio Azevedo (Brazil), Eugenio Cambaceres (Argentina), and Federico Gamboa (Mexico). Standing above them all, both combining and surpassing these trends, was the Brazilian Joaquim Maria Machado de Assis, whose work already pointed in the direction that the novel would take in the 20th century.

The move away from romanticism in poetry came about through the influence of French parnassianism and symbolism. In Brazil, it led to two movements under the same names and the poetry of Olavo Bilac, Alberto de Oliveira, João de Cruz e Sousa, and Alphonsus de Guimaraens, among others. In Spanish America, the same influences gave rise to *modernismo*, a term not to be confused with Brazilian modernism, which refers to a 20th-century avant-garde movement, or with the English term "modernism," used to refer to styles in art and culture in the late 19th and early 20th centuries that reflected the new technologies and growing industrialization of the age. Spanish American *modernismo* was an aesthetic movement that had its greatest impact on poetry, but was also felt in prose writing. With its cultivation of elegance and exoticism, the ideal, and the themes of mortality and melancholy, it shared some of the characteristics of the belle epoque and end-of-century decadence. It is associated above all with the Nicaraguan Rubén Darío and was at its peak during his lifetime, but it spread to all countries of Spanish America and influenced writers as diverse as the Peruvian Ricardo Jaimes Freyre, the Argentinean Enrique Larreta, the Mexican Amado Nervo, and the Colombian Guillermo Valencia. As Latin America's first homegrown literary movement, emerging as the 19th century ended, it also demonstrated a certain cultural maturity, a capacity to surpass the status of culturally dependent colony and produce a movement grown from within.

In contrast to 19th-century poetry and prose, which soon responded to the new social and political reality of Latin America's first post-colonial century, even while remaining under the influence of European literary trends, the theater reacted more slowly. The building of theaters since the late 18th century contributed to the development of the genre as a public institution, but foreign plays or plays written in imitation of foreign models dominated the stage for much of the 19th century. Notable 19th-century dramatists included the Mexican Manuel Eduardo de Gorostiza and the Peruvians Felipe Pardo y Aliaga and Manuel Ascensio Segura, and the Brazilians José Joaquim França Jr. and Luís Carlos Martins Pena, whose satires and comedies of manners reflected the European heritage of neoclassicism, romanticism, *costumbrismo*, and realism. The emergence of a theater more attuned to social crises and movements in national politics would not take place until the end of the 19th century and the beginning of the 20th.

The 20th and 21st Centuries

Latin America's second century of independence has, in its way, been as tumultuous as the first. Populations have grown enormously, the result of both massive immigration and a surging birthrate. Traditional lifestyles have waned in the wake of widespread urbanization and the massification of culture. Economies have endured the roller coaster of repeating cycles of boom and bust, affected by movements in economic nationalism as well as by trends in world markets and neocolonial intervention and control. Political stability, challenged by periods of militarism, populism, socialism, and other forces, has often seemed fragile. Amid such times, while benefiting from prosperity and contending with the reversals of upheaval, literature in Latin America has developed extraordinarily. In the world at large, it has lost its marginal status as a lesser known regional literature and has become widely known, with some of its authors recognized as icons of international culture.

Poetry

Although *modernismo* in Spanish America had passed its peak by 1920, its influence continued to be felt during the first decades of the 20th century and was manifested in the work of several notable poets, including, for example, Alfonsina Storni, Juana de Ibarbourou, Delmira Agustini, and Leopoldo Lugones. The first half of the 20th century was also the time of Gabriela Mistral, Latin America's first Nobel laureate, but a major shift began in the 1920s with the rise of the avant-garde through the influence in art and literature of cubism, surrealism, Dadaism, futurism, and other movements. In Latin America the literary avant-garde flourished in national groups of writers clustered around journals and other periodicals that served as vehicles for the publication of their work and the dissemination of their ideas. Among the more prominent trends were *estridentismo* in Mexico, *ultraísmo* in Argentina, and *creacionismo* in Chile. *Modernismo* in Brazil, celebrated in 1922 during the Week of Modern Art in São Paulo, signaled the demise of parnassianism and symbolism in favor of a modern aesthetic more attuned to contemporary life at the same time that it heralded an examination of Brazilian identity.

The avant-garde gave rise to poets of the stature of Carlos Drummond de Andrade, César Vallejo, and Vicente Huidobro. Others, among them Pablo Neruda and João Cabral de Melo Neto, although nurtured by the avant-garde, eventually followed paths dictated by their own inclinations and are celebrated for the richness and diversity of their oeuvre rather than for their attachment to a particular trend. In due course, particular avant-garde movements lost their capacity to serve as focal points, but the impact and freedom they brought to language and poetic structures remained. The post-avant-garde period has produced a number of oustanding poets, of whom Octavio Paz has achieved the highest recognition. Others include Claribel Alegría, Germán Belli, Gioconda Belli, Ernesto Cardenal, Antonio Cisneros, Nicanor Parra, Alejandra Pizarnik, and Vinícius de Moraes.

The Novel

The realist trend that had already begun to set the course of the Latin American novel during the last decades of the 19th century remained strong for much of the first half of the 20th. The novel of the land, regionalism, and *mundonovismo* have been variously used to describe novels of this period, which document and typify the events, the life, and the geography of Latin America at a time when social and political change brought a heightened sense of cultural and national identity. In

Mexico such tendencies were represented in narratives of the revolution; in Venezuela, Colombia, and Argentina they appeared in novels by Rómulo Gallegos, Eustasio Rivera, and Ricardo Güiraldes, which portrayed the relation between life and the land; in Brazil, Euclides da Cunha's 1902 account of the backlands of the Northeast heralded further 20th-century explorations of the region; and in the *indigenismo* of countries of the Andean region writers sought to offer a more realistic view of native peoples than was to be found in 19th-century *indianismo* and would culminate in due course in the work of the Peruvians José María Arguedas and Manuel Scorza.

Yet Latin American fiction in the first half of the 20th century was more diverse than the various forms of realism. It also included explorations of inner landscapes and urban environments, as in novels by Roberto Arlt, Eduardo Barrios, Eduardo Mallea, Leopoldo Marechal, and Juan Carlos Onetti. The experimentalism of the avant-garde that had left its mark so clearly on poetry was equally felt in fiction. The Brazilians Mário de Andrade and Oswald de Andrade would both be included in a representative group, as would the Chilean María Luisa Bombal and the Venezuelan Teresa de la Parra, both of whom also anticipated the surge in writing by women and the representation of female subjectivity that would occur before the end of the century. In effect, the late 1940s, the 1950s, and the 1960s were a period of ferment in fiction that saw the publication of important works by Miguel Ángel Asturias, Elena Garro, João Guimarães Rosa, Juan Rulfo, Agustín Yáñez, and others. They were all innovative writers and heralded the breakthrough in international recognition of the Latin American novel that came with the boom.

As much as it was a product of the creativity of a group of writers, the boom was also a creation of the publishing industry and its capacity to successfully market authors internationally. As a literary phenomenon, the boom belongs above all to the 1960s. Its principal authors were Julio Cortázar, Carlos Fuentes, Mario Vargas Llosa, and Gabriel García Márquez, whose *Cien años de soledad* (1967; *One Hundred Years of Solitude*), now a classic of universal literature, is identified with magic realism, a style that also came to be identified with Latin America itself. The success of these writers is owed in part to the attention and interest sparked by Latin America immediately after the triumph of the Cuban Revolution in 1959 and their ability to create a vision of the region that seemed to give an international readership a vision of the uniqueness of its histories, mythologies, and quintessential identity. At the same time, they incorporated the influences of Anglo-American modernism and the French new novel fully into their work and furthered the renovation of fiction in Latin America that the previous generation had initiated.

Long after the euphoria of their first triumphs declined, the boom writers have continued to publish successfully during a phase often referred to as the post-boom. Throughout both periods, boom and post-boom, they have been accompanied by numerous other writers, including Jorge Amado, Roberto Bolaño, Diamela Eltit, Clarice Lispector, Manuel Puig, Cristina Peri Rossi, Antonio Skármeta, Lygia Fagundes Telles, and Luisa Valenzuela. The later period has also been marked by considerable successes, including some international best sellers, such as Isabel Allende's *La casa de los espíritus* (1982; *The House of the Spirits*) and Laura Esquivel's *Como agua para chocolate* (1989; *Like Water for Chocolate*), both hailed for their magic realism and Latin Americanness. At the same time, the post-boom novel has morphed into the postmodern novel, which has seen the full emergence of the self-conscious narrative (i.e., one that refers to itself and the process of its composition); an emphasis on mass popular cultures, especially music and film; and the representation of hitherto marginalized points of view, including those of youth, gays, lesbians, and women. The scope of all these changes is no better illustrated than in the Latin American new historical novel, which not only incorporates the stylistic changes fostered by postmodernism but, in the wake of the collapse of the authoritarian regimes of the 1960s, 1970s, and 1980s, also offers a far more inclusive view of society and versions of history that challenge those of officialdom. The contemporary novel in Latin America has thus become a more open genre. Like its counterparts in Europe and North America, it responds to local issues and conditions, but its direction is also set by the twists and turns of taste and fashion, sometimes determined by the influence of the media and sometimes by the publishing industry and the marketability of authors and their work.

The Short Story

Although not without some antecedents, the short story in Latin America is often considered as having begun in the 19th century with

Esteban Echeverría's "El matadero" (1838; *"The Slaughter House"*), an allegory of life in Argentina under Juan Manuel Rosas. Echeverría, of course, is equally well known as a romantic poet, one of many writers who have won recognition in more than one genre. Indeed, given that most of the authors who figure in the history of the novel in Latin America also wrote shorter fiction, the history of the short story parallels that of longer fiction in terms of both the themes developed and the modes of writing. Among the major novelists who have also published significant and influential collections of short stories, José María Arguedas, Joaquim Maria Machado de Assis, Julio Cortázar, Rubem Fonseca, Clarice Lispector, Gabriel García Márquez, and Juan Rulfo stand out in particular.

Although the short story was a way for writers to hone their craft as novelists, many authors have devoted themselves to it almost to the exclusion of other genres and are recognized for the high level of their accomplishments. One of the first was the Uruguayan Horacio Quiroga, whose tales of the supernatural and the jungle established the influence of Edgar Allan Poe in Spanish America and made the short story a genre to be recognized in the 20th century. Others who have followed him include the Mexican Juan José Arreola, the Brazilian Dalton Trevisan, the Uruguayan Felisberto Herández, the Peruvian Julio Ramón Riberyo, and the Guatemalan Augusto Monterroso, but no comments on the short story would be complete without mentioning Jorge Luis Borges. Not only was he one of Latin America's major literary figures of the 20th century, but his short fictions, many of them microtales and some of them fictive essays, revolutionized the short story and the literary representation of reality.

Nonfiction Prose

Having had some of its origins in the narratives of the personal experiences and observations of the conquistadors and colonists, nonfiction prose had already found a place in Latin American literature long before the rise of the *testimonio* (eyewitness account or testimonial novel) and the urban chronicle in the 20th century. The *testimonio* not only features life-writing, and in this sense overlaps with autobiography, but is also a vehicle for the voiceless and the marginalized. Thus, Rigoberta Menchú speaks for indigenous people, Domitila Barrios de Chungara for mine workers and their families, Jacobo Timerman for political prisoners, Paulo Lins for the urban poor, and Elena Poniatowska for women. *Testimonios* customarily benefit from the anthropological or journalistic research into their subjects undertaken by their authors, whose representations of the subaltern also played into the postmodern trend in literature toward greater social inclusivity. In this respect, the contemporary urban chronicle, with its emphasis on mass culture and city life, is also an eminently postmodern genre, especially as exemplified by authors such as the Mexican Carlos Monsiváis, the Brazilian Rubem Braga, and the Chilean Pedro Lemebel. The chronicle has a much longer history, however. It may be associated with the 19th-century interest in local or regional customs, and its growth may be connected to the rise of mass-circulation newspapers in the late 19th and early 20th centuries, a period that corresponds in Latin America to one of the first periods of rapid urbanization. Indeed, the most common form of the publication of chronicles as books is as anthologies of columns first written for the daily press.

In contrast to the *testimonio* and the chronicle, both of which, but especially the former, are characterized by their narrative structures and in this sense have a clearly literary constitution, the essay adopts a more direct and argumentative approach to description and analysis. It may be equated with the treatises on philosophy, medicine, law, or natural science published in the colonial period. During the revolutionary wars and in the two centuries since independence, however, the essays that have resonated most are those more concerned with political institutions in Latin America, the interpretation of national histories, and the character of national identities. From the early 19th century, the name of the Great Liberator Simón Bolívar stands above others. In the last years of the same century, José Enrique Rodó's spiritual conceptualization of Latin American culture not only initiated a lingering debate, but established him as a founding figure of the modern Latin American essay. Among those who followed and whose work has had influence beyond the borders of their own countries, José Vasconcelos, José Carlos Mariátegui, Ezequiel Martínez Estrada, Gilberto Freyre, and Octavio Paz had considerable impact in the first half of the 20th century, whereas the likes of Ángel Rama, Silviano Santiago, and Beatriz Sarlo, who published in the second half, have been widely read as both cultural commentators and literary critics.

Theater

The evolution of the theater in Latin America between the late 19th century and the first half of the 20th century took place in the context of significant changes undergone by Latin American society during the same period and the transformation of theater as a cultural institution in the world at large. By this time, however, Latin American writers in all genres were learning to respond more creatively and critically to influences from outside and to look at the world around them from perspectives more attuned to their own realities and experiences. Though following the trends from abroad, writers for the stage were far less slavish in their adoption of new models. Thus, plays written for the popular theaters in Buenos Aires by dramatists such as Florencio Sánchez in the early 1900s embodied the points of view of the urban populations for which they were written. The experimental plays of the Argentinean Roberto Arlt and the Mexican Xavier Villaurrutia of the 1930s incorporated local perceptions and avant-garde practices. Above all, theater came to be used to explore pressing questions of nationalism and identity, whether among Mexican playwrights such as Rodolfo Usigli, Celestino Gorostiza, and Vicente Leñero, or among their Brazilian counterparts, such as Nelson Rodrigues or Ariano Vilar Suassuna. Since the second half of the 20th century, dramatists and directors in each of the countries of Latin America have explored ways to use theater as a vehicle for representing and critiquing their own histories and contemporary life.

The recent history of theater in Latin America has become the history of a multitude of theatrical projects, some quite ephemeral, others more durable, through which professionals associated with the stage have endeavored to pursue their craft. At the same time, for all the progress it has made, the theater in Latin America remains more vulnerable than either poetry or prose. As an institution that depends on public performance, it is highly susceptible to censorship during periods of conflict, and it has had to compete, more so than other genres, with other forms of entertaining and engaging the public, such as cinema, television, and video. Nevertheless, the theater is a thriving and creative force in many of Latin America's major urban centers, and the work of its more prominent authors is increasingly translated and performed internationally.

The Dictionary

– A –

ABREU, CAIO FERNANDO (Brazil, 1948–1996). Novelist, short story writer, journalist, and dramatist. Considered a spokesperson of his generation, Abreu's narrative, often direct and confessional, portrays contemporary anxieties and fears surrounding loneliness and sexuality. A homosexual who died from AIDS-related complications, he was persecuted by the government and sought refuge in the Campinas home of writer **Hilda Hilst**. His early short story collections include *Inventário do Irremediável* (1970; Inventory of Irretrievables) and *Pedras de Calcutá* (1977; Stones of Calcutta). His novel *Morangos Mofados* (1982; Musty Strawberries) earned him considerable success and *Triângulo das Águas* (1983; Triangle of the Waters) the **Jabuti Prize**. The topic of AIDS is touched upon with traces of black humor in his unpublished plays *Zona Contaminada* (Contaminated Zone) and *O Homem e a Mancha* (The Man and the Stain). *See also* GAY AND LESBIAN WRITERS AND WRITING; THEATER.

ABREU, CAPISTRANO DE (Brazil, 1853–1927). Historian and critic. He was the author of important studies of the Brazilian colonial era, including *Capítulos de História Colonial* (1907; Chapters of Colonial History) and the posthumous volumes *O Descobrimento do Brasil* (1929; The Discovery of Brazil) and *Caminhos Antigos e Povoamento do Brasil* (1930; Old Roads and Settlement of Brazil).

ABREU, CASIMIRO JOSÉ MARQUES DE (Brazil, 1839–1860). Poet. Author of fewer than 100 poems, Marques de Abreu led a bohemian life in Rio after a brief sojourn in Portugal. Despite an early death from tuberculosis, he became an icon of **romanticism**, thanks to the successful volume *Primaveras* (1859; Springs), on the themes of longing, love, and pessimism. *See also* ASSIS, JOAQUIM MARIA MACHADO DE.

ACADEMIAS. Societies created in colonial Brazil for the study of language, literature, history, and science. Famous ones include Academia Brasílica dos Esquecidos (Bahia, 1724; Brazilian Academy of the Forgotten), Academia dos Felizes (Rio, 1736; Academy of the Felicitous), Academia dos Seletos (Rio, 1752; Academy of the Select), and Academia Brasileira dos Renascidos (Bahia, 1759; Brazilian Academy of the Reborn). The Academia Brasileira de Letras (Rio, 1896; Brazilian Academy of Letters) is a modern heir to this tradition. Among its cofounders are the writers **Joaquim Maria Machado de Assis, Afonso Celso, Henrique Maximiano Coelho Neto**, and **Alberto de Oliveira**, and the critics **Sílvio Romero** and **José Veríssimo Dias de Matos**. In 1977, **Raquel de Queirós** became the first female member, and in 1996, **Nélida Piñon** was elected its first female president. Membership has sometimes been controversial, as in the cases of **João Guimarães Rosa**, perhaps the most respected icon of 20th-century Brazilian literature, who was admitted only three days before his death, and **Paulo Coelho**, a writer of what some deem to be low-brow best sellers, who was elected to the academy in 2002.

ACEVEDO DÍAZ, EDUARDO (Uruguay, 1851–1921). Novelist. After an initial, somewhat unsuccessful, foray into **romanticism** in his first literary undertakings, he turned to the **historical novel** in the style of **realism**, influenced by Sir Walter Scott (1771–1832) and the *Episodios nacionales* (Episodes from National History) of the Spanish novelist Benito Pérez Galdós (1843–1920), and produced a tetralogy concerned with the period of Uruguay's emergence as a nation. The most successful of the four works is the first *Ismael* (1888; Ismael), covering the war with Spain (1808–1811). *Nativa* (1890; Native) and *Grito de Gloria* (1893; Cry of Glory) address the period from 1823 to 1825, which includes part of the occupation of Uruguay by **Brazil** and its liberation by a group of exiles known as the "thirty-three Orientales." The last novel, *Lanza y sable* (1914; Lance and

Saber), is about the years 1834–1838 and internal struggles for power after independence. *See also* RODRÍGUEZ MONEGAL, EMIR.

ACOSTA, DELFINA (Paraguay, 1956–). Poet and short story writer. She has published three collections of poetry—*Todas las voces, mujer. . .* (1986; All the Voices, Woman . . .); *La cruz del colibrí* (1993; The Hummingbird's Cross); and *Romancero de mi pueblo* (1998; Ballads of My People)—as well as *El viaje* (1995; The Journey), a volume of short stories.

ACOSTA, JOSÉ DE (Spain, 1540–1600). Chronicler. A member of the Jesuit Order, he was sent to Lima in 1569 and remained in the Americas until 1587. He traveled extensively and became familiar with parts of the territories now known as **Mexico, Peru, Bolivia,** and **Chile.** In addition to religious writings, he also wrote the **chronicle** *Historia natural y moral de las Indias* (1590; *The Natural and Moral History of the Indies*), which incorporated an earlier work written in Latin, *De natura Novi Orbis* (1588; On the Nature of the New World). The *Historia natural y moral* was widely read in its day and was translated into several languages. It is recognized today as one of the earliest attempts to undertake a systematic understanding of natural phenomena in the Americas.

ACOSTA DE SAMPER, SOLEDAD (Colombia, 1833–1913). Novelist and journalist. Among 19th-century Latin American **women** writers, she was one of the most significant. She founded newspapers and magazines and published a number of books in a variety of genres. Her narratives, written in the style of 19th-century **realism,** tell stories of the everyday lives of ordinary women. *Novelas y cuadros de la vida sur-americana* (1869; Novels and Sketches of South American Life) is a collection of short pieces that also includes two texts originally published separately: *Dolores: cuadros de la vida de una mujer* (1867; Dolores: Scenes from a Woman's Life), about a woman who encounters her long-lost father only to learn that he has leprosy and that she too has contracted the disease, and *Teresa la limeña: páginas de la vida de una peruana* (1869; Teresa from Lima: Pages in the Life of a Peruvian Woman), about the limitations of marriage and other choices in life for a woman who discovers self-fulfillment in writing. *El corazón de la mujer* (1869; The Heart of a Woman) belongs to the same period in Acosta's life and shows the emotional transformations undergone by women from youth to old age. A later work, *Una holandesa en América* (1888; A Dutch Woman in America), documents the return of a woman to Colombia after being raised in Holland. Its uniqueness as a travel narrative lies in the presentation of a journey by a woman through the worlds of women, and its **costumbrismo** reflects a characteristic of Acosta's other writings.

ACUÑA DE FIGUEROA, FRANCISCO (Uruguay, 1791–1862). Poet. Considered one of the originators of Uruguayan literature, he wrote an impressive amount of satirical and burlesque verse and is also known for his celebratory poems, which include the lyrics for the national anthems of Uruguay and **Paraguay**. Among his works are *Malambrunada* (ca. 1829), a comic piece of **epic poetry** narrating a battle between young and old **women** as representatives, respectively, of **romanticism** and classicism; the licentious miscellany *Nomenclatura y apología del carajo* (n.d.; Name and Apology for the Prick); and *Mosaico poético* (1857; Poetic Mosaic), a collection of his shorter verse.

ADÁN, MARTÍN (Peru, 1907–1985). Poet. Adán Martín was the pseudonym of Rafael de la Fuente y Benavides. The influence of the Spanish **avant-garde** and **ultraísmo** is to be found in the striking images and wordplay of his early poetry and in a short novel, *La casa de cartón* (1928; The Cardboard House), which describes a young man's awakening to life and is considered in Peruvian literature as one of the best novels of his generation. At the same time, Adán was drawn to the traditional. *La rosa de la espinela* (1939; The Rose of the Espinela) is a collection of *décimas* or *espinelas* (stanzas of 10 lines of octosyllabic verses), and one of his best-known collections, *Travesía de extramares* (1950; Voyage Beyond the Seas), is a book of sonnets written in strict form while also exploring the limits of the genre. In *Escrito a ciegas* (1961; Blindly Written), he ventured into free verse for the first time, and in *La mano desasida (Canto a Macchu Picchu)* (1964; The Relinquished Hand: A Song to Macchu Picchu) and *La piedra absoluta* (1966; The Absolute Stone), he produced much longer poems than he had been accustomed to write. In *Mi Darío* (1967; My Darío) and *Diario de poeta* (1975; Diary of a Poet), he returned to the sonnet. Much of Adán's verse is profoundly metaphysical, an exploration of the inner self and of the role of poetry as an expression of the poet's form of being.

ADOUM, JORGE ENRIQUE (Ecuador, 1926–2009). Poet, dramatist, and novelist. In whatever genre he chose, he was an experimental, **avant-garde** writer. He was also ardently Marxist and an advocate of the social origin and role of literature. The central theme of much of his work is the invasion and colonization of the Americas, which he denounces defiantly and combattively. It is the theme of his first collection of poetry, *Ecuador amargo* (1949; Bitter Ecuador), and his four-part **epic** *Los cuadernos de la tierra* (1952–1961; Notebooks of the Land), a history of violence in the region of contemporary Ecuador from pre-Hispanic times to the 18th century. Later collections of poetry, such as *Yo me fui con tu nombre por la tierra* (1964; I Left with Your Name Across the Land) and *Prepoemas en postespañol* (1979; Pre-poems in Post-Spanish), are less didactic and place more emphasis on the exploration of language.

Adoum's political stance is equally strong in his **theater**, such as *El sol bajo las patas de los caballos* (1972; *The Sun Trampled Beneath the Horses' Hooves*) and *La subida a los infiernos* (1976; Ascent to Hell), which are, respectively, an attack against conquests of all kinds in all places and an attack against bourgeois suppression of religious and human rights. Aside from his poetry and theater, however, the work by Adoum that has brought him most celebrity is his novel *Entre Marx y una mujer desnuda* (1976; Between Marx and a Naked Woman). It is a complex novel, constructed in concentric circles, featuring an author writing a book about another author contemplating writing a book about yet another author. The novel embodies the customary thematics of Adoum's work and is considered one of the most remarkable examples of the **new novel** in Latin America.

AGUILERA MALTA, DEMETRIO (Ecuador, 1909–1981). Novelist. He is considered one of Ecuador's most important 20th-century writers. His early work, including *Don Goyo* (1933; Don Goyo) and *Canal zone* (1935; Canal Zone), was produced during his association with the **Grupo de Guayaquil**. The realist style of those works also characterized his historical novels, among them *Una cruz en la Sierra Maestra* (1960; A Cross in the Sierra Maestra), on the Cuban Revolution; *La caballeresa del sol* (1964; The Lady of the Sun), on Simón Bolívar's lover Manuela Sáenz; *El Quijote de El Dorado* (1964; The Quixote of El Dorado), on Francisco de Orellana (1500–ca. 1549), the first European to navigate the Amazon; and *Un nuevo mar para el rey* (1965; A New Ocean for the King), on Vasco Núñez de Balboa (1475–1519), the European discoverer of the Pacific Ocean. In contrast to these works, the novel for which Aguilera Malta is best known, *Siete lunas y siete serpientes* (1970; *Seven Serpents and Seven Moons*), departs considerably from the social realism of his earler style. It is set in a jungle town and pits good against evil and tradition against modernity in the style of **magic realism**. A later novel, *El secuestro del general* (1973; Kidnapping the General), belongs to the Spanish American **dictator novel**, but did not achieve the same success. Aguilera Malta also wrote four pieces for the **theater**.

AGUIRRE, ISIDORA (Chile, 1919–). Dramatist. Much of her work is socially committed and written in the manner of **Brechtian theater**, but she has also written in many other styles. *La pérgola de las flores* (1960; The Flowering Pergola) is a muscial comedy. *Los papeleros* (1963; The Paper Pickers) dramatizes the plight of those who survive by scavenging for paper. *Los que van quedando en el camino* (1969; Those Left by the Wayside) also deals with the socially marginalized and earned her a **Casa de las Américas** prize. *Lautaro: epopeya del pueblo mapuche* (1982; Lautaro: Epic of the Mapuche) is a historical play that dramatizes resistance to the Spanish conquest of Chile. Aguirre has also written two novels and is both a writer and illustrator of **children's literature**. *See also* THEATER; WOMEN.

AGUSTÍN, JOSÉ (Mexico, 1944–). Novelist. He was the prime force in the literary movement of the 1960s known in Mexico as **la onda**, or new wave, which professed an affiliation for pop culture and a rebellious attitude toward conventions. His first novel, *La tumba* (1964; The Tomb), written in that vein, expresses the disaffection of youth with the establishment through the theme of the lack of communication between parents and children. Its language was thought to be indecent by some readers and was the source of considerable controversy. His second novel, *De perfil* (1966; In Profile), uses the same kind of uninhibited, and very humorous, language in a fast-paced, coming-of-age novel covering three days in the life of its protagonist. In a later novel, *Ciudades desiertas* (1982; Deserted Cities), Agustín also reacted to the status quo by giving a voice to a new generation of **women**. In *Dos horas de sol* (1994; Two Hours of Sun), he used the format of a journalistic report to denounce discrimination against minorities and the negative consequences of the North American Free Trade Agreement (NAFTA) signed by Canada, the United States, and Mexico. Other novels by Agustín include *Se está haciendo tarde* (1973; It's Getting Late), *El rock de la cárcel* (1985; Jailhouse Rock), and *La miel derramada* (1992; Spilt Honey).

AGUSTINI, DELMIRA (Uruguay, 1886–1914). Poet. She wrote in the style of **modernismo**, although her relative isolation in Uruguay set her apart from the major figures of the time. Three collections of poetry were published during her lifetime: *El libro blanco (Frágil)* (1907; The White Book: Fragile), *Cantos de la mañana* (1910; Songs of the Morning), and *Los cálices vacíos* (1913; Empty Chalices). Two more appeared posthumously: *Los astros del abismo* (1924; The Stars of the Abyss) and *El Rosario de Eros* (1924; Eros's Rosary). She wrote personal, intimate verses. Her erotic themes, developed in part in relation to the writings of Spanish 16th-century mystics, often attracted more attention to her than to her work and resulted in a superficial criticism of her writing, both in her lifetime and after, which her death, at the age of 28 and at the hands of her estranged husband, did little to dispel. *See also* MARTÍNEZ MORENO, CARLOS; VAZ FERREIRA, MARÍA EUGENIA; WOMEN.

AIRA, CÉSAR (Argentina, 1949–). Novelist, short story writer, essayist. Although he has had limited public recognition, especially outside Argentina, he is considered one of his country's most important contemporary writers. He is the author of more than 50 books. Most are works of fiction, but he has also published essays, notably *Copi* (1991; Copi), on the Franco-Argentinean author Raúl Damonte

Botana (1939–1987), and *Alejandra Pizarnik* (1998; Alejandra Pizarnik), a study of the Argentinean poet. He is also the author of *Diccionario de autores latinoamericanos* (2001; Dictionary of Latin American Authors).

The content of Aira's fiction is varied. He has written on historical themes in *Ema, la cautiva* (1981; Emma the Captive), a spoof of 19th-century captive literature, such as **Esteban Echeverría**'s *La cautiva*, *La liebre* (1991; *The Hare*), and *Un episodio en la vida de un pintor viajero* (2000; *An Episode in the Life of a Landscape Painter*). His hometown, Coronel Pringles in Buenos Aires province, figures in works like *Como me hice monja* (1993; *How I Became a Nun*) and *Las curas milagrosas del doctor Aira* (2007; The Miraculous Cures of Dr. Aira). Other novels, *El sueño* (1998; The Dream) and *La villa* (The Slum), are set in the district of Flores in Buenos Aires.

Many of Aira's novels are short. Humor plays an important role in his fiction, much of it not easily classified because he frequently crosses boundaries between genres. His plots often begin simply but become extraordinarily complicated and may remain open-ended or have very extravagant endings, which gives his writing the quality of a particular kind of **magic realism**. See also LAMBORGHINI, OSVALDO.

AIRES RAMOS DA SILVA DE EÇA, MATIAS (Brazil, 1705–1763). Essayist and moral philosopher. He was born in Brazil but emigrated young to Portugal, where he was educated. Dedicated to the king of Portugal, his didactic *Reflexões sobre a Vaidade dos Homens* (1752; Reflections on the Vanity of Men) allies him with French moralists such as Michel de Montaigne (1533–1592), Blaise Pascal (1623–1662), and François de la Rochefoucauld (1613–1680). Other works include *Lettres bohèmiennes* (1759; Bohemian Letters) and *Problema de Arquitetura Civil* (1770; Problem of Civil Architecture).

AJZENBERG, BERNARDO (Brazil, 1959–). Journalist and novelist. His urban fiction portrays uprooted characters entangled in intimate dramas, such as *Variações Goldman* (1998; The Goldman Variations), set in the overwhelming environment of São Paulo, and *A Gaiola de Faraday* (2001; Faraday's Cage), the story of an unemployed civil engineer who abandons his family in a self-imposed exile.

ALBERDI, JUAN BAUTISTA (Argentina, 1810–1884). Essayist. He was a prominent 19th-century intellectual and is remembered mainly for political rather than literary writings. His *Bases y puntos de partida para la organización de la República Argentina* (1852; Foundations and Beginnings for Organizing the Argentinean Republic) was highly influential in Argentina and elsewhere in Latin America.

ALEGRÍA, ALONSO (Peru, 1940–). Dramatist. He was the director of the Teatro Nacional Popular in Lima from its founding in 1971 until 1978. Alegría's first play was *Remigio el huaquero* (1965; *The Buried Palace*), the story of a man who makes his living finding and selling artefacts mainly from pre-Hispanic graves. His best-known work, however, is *El cruce sobre el Niágara* (1974; Crossing Niagara), about the Frenchman known as Charles Blondin (1824–1897), who was celebrated for his crossings over Niagara Falls on a tightrope. Other plays by Alegría include *El color de Chambalén* (1981; The Color of Chamberlain) and *Daniela Frank* (1982; Daniela Frank). *See also* THEATER.

ALEGRÍA, CIRO (Peru, 1909–1967). Novelist. His involvement in Peru in the Alianza Popular Revolucionaria Americana (APRA; American Popular Revolutionary Alliance) resulted in periods of imprisonment and exile. He wrote three novels, which show the influence of his politics and the teachings of two prominent Peruvians, **José Carlos Mariátegui** and **Víctor Raúl Haya de la Torre**. *La serpiente de oro* (1933; *The Golden Serpent*), the first of the novels, is an episodic work constructed from scenes in the lives of communities living on the banks of the Marañón River. In *Los perros hambrientos* (1935; The Hungry Dogs), his second novel, Alegría focused on the poverty and violence of rural life using the metaphor of a pack of sheep dogs. Although both novels were successful, the author's fame rests above all on his third novel, *El mundo es ancho y ajeno* (1941; *Broad and Alien Is the World*), a narrative about the trials of an Indian community in the Peruvian highlands. It explores the community's history, culture, and connections to the land and the sufferings caused by persecution and encroachment from outsiders. The novel is one of the main works of Peruvian **indigenismo** and received a prize sponsored by the U.S. publisher Farrar & Rinehart. Aside from a collection of short stories *Duelo de caballeros* (1963; A Duel of Gentlemen), Alegría published no other books during his lifetime, but three books appeared posthumously: a portrait of **Gabriela Mistral,** a memoir of the Cuban Revolution (1973), and an unfinished novel, *Lázaro* (1973; Lazarus). See also LÓPEZ AL-BÚJAR, ENRIQUE.

ALEGRÍA, CLARIBEL (El Salvador, 1924–). Poet, novelist, short story writer. She was born Clara Isabel Alegría Vides in **Nicaragua,** but grew up in El Salvador, where she is a citizen. Much of her writing emerges from her social and political commitment to Nicaragua. Some of it was written in collaboration with her husband, Darwin Flakoll, who has also been her translator. Her prose writings include *Cenizas de Izalco* (1966; *Ashes of Izalco*), a story of the genocide of the Izalco Indians; *Album familiar* (1982; *Family Album: Three Novellas*); *No me agarran viva: la mujer salvadoreña en lucha* (1983; *They Won't Take Me Alive: Salvadoran Women in Struggle for National Liberation*), a **testimonio** based on the life of a *guerrillera*; *Para romper el silencio* (1984; To Break the Silence), also a testimonio, based on interviews with Salvadoran prisoners; and *Despierta, mi bien, despierta* (1986; Awake, My Love, Awake). *Luisa en el país de la realidad* (1987; *Luisa in Realityland*) is an autobiographical work that combines verse and prose.

Alegría has also written **children's literature** and has published more than 15 books of poetry since 1948. Her earlier collections, *Anillo de silencio* (1948; Ring of Silence), *Vigilias* (1953; Vigils), *Anuario* (1955; Yearbook), and *Huésped de mi tiempo* (1961; Guest of My Time), are lyrical, introverted, and sensuous. Some of her later collections show more of her political commitment. These include *Sobrevivo* (1978; I Survive), which won a **Casa de las Américas** prize; *La mujer del río Sumpul* (1987; *Women of the River*); *Fuga de canto grande* (1992; *Fugues*); and *Umbrales* (1996; Thresholds). *See also* WOMEN.

ALEGRÍA, FERNANDO (Chile, 1918–2005). Poet, novelist, and critic. He lived much of his life in the United States and was the author of over two dozen books, including several significant works of criticism. Among his novels, his first, *Recabarren* (1938; Recabarren), is based on the life of the Chilean politician Luis Emilio Recabarren. *Caballo de copas* (1957; *My Horse González*) is a humorous narrative about a Chilean jockey who emigrates to the United States. *Coral de guerra* (1979; War Chorale) and *El paso de gansos* (1980; Goose Step) are both critiques of the military regime in Chile. His last work of fiction was *La rebelión de los placeres* (1990; The Revolt of the Pleasures).

ALENCAR, JOSÉ DE (Brazil, 1829–1877). Novelist, journalist, dramatist, essayist, and poet. A prominent figure of Brazilian **romanticism**, Alencar was born and raised in Ceará, Northeastern Brazil, where his father participated in revolutionary struggles. He studied law at São Paulo and Recife before settling in Rio to work as a journalist for major dailies and publishing his early *Cartas sobre "A Confederação dos Tamoios"* (1856; Letters on "The Tamoio Confederation"), critical articles on a poem by **Domingos José Gonçalves de Magalhães** that launched a debate on the poet and the role of indigenous people in Brazilian culture. Alencar's seminal works inspired by **indianismo** include the novels *O Guarani* (1857; The Guaraní), *Iracema* (1865; *Iracema*), and *Ubirajara* (1874, Ubirajara), and his **epic poem** *Os Filhos de Tupã* (written 1863; published 1910–1911; The Sons of Tupã).

His vast narrative oeuvre included the serial novels *Cinco Minutos* (1856; Five Minutes) and *A Viuvinha* (1860; The Little Widow); urban novels dealing with social issues, *Senhora* (1875; *Senhora: Profile of a Woman*) and *Encarnação* (1893; Encarnação); the regional novels *O Gaúcho* (1870; The Gaucho), *O Tronco do Ipê* (1871; The Trunk of the Catalpa), *Til* (1872; Tide), and *O Sertanejo* (1875; The Backlander); and the **historical novels** *As Minas de Prata* (1862/1865–1866; The Silver Mines), *Alfarrábios: Crônicas dos Tempos Coloniais* (1873; Old Books: Chronicles of Colonial Times), and *A Guerra dos Mascates* (1873–1874; The War of the Street Peddlers). His writing for the **theater** includes one historical play, *O Jesuíta* (1875; The Jesuit), and several comedies and dramas that were staged in Rio de Janeiro: *O Demônio Familiar* (1857; The Familiar Demon), *O Rio de Janeiro: Verso e Reverso* (1857; Rio de

Janeiro: Back and Front), *As Asas de um Anjo* (1860; The Wings of an Angel), and *Mãe* (1862; Mother).

Alongside his literary career, Alencar had an active political life as regional representative for Ceará and minister of justice. A staunch opponent of Emperor Pedro II (1840–1889), his critiques include *Ao Imperador: Cartas Políticas de Erasmo* (1865; To the Emperor: Political Letters by Erasmus) and *Ao Emperador: Novas Cartas Políticas de Erasmo* (1866; To the Emperor: New Political Letters by Erasmus). Suffering from tuberculosis, Alencar traveled to Europe in 1877 to attempt a cure, but died that same year. His autobiography is entitled *Como e Porque Sou Romancista* (1893; How and Why I Became a Novelist). Alencar's wide-ranging oeuvre produced the most complete portrait of Brazil available at the time and laid the literary groundwork for the creation of Brazil's cultural identity. *See also* ALVES, ANTÔNIO FREDERICO DE CASTRO.

ALLENDE, ISABEL (Chile, 1942–). Novelist. She is a widely translated author of **best sellers**, noted for her storytelling, romanticism, and rich language. She has lived outside her native Chile since 1975, mainly in the United States. Her literary popularity began with *La casa de los espíritus* (1982; *The House of the Spirits*), a work with elements of **magic realism** telling the history of Chile through a line of female characters, drawing on her own life and the political and cultural figures of her country. It has been compared with *Cien años de soledad* (*One Hundred Years of Solitude*) by **Gabriel García Márquez**, not always very favorably. Her second novel, *De amor y de sombras* (1984; *Of Love and Shadows*), deals with Chile after the overthrow of Salvador Allende's government in 1973.

Since then, she has published over a dozen books. *Eva Luna* (1987) and *Cuentos de Eva Luna* (1989; *The Stories of Eva Luna*) are both set in the tropics. *Paula* (1994; *Paula*), *Afrodita: cuentos, recetas y otros afrodisíacos* (1997; *Aphrodite: A Memoir of the Senses*), and *La suma de los días* (2007; *The Sum of Our Days*) are all memoirs, the first about her life in Santiago written as a letter to her daughter, who was dying of porphyria. Allende has also set novels in California, where she now lives, including *El plan infinito* (1991; *The Infinite Plan*), *Hija de la fortuna* (1999; *Daughter of Fortune*), and *Retrato en sepia* (2000; *Portrait in Sepia*), the last about links between California and Chile in the 19th and early 20th centuries. Among her more recent novels are *Zorro* (2005; *Zorro*), about the legendary comic-book and Hollywood film hero, and *Inés del alma mía* (2006; *Inés of My Soul*), based on the life of **Sor Juana Inés de la Cruz.**

Allende's literary output also includes books such as *El reino del dragón de oro* (2004; *Kingdom of the Golden Dragon*) and *El bosque de los pigmeos* (2005; *Forest of the Pygmies*), both works of **children's literature,** a genre she had already cultivated in Santiago. *See also* WOMEN.

ALMEIDA, GUILHERME DE (Brazil, 1890–1969). Journalist, essayist, poet, and translator. Almeida received his law degree in 1912 in São Paulo, where he wrote for major daily newspapers such as *O Estado de São Paulo*. He participated in the **Week of Modern Art** in 1922 alongside **Mário de Andrade,** who praised his early poetry, such as *Nós* (1917; Us), *Messidor* (1919; Messidor), *A Dança das Horas* (1919; The Dance of the Hours), and *Livro de Horas de Sóror Dolorosa* (1920; The Book of Hours of Sister Dolorous). *A Frauta que Eu Perdi* (1924; The Flute I Lost) and *A Flor que Foi um Homem: Narciso* (1925; The Flower That Was a Man: Narcissus) followed the models of **parnassianism** and **symbolism,** privileging the sonnet and sensual images or images based on Greek themes. They gave way to *Meu* (1925; Mine) and *Raça* (1925; Race), modernist works inspired by nationalism. But Almeida's affiliation with **Brazilian modernism** was temporary. His later poetry, *Você* (1931; You) and *Acaso* (1939; Chance), displays his gift for versification and traditional forms and themes. *Acalanto de Bartira* (1954; Bartira's Lullaby) was written in praise of the city of São Paulo, and *Camoniana* (1956; Camoniana) is a eulogy of the Portuguese renaissance poet Luís de Camões (1524–1580). He also wrote haikus and translated Sophocles, Rabindranath Tagore (1861–1941), and Charles Baudelaire (1821–1867).

ALMEIDA, JÚLIA LOPES DE (Brazil, 1862–1934). Dramatist, journalist, novelist, and short story writer. Married to the Portuguese writer Felinto de Almeida, Lopes de Almeida had three children who were also writers and devoted 40 years of her life to a literary career, writing extensively for newspapers in São Paulo and Rio, occasionally on women's issues. Her major novels in the style of **realism,**

A Família Medeiros (1892; The Medeiros Family) and *A Falência* (1901; The Bankruptcy), and the book of short stories, *Ânsia Eterna* (1903; Eternal Longing), depict the mores of the period and her support for abolitionism. She also wrote plays and didactic works. *See also* WOMEN.

ALMEIDA, MANUEL ANTÔNIO DE (Brazil, 1831–1861). Journalist and novelist. Orphaned at age 10, Almeida grew up in a family of modest means. Early training in drawing was followed by an interest in medicine. While still a student, he began to collaborate with Rio's daily newspaper *Correio Mercantil*, where he published his serial novel, *Memórias de um Sargento de Milícias* (1853–1855; *Memoirs of a Militia Sergeant*), under the pseudonym "Um Brasileiro" ("A Brazilian"). Despite his lack of literary pretensions, this memoir-like social novel of customs in the style of **realism** became a landmark document of life in Rio de Janeiro in the early days of the 19th century through its depiction of types and its use of a personal narrative voice in the manner of the **picaresque novel**. This literary line would be followed by **Joaquim Maria Machado de Assis**, who was Almeida's apprentice typographer at the National Press. Almeida had a brief stint in politics, but died young during a pre-electoral trip when his ship capsized off the coast of Rio de Janeiro. *See also* REBELO, MARQUES.

ALTAMIRANO, IGNACIO MANUEL (Mexico, 1834–1893). Novelist. He was of indigenous heritage and a prominent national figure in literature, education, and journalism during the period following the French occupation of Mexico (1864–1867). His work belongs to a variety of genres: journalism, poetry, **costumbrismo** sketches, and short narratives, of which *La navidad en las montañas* (1871; Christmas in the Mountains) is the most popular. Altamirano's two best-known novels are *Clemencia* (1869; *Clemencia*), a sentimental narrative set in the time of the French occupation, and the **historical novel** *El Zarco* (completed 1889, published 1901; *El Zarco the Blue-eyed Bandit*). Both are didactic novels, conforming to the characteristics of **romanticism**, and served to promote ethical conduct and a sense of Mexican nationalism. *See also* VALLE, RAFAEL HELIODORO.

ALVARADO TEZOZOMOC, HERNANDO (Mexico, active 1598– early 17th century). Chronicler. His **chronicle** *Crónica mexicana* (first published in 1878; Mexican Chronicle) tells the story of the Aztec nobility from its mythic origins to the Spanish conquest from an indigenous perspective.

ALVARENGA, MANUEL INÁCIO DA SILVA (Brazil, 1749– 1814). Journalist and poet. Son of a mulatto and an unknown mother, Silva Alvarenga studied in Rio and Coimbra (Portugal), where he received a degree in canon law. His satiric poem *O Desertor* (1774; The Deserter) justified university reforms introduced by the Portuguese minister at the time, the Marquis of Pombal (1750–1777). Back in Brazil, he worked as a lawyer and professor of poetics and rhetoric and was jailed between 1795 and 1797 for his sympathies with French revolutionary ideas. *Glaura: Poemas Eróticos* (1799; Glaura: Erotic Poems) explores bucolic themes in rondo and madrigal poetic forms using names of Brazilian trees, which, according to **Ronald de Carvalho,** makes Silva Alvarenga "the link between **Arcadians** and **Romantics.**"

ÁLVAREZ, JOSÉ (Argentina, 1858–1903). Essayist and journalist. A tireless contributor to the magazines and newspapers of his day, he was more popularly known as Fray Mocho, the pseudonym with which he signed his essays on Buenos Aires written in the style of **costumbrismo.** He also wrote *Vida de los ladrones célebres de Buenos Aires y sus maneras de robar* (1887; Lives of Celebrated Thieves of Buenos Aires and How They Stole); *Memorias de un vigilante* (1897; Memoirs of a Constable), derived from his experiences as an administrator working for the police service; and an imaginary account of a journey on a whaler, *En el mar austral: croquis fueguinos* (1898; In the Southern Sea: Fuegian Sketches). He was the first editor of the magazine *Caras y caretas,* founded in 1898, one of Argentina's significant news magazines of the first half of the 20th century. An anthology of his writings, *Cuentos de Fray Mocho* (1906; Tales by Fray Mocho), has been reprinted many times.

ÁLVAREZ GARDEAZÁBAL, GUSTAVO (Colombia, 1945–). Novelist. His most celebrated novel, *Cóndores no entierran todos los* *días* (1971; Condors Are Not Buried Every Day), is about **la violencia** and was the basis for a 1984 film. Other novels include *La tara del papa* (1971; The Pope's Phobia), *El bazar de los idiotas* (1947; *Bazar of Idiots*), *Los míos* (1981; My People), *El último gamonal* (1987; The Last Chief), *Los sordos ya no hablan* (1991; The Deaf No Longer Speak), and *La resurrección de los malditos* (2007; Resurrection of the Accursed). In addition to Colombia's history of violence, he criticizes society, religion, and corruption. He is also a newspaper and radio commentator and has held political office, as mayor of Tuluá and as governor for Valle del Cauca. He was imprisoned in 1999 for involvement with drug traffickers in a case that many believe was politically motivated.

ALVES, ANTÔNIO FREDERICO DE CASTRO (Brazil, 1847–1871). Dramatist and poet. The son of a doctor, Castro Alves studied law in Recife, where he came in contact with liberal abolitionists and fell in love with the actress Eugênia Câmara, who performed in the play he wrote for her, *Gonzaga ou a Revolução de Minas* (1875; Gonzaga or The Minas Revolution). He moved to São Paulo, where he met important young academics like **Joaquim Nabuco** and Rui Barbosa, and during a visit to Rio his poetic talent impressed **Joaquim Maria Machado de Assis** and **José de Alencar**. After his breakup with Câmara, Castro Alves took up hunting and accidentally shot himself in the foot, which had to be amputated, aggravating his childhood tuberculosis. Retiring to convalesce in the interior of Bahia, he devoted his energies to the publication of *Espumas Flutuantes* (1870; Floating Foams), a poetry volume influenced by Alphonse de Lamartine (1790–1869) and Victor Hugo (1802–1885). He is also known as a member of the literary school of *condoreirismo*, which emphasized a poetry of egalitarianism and social concerns. He died before he could publish several important volumes of antislavery poetry—*Vozes d'África: Navio Negreiro* (1880; Voices from Africa: The Slave Ship), *Os Escravos* (1883; The Slaves), and *A Cachoeira de Paulo Afonso* (1876; The Paulo Afonso Falls)—which, significantly, appeared before the abolition of slavery in Brazil in 1888. For decades, much of his reputation was due to word of mouth, as many of his works only saw the light of day 50 years after his death. *See also* ROMERO, SÍLVIO; THEATER.

ALVIM, FRANCISCO (Brazil, 1938–). Poet. A career diplomat, Alvim has lived in Paris, Barcelona, Rotterdam, and **Costa Rica**. Associated with post-**avant-garde** poetry and later with **poesia marginal**, Alvim's early works, *Sol dos Cegos* (1968; Sun of the Blind), *Passatempo* (1974; Pastime), and *Lago, Montanha* (1981; Lake, Mountain), alternate inner meditation with external observation. *Elefante* (2000; Elephant) uses a ready-made aesthetic, collecting snippets of everyday speech. He earned the **Jabuti Prize** twice, in 1981 and in 1988, for his *Poesias Reunidas, 1968/1988* (1988; Collected Poems).

AMADO, JORGE (Brazil, 1912–2001). Biographer, dramatist, novelist, journalist, and poet. One of Brazil's most translated and internationally known writers, Amado was born on a farm in the interior of Bahia. He studied in Rio and Salvador, before settling there as a journalist in the 1920s and becoming acquainted with the bohemian modernist intelligentsia. After an early novel, *O País do Carnaval* (1931; The Country of Carnival), Amado traveled extensively in the countryside of Bahia and Sergipe, the setting of his rural and urban proletarian works, *Cacau* (1933; Cacao), *Suor* (1934; Sweat), *Jubiabá* (1935; *Jubiabá*), *Mar Morto* (1936; *Sea of Death*), and *Capitães da Areia* (1937; *Captains of the Sands*), the latter three lyrical portrayals of quarrelling sailors and love.

In the 1930s, Amado toured Latin America and became a politically committed writer, collaborating with **José Lins do Rego Cavalcanti, Graciliano Ramos, Aníbal Machado**, and **Raquel de Queirós** on *Brandão entre o Mar e o Amor* (1942; Brandão Between the Sea and Love). Opposed to the Estado Novo authoritarian regime (1937–1945) of President Getúlio Vargas, he was jailed briefly in 1942, and in 1945 joined the Communist Party. During World War II, Amado wrote propaganda novels such as *Terras do Sem Fim* (1943; *The Violent Lands*), *São Jorge dos Ilhéus* (1944; São Jorge of Ilhéus), and *Seara Vermelha* (1946; Red Harvest), and biographies such as *ABC de Castro Alves* (1941; ABC of Castro Alves) and *Vida de Luís Carlos Prestes, O Cavaleiro da Esperança* (1942; Life of Luis Carlos Prestes, Knight of Hope). After the war, a long sojourn in Europe and Asia (1948–1952) inspired his travel memoir *Os Subterrâneos da Liberdade* (1954; The Freedom Underground).

Amado's later novels chronicle life in the provinces, particularly through the invention of free-spirited, sexually active **women** characters who emblematize the Brazilian people: *Gabriela, Cravo e Canela* (1958; *Gabriela, Clove and Cinnamon*), *Dona Flor e Seus Dois Maridos* (1966; *Dona Flor and Her Two Husbands*), *Tenda dos Milagres* (1969; *Tent of Miracles*), *Tereza Batista, Cansada de Guerra* (1969; *Tereza Batista: Home from the Wars*), and *Tieta do Agreste, Pastora de Cabras* (1977; *Tieta, the Goat Girl*). *Gabriela, Dona Flor,* and *Tieta do Agreste* have all been adapted for the screen. Some of these novels became **best sellers** and earned him considerable success—prizes and countless translations and reprints—as well as some notoriety; because of threats due to the alleged morally offensive content of his novels, he was unable to visit Ilhéus for years.

Os Velhos Marinheiros (1961; *Home Is the Sailor*)—a volume that contains two novellas, *A Morte e a Morte de Quincas Berro D'Água* (*The Two Deaths of Quincas Wateryell*) and *A Completa Verdade sobre as Discutidas Aventuras do Comandante Vasco Moscoso de Aragão, Capitão de Longo Curso* (*The Whole Truth Concerning the Redoubtful Adventures of Captain Vasco Moscoso de Aragão, Master Mariner*)—and Os *Pastores da Noite* (1964; *Shepherds of the Night)* are somewhat different, shorter narratives with interconnected characters. Subsequent novels, *Farda, Fardão, Camisola de Dormir* (1979; *Pen, Sword, Camisole*) and *Tocaia Grande: A Face Obscura* (1984; *Showdown*), also had great commercial success.

The author's last books include *O Sumiço da Santa* (1988; *The War of the Saints*), *A Descoberta da América pelos Turcos* (1994; How the Turks Discovered America), the memoir *Navegação de Cabotagem* (1992; Coastal Navigation), and *O Compadre de Ogum* (1995; Companion of the God Ogum). He also wrote the travel guide *Bahia de Todos os Santos* (1945; Bahia de Todos os Santos). A writer of great popular appeal, Amado also received numerous homages from samba schools and Afro-Brazilian religious communities as well as academic honors. A foundation was established in 1987 to promote his literature and Bahian culture in general. Although he was often a **Nobel Prize** hopeful, he died without receiving it. *See also* RIBEIRO, JOÃO UBALDO.

AMÂNCIO, MOACIR (Brazil, 1949–). Journalist, essayist, and poet. For many years the head of the culture section of the newspaper *O Estado de São Paulo*, Amâncio's early fiction includes *Chame o Ladrão* (1978; Call the Thief) and *O Riso do Dragão* (1981; The Dragon's Laughter). Better known as a poet, he has published *Do Objeto Útil* (1993; The Useful Object), *Figuras na Sala* (Figures in the Room, 1995), *O Olho do Canário* (1998; The Canary's Eye), *Colores Siguientes* (1999; Following Colors), *Contar a Romã* (2001; Counting the Pomegranate), *Óbvio* (2004; Obvious), and *Ata* (2007; Ata), his collected poems. Amâncio employs a synthetic and elliptic style and has also written poems in Spanish, English, and Hebrew.

AMBROGI, ARTURO (El Salvador, 1875–1936). Short story writer and chronicler. Although at first drawn to **modernismo**, he turned more to the **realism** of **costumbrismo** and **naturalism** as he matured and published many of his sketches of Salvadoran life in *El libro del trópico* (1907; Book of the Tropics) and *El segundo libro del trópico* (1916; Second Book of the Tropics). Other books, some of which also reflect his travels in Asia, include *Cuentos y fantasías* (1895; Tales and Fantasies), *Máscaras, manchas y sensaciones* (1901; Masks, Blots, and impressions), *Sensaciones del Japón y de la China* (1915; Impressions of Japan and China), and *El jetón* (1936; Thick-lips).

AMORIM, ENRIQUE (Uruguay, 1900–1960). Novelist, short story writer, and poet. Although he published 10 books of poetry, his literary reputation rests primarily on his fiction, which consists of 15 novels and 14 collections of short stories. His fiction belongs mainly in the tradition of **realism**, but he often gives a new twist to established tradition. In an early collection of short stories, *Horizontes y bocacalles* (1926; Horizons and Street Entrances), he introduced the urban and rural worlds that would occupy most of his fiction. In *La carreta* (1932; The Wagon), he brought sexuality into the rural realist novel through a story about traveling prostitutes. In *El paisano Aguilar* (1934; The Compatriot Aguilar), his contribution to **gaucho literature**, he attempted a new description of the gaucho, and he wrote about the conflicts between landowners and immigrants in *El caballo y su sombra* (1941; *The Horse and His Shadow*). Amorim wrote two works of **crime fiction**, *El asesino desvelado* (1945; The Murderer Unveiled) and *Feria de farsantes* (1952; Fair of Frauds), both published in a series edited by **Jorge Luis Borges** and **Adolfo Bioy Casares**. His last novels include *Corral abierto* (1956; Open Corral), about youth in the collar of shantytowns surrounding Montevideo and cities of the interior; *Los montaraces* (1957; The Wild Men), on rural themes; and *La desembocadura* (1958; The Culmination), a retrospective on the first half of the 20th century.

ANCHIETA, JOSÉ DE (Brazil, 1534–1597). Chronicler, dramatist, and poet. Often deemed Brazil's first writer, Anchieta was born in the Canary Islands but arrived as a Jesuit novice in Brazil, where he founded schools and taught Latin. Captured by the Tamoyo Indians, in 1563 he composed the Latin poem *De Beata Virgine Dei Matre Maria* (1663; Of the Blessed Virgin Mary, Mother of God). He catechized and served as conflict negotiator for various native peoples, whose languages he learned. He authored **chronicles**, prayers, and religious plays, or **autos**, in Portuguese, Tupi, and Spanish, featuring Indian myths and rituals. Other works include *Arte de Gramática da Língua Mais Usada na Costa do Brasil* (1595; Grammar of the Most Used Language on the Coast of Brazil); *Cartas, Informações, Fragmentos Históricos e Sermões* (1933; Letters, Reports, Historical Fragments, and Sermons); and the **epic poem** *De Rebus Gestis Mendi de Saa* (1958; History of Mem de Sá), on the Portuguese conquest of Brazil. *See also* THEATER.

ANCONA, ELIGIO (Mexico, 1836–1893). Novelist. He was a prominent politician of the Yucatán whose literary reputation derives from a half dozen **historical novels** set mainly in the colonial period. Among them are *Los mártires de Anáhuac* (1870; Martyrs of Anahuac), concerned with the period of the Spanish conquest (1519–1521); *El filibustero* (1866; The Buccaneer), dealing with political events in the Yucatán in the late 17th and early 18th centuries, notwithstanding its apparently nautical title; and *Memorias de un alférez* (1904; Memoirs of an Army Lieutenant), a novel of love and intrigue set principally in the 1820s, the early years of Mexican independence. Ancona also wrote *Historia de Yucatán* (4 vols., 1878–1880; History of the Yucatan).

ANDERSON IMBERT, ENRIQUE (Argentina, 1910–2000). Novelist, short story writer, and critic. He emigrated to the United States in 1946, where he became a prominent university professor and critic of Spanish American literature. He wrote a large number of critical studies, including books on **Roberto Jorge Payró, Domingo Faustino Sarmiento**, and **Rubén Darío**. One of his most successful publications was *Historia de la literatura hispanoamericana* (2 vols., 1954–1961; *Spanish-American Literature: A History*), which became a standard reference work and was published in several editions. His literary work consists of three novels and seven collections of short stories. Many of the latter are written in the mode of **fantastic literature**, and some of the best examples of his writing are contained in the collection *La locura juega al ajedrez* (1971; Madness Plays Chess).

ANDRADE, CARLOS DRUMMOND DE (Brazil, 1902–1987). Journalist, poet, and short story writer. Considered one of Brazil's greatest poets, Drummond grew up on a farm. He received a degree in pharmacy and taught geography for a while in Belo Horizonte, where he founded the **journal** *A Revista* in 1925, the main organ of **Brazilian modernism** in Minas Gerais. In 1924 he met the movement's leading exponents, **Mário de Andrade**, Tarsila do Amaral, and **Oswald de Andrade**, who published Drummond's famous poem "No Meio do Caminho" ("In the Middle of the Road") in *Revista de Antropofagia* (Cannibal Review) in 1928. His first book of poetry, *Alguma Poesia* (1930; Some Poetry), attempted to record everyday experience in a pure way, at times in a tone of ironic self-deprecation.

Drummond moved to Rio in 1933, where he wrote for dailies and served in the Ministry of Public Education and Health, and later as director of the National Historical and Artistic Heritage Service of Brazil. *Brejo das Almas* (1934; Morass of Souls), his second book of poetry, emphasized humor and turned away from the observation of the outside world to more pessimistic meditations on the lack of meaning and the poet's powerlessness. The devastation of World War II inspired *Sentimento do Mundo* (1940; Feeling of the World), which portrays life's pain and a sense of solidarity with others, feelings that would be accentuated in *José* (1942; Joseph) and the politically committed *A Rosa do Povo* (1945; The Rose of the People), albeit with more hope in a better world. At this time, Drummond briefly wrote for the Communist paper *Tribuna Popular*. His work before 1942 was little known, until *Poesias* (1942; Poems) reached a wider audience.

A departure from strictly political poetry is seen in *Novos Poemas* (1948; New Poems) and *Claro Enigma* (1951; Clear Enigma), which focus more on a poetic search for the real, and, notably, in "A Máquina do Mundo" ("World Machine"), an ambitious metaphysical poem on the search for knowledge that references the renaissance epic *The Lusiads* (1572) by Luis de Camões (1524–1580). An edition of selected poems also appeared in Spanish in 1951, and since then he has been published in English, French, Italian, German, Swedish, Czech, and other languages. Drummond translated works by François Mauriac (1885–1970), Pierre Choderlos de Laclos (1741–1803), Marcel Proust (1871–1922), Honoré de Balzac (1799–1850), and Federico García Lorca (1898–1936), among others.

A Vida Passada a Limpo (1959; Clean Draft of Life) and *Lição de Coisas* (1962; Lesson of Things) display Drummond's forays into the object-poem and other formal and semantic experimentation. His collected poems in *Fazendeiro do Ar e Poesia até Agora* (1954; Farmer of the Clouds and Poetry Until Now) sealed his reputation as one of Brazil's foremost modernist poets. In addition, he reprinted his works in three volumes: *Reunião* (1969; Collected Poems), *Nova Reunião* (1983; New Collected Poems), and *Obra Completa* (1967; Complete Works). Later poetry books, some inspired by childhood reminiscences and others by meditations on poetry, include *Boitempo* (1968; Oxtime), *As Impurezas do Branco* (1973; The Impurities of White), *Menino Antigo* (1973; Oldtime Boy), *Discurso de Primavera* (1977; Springtime Address), *Esquecer para Lembrar* (1979; To Remember in Order to Forget), *A Paixão Medida* (1980; A Passion for Measure), *Corpo* (1984; Body), and *Amar se Aprende Amando* (1985; Love Is Learned by Loving).

As a prose writer, Drummond published brief literary essays and short stories: *Confissões de Minas* (1944; Minas Confessions), *Contos de Aprendiz* (1951; Tales from an Apprentice), *Passeios na Ilha* (1952; Island Promenades), *Fala, Amendoeira* (1957; Speak, Peanut Tree), *Contos Plausíveis* (1981; Plausible Stories), *Boca de Luar* (1984; Moonlight Mouth), and *O Observador no Escritório* (1985;

The Observer in His Study). A collection of his erotic poetry, *O Amor Natural* (1992; Love au Naturel), was published posthumously. *See also* ANTROPOFAGIA; AZEVEDO, CARLITO; GUIMARÃES, JÚLIO CASTAÑON; MACHADO, ANÍBAL; PRADO, ADÉLIA; SABINO, FERNANDO.

ANDRADE, JOSÉ OSWALD DE SOUSA (Brazil, 1890–1954). Dramatist, essayist, novelist, and poet. Perhaps the most revolutionary figure of **Brazilian modernism**, Andrade was born into a well-to-do, land-owning family from São Paulo. In 1912 he traveled to Europe for the first time, where he came into contact with European **avant-garde** trends. He graduated with a law degree in 1917, the same year he met **Mário de Andrade**, another seminal figure of the modernist movement, with whom he participated in the 1922 **Week of Modern Art**. That year he published the first novel in *A Trilogia do Exílio* (1922; Trilogy of Exile), *Os Condenados* (1922; The Damned), later completed by *A Estrela de Absinto* (1927; The Absinthe Star) and *A Escada Vermelha* (1934; The Red Staircase).

During this period, he wrote for the dailies *Jornal do Comércio* and *Correio Paulistano* and began publishing in literary magazines such as *O Pirralho*, *A Cigarra*, *Papel e Tinta*, and *Klaxon*. For a year, in 1923, Andrade settled with the painter Tarsila do Amaral in Paris, where he also wrote and published his first literary works in French and met major European avant-garde figures, including the Swiss poet Blaise Cendrars (1887–1961), who visited the couple in Brazil. In 1926–1929, he traveled to the Middle East and several times to Europe. He married Tarsila do Amaral in 1926; the couple separated in 1930.

Andrade's "Manifesto da Poesia Pau-Brasil" (1924; "Brazilwood Poetry Manifesto") preceded his book of poetry *Pau Brasil* (1925; Brazilwood), published in Paris during his next sojourn there. *Pau Brasil* was a radical departure from former poetic models, introducing an unprecedented synthetic collage aesthetic that made humorous use of the *objet trouvé* (found object) and advocated a truly Brazilian "poetry for export." Similar experimental methods were employed in his two important novels, *Memórias Sentimentais de João Miramar* (1924; *Sentimental Memoirs of John Seaborne*) and *Serafim Ponte Grande* (1933; *Seraphim Grosse Pointe*), and in *Pri-*

meiro Caderno de Poesia do Aluno Oswald de Andrade (1927; First Poetry Notebook of the Student Oswald de Andrade). His important "Manifesto Antropófago" (1928; "Cannibal Manifesto") began an avant-garde trend of nationalist aesthetics that became known as **antropofagia**, the leitmotif of *Revista de Antropofagia* (1928–29; Cannibal Review), which he founded with **Raul Bopp** and **António de Alcântara Machado**.

The fall of the stock exchange in 1929 and a reversal of his family fortune steered Andrade toward more radical political ideas and writing, such as the experimental plays *O Homem e o Cavalo* (1934; The Man and the Horse), *A Morta* (1937; The Dead Woman), and *O Rei da Vela* (1937; The King of the Candle). In the 1930s, he had a relationship with the radical writer and activist **Patrícia Galvão** and joined the Communist Party and the PEN club of Brazil. In his last years he produced mainly essays, many of which were published posthumously: *Ponta de Lança* (1944; Spearhead); *A Crise da Filosofia Messiânica* (1950; The Crisis of Messianic Philosophy); *Marco Zero* (Zero Milestone), series I—*A Revolução Melancólica* (1943; The Melancholy Revolution) and series II—*Chão* (1945; Ground); *Um Homem sem Profissão* (1954; A Man without a Profession); and *A Marcha das Utopias* (1953; The Course of Utopias). Largely ignored at that point, Andrade died in São Paulo in 1954. His poetry was not given serious attention until **Haroldo de Campos** and **Augusto de Campos** published an anthology of his work in 1966, recovering his legacy. His poetry is collected in *Poesias Reunidas* (1945, 1966; Collected Poetry), and the publishing house Globo began the definitive edition of his works in 2000. *See also* ANDRADE, CARLOS DRUMMOND DE; GULLAR, FERREIRA; PICCHIA, PAULO MENOTTI DEL; TELLES, LYGIA FAGUNDES; THEATER.

ANDRADE, MÁRIO RAUL DE MORAIS (Brazil, 1893–1945). Essayist, novelist, and poet. A pivotal figure of **Brazilian modernism**, Mário de Andrade was born in São Paulo, where he received a degree in music. In a radical departure from his first conventional book of poems, *Há uma Gota de Sangue em Cada Poema* (1917; There Is a Drop of Blood in Every Poem), *Paulicéia Desvairada* (1922; Hallucinated City) inaugurated modern poetry in Brazil through a new aesthetic based on syntactic experimentation and a focus on local themes, namely the modern city of São Paulo. The preface-manifesto in this book, later expanded into the essay on aesthetics, *A Escrava que não é Isaura* (1925; The Slave Who Is Not Isaura), explored and ridiculed the founding of new **avant-garde** "isms" and searched for an authentic Brazilian modern expression.

Andrade further pursued the use of native themes and vocabulary in subsequent collections of poems that combined everyday chronicles with the modernist *poema-piada* ("joke poem"): *Losango Cáqui* (1926; Khaki Rhombus); *Clã do Jabuti* (1927; The Turtle's Clan), which includes "Carnaval Carioca" ("Rio Carnival"); and *Remate de Males* (1930; Culmination of Evils). With **Oswald de Andrade** and others he participated actively in the **Week of Modern Art** in 1922, and he became a chief animator of this movement, often serving as critic and mentor to others.

From 1934 to 1937, Andrade served at the Department of Culture of São Paulo, where he instituted important policies regarding art education, the creation of libraries, and preservation of folklore. He moved to Rio in 1938, holding appointments at local universities and collaborating with the Ministry of Education and Culture. As part of this mandate, he actively promoted the study and dissemination of Brazilian folklore, music, dance, and literature, in particular.

Many aspects of the folklore he had begun collecting in the early 1920s were used in his seminal avant-garde novel *Macunaíma* (1928; *Macunaíma*), a narrative centered on Macunaíma, the "hero without a character," which combines native mythology with humor and satire and is widely considered a modernist landmark. Other, less experimental fiction includes the Freudian novel *Amar, Verbo Intransitivo* (1927; *Fräulein*) and the books of short stories *Primeiro Andar* (1926; First Floor), *Belazarte* (1934; Belazarte), and *Contos Novos* (1947; New Stories), lyrical narratives with loose plots.

Andrade wrote extensive essays on Brazilian literature, folklore, and music, including *O Movimento Modernista* (1942; The Modernist Movement) and *Aspectos da Literatura Brasileira* (Aspects of Brazilian Literature, 1943). In 1940, he returned to São Paulo, where he died in February 1945. His last book of poetry, *Lira Paulistana* (1946; São Paulo Lyre), once more praises the city where he spent most of his life. Besides his formal writings, Andrade was a prodigious correspondent, leaving behind thousands of letters, including correspondence with important figures such as **Manuel Bandeira**. His complete works span some 20 volumes. *See also* ALMEIDA, GUILHERME DE; ANDRADE, CARLOS DRUMMOND DE; PICCHIA, PAULO MENOTTI DEL; RICARDO LEITE, CASSIANO; RODRÍGUEZ MONEGAL, EMIR; SABINO, FERNANDO; TELLES, LYGIA FAGUNDES.

ÁNGEL, ALBALUCÍA (Colombia, 1939–). Novelist. She is one of Colombia's prominent **women** writers, although her first three novels were written while living in Europe. The first of these, *Los girasoles en invierno* (1970; Sunflowers in Winter), written as a reaction to the rural novel of Colombia, is set in France and Italy and conveys the random thoughts and conversations of characters, with little plot or psychological insight. *Dos veces Alicia* (1972; Two Times Alice) is set in London and uses the tradition of **crime fiction** to describe the breakup of a family. Like these two novels, Ángel's third, *Estaba la pájara pinta sentada en el verde limón* (1982; The Piebald Bird Sat in the Green Lemon Tree), is also a disjointed work, consisting of a memoir of its principal character that includes both private and public history in Colombia.

Among the author's more recent writings are *Misiá señora* (1983; Madam Lady) and *Las andariegas* (1984; The Wandering Women), both self-consciously feminist and radical experiments in fiction in which conventional narrative is abandoned. The former presents the struggle of the protagonist Mariana to be herself, in contrast to the conventional expectations placed on her as a woman in a traditional society; the latter is a collection of episodes describing the journeys of women at different times and through different spaces.

ANJOS, AUGUSTO DOS (Brazil, 1884–1914). Poet. Dos Anjos was born on a sugar plantation in the Northeast of Brazil during a period of utter decline. In addition to financial ills, the dos Anjos family was plagued by mental and physical disease: his mother was clinically insane and his father died of general paralysis. Despite these misfortunes, dos Anjos excelled in school, received a law degree with distinction in Recife in 1907, and later moved to Paraíba to become a teacher. During his time in Recife, dos Anjos came under the spell of **positivism** and the ideas of Auguste Comte (1798–1857), Charles

Darwin (1809–1882), Herbert Spencer (1820–1903), and Ernest Haeckel (1834–1919), among others, introduced by the philosopher **Tobias Barreto de Meneses**. Anjos's work, gathered in a single volume eccentrically entitled *Eu* (1912; I), can be read not just as the product of a belated *poète maudit* (accursed poet) after the influences of French **symbolism** and **parnassianism**, but also as a powerful attack on a deceitfully blithe view of modernity. Appropriating scientific vocabulary and images popular in his day, his poetry deals obsessively with disease, processes of physical and moral decay, and the metaphysical angst produced by the impotence of positivist science vis-à-vis these realities. Dos Anjos died at age 30 from pneumonia. His posthumous collected poems, *Eu e Outras Poesias* (1920; I and Other Poems), have seen countless reprints.

ANNALS OF THE CAKCHIQUEL. One of the most significant accounts of the history and traditions of the highland Maya of **Guatemala**, covering the period from the preconquest foundation of the Cakchiquel people to 1601.

ANTIPOETRY. The term, *antipoesía* in Spanish, is associated above all with the poet **Nicanor Parra (Chile)**, who used it to refer to the ordinariness of the experience of the poet and to a poetic language that eschewed a high-flying rhetoric. He is thought to have applied it to his own iconoclastic verse to differentiate it from the **avant-garde** style of **Pablo Neruda**. Parra's compatriot **Enrique Lihn** also adopted the concept, and other poets, such as **Adalberto Ortiz (Ecuador)**, have also invoked it, sometimes to separate their work from traditions that preceded the avant-garde.

ANTROPOFAGIA. Designating an aesthetic notion of **Brazilian modernism**, this term was coined in **Brazil** by **Oswald de Andrade** in his "Manifesto Antropófago" (1928; "Cannibalist Manifesto"), published in the **journal** *Revista de Antropofagia* (1928–1929; Cannibal Review). Based on the myths and documented cases of cannibalism of Europeans by native Brazilians, Andrade proposed a metaphorical "law of the cannibal," whereby Brazil (and by extension the New World) would "cannibalize" European cultural products as a way both to enrich itself and acquire its energies, simultaneously paying homage to its ancestry and overcoming dependency. This powerful metaphor was taken up again by Brazilian **avant-garde** movements in the late 1960s and early 1970s and remains a reference in Brazilian culture to this day. Among the most important early writers in this trend are Oswald de Andrade and **António de Alcântara Machado**. The most representative literary work is **Raúl Bopp**'s *Cobra Norato*. *See also* ANDRADE, CARLOS DRUMMOND DE; CAMPOS, AUGUSTO DE; CAMPOS, HAROLDO DE; GALVÃO, PATRÍCIA; INDIGENOUS TRADITIONS; MENDES, MURILO.

ANTUNES, ARNALDO (Brazil, 1960–). Lyricist and poet. Antunes began his career as a rock musician. His early work explored the material aspects of language under the influence of **concrete poetry**. In later **avant-garde** works he employs minimalist and pop culture aesthetics as well as multimedia experimentation. His major poetry books are *Psia* (1986; Psia), *Tudos* (1990; All of Them), *As Coisas* (1992; Things), *2 ou + Corpos no Mesmo Espaço* (1997; 2 or More Bodies in the Same Space), and *ET EU TU* (2003; ET I YOU).

AQUINO, MARÇAL (Brazil, 1958–). Journalist, novelist, and short story writer. Aquino is known for narratives that focus on criminality in the periphery of large cities, including *O Amor e outros Objetos Pontiagudos* (1999; Love and Other Sharp Objects), *Faroestes* (2001; Far Wests), and *Famílias Terrivelmente Felizes* (2003; Terribly Happy Families). He has also adapted some of his novels, such as *O Invasor* (2002; The Invader), for the screen and written original screenplays. He won the **Jabuti Prize** in 2000.

ARANHA, JOSÉ PEREIRA DA GRAÇA (Brazil, 1868–1931). Essayist and novelist. A native of Maranhão, Graça Aranha practiced law before joining Brazil's foreign service, residing in Europe for 20 years. Back in Brazil in 1920, he endorsed the 1922 **Week of Modern Art** and wrote *Estética da Vida* (1921; Aesthetics of Life) and *Espírito Moderno* (1924; Modern Spririt). His premodernist narrative *Canaã* (1902; Canaan), perhaps Brazil's first ideological novel, portrayed the nature/culture conflict and the theme of **civilization and barbarism** through the story of German immigrants in Espírito Santo.

ARCADIANISM. As a reaction to the so-called excesses of **baroque** literature, arcadianism in **Brazil** was a literary idealization of pastoral values and life that also sought simplicity of expression. The Brazilian Arcadia followed the Portuguese model, in which poets assumed shepherd names and behaved accordingly in the eclogues they wrote. Arcadianism did not imitate nature directly, but rather the famous imitators of nature such as Virgil, Ovid, and Camões. Among the Brazilian arcadians are **Manuel Inácio da Silva Alvarenga, Cláudio Manuel da Costa, José de Santa Rita Durão, José Basílio da Gama, Tomás Antônio Gonzaga,** and **Inácio José de Alvarenga Peixoto.** *See also* BRAZIL; INDIANISMO.

ARCINIEGAS, GERMÁN (Colombia, 1900–1999). Essayist. He was a historian, diplomat, and prominent Latin American intellectual of the 20th century who authored more than 50 books on a wide range of topics concerning Latin American cultural and literary history. They include *Los alemanes en la conquista de América* (1941; *Germans in the Conquest of America*), *Biografía del Caribe* (1945; *Caribbean: Sea of the New World*), *Cosas del pueblo: crónica de la historia vulgar* (1962; *Latin America: A Cultural History*), and *América en Europa* (1975; *America in Europe*). He also edited *The Green Continent: A Comprehensive View of Latin America by Its Leading Writers* (1944), an anthology for English readers that had wide circulation in its day.

ARÉVALO MARTÍNEZ, RAFAEL (Guatemala, 1884–1975). Novelist, short story writer, and poet. He wrote poetry in the style of **modernismo,** but is remembered most for his fiction. Among his pieces that have had most impact is a short story, "El hombre que parecía un caballo" (1914; "The Man Who Looked Like a Horse"), which is thought to have prefigured the **boom** writers and **magic realism.** The same title also appeared as the title to his later collections of short stories. Two of his early novels, *Una vida* (1914; A Life) and *Manuel Aldano* (1922; Manuel Aldano), are both autobiographical. *El mundo de los maharachías* (1938; The World of the Maharachías) and its sequel *Viaje a Ipanda* (1939; Journey to Ipanda) are works of science fiction fantasy. Other novels have political themes. *La oficina de la paz en Orolandia* (1925; The Office of Peace in

Orolandia) concerns corruption in Central America and the cynicism of the United States; *¡Ecce Pericles!* (1945; Behold Pericles) is about the Guatemalan dictator Manuel Estrada Cabrera (1898–1920) and anticipates later Latin American **dictator novels**.

ARGENTINA. The diversity and productivity of modern Argentinean literature places it on a par with other major literatures in Latin America, such as those of Brazil or Mexico. Yet, unlike both those countries and several other Latin American nations, Argentina lacks a strong literary tradition going back to colonial times. There were no great campaigns of conquest against Native American empires to inspire a legacy of historical narrative as the foundation of a national story. Moreover, Buenos Aires was principally a center for colonial trade, not one of the centers of American culture, even after its elevation as the capital of the Viceroyalty of La Plata in 1776. Hence, although some texts from colonial Argentina survive, Argentinean literature essentially begins in the 19th century. When searching for the context in which the national story, as expressed through its literature, began to take shape, modern writers are more inclined to look to the War of Independence and the years of civil war that followed, when Federalists and Unitarians fought each other during the dictatorship of **Juan Manuel Rosas**, rather than to the colonial period.

Among local cultural practices formed in pre-Independence Argentina, the oral traditions of the interior northern provinces, represented in the rural narratives and songs of the *payador* (troubador), formed the basis of a tradition in **gaucho literature** that contributed to the formation of a national literary identity and maintained its currency well into the 20th century, long after the lifestyle it represented had disappeared. The work of the Uruguayan-born **Bartolomé Hidalgo,** one of the earliest literary manifestations of this tradition, was followed by that of the Argentineans **Hilario Ascasubi** and **Estanislao del Campo**, and culminated in the 19th century in the two parts of **José Hernández**'s classic work *Martín Fierro* (1872 and 1878). In the 20th century, the figure of the gaucho was sustained in fiction through **Eduardo Gutiérrez**, **Alberto Gerchunoff**, and **Ricardo Güiraldes**, and became a staple in the popular **theater** of Buenos Aires as well as a constant source of reference in more recent literature.

Rural themes, or more notably, the conflict between the city and the country, represented in the opposition between **civilization and barbarism**, are also prominent features of 19th-century Argentinean **romanticism**. **Esteban Echeverría**'s *La cautiva* (1837; The Captive), a tale of captivity among Indians, is a fine example, although his satire of Buenos Aires under Rosas in *El matadero* (1839; *The Slaughter House*) is an equally eloquent statement about the barbarism of the city. The work that most embodies the spirit and politics of the first half of the 19th century, however, is *Facundo* (1845) by **Domingo Faustino Sarmiento**, who, with other public intellectuals such as **Juan Bautista Alberdi** and **Juan María Gutiérrez**, contributed to the foundations of a national ideology. The novel added to this legacy, especially through **José Mármol**'s *Amalia* (1855), considered Argentina's first major novel. Other prominent novelists of the time were **Juana Manuela Gorriti** and **Vicente Fidel López**.

By 1880, the internal conflicts that had afflicted the country since independence were over, and the interior provinces were becoming more settled. **Lucio V. Mansilla** offered a late, humanistic view of indigenous life in 1870, but its time was already drawing to a close. Stimulated by agricultural wealth and waves of immigration, Buenos Aires asserted its economic and cultural dominance as the nation's federal capital. In the late 19th and early 20th centuries, the modes of **costumbrismo, realism,** and **naturalism** in the prose of the likes of **José Álvarez, Roberto Arlt, Eugenio Cambaceres, Manuel Gálvez, Benito Lynch, Roberto J. Payró, Manuel T. Podestá**, and **Hugo Wast** stood out as ways of representing the forms of social life taking shape, especially in the new urban environment. The aestheticism of **modernismo** made some impression in replacing those trends, notably through the work of **Leopoldo Lugones** and **Enrique Larreta**, but a greater impact was felt by the arrival of the **avant-garde** following the return of **Jorge Luis Borges** from Spain in 1923 and the introduction of **ultraísmo** to Buenos Aires.

Members of the avant-garde became known as the **Grupo de Florida**, identified with the upper-class district of the city, in contrast to the realists, who were known as the **Grupo de Boedo** and were identified with the more working-class areas. Both groups produced their own literary **journals**, among which the avant-garde *Proa* and

Martín Fierro figured prominently as the voices of ultraísmo. In addition to Borges, among the main avant-garde or post-modernismo poets were **Oliverio Girondo, Eduardo González Lanuza, Norah Lange, Raúl González Tuñón, Ricardo Molinari, Aldo Pellegrini,** and **Alfonsina Storni.**

Since about 1930, the year of the first of the 20th-century military coups in Argentina, literary activity has been more splintered, less organized according to groups or schools. In 1931 the journal *Sur,* founded by **Victoria Ocampo,** represented this change by becoming a focal point for literary culture in general and publishing contributions from writers of every kind. Since the avant-garde, Argentina has produced a distinguished number of poets of varying trends, including **Sara Gallardo, Juan Gelman, Alberto Girri, Roberto Juárroz, Osvaldo Lamborghini, Francisco Madariaga, Olga Orozco, Juan L. Ortiz, Néstor Perlongher,** and **Alejandra Pizarnik.** At the same time, writers in prose, essayists and literary critics, and historians, including **José Ingenieros, Arturo Jauretche, Ezequiel Martínez Estrada, Héctor A. Murena,** and **Ricardo Rojas,** following in the footsteps of their 19th-century counterparts, have maintained the tradition of the essay as a vehicle for analyzing the state of the nation and its cultural institutions. In more recent times, the description of historical events and the analysis of social change have been complemented by other genres characterized by a more documentary style of writing, such as the **testimonios** of **Rodolfo Walsh** and **Jacobo Timerman** and the urban **chronicles** of **Beatriz Sarlo.**

Although the avant-garde had its greatest effect on poetry, **Juan Filloy** and **Macedonio Fernández** are among avant-garde prose writers whose work stands out for its idiosyncrasy. Borges is one of several writers to have acknowledged the influence of Macedonio Fernandez, and Borges himself had an undeniable impact on several trends in prose writing. His short narratives, **microtales,** and fictive essays enhanced the popularity of the short story. His interest in the **fantastic** was shared by his contemporaries **Adolfo Bioy Casares** and **Silvina Ocampo** and would lead in due course to **Enrique Anderson Imbert** and, above all, to the short stories of **Julio Cortázar,** published between the 1950s and 1980s. **Crime fiction** also figured in Borges's oeuvre and contributed to the popularity of a genre taken up by other writers such as **Manuel Peyrou** and **Marco Denevi**. The focus that Borges and his contemporaries brought to bear on Argentinean society was sustained by novelists in the middle decades of the century, such as **Bernardo Kordon, Eduardo Mallea, Leopoldo Marechal, Manuel Mujica Láinez, Ernesto Sábato, Bernardo Verbitsky**, and Julio Cortázar, each of whom looked at society from his own particular aesthetic and angle. Cortázar's novel *Rayuela* (1966; *Hopscotch*) achieved particular international celebrity and associated him with the **new novel** and the **boom** in Latin American writing.

Since the 1970s, the Argentinean novel has become a very diverse genre and has been affected considerably by the waves of political turmoil and social change that have befallen the country. The immediate **post-boom** period saw an engagement in fiction with different forms of popular culture, such as cinema, crime fiction, popular music, and sport, in the work of **Mempo Giardinelli, Manuel Puig**, and **Osvaldo Soriano. Mario Szichman**, writing during the same period, focused on Argentinean **Jews**. The 1976–1983 dictatorship was a watershed in at least two ways. It separated the work of those who remained in the country, such as **Luis Gusmán** and **Ricardo Piglia**, from those who wrote from exile, such as **Daniel Moyano, Héctor Tizón, David Viñas,** and **Juan José Saer**. Above all, it confronted writers with the need to face the events of the dictatorship and their implications. In some cases, this has meant an examination of both the recent and more distant past, as in **new historical novels** by **Sylvia Iparraguirre, Tomás Eloy Martínez, Abel Posse**, and **Andrés Rivera**, which have described history in a new light. In other cases, as in fiction by **César Aira, Jorge Asís, Rodolfo Enrique Fogwill, Rodrigo Fresán**, or **José Pablo Feinmann**, it has resulted in works that highlight the characteristics of postdictatorship society and the challenges posed by the recent history of violence, technological changes, and a globalized culture and economy. Trends in fiction since the dictatorship are also marked by an increase in the number of publications by **women**. This development had already begun much earlier, as evidenced by writers such as **Slvina Bullrich, Beatriz Guido**, and **Marta Lynch**. However, the work of the more recent generation, including **Luisa Futoransky, Angélica Gorodischer, Martha Mercader, Tununa Mercado, Reina Roffé, Marta Traba,** and **Luisa Valenzuela**, is marked not just by the violence of the recent regime, but also by a militant feminism and a coming to terms with the consequences of exile and return experienced by the authors themselves. Among this group of contemporary women, other writers such as **María Elena Walsh** and **Syria Poletti** have also made important contributions to **children's literature**.

Theater in Argentina did not become a thriving institution until the late 19th century. Before that time, although there were buildings that served as permanent theaters, popular plays were often performed at improvised locations, and the genre was slow to become fully established. The development of theater was affected by adverse political conditions and by the dominance of foreign productions and opera. To some extent, its history, even during much of the 20th century, is one of repeating cycles of renovation, boom, and decline due to periods of instability created by fluctuating economic and political conditions.

As in other literary genres, the figure of the gaucho contributed to the birth of the modern theater in Argentina. The dramatization of **Eduardo Gutiérrez**'s *Juan Moreira* in 1884 by the actor **José J. Podestá** initiated a cycle of gaucho plays, many performed in association with circuses. At about the same time, the *sainete* began a sustained period of popularity that would last from about 1880 to 1930. This form of one-act farce, often incorporating musical performances, grew up in conjunction with the tango in Buenos Aires and was one of the favored sources of entertainment among the thousands of immigrants who flooded into the city. **Nemesio Trejo** was one of the most popular writers, although the *sainete* eventually came to be represented through several subgenres: comedy in the plays by **Roberto Payró**, drama in the work of the Uruguayan-born **Florencio Sánchez**, and musical plays by **Alberto Vacarezza**.

When the golden age of Argentinean theater ended in 1930, it entered a period of fluctuating stability and was characterized by a series of movements in which groups of dramatists sought to give it new life and new directions. The first of these consisted of **Roberto Arlt**, **Francisco Defilippis Novoa, Samuel Eichelbaum,** and **Armando Discépolo**. This group, influenced by trends in European theater represented by Luigi Pirandello, gave rise to the *grotesco criollo*. During the late 1940s and early 1950s, **Conrado Nalé Roxlo** and

Carlos Gorostiza used an imaginative theater to keep it alive during the difficult times of the presidency of **Juan Domingo Perón**. This was followed by a greater trend toward realism by **Osvaldo Dragún** and especially by **Roberto Cossa** in the 1960s. One notable piece of theater was *El avión negro* (1971; The Black Plane), a collaborative work by Roberto Cossa, **Ricardo Talesnik**, **Carlos Somigliana**, and **Germán Rozenmacher**, which finally brought **Peronism** openly onto the stage.

The formation of a movement toward the avant-garde in theater was fostered by the foundation of the Instituto Torcuato Di Tella in 1958. Among the most significant dramatists to emerge from this context were **Griselda Gambaro** and **Eduardo Pavlovsky**. Along with writers such as **Diana Raznovich**, they wrote against authoritarianism and oppression at a time when to do so invited reprisals and the closure of theaters. The themes they wrote about were also among those taken up by the **Teatro Abierto** beginning in 1981, which sought to question abuses committed by those in positions of power.

In the period immediately following the return to democracy in 1983, the atrocities committed during the dictatorship were common subjects for the theater. As time has passed, however, the theater has become more open in its themes and styles. The traditional forms remain, but there are new themes, especially those related to gender (machismo, feminism, gay and lesbian topics), and there is greater experimentation in phenomena such as dance theater, rock theater, and new media. See also BEST SELLER; BOAL, AUGUSTO; BOLIVIA; CASA DE LAS AMÉRICAS; CRIOLLISMO; DARÍO, RUBÉN; DÍAZ DE GUZMÁN, RUY; DORFMAN, ARIEL; GÓMEZ CARRILLO, ENRIQUE; HIDALGO, ALBERTO; HISTORICAL NOVEL; INDIANISMO; JAIMES FREYRE, RICARDO; MAGIC REALISM; MIGUEL DE CERVANTES PRIZE; MOOCK, ARMANDO; NEO-BAROQUE; NOVEL OF THE LAND; PARAGUAY; PICARESQUE NOVEL; PLA, JOSEFINA; POSITIVISM; QUIROGA, HORACIO; REYES, ALFONSO; TABOADA TERÁN, NÉSTOR; THEATER OF CRUELTY; THEATER OF THE ABSURD; URUGUAY.

ARGUEDAS, ALCIDES (Bolivia, 1879–1946). Novelist and historian. His social essay *Pueblo enfermo* (1909; Infirm People) and his novel *Raza de bronce* (1919; Bronze Race), for which he is best known, established him as one of the early proponents of **indigenismo**. Other works of fiction include *Wata-Wara* (1904; Wata-Wara) and *Vida criolla, la novela de la ciudad* (1905; Creole Life: Novel of the City). Yet, although interested in the life and customs of indigenous peoples of the Andean highlands, he wrote about them from the deterministic perspectives of race and environment, influenced by **naturalism**, and thought their salvation lay in Europeanization at the expense of their own culture. As a historian, he also undertook a monumental *Historia de Bolivia* (History of Bolivia), several volumes of which were published between 1922 and 1929, a work that lacks historical objectivity and reveals the beliefs and prejudices of its author. See also TAMAYO, FRANZ.

ARGUEDAS, JOSÉ MARÍA (Peru, 1911–1969). Novelist, short story writer, and ethnographer. He is considered one of the major figures of 20th-century Peruvian literature, whose writing had a profound impact on **indigenismo** and ushered in **neo-indigenismo**. Much of his writing has autobiographical roots and derived from the familiarity with Quechua, indigenous culture, and the marginalized state of native peoples in Peru he obtained during his childhood. These characteristics are already evident in his first collections of short stories, *Agua* (1935; Water) and *Diamantes y pedernales* (1954; Diamonds and Flints), and in his first novel, *Yawar fiesta* (1940; *Yawar fiesta*).

The novel that firmly established Arguedas's reputation was *Los ríos profundos* (1958; *Deep Rivers*). Here, as in some of his earlier work, he adopted the perspective of a child; explores the interactions of Quechua and Spanish; and focused on the internal, psychological dimensions of indigenous culture in ways that shed new light on the conflicts between indigenous and European ways of life. In his next novel, *Todas las sangres* (1964; All the Bloods), he examined the social, economic, and racial divisions of Peruvian society, a theme that figured significantly in his own preoccupations about his country. In his last novel, *El zorro de arriba y el zorro de abajo* (1971; *The Fox from Up Above and the Fox from Down Below*), Arguedas intended to describe the life of indigenous workers in the port of Chimbote. The novel remained unfinished, however, when the author took his own life in 1969. His state of mind and his decision to kill himself, not the first time Arguedas attempted suicide, are part of the problematic of the novel.

ARGUETA, MANLIO (El Salvador, 1936–). Novelist and poet. The novels for which Argueta is best known are characterized by changing points of view, flashbacks, first person narratives, and interior discourse. *El valle de las hamacas* (1970; Valley of the Hammocks), a title that refers to the city of San Salvador, is a fragmented story about a *guerrillero* in search of a cache of arms. Similarly, *Caperucita en la zona roja* (1977; Little Red Riding Hood in the Red Zone) is an opaque, experimental novel set in an urban milieu and based on the life of **Roque Dalton**. It received a **Casa de las Américas** prize. *Un día en la vida* (1980; *One Day of Life*) compresses the history of El Salvador into one day in the life of its protagonist, Lupe Fuentes. It has some of the character of a **testimonio,** as does *Cuzcatlán: donde bate la mar del sur* (1986; *Where the Southern Sea Breaks*), which also contains elements of **magic realism** and is based on the testimonies of four generations traveling together on the same bus. Cuzcatlán is an Indian name for El Salvador.

ARIDJIS, HOMERO (Mexico, 1940–). Poet and novelist. Aridjis has served as president of International PEN and founded the Grupo de los Cien (Group of 100), an association of artists and intellectuals working for environmental protection. His poetry often draws from the natural world. *Mirándola dormir* (1964; Seeing Her Sleep), *Perséfone* (1967; Persephone), and *Espacios azules* (1968; *Blue Spaces*) are representative early collections; *Ojos de otro mirar* (2002; *Eyes to See Otherwise*) is an anthology of his verse from 1960 to 2000. He has also written for the **theater** and, as a novelist, has established a reputation as the author of **new historical novels.** These include *Memorias del Nuevo Mundo* (1988; Memories of the New World) and *1492: vida y tiempos de Juan Cabezón de Castilla* (1985; *1492: The Life and Times of Juan Cabezón de Castilla*), which evokes a century of persecution in Spain before the expulsion of the Jews from the country in 1492, a date that also marks the beginning of Spain's imperial ventures in the New World.

ARIELISMO. The term refers to the aesthetic and political positions developed by the Uruguayan **José Enrique Rodó** in his 1900 essay *Ariel*, which was widely read and had considerable influence on early 20th-century debates about Latin American identity. The title of Rodó's essay derives from Ariel, Shakespeare's spirit character in *The Tempest*, which is intended to symbolize the spiritual nature of Latin America in contrast to the pragmatism of **positivism** and the growing economic influence of North America. Arielism had a number of followers in Mexico, headed by **Alfonso Reyes**, and also influenced writers in other parts of Latin America, including **Mariano Picón Salas** in **Venezuela, Pedro Prado** in **Ecuador, Luis Alberto Sánchez** in **Peru**, and **Alberto Zum Felde** in **Uruguay**. *See also* DÍAZ RODRÍGUEZ, MANUEL; ZORILLA Y SAN MARTÍN, JUAN.

ARLT, ROBERTO (Argentina, 1900–1942). Novelist, short stort writer, dramatist, and journalist. Although his importance was not acknowledged during his lifetime, his impact on other writers, notably **Julio Cortázar** and **Juan Carlos Onetti**, was considerable, and he has come to be recognized as one of the formative figures of 20th-century Argentinean literature. His language is a rich mixture of the vocabulary and different registers of everyday speech in Buenos Aires, and his writing is populated by immigrants and other socially marginalized characters. Poverty, violence, and urban alienation are consistent features of his work, making him one of the most prominent writers of social **realism** of his generation. His first novel, *El juguete rabioso* (1926; *Mad Toy*), is a semiautobiographical account of survival in an urban world, later explored on a larger scale in *Los siete locos* (1929; *The Seven Madmen*) and its sequel, *Los lanzallamas* (1931; The Flamethrowers). *El amor brujo* (1932; Love the Magician), his last novel, traces the antisocial behavior and growing psychoses of its protagonist. A number of short stories are collected in *El jorobadito* (1933; The Little Hunchback) and *El criador de gorilas* (1951; The Gorilla Breeder), and his **chronicles** of everyday life, written mainly for the Buenos Aires newspaper *El Nacional*, have been anthologised under various titles. The earliest collection was called *Aguafuertes porteñas* (1933; Buenos Aires Etchings).

Arlt's writing for the theater shows a similar brand of social realism, presented through liminal characters and situations. He contributed to the renovation of Argentine theater of the early 20th century, and works such as *Trescientos millones* (1932; Three Hundred Million) and *Saverio el cruel* (1933; Saverio the Cruel) associate him with the **avant-garde** and are thought to show the influence of the Italian dramatist Luigi Pirandello (1867–1936). *See also* GUIDO, BEATRIZ.

ARRÁIZ LUCCA, RAFAEL (Venezuela, 1957–). Poet and essayist. One of Venezuela's prominent contemporary poets, he has published a number of collections, including *Terrenos* (1985; Plots of Land), *Almacén* (1988; Store), *Litoral* (1991; Shoreline), *Pesadumbre en Bridgetown* (1992; Sorrow in Bridgetown), *Batallas* (1995; Battles), *Poemas ingleses* (1997; English Poems), and *Plexo solar* (2002; Solar plexus). As an essayist, he has published books on Venezuela, poetry, and topics of contemporary interest, including *Venezuela en cuatro asaltos* (1993; Venezuela in Four Tries), *Trece lecturas venezolanas* (1997; Thirteen Readings of Venezuela), *El coro de las voces solitarias, una historia de la poesía venezolana* (2002; The Chorus of Solitary Voices: A History of Venezuelan Poetry), and *¿Qué es la globalizacion?* (2002; What Is Globalization?).

ARREOLA, JUAN JOSÉ (Mexico, 1918–2001). Short story writer. His short stories show elements of **fantastic literature** used to explore life as an unpredictable and sometimes absurd condition. His **existentialism** is sometimes confusing, but humorous, and often compared to that of Franz Kafka (1883–1924) and Alberta Camus (1913–1960). Collections of stories appeared under the titles *Varia invención* (1949; Various Inventions) and *Confabulario* (1952; Confabulation and Other Inventions), both published again with other stories and new material in *Confabulario total* (1962; Complete Confabulation). "El guardagujas" ("The Switchman"), using the metaphor of a train journey to describe the absurdity of existence, is one of his most widely read pieces. Although best known as the author of short stories, Arreola also wrote a novel, *La feria* (1980; The Fair), and two plays, *La hora de todos* (1955; Moment of Truth) and *Tercera llamada ¡tercera! o empezamos sin usted* (1971; Last Call, Last Call! Or We Start Without You). The second of these is an innovative piece that brings together elements of the religious *auto* and the **theater of the absurd**. *See also* THEATER.

ASCASUBI, HILARIO (Argentina, 1807–1875). Poet. His involvement in the political and military turmoil of postindependence Argentina is represented in the periods of military service and exile that punctuated his life. Through his writing, the history of those times is reflected in poetry that drew on rural traditions and the figure of the gaucho. His most celebrated achievement was *Santos Vega, o Los mellizos de la Flor* (1872; Santos Vega, or The Twins from La Flor), which, along with **José Hernández**'s *Martín Fierro*, ignited the trend in **gaucho literature** of the late 19th century and beyond. *See also* MUJICA LÁINEZ, MANUEL.

ASCHER, NELSON RONNY (Brazil, 1958–). Journalist, poet, and translator. Trained in administration and semiotics, Ascher has written on culture and politics for *Folha de São Paulo* since the 1980s. He founded the **journal** *Revista USP* in 1988–1989, serving as main editor until 1994. His books of poems include *Ponta da Língua* (1983; Tip of the Tongue), *Sonho da Razão* (1993; Dream of Reason), *Algo de Sol* (1996; Some Sun), and *Parte Alguma* (2005; Some/ No Part). A prolific translator, particularly from Eastern European languages, he collaborated with Boris Schnaidermann on the translation of *Queen of Spades* (1834) by Alexander Pushkin (1799–1837). *O Lado Obscuro* (1996; The Dark Side) and *Poesia Alheia* (1998; Another's Poetry) gather his translations, and *Pomos da Discórdia* (1993; Apples of Discord) gathers his essays.

ASÍS, JORGE (Argentina, 1946–). Novelist. He is a diplomat, was a candidate for the vice presidency of Argentina in 2007, and has written several successful novels. These include *Don Abdel Zalim, el burlador de Dominico* (1972; Don Abdel Zalim, Dominico's Deceiver), *Sandra, la trapera* (1996; Sandra, Vendor of Secondhand Clothes), and *Flores robadas en los jardines de Quilmes* (1980; Flowers Stolen from Gardens in Quilmes), a novel about youth in Buenos Aires, which was a **best seller** in Argentina and the source of a successful film.

ASSIS, JOAQUIM MARIA MACHADO DE (Brazil, 1839–1908). Dramatist, essayist, journalist, novelist, and short story writer. Perhaps Brazil's most celebrated writer, Machado de Assis came from very humble origins, the son of a mulatto painter and a Portuguese washerwoman. Orphaned in childhood, he was mostly self-taught, acquiring a vast literary culture through reading Jonathan Swift (1667–1745), Laurence Sterne (1713–1768), and Giacomo Leopardi (1798–1837). He became fluent in French and English, and translated Edgar Allan Poe (1809–1849) and Shakespeare, whom he quoted extensively in his work.

Employed as a typographer, he began publishing his first works in the literary magazine *A Marmota* and met writers such as **Casimiro de Abreu** and **Manuel Antônio de Almeida**, whom he befriended. He worked briefly for Rio dailies but later secured government jobs that allowed him to devote himself to writing. In the 1860s, he married a Portuguese woman; gained fame for *Crisálidas* (1864; Chrysalis), a book of poetry in the manner of **romanticism**; and composed comedies that are only valued by critics as exercises for his subsequent narratives, the short story collections *Contos Fluminenses* (1870; Rio Stories) and *Histórias da Meia-Noite* (1873; Midnight Stories) and the novels *Ressureição* (1872; Resurrection), *A Mão e a Luva* (1874; *The Hand and the Glove*), *Helena* (1876; *Helena*), and *Iaiá Garcia* (1878; *Iaiá Garcia*).

All these works, however, are still in the early, more conventional romantic style that he broke with in his next important novel, *Memórias Póstumas de Brás Cubas* (1881; *Posthumous Memoirs of Brás Cubas*; also translated as *Epitaph of a Small Winner)*, turning instead to the narrative mode of **realism**, although not without some irony and pessimism about this new style. Other important works in which Machado de Assis displayed his gift for a new, fragmented narrative style, psychological analysis, and a tragicomic view of human nature are the novels *Dom Casmurro* (1899; *Dom Casmurro*), *Esaú e Jacó* (1904; *Esau and Jacob, a Novel*), and *Memorial de Aires* (1908; *The Wager: Aires' Journal*), and the short story collections *Várias Histórias* (1896; Several Stories), *Páginas Recolhidas* (1899; Collected Pages), and *Relíquias de Casa Velha* (1906; Relics from the Old House).

Machado de Assis theorized his views on national art and literature in two essays, "Instinto de Nacionalidade" (1873; "Nationality Instinct") and "A Nova Geração" (1879; "The New Generation"), both published in the New York Portuguese-language newspaper *O Novo*

Mundo. Machado de Assis founded the Brazilian Academy of Letters in 1896 (*see* ACADEMIAS) and was its first president when he died from a cancerous ulcer. *See also* ALVES, ANTÔNIO FREDERICO DE CASTRO; FONSECA, RUBEM; ROMERO, SÍLVIO.

ASTURIAS, MIGUEL ÁNGEL (Guatemala, 1899–1974). Novelist. A decade in Paris (1923–1933) brought him into contact with the French literary scene, **surrealism**, and the Sorbonne lectures of Georges Raynaud on Mayan religions, elements that, in combination with Jungian psychoanalysis, informed much of his writing. *Leyendas de Guatemala* (1930; *Legends of Guatemala*) was his first major literary work, and by 1933 he had completed *El señor presidente* (1946; *The President*), a **dictator novel** on political corruption, although it was not published for over a decade, until a regime change in Guatemala.

Hombres de maíz (1949; *Men of Maize*), incorporating the mythic origins and legends of the Mayan people and their modern political and social travails, consolidated the place of Asturias in **neo-indigenismo**. It also established the role of myth creation as a device for approaching the narrative of Latin American history, which would figure prominently in the work of members of the **boom** generation. Other novels followed, including his "banana trilogy": *Viento fuerte* (1950; *Stong Wind*), *El papa verde* (1954; *The Green Pope*), and *Los ojos de los enterrados* (1960; *The Eyes of the Interred*), on the United Fruit Company's exploitation of Guatemala; *El alhajadito* (1961; *The Bejeweled Boy*); *Mulata de tal* (1963; *Mulata and Mister Fly*); and *Viernes de dolores* (1972; Good Friday).

Asturias also wrote five experimental plays, whose meanings are often elusive: *Soluna* (1955; Sunmoon) about old myths and modern life and the need for cultural continuity with the past; *La audiencia de los límites* (1957; Frontier Tribunal), on the courts in colonial times and the maltreatment of Indians in history; *Cuculcán* (1948; Cuculcan), a balletic representation of aspects of the sun taken from pre-Columbian sources; *Chantaje* (1964; Blackmail), a drama of the absurd; and *Dique seco* (1964; Dry Dock), a farse set in Italy. Asturias received the Lenin Peace Prize in 1966 and the **Nobel Prize for Literature** in 1967. *See also* THEATER.

ATAÍDE, TRISTÃO DE, pseudonym of **ALCEU AMOROSO LIMA (Brazil, 1893–1983).** Essayist and critic. Considered one of Brazil's most important critics of the 20th century, Ataíde (whose name is also spelled Tristão de Athayde) first assumed an aesthetic position vis-à-vis criticism. His conversion to Catholicism produced a shift toward more doctrinaire and moralistic views, although he was still respected as a perceptive critic, especially in the study of **Brazilian modernism.** In later years, he wrote essays on philosophical, moral, religious, political, and pedagogical topics. An extremely prolific writer, his works on literature include *Estudos* (1927–1933; Studies), *O Espírito e o Mundo* (1936; The Spirit and the World), *Contribuição à História do Modernismo 1: O Premodernismo* (1939; Contribution to the History of Modernism 1: Premodernism), *Poesia Brasileira Contemporânea* (1941; Contemporary Brazilian Poetry), *Três Ensaios sobre Machado de Assis* (1941; Three Essays on Machado de Assis), *O Crítico Literário* (1945; The Literary Critic), *A estética literária e o crítico* (1945; Literary Aesthetics and the Critic), *Primeiros Estudos: Contribuição à História do Modernismo Literário* (1948; First Studies: Contribution to the History of Literary Modernism), *Introdução à Literatura Brasileira* (1956; Introduction to Brazilian Literature), *Quadro Sintético da Literatura Brasileira* (1956; Survey of Brazilian Literature), and *A Crítica Literária no Brasil* (1959; Literary Criticism in Brazil). His collected literary and critical writings appeared as *Tristão de Athayde: Teoria, Crítica e História Literária* (1980; Tristão de Athayde: Literary Theory, Criticism, and History).

AUTO. When used in the context of the **theater,** *auto* commonly refers to a short religious play, usually of one act. *Autos* originated in Spain and Portugal and were performed to commemorate religious occasions and feast days such as Christmas or Corpus Christi, although they might also be staged to mark secular events. Their content was often allegorical, and when they had a religious purpose, they were used to convey a moral or to explain a particular aspect of Christianity. In the Americas, they were widely used in the Christianization of local populations, frequently through performances in local languages. Among *autos* from the colonial period that have survived are several by notable authors, including **José de Anchieta (Brazil)**, **Juan de Espinosa Medrano (Peru)**, and **Fernán González de Eslava** and **Sor Juana Inés de la Cruz (Mexico)**. Dramatists in modern times, such as **Juan José Arreola** and **Sergio Magaña** (Mexico), **Luis Albert Heiremans (Chile)**, and **Ariano Vilar Suassuna** (Brazil), have also used the form and its traditions to frame their own work. See also THEATER IN QUECHUA.

AVANT-GARDE. Although used in general to refer to artists and their work in the forefront, or vanguard, of change in relation to established traditions of expression, the term also has a particular historical connotation and refers to changes in the representation of reality and the human experience that took place in the early 20th century. These changes were part of what was happening in the world at large, such as shifts in politics with the rise of Marxism and related philosophies, growing industrialization and technological innovation, cultural massification, and even new perceptions of the physical universe.

In literature the historical avant-garde entailed an aesthetic revolution that introduced a greater emphasis on the literary work itself rather than on how the world was mimetically represented. Literature became a place for experimentation with new forms and structures and the exploration of new ways to use language. Established genres were transformed with the abandonment of traditional rhetorics, metrical structures, and even typographical layout in poetry, and the introduction of different ways to structure and present narratives in fiction and **theater**. Above all, the avant-garde made full use of developments in the understanding of subjectivism and the individual psyche, such that the literary work placed more emphasis on the irrational, interior vision of the subject than on the objective external world.

These changes began to be felt in Spanish America in the 1920s, largely as a consequence of the influence of developments in Europe. **Surrealism**, in its varying manifestations, was the most widely felt phenomenon. However, although influences from Europe were strongly felt, Latin America also experienced the avant-garde in its own fashion and responded to it in its own ways. The novelty of the avant-garde was perceived in relation to the aesthetics of **criollismo** and **modernismo**, and it was expressed through particular local manifestations. **Estridentismo** and **Los Contemporáneos** in **Mexico** are associated with **José Gorostiza, Germán List Arzubide, Manuel Maples Arce, Salvador Novo, Jaime Torres Bodet, Carlos Pellicer**, and **Xavier Villaurrutia.** In Chile, **creacionismo** is associated above all with **Vicente Huidobro.** In **Argentina**, the most significant movement was **ultraísmo**, whose members are often conventionally aligned in two contrasting groups, the **Grupo de Florida**, and the **Grupo de Boedo.** Its contributors included **Jorge Luis Borges, Oliverio Girondo, Alberto Hidalgo, Norah Lange, Ricardo E. Molinari**, and **Leopoldo Lugones.**

The avant-garde influenced all genres and affected writers who were not necessarily affiliated with a particular movement. Among prominent avant-garde poets were **José Juan Tablada** (Mexico); **José Coronel Urtecho, Pablo Antonio Cuadra**, and **Joaquín Pasos (Nicaragua); Eunice Odio (Costa Rica); Rogelio Sinán (Panama); Martín Adán, Carlos Oquendo de Amat**, and **César Vallejo (Peru); Pablo Neruda** and **Pablo de Rokha** (Chile); and **Aldo Pellegrini** (Argentina). Prominent prose writers included **Jorge Enrique Adoum (Ecuador), Julio Cortázar, Macedonio Fernández,** and **Leopoldo Marechal** (Argentina); and **Felisberto Hernández (Uruguay). Roberto Arlt** and **Eduardo Pavlosvsky** (Argentina) and **Isaac Chocrón (Venezuela)** were some of the notable dramatists.

The term "avant-garde" is less commonly used in relation to literature in **Brazil**, where the trends to which it refers are collectively covered by **Brazilian modernism**, a broad movement whose beginning is conventionally dated from the **Week of Modern Art** celebrated in 1922. **Antropofagia** and **concrete poetry** are two of the trends included under the umbrella of this term, and among the most significant authors who contributed to Brazilian modernism and the avant-garde are **Carlos Drummond de Andrade, Oswald de Andrade, Mário de Andrade, Manuel Bandeira, Raul Bopp, Augusto de Campos, Haroldo de Campos, Paulo Leminski, João Cabral de Melo Neto, Paulo Menotti del Picchia, Décio Pignatari, Cassiano Ricardo Leite, Plínio Salgado,** and **Pedro Xisto.** *See also* ALVIM, FRANCISCO; ANTIPOETRY; ANTUNES, ARNALDO; BONVINCINO, RÉGIS; CAMPOS CERVERA, HERIB; CHAMIE, MÁRIO; COLOMBIA; CORREA, JULIO; D'HALMAR, AUGUSTO; EGURÉN, JOSÉ MARÍA;

FILHO, ARMANDO FREITAS; GARMENDÍA, JULIO; GIRRI, ALBERTO; GRUPO DE GUAYAQUIL; GUATEMALA; HOLANDA, SÉRGIO BUARQUE DE; LAMBORGHINI, OSVALDO; LÓPEZ, LUIS CARLOS; LÓPEZ VELARDE, RAMÓN; MUJICA LÁINEZ, MANUEL; NEO-INDIGENISMO; NUEVO GRUPO; ROMANTICISM; SELVA, SALOMÓN DE LA; USLAR PIETRI, ARTURO; WOMEN.

AVELLÁN FERRÉS, ENRIQUE (Ecuador, 1908–). Novelist and dramatist. Although he wrote several novels, the first titled *La enorme pasión* (The Great Passion), his **theater** won him more attention. *Manos de criminal* (1939; Criminal Hands) is a dark psychological drama that consolidated the presence of social realism on the Ecuadorian stage. Other plays by Avellán Ferrés include *Como los árboles* (1927; Like the Trees) and *El mismo caso* (1938; The Same Case). In a different vein, he also wrote theater for children, including *Clarita la negra* (1966; Clarita the Black Woman) and *La rebelión del museo* (1969; Rebellion in the Museum), a musical fantasy.

ÁVILA, AFFONSO (Brazil, 1928–). Poet. Ávila published his first poetry collection, *O Açude e Sonetos da Descoberta* (1953; The Dam and Sonnets of the Discovery), before meeting the São Paulo poets **Haroldo de Campos** and **Augusto de Campos** and joining the **concrete poetry** movement. Among his poetry collections are *Carta do Solo* (1961; Letter from the Ground) and *Frases Feitas* (1963; Standard Expressions), which exhibit linguistic experimentation and erotic and ideological themes. Associated mostly with the concrete poetry movement, he won the 1991 **Jabuti Prize** for *O Visto e o Imaginado* (1990; The Seen and the Imagined) and again in 2007 for *Cantigas do Falso Alfonso el Sabio* (2006; Songs of the False Alfonso the Wise).

AZEVEDO, ALUÍSIO (Brazil, 1857–1913). Dramatist, novelist, short story writer. The son of the Portuguese viceconsul in Maranhão, Azevedo had a comfortable childhood, displaying an early artistic inclination when designing sets for the plays his brother, Artur, wrote in his youth. He followed his brother to Rio, where he established himself as a journalist for *O Mequetrefe*, *Fígaro*, and *Zig-Zag*, but when his father died, he had to return to Maranhão. There he wrote articles for the press and published his first conventionally romantic novel, *Uma Lágrima de Mulher* (1879; A Woman's Tear), neither of which would earn him his current reputation. Azevedo combined his close observation of racial prejudice in Maranhão and his knowledge of European **naturalism** in his next novel, *O Mulato* (1881; *Mulatto*), a tale involving explicit sexuality, which earned him financial and literary success, but socially alienated him in his home state. He therefore moved to Rio, where he made a living as a writer from 1882 to 1895, producing two other important naturalist novels deterministically portraying urban poverty: *Casa de Pensão* (1884; Boarding House) and *O Cortiço* (1890; *A Brazilian Tenement*).

Azevedo also wrote the serial novels *Mistérios da Tijuca* (1883; Tijuca Mysteries), subsequently known as *Girândola de Amores* (1900; Pinwheel of Love), and *A Mortalha de Alzira* (1894; Alzira's Shroud), in the style of **romanticism**, as well as many plays and revues in collaboration with his brother and others. Despite his success, Azevedo resented the stress of a literary life and sought instead diplomatic posts in Vigo, Naples, Tokyo, and Buenos Aires, where he died. After joining the Foreign Service, he lost his interest in literature and never published another book. *See also* AZEVEDO, ARTUR NABANTINO GONÇALVES; THEATER.

AZEVEDO, ARTUR NABANTINO GONÇALVES (Brazil 1855–1908). Chronicler, dramatist, and short story writer. Brother of the novelist **Aluísio Azevedo**, Artur Azevedo moved from Maranhão to Rio, where he became a journalist and comic playwright. Azevedo is seen as the continuator of **Luís Carlos Martins Pena**'s satirical dramas, particularly aimed at chastising contemporary Rio society. He excelled in the *teatro de revista* or *teatro ligeiro*, genres that combined elements of vaudeville and the musical, parodies of foreign dramas, and satirical sketches on the important events of the previous year, focusing on the capital, Rio de Janeiro. Among his most important works are the comedies *Amor por Anexins* (1872; The Love of Proverbs), *A Jóia* (1879; The Jewel), *O Badejo* (1898; The Stockfish), and *A Capital Federal* (1897; The Federal Capital). Besides plays, Azevedo also wrote **theater chronicles** and the humorous short story collections *Contos Possíveis* (1889; Possible Stories),

Contos Fora da Moda (1893; Passé Stories), *Contos Efêmeros* (1897; Ephemeral Stories), and *Contos em Verso* (1909; Stories in Verse).

AZEVEDO, CARLITO (Brazil, 1961–). Critic, editor, translator, and poet. Although Azevedo's poetic sources can be traced to **poesia marginal, concrete poetry,** and **João Cabral de Melo Neto,** he quickly attempted to establish his own style. His first book, *Collapsus Linguae* (1991; Collapsus Linguae), earned him the **Jabuti Prize.** *As Banhistas* (1993; The Bathers) presents a reflection on his own poetics influenced by **Carlos Drummond de Andrade** and the urban *flâneur* of Charles Baudelaire (1821–1867). Other works include *Sob a Noite Física* (1996; Under the Physical Night) and *Versos de Circunstância* (2001; Occasional Poems). He has published an anthology of his work, *Sublunar* (2001; Sublunar). In 1997, he founded the well-known poetry review *Inimigo Rumor,* which he coedits to this day. He has also translated poetry from the French.

AZEVEDO, MANUEL ANTÔNIO ALVARES DE (Brazil, 1831–1852). Poet, dramatist, and short story writer. Alvares de Azevedo studied law in Rio and Niterói and participated actively in the intellectual and literary circles of his day. He was the most gifted poet of his generation, writing poems under the influence of the pessimistic **romanticism** of Lord Byron (1788–1824). Other themes include virginal love, *ennui* and *mal du siècle,* and misunderstood genius. He died from tuberculosis at age 21 before he could publish *Lira dos Vinte Anos* (1853; The Lyre at Age Twenty). Other works include the **fantastic** narrative *A Noite na Taverna* (1855; Night in the Tavern), journalistic prose in *Livro de Fra Gondicairo* (1962; Fra Gondicario's Book), and the narrative/dialogue piece *Macário* (Macario) in his *Obras Completas* (1944; Complete Works). *See also* GUIMARÃES, BERNARDO JOAQUIM DA SILVA.

AZUELA, MARIANO (Mexico, 1875–1952). Novelist. He is considered to have founded the **novel of the Mexican Revolution** with *Los de abajo* (1915; *The Underdogs*), a work developed from the author's experience of the conflict as a field doctor attached to **Francisco Villa**'s campaign. Although it passed almost unnoticed when it first appeared, *Los de abajo* has since become an established classic, noted for its style, **realism**, and the ambiguity of its representation of the revolutionary movement. Azuela had already written other novels before *Los de abajo*, notably *María Luisa* (1907; María Luisa) and *Mala yerba* (1909; *Marcela: A Mexican Love Story*), and would eventually publish 25 novels. Those related to the revolution include *Los caciques* (1917; *The Bosses*) and *Las moscas* (1918; *The Flies*), and he also wrote about postrevolutionary society, as in *Las tribulaciones de una familia decente* (1918; *The Trials of a Respectable Family*). He viewed the revolution as an uncontrollable force caused by oppression. He sympathized with the "underdogs," and his works show some of the characteristics of **indigenismo**, but he maintains an essentially middle-class perspective, not entirely able to identify with his literary characters. In *La malhora* (1923; *Evil Hour*), *El desquite* (1925; *Recovery*), and *La luciérnaga* (1932; *The Firefly*), he attempted a more "contemporary" style, but his reputation rests on the realist mode of **naturalism** pursued in his earliest works, including *Los de abajo*.

– B –

BACCINO PONCE DE LEÓN, NAPOLEÓN (Uruguay, 1947–). Novelist. He is the author of *Maluco: novela de los descubridores* (1989; *Five Black Ships: A Novel of Magellan*), a **new historical novel** in which the story of the first circumnavigation of the globe is told in a letter to Charles V of Spain written by a court jester who claims to have been a member of the expedition. Baccino Ponce de León has also published *Un amor en Bangkok* (1994; Love in Bangkok) and *Arte de perder* (1995; *The Art of Losing*).

BALBUENA, BERNARDO DE (Mexico, ca. 1562–1672). Poet. Although born in Spain, he was raised in Mexico, and his religious career took him to several parts of the New World, where he served as bishop in Jamaica and Puerto Rico. His work belongs to the **baroque** and includes *Grandeza mexicana* (1604; The Grandeur of Mexico), a lyric poem on Mexico City; a pastoral romance, *Siglo de Oro en las selvas de Irílife* (1608; Golden Age in the Woodlands of Irilife), written in verse and prose; and *El Bernardo o victoria de Roncesvalles*

(1624; Bernardo or Victory at Roncesvalles), an **epic poem** of the time of Charlemagne. *See also* NOVO, SALVADOR.

BANDEIRA, MANUEL (Brazil, 1886–1968). Journalist, essayist, poet, and translator. A major figure of **Brazilian modernism** and one of Brazil's most cherished poets, Bandeira was born in Recife but as a boy moved to Rio, where he completed his secondary education. He relocated later to São Paulo for a career in architecture, which was interrupted by tuberculosis. He sought a cure in a Swiss sanatorium in 1913, where he became acquainted with French post-**symbolist** poetry and met the French poet Paul Éluard (1895–1952). Around this time he attempted to publish *Poemetos Melancólicos* (Melancholy Little Poems) in Portugal, but the manuscript was lost in the sanatorium. Returning to Brazil in 1917, he began to write for newspapers and published his first poetry collections, *A Cinza das Horas* (1917; Ash of Hours) and *Carnaval* (1919; Carnival), which already demonstrated a modern poetic sensibility and caught the attention of critics and modernist artists in Rio and São Paulo. Although he did not attend the **Week of Modern Art** in 1922, his satirical poem "Os Sapos" ("The Toads") was famously read by **Ronald de Carvalho** during one of the events.

In 1924, Bandeira reprinted his two previous books in the volume *Poesias* (1924; Poems), along with a new one, *O Ritmo Dissoluto* (1924; Scattered Rhythm), in which the use of free verse was ubiquitous. His professional journalistic activity intensified, as he began to write cultural criticism for **journals** such as *O Mês Modernista*, *A Noite*, *A Idéia ilustrada*, and *Ariel*, and traveled extensively throughout Brazil. *Libertinagem* (1930; Debauchery) is perhaps Bandeira's most modernist work, exhibiting a self-ironic diction. On this 50th birthday, Bandeira was feted with the critical volume *Homenagem a Manuel Bandeira* (1936; Homage to Manuel Bandeira). The same year, he also published another poetry collection, *Estrela da Manhã* (1936; Morning Star), and, shortly after, the book of **chronicles** *Crônicas da Província do Brasil* (1937; Chronicles of the Province of Brazil).

His poetry collections from later years include *Lira dos Cinqüent' Anos* (1940; Lyre at Age Fifty) in his *Poesias Completas* (Complete Poems), *Belo Belo* (1948; Lovely, Lovely), *Mafuá do Malungo*

(1948; Carnival of the Malungo), *Opus 10* (1952: Opus 10), and *Estrela da Tarde* (1960; Evening Star). In the 1940s and through the 1960s, Bandeira taught Spanish American literature at the University of Rio and wrote several important works of literary criticism, among which were *Noções de História das Literaturas* (1940; Concepts on the History of Literatures), *Aprensentação da Poesia Brasileira* (1946; Introduction to Brazilian Poetry), *Literatura Hispano-Americana* (1949; Spanish American Literature), *Gonçalves Dias: Esboço Biográfico* (1952; Gonçalves Dias: Biographical Sketch), and *De Poetas e de Poesia* (1954; Of Poets and Poetry).

Other writings include chronicles and memoirs, such as *Itinerário de Parsárgada* (1954; Itinerary of Pasárgada), *Guia de Ouro Preto* (1938; Guide to Ouro Preto), *Flauta de Papel* (1957; Paper Flute), *Andorinha, Andorinha* (1966; Little Swallow), *Os Reis Vagabundos e Mais 50 Crônicas* (1966; The Vagabond Kings and 50 More Chronicles), and *Colóquio Unilateralmente Sentimental* (1968; Unilaterally Sentimental Colloquy). Many of his chronicles were broadcast on national radio. A prolific translator, Bandeira also published a volume of translations, *Poemas Traduzidos* (1958; Translated Poems). On his 80th birthday, he was honored with the publication of another poetry collection, *Estrela da Vida Inteira* (1966; *Star of His Entire Life*), and he received several distinctions, among them The National Order of Merit. *See also* ANDRADE, MÁRIO RAUL DE MORAIS; FERRAZ, HEITOR; FREYRE, GILBERTO DE MELO; GUIMARÃES, BERNARDO JOAQUIM DA SILVA; PRADO, ADÉLIA.

BARBOSA, FREDERICO (Brazil, 1961–). Poet. A contemporary poet who emerged from the lessons of the **concrete poetry** movement, Barbosa has established himself as a major dissenting voice in contemporary poetry. His principal works include *Rarefato* (1990; Rarefact), *Nada Feito Nada* (1993; Nothing Made Nothing), *Contracorrente* (2000; Countercurrent), and *Louco ou Oco Sem Beiras: Anatomia da Depressão* (2001; Crazy or Hole without Edges: Anatomy of Depression).

BAREIRO SAGUIER, RUBÉN (Paraguay, 1930–). Poet and short story writer. Most of his writing was produced in exile in France, where he lived after a year in prison in Paraguay for his involvement in opposition to the government. His poetry includes *A la víbora de la mar* (1977; London Bridge Is Falling Down) and *Estancias/errancias/querencias* (1982; Visits/Wanderings/Longings), as well as *Biografía de ausente* (1964; Biography of a Missing Person), published in Paraguay before he went into exile. His collections of short stories, *Ojo por diente* (1972; An Eye for a Tooth) and *El séptimo pétalo del viento* (1984; The Seventh Petal of the Wind), contributed to the development of a more socially critical tone in Paraguayan fiction. *Ojo por diente* received a **Casa de las Américas** prize.

BAROQUE. Derived from Europe, the baroque was the dominant style of the colonial period and was especially prevalent in the 17th and 18th centuries. It affected all forms of expression, including architecture, painting, music, literature, and **theater**. In literature, the baroque is often characterized by complex language and highly imaginative metaphors, sharp contrasts, and the conflict between a secular and a religious view of the world. Among its prominent exponents in Spanish America were **Bernardo de Balbuena**, **Sor Juana Inés de la Cruz**, **Eusebio Vela**, and **Carlos de Sigüenza y Góngora** from **Mexico**, and from **Peru**, **Juan de Espinosa Medrano** and **Juan del Valle y Caviedes**. In **Brazil** it includes the satirical poetry and drama of **Gregório de Mattos e Guerra**, the comedies and secular love poetry of **Manuel Botelho de Oliveira**, and the sermons of **Antônio Vieira**. *See also* ARCADIANISM; COLOMBIA; COSTA, CLÁUDIO MANUEL DA; LEMINSKI, PAULO; LINS, OSMAN; MADARIAGA, FRANCISCO; SALOMÃO, WALY; VENEZUELA.

BARRETO DE MENESES, TOBIAS (Brazil, 1839–1889). Essayist and philosopher. Of modest and mixed-race origin, Barreto learned Latin in his native Sergipe and became a teacher at age 15. He then studied law in Recife and began writing poetry in the style of Victor Hugo (1773–1828), engaging in a polemic with **Antônio Frederico de Castro Alves**. A declared enemy of traditional philosophy and law, Barreto attempted to stir Brazil's outdated monarchical society through an appropriation of Darwinism and French **positivism**, as in his *Estudos de Filosofia e Crítica* (1875; Studies in Philosophy and Criticism) and *Questões Vigentes de Filosofia e de Direito* (1888; Current Issues in Philosophy and Law). The intellectual movement of renovation Barreto spearheaded became known as the School of Recife, and one of his disciples was the literary critic **Sílvio Romero**. Barreto also taught himself German in order to read Ernst Haeckel (1834–1919) and other philosophers in the original, and he published some works on German subjects, including *Estudos Alemães* (1881; German Studies) and some articles written in German. His posthumous works include the poetry of *Dias e Noites* (1893; Days and Nights) and the essays of *Vários Escritos* (1900; Selected Writings) and *Obras Completas* (1926; Complete Works). *See also* ANJOS, AUGUSTO DOS; ROMERO, SÍLVIO.

BARRIOS, EDUARDO (Chile, 1884–1963). Novelist. He wrote introspective, psychological novels of the abnormal, of which the most enduring is *El niño que enloqueció de amor* (1915; *The Child Who Went Crazy with Love*), about an adolescent's feelings for an older woman. Other prominent novels are *Un perdido* (1918; A Lost Soul); *El hermano asno* (1922; *Brother Ass*), concerning the spiritual and sexual conflicts of two monks; and *Gran señor y rajadiablos* (1948; Great Lord and Hellraiser), a saga of life in rural Chile spanning the late 19th and early 20th centuries, having some of the characteristics of **criollismo**.

BARRIOS DE CHUNGARA, DOMITILA (Bolivia, 1937–). Her life and the struggles of Bolivian tin miners and their families figure in the **testimonio** *Si me permiten hablar: testimonio de Domitila, una mujer de las minas de Bolivia* (1978; *Let Me Speak! Testimony of Domitila, a Woman of the Bolivian Mines*), written with Moema Viezzer. *See also* WOMEN.

BARROS, MANOEL DE (Brazil, 1916–). Poet. Although Barros began publishing early with his first book, *Poemas Concebidos Sem Pecado* (1937; Poems Conceived Without Sin), he only gained recognition in the 1980s. Born and raised in the rural area of Pantanal in southwestern Brazil, Barros writes a poetry of the quotidian, mainly inspired by his homeland and nature, the observation of which leads to more profound existential reflections. His poetry attempts to recuperate the notion of a primordial Edenic language, such as *Gramática Expositiva do Chão* (1966; Expository Grammar of the Ground) and

O Livro das Ignorãças (1993; The Book of IgnoRa(n)ces). Other books include *Arranjos para Assobio* (1980; Arrangements for a Whistle), *O Guardador de Águas* (1989; The Keeper of Waters), *Livro Sobre Nada* (1996; Book on Nothing), *Ensaios Fotográficos* (2000; Photographic Essays), *Tratado Central das Grandezas do Ínfimo* (2001; Central Treaty on the Greatness of the Negligible), and *Memórias Inventadas: A Infância* (2003; Invented Memories: Childhood).

BARROS, PÍA (Chile, 1956–). Short story writer. Focusing on the themes of identity, the erotic, and the culture and politics of Chile, Barros has published several collections of stories. These include *Miedos transitorios* (1986; Transitory Fears), *A horcajadas* (1995; Astride), *Signos bajo la piel* (1995; Signs Beneath the Skin), *Los que sobran* (2002; Those Left Over), and *Llamadas perdidas* (2008; Lost Calls), a collection of **microtales**. She has also written a novel, *El tono menor del deseo* (1991; The Undertone of Desire).

BARROS GREZ, DANIEL (Chile, 1834–1904). Novelist and dramatist. He introduced the serial novel to Chile and wrote a number of **historical novels** that have become a mine of information about the customs and folklore of Chile. His best-known novel is *Pipiolos y pelucones* (1876; Liberals and Conservatives), a historical novel set in the first half of the 19th century. Later works include *El huérfano* (1881; The Orphan), a mammoth **picaresque** tale in six volumes based in part on the author's own life; *La academia político-literaria* (1890), a miscellany of narratives and poetry; and *Primeras aventuras maravillosas del perro Cuatro Remos en Santiago* (1898; The First Marvelous Adventures of the Dog Four Oars in Santiago), a tale built around a dog belonging to a group of Santiago firemen. As a dramatist, he is best known for plays written in the style of **costumbrismo**, poking fun at the middle class, several of which have been revived for 20th-century performances. His first play was *La beata* (1859; The Devout Woman), a satire of religious excess. *El ensayo de la comedia* (1889; The Rehearsal) uses the strategy of the "play within the play," and one of his best-known works is *Como en Santiago* (1875; As in Santiago), a comedy of manners about the imitation of the ways of the capital in the provinces. *See also* THEATER.

BASURTO, LUIS G. (Mexico, 1921–1990). Dramatist. Although he qualified as a lawyer, Basurto went to Hollywood in 1942 to study cinematography and devoted much of his life to writing and directing for the stage and cinema. He often worked in collaboration with **Xavier Villaurrutia** and became one of the most successful dramatists of the second half of the 20th century, appreciated for his humorous works of social criticism. *Cada quien su vida* (1955; Each to His Own Life) is one of the most frequently performed plays in the history of Mexican theater. Other plays include *Los diálogos de Suzette* (1940; Suzette's Dialogues), *Voz como sangre* (1942; Voice Like Blood), *La que se fue* (1946; The Woman Who Left), *Frente a la muerte* (1952; Facing Death), *Toda una dama* (1954; The Complete Lady), *Miércoles de ceniza* (1956; Ash Wednesday), *La locura de los ángeles* (1957; The Madness of the Angels), *Los reyes del mundo* (1959; Kings of the World), *El escándalo de la verdad* (1960; The Truth Scandal), *Bodas de plata* (1960; Silver Wedding), *La gobernadora* (1963; The Lady Governor), *Y todos terminaron ladrando* (1964; And They All Ended Up Barking), *Cadena perpetua* (1965; Life Sentence), and *Con la frente en el polvo* (1967; Head in the Dust).

BATRES MONTÚFAR, JOSÉ (Guatemala, 1809–1844). Poet. One of his country's most important 19th-century poets. His *Poemas* (1845; Poems) were published posthumously with an introduction by **José Milla y Vidaure**. He wrote lyric verse, but is best remembered for verse narratives that have retained their popularity for over a century and a half. Taken from colonial times and with some of the characteristics of **romanticism** and the style of Spanish authors such as José Zorilla (1817–1893), his narratives also anticipate the *tradiciones* of **Ricardo Palma**.

BAYLY, JAIME (Peru, 1965–). Novelist. His novels on contemporary society deal with themes of desire and sexual repression. His works include *No se lo digas a nadie* (1994; Don't Tell Anyone); *Fue ayer y no me acuerdo* (It Was Yesterday and I Don't Remember), which includes episodes of bisexuality and homosexuality; *Los últimos días de La Prensa* (1996; The Last Days of La Prensa), a novel about the banning of a major Peruvian newspaper; *Yo amo a mi mamá* (1999;

I Love My Mummy); *La mujer de mi hermano* (2002; My Brother's Wife); *El huracán lleva tu nombre* (2004; The Hurricane Bears Your Name); and *Y de repente, un ángel* (2005; And Suddenly an Angel). Bayly is a televsion personality, and his first and most recent novels have served as the basis for movies. *See also* GAY AND LESBIAN WRITERS AND WRITING.

BELLI, CARLOS GERMÁN (Peru, 1927–). Poet. In contrast to others of his generation, whose work tends to be simpler, Belli's poetry is more hermetic. It develops its own system of symbols and often refers to writers of the Spanish Renaissance and baroque. At the same time, Belli evokes the horror of life in contemporary Lima while longing for a brighter future for himself and his country. His major works include *¡Oh, Hada Cibernética!* (1961; Oh, Cybernetic Muse!), *El pie sobre el cuello* (1964; With a Foot on the Neck), *Por el monte abajo: poemas* (1966; Down the Mountain: Poems), *En alabanza del bolo alimenticio* (1979; In Praise of the Bolus), *Más que señora humana* (1986; More Than Human Lady), and *En el restante tiempo terrenal* (1988; In the Remaining Time on Earth).

BELLI, GIOCONDA (Nicaragua, 1948–). Novelist and poet. Her affiliation with the Sandinista Revolution (1970–1979) in Nicaragua colors much of her writing, especially her autobiographical work *El país bajo mi piel: memorias de amor y guerra* (2001; *The Country Under My Skin: A Memoir of Love and War*), although her support for the revolutionary party in Nicaragua has since declined. Her first novel, *La mujer habitada* (1988; *The Inhabited Woman*), became an international **best seller** and gave the author a prominent place among contemporary Latin American **women** writers. It was one of the first novels to raise the question of gender in narratives of the Sandinista Revolution. Her second novel, *Sofía de los presagios* (1990; Sofía and Her Premonitions), sustains a focus on women in society and female liberation. Her later novels include *El pergamino de la seducción* (2005; *The Scroll of Seduction*). Women and the revolution have also figured as prominent themes in her poetry, of which she has several collections, including *Sobre la grama* (1974; On the Grass); *Línea de fuego* (1978; Line of Fire), which received a **Casa de las Américas** prize; *De la costilla de Eva* (1987; *From Eve's Rib*); and *Apogeo* (1997; Apogee). *Truenos y arco iris* (1982; Thunder and Rainbow) concerns the period of reconstruction in Nicaragua. An anthology of her poetry has been collected in *El ojo de la mujer* (1991; The Woman's Eye). *See also* CORONEL URTECHO, JOSÉ.

BELLO, ANDRÉS (Venezuela/Chile, 1781–1865). Poet, grammarian, historian, and journalist. He was one of Latin America's most significant 19th-century intellectuals and a prominent figure in the cultural and political life of Venezuela, where he was born, and Chile, where he lived the latter half of his life. In addition to his poetry, he authored books on law, geography, the Spanish language, and history. His poetry includes his *Alocución a la poesía* (1823; Invocation to Poetry) and *Silva a la agricultura de la zona tórrida* (1826; Silva to Agriculture in the Torrid Zone), his most frequently cited literary works. Both were written in the style of **neo-classicism** while living in London (1810–1829), and praise the natural world of the Americas as a fit subject for poetry. His *Gramática de la lengua castellana destinada al uso de los americanos* (1847; Grammar of the Spanish Language Intended for the Use of Americans) and other writings on language reflect the importance he attached to education for the newly independent countries of Spanish America and his belief that language could serve to unify them. *See also* LASTARRIA, JOSÉ VICTORINO; RODRÍGUEZ MONEGAL, EMIR.

BENAVENTE, TORIBIO DE (MOTOLINÍA) (Mexico, ca. 1500–1568). Chronicler. A Franciscan friar, he was among the first group of missionaries sent to Mexico to undertake the conversion of the native population. Of the writings he left, the most substantial is his **chronicle** *Historia de los indios de la Nueva España* (History of the Indians of New Spain), which he began in 1536, although it was not published until 1858. It has sections on Aztec religion, the conversion to Christianity, and the New World in general, and is an important historical resource concerning the early years of colonization. Motolinía, the Nahuatl name adopted by Fray Toribio, means "poor."

BENEDETTI, MARIO (Uruguay, 1920– 2009). Novelist, short story writer, poet, and essayist. Fiction and poetry predominate in his work, but he is a prolific writer in all the genres he cultivates. His first collection of short stories, *Esta mañana* (1949; This Morning), shows the influence of wide reading in modern fiction, including the work of **Juan Carlos Onetti**, and the presence of themes he continued to develop in his subsequent publications. In the novel *Quién de nosotros* (1953; Who Among Us), the verse in *Poemas de la oficina* (1956; Office Poems), and the short stories in *Montevideanos* (1959; Montevideans), Benedetti began to examine the growing social crisis in Uruguay in the 1950s and to focus on everyday life and the urban middle class. These concerns continue in *La tregua* (1960; *The Truce*), the author's most enduring novel, about an older man experiencing a brief moment of happiness, and in *Gracias por el fuego* (1965; Thanks for the Light), his third novel, based on his experiences in the United States.

Benedetti's involvement in the political opposition in Uruguay during the 1970s was expressed in writing as well as in actions. His political speeches and articles were collected in *Crónicas del 71* (1972; Chronicles from 71), and in *El cumpleaños de Juan Ángel* (1971; Juan Angel's Birthday), he wrote a novel in verse that tells how the life of its protagonist led him to become a revolutionary. Forced into exile, Benedetti continued to write. He renewed his interest in **theater**. He had already had some success with *Ida y vuelta* (written 1955, published 1963; Round Trip) before his play *Pedro y el capitán* (1979; Peter and the Captain), dealing with the military regime, was first performed by a theater company in exile.

His experience of exile is expressed in the novel *Primavera con un esquina rota* (1982; Spring with a Broken Corner), in which Benedetti uses different narrative lines to convey a range of circumstances, including imprisonment and repression; in *Geografías* (1984; Geographies), a collection of short stories that includes both poetry and prose; and in the novel *Recuerdos olvidados* (1988; Forgotten Memories). Benedetti's essays of that time, such as *Letras de emergencia* (1981; Urgent Writings) and *Crítica cómplice* (1981; Committed Criticism), on political, literary, and social themes, are in a direct, straightforward style and convey his political engagement. His collected poetry has appeared in a volume titled *Inventario* (1963; Inventory), which has had numerous expanded editions to include more recent work. His fiction and poetry have also served as a basis for numerous films, and many of his poems have been set to music and recorded, notably by the Catalan singer Joan Manuel Serrat.

BERMAN, SABINA (Mexico, 1953–). Dramatist. Berman is one of Mexico's most successful contemporary playwrights. She often focuses on the enigmas of life centered on questions of identity and power relationships, in plays that are open-ended or highly ambiguous. Her major works for the stage include *El suplicio del placer* (1978; *The Agony of Ecstasy*); *Yanqui* (1979; *Yankee*), about the shifting identity of an American and his influence; *Rompecabezas* (1982; *Puzzle*), on the assassination of Leon Trotsky in Mexico in 1942; *Herejía* (1983; *Heresy*), about a family of *conversos* (Jews converted to Christianity) in colonial times; and *Krisis* (1996; Krisis), a play attacking the Partido Revolucionario Institucional (Institutional Revolutionary Party), which governed Mexico from 1929 until 2000. *See also* THEATER; WOMEN.

BEST SELLER. The term began to be used in the 1960s, especially in association with the major writers of the **boom** in Spanish American fiction such as **Julio Cortázar, Carlos Fuentes, Gabriel García Márquez,** and **Mario Vargas Llosa,** whose works were among the first to be aggressively marketed and to have high international sales. After their early successes, their later novels were often published simultaneously in multiple languages. Once the popularity of Latin American writing had been established, other writers also obtained wide international sales. **Isabel Allende (Chile)** and **Laura Esquivel (Mexico)** are among **women** writers whose books have achieved notable success and were promoted further by film versions. Other internationally successful authors include **Gioconda Belli (Nicaragua)** and **Tomás Eloy Martínez** and **Manuel Puig (Argentina).** On a different scale, as in the case of novels by authors such as **María Elena Walsh** and **Jorge Asís** (Argentina), **Enrique Lafourcade** (Chile), or **Ángeles Mastretta** (Mexico), the term "best seller" is also used to refer to books that have won recognition through their sales in national markets.

Brazil had best-selling authors even before the 1960s boom, which is often considered mainly a Spanish American phenomenon. Authors such as **Dinah Silveira de Queirós** and **Érico Veríssimo** in the 1930s and 1940s anticipated the success of **Jorge Amado**, who began writing before the boom and became known internationally later thanks to translations of his works and film adaptations. More recently, **Rubem Fonseca, Luis Fernando Veríssimo**, and **João Ubaldo Ribeiro** have also achieved best-selling status. Yet none of them matches **Paulo Coelho**, Brazil's all-time best-selling author, who has 100 million copies to his credit and in 2003 was the most sold author worldwide.

BILAC, OLAVO BRÁS MARTINS DOS GUIMARÃES (Brazil, 1865–1918). Essayist and poet. Brazil's parnassian poet par excellence, Bilac attained greater prestige and popular esteem while alive than any other poet. He was also a journalist and civic activist at the time when the monarchy and slavery were abolished and the republic proclaimed. Bilac traveled extensively in Brazil and abroad, charged with public missions, and was elected the first "Prince of Poets" of Brazil. A consummate wordsmith, his poetry sought the perfection of form and the understatement of feeling promoted by **parnassianism**. Besides several poetry collections, including *Poesias* (1888; Poems), a volume gathering *Panóplias* (Panoplies), *Via Láctea* (Milky Way), and *Sarças de Fogo* (Fire Brambles), with a second edition in 1902 that added *Alma Inquieta* (Restless Soul), *As Viagens* (Travels), and *O Caçador de Esmeraldas* (The Emerald Hunter), Bilac also authored a rhyming dictionary and a treatise on versification. *See also* CORREIA, RAIMUNDO; MEIRELES, CECÍLIA; POMPÉIA, RAUL D'ÁVILA.

BIOY CASARES, ADOLFO (Argentina, 1914–1999). Novelist and short story writer. He often explores the nature of reality and human existence by combining elements of the fantastic, terror, and science fiction in the manner of **fantastic literature**. His first novel, *La invención de Morel* (1940; *The Invention of Morel*), a classic of Latin American literature, is the story of a fugitive on an island who discovers the world around him to be a projection. *Plan de evasión* (1945; *A Plan for Escape*), his second novel, also set on an island, describes the unsuccessful attempts by a prison governor to control inmates' lives using similar kinds of projections. In *El sueño de los héroes* (1954; *The Dream of Heroes*), set in Buenos Aires, the protagonist tries to learn whether part of his life is a repetition of what he has already lived.

The author turned to different issues in *Diario de la guerra del cerdo* (1969; *Diary of the War of the Pig*) and *Dormir al sol* (1973; *Asleep in the Sun*), which deal, respectively, with generational conflict and personality manipulation, but he returns to the relation between images and reality in his last novel, *La aventura de un fotógrafo en La Plata* (1985; A Photographer's Adventure in La Plata). His short stories explore the same kinds of themes and styles as his novels. He published nine collections in total, including *La trama celeste* (1948; The Celestial Plot), *Guirnalda con amores* (1959; Bouquet with Love), *Historias de amor* (1972; Tales of Love), and *Historias fantásticas* (1972; Tales of the Fantastic).

Bioy Casares also wrote in collaboration with his wife, **Silvina Ocampo**, and **Jorge Luis Borges**. Among his collaborations with the latter is a collection of crime stories, *Seis problemas para don Isidro Parodi* (1942; *Six Problems for Don Isidro Parodi*), and the two writers also edited a **crime fiction** series called Séptimo Círculo (Seventh Circle). Bioy Casares received the **Miguel de Cervantes Prize for Literature** in 1990. *See also* AMORIM, ENRIQUE.

BIVAR, ANTÔNIO (Brazil, 1940–). Dramatist and nonfiction writer. Best known for his political plays set in an authoritarian society, Bivar participated in the counterculture movements of the 1960s, 1970s, and 1980s. He received prizes for his play *Cordélia Brasil* (1967; Cordelia Brazil) and his autobiographical narrative *Verdes vales do fim do mundo* (1984; Green Valleys at the End of the World). *See also* THEATER.

BLANCO FOMBONA, RUFINO (Venezuela, 1874–1944). Poet, novelist, and essayist. He was a prolific writer, and much of what he wrote responded to his unfailing interest in Spanish America or his antagonism toward the dictatorial regimes of his native country. He published five collections of poetry. Of these, *Cantos de la prisión y del destierro* (1911; Songs of Prison and Exile) was written in defiance of the dictator General Juan Vicente Gómez (1908–1935) at the beginning of a long period of exile the author spent in Europe (1910–1936). He also wrote five biographical novels that tell the lives of strong, driven personalities. In both *El hombre de hierro* (1907; The Man of Iron) and *El hombre de oro* (1915; *The Man of Gold*), for example, his protagonists are Darwinian characters, whose actions yield success in the first novel and failure in the second.

Blanco Fombona is perhaps best remembered, however, for his essays. He wrote several books on Simón Bolívar (1783–1830), whose speeches and letters he also edited. Among his historical writings are *La evolución política y social de Hispanoamérica* (1911; The Political and Social Evolution of Spanish America) and *El conquistador español del siglo XVI* (1921; The Spanish Conqueror of the Sixteenth Century). His literary criticism includes *Grandes escritores de América* (1917; Great Writers of America) and *El modernismo y los poetas modernistas* (1929; Modernism and the Modernist Poets), in which he established the critical foundations of **modernismo**.

BLEST GANA, ALBERTO (Chile, 1830–1920). Novelist. One of the first novelists in Spanish America to adopt European **realism**, he applied what he read in the works of French author Honoré de Balzac (1799–1850) to a description of the emerging middle class in Chile and the power of money as the force underlying 19th-century society. His novels reflect his capacity for social observation, but have been criticized for their adherence to romantic plot conventions, as in *Martín Rivas* (1862; *Martin Rivas*), his best-known work and one of the classics of 19th-century Latin American literature, in which the drama of the hero's political gesture is a consequence of his frustration in love. Other works include *La aritmética en el amor* (1860; The Arithmetic of Love), *El ideal de un calavera* (1863; A Rake's Ideal), and a **historical novel**, *Durante la conquista* (1897; During the Conquest). *See also* GREZ, VICENTE; ORREGO LUCO, LUIS.

BOAL, AUGUSTO (Brazil, 1931–2009). Dramatist, essayist, and theater director. An internationally recognized innovative director and cultural activist, Boal came into conflict with the military government after the staging of his nationalist plays *Arena Conta Zumbi* (1965; Arena Retells Zumbi) and *Arena Conta Tiradentes* (1967; Arena Retells Tiradentes), both coauthored with **Gianfrancesco Guarnieri** and based on controversial historical figures. Boal was exiled in **Argentina**, where he published his influential reflections on **theater** technique, *Teatro del oprimido y otras poéticas políticas* (1974; *Theater of the Oppressed and Other Political Poetics*), inspired by *Pedagogy of the Oppressed* (1968) by Paulo Freire (1921–1997), and *Técnicas latinoamericanas de teatro popular* (1975; Latin American Popular Theater Techniques). In the former, following the concepts of **Brechtian theater**, Boal critiqued Aristotelian poetics as oppressive. His influential *Jeux pour acteurs et non-acteurs* (1978; *Games for Actors and Non-Actors*), published while he lived in Paris, contains practical exercises for drama performance. Boal developed a "Joker system," in which all actors play all roles and the action is narrated by the "Joker," an analytical observer. More recently, Boal had an active career in local politics in Brazil.

BOLAÑO, ROBERTO (Chile, 1953–2003). Novelist and short story writer. Bolaño is considered by many to be one of the greatest prose writers of his generation. He lived outside Chile after 1973 and eventually settled in Spain, where some of his fiction is set. His two major novels are both epic in scope. *Los detectives salvajes* (1998; *The Savage Detectives*), which won the 1999 **Rómulo Gallegos Prize**, is a meandering narrative with multiple voices and testimonies structured around the wanderings of its two main characters and the intricacies of a movement called "Visceral Realism." *2666* (2004; *2666*) focuses on serial murders committed in the fictive Mexican town of Santa Teresa, first introduced in *Los detectives salvajes*. It has over 1,000 pages and offers an apocalyptic view of the 20th century. Bolaño's other novels include *La pista de hielo* (1993; The Ice Trail), a story of crime on the Spanish Mediterranean that includes his own literary persona, Arturo Belano, and anticipates the multiple narratives characteristic of later work; *Literatura nazi en América* (1996; *Nazi Literature in the Americas*), an encyclopedia of fictional authors; *Estrella distante* (1996; *Distant Star*) and *Amuleto* (1999; *Amulet*), both developed from earlier novels; and *Nocturno de Chile* (2000; *By Night in Chile*), about a priest and a literary critic connected to the regime of Augusto Pinochet (1973–1990) in Chile. Bolaño's short stories have appeared in *Llamadas telefónicas* (1997; Telephone Calls), *Putas asesinas* (2001; Killer Whores), and *El gaucho insufrible* (2003; The Intolerable Gaucho). A selection from the first two of these was published in English translation in *Last Evenings on Earth*

(2006). Bolaño also wrote poetry and journalism, but his reputation is founded on his fiction.

BOLÍVAR, SIMÓN (Venezuela, 1783–1830). Although celebrated most for his military and political activities at the time of the Wars of Independence and after, some of his writings are among the most important foundational texts of Spanish America. They include his call to arms in *El Manifiesto de Cartagena* (1812; The Cartagena Manifesto) and his reflections on the War in *Carta de Jamaica* (1815; *Letter from Jamaica*). *See also* GARCÍA MÁRQUEZ, GABRIEL; OLMEDO, JOSÉ JOAQUÍN; VARGAS TEJADA, LUIS.

BOLIVIA. In comparison with that of its neighbors **Argentina**, **Brazil**, and **Chile**, the literary output of Bolivia is relatively small. Some have seen this as the result of a history of isolation, separated from the cultural centers of South America during the colonial period and subsequently landlocked following the loss of an outlet to the sea after the War of the Pacific (1879–1884). With Quechua and Aymara-speaking Amerindians constituting over 50 percent of the population, Bolivia is also thought of as less disposed to enter the main literary systems of Latin America. Moreover, the country has endured political and economic instability for much of its history since independence, including the loss of over half of its national territory through wars and secession.

Notwithstanding these conditions, Bolivia has chronicled its social and political life in literature and produced a body of important writers who are part of the Latin American canon. In poetry, **Ricardo Jaimes Freyre** was a significant representative of **modernismo**, as was **Franz Tamayo**, albeit a late, aestheticized practitioner of the style. By contrast, **Jaime Saénz**, a younger poet than either of these two modernists, wrote successfully in a hermetic style akin to **surrealism**. In prose writing, one of the first Bolivians to be widely read outside his country was the novelist and historian **Alcides Arguedas**, whose negative **indigenismo** found an equally extreme but opposite counterpart in the essays of the poet Franz Tamayo. A more sympathetic view of indigenous life and culture was in due course found in the work of **Jesús Lara**. As a country whose economy has been dominated by resource extraction—first silver, then tin—both before and after independence, Bolivia also has a tradition of prose writing related to mining, within which the **testimonio** by **Domitila Barrios de Chungara** is an important example. Mining also figures in the **historical novels** of **Néstor Taboada Terán**, Bolivia's most important contemporary novelist, who has written on the theme of the Chaco War (1932–1935) between Bolivia and **Paraguay**, which had disastrous consequences for Bolivia and also gave rise to a body of literary writing.

With respect to **theater**, there was a tradition of theatrical performance in Quechua and Aymara, which was used by the Spanish missionaries as a strategy for teaching Christianity. As early as the 16th century, there was a secular theater in the mining city of Potosí. The development of a Bolivian theater did not progress significantly, however, until the 19th century, with the writing and staging of plays on historical themes, although not necessarily from Bolivian history. **Ricardo Jaimes Freyre** was among the contributors to this trend. The Chaco War also served later as a source of inspiration for dramatists. In the 1950s and 1960s, there were some notable writers for the stage, such as **Guillermo Francovich** and **Raúl Botelho Gonsálvez**, but they did not transcend their enviroment. The same might be said of subsequent decades. Original plays draw on historical sources and deal with politics and social injustice, but often in rather didactic terms at the expense of artistic merit. In effect, the theater in contemporary Bolivia does not have a strong presence, its impact is local, and there is also some tendency to favor the staging of foreign plays. See also ACOSTA, JOSÉ DE; GORRITI, JUANA MANUELA; MARÍN CAÑAS, JOSÉ; PARAGUAY; ROA BASTOS, AUGUSTO; WOMEN.

BOMBAL, MARÍA LUISA (Chile, 1910–1980). Novelist. She is known principally for her two novels, *La última niebla* (1935; *The Final Mist*) and *La amortajada* (1938; *The Shrouded Woman*). Both are highly introspective works that explore inner fantasies in the manner of **surrealism** and break with the predominantly realistic style of the times. They also place the author in the vanguard of 20th-century **women** writers whose fiction served to explore female subjectivity.

BONASSI, FERNANDO (Brazil, 1962–). Dramatist, novelist, and short story writer. Born in the working-class district of Mooca in São Paulo, Bonassi studied cinema and wrote his first play in 1989, but then turned to narrative. He became famous with his novel *Subúrbio* (1994; Suburb), a tale of people suffering solitude, failure, degradation, and violence in an urban industrial neighborhood. *Subúrbio* shocked the reading public and inaugurated a new trend in Brazilian fiction. His realistic and candid portrayal of underclass social types links him to his predecessor in the genre of **crime fiction**, **Rubem Fonseca**. Other works in this style, which also re-create popular urban speech, include *Um Céu de Estrelas* (1991; A Sky of Stars), *Crimes Conjugais* (1994; Conjugal Crimes), and the very short narratives of *100 Histórias Colhidas na Rua* (1996; 100 Stories Gathered on the Streets). In *Passaporte* (2001; Passport), Bonassi compared European genocides to everyday crimes in Brazil. His play *Apocalipse 1,11* (2002; Revelation 1:11), partly based on St. John's *Revelation*, was adapted as the screenplay for the blockbuster *Carandiru*. *See also* THEATER.

BONVINCINO, RÉGIS (Brazil, 1955–). Poet and translator. Emerging from the **concrete poetry** movement in the mid-1970s, Bonvincino's career soon took a different route through early experimentation with pop music, humor, comic strips, and the vernacular in *Régis Hotel* (1978; Hotel Régis) and *Más Companhias* (1987; Bad Company). Still retaining a youthful diction, *33 Poemas* (1990; 33 Poems) gave way to *Outros Poemas* (1993; Other Poems), *Ossos de Borboleta* (1996; Butterfly Bones), and *Céu-Eclipse* (1999; Sky-Eclipse), which display a more mature voice and a sober, linguistically minimal observation of reality. A restless innovator, Bonvicino has often sought inspiration in non-Brazilian models, particularly American **avant-garde** poets such as Charles Bernstein (1950–) and Robert Creeley (1926–2005), whose work he he translated. His *Remorso do Cosmos (de Ter Vindo ao Sol)* (2003; Remorse of the Cosmos [for Having Arrived at the Sun]) and *Página Órfã* (2007; Orphan Page) are collections in which postmodern images from the media collide with the harsh reality of life in the megalopolis of São Paulo. Bonvicino also directs the poetry review *Sibila* (Sybil).

BOOKS OF CHILAM BALAM. A collection of documents relevant for a consideration of **indigenous traditions**. They are hybrid texts from **Guatemala** that integrate Maya and Christian concepts. Among the most significant are the *Books of Chilam Balam of Chumayel*.

BOOM. This term, coined by **Emir Rodríguez Monegal**, refers to the rise in international popularity of the Latin American novel that began in the 1960s. The boom was marked by the emergence of a group of especially talented writers, but was also the product of successful marketing that gave them increased visibility and turned some of their books into **best sellers**. It did not constitute a formal movement, although some of the novels shared certain characteristics in that they experimented with narrative conventions; told epic tales that attempted to capture the history, geography, and culture of the country to which they referred; and were thought of as having a particularly Latin American style often associated with **magic realism**. In Spanish America, the principal authors were **Julio Cortázar** (Argentina), **Carlos Fuentes** (Mexico), **Gabriel García Márquez** (Colombia), and **Mario Vargas Llosa** (Peru), with others such as **José Donoso** (Chile), **Alfredo Bryce Echenique** and **Manuel Scorza** (Peru), and **Manuel Puig** (Argentina) also associated with the phenomenon. In **Brazil, Jorge Amado, João Guimarães Rosa**, and **Clarice Lispector** are often seen as part of the boom, but the attribution is controversial because of the different characteristics of their work and their own sense of autonomy. Moroever, the boom is often considered a Spanish American phenomenon. *See also* ARÉVALO MARTÍNEZ, RAFAEL; ASTURIAS, MIGUEL ÁNGEL; POST-BOOM.

BOPP, RAUL (Brazil, 1898–1984). Poet. One of the main exponents of **antropofagia**, Bopp traveled and worked at odd jobs before coming into contact with figures of **Brazilian modernism**. Initially attracted by the nationalist conservative vanguard led by **Plínio Salgado**, he coauthored the *Manifesto do Verdeamarelismo ou da Escola da Anta* (1929; Manifesto of the Green-Yellow Movement or The School of the Tapir). He later joined the opposing group led by **Oswald de Andrade** and his *Revista de antropofagia*. Bopp is best known for his Amazonian **epic-magic poem**, *Cobra Norato* (1931; Cobra Norato), one of the most representative works of the mixture of nationalism and primitivism characteristic of antropofagia. It features a snake named Cobra Norato and magical beings who inhabit the rain forest and was inspired by native Brazilian legends from the Amazon. Another of Bopp's poems, *Urucungo* (1933; Urucungo), drew from elements of Afro-Brazilian culture. *See also* GALVÃO, PATRÍCIA; RICARDO LEITE, CASSIANO; VERDEAMARELISMO.

BORGES, JORGE LUIS (Argentina, 1899–1986). Poet, short story writer, and essayist. Borges is one of Latin America's foremost and most internationally recognized literary figures of the 20th century. His wide reading in European and American literature and in Eastern and Western philosophy and religions is reflected in his work, but unlike many of his contemporaries, he was not overtly political in his writing. In carefully crafted short pieces (stories, **microtales**, fictive-essays), he was drawn more to the universal dimensions of life and its character as a riddle represented by metaphors such as the labyrinth, mirror images, or the circularity of time, often in the manner of **fantastic literature**. Returning to Argentina in 1923 after seven years in Europe, he wrote for the **avant-garde** review *Martín Fierro*, was cofounder of the **journal** *Proa* in 1924, and contributed to *Sur*, Argentina's most important literary journal. His first collection of verse, *Fervor de Buenos Aires* (1923; The Fervor of Buenos Aires), an exploration of existence through a sensitive evocation of the city, followed the precepts of **ultraísmo** adopted by Borges while in Spain. Later volumes, *Poemas 1922–1943* (1944; Poems 1922–1943), *Poemas 1923–1953* (1954), *Poemas 1923–1958* (1958), and *Obra poética 1923–1977* (1983; Poetic Work 1923–1977), successively added to and revised earlier collections. The last of his collections of verse, *Los conjurados* (1985; The Conspirators), appeared the year before he died.

Borges's early prose works were essays, published in *Inquisiciones* (1925; Inquisitions), *Discusión* (1932; *Discussion*), *Historia universal de la infamia* (1935; *A Universal History of Infamy*), and *Historia de la eternidad* (1936; *History of Eternity*), in which he often presented arguments based on false logic or a hoax. His first collection of stories was *El jardín de senderos que se bifurcan* (1941; *The Garden of Forking Paths*), followed by *Ficciones* (1944; *Fic-*

tions) and *El Aleph* (1949; *The Aleph and Other Stories*). These collections were remarkable. In stories such as "Pierre Menard, autor del Quijote" ("Pierre Menard, Author of Don Quixote"), "Las ruinas circulares" ("The Circular Ruins"), "El jardín de senderos que se bifurcan" ("The Garden of Forking Paths"), and "El sur" ("The South"), he showed the multidimensional nature of reality. He focused on the circular or cyclical nature of events, the interconnectedness of phenomena, and the labyrinthine quality of life. The complexity of his work was original and introduced innovative ways of looking at literature and how it represented the world.

Although Borges's progressive blindness would eventually affect his writing, he remained productive. His later prose works included further collections, *El hacedor* (1960; *The Doer*), *Elogio de la sombra* (1969; *In Praise of Darkness*), *El informe de Brodie* (1970; *Dr. Brodie's Report*), and *El libro de arena* (1975; *The Book of Sand*). Earlier in his career he also wrote in collaboration with several other writers, notably **Adolfo Bioy Casares**, with whom he published *Seis problemas para don Isidro Parodi* (1942; *Six Problems for Don Isidro Parodi*) and *Crónicas de Bustos Domecq* (1967; *Chronicles of Bustos Domecq*) and edited an extensive, and very popular, **crime fiction** series called Séptimo Círculo (Seventh Circle). With Bioy Casares and **Silvina Ocampo**, he also edited the celebrated *Antología de la literatura fantástica* (1940; *The Book of Fantasy*). Although he had a profound impact on literature both in Argentina and beyond, he was not a recipient of the **Nobel Prize**. He shared the **Miguel de Cervantes Prize for Literature** with the Spanish poet Gerardo Diego in 1979. *See also* AMORIM, ENRIQUE; COBO BORDA, JUAN GUSTAVO; FERNÁNDEZ, MACEDONIO; GIRONDO, OLIVERIO; GONZÁLEZ LANUZA, EDUARDO; GROUSSAC, PAUL; LANGE, NORAH; MONTERROSO, AUGUSTO; OCAMPO, VICTORIA; PACHECO, JOSÉ EMILIO; PIGLIA, RICARDO; RAMOS SUCRE, JOSÉ ANTONIO; RODRÍGUEZ MONEGAL, EMIR; SAER, JUAN JOSÉ; SOCA, SUSANA; TEITELBOIM, VOLODIA.

BOTELHO GONSÁLVEZ, RAÚL (Bolivia, 1917–1967). Novelist and dramatist. In his fiction he wrote mainly about social injustice, partly in the manner of **costumbrismo**, with ample reference to the Bolivian landscape. His titles include *Borrachera verde* (1938;

Green Binge), *Coca* (1941; Coca), *Altiplano* (1945; Uplands), *Vale un Potosí* (1949; It's Worth Potosí), *Tierra chúcara* (1957; Hostile Ground), *Los toros salvajes y otros cuentos* (1965; Wild Bulls and Other Stories), and *El tata Limachi* (1967; Grandpa Limachi). He also wrote essays on Bolivian history and politics, and an essay on **José Enrique Rodó**, *Reflexiones sobre el cincuentenario de "Ariel" de José Enrique Rodó* (1950; Reflections on the 50th Anniversary of José Enrique Rodó's "Ariel"). As a dramatist, he is known for his historical play *La lanza capitana* (1961; The Leading Lance), about the last Indian rebellion against the Spanish, led by the Aymara Tupai Katari. *See also* THEATER.

BOULLOSA, CARMEN (Mexico, 1954–). Novelist, poet, and dramatist. She is a prolific writer and a significant figure among contemporary **women** writers in Mexico. The content of her work is eclectic, although she often writes on issues of gender and feminism. She experiments with language in all the genres she pursues and is known for the highly imaginative content of her writing. Her first success in fiction was *Son vacas, somos puercos* (1991; *They're Pigs, We're Cows*), a novel in which an old man looks back at the past and recounts his life as a pirate in a way that highlights social difference. Several of her novels are similarly set in historical contexts. *La milagrosa* (1993; *The Miracle Worker*) tells the story of a young woman who falls for the man sent to discredit her ability to perform miracles. *Treinta años* (1999; *Leaving Tabasco*) is a coming-of-age story of Delmira Ulloa, who was raised in Tabasco in an all-female household. *De un salto descabalga la reina* (2002; *Cleopatra Dismounts*) presents alternative versions of the life of the Egyptian queen. Other novels include *Duerme* (1995; Sleep), *Antes* (2001; Before), *La otra mano de Lepanto* (2005; The Other Hand at Lepanto), and *El Velázquez de París* (2007; The Parisian Velazquez).

Boullosa's work for the **theater** is related in part to her own activities as an actor and owner of a popular theater locale in Mexico City. Among her successes are *Cocinar hombres* (1983; Cook Men), about two girls turned into witches so that they can fly over the earth at night in order to tempt, but not satisfy, men; *Aura y las once mil vírgenes* (1986; Aura and the Eleven Thousand Virgins), the story of a man commanded by God to seduce 11,000 virgins, who turns his adventures into a source of television commercials; and *Propusieron a María* (1987; They Proposed to Mary), in which Mary and Joseph talk about the impending birth of Jesus. Other plays include *Trece señoritas* (1983; Thirteen Young Ladies) and *Mi versión de los hechos* (1987; My Version of Events).

Boullosa has also published more than 10 books of poetry, of which some of the most recent are *Niebla* (1997; Mist), *Los delirios* (1998; Deliriums), *Agua* (2000; Water), and *La bebida* (2002; The Draught).

BRAGA, RUBEM (Brazil, 1913–1990). Chronicler. Born in Espírito Santo, Braga is the only Brazilian author to have become famous solely for the **chronicle**. He studied law in Belo Horizonte, but soon left his studies to become a journalist, and published his first book of chronicles, the autobiographical *O Conde e o Passarinho* (The Count and the Little Bird) in 1936. During World War II, Braga traveled to Italy with the Brazilian Expeditionary Force, an experience that inspired his book *Com a FEB na Itália* (1945; With the BEF in Italy). His success as a chronicler is due to his poetic and even lyrical reflections on people, objects, events, and places, all marked by a simplicity of language. Braga is said to have renewed the chronicle as a genre in Brazil and to have contributed to its rehabilitation. Other works include *O Morro do Isolamento* (1944; The Hill of Isolation), *Um Pé de Milho* (1948; A Cornstalk), *O Homem Rouco* (1949; The Hoarse Man), *Cinqüenta Crônicas Escolhidas* (1951; Fifty Selected Chronicles), *A Borboleta Amarela* (1956; The Yellow Butterfly), *A Cidade e a Roça* (1957; The City and the Countryside), *Cem Crônicas Escolhidas* (1958; One Hundred Selected Chronicles), *Ai de Ti, Copacabana!* (1960; Woe Is You, Copacabana!), *A Traição das Elegantes* (1967; The Betrayal of the Elegant), *200 Crônicas Escolhidas* (1977; 200 Selected Chronicles), *As Boas Coisas da Vida* (1988; The Good Things in Life), and *O Verão e as Mulheres* (1990; The Summer and Women). *See also* SABINO, FERNANDO.

BRAÑAS, CÉSAR (Guatemala, 1900–1976). Novelist and poet. His fiction is affiliated mainly with **costumbrismo** and includes the novels *Alba emérita* (1920; Emeritus Dawn), *Tú no sirves* (1926; You're No Use), and *La vida enferma* (1926; Sick Life). Other writings in prose include a number of essays on cultural, historical, and literary subjects and a series of diaries, all similarly titled in the manner of *Diario de un apréndiz de cínico* (1945; Diary of an Apprentice as Cynic) and *Diario de un apréndiz de viejo* (1962; Diary of an Apprentice as an Old Man). As a poet, Brañas published more than a dozen collections of his verse. Notable among them are *Viento negro* (1938; Black Wind), a widely read elegy on the death of his father, and *Lecho de Procrusto* (1945; Procrustean Bed), a collection of sonnets.

BRAZIL. With a population almost five times that of **Argentina** and twice that of **Mexico**, Brazil is South America's largest country and boasts a diverse, 500-year literary history that nevertheless is far less known abroad than the literature of those other countries. Part of the reason for this may be the relative linguistic isolation of Brazil, the only Portuguese-speaking country on the continent, which has also led to the strong sense of national identity pervading many of its literary endeavors. Still, the literature of Brazil has many parallels with that of Spanish America, as well as its own idiosyncrasies and regional differences created by a large territory and settlement over different periods of history.

Economics have often shifted the centers of both commercial and cultural exchange within Brazil. In the early 1500s and 1600s, Europeans settled along the northeastern coast, setting up profitable sugar plantations, which fostered commerce and the slave trade. In the 18th century, diamonds and precious metals were discovered in Minas Gerais, making that region prosperous and sophisticated. The 19th century saw the growth of cities like Rio, when the Portuguese court settled there, and in the late 19th century the rubber trade brought economic activity to the heart of the Amazon. In the early 20th century, the coffee industry made the state of São Paulo and its capital city the largest metropolitan region of South America, a status they retain to this day.

The earliest writings in Brazilian literature, as in Spanish America, were texts or **chronicles**, informing about the discovery and exploration of the territory by European (primarily Portuguese) colonizers, such as **Pero Vaz de Caminha**'s letter written to King Dom Manuel in 1500 upon the arrival of Pedro Alvares Cabral's expedition. Other important chroniclers, who not only charted the territories but also described local populations and customs, include **Pero de Magalhães Gândavo, Frei Vicente do Salvador, Gabriel Soares de Sousa, Fernão Cardim**, and **Manuel da Nóbrega**.

The influence of the Counter-Reformation was felt in the literature of the 17th century, when the first properly "literary" texts saw the light. A contrast of opposites characteristic of European **baroque** authors such as Luis de Góngora (1561–1827), Francisco de Quevedo (1580–1645), and Luís de Camões (1524–1580), and the establishment of a colonial society in which religious and secular views clashed informs the satirical poetry and drama of the Bahian **Gregório de Mattos e Guerra**, the poetry of the first Brazilian to publish his work, **Manuel Botelho de Oliveira**, and the fiery sermons of the Portuguese-born Jesuit **Antônio Vieira**.

As a reaction to the excesses of the baroque, **neo-classicism** in Brazil revived models from Greek and Roman mythology and reflected the rationalist values of the Enlightenment, thereby countering the religious views of the Counter-Reformation. A landmark of the period is the volume of collected poems by **Cláudio Manuel da Costa**, who wrote in the bucolic style of **arcadianism**. **José de Santa Rita Durão, Basílio da Gama, Tomás Antônio Gonzaga, Inácio José de Alvarenga Peixoto**, and **Manuel Inácio da Silva Alvarenga** are also associated with this trend, and some of them politically with the Minas Gerais Conspiracy, which sought independence from Portugal for this rich mining region of Brazil. Gonzaga was equally noted for his love poetry and his satirical prose fiction. Da Gama and Santa Rita Durão also wrote **epic poetry**. Born in Brazil, but living most of his life in Portugal, **Matias Aires Ramos da Silva de Eça** wrote tracts on moral philosophy. Likewise, in this period literary associations called **academias** were founded by writers and intellectuals to reflect on problems of identity in the Portuguese colonies.

The issue of national identity came to the forefront as neo-classical models were depleted and the winds of **romanticism** swept Brazil. Officially, romanticism was launched by **Domingos José Gonçalves de Magalhães** with his first volume of poetry in 1836. In this search for national expression, writers focused on the figure of the Indian in a highly idealized way, giving rise to **indianismo**. The main exponents of this tendency were **Antônio Gonçalves Dias** in poetry and **José de Alencar** in narrative. Romantic lyric poetry influenced by Lord Byron (1788–1824) also flourished in this period, with **Casimiro de Abreu** and **Manuel Antônio Alvares de Azevedo** as representative voices. Socially concerned poets such as **Antônio de Castro Alves** wrote antislavery poetry in a hyperbolic style. The late romantic **Joaquim de Sousândrade** wrote an epic in a style that was ahead of his time, and he was later revived as an **avant-garde** poete *avant-la-lettre*. Alencar was one of the initiators of the tradition of **regionalism**, with novels that reflected the way of life of various regions of Brazil. Other writers in this style include **Joaquim Manuel de Macedo, Bernardo Joaquim da Silva Guimarães,** and **Alfredo d'Escragnolle, Visconde de Taunay.** Alencar's urban and **historical novels** served as models for subsequent generations; another important project in this period, coinciding with the regency of the Portuguese prince Pedro (1831–1841), was the historical research carried out in defining Brazil's national character, by **Francisco Adolfo de Varnhagen.**

Following the idealizing excesses of romanticism, a new focus on science and an objective view of reality took hold of intellectual and literary currents. In prose this produced the trends of **realism** and **naturalism**, and in poetry it spawned **parnassianism** and **symbolism**. An early precursor of realism, **Manuel Antônio de Almeida**'s fiction portrayed the life and customs of early 19th-century Rio, influencing **Joaquim Maria Machado de Assis,** the greatest Brazilian writer of this period, who distinguished himself for his early romantic novels and his mature, more psychologically introspective fiction. **Aluísio Azevedo** is considered the initiator of **naturalism** in Brazil, with novels that frankly portray racial, sexual, and social issues, whereas **Adolfo Caminha**'s narrative depicted homosexuality for the first time and is recognized as the purest of the naturalists. In poetry, parnassianism emphasized formal perfection, particularly the use of fixed forms such as the sonnet, a revival of Greek and Latin motifs, and the ideal of "art for art's sake." The main exponents of this trend were **Alberto de Oliveira, Raimundo Correia,** and **Olavo Bilac.** In 1893, **João da Cruz e Sousa** officially launched symbolism, a style that includes the voices of **Augusto dos Anjos,** who experimented with scientific vocabulary, and **Alphonsus de Guimaraens** and **Pedro Kilkerry,** who wrote, respectively, and insistently, about death and about dreams and mysticism. Free verse in symbolism was introduced by **Adalberto Guerra Duval**.

In the period of transition to **Brazilian modernism** often called premodernism, realism and naturalism still continued to influence major works such as **Euclides da Cunha**'s monumental account of the Canudos War, also noted for its Darwinism. **Henrique Maximiano Coelho Neto, Raul d'Ávila Pompéia**, and **Afonso Henriques de Lima Barreto** are important fiction writers who depicted the urban and suburban life of Rio de Janeiro. In this period too, **Tobias Barreto** founded the School of Recife, which introduced **positivism** in Brazil, influencing the work of literary critics such as **Sílvio Romero** and **José Veríssimo**. Historian **Capistrano de Abreu** contributed work on colonial Brazil.

Regionalism was taken up again in this period of transition to modernism by **José Bento Monteiro Lobato**, in novels that portray rural characters and in his **children's literature**. Other authors in this period include **Afonso Celso**, author of an essay praising Brazil's beauty; **Catulo da Paixão Cearense**, a popular poet, lyricist, and musician; **João do Rio**, chronicler and dramatist of Rio par excellence; the essayist, diplomat, and biographer **Joaquim Nabuco**; and **Júlia Lopes de Almeida** and **Gilka Machado**, whose work focuses on **women**.

The **Week of Modern Art**, presided over by **José Pereira da Graça Aranha**, gathered artists and writers to launch Brazilian modernism officially in São Paulo in 1922. Modernism introduced European avant-garde trends into Brazil and sought to construct models for a national literature. Literature was profoundly altered by the avant-garde poetry and prose written by some of the participants in the week, such as **Mário de Andrade** and **Oswald de Andrade**. Oswald de Andrade later founded **antropofagia**, to which he and **Raul Bopp** and **António de Alcântara Machado** contributed. Other modernist poets include **Guilherme de Almeida, Manuel Bandeira, Ronald de Carvalho**, and **Rui Ribeiro Couto**. **Paulo Menotti del Picchia, Cassiano Ricardo Leite**, and **Plínio Salgado** also founded a nationalist vanguard called **verdeamarelismo**. Radical political activist and writer **Patrícia Galvão**, who was married to Oswald de Andrade for several years, published proletarian fiction. In this period also a number of fine essayists emerged, among them **Sérgio Milliet da Costa e Silva, Paulo Prado,** and in the Northeast, **Gilberto Freyre,** who began a tradition of reflection on the Brazilian national character, continued in the next generation by **Sérgio Buarque de Holanda.**

Critics and writers who opposed the modernism of São Paulo include **Afrânio Peixoto** and **Graciliano Ramos,** who devised another model for literature based not on the urban but on the rural landscape of Northeastern Brazil. This movement was spearheaded by Freyre, whose important work on the contribution of slaves to Brazilian culture instigated a brilliant generation of novelists in this region, including **José Lins do Rego Cavalcanti, Raquel de Queirós,** and **Jorge Amado.** Their work depicts periodic droughts, poverty, and social issues afflicting the Northeast. Other heirs of this tradition include the novelists **Adonias Filho, Aníbal Machado, Dionélio Machado, José Geraldo Vieira,** and **Marques Rebelo.**

In the late 1930s and early 1940s, under the dictatorial regime of Getúlio Vargas, the urban novels and poetry of **Érico Veríssimo** represented a return to classical forms and religious concerns, as in romanticism and symbolism. Perhaps the most important poet of Brazil in the 20th century, **Carlos Drummond de Andrade,** published some of his main works during that period. Other important late modernist poets and novelists include **Otávio de Faria, Jorge de Lima, Murilo Mendes, Cecília Meireles, Vinícius de Moraes, Augusto Frederico Schmidt, Mário Quintana, Augusto Meyer, Henriqueta Lisboa,** and **Tristão de Ataíde.**

A formalist poetic trend known as the **Generation of '45** included **Geir Campos, Ledo Ivo,** and **João Cabral de Melo Neto,** a major poet who later introduced social themes into a work characterized by its formal rigor and emotional restraint. In prose, a new linguistic experimentalism is evident in the next generation, especially in the work of **João Guimarães Rosa,** whose fiction renders the Brazilian backland at once regional and universal. **Clarice Lispector** wrote **existential** novels and short stories of deep psychological exploration, a vein also mined by the novelists **Lúcio Cardoso, Fernando Sabino,** and **Dinah Silveira de Queirós. Rubem Braga** excelled in the chronicle.

The 1950s was a period of modernization in Brazil under the government of Juscelino Kubitschek, with the construction of the new capital, Brasília. All this inspired **concrete poetry**, founded by **Haroldo de Campos**, **Augusto de Campos**, and **Décio Pignatari**, which revived the modernism of 1922 and countered the Generation of '45, gaining followers such as **Affonso Ávila** and **Pedro Xisto**, and opposition from **Mário Chamie**. A predecessor of concrete poetry who died young was the poet and critic **Mário Faustino**. The literary criticism of **Afrânio Coutinho** and **Antonio Candido** emerged in the 1950s and 1960s, and the **Jabuti Prize**, Brazil's most prestigious literary award, was established. Other writers in this period include **Murilo Rubião** and **Millôr Fernandes**, who excelled in the genres of **fantastic literature** and humorous fiction, respectively.

After Kubitschek's brief era of optimism, the economy took a downturn in the 1960s and 1970s, precipitating takeover by a military regime through a bloodless coup in 1964. Censorship and political repression ensued. In this period some novelists, such as **Antônio Callado** and **Ignácio de Loyola Brandão**, focused on this new social reality, while other writers, such as **Raduan Nassar, Lygia Fagundes Telles, Autran Dourado**, and **Osman Lins**, turned to stories and novels of psychological introspection and narrative experimentalism. **Darcy Ribeiro** focused on indigenous subjects in fiction and nonfiction, and **Dalton Trevisan**, a master of the short story, mixed the quotidian with grim satire. Another concrete poetry dissident, **Ferreira Gullar**, gained new impetus with his engagé poetry. In the late 1970s, the counterculture movement Tropicália, headed by popular musicians such as **Caetano Veloso**, had an impact on a political and popular **poesia marginal**, represented by **Glauco Mattoso, Ana Cristina César, Paulo Leminski, Francisco Alvim**, and **Waly Salomão**. Another popular musician, **Chico Buarque**, also authored satirical novels.

In the 1980s, following the dismantling of the military regime and the return to democracy, a number of voices emerged expressing contrasting views and positions. The militant political attitude of the 1970s disappeared and was replaced by experimentation in narrative and poetic techniques and a focus on the urban setting. Along such lines, **Rubem Fonseca** wrote **crime fiction** that also explored the social and psychological effects of violence in big cities. In both fiction and poetry, female writers such as **Hilda Hilst, Nélida Piñon, Sônia Coutinho,** and **Adélia Prado** focused on the feminine from various perspectives, from the sexual to family histories of immigration and the everyday life of women. **Caio Fernando Abreu** also wrote urban fiction exploring homosexuality, and **João Ubaldo Ribeiro** revisited the theme of Brazilian identity from a postmodern perspective.

In the 1990s, several authors who had begun writing much earlier came to the fore: **Milton Hatoum** wrote on Lebanese immigrants in Northeastern Brazil, **Manoel de Barros** linked his elemental poetry to the Pantanal region, **Bruno Tolentino** wrote conservative poetry, **Moacyr Scliar** explored **Jewish** identity and fantastic literature, **Silviano Santiago** wrote criticism and gay fiction, **Luís Fernando Veríssimo** produced humorous **best sellers,** and **Sebastião Uchoa Leite** wrote eclectic poetry. Notably, **Paulo Coelho,** writer of spiritualist fiction best sellers, became Brazil's most widely read author.

In the late 1990s and early 21st century, a new generation of poets emerged, seeking either the complete rejection of concrete poetry or a more gradual evolution away from it. This generation includes poets as varied as **Moacir Amâncio, Nelson Ascher, Carlito Azevedo, Frederico Barbosa, Paulo Henriques Britto, Régis Bonvicino, Age de Carvalho, Horácio Costa, Antônio Cícero, Fernando Paixão, Duda Machado, Júlio Castañon Guimarães,** and **Armando Freitas Filho.** Among poets born after 1960, **Heitor Ferraz** and **Arnaldo Antunes** are of note. In contemporary prose, **Wilson Bueno, Nuno Ramos, Paulo Lins, Bernardo Carvalho, Fernando Bonassi, Marçal Aquino,** and **Bernardo Ajzenberg** represent everything from a crude realism in the manner of Rubem Fonseca, to a more experimental metaphorical prose written in a mix of Portuguese, Guarani, and Spanish. Women writers focusing on female psychological and social space include **Joyce Cavalcante** and **Helena Parente Cunha.**

Brazilian **theater** originated in the 16th century with the *autos* created by Jesuits, such as the European-born **José de Anchieta,** whose works, in Portuguese, Spanish, and Tupi are the only ones that have survived. Their purpose was didactic and religious, aiming both at curbing the greed and cruelty of the colonizers and converting the indigenous populations to Christianity. The 17th and 18th centuries saw works such as the comedies in Spanish by Manuel Botelho de

Oliveira and the light drama of Cláudio Manuel da Costa, neither of whom left much of a mark on the history of Brazilian theater because they did not address the local reality per se.

As with prose and poetry, the nationalist spirit of the romantic movement also inspired a renovation in theater, and Domingos Gonçalves de Magalhães is credited with writing the first Brazilian tragedy on a national subject, but the satirical plays and comedies of manners by **Luís Carlos Martins Pena** were more successful and have better stood the test of time. Antônio Gonçalves Dias also wrote historical dramas, but they are less known than his poetry. Although set in Brazil, José de Alencar's comedies in this period are much more concerned with moralizing, and Joaquim Manuel de Macedo's are less a document of the period than a satire of vices in general.

In the late 19th century and in the vein of realism, **Artur Azevedo** continued the tradition of the comedy of manners initiated by Martins Pena, writing original comedies as well as parodies of dramas and humorous sketches of recent events, combining elements of the musical and vaudeville. **Joaquim José da França Jr.** was a precursor to Azevedo, with his light comedies that often satirized Rio society. Joaquim Maria Machado de Assis also wrote comedies, which were not however performed publicly in his time, and he is understandably better known for his prose. **Qorpo-Santo**'s plays, on the contrary, though marginalized in his time, are now recognized as precursors of the **theater of the absurd**.

The popularity of the comedy of manners continued throughout the early 20th century, focusing on Rio society. **João do Rio**, also the author of chronicles, staged a successful drama in this vein. Brazilian modernists such as Oswald de Andrade and Otávio de Faria introduced innovations in theater that were not, however, adopted by the mainstream. The real breakthrough arrived in the 1930s, with the realist and psychological dramas of **Nelson Rodrigues**, Brazil's most prominent playwright of the 20th century. Rodrigues's path was followed by **Gianfrancesco Guarnieri** and **Alfredo Dias Gomes**, who sought to portray social realities and class struggle on the stage, the latter in collaboration with Ferreira Gullar. Both Guarnieri and Dias Gomes eventually also had careers writing and directing soaps for television. **Ariano Suassuna** is a unique dramatist who mixed medieval and Commedia dell'Arte traditions together with innovation in his plays, but eventually turned to narrative. Osman Lins, though mostly a novelist, wrote a well-known drama. **Abdias do Nascimento, Augusto Boal**, Chico Buarque, and **Antônio Bivar** wrote and staged plays inspired by black social movements, **Brechtian theater**, and popular music. Millôr Fernandes has written cosmopolitan comedies. Among female dramatists, Hilda Hilst wrote dramas inspired by the urban environment of São Paulo, many of which, though staged, were not published. Among contemporary playwrights, Fernando Bonassi's plays have been successfully adapted for the screen. *See also* ACEVEDO DÍAZ, EDUARDO; ARCADIANISM; CIVILIZATION AND BARBARISM; JOURNALS; MICROTALES; PARAGUAY; PERLONGHER, NÉSTOR; PICARESQUE NOVEL; PLA, JOSEFINA; POESIA MARGINAL.

BRAZILIAN MODERNISM. Following the **Week of Modern Art** in 1922, **avant-garde** literary and artistic movements in Brazil were labeled "modernismo" in Portuguese, a term best translated as "Brazilian modernism" and not to be confused with the Spanish American literary movement called **modernismo**. Spanish American modernismo and Brazilian modernism are not contemporaneous. The former roughly corresponds to late 19th- and early 20th-century **parnassianism** and **symbolism** in Brazil, whereas Brazilian modernism corresponds to the Spanish American avant-gardes of the 1920s and 1930s.

In Brazilian modernism, various European avant-garde movements such as futurism, expressionism, and cubism were fused into a movement that was also seeking to represent the national character. Its first, so-called heroic phase thrived from 1922 to 1928, its endpoints being the Week of Modern Art and the creation of **antropofagia** by **Oswald de Andrade**. This early combative period was characterized by bombastic manifestos and debates and a focus on innovative poetry such as *Paulicéia Desvairada* (1922; *Hallucinated City*) by **Mário de Andrade** and *Pau Brasil* (1926; Brazilwood) by Oswald de Andrade, as well as the publication of literary **journals** such as *Klaxon* and *Revista de Antropofagia*. Among other participants in the early phase of this movement were **Guilherme de Almeida, Raul Bopp, Ronald de Carvalho, Patrícia Galvão, António de Alcântara Machado**, and **Sérgio Milliet da Costa e Silva**. After the incorporation of international trends, a focus on the creation of a national literary idiom was the concern of the two Andrades and other more nationalist writers, such as **Plínio Salgado**, **Menotti del Picchia**, and **Cassiano Ricardo Leite**. From 1928 to 1939, the focus was the **novel of the land**, mainly rooted in Northeastern Brazil, with writers such as **Jorge Amado**, **Graciliano Ramos**, and **José Lins do Rego Cavalcanti**, and the urban psychological fiction of **Érico Veríssimo**, **Otávio de Faria**, and **Marques Rebelo**. A third period, continuing until 1945, is characterized by the production of literary critics such as Alvaro Lins and **Antonio Candido**, heirs of other earlier modernist essayists such as **Gilberto Freyre** and **Paulo Prado**.

In its renovation of language, creation of new forms, and establishment of an independent Brazilian literary expression, Brazilian modernism paved the way for Brazil's great universal writers of the 20th century, such as **João Guimarães Rosa**, **Clarice Lispector**, **Manuel Bandeira**, and **Carlos Drummond de Andrade**, as well as the postwar avant-gardes movements such as **concrete poetry**. *See also* ADONIAS FILHO; ATAÍDE, TRISTÃO DE; BEST SELLERS; CAMPOS, GEIR; CARDOSO, LÚCIO; COELHO NETO, HENRIQUE MAXIMIANO; GENERATION OF '45; GULLAR, FERREIRA; HOLANDA, SÉRGIO BUARQUE DE; INDIGENOUS TRADITIONS; LIMA, JORGE DE; LISBOA, HENRIQUETA; MACHADO, ANÍBAL; MEIRELES, CECÍLIA; MENDES, MURILO; MEYER, AUGUSTO, JR.; PEIXOTO, AFRÂNIO; QORPO-SANTO; QUINTANA, MÁRIO; RIBEIRO, JOÃO UBALDO; ROMANTICISM; SALOMÃO, WALY; SANTIAGO, SILVIANO; SCHMIDT, AUGUSTO FREDERICO; TELLES, LYGIA FAGUNDES; VIEIRA, JOSÉ GERALDO.

BRECHTIAN THEATER. The theories of the German dramatist Bertold Brecht (1898–1956), often referred to as "epic **theater**," have been widely practiced in Latin America. The notion of an epic in this context not only refers to the scope of the topics dramatized, but also to the representation of human struggles. Brechtian theater is characteristically political, espousing Marxism and the politics of the Left. It seeks to address the audience directly by using techniques that break the convention of theater as an illusion of reality, making the audience aware that it is watching a performance and inviting it to reflect on what it is watching. Spanish American dramatists who have followed Brecht's precepts in one form or another and have been particularly successful include **Isidora Aguirre (Chile)**, **Enrique Buenaventura (Colombia)**, **Pablo Antonio Cuadra (Nicaragua)**, and **Osvaldo Dragún (Argentina)**. In **Brazil**, **Augusto Boal** employed Brechtian poetics in developing his concept of the Theater of the Oppressed, and the Italian-Brazilian **Gianfrancesco Guarnieri** used Brechtian and Marxist techniques in work staged at Teatro de Arena.

BRITTO, PAULO HENRIQUES (Brazil, 1951–). Translator and poet. A native of Rio, Henriques Britto has translated more than 80 books of poetry and prose, including works by Elizabeth Bishop (1911–1979), John Updike (1932–2009), Don DeLillo (1936–), and Philip Roth (1933–). A respected poet as well, he has also published the poetry collections *Liturgia da Matéria* (1982; Liturgy of Matter), *Mínima Lírica* (1989; Minima Lyrica), *Trovar Claro* (1997; Plain-chant), and *Macau* (2003; Macau).

BRITTON, ROSA MARÍA (Panama, 1936–). Novelist, short story writer, and dramatist. As well as an accomplished writer, she has an established reputation in medicine, notably in the treatment of cancer. Her first novel, *El ataúd de uso* (1983; The Usual Coffin), is a historical work that traces the story of a coastal family from independence in 1903 to the beginning of World War II. Her second novel, *El señor de las lluvias y el viento* (1984; Lord of the Rains and the Wind), is a more intimate story in which three narratives are interconnected. In *No pertenezco a este siglo* (1989; I Don't Belong to This Century), Britton returns to the time of Panamanian independence, and in *Todas íbamos a ser reinas* (1997; We Were All to Be Queens), she tells a story of pre-Castro Cuba, drawing on her experiences as a student in Havana. Her more recent novels include *Laberintos de orgullo* (2002; Labyrinths of Pride) and *Suspiros de fantasmas* (2005; Sighs from Ghosts). Her fiction also includes two collections of short stories, *La muerte tienen dos caras* (1988; Death Has Two Faces) and *Semana de la mujer y otras calamidades* (1995; Women's Week and Other Calamities). Britton's work for the **theater** consists of *Esa esquina del paraíso* (1986; That Corner of Paradise); *Banquete de* *despedida* (1987; Farewell Banquet), a critique of racism in Panama and the United States; and *Miss Panamá Inc* (1992; Miss Panama Inc), a critique of beauty pageants. *See also* WOMEN.

BRUNET, MARTA (Chile, 1897–1967). Novelist and short story writer. Her writing is noteworthy for her representation of **women**. Having grown up in a rural environment in southern Chile, her first works of fiction are located in the region she knew well from childhood. These include the novels *Montaña adentro* (1923; Back Country), *Bestia dañina* (1926; Harmful Beast), *María Rosa, flor del Quillén* (1927; María Rosa, Flower of Quillén), and *Bienvenido* (1929; Welcome), as well as the short story collections *Don Florisondo* (1926; Don Florisondo) and *Reloj de sol* (1930; Sundial). Her account of rural life, detailed descriptions of the landscape, and introduction of the conflicts between modernization and tradition place her work within the frame of **criollismo** and approaches to reality typical of **realism** and **naturalism**. At the same time, however, her fiction already showed some of the characteristics that were developed more strongly in later works, including the psychological portrayal of her characters, the tension between interior worlds and society, sexuality, and the struggle of women against social expectations.

Such elements figure in *Aguas abajo* (1943; Downstream), a set of three rural tales, and the novel *Humo hacia el sur* (1946; Smoke in the South), Brunet's most successful work, in which she locates her story in a more urban environment and covers the social spectrum of a booming lumber town. In her final works, which include the short stories in *Raíz del sueño* (1949; Root of the Dream) and the novels *La mampara* (1946; The Screen), *María nadie* (1957; Mary Nobody), and *Amasijo* (1962; Dough), she continued to explore the predicaments of female characters arising from their social situations. The last of these was also her most controversial on account of her treatment of homosexuality. Marta Brunet also wrote **children's literature**, including *Cuentos para Mari-Sol* (1934; Tales for Mari-Sol), a popular collection of stories, and *Aleluyas para los más chiquitos* (1960; Alleluyas for the Very Small), a collection of verses.

BRYCE ECHENIQUE, ALFREDO (Peru, 1939–). Novelist and short story writer. Much of his life has been spent outside Peru, mainly in France. He is customarily located on the fringes of the **boom** generation. An early collection of stories, *Huerto cerrado* (1968; Closed Garden), chronicled the initiation of a young man into adulthood. It paved the way for *Un mundo para Julius* (1970; *A World for Julius*), Bryce Echenique's most successful novel, the story of a young boy born into an upper-class Peruvian family. Publication of the novel coincided with the beginning of the left-leaning presidency of General Juan Velasco Alvarado (1968–1975) and the collapse of the oligarchy and was acclaimed as representative of the times. It also introduced many of the characteristics that would reappear in Bryce Echenique's subsequent fiction: the antihero, the orality of his narratives, a sense of humor that runs the gamut from the hilarious to the grotesque, hyperbole, biting irony and satire, and a highly playful use of language.

Un mundo para Julius was followed by a collection of short stories, *La felicidad, ja-ja* (1974; Happiness, Ha-ha), which also dealt with the world of the oligarchy in Peru, but a number of other novels have appeared since then. In *La pasión según San Pedro Balbuena, que fue tantas veces Pedro, y que nunca pudo negar a nadie* (1977; The Passion According to Saint Pedro Balbuena, Who Was Pedro So Many Times and Never Could Refuse Anyone), the author abandons the Peruvian setting for Europe to tell the story of a failed writer who reflects on the problems of the creative process. *La vida exagerada de Martín Romaña* (1981; The Exaggerated Life of Martín Romaña) narrates the Peruvian misadventures of a writer and describes what Paris means to him. Here, as in Bryce's other novels, there is a strong autobiographical dimension. *El hombre que hablaba de Octavia de Cádiz* (1985; The Man Who Spoke of Octavia de Cádiz) forms a diptych with *La vida exagerada de Martín Romaña*, but was written after the author had moved from Paris to Barcelona. *La última mudanza de Felipe Carrillo* (1988; Felipe Carrillo's Last Change) dwells on the role of memory and the reconstruction of a love affair. It is also characterized by a particularly oral narrative and by references to popular music, notably traditional Peruvian waltzes and boleros.

In his next two novels, Bryce Echenique returned to Peruvian settings. *Dos señoras conversan* (1990; Two Women Chat) consists of two novellas referring to the 1960s and the 1970s and the rise of the terror that afflicted Peruvian society during the 1980s; *No me esperen en abril* (1995; Don't Wait for Me) takes up the story of the Peruvian oligarchy once more to describe what has become of them in the second half of the century. *Reo de nocturnidad* (1997; Thief of Nocturnity) and *La amigdalitis de Tarzán* (1999; *Tarzan's Tonsillitis*) are both love stories, the former set in Montpellier, France, where Bryce Echenique was a professor of Latin American literature for several years; the latter is the story of a singer-songwriter's 30-year love affair.

Bryce Echenique returned to Peru in 1999, not long after he published *Guía triste de París* (1998; *A Sad Tour of Paris*), stories of the misadventures of Latin Americans in Paris. He has also published two volumes of his autobiography: *Permiso para vivir: antimemorias I* (1993; Permission to Live: Antimemoirs I) and *Permiso para sentir: antimemorias II* (2005; Permission to Feel: Antimemoirs II). *See also* DIEZ CANSECO, JOSÉ; RIBEYRO, JULIO RAMÓN.

BUARQUE, CHICO (Brazil, 1944–). Dramatist, songwriter, and novelist. A world-renowned singer and songwriter, Chico Buarque belongs to a family of intellectuals and performers. His father was the historian and modernist writer **Sérgio Buarque de Holanda**, and his three sisters are singers. Buarque has been a distinct presence in Brazilian cultural and political life since the early 1960s, when he emerged first as a composer of romantic ballads and later of political songs. During military rule in Brazil (1964–1988), he was an outspoken artist and activist, writing and staging several key social and political plays that critiqued the dictatorship, including *Roda Viva* (1967; Wheel of Life); *Calabar: O Elogio da Traição* (1973; Calabar, Eulogy of Treason), written with Ruy Guerra; *Gota d'Água: Uma Tragédia Carioca* (1975; The Last Straw, a Rio Tragedy), written with Paulo Pontes; and *Ópera do Malandro* (1978; Malandro's Opera). He has also excelled as a novelist with *Fazenda Modelo* (1974; Model Farm), *Estorvo* (1991; Hindrance), *Benjamin* (1995; Benjamin), and *Budapeste* (2003; *Budapest*). *See also* THEATER.

BUENAVENTURA, ENRIQUE (Colombia, 1925–2003). Dramatist. He was involved in all aspects of the **theater**, including management and production. One of his major achievements was the foundation and direction of the Teatro Experimental de Cali (TEC; Cali Experimental Theater), which flourished for more than 30 years (1955–1990). It had many notable productions and was a source for the dissemination of theater from other countries. At the same time, its members engaged in collective creation, often taking their ideas from folktales or fiction. In his theater practice, Buenaventura implemented the theories of epic from **Brechtian theater**. In *A la diestra deDios Padre* (1958; At the Right Hand of God the Father), he wrote a version of the Faust theme, and in *Los papeles del infierno* (1968; The Papers of Hell), he dramatized the plight of individuals affected by political violence in Colombia. His plays on historical themes include *Un requiem por el padre Las Casas* (1963; A Requiem for Father Las Casas), on the devastating effects of the Spanish conquest and colonization, and *La denuncia* (1973; The Denunciation) on the impact of strikes against foreign banana companies in Colombia. See also GARCÍA, SANTIAGO.

BUENO, WILSON (Brazil, 1949–2010). Novelist, short story writer, and poet. Bueno first became known for his novel *Mar Paraguayo* (1992; Paraguayan Sea), an experimental text written in "Portunhol," a mix of Spanish, Portuguese, and Guarani, whose characters enact an allegory of Latin American dictatorships. Other narrative texts, marked by their brevity, include *Bolero's Bar* (1986; Bolero's Bar), *Manual de Zoofilia* (1991; Zoophilia Handbook), and *Jardim Zoológico* (1999; Zoological Garden). *Meu Tio Roseno, a Cavalo* (2000; My Uncle Roseno, on Horseback) is a novel that explores the issue of landownership in Brazil, and *Pequeno Tratado de Brinquedos* (1996; Small Treatise on Toys) is a collection of short poems. *A Copista de Kafka* (2007; Kafka's Copyist) is his most recent volume of short stories. He died in Curitiba, where he had lived since the 1970s.

BUITRAGO, FANNY (Colombia, 1940–). Novelist and short story writer. Although her writing is not overtly political, the protracted periods of civil strife in her native Colombia are symbolically represented through the dysfunctional relations represented in her fiction. Among **women** writers, her writing stands out in Colombia for its attention to patriarchy and violence against women, and the problems of both childbearing and infertility. Her novels include *El hostigante* *verano de los dioses* (1963; The Irritating Summer of the Gods), a story of the spiritual exhaustion of young people, which has been re-edited several times; *Cola de zorro* (1970; Foxtail), a tale of three generations; and *Los pañamanes* (1979; The Spanish Men), set on a Caribbean island where the traditions of the past conflict with modernization. Buitrago has published five collections of short stories, notably the love stories in *Los amores de Afrodita* (1983; Aphrodite's Loves) and *¡Líbranos de todo mal!* (1989; Deliver Us from All Evil), a more politically inclined collection. Buitrago has also written **children's literature**.

BULLRICH, SILVINA (Argentina, 1915–1990). Novelist. Although she was one of Argentina's most prolific female authors, was well known in literary circles, and had some commercial successes with some of her fiction, her work overall has never achieved great critical acclaim. She is best known for the novel *Los burgueses* (1964; The Bourgeoisie), in which the history, secrets, and drama of a middle-class family are revealed by an unidentified first person narrator during a celebration dinner. The novel was part of a trilogy that included *Los salvadores de la patria* (1965; Saviors of the Fatherland) and *Los monstruos sagrados* (1971; Sacred Monsters) and was intended to represent contemporary Argentina. Among her other notable works of fiction are *La redoma del primer ángel* (1944; The Flask of the First Angel), *Bodas de cristal* (1951; Crystal Wedding Anniversary), and *Los pasajeros del jardín* (1971; Passengers in the Garden). *See also* WOMEN.

– C –

CABALLERO CALDERÓN, EDUARDO (Colombia, 1910–1993). Novelist. He wrote 10 novels that focus for the most part on Colombian themes: the urban/rural divide, rural life, and the condition of the landless during Colombia's endemic political violence between Liberals and Conservatives, known as **la violencia**. Three of his best-known novels are set in this context. *El Cristo de espaldas* (1952; Christ with His Back Turned) is the story of a liberal son accused of having killed his conservative father and the attempts of a priest, newly arrived in the town, to mediate the conflict. In *Siervo sin tierra* (1954; Slave Without Land), the protagonist is a victim of violence before he is able to realize his dream of owning land. *Manuel Pacho* (1962; Manuel Pacho) is the tale of a humble man given the opportunity to be a hero. In contrast to these novels, *El buen salvaje* (1965; The Good Savage) is set in Paris and is concerned with the struggles of a failed writer to produce a novel. Caballero Calderón's other novels include *La penúltima hora* (1955; The Penultimate Hour), *Caín* (1969; Cain), and *Historia de dos hermanos* (1977; Story of Two Brothers). He also published several books of short stories and essays. Among the latter is an essay on *Don Quijote* by Miguel de Cervantes that demonstrates a wide-ranging knowledge of literature in Spanish.

CABELLO DE CARBONERA, MERCEDES (Peru, 1845–1909). Novelist. She attended the salons of **Juana Manuela Gorriti** and was a friend of **Clorinda Matto de Turner** and **Manuel González Prada**, whose political ideas she also accepted. Cabello de Carbonera was an outspoken social critic in her newspaper articles and public presentations, in which she professed her support for **positivism**. By contrast, her early novels, *Los amores de Hortensia, biografía de una mujer superior* (1886; Hortensia's Loves: Biography of a Superior Woman), *Sacrificio y recompensa* (1886; Sacrifice and Reward), and *Eleodora* (1887; Eleodora), later revised and published as *Las consecuencias* (1889; Consequences), all bear the stamp of **romanticism**. They are sentimental stories dependent on the conventional plot devices of the romantic novel and still owe much to **costumbrismo**. In her two last novels, however, the level of social criticism is appreciably higher. *Blanca Sol* (1888; Blanca Sol) is a critique of marriage through the story of a "fallen woman" that chronicles her rise through society and descent into prostitution. *El conspirador* (1892; The Conspirer) is a story told from a male viewpoint that shows the machinations of political life as a way to critique militarism and corruption in government. *See also* WOMEN.

CABEZAS, OMAR (Nicaragua, 1950–). Memorialist. He fought in the guerrilla war in Nicaragua against Anastasio Somoza (1967–

1979) and was a member of the Sandinista government after the triumph of the revolution. *La montaña es algo más que una inmensa estepa verde* (1982; *Fire from the Mountain*) is both a coming-of-age narrative and a **testimonio**. It is both the story of the author's youth, how he came to recognize social injustice in his country and joined the revolution against the Somoza dictatorship to fight it, and an account of his life in the guerrilla army. Several years later, he published *Canción de amor para los hombres* (1988; Song of Love of Humanity), also drawing on his experiences, but it is more reflective, without the fire of his earlier military narrative.

CABRUJAS, JOSÉ IGNACIO (Venezuela, 1937–1995). Dramatist. A member of the **Nuevo Grupo**, he was one of several dramatists who sustained the revival of Venezuelan **theater** in the mid-20th century with a brand of social commentary characterized by humor and a focus on the common people. His best-known play is *El día que me quieras* (1979; *The Day You'll Love Me*), about the dreams of a committed communist living for the future. Other plays include *El extraño viaje de Simón el Malo* (1960; The Strange Journey of Simon the Bad); *Los insurgentes* (1960; The Insurgents); *En nombre del rey* (1963; In the Name of the King); *Días de poder* (1964; Days of Power), written with **Román Chalbaud**; *Testimonio* (1967; Testimony); *El tambor mágico* (1970; The Magic Drum); *La soberbia milagrosa del general Pío Fernández* (1974; The Miraculous Pride of General Pío Fernández); and *Una noche oriental* (1983; An Oriental Night). He also wrote a number of screenplays, including one for *El día que me quieras*, and in his work for telelvision he raised the quality of scripts for soap operas.

CADENAS, RAFAEL (Venezuela, 1930–). Poet. His early poetry, written as a member of a group known as Tabla Redonda, has some of the characteristics of North American beat poetry, whereas his later work is more reflective. Collections of his work include *Cantos iniciales* (1946; First Songs), *Los cuadernos del destierro* (1960; Notebooks from Exile), *Falsos maniobras* (1966; False Maneuvers), *Realidad y literatura* (1972; Reality and Literature), *Intemperie* (1977; The Elements), *Memorial* (1977; Memoir), and *Anotaciones* (1983; Notations).

CALLADO, ANTÔNIO (Brazil 1917–1997). Novelist, journalist, and dramatist. Callado began his career at major dailies in Rio and worked for BBC radio in Europe from 1941 until 1947. Back in Brazil, he resumed his journalistic activities and published his first novels, *Assunção de Salviano* (1954; Salviano's Assumption) and *A Madona de Cedro* (1957; The Cedar Madonna), both influenced by religious themes. Set against the backdrop of Brazil's military regime, his best-known novel, *Quarup* (1967; *Quarup*), recounts the story of a priest who becomes a left-wing revolutionary. Two more novels, *Bar Don Juan* (1971; Bar Don Juan) and *Reflexões do Baile* (1976; Meditations on the Dance), also critiqued the military government that followed the 1964 coup. His play *Pedro Mico* (1957; Pedro Mico) was adapted for the screen, featuring the soccer star Pelé. *See also* THEATER.

CAMBACERES, EUGENIO (Argentina, 1843–1889). Novelist. He was born into the Argentinean upper class and turned to literature more fully after it became clear that his radical opinions ensured he would have no success in politics. His four novels, all strongly influenced by **naturalism** and the French writer Emile Zola (1840–1902), broke many social taboos and prompted harsh criticism, but they also portrayed some of the wretchedness and violence of society in his time. *Potpourri* (1882; Hodgepodge) is a tale of adultery that serves as a vehicle to expose the corruption of Buenos Aires society. *Música sentimental* (1884; Sentimental Music) follows the dissolute life of a wealthy Argentinean in Paris and his relationship with a prostitute. *Sin rumbo* (1885; Shiftless), perhaps the most successful of the four novels, is the story of Andrés, a wealthy but pessimistic city man who takes his own life after the death of both the innocent country girl he seduced and the daughter he had with her. *En la sangre* (1887; In the Blood), a novel reflecting the xenophobia of the time toward immigrants in Argentina, is about Genaro, the son of a poor Italian immigrant who has few scruples about how to make his way in society.

CAMINHA, ADOLFO (Brazil, 1867–1897). Novelist. Born in the Northeast of Brazil, Caminha moved to Rio as a young man, where he joined the navy. Although he rose to the rank of second lieutenant, he was forced to leave the navy because of his scandalous affair with a married woman, whom he later married. Caminha is one of the main exponents of **naturalism** in Brazil. His novel *Bom-Crioulo* (1895; *The Black Man and the Cabin Boy*), a tragic love story between a black sailor and a white teenage cabin boy, shocked audiences at the time for its explicit treatment of homosexual love and interracial relationships, but is seen today as a precursor of the open presentation of such themes. *A Normalista* (1892; The School Teacher) also deals with themes of social pessimism and social determinism.

CAMINHA, PERO VAZ DE (Brazil, 1450–1500). Chronicler. The secretary to Portuguese navigator Pedro Álvares Cabral (ca. 1467–ca. 1520), Pero Vaz de Caminha wrote *Carta do Descobrimento do Brasil* (1500; Letter on the Discovery of Brazil), first published by Manuel Aires do Casal in *Corografia Brasílica* (1817; Chorography of Brazil), a day-by-day account describing the Portuguese exploration of the territory of Brazil. This 27-page document, now housed at the Arquivo Nacional da Torre do Tombo in Lisbon, was addressed to King Manuel I of Portugal (1469–1521). It is the first European **chronicle** from Brazil and is considered the founding document of both Brazilian history and literature.

CAMPO, ÁNGEL DE (Mexico, 1868–1908). Chronicler and journalist. He wrote two novels but is best remembered for the volumes of collected articles, or **chronicles**, *Ocios y apuntes* (1890; Idle Writings and Notes), *Cosas Vistas* (1894; Things Seen), and *Cartones* (1897; Cartoons), written in the manner of **costumbrismo** and **realism**, which give an image of Mexico in the late 19th century.

CAMPO, ESTANISLAO DEL (Argentina, 1834–1880). Poet. His place in the literary history of Argentina is secured by his contribution to **gaucho literature** in *Fausto: impresiones del gaucho Anastasio el Pollo en la representación de esta ópera* (1866; *Fausto*). His poem is a parody of the story of Doctor Faustus, told in the manner of a gaucho and conceived after attending a performance of the opera *Faust* by Charles-François Gounod (1818–1893) in Buenos Aires. *See also* MUJICA LÁINEZ, MANUEL.

CAMPOBELLO, NELLIE (Mexico, 1900–1986). Novelist. Although first known as a dancer and choreographer, it is her reputation as a writer that has lasted. She is the author of two novels that have made her the only significant female writer to be recognized in the canon of the **novel of the Mexican Revolution**. Both are derived from personal experiences while living with her family in the Mexican states of Chihuahua and Durango. The first of these, *Cartucho: relatos de la lucha en el norte de México* (1931; *Cartucho: Tales of the Struggle in Northern Mexico*), is a collection of scenes from the revolutionary period from the perspective of a child that portray the violence and arbitrariness of the times. The second work, *Las manos de mamá* (1937; *My Mother's Hands*), is a more lyrical, autobiographical collection, mainly of scenes from her childhood, and reminiscences of her mother. Like *Cartucho*, it is an episodic work without a linear plot and the conventional narrative structure of a novel. Both works reflect support, shared by her family, for **Francisco Villa**, about whom she also wrote a somewhat partisan account, *Apuntes sobre la vida militar de Francisco Villa* (1940; Notes on the Military Life of Francisco Villa). *See also* WOMEN.

CAMPOS, AUGUSTO DE (Brazil, 1931–). Poet, translator, and critic. Founder, with his brother **Haroldo de Campos** and fellow poet **Décio Pignatari**, of the **journal** *Noigandres* and of Brazilian **concrete poetry**, Augusto de Campos is one of his country's most innovative **avant-garde** figures. An early book of nonconcrete verse, *O Rei Menos o Reino* (1951; The King Minus the Kingdom), was followed by *Poetamenos* (1954; Minuspoet), his first book of concrete poetry, inspired in part by the techniques in musical composition of Anton Webern (1883–1945) known as *Klangfarbenmelodie,* based on passing a melody from one instrument to another. His concrete poems, first published in various journals, were collected in *Viva Vaia: Poesia 1949–1979* (1979; Long-live Boo: Poetry 1949–1979) and *Despoesia: 1979–1993* (1994; Unpoetry).

After working with graphic space, de Campos began experimenting with new visual media such as electric billboards, videotext, neon, hologram and laser, computer graphics, and multimedia events. These experiments were published in *Poesia é Risco* (1995; Poetry is Risk), a CD-book of music and poetry issued in collaboration with his son, Cid Campos (1958–). His more recent *Não* (2003; No) also features a multimedia CD. As a critic, he was fundamental in theorizing concrete poetry, recovering past masters of literary experimentation in Brazil, and introducing international avant-garde figures to the Brazilian context, in volumes of essays such as *Teoria da Poesia Concreta*, (1965; Theory of Concrete Poetry), written with Haroldo de Campos and Décio Pignatari; *Revisão de Sousândrade* (1964; Revision of Sousândrade); *Poesia, Antipoesia, Antropofagia* (1978; Poetry, Antipoetry, Anthropophagy); *O Anticrítico* (1986; The Anticritic); *Linguaviagem* (1987, Languavoyage); and *À Margem da Margem* (1989; At the Edge of the Edge).

De Campos's translations of avant-garde poets include "Mauberley" and selections from the *Cantos* of Ezra Pound (1885–1972); fragments of *Finnegan's Wake* by James Joyce (1882–1941); and poems by Gertrude Stein (1874–1946), e.e. cummings (1894–1962), Vladimir Mayakovsky (1893–1930), and Velimir Khlebnikov (1885–1922). He also translated some of the great "inventors" of the past: Arnaut Daniel (12th century) and other medieval troubadours, John Donne (1572–1631) and the metaphysical poets, and Stéphane Mallarmé (1842–1898) and the French symbolists. His translations are included in the volumes *Verso Reverso Controverso* (1978; Verse Reverse Controverse), *Rimbaud Livre* (1992; Free Rimbaud), *Hopkins: A Beleza Difícil* (1997; Hopkins: The Difficult Beauty), *Coisas e Anjos de Rilke* (2001; Things and Angels of Rilke), *Poesia da Recusa* (2006; Poetry of Refusal), and *Emily Dickinson: Não Sou Ninguém* (2008; Emily Dickinson: I'm Nobody). *See also* ANDRADE, JOSÉ OSWALD DE SOUSA; ANTROPOFAGIA; ÁVILA, AFFONSO; GULLAR, FERREIRA; KILKERRY, PEDRO; SOUSÂNDRADE, JOAQUIM DE; TOLENTINO, BRUNO.

CAMPOS, GEIR (Brazil, 1924–1997). Poet, journalist, and translator. Associated with the **Generation of '45** that followed **Brazilian modernism**, Geir Campos's attention to the literary craft in his poetry earned him the title "artisan of the word." Among his works are his early *Rosa dos Rumos* (1950; Rose of the Winds), *Arquipélago* (1952; Archipelago), and the rare *Coroa de Sonetos* (1953; Crown of Sonnets). He also translated works by Rainer Maria Rilke (1875–1926), Bertolt Brecht (1898–1956), Johann Wolfgang von Goethe

(1749–1832), William Shakespeare (1564–1616), Sophocles (496–406 BCE), and Walt Whitman (1819–1892), and published *Pequeno Dicionário de Arte Poética* (1960; Small Dictionary of Poetic Art).

CAMPOS, HAROLDO DE (Brazil, 1929–2003). Poet, translator, and critic. One of the key **avant-garde** figures to emerge from Brazil in the postwar period, Haroldo de Campos was the founder of Brazilian **concrete poetry** together with his brother **Augusto de Campos** and fellow poet **Décio Pignatari**. With them he directed the poetry journal *Noigandres*, in which he published *Servidão de Passagem* (1962; Servitude of Passage), following his earlier *Auto do Possesso* (1950; Act of the Possessed). His experimentation with graphic space and other material properties of language led to a revolution in Brazilian poetry, away from traditional poetic forms and toward innovative texts, many of which are gathered in his book *Xadrez de Estrelas: Percurso Textual, 1949–1974* (1976; Chess of Stars, Textual Itinerary 1949–1974).

Further work with fragmentation and spatialization of language is evident in his *Signantia Quase Coelum/Signância Quase Céu* (1979; *Paradisiacal Signifiers*), in contrast to a return to more traditional writing in lines in his later volumes of poetry, such as *A Educação dos Cinco Sentidos* (1985, *The Education of the Five Senses*), *Crisantempo* (1998; Chrysantempus), and *A Máquina do Mundo Repensada* (2000; The World's Machine Rethought). Already in the mid-1960s, while the concrete poetry movement in Brazil was still in full swing, de Campos began the first fragments of what would become arguably his most original and innovative work, *Galáxias* (1984; *Galáxias*), an impressive poetic prose travelogue, in the style of *Finnegan's Wake* by James Joyce (1882–1941), charting de Campos's journeys in life and literature.

De Campos was also chiefly responsible for theorizing the concrete poetry movement in volumes of essays such as *Teoria da Poesia Concreta* (1965; Theory of Concrete Poetry), written with Augusto de Campos and Décio Pignatari; *A Arte No Horizonte do Provável* (1969; Art in the Horizon of the Probable); *Metalinguagem* (1970; Metalanguage); and *A Operação do Texto* (1977; Textual Operations). Other criticism focuses on recovering the legacy of past masters and arguing against the cultural dependency of Latin America:

Ruptura dos Gêneros na Literatura Latino-Americana (1977; Breaking Genres in Latin American Literature), "Da Razão Antropofágica: a Europa sob o Signo da Devoração," in issue 62 of *Colóquio-Letras* (July 1981; "*Anthropophagous Reason: Dialogue and Difference in Brazilian Culture*"), and *O Sequestro do Barroco na Formação da Literatura Brasileira: o Caso Gregório de Matos* (1989; *Disappearance of the Baroque in Brazilian Literature: The Case of Gregório de Matos*).

A gifted translator, in collaboration with his brother Augusto he translated the works of Ezra Pound (1885–1972), James Joyce (1882–1941), Gertrude Stein (1874–1946), e.e. cummings (1894–1962), Vladimir Mayakovsky (1893–1930), Velimir Khlebnikov (1885–1922), Arnaut Daniel (12th century), and Stéphane Mallarmé (1842–1898). De Campos theorized the translation of creative texts as "transcreations" or translations that re-create the features of the original as an independent creation. In this vein, he produced radical and brilliant translations of Homer, Dante (1265–1321), Octavio Paz (1914–1998), the *Ecclesiastes*, Chinese poetry, and Japanese classical theater, among others. De Campos received numerous honors both at home and abroad, including the **Jabuti Prize** and many honorary doctorates. *See also* ANDRADE, JOSÉ OSWALD DE SOUSA; ÁVILA, AFFONSO; ANTROPOFAGIA; GULLAR, FERREIRA; SOUSÂNDRADE, JOAQUIM DE; TOLENTINO, BRUNO.

CAMPOS, JULIETA (Mexico, 1932–2007). Novelist and critic. Although born in Cuba, Campos became a Mexican citizen and lived in Mexico from 1955. Her literary practice is underscored by her work as a critic and theorist of fiction, a field in which she published several studies, notably *La imagen en el espejo* (1967; The Image in the Mirror), *Oficio de leer* (1971; The Task of Reading), and *Función de la novela* (1973; The Function of the Novel). Her first two works of fiction, *Muerte por agua* (1965; Death by Water) and *Celina o los gatos* (1968; Celina, or the Cats), explore the inner worlds of her characters. The former, a novel, explores the lack of communication among the members of a family living in a house by the sea where it always rains. The latter is a collection of five narratives, in which changing perceptions about cats in the course of history are used to situate the conditions and conflicts of the characters in her stories. Her later novels are also explorations of the nature of fiction. *Tiene* *los cabellos rojizos y se llama Sabina* (1974; She Has Reddish Hair and Is Called Sabina), with several narrators, one of whom is writing a novel about someone who is writing a novel, is a self-reflexive work that examines the art of narrating. Similarly, *El miedo de perder a Eurídice* (1979; Fear of Losing Eurydice) is also about a writer engaged in writing, one whose efforts in this instance also relate his activity to that of other writers in history. *See also* WOMEN.

CAMPOS CERVERA, HÉRIB (Paraguay, 1905–1953). Poet. Like others of his generation, much of his writing was produced in exile, a theme strongly represented in his work. His output was small, consisting of one collection of poems, *Ceniza redimida* (1950; Ashes Redeemed), published in Buenos Aires during his lifetime, and *Palabras del hombre secreto* (1955; Words of the Secret Man), published after his death. Nevertheless, his work influenced his compatriots and marked a turn toward **surrealism** and the **avant-garde**.

CANDIDO, ANTONIO (Brazil, 1918–). Critic. One of Brazil's foremost intellectuals, Candido was an influential literary critic and educator. Among his volumes of essays that for the first time approached literature from a sociological perspective are *Formação da Literatura Brasileira: Momentos Decisivos* (1957; Formation of Brazilian Literature: Decisive Moments), and, with José Aderaldo Castello, *Presença da Literatura Brasileira* (1964; Presence of Brazilian Literature).

CARBALLIDO, EMILIO (Mexico, 1925–2008). Dramatist. He was a prolific writer, the author of more than 100 dramatic texts, including full-length and one-act plays, librettos, and film scripts. His work embraces the major trends in Western **theater** and was influenced by religious themes. He often incorporated elements of different trends within the same piece. At the same time, he was an active presence in Mexican theater as a **journal** editor, anthologist, director, and producer.

Carballido's first full-length play was *Rosalba y los llaveros* (1950; Rosalba and the Keyrings), about the intrusion of a city-bred woman into the lives of her provincial relatives. Other works in a realistic mode followed: *La danza que sueña la tortuga* (1955; The Dance That the Turtle Dreams), *Felicidad* (1957; Happiness), and

Las estatuas de marfil (1960; The Ivory Statues). He also wrote in a more fantastic vein, but with *La hebra de oro* (1955; *The Golden Thread*), about the loneliness and dreams of two old women, began to combine the real and the imagined, or the fantastic, in the same work.

Other examples of this style are *El relojero de Córdoba* (1960; *The Clockmaker from Córdoba*), in which the clockmaker finds himself caught between reality and his inventions; *Un pequeño día de ira* (1962; A Small Day of Anger), an example of political realism, with a narrator whose role is to address the audience, but who also enters the world onstage; *El día que se soltaron los leones* (1963; *The Day They Let the Lions Loose*); and *Yo también hablo de la rosa* (1965; *I, Too, Speak of the Rose*), a one-act play about two young people faced with the consequences of accidentally derailing a train, considered one of Carballido's best-known works in this style. His one-act plays have appeared in *D.F.* (1957; D.F.), a volume published in a series of revised and expanded editions. He also published several novellas and short stories in which, in scene-wise structures comparable to theater, he narrated the themes of family relationships and undertook the same kinds of psychological studies characteristic of his drama. See also MAGAÑA, SERGIO.

CARDENAL, ERNESTO (Nicaragua, 1925–). Poet. Coming from the same family as the Nicaraguan poets **Pablo Antonio Cuadra** and **José Coronel Urtecho**, poetry seems to run in his genes. His work is voluminous and, in part, a response both to events in Nicaragua and his own political and spiritual development. Although he wrote poetry from an early age, his first significant volume was *Hora cero* (written 1954–1956, published 1960; *Zero Hour*), produced after he felt the influence of poetry in English while living in New York between 1947 and 1949, and after his participation in 1954 in a failed revolt against the Nicaraguan dictator Anastasio Samoza García (1936–1956). *Hora cero* is a predominantly political work. It contains some autobiographical elements, but focuses principally on Central America under dictatorships, the role of the United Fruit Company in the region, and the war of Augusto César Sandino (1895–1934) against the U.S. military presence (1926–1933).

After experiencing a crisis and spiritual transformation, Cardenal spent two years (1957–1959) at a Trappist monastery in Kentucky, where he met the influential religious writer and activist Thomas Merton (1915–1968). From this period came *Gethsemani Ky* (1960; Gethsemani Kentucky), a collection of haiku-type poems and sketches, and *Epigramas* (1961; Epigrams), followed by *Salmos* (1964; *Psalms*), a recasting of biblical texts to highlight the themes of poverty, oppression, and social injustice that anticipated liberation theology. In 1965, he was ordained a Catholic priest, and in 1966 he founded the religious and art communities of Solentiname in Nicaragua. The activities and spiritual orientation of that endeavor would be reflected in *El evangelio de Solentiname* (1975; *The Gospel in Solentiname*).

Cardenal's poetry maintained its political focus during these years. *Oración por Marilyn Monroe, y otros poemas* (1965; *Marilyn Monroe and Other Poems*), one of the works for which he is best known outside his own country, is a critique of consumerism, advertising, and the kind of exploitation to which Marilyn Monroe was subjected by the movie industry. In *El estrecho dudoso* (1966; *The Doubtful Strait*) he reinterpreted history in the same way that he had reinterpreted biblical texts in *Salmos*, drawing on indigenous traditions and the **chronicles** of the conquest. *Homenaje a los indios americanos* (1969; *Homage to the American Indians*) sustains his interest in indigenous traditions and attempts to describe the cultures of pre-Columbian societies throughout the Americas.

His poetry contains an eclectic mix of sources in a collage of elements that takes from both high and low culture. He also maintains a focus on events in his own country. *Canto nacional* (1972; National Song), showing the influence of the *Canto general* by **Pablo Neruda** in its title, is a lyical composition that evokes the Nicaraguan countryside, but is also concerned with the Sandinista Revolution against the government of Anastasio Somoza (1967–1979) and his American backers. *Oráculo sobre Managua* (1973; Prophesy About Managua) is a response to the earthquake that devastated the Nicaraguan capital on 23 December 1972 and an indictment of the government's mismanagement and corruption during the recovery from the disaster. As these books reveal, Cardenal had become increasingly militant. He was a member of the Sandinista National Liberation Front (FSLN), but remained nonviolent, although he allowed his community at Solentiname to be used as a base of operations, for which it was attacked and destroyed by Somoza's forces. With the triumph of the Sandinista Revolution in 1979, Cardenal was named minister of culture, a position he held until 1988.

His political involvement brought criticism from his Church superiors in Rome and a public admonishment by Pope John Paul II on the occasion of the latter's visit to Nicaragua in 1983. Cardenal's state duties did not curtail his literary activity, however. Poetry published while in government office included *Tocar el cielo* (1981; Touch the Sky); *Vuelos de victoria* (1984; *Flights of Victory*), on the triumph of Sandinismo; and *Los ovnis de oro: poemas indios* (1988; *Golden UFOs: The Indian Poems*), a continuation of the project begun in *Homenaje a los indios americanos*. The year after he left office he published *Cántico cósmico* (1989; *Cosmic Canticle*), a long, theological poem that seeks to achieve a unified view of creation by reconciling religion and science and by understanding the problems of human society.

Since the electoral defeat of the Sandinistas in 1990 in Nicaragua, Cardenal has been removed from the political spotlight. He resigned his membership in the FSNL over disagreement with directions it had taken, but has continued to write and publish. Recent books include *Del monasterio al mundo: correspondencia entre Ernest Cardenal y Thomas Merton*, 1959–1968 (2004; From the Monastery to the World: Correspondence Between Ernesto Cardenal and Thomas Merton), volumes of his memoirs (in 1999, 2001, 2002, and 2004), and more of his poetry, *Versos del pluriverso* (2005; *Pluriverse: New and Selected Poems*). *See also* ZAMORA, DAISY.

CARDIM, FERNÃO (Brazil, 1548?–1625). Chronicler. After joining the Jesuits in Portugal, Cardim sailed for Brazil as secretary to a visiting Jesuit official and traveled throughout the country. Captured by English pirates, he was eventually liberated and became provincial representative of the Jesuit Order in Brazil. His **chronicles** *Narrativa epistolar* (1583; Epistolary Narrative) and *Tratados da Terra e Gente do Brasil* (1925; Treatise of the Land and People of Brazil), are early historical, geographic, and ethnographic descriptions of Brazil.

CARDOSO, LÚCIO (Brazil, 1913–1968). Novelist. Cardoso belongs to the second generation of **Brazilian modernism**, adapting modern narrative techniques to regional themes yet related to the national political context. Set in the interior of Minas Gerais, his novel *Crônica da Casa Assassinada* (1959; Chronicle of the Murdered House) is a Faulknerian tale of passion and perversion, violence and incest, recounting the downfall of a family.

CARDOZA Y ARAGÓN, LUIS (Guatemala, 1904–1992). Poet, novelist, and essayist. He is acclaimed as one of Guatemala's prominent 20th-century intellectuals, although he lived much of his life outside the country, the last 40 years of it in **Mexico**. His early poetry, *Luna Park* (1923; Luna Park), *Maelstrom: films telescopiados* (1926; Maelstrom: Telescoped Films), *Torre de Babel* (1930; Tower of Babel), and *Sonámbulo* (1937; Sleepwalker), shows the influence of **surrealism**, to which he was drawn while living in France for several years. In his later poetry, such as *Pequeña sinfonía del Nuevo Mundo* (1948; Small New World Symphony), his outlook is much more Americanist. His fiction includes *Retorno al futuro* (1948; Back to the Future), *Nuevo Mundo* (1960; New World), and a long autobiographical novel, *El río: novelas de caballería* (1986; The River: Novels of Chivalry). As an essayist, he wrote on a variety of topics. He became an established authority on Mexican painting and wrote on a number of movements and artists, including José Guadalupe Posada (1852–1913) and Diego Rivera (1886–1957). He touches on Guatemalan history, culture, and politics in *La revolución guatemalteca* (1955; The Guatelmalan Revolution) and *Guatemala: las líneas de su mano* (1955; Guatemala: The Lines on Its Hand), his most celebrated essay, and on literature in *Miguel Ángel Asturias, casi novela* (1991; Miguel Ángel Asturias, Almost a Novel). Cardoza y Aragón was also the first to make the ***Rabinal Achí*** available in Spanish by translating it from a version in French.

CARRASQUILLA, TOMÁS (Colombia, 1858–1940). Novelist and short story writer. He was a **regionalist** whose fiction is set mainly in the Colombian Department of Antioquía, where he was born and from which he rarely traveled. His short stories and novels both portray regional types and customs in the manner of **costumbrismo** and **realism**. Autobiography is a feature of some of his fictional world, as is the conflict of interests between the capital and the provinces. Children and strong female characters also figure prominently. *Frutos de mi tierra* (1896; Fruits of My Land), his first novel and also one of his best known, establishes the kinds of family dramas developed in his later writing. Many of these familiar elements are found in Carrasquilla's **historical novel** *La marquesa de Yolombó* (1928; The Marchioness of Yolombó). Set in the time of Colombian independence, it has a female protagonist who struggles to overcome both the social limitations imposed on her by her gender and the exploitation of mining interests for the benefit of the mine owners rather than the local population. In another historical work, the trilogy published under the general title *Hace tiempos: memorias de Eloy Jamboa* (1935–1936; Times Long Ago: Memoirs of Eloy Jamboa), Carrasquilla examines the transformation of Colombia in the 19th century from a mining to an agricultural economy.

CARRERA ANDRADE, JORGE (Ecuador, 1902–1978). Poet and essayist. As affirmed by his writing both in verse and prose, Carrera Andrade was an inveterate traveler. His prose works fall into three main areas: travel, the history and culture of Ecuador, and Ecuadorian and Latin American poetry. His own poetry is predominantly lyrical and focused on the world of nature, which he endeavors to interpret through a pantheistic approach. His publications include *Boletines de mar y de tierra* (1930; Bulletins from Sea and Land); *La hora de las ventanas iluminadas* (1937; The Hour of the Illumninated Windows); *Microgramas* (1940; Micrograms), short, haiku-like and epigrammatic pieces; *Lugar de origen* (1945; Place of Origen); and *Hombre planetario* (1959; Planetary Man).

CARRILLO, HUGO (Guatemala, 1928–1994). Dramatist. He was a prominent figure during a period of relative stability in Guatemalan **theater** between the 1950s and 1970s. Among his major successes was the dramatization of *El señor presidente* (1974; Mr. President), by the novelist **Miguel Ángel Asturias**. He also adapted a number of classic Latin American novels for school and college students, including another novel by Asturias, *Viernes de dolores* (Good Friday). Among his other works are *El corazón del espantapájaros* (1962; The Scarecrow's Heart), *La herencia de la Tula* (1964; Tula's

Inheritance), and *Mortaja, sueño y autopsia para un teléfono* (1972; Shroud, Dream, and Autopsy for a Telephone).

CARRIÓ DE LA VANDERA, ALONSO (Spain, 1715?–1783). Chronicler. Also known by the pseudonym Concolorcorvo, Carrió de la Vandera was a functionary of the Spanish crown who wrote *El lazarillo de ciegos caminantes* (1775 or 1776; *El lazarillo. A Guide for Inexperienced Travelers Between Buenos Aires and Lima*), which informs travelers about local customs and conditions likely to be met on their journey and is occasionally critical of colonial authorities. The **chronicle** of his journey is an invaluable account of life in late colonial South America and in both in its title and its content shows the influence of the **picaresque novel**.

CARVALHO, AGE DE (Brazil, 1958–). Poet. Born and raised in Belém do Pará, in northern Brazil, de Carvalho moved to Europe in 1986, living and working as a graphic designer in Vienna and Munich since then. His poetry is influenced by German-language modernist poets such as Paul Celan (1920–1970) and Georg Trakl (1887–1914), whom he translated. His early books of poetry are gathered in *Ror: 1980–1990* (1990; Ror: 1980–1990). His most recent volume is *Caveira 41* (2003; Skull 41).

CARVALHO, BERNARDO (Brazil, 1960–). Journalist and novelist. A Paris and New York correspondent for the daily newspaper *Folha de São Paulo*, Carvalho has published nine novels since 1993, among which are *Medo de Sade* (2000; *Fear of De Sade*), a postmodernist murder story inspired by the Marquis de Sade, and *Nove Noites* (2002; *Nine Nights*), the semifictional account of an American anthropologist's suicide in the Brazilian Amazon, a tale reminiscent of Joseph Conrad (1857–1924) and Claude Lévi-Strauss (1908–2009).

CARVALHO, RONALD DE (Brazil, 1893–1935). Poet. A career diplomat, de Carvalho was an important link between **Brazilian modernism** and cultural movements in Europe and the Americas. After an early stint as a journalist, he studied philosophy and sociology in Paris, where he also published: *Luz Gloriosa* (1913; Glorious Light), poetry influenced by Charles Baudelaire (1821–1867) and

Paul Verlaine (1844–1896). Back in Brazil, he joined the Foreign Service, which took him to Lisbon, where he met Portuguese futurists gathered around the review *Orpheu.* After publishing *Poemas e Sonetos* (1919; Poems and Sonnets) in the style of **parnassianism**, he participated in the famous **Week of Modern Art**, where he read **Manuel Bandeira**'s satirical poem "Os Sapos." His later books, *Epigramas Irônicos e Sentimentais* (1922; Ironic and Sentimental Epigrams) and *Toda a América* (1926; All of America), display a modernist idiom, and the latter a Whitmanian pan-American impulse. His *Pequena História da Literatura Brasileira* (1919; Brief History of Brazilian Literature) is a classic among literary histories in Brazil. De Carvalho died an untimely death as a result of a car accident. *See also* ALVARENGA, MANUEL INÁCIO DA SILVA.

CASA DE LAS AMÉRICAS. Founded in Havana in 1959 after the triumph of the Cuban Revolution at the beginning of that year, this cultural institute has awarded prizes in a wide range of genres to Latin America writers. Those recognized include **Claribel Alegría** and **Roque Dalton (El Salvador), Antonio Cisneros (Peru), Roberto Ibáñez (Uruguay),** and **Jorge Zalamea (Colombia)** for poetry; **Manlio Argueta** (El Salvador), **Gioconda Belli (Nicaragua), Roberto Sosa (Honduras), Rubén Bareiro Saguier (Paraguay), Luis Gusmán, Ricardo Piglia,** and **Marta Traba (Argentina), Jorge Ibargüengoitia (Mexico),** and **Antonio Skármeta (Chile)** for fiction; **José de Jesús Martínez (Panama)** for biography; and **Isidora Aguirre** (Chile) for **theater**.

CASACCIA, GABRIEL (Paraguay, 1907–1980). Novelist and short story writer. Considered the founder of modern Paraguayan fiction, his first book was the novel *Hombres, mujeres, y fantoches* (1929; Men, Women, and Puppets), but it was a collection of stories, *El guajhú* (1938; The Howl), that established his reputation. He later published another collection of stories, *El pozo* (1947; The Pit), which had a somewhat Kafkaesque atmosphere, as did much of his later work, but he also became known for a series of novels centered on the town of Areguá, not far from Asunción. This place first figured in the novel *Mario Pareda* (1940; Mario Pareda) and occupied a more central place in *La babosa* (1952; The Dimwit), his best-known work and one of the most remarkable novels produced hitherto in Paraguay, and in *La llaga* (1963; The Wound), a dark, psychological novel. Other novels include *Los exiliados* (1966; The Exiles), set in a brothel in a frontier region where political exiles have sought refuge; *Los herederos* (1976; The Inheritors); and *Las Huertas* (1981; The Orchards). Casaccia also wrote *Los bandoleros* (1932; The Bandits) for the **theater**.

CASTELLANOS, JUAN DE (Colombia, 16th century). Chronicler. His *Elegías de varones ilustres de Indias* (1589; Elegies for the Illustrious Men of the Indies) is based on biographies of prominent figures from the conquest and early colonization, beginning with **Christopher Columbus**, and is one of the longest verse **chronicles** of the period. It is often included in the **epic poetry** of the colonial period.

CASTELLANOS, ROSARIO (Mexico, 1925–1974). Essayist, poet, novelist, and short story writer. She was one of Mexico's most important 20th-century **women** writers. Many of her essays, written for some of Mexico's major newspapers and magazines, have been collected in books such as *Juicios sumarios* (1966; Summary Judgements). In her essays, as well as in her poetry and fiction, she explored and developed her ideas about Mexican culture, gender, and the social exclusion of women and other groups. Her poetry was collected in *Poesía no eres tú: obra poética 1948–1971* (1972; Poetry Is Not You: Poetic Works 1948–1971), which brought together hitherto published and unpublished collections.

In her major works of fiction, Castellanos focused on conflicts between Indian and Spanish populations, representing indigenous myths and legends, native languages, and daily customs in a way that moved beyond the social **realism** of the past toward **neo-indigenismo**. The novel *Balún canán* (1957; *The Nine Guardians*) is set in the state of Chiapas during a period of land reform under the presidency of Lázaro Cárdenas (1934–1940), and *Oficio de tinieblas* (1962; *The Book of Lamentations*), also a novel, is based on a 19th-century Indian rebellion. In two collections of short stories, *Los convidados de agosto* (1964; The Guests of August) and *Álbum de familia* (1971; Family Album), she wrote about middle-class women in Chiapas and about the alienation and frustrations of urban women. Castellanos also wrote for the **theater**, but without the same impact of her essays, poetry, and fiction.

CASTILLO, ANDRÉS (Uruguay, 1920–). Dramatist. After training as a lawyer, he turned to the **theater** and wrote a number of plays on social themes. *La cauta* (1957; Cautious) and *La jaula* (1963; The Cage) are about wayward adolescents. *La noche* (1959; The Night) and *La bahía* (1960; The Bay) are comments on the lack of social justice for the poor. *Cinco goles* (1963; Five Goals) is concerned with the commercialization of sport, and *El negrito del pastoreo* (1969; Black Boy from the Pasture Land) has an African Uruguayan theme.

CASTILLO, MADRE (Colombia, 1671–1742). Mystic. Her works are an example of conventual writing in colonial Latin America. Francisca Josefa Castillo y Guevara, known by her name in religion, Madre Castillo (Mother Castillo), left several writings. She is best known for her spiritual exercises and autobiography, which were written for her community but not published in her lifetime: *Vida* (1817; Life) and *Sentimientos espirituales* (1843; Spiritual Feelings). *See also* WOMEN.

CASTILLO, OTTO RENÉ (Guatemala, 1936–1967). Poet. His poetic output is small and consists mainly of two collections: *Vámonos patria a caminar* (1965; Let's Walk Together, My Country), the title poem of which has become widely known, and *Informe de una injustica* (1975; Report on an Injustice). However, he was the most significant poet of his generation and one of those who most successfully caught the revolutionary spirit of Guatemala in simple, lyrical verses expressing the romantic idealism of love and death. He spent much of the last half of his life in exile, but was captured, tortured, and killed by the army after reentering the country in 1967.

CASTRO CAYCEDO, GERMÁN (Colombia, 1940–). Journalist. He has written numerous nonfiction narratives, using the techniques of a novelist to tell his stories, but anchoring himself in reality and scrupulous documentation. The subjects he covers are varied and are drawn from the different regions and social sectors of Colombia.

Colombia amarga (1976; Bitter Colombia) is an anthology of stories collected from throughout the country. *Mi alma se la dejo al diablo* (1982; I Leave My Soul to the Devil) is about a dying man, the title having been taken from the last line of the diary in which he recorded his approaching death. *La bruja: coca, política y demonio* (1994; The Witch: Cocaine, Politics and the Devil) tells of the mix of politics and drug trafficking in Colombia. *La muerte de Giacomo Turra* (1997; The Death of Giacomo Turra) is about a police incident set in Venice and Cartagena. *Con las manos en alto: episodios de la guerra en Colombia* (2001; Hands Up: Episodes from the War in Colombia) is a collection of narratives about military conflicts in Colombia. *El palacio sin máscara* (2008; Palace Without a Mask) is an account of the assault by guerrillas on the Palace of Justice in Bogotá in November 1985 that took the lives of 115 people. These books may be classified as **chronicles** or **testimonios**, and they have made Castro Caycedo one of Latin America's most widely read contemporary nonfiction authors.

CAVALCANTE, JOYCE (Brazil, 1949–). Novelist and short story writer. Cavalcante's fiction focuses on female issues, often exploring eroticism and sexuality. Among her works are the short story collection *O Discurso da Mulher Absurda* (1985; The Discourse of the Absurd Woman) and the novel *Inimigas Íntimas* (1993; Intimate Enemies), the saga of a family, set in Northeastern Brazil. *See also* WOMEN.

CEARENSE, CATULO DA PAIXÃO (Brazil, 1863–1946). Poet and lyricist. A popular musician from the Northeast of Brazil and hailed by many as the greatest popular poet of Brazil, da Paixão Cearense is also remembered for hundreds of popular lyrics he wrote for *modinhas*, a musical form he also helped revive. Among his most famous compositions are "Luar do Sertão" (1908; "Moonlight in the Backlands") and "Flor Amorosa" (n.d.; "Flower of Love").

CELSO, AFONSO (Brazil, 1860–1938). Poet and essayist. A politician, journalist, and educator, Celso was one of the founding members of the Brazilian Academy of Letters (*see* ACADEMIAS). He also published a number of books of romantic poetry, among them

Rimas de Outrora (n.d.; Rhymes from Long Ago), as well as fiction, including *Um Invejado* (1895; The Envy of Some) and *Giovanina* (1896; Giovanina), but he is best known for *Por Que Me Ufano do Meu País* (1900; Why I Boast About My Country), an essay celebrating Brazil's beauty and alleged superiority that gave rise to the nationalist trend in Brazilian essay writing.

CÉSAR, ANA CRISTINA (Brazil, 1958–1983). Poet. Born into a middle-class family, César, who signed her name as Ana C., grew up in Rio, where she studied between travels and sojourns abroad, particularly in London, where she pursued an M.A. in translation and read the poetry of Sylvia Plath (1932–1963), whom she admired and emulated. Associated with **poesia marginal**, César also worked as a journalist and published *A Teus Pés* (1982; At Your Feet), a volume of confessional poems that also play with irony. She committed suicide by jumping out of a window of her parents' apartment in Rio. *See also* WOMEN.

CEVALLOS, PEDRO FERMÍN (Ecuador, 1812–1893). Historian. His five-volume *Resumen de la historia de Ecuador* (1870; Summary of the History of Ecuador) is a straightforward, factual account, the first history of the country to have been written, and widely read in its time.

CHALBAUD, ROMÁN (Venezuela, 1931–). Dramatist. He was a member of the **Nuevo Grupo** that contributed to the renaissance in Venezuelan **theater** begun in the 1950s and has contributed extensively as a writer and director to cinema and television. His stories often examine urban environments. They have a strong social message, dealing with poverty and people on the social margins. *Caín adolescente* (1955; Cain as an Adolescent) is about the movement of people from the country to the city, in which the two main characters are a virgin and a prostitute, and is concerned with alienation and the social decay brought on by violence. His other plays include *Los adolescentes* (1951; The Adolescents); *Muros horizontales* (1953; Horizontal Walls); *Réquiem para un eclipse* (1957; Requiem for an Eclipse); *Sagrado y obsceno* (1961; Sacred and Obscene); *Café y orquídeas* (1962; Coffee and Orquids); *Días de poder* (1964; Days of

Power), written with **José Ignacio Cabrujas**; *Los ángeles terribles* (1967; Terrible Angels); *La quema de Judas* (1974; The Burning of Judas); and *El viejo grupo* (1981; The Old Gang).

CHAMIE, MÁRIO (Brazil, 1933–). Poet. Critical of the **concrete poetry** movement, Chamie founded a new **avant-garde** movement with the manifesto *Poesia Praxis* (Praxis Poetry), published in his poetry volume, *Lavra Lavra* (1962; Till, Till). Influenced by Marxism, praxis poetry rejects an aesthetic of art for art's sake and attempts instead to create poetry based on the practice of life. Other books by Chamie include *Now Tomorrow Man* (1963; Now Tomorrow Man); *Indústria* (1967; Industry), his collected works; *Objeto Selvagem* (1977; Savage Object); and the more recent *Natureza da Coisa* (1993; Nature of the Thing) and *Caravana Contrária* (1997; Contrary Caravan). *See also* FILHO, ARMANDO FREITAS.

CHILDREN'S LITERATURE. The development of children's literature as a specialized area of publishing for writers who produce exclusively in that area is a relatively new phenomenon in Latin America. However, a number of mainstream literary authors have also written for children. In Spanish America these include **Claribel Alegría (El Salvador)**, **Carmen Lyra (Costa Rica)**, **Isabel Allende** and **Marta Brunet (Chile)**, **Fanny Buitrago (Colombia)**, **Sara Gallardo**, **Griselda Gambaro**, **Silvina Ocampo**, **Syria Poletti**, **Alfonsina Storni**, and **María Elena Walsh (Argentina)**. A number of dramatists have written plays for children, including **Enrique Avellán Ferrés (Ecuador)**, **Jorge Díaz (Chile)**, **Carlos Gorostiza (Argentina)**, **Mauricio Rosencof (Uruguay)**, and **Sergio Magaña (Mexico)**.

Many writers in **Brazil** have also written children's books alongside their adult fiction and poetry, but **José Bento Monteiro Lobato** is by far the most important Brazilian author of children's literature in the 20th century. With 20 books to his credit, many set on the imaginary *Sítio do Picapau Amarelo* ("Yellow Woodpecker Ranch"), they have been read by generations and were adapted for television. *See also* JABUTI PRIZE; LISBOA, HENRIQUETA; LISPECTOR, CLARICE; MACHADO, DUDA; MENDOZA, MARÍA LUISA; MISTRAL, GABRIELA; PUGA, MARÍA LUISA; QUEIRÓS,

DINAH SILVEIRA DE; RAMOS, GRACILIANO; SINÁN, RO-
GELIO; THEATER; VERÍSSIMO, ÉRICO.

CHILE. Among the earliest documents in Spanish having to do with
Chile are the letters of the conquistador **Pedro de Valdivia** sent
to Spain in 1552. However, Chilean literature is often considered
as having its beginning in the **epic poetry** of **Alonso de Ercilla y
Zúñiga** and his narrative of the conquest, including the resistance to
occupation by the native population. Among those who also wrote
of the conquest in the 16th century, following in the footsteps of
Ercilla were **Pedro de Oña** and **Alonso de Góngora Marmolejo,**
the former in verse, the latter in prose. A later episode of the conflict
between the Spanish and indigenous inhabitants was recorded by
Francisco Núñez de Pineda y Bascuñán in the 17th century.

In the decades following independence from Spain, the development of letters in Chile felt the impact of two of Latin America's major literary figures. The Argentinean **Domingo Faustino Sarmiento**
wrote and published parts of his *Facundo* during a period of exile in
Chile, and the Venezuelan-born **Andrés Bello** took up residence in the
country in 1829. Bello set the tone of **neo-classicism** of the first half
of the 19th century and had a profound influence on subsequent generations, notably on **José Victorino Lastarria.** As Chilean literature
came into its own, **costumbrismo** was the dominant trend in prose
writing and, in the first half of the century, had its most representative
figure in **José Joaquín Vallejo.** Other costumbristas included **José
Zapiola** and **Vicente Pérez Rosales.** Then, through writers such as
Daniel Barros Grez and **Vicente Grez,** the costumbrista sketch gave
way to the novel and **realism,** of which the most outstanding exponent
was **Alberto Blest Gana.** His novel *Martín Rivas* (1862) remains
Chile's most read work of fiction. The same realist vein was also exploited by **Luis Orrego Luco,** but as the novel developed in the first
decades of the 20th century it became more diverse and acquired elements of **modernismo,** psychology, **regionalism (mundonovismo** or
criollismo), and **naturalism.** The prominent writers were **Marta
Brunet, Eduardo Barrios, Joaquín Edwards Bello, Augusto
D'Halmar,** and **Pedro Prado.** Like many novelists, these authors also
wrote short stories, unlike **Baldomero Lillo,** who concentrated on the
genre and wrote a number of exceptional naturalist stories.

Poetry in Chile in the 19th century was inspired by **romanticism** but produced no major figures. By contrast, 20th-century Chilean poetry is notable for the number of significant contributors to the genre. Although modernismo had some impact, and the influence of **Rubén Darío** was felt, the most recognized poet of the first half of the century was **Gabriela Mistral**, Latin America's first **Nobel** laureate, who developed a subjective, intimate style. The **avant-garde** made its entry into Chilean poetry with **Vicente Huidobro** and **creacionismo** and the work of **Pablo de Rokha**. Chile's most important poet of the 20th century, however, was **Pablo Neruda**, the country's most widely known author and second Nobel laureate. Neruda's literary career began with love poetry, moved into the avant-garde, and was eventually characterized by a more eclectic and more accessible style. Later avant-garde generations include **Nicanor Parra** and **antipoetry**, **Gonzalo Rojas**, and **Enrique Lihn**. The new, postdictatorship generation is represented by **Raúl Zurita,** and the poetry of folklore and song lyrics in the 20th century by **Violeta Parra** and **Patricio Manns**.

The realist novel continued into the first decades of the 20th century in the fiction of **Manuel Rojas** and **Volodia Teitelboim**. The **historical novel** was represented in popular works by **Benjamín Subercaseaux** and **Magdalena Petit**, and **Fernando Alegría** is an example of the writer in exile. In the 1940s, however, the novel also felt the impact of the avant-garde and European modernism, trends apparent in the works of **Carlos Droguett** and **María Luisa Bombal**. Chile's major novelist of the 20th century and member of the Latin American **boom** generation was **José Donoso**, whose first important works began to appear in the 1950s and 1960s. Other members of his generation were **Jorge Edwards** and **Enrique Lafourcade**. By the 1980s, a new generation had emerged, including **Antonio Skármeta**, **Roberto Bolaño**, **Isabel Allende**, and **Diamela Eltit**. They were writers in exile for the most part, forced to abandon their country after the 1973 military coup of Augusto Pinochet, affected in some cases by a Latin American trend in **magic realism**, and also by a less militantly divisive approach to Chilean politics. Recent decades have also seen a rise in the number of significant **women** writers. **Pía Barros, Ana María del Río**, and **Marcela Serrano** are among those who should be added to those already mentioned.

A list of prominent essayists from Chile should include Volodia Teitelboim, **Arturo Torres-Rioseco**, and **Cedomil Goic**, who have written extensively on Chilean literature, and Jorge Edwards and **Ariel Dorfman**, whose essays have a more political focus. In the contemporary urban **chronicle, Pedro Lemebel**'s writing about Santiago has had significant impact.

The Chilean **theater** began in the 19th century. Translations of foreign plays were popular, but there was also a demand for locally written plays on themes particular to Chile. With works by Daniel Barros Grez, **Armando Moock**, and **Germán Luco Cruchaga**, there developed a repertoire that included comedies of manners (costumbrismo) and historical dramas, which were performed well into the 20th century. In the 1940s, theater received another significant boost through the founding of university theater programs. It led to a boom period and the emergence of a group of dramatists, including **Isidora Aguirre**, **Jorge Díaz**, **Luis Alberto Heiremans**, and **Egon Wolff**, who became the backbone of Chilean theater. Their work covered a wide spectrum in styles and content: history, folklore, psychology, social realism, **Brechtian theater**, and **theater of the absurd**.

The boom collapsed with the rise of television and other forms of popular entertainment, although some new writers, Ariel Dorfman and Antonio Skármeta among them, had already begun to write for the stage in the years immediately before the 1973 coup. The coup itself had a devastating effect. Censorship restrained the theater at home, and many writers, directors, and performers went into exile. Faced with this situation, conscious efforts to rebuild were made between the mid-1970s and mid-1980s. Established dramatists such as Jorge Díaz and Egon Wolff contributed, but in **Marco Antonio de la Parra**, **Ramón Griffero**, and **Juan Radrigán** significant new voices also appeared. Once the dictatorship began to loosen its grip, dramatists like Isidora Aguirre and Ariel Dorfman begfan to stage and interpret what had transpired during the coup. Since the late 1980s and 1990s, there has been considerable experimentation with new forms of theatrical representation using music, dance, lighting, and recently developed audiovisual technologies. New writers have emerged, while the older generations remain productive, giving Chile a firm place in contemporary Latin American theater. *See also* ACOSTA, JOSÉ DE; BEST SELLER; BOLIVIA; CASA DE LAS

AMÉRICAS; CHILDREN'S LITERATURE; DARÍO, RUBÉN; GÓMEZ CARRILLO, ENRIQUE; GULLAR, FERREIRA; JOUR-NALS; LÓPEZ, VICENTE FIDEL; MONTERROSO, AUGUSTO; MICROTALES; MIGUEL DE CERVANTES PRIZE; PERU; PI-CARESQUE NOVEL; PICÓN SALAS, MARIANO; POSITIVISM; RULFO, JUAN; SARMIENTO, DOMINGO FAUSTINO.

CHOCANO, JOSÉ SANTOS (Peru, 1875–1934). Poet. He led a very adventurous life, characterized by travel; association with some unsavory political regimes, particularly in **Guatemala**; and engagement in money-making schemes that were not always entirely legal, one of which would lead him to a violent death in Santiago de Chile. Although his early work, such as *Iras santas* (1895; Sacred Angers), shows an affinity with the **romanticism** of the French writer Victor Hugo (1802–1885), he was soon drawn to the aesthetic and political tendencies associated with **modernismo** and represented by the work of **Rubén Darío**. Written in a very boisterous style, his poetry touches on the themes of nationalism and the history and landscapes of America. His collections include *Selva virgen* (1896; Virgin Jungle), *Los cantos del Pacífico* (1904; Songs of the Pacific), and *Ayacucho y los Andes* (1925; Ayacucho and the Andes). The work that established his reputation and made him highly celebrated throughout Latin America was *Alma América* (1906; American Soul), in which he wrote of both the American and Peruvian landscapes, evoked the past and future of the continent, and meditated on the lives of its indigenous and mestizo populations.

CHOCRÓN, ISAAC (Venezuela, 1932–). Dramatist. He was an important contributor to the revitalization of **theater** in Venezuela in the 1960s. His early work, *Animales feroces* (1963; Wild Animals) and *Asia y Lejano Oriente* (1966; Asia and the Far East), is highly realistic. In *Tric-trac* (1967; Tick-Tock), the play that marked the initiation of the **Nuevo Grupo**, he adopted a more **avant-garde** style, turning to the **theater of the absurd** and **total theater** in the manner of the French dramatist Antonin Artaud (1896–1948).

CHRONICLE. The term refers to two different genres. The first of these refers to accounts of the conquest and early colonization written, in many cases, by witnesses to the events. The importance of these documents lies in their role as foundational texts, as accounts of the origins of the modern nations of Latin America and the earliest descriptions in a European language of the land, its people, and the deeds of the newly arrived conquerors. Among the more prominent authors in Spanish America were **Juan de Castellanos, Christopher Columbus, Gonzalo Fernández de Oviedo, Bartolomé de las Casas,** and **Pedro Mártir de Anglería** for Spanish America in general; **Fernando de Alva Ixtlilxochitl, Toribio de Benavente (Motolinía), Hernán Cortés, Bernal Díaz del Castillo, Diego de Landa,** and **Bernardino de Sahagún** for **Mexico; Juan Rodríguez Freyle** for **Colombia; José Agustín Oviedo y Baños** for **Venezuela; Pedro de Cieza de León, El Inca Garcilaso de la Vega, Felipe Guaman Poma de Ayala,** and **Agustín de Zárate** for **Peru;** and **Alonso de Góngora de Marmolejo** and **Pedro de Valdivia** for **Chile.** For **Brazil,** the main authors of early chronicles are **José de Anchieta, Pero Vaz de Caminha, Fernão Cardim, Pero de Magalhães Gândavo, Manuel da Nóbrega,** and **Gabriel Soares de Sousa.** *See also* ACOSTA, JOSÉ DE; ALVARADO TEZOZOMOC, HERNANDO; DÍAZ DE GUZMÁN, RUY; INDIANISMO; LASSO DE LA VEGA, GABRIEL LOBO; LÓPEZ DE GÓMARA, FRANCISCO; NÚÑEZ CABEZA DE VACA, ALVAR; NÚÑEZ DE PINEDA Y BASCUÑÁN, FRANCISCO; PALMA, RICARDO; PARAGUAY; SALVADOR, VICENTE DO; SOUSA, GABRIEL SOARES DE.

The second use of the term is to refer to short essays about contemporary life and culture. More often than not they are concerned with urban life and often appear first as columns in daily newspapers before being collected and published as a book. In Spanish America, from 19th- and early-20th-century **modernismo** to more recent styles of writing about contemporary life and the urban scene, prominent chroniclers include **Carlos Monsiváis, Manuel Gutiérrez Nájera, Salvador Novo,** and **Luis G. Urbina** from **Mexico; Rubén Darío** and **Enrique Gómez Carrillo** from **Guatemala; José Marín Cañas** from **Costa Rica; Germán Castro Caycedo** from **Colombia; Enrique Bernardo Núñez** from Venezuela; **Ventura García Calderón** from Peru; **Roberto Arlt** from **Argentina;** and **Joaquín Edwards Bello** and **Pedro Lemebel** from Chile. Brazil also has an extensive history of social and political chronicles. In the 19th and early 20th centuries, **António de Alcântara Machado, Henrique Maximiano Coelho Neto, Joaquim José da França Jr.**, **Afonso Henriques de Lima Barreto**, and **João do Rio** were notable practitioners of the genre. Many poets and prose writers in the 20th century, such as **Cecília Meireles, Vinícius de Moraes, Manuel Bandeira, Hilda Hilst, Clarice Lispector, Dinah Silveira de Queirós, Raquel de Queirós**, and **Fernando Sabino**, have also written in this genre, but **Rubem Braga** is the only Brazilian to have become famous solely for his chronicles. See also AZEVEDO, ARTUR NABANTINO GONÇALVES; CAMPO, ÁNGEL DE; CARDENAL, ERNESTO; CARRIÓ DE LA VANDERA, ALONSO; COSTUMBRISMO; FRANÇA, JR., JOAQUIM JOSÉ DA; LAFOURCADE, ENRIQUE; LEÑERO, VICENTE; LÓPEZ VELARDE, RAMÓN; MENDOZA, MARÍA LUISA; MORAES, VINÍCIUS DE; PENA, LUÍS CARLOS MARTINS; PUGA, MARÍA LUISA; SANTIAGO, SILVIANO; URBINA, LUIS G.; VALDELOMAR, ABRAHAM.

CHUMACERO, ALÍ (Mexico, 1918–). Poet. His first book of poetry, *Páramo de sueños* (1944; Desert of Dreams), shows the influence of **Xavier Villaurrutia** in the representation of dream as the foundation of existence. In *Imágenes desterrados* (1947; Exiled Images), his verses reflect a more nihilistic attitude toward life. However, his most recognized collection, *Palabras en reposo* (1956; Words at Rest), is more realistic than his earlier work. It lacks the same degree of interiorization and focuses more on social types than on the self.

CÍCERO, ANTÔNIO (Brazil, 1945–). Poet. Cícero began writing poetry and prose as a teenager, but did not publish any books in his early years. His poetry circulated instead as song lyrics, sung by his sister Marina Lima and others. Finally, he gathered a number of his older poems and some new ones in the volume *Guardar* (1996; To Keep). Although he is an admirer of the vanguards such as **concrete poetry**, his own poetry is discursive and makes use of traditional poetic forms and devices. His most recent poetry book is *A Cidade e os Livros* (2002; The City and the Books).

CIEZA DE LEÓN, PEDRO DE (Spain, c. 1520–1554). Chronicler. He was the author of one of the earliest histories of the Viceroyalty of

Peru. Cieza de León was named official **chronicler** of Peru in 1548 and devoted the next two years to research and writing. Of the four volumes he wrote, *La crónica del Perú* (1553; *Chronicle of Peru*), a title given to both the entire work and its first volume, only the first volume appeared in his lifetime. The remaining three, *El señorío de los Incas* (*The Domain of the Incas*), *Descubrimiento y conquista del Perú* (*The Discovery and Conquest of Peru*), and *Las guerras civiles del Perú* (*The Peruvian Civil Wars*), were not published until the 19th century, although they were known to earlier historians. Cieza de León was an enthusiastic supporter of the Spanish mission in the Americas, but was sympathetic to the plight of the indigenous people and favored a process of pacification rather than conquest.

CISNEROS, ANTONIO (Peru, 1942–). Poet. He was a significant figure in Latin America's 1960s generation and, like his contemporaries, felt the influence of the Cuban Revolution (1959) and other revolutionary movements of the time, in Peru and elsewhere. His writing reflects this mood and is often iconoclastic and acerbic, showing his affiliation with the politics of the Left. His first major work was *Comentarios reales de Antonio Cisneros* (1964; Antonio Cisneros' Royal Commentaries). The title refers to the historical work of **El Inca Garcilaso de la Vega**, although Cisneros offers a view of history from the perspective of the common people rather than a narrative of the nation's great events and the deeds of its leaders. *Canto ceremonial contra un oso hormiguero* (1968; Ceremonial Song Against an Ant Eater), which received a **Casa de las Américas** prize, is a response to the new cultures of contemporary Europe and a shift in the poet's political stance from the traditional left toward alternatives. This change became more pronounced in *El libro de Dios y de los húngaros* (1978; The Book of God and the Hungarians), in which Cisneros revealed a turn to Christianity. His poetry of the 1980s endorsed that change. *Crónica de Niño Jesús de Chilca* (1981; Chronicle of Child Jesus of Chilca) is the history of a religious community not far from Lima, which Cisneros researched through interviews with its members, subsequently including elements of their speech in his work. *Monólogo de la casta Susana* (1986; Monologue of the Chaste Susana) was inspired by the Old Testament. More recent collections by Cisneros include *Postales para Lima*

(1991; Postcards for Lima), *Las inmensas preguntas celestes* (1992; Immense Celestial Questions), and *Un crucero a las Islas Galápagos* (2005; A Cruise to the Galapagos Islands).

CIVILIZATION AND BARBARISM. The opposition between these two concepts is most famously recorded in the title of **Domingo Faustino Sarmiento**'s *Facundo: civilización y barbarie* (1845; *Facundo: Civilization and Barbarism*), a biography of the **gaucho** chieftain Juan Facundo Quiroga intended to be read as a denunciation of the barbarism of the **Argentinean** dictator **Juan Manuel Rosas**. The notion that nature in Latin America was so inherently barbaric that it affected its inhabitants and theatened to displace the civilizing influence of European culture was explored by some of Sarmiento's fellow Argentineans, including **Esteban Echeverría, Lucio V. Mansilla, José Mármol**, and **Ezequiel Martínez Estrada**, while the opposition between the two concepts was also taken up by writers in other contexts such as **José Pereira da Graça Aranha (Brazil), Agustín Yáñez (Mexico), Mario Monteforte Toledo (Guatemala), Rómulo Gallegos (Venezuela)**, and **Tomás de Mattos (Uruguay)**.

COBO BORDA, JUAN GUSTAVO (Colombia, 1948–). Poet and essayist. His first book of poetry, *Consejos para sobrevivir* (1974; Advice for Surviving), has been followed by a dozen other collections, including *Ofrenda en el altar del bolero* (1981; Offering on the Altar of Bolero), *Todos los poetas son santos e irán al cielo* (1983; All Poets Are Saints and Will Go to Heaven), and, more recently, *La musa inclemente* (2001; The Merciless Muse). His verse is characterized by humor, sarcasm, and a self-deprecating sense of irony. He has read very widely, and the depth of his cultural knowledge is reflected in both his poetry and essays. These include pieces on painting and on literary giants such as **Jorge Luis Borges** and **Gabriel García Márquez**, in which he shows the facility of expression and breadth of knowledge that already appeared in his earliest prose works on literature: *La alegría de leer* (1976; The Delight of Reading) and *La tradición de la pobreza* (1980; The Tradition of Poverty).

COELHO, PAULO (Brazil, 1947–). Novelist and lyricist. A writer of **best sellers** and Brazil's most widely read author in terms of copies sold, Coelho was born in Rio, where he attended school. He had a troubled youth and was committed to a mental institution, from which he escaped. When eventually released, he traveled across several continents after dropping out of law school and becoming involved in the drug culture. During Brazil's military regime, he was jailed and tortured. He wrote lyrics for Raul Seixas and other popular singers and worked in **theater** and as a journalist. His first book, *Arquivos do Inferno* (1982; Hell's Archives), was not very successful. After a journey on foot to Santiago de Compostela in Spain, he experienced a conversion, which he recounted in his novel *O Diário de um Mago* (1982; *The Pilgrimage*), and decided to carry out his childhood dream of becoming a writer. His next book, *O Alquimista* (1986; *The Alchemist*), after disappointing initial sales, became the most sold and most translated book ever, earning him a contradictory reputation. Some criticize his fiction on spiritualist, occult, and self-help themes for being facile and commercial, whereas others praise him as a messenger of peace. Nevertheless, he has been admitted as a member of the Brazilian Academy of Letters (*see* ACADEMIAS).

Other titles by Coelho include *Brida* (1990; *Brida*); *As Valkírias* (1992; *The Valkyries*); *Na Margem do Rio Piedra Eu Sentei e Chorei* (1994; *By the River Piedra I Sat Down and Wept*), a selection of his columns for the daily *Folha de São Paulo*; *Maktub* (1994; *Maktub*); *O Monte Cinco* (1996; *The Fifth Mountain*); *O Manual do Guerreiro da Luz* (1997; *Warrior of the Light: A Manual*); *Veronika Decide Morrer* (1998; *Veronika Decides to Die*); *O Demônio e a Srta. Prym* (2000; *The Devil and Miss Prym*); *Onze Minutos* (2003; *Eleven Minutes*); *O Zahir* (2005; *The Zahir*); *A Bruxa de Portobello* (2006; *The Witch of Portobello*); and *Ser Como o Rio que Flui* (2006; *Like a Flowing River*).

COELHO NETO, HENRIQUE MAXIMIANO (Brazil, 1864–1934). Novelist, journalist, and short story writer. Perhaps the most widely read Brazilian prose writer in the beginning of the 20th century, Coelho Neto was also a politician and journalist. His work fell into oblivion due to attacks by members of **Brazilian modernism** following the **Week of Modern Art**. Some of his works of fiction, such as *A Conquista* (1899; The Conquest) and *Fogo-Fátuo* (1928; St. Elmo's Fire), describe the artistic and bohemian environment in mid-19th-century Rio de Janeiro. He was a prolific writer who cultivated many premodernist styles in his numerous urban **chronicles** and fiction, including **naturalism**, impressionism, **regionalism**, and **realism**. He also wrote the first script for a Brazilian movie, *A Cidade Maravilhosa* (1928; The Marvelous City), and was a founding member of the Brazilian Academy of Letters (see ACADEMIAS).

COLLAZOS, ÓSCAR (Colombia, 1942–). Novelist and short story writer. Political themes and questioning of the authority of the ruling oligarchy, emerging from the history of violence in Colombia and Latin America, figure strongly in his earlier works, such as *Crónica de un tiempo muerto* (1975; Chronicle of a Dead Time), *Los días de la paciencia* (1976; Days of Patience), *Todo o nada* (1979; All or Nothing), and *Tal como el fuego fatuo* (1986; Like the Will-o'-the-Whisp). In later works, Collazos's themes are more varied, but contemporary life and Colombia are still present. *La ballena varada* (1997; The Beached Whale) provides a context in which to confront the dreams of a child with the world of adults and ecological preservation with short-term economic gain. *La modelo asesinada* (1999; The Murdered Model) is a thriller, and *Batallas en el Monte de Venus* (2003; Battles on the Mount of Venus) flirts with the traditions of the erotic novel to focus on female preoccupation with beauty. His most recent collection of short stories, *Adiós Europa, adiós* (2000; Farewell Europe, Farewell), deals with the passages in time and space experienced by various protagonists.

COLOMBIA. The literary world of New Granada, as colonial Colombia was called, may be represented by three texts, each with an established place in Latin American literature. The *Elegías de varones ilustres* (Elegies for the Illustrious Men of the Indies), by **Juan de Castellanos**, is a notable example of a 16th-century verse **chronicle** of the conquest period. By contrast, **Juan Rodríguez Freyle**'s 17th-century narrative, known as *El carnero*, offers a picture of social life in the early colonial period, and in the autobiographical and reflective works of **Madre Castillo**, conventual life and religious writing of the 18th-century **baroque** are exemplified.

As Colombian literature developed after independence in the 19th century, it did not lead immediately to a coherent view of the country. This would emerge only with the kind of national mythology formulated in the fictions of **Nobel Prize** winner **Gabriel García Márquez**. Like other aspects of culture in Colombia, literature was highly regionalized and more inclined to address local worlds than the national arena, the consequence in part of internal separations and differences imposed by geography. Literature was also affected by the country's political divisions, embedded in differences between Liberals and Conservatives that erupted periodically into periods of prolonged conflict. In 1948, the assassination of the Liberal candidate for the presidency, Jorge Eliécer Gaitán, prompted the *bogotazo*, a violent reaction in the capital, that was the prelude to a conflict known as **la violencia**, which was not ended until 1965. Since then, Colombia has also endured guerrilla insurgency from both sides of the political spectrum as well as the wars between and against drug cartels.

Colombia's most important 19th-century novel, **Jorge Isaacs**'s *María* (1867), was also one of the most widely read works of Latin American **romanticism**. Prose in the 19th century also included the **costumbrismo** of **Soledad Acosta de Samper**, a trend continued into the early 20th century in the work of **Tomás Carrasquilla**, who wrote mainly about the region of Atioquía. **Modernismo** was a characteristic of the popular novels of **José María Vargas Vila**. The most significant Colombian novel of the first half of the 20th century, however, was *La vorágine* (1926; *The Vortex*), **José Eustasio Rivera**'s **novel of the land** set in the jungle. After the mid-century, the theme of la violencia began to enter works of fiction and featured in novels by **Manuel Mejía Vallejo** and **Eduardo Caballero Calderón**, the former writing about Antioquía, the latter about Bogotá and the highlands. Writing on African Colombian themes by the brothers **Juan** and **Manuel Zapata Olivella** also belongs to this time. The publication of *Cien años de soledad* by Gabriel García Márquez in 1967, however, radically changed the literary landscape in Colombia. **Regionalism** and a concern for Colombia's violent history did not disappear, but García Márquez and his contemporaries, known as the Baranquillo Group, were influenced by North American and European writers, and brought new perspectives to established themes.

Pedro Gómez Valderrama and **Álvaro Mutis** are both of the same generation as García Márquez. **Óscar Collazaos** and **Gustavo**

Alvárez Gardeazábal are younger, however, as are **Fernando Vallejo** and **Germán Castro Caycedo**. Born in the 1940s, their writings have documented more recent social conflicts in Colombia. **Fanny Buitrago** and **Albalucía Ángel** are Colombia's most prominent 20th-century **women** writers of fiction, and the essay in Colombia is well represented through **Germán Arciniegas, William Ospina**, and **Juan Gustavo Cobo Borda**.

Colombia has produced few poets with a stature comparable to that of some of the country's novelists. **Rafael Núñez** is a representative of romanticism, but is not well known outside Colombia. By contrast, **José Asunción Silva** has had considerable influence and is one of Latin American literature's recognized poets, notwithstanding his small output. He is of the same generation as **Guillermo Valencia** and bridges the movement between romanticism and modernismo. Between modernismo and the **avant-garde** stands the work of **Luis Carlos López**. The avant-garde movements in poetry are represented by **León de Greiff**, who belonged to a group known as *los nuevos* (the new ones) and was followed by the likes of **Rafael Maya** and **Jorge Zalamea**. Contemporary poetry has a voice in Juan Gustavo Cobo Borda and William Ospina.

In Colombia, as elsewhere in preconquest America, the performance of rituals involving song, dance, and ceremony had a certain theatrical character. During the colonial period and the 19th century, Spanish and other foreign **theaters** dominated the stages. The best-known Colombian play of that time was *Las convulsiones*, a comedy of manners by **Luis Vargas Tejada**. Until the 1960s, however, the theater lacked the commercial and institutionalized support that would allow it to thrive. Affected by the influence of avant-garde movements and by a desire to introduce changes that had already become commonplace, efforts were made at that time to bring Colombian theater into the mainstream. Among the measures that had the most impact were the foundation of the Teatro Experimental de Cali under the direction of **Enrique Buenaventura** in 1963 and the subsequent formation in 1966 of the Candelaria collective in Bogotá under **Santiago García**. Theater has since become established in the universities. Groups and companies, supported by festivals and workshops, have increased in number, and there is an active cohort of dramatists, such as **Henry Díaz Vargas**, who are in tune with what is happening in the world of theater at large and are writing on Colombian themes. *See also* BRECHTIAN THEATER; CASA DE LAS AMÉRICAS; CHILDREN'S LITERATURE; HISTORICAL NOVEL; MIGUEL DE CERVANTES PRIZE; NEW HISTORICAL NOVEL; PANAMA; PICARESQUE NOVEL; REALISM; TRABA, MARTA.

COLONIAL NOVEL. A term used in **Mexico** to refer to the **historical novel** based on a narrative of events taken from colonial times, which flourished in the 19th and early 20th centuries. Its principal practitioners were **Eligio Ancona**, **José Tomás de Cuéllar**, **Justo Sierra O'Reilly**, **Vicente Riva Palacio**, and **Artemio de Valle Arizpe**.

COLUMBUS, CHRISTOPHER (Italy, 1451–1506). Navigator and diarist. A number of documents of the life and travels of Columbus have survived. Among the most significant are the diaries of his voyages from Europe to the Americas in 1492, 1493, 1498, and 1502. His *Diario de a bordo* (*Diary of Christopher Columbus's First Voyage to America, 1492–1493*), preserved in a transcription made by **Bartolomé de las Casas**, is a **chronicle** of his first transatlantic journey that displays all the sense of wonder felt by the navigator on his first encounter with the New World and the benefits he anticipated would accrue to the Spanish crown and to himself. *See also* GÓMEZ VALDERRAMA, PEDRO; POSSE, ABEL; ROA BASTOS, AUGUSTO

CONCRETE POETRY. An exhibit of visual poems and "concrete" paintings and sculptures in the Museum of Modern Art in São Paulo in 1956 officially launched the **avant-garde** movement in **Brazil** known as concrete poetry, although the adjective "concrete" had already been used in connection with abstract painting and experimental music. In 1958, **Haroldo de Campos**, **Augusto de Campos**, and **Décio Pignatari** launched the manifesto "Plano Piloto Para Poesia Concreta" (Pilot Plan for Concrete Poetry), in which they declared the end of the historical cycle of verse and proposed instead a "verbivoco-visual" poetry that focused on the material aspects of language and incorporated the media and methods of modern advertising.

Concrete poetry fuses a number of influences, from the international avant-gardes, such as Stéphane Mallarmé (1842–1898) in "Un Coup de Dés," e.e. cummings (1894–1962), Ezra Pound (1885–1972), Guillaume Apollinaire (1880–1918), James Joyce (1882–1941), Vladimir Mayakovsky (1893–1930), and Sergei Eisenstein (1898–1948), to Brazilian premodernist and modernist writers, such as **Joaquim de Sousândrade, Oswald de Andrade,** and **João Cabral de Melo Neto.** The concrete poets published five issues of the **journal** *Noigandres* starting in 1952 and established contact with poets in Germany, Great Britain, and Japan, among others. Among early adherents to this group were Ronaldo Azeredo, **Pedro Xisto,** Wlademir Dias Pino, and **Ferreira Gullar,** who went on to found the dissident neo-concrete movement. **Mário Chamie,** another dissident, founded "poesia praxis." In later stages, the concrete poets published their work in the review *Invenção. See also* ANTUNES, ARNALDO; ÁVILA, AFFONSO; AZEVEDO, CARLITO; BARBOSA, FREDERICO; BONVINCINO, RÉGIS; BRAZIL; BRAZILIAN MODERNISM; CÍCERO, ANTÔNIO; FAUSTINO, MÁRIO; FILHO, ARMANDO FREITAS; GUIMARÃES, JÚLIO CASTAÑÓN; LEMINSKI, PAULO; MACHADO, DUDA; MATTOSO, GLAUCO; RICARDO LEITE, CASSIANO; TOLENTINO, BRUNO; VELOSO, CAETANO; ZURITA, RAÚL.

CONTI, HAROLDO (Argentina, 1925–1976). Novelist and short story writer. His first novels, *Sudeste* (1962; Southeast) and *En vida* (1971; Alive), evoke the sea and river, environments that Conti knew. They are somewhat reminiscent of tales such as *Moby Dick* (1851) by Herman Melville (1819–1891) and *The Old Man and the Sea* (1952) by Ernest Hemingway (1899–1961) for their encounters with marine creatures. *Mascaró, el cazador americano* (1975; Mascaró, the American Hunter), his last novel, shows aspects of **magic realism.** His collections of short stories include *Todos los veranos* (1964; Every Summer), *Con otra gente* (1967; With Other People), and *La balada del álamo carolina* (1975; The Ballad of the Caroline Poplar). Conti's work became increasingly political, and in 1976, he "disappeared" after being taken into custody from his home in Buenos Aires by agents of the armed forces.

CORONEL URTECHO, JOSÉ (Nicaragua, 1906–1994). Poet and dramatist. He was one of Nicaragua's most influential intellectuals and writers. His break with the tradition of **Rubén Darío** brought the **avant-garde** to his country and persuaded others of his generation, notably **Pablo Antonio Cuadra** and **Joaquín Pasos**, to follow him. His influence has been felt equally by later writers, including authors such as **Gioconda Belli**. One of his best-known collections is *Pól-la-d'anánta katánta paránta: imitaciones y traducciones* (1970; Pól-la-d'anánta katánta paránta: Imitations and Translations), a title indicative of the experimentalism of its contents. He also courted the avant-garde as a dramatist and explored the **theater of the absurd** in the vein later pursued by the French writer Eugene Ionesco (1909–1994). *La chinfonía burguesa* (1939; The Bourgeois Chinphony), co-written with **Joaquín Pasos**, and *La petenera* (n.d.; Petenera) both engage in verbal games and use nursery rhymes and popular sayings to create an effect. *See also* CARDENAL, ERNESTO; THEATER.

CORREA, JULIO (Paraguay, 1890–1953). Poet and dramatist. His one collection of poems, *Cuerpo y alma* (1943; Body and Soul), is mainly on political themes and falls aesthetically between **modernismo** and the **avant-garde**. By that time, however, he had already begun to write for the **theater** in Guaraní on themes related to everyday life and the Chaco War. His plays include *Sandia yvyguy* (Deserter), *Terejó yeby frente* (Back to the Front), and *Guerra ayá* (After the War). Such was their impact, they have earned him the title of founder of the theater in Paraguay.

CORREIA, RAIMUNDO (Brazil, 1859–1911). Poet. A diplomat and politician, Correia's early poetry, *Primeiros Sonhos* (1879; First Dreams), in the style of **romanticism**, soon gave way to a refined **parnassianism**. With **Olavo Bilac** and **Alberto de Oliveira**, he forms a "trinity" as one of the best Brazilian poets in this vein. Correia is especially known for sonnets that manifest a nihilist disillusion. His works include *Sinfonias* (1883; Symphonies); *Versos e Versões* (1887; Verses and Versions), which includes translations; and *Aleluias* (1891; Hallelujahs), all collected in his two-volume *Poesias Completas* (1948; Collected Poems).

CORTÁZAR, JULIO (Argentina, 1914–1984). Novelist, short story writer, and essayist. He belonged to the **boom** generation, was one of the major figures of 20th-century literature, and has been very widely translated and read. He lived much of his life in France, where he took up residence in 1951 and flourished. Although Argentina and Latin America remained constant points of reference and he wrote in Spanish, he was culturally drawn to Europe, especially France. He published five novels. *El examen* (written 1950, published 1986; The Exam) evokes the tension of Buenos Aires under **Juan Domingo Perón**. *Los premios* (1960; *The Winners*) is a psychological thriller set on a cruise ship among a group of characters who have won the cruise as a lottery prize and are subject to an unidentified threat. Cortázar had already begun to experiment with the structure of the novel in these early works, but took his experimentation much further in the remaining three. *Rayuela* (1966; *Hopscotch*), the most celebrated of these, concerns the experiences of Horacio Oliveira, in Paris and in Buenos Aires, narrated after his return to Argentina. *Rayuela* is an open-ended anti-novel. In addition to a linear reading, the reader is invited to read it in a nonlinear order, following a different organization among the chapters and incorporating supplementary or dispensable chapters. This kind of structure also underlies *62, modelo para armar* (1968; *62: A Model Kit*), but the author turned away from it in *Libro de Manuel* (1973; *A Manual for Manuel*), a political novel, written to denounce torture in Latin America, which is based on fiction and excerpts from real newspapers.

Cortázar is equally celebrated for his 10 volumes of short stories. The first collection, *Bestiary* (1951; Bestiary), appeared shortly after he left for Paris; the last, *Deshoras* (1982; *Unreasonable Hours*), two years before his death. Among his other collections are *Final del juego* (1956; *End of the Game and Other Stories*), *Todos los fuegos el fuego* (1966; *All Fires the Fire and Other Stories*), *Alguien que anda por ahí* (1977; *A Change of Light and Other Stories*), and *Queremos tanto a Glenda* (1980; *We Love Glenda So Much and Other Tales*). His short stories show the influence of **surrealism**, **fantastic literature**, **Horacio Quiroga**, **Macedonio Fernández**, and Edgar Allan Poe (1809–1849), whose work he translated into Spanish, but his own writing is far from imitative. Cortázar developed his own voice and is said to have renovated fantastic literature by producing a style sometimes referred to as neo-fantastic, in which the effect is obtained not by the emergence of the supernatural, but by an unexpected shift in reality.

In addition to his fiction, the author's creative work includes books such as *Historias de cronopios y de famas* (1962; *Cronopios and Famas*), *La vuelta al día en ochenta mundos* (1967; *Around the Day in Eighty Worlds*), and *Último round* (1969; Last Round), miscellaneous collections, or collages, of notes and stories, presented in a playful and sometimes surreal style. He also published some poetry, and his political essays include discussions of some of the topical issues of the time with respect to Latin America. *Nicaragua tan violentamente dulce* (1983; Nicaragua So Violently Gentle) and *Argentina: años de alambradas culturales* (1984; Argentina: Years of Cultural Barbed Wire) are notable examples. *See also* ARLT, ROBERTO; FILLOY, JUAN; HERNÁNDEZ, FELISBERTO; JUÁRROZ, ROBERTO; LINS, OSMAN; MARECHAL, LEOPOLDO; SAER, JUAN JOSÉ; WALSH, RODOLFO.

CORTÉS, HERNÁN (Spain, 1485–1547). Conquistador and chronicler. The five *Cartas de relación* (1520–1526; *Letters from Mexico*), written by the conqueror of Mexico to Charles V of Spain, are both a **chronicle** of the military campaign and an attempt by Cortés to exalt his accomplishments and justify his conduct against any criticism or perceptions of shortcomings. The chronicle by Cortés's secretary, **Francisco López de Gómara**, has similar purposes. *See also* DÍAZ DEL CASTILLO, BERNAL; ESQUIVEL, LAURA; GOROSTIZA, CELESTINO; VALLE, RAFAEL HELIODORO.

COSSA, ROBERTO (Argentina, 1934–). Dramatist. He was an active member of the **Teatro Abierto** in Argentina and has been one of Argentina's most productive contemporary dramatists. With **Germán Rozenmacher, Carlos Somigliana**, and **Ricardo Talesnik**, he collaborated in the writing of *El avión negro* (1970; The Black Airplane), a new approach to the representation of reality and **Peronism** through the use of humor and the grotesque. During the military dictatorship of 1976–1983 in Argentina, Cossa continued to write a critical **theater**. *La nona* (1977; The Grandmother) and *Gris de ausencia* (1981; Grey Absence), both of which had considerable commercial success, were two plays on immigration, the search for success among immigrants, and the impact of cultural fragmentation on families. His recent works include *Pingüinos* (2001; Penguins), *Definitivamente adiós* (2003; Absolutely Farewell), and *De cirujas, putas y suicidas* (2005; Rag Pickers, Whores, and Suicides).

COSTA, CLÁUDIO MANUEL DA (Brazil, 1729–1789). Poet. Born in Minas Gerais and educated in Rio de Janeiro and Coimbra (Portugal), da Costa is considered one of Brazil's best poets of **neoclassicism**. His early works, written while still in Portugal under the influence of the **baroque**, include the heroic romance *Munúsculo Métrico* (1751; Small Metric Gift), the elegy *Epicédio* (1753; Epicedium), and *Culto Métrico* (ca. 1751–1753; Metrical Cult). In the tradition of **arcadianism**, da Costa wrote bucolic poetry under the pseudonym Glauceste Satúrnio. He published an edition of his *Obras* (1768; Works) in Portugal and composed a musical drama, *O Parnaso Obsequioso* (1931; Courteous Parnassus). Jailed for his participation in the so-called Inconfidência Mineira (Minas Gerais Conspiracy) favoring the independence of this rich mining region of Brazil, da Costa is said to have committed suicide in his prison cell. He also wrote the **epic poem** *Vila Rica* (1839; Vila Rica), celebrating the founding of the city of Ouro Preto. *See also* PEIXOTO, INÁCIO JOSÉ DE ALVARENGA.

COSTA, HORÁCIO (Brazil, 1954–). Poet, essayist, and translator. Costa is also a militant activist for **gay** rights. He studied architecture as an undergraduate but obtained graduate degrees in letters from American universities. He taught literature in **Mexico** from 1987 to 2001 and was instrumental in promoting literary and cultural exchanges between Brazil and Mexico. Influenced by Brazilian **concrete poetry**, his work is, however, better placed within postmodernism. Fragmentation, citation, and personal memory are some of the elements in works such as *Satori* (1989; Satori), *O Livro dos Fracta* (1990; The Book of the Fracta), *O Menino e o Travesseiro* (1994; The Boy and the Pillow), and *Quadragésimo* (1999; Fortieth). He has also published essays on literature: *José Saramago: O Periodo Formativo* (1997; José Saramago: The Formative Period) and *Mar abierto: Ensayos sobre literatura brasileña, portuguesa e hispano-*

americana (2001; Open Sea: Essays on Brazilian, Portuguese, and Spanish American Literature).

COSTA RICA. As a small country, Costa Rica has not figured significantly in Latin American cultural history. As a relatively peaceful country, however, it has often been a place of refuge for writers from other Central American countries. The Nicaraguans **Rubén Darío**, **Sergio Ramírez**, and **Daisy Zamora**, and the Salvadoran **Manlio Argueta** all lived there for periods of time. By contrast, significant Costa Rican authors, such as **Yolanda Oreamuno** and **Eunice Odio**, found it necessary to abandon their country to pursue their writing.

Costa Rican literature itself began to take shape in the second half of the 19th century with a focus on the life and customs of the country through **costumbrismo** and authors such as **Aquileo J. Echeverría** writing in verse and **Manuel González Zeledón** in prose. The evolution from the costumbrista sketch to **realism, naturalism**, and the novel came through the work of **Joaquín García Monge** and was sustained by other 20th-century writers such as **Carmen Lyra, Carlos Luis Fallas**, and **José Marín Cañas**. The break with this style came with Yolanda Oreamuno and with the short stories and novels of **Carmen Naranjo**. One of the country's first significant black writers is **Quince Duncan**. Costa Rica has produced several poets of note, but no highly recognized figures save for Eunice Odio, who was Costa Rica's most important 20th-century writer in this genre.

The history of commercial **theater** in Costa Rica begins in the 18th century. The plays most commonly performed had religious or pro-government themes and for much of the 19th and 20th centuries stages were dominated by foreign productions. Indeed, when plays with local topics began to appear in the second half of the 19th century, they were still subject to religious censorship and were written in the manner of costumbrismo. As an institution, theater in Costa Rica did not establish a firm basis for training and professionalism until the foundation of the Teatro Universitario in 1950. A number of home-grown dramatists came onto the scene during the 20th century, including some recognizable figures such as José Marín Cañas; Carmen Lyra, who wrote theater for children; and Carmen Naranjo. Nevertheless, Costa Rica has yet to establish its own theater and to explore its identity fully on the stage. *See also* ALVIM, FRANCISCO;

CHILDREN'S LITERATURE; CHRONICLE; CREACIONISMO; SELVA, SALOMÓN DE LA.

COSTUMBRISMO. Rather than a literary movement, costumbrismo was a style of representing reality in Spanish America through a description of the traditions and customs associated with places, people, and their culture and is linked to endeavors to capture and categorize national characteristics. In Europe, where it originated, it preceded the great realist novels of the 19th century. In Latin America, it coexisted with other forms of **realism** as one of the dominant styles of prose writing during the second half of the 19th century, retaining its attraction until well into the first decades of the 20th century. It is often associated with **criollismo** and **regionalism**. The *artículo de costumbres*, or costumbrista essay, a feature of the daily press during that time, evolving in due course into the **chronicle**, could be descriptive, humorous, or satirical. It might focus on either rural or urban life, and an author's newspaper columns were often collected for publication as a book. Costumbrismo also occurred in fiction through novels and short stories offering a somewhat stereotypical view of reality.

Prominent prose costumbristas include **Manuel Ignacio Altamirano, Ángel de Campo, José Tomás de Cuéllar, Rafael Delgado, Luis G. Inclán**, and **Manuel Payno** in **Mexico; César Brañas** and **José Milla y Vidaure** in **Guatemala; Arturo Ambrogi, José María Peralta Lagos**, and **Salarrué** in **El Salvador; Manuel González Zeledón** in **Costa Rica; Tomás Carrasquilla** in **Colombia; José Álvarez** in **Argentina; Mercedes Cabello de Carbonera** and **Ricardo Palma** in **Peru; Raúl Botelho Gonsálvez** in **Bolivia**; and **Vicente Pérez Rosales, José Joaquín Vallejo**, and **José Zapiola** in **Chile**.

There was also a costumbrista **theater** that figured in the work of dramatists such as **Hernán Robledo** (**Nicaragua**), the Argentinean **Samuel Eichelbaum**, the Peruvians **Felipe Pardo y Aliaga** and **Manuel Ascensio Segura**, and the Chileans **Daniel Barros Grez** and **Armando Moock**. In poetry the objectives of costumbrismo are reflected in the work of **Guillermo Prieto** from Mexico and **Aquileo J. Echeverría** from Costa Rica. *See also* ACOSTA DE SAMPER, SOLEDAD; DRAGÚN, OSVALDO; HONDURAS; INDIGENISMO; MODERNISMO; VENEZUELA.

COUTINHO, AFRÂNIO (Brazil, 1911– 2000). Critic. Coutinho studied medicine but then devoted himself instead to literature and journalism. He taught at Brazilian and U.S. universities and was notable for his adoption of new criticism techniques and their application to Brazilian literature, which influenced subsequent Brazilian critics. Among his works are *A Filosofia de Machado de Assis* (1940; The Philosophy of Machado de Assis), *Aspectos da Literatura Barroca* (1950; Aspects of Baroque Literature), *Introdução à Literatura no Brasil* (1959; Introduction to Literature in Brazil), and *A Tradição Afortunada* (1968; The Fortunate Tradition).

COUTINHO, SÔNIA (Brazil, 1939–). Novelist and short story writer. Coutinho, who has also worked as a journalist and translator, is known for her fiction centered on **women**. Her collections of short stories include *Do Herói Inútil* (1966; Of the Useless Hero), *Nascimento de uma Mulher* (1970; Birth of a Woman), *Uma Certa Felicidade* (1976; A Certain Happiness), and *Os Venenos de Lucrécia* (1978; Lucretia's Poisons). Her novels are *O Ultimo Verão de Copacabana* (1985; Last Summer in Copacabana), *Atire em Sofia* (1989; Shoot Sophia), and *O Caso Alice* (1991; The Alice Case).

COUTO, RUI RIBEIRO (Brazil, 1898–1963). Poet and short story writer. Ribeiro Couto worked as a journalist and civil servant before becoming a diplomat and serving in various European countries. His early poetry, influenced by **symbolism**, included volumes such as *O Jardim das Confidências* (1921; The Garden of Confessions) and *Poemetos de Ternura e de Melancolia* (1924; Little Poems of Tenderness and Melancholy), in which he reflects on everyday life. He recited poems during the **Week of Modern Art** and later wrote, in free verse and influenced by Paul Verlaine (1844–1896), poetry based on his experiences in various parts of Brazil: *Um Homem na Multidão* (1926; A Man in the Crowd), *Província* (1933; Province), and *Noroeste e Outros Poemas do Brasil* (1933; Northeast and Other Poems of Brazil). He also employed popular lyric forms in *Correspondência de Família* (1933; Family Correspondence), *Cancioneiro do Dom Afonso* (1939; Songbook of Dom Afonso), and *Cancioneiro do Ausente* (1943; Songbook of the Absent One). *Longe* (1961; Faraway) has been noted for some of the best sonnets in Portuguese. His fiction depicts the anonymous existence of humble people.

CREACIONISMO. A movement in **avant-garde** poetry associated mainly with **Vicente Huidobro (Chile)**, whose *Manifiesto creacionista* (Creationist Manifesto) was published in 1925. He applied its precepts most notably in his major work *Altazor, o el viaje en paracaídas* (1931; *Altazor, or A Voyage in a Parachute*). According to creacionismo, each poem and its language are entirely new creations, with no referent other than themselves. The poet is thus entirely freed from the conventions of language and at liberty to shock, neologize, and suggest new combinations. The movement was short-lived and had only a few adherents, including **Eunice Odio (Costa Rica)** and **Carlos Oquendo de Amat (Peru)**. It has some similarities with **ultraísmo**, with which Huibodro was briefly associated in Spain.

CRIME FICTION. Although conventionally considered a genre of popular literature, crime fiction has also attracted the attention of mainstream writers. This has especially been the case in **Argentina**, where **Eduardo Gutiérrez** was an early practitioner of the genre. **Jorge Luis Borges, Adolfo Bioy Casares**, and **Manuel Peyrou** were all drawn to the English cerebral tradition. More recently, **José Pablo Feinmann, Mempo Giardinelli, Luis Gusmán, Ricardo Piglia, Andrés Rivera, Juan José Saer, Osvaldo Soriano**, and **Rodolfo Walsh**, all Argentineans, have taken to the North American hard-boiled tradition and have revived the genre as a vehicle through which to comment on contemporary society and politics. Beyond Argentina, other notable authors of crime fiction include **Paco Ignacio Taibo II (Mexico), Sergio Ramírez (Nicaragua)**, and **Enrique Amorim (Uruguay)**. In **Brazil**, the most successful crime fiction writer is **Rubem Fonseca**, although others, such as **Dinah Silveira de Queirós**, before him, and **Fernando Bonassi**, more recently, have also written in the genre. *See also* ÁNGEL, ALBALUCÍA; USIGLI, RODOLFO.

CRIOLLISMO. The term derives from *criollo* (Spanish for "creole"), referring to the people and their cultures descended from the Old

World settlers in the New World. It alludes in particular to the traditions and a sense of national identity belonging to a period before mass immigration to the Americas in the late 19th and early 20th centuries changed the demographic complexity of the continent. It has many of the characteristics of **costumbrismo**, and the terms **regionalism**, **mundonovismo**, and nativismo are sometimes used synonymously. In fiction it is associated especially with the **novel of the land** and with authors such as **Carlos Wyld Ospina (Guatemala)**, **Salarrué (El Salvador)**, **Arturo Uslar Pietri (Venezuela)**, **Benito Lynch (Argentina)**, **Javier de Viana (Uruguay)**, and **Eduardo Barrios** and **Marta Brunet (Chile)**. *See also* EDWARDS, JORGE; HONDURAS; REALISM; REGIONALISM; WOMEN.

CUADRA, JOSÉ DE LA (Ecuador, 1903–1941). Novelist and short story writer. He was an active member of the **Grupo de Guayaquil**, who wrote mainly about the *montuvio*, the coastal lowlands of Ecuador. His novel *Los Sangurimas* (1934; The Sangurimas) is a family saga set in this region. As a work that incorporates several levels of reality (myth, legend, history, the symbolic), it anticipates **magic realism** by several decades. It also embodies certain sociological principles that the author described in *El montuvio ecuatoriano* (1937; The Ecuadorian Lowlands). Moreover, his collections of short stories—*Repisas* (1931; Display Cabinet), *Horno* (1932; Oven), and *Guasintón* (1938; Guasintón)—all contribute to the development of his fictional representation of the *montuvio*. A second novel, *Los monos enloquecidos* (1951; The Crazed Monkeys), was left unfinished at his death and was published posthumously.

CUADRA, PABLO ANTONIO (Nicaragua, 1912–2002). Poet and dramatist. Influenced by **José Coronel Urtecho**, he was an early exponent of **avant-garde** poetry that represented a reaction to **modernismo** and **Rubén Darío**. His verse reflects a preoccupation with Nicaraguan and Latin American identity, as expressed in *Poemas nicaragüenses* (1933; Nicaraguan Poems) and in later collections, such as *El jaguar y la luna* (1959; *The Jaguar and the Moon*) and *Cantos de Cifar* (1971; *Songs of Cifar and the Sweet Sea*), through themes concerned with history, myth, the landscape, the people, and politics.

Cuadra was also an essayist, critic, playwright, and graphic artist. He was Nicaragua's major poet before the advent of Ernesto Cardenal, although his association with the governments of Anastasio Somoza (1967–1972, 1974–1979) and opposition to the Sandinista Revolution distanced him both from Ernesto Cardenal and José Coronel Urtecho. Among his contributions to the **theater** are *Satanás entra en escena* (1948; Satan Comes on Stage), about religious and political freedom, and the play *Por los caminos van los campesinos* (1957; Along the Roads Go the Peasants), in the epic style of **Brechtian theater**, which tells the story of civil war, foreign intervention, and revolution in Nicaragua and has become one of the standards of Latin American theater. His other plays include *Pastorela* (1940; Nativity Play), *El bailete del oso burgués* (1942; The Dance of the Bourgeois Bear), and *El que parpadea pierde* (1943; Whoever Blinks Loses). *See also* CARDENAL, ERNESTO.

CUÉLLAR, JOSÉ TOMÁS DE (Mexico, 1830–1894). Novelist. He first wrote *El pecado del siglo* (1869; The Sin of the Century), a **historical** or **colonial novel** of crime and intrigue, and other early writings include several works for the **theater**. He is best known, however, for a collection of short narratives written in the manner of **costumbrismo**. These were published under the title *La linterna mágica* (1871; The Magic Lantern) in a collection that would eventually amount to 24 volumes. Cuéllar portrayed social types and made fun of the foibles of the petite bourgeoisie. Among his most successful narratives are "Ensalada de pollos" ("A Mixture of Young Coves") and "Historia de Chucho el Ninfo" ("The Story of Chucho the Nymph").

CUESTA, JORGE (Mexico, 1903–1942). Poet. He was a member of **Los Contemporáneos**, the theorist of the group who compiled the work of his fellows in *Antología de la poesía mexicana moderna* (1928; Anthology of Modern Mexican Poetry). He did not publish any books of his own work. His collected poetry appeared posthumously in 1958 and has since been re-edited in *Poemas y ensayos* (1964; Poems and Essays) and *Obras reunidas* (2003; Collected Works). His early death was the result of suicide.

CUNHA, EUCLIDES DA (Brazil, 1866–1909). Journalist and essayist. Da Cunha lost his mother at age three. His father then entrusted his upbringing to relatives, and he was sent to various schools. Witnessing the abolition of slavery and the fall of the monarchy in 1888 and 1889, respectively, fostered his abolitionist and liberal tendencies. In 1888, he was expelled from a military school for organizing a republican protest, which also landed him briefly in jail. He then took up journalism, writing articles on social issues for newspapers in São Paulo and Rio. After completing his military education and becoming an engineer, da Cunha alternated engineering with journalism. In 1898 he was sent to cover the final phase in the War of Canudos, which began in 1897 in the state of Bahia. The articles he wrote about this rebellion are the backbone of his posthumously published masterpiece, *Os Sertões (Canudos, diário de uma expedição)* (1939; *Rebellion in the Backlands*), a classic of Brazilian literature.

In *Os Sertões*, through a thorough analysis of the region in all of its aspects, from geography, botany, and zoology, to ethnography, sociology, and psychology, da Cunha attempted to demonstrate why the Brazilian army could not quell the rebellion led by the charismatic religious leader Antonio Conselheiro. Influenced by Darwinism and **naturalism**, Da Cunha's extensive, fatalistic tableau of the *sertão* (backlands) blames the republic for the poverty and ignorance that had led to such fanaticism and violence. Although essentially nonfiction, *Os Sertões* has also been noted for its matchless literary expression. Other works include *Peru versus Bolívia* (1907; Peru vs. Bolivia), on the border dispute between these two countries, and the historical essays *Contrastes e Confrontos* (1907; Contrasts and Comparisons) and *À Margem da História* (1909; On the Margins of History). Da Cunha died from wounds received in a duel he insisted on fighting against his wife's lover. *See also* VARGAS LLOSA, MARIO.

CUNHA, HELENA PARENTE (Brazil, 1930–). Novelist and short story writer. Parente Cunha's postmodern fiction blends autobiography and psychoanalysis to question the traditional representation of **women**, especially female artists. Among her books are the short story collections *Os Provisórios* (1980; The Provisional Ones) and

Cem Mentiras de Verdade (1985; One Hundred Lies About the Truth) and the novels *A Mulher no Espelho* (1985; The Woman in the Mirror), and *As Doze Cores do Vermelho* (1998; The Twelve Colors of Red).

– D –

DALTON, ROQUE (El Salvador, 1935–1975). Poet and prose writer. Along with Ernesto "Che " Guevara (1928–1967), Roque Dalton is an archetypal revolutionary intellectual whose endeavors embrace both theory and practice. His political activity in revolutionary movements in El Salvador led to periods of imprisonment, exile, and eventually death by execution by one of the revolutionary factions. His writing engages his revolutionary work entirely. His poetry is humane, political, but bitingly humorous, as in *Taberna y otros lugares* (1969; Tavern and Other Places), which won a **Casa de las Américas** prize. *Las historias prohibidas del Pulgarcito* (1974; The Forbidden Tales of Tom Thumb) is a collection of pieces in verse and prose that convey the history of El Salvador from the conquest to 1969. The name Tom Thumb refers to the smallness of the country and comes from a remark by the Chilean poet **Gabriela Mistral**. In *¡Pobrecito poeta que era yo!* (1976; The Poor Little Poet I Was), Dalton wrote a semiautobiographical novel. *Poemas clandestinos* (1980; *Poemas clandestinos*) are expressions of commitment and idealism. They were written in voices different from that of the author in order to escape detection by the authorities and were collected and published posthumously. They have been republished several times. Selected poems in English translation appear in *Small Hours of the Night* (1996). Among Dalton's prose writings, *Miguel Mármol y los sucesos de 1932 en El Salvador* (1972; *Miguel Mármol: A Testimony*) is a celebrated **testimonio** of the life of a Salvadoran revolutionary. It is not just the biography of an old guard political warrior; the ideas of Miguel Mármol and Roque Dalton are fully integrated. *See also* ARGUETA, MANLIO.

DARÍO, RUBÉN (Nicaragua, 1867–1916). Poet and journalist. Darío produced a large body of cultural writing through his journalism, but his celebrity rests on his reputation as a poet. He is considered the "father" of **modernismo** and was the most influential writer in Latin America in the late 19th and early 20th centuries, although he is still not widely known outside Spain and Latin America. Darío traveled extensively and spent productive periods of his life in **Chile**, Spain, and **Argentina**. His poetry brought the literatures of Europe and America together. Combining **romanticism**, **symbolism**, and **parnassianism**, he renovated poetic language and meter in Spanish, giving them new levels of sophistication that were felt throughout Latin America and profoundly changed writing in verse and prose. Success first came with the collection *Azul . . .* (1888; *Blue*) and was consolidated and matured in a second, expanded edition of the same book in 1890. *Prosas profanas y otros poemas* (1896; Profane Prose and Other Poems), *Cantos de vida y esperanza* (1905; *Songs of Life and Hope*), and *El canto errante* (1907; The Wandering Song) followed, which all made his work a watershed in poetic writing and contributed to establishing his place as the leader of the new style at the beginning of the century. *See also* ANDERSON IMBERT, ENRIQUE; CORONEL URTECHO, JOSÉ; CUADRA, PABLO ANTONIO; DÍAZ MIRÓN, SALVADOR; ECHEVERRÍA, AQUILEO J.; GAVIDIA, FRANCISCO; HERRERA, DARÍO; JAIMES FREYRE, RICARDO; LASTARRIA, JOSÉ VICTORINO; MIRÓ, RICARDO; NÚÑEZ, RAFAEL; RAMA, ÁNGEL; RODÓ, JOSÉ ENRIQUE; TORRES-RIOSECO, ARTURO; VILARIÑO, IDEA.

DEFILIPPIS NOVOA, FRANCISCO (Argentina, 1891–1930). Dramatist. The first of his plays to be staged in Buenos Aires was *El diputado por mi pueblo* (1918; The Representative for My Town). During the 1920s, he was an important presence in the Argentinean capital and often had more than one play running in different **theaters** at the same time. He represented the dark reality of urban life in *grotescos criollos* and *sainetes* such as *Puerto Madero* (1924; Port Madero), about anarchism and a dock strike in Buenos Aires, and *María la tonta* (1927; Crazy Mary), in which the Virgin Mary is represented as a madwoman in a city of criminals, pimps, prostitutes, and beggars. Defilippis felt the influence of Henrik Ibsen (1828–1906), August Strindberg (1849–1912), and Eugene O'Neil

(1888–1953) in his later writing. He also translated the work of Luigi Pirandello (1867–1936) and other dramatists.

DELGADO, RAFAEL (Mexico, 1853–1914). Novelist. Although he wrote several plays in the early part of his literary career, he is remembered most for several novels that conform to the norms of **realism**. *La calandria* (1891; The Lark) is the drama of a woman caught between her affections for two different men, one a stable, moral person, the other a rogue. *Angelina* (1895; Angelina) is a tale about a young man who attempts, and fails, to regain a rural idyll after living in the city. *Los parientes ricos* (1902; Rich Relations) is a satire on wealth told through the story of the poor side of a family that seeks protection from wealthy relations. Delgado also wrote the short novel *Historia vulgar* (1904; A Vulgar Tale), and in *Cuentos y notas* (1902; Stories and Notes) left a collection of sketches in the manner of **costumbrismo**.

DENEVI, MARCO (Argentina, 1922–1998). Novelist and short story writer. He entered the literary world with a prize-winning first novel, *Rosaura a las diez* (1955; Rosa at Ten O'Clock), a mystery novel about a woman murdered in a seedy Buenos Aires hotel. The novella-length *Ceremonia secreta* (1960; Secret Ceremony) is also a story of crime and violence, as is a later novel, *Los asesinos de los días de fiestas* (1972; The Holiday Murderers). Denevi's novels are marked by considerable technical virtuosity involving multiple points of view and narrative voices, fragmented chronologies, and embedded narratives. He was equally successful with his short stories and **microtales**, which show his creativity and playfulness. The first collection of these was *Falsificaciones* (1966; Falsifications), a series of apocryphal versions of literary works and historical events. It was followed by *El emperador de China y otros cuentos* (1970; The Emperor of China and Other Stories) and *Parque de diversiones* (1970; Amusement Park). Later collections, *Hierba del cielo* (1973; Herb of Heaven) and *Reunión de desaparecidos* (1977; A Gathering of the Disappeared), are more serious and represent a coming to terms with life's disappointments and the urban environment of Buenos Aires.

During the 1980s, Denevi wrote extensively for television and acquired a popular following through a column he contributed to the

Argentinean daily newspaper *La Nación.* Several of his novels have been turned into films or dramatized for television, and Denevi ventured into the **theater**, but without the success of his prose fiction. Among his last books were *Araminta, o El poder* (1982; Araminta, or The Power), a miscellaneous, autobiographical collection of sketches, essays, and stories, and a novel, *Manuel de historia* (1985; Manuel of History), admonishing Argentina to put its house in order.

D'HALMAR, AUGUSTO, pseudonym of **AUGUSTO GOEMINE THOMSON (Chile, 1882–1950).** Novelist and essayist. He was a highly cultured man, and the influences of his reading are often evident in his writing. Among the most noticeable are Leo Tolstoy (1828–1910), Óscar Wilde (1854–1900), Alphonse Daudet (1840–1897), and Pierre Loti (1850–1923). The impact of Tolstoy was such that D'Halmar sought, in 1904, to found a Tolstoyan cultural community based on the Russian writer's philosophy. D'Halmar's aesthetic outlook was similarly eclectic, and from his early **naturalism** he moved first to **modernism** and then to the **avant-garde**.

D'Halmar's novel *Juana Lucero, o los vicios de Chile* (1902; Juana Lucero, or the Vices of Chile), an imitation of *Nana* (1880) by Emile Zola (1840–1902), about the life of a prostitute, introduced naturalism to Chile and is one of the author's most read works. In *La lámpara en el molino* (1914; The Lamp in the Mill), however, based on events surrounding his sister's marriage, he abandoned naturalistic realism in favor of a more surreal and imaginative style. His later novels include *La pasión y muerte del cura Deusto* (1924; The Passion and Death of Father Deusto). Considered his most accomplished work, it is a story of **homosexual** desire, set in Seville, Spain, and one of the first works of fiction in Spanish to deal openly with homoeroticism. D'Halmar's essays include several he wrote during a 26-year period away from his native Chile that reflect some of his travels. Among them are *Nirvana* (1918; Nirvana), about the Far East, and *La Mancha de Don Quijote* (1934; Don Quixote's La Mancha), a reflection of his experiences in Spain.

DIAS, ANTÔNIO GONÇALVES (Brazil, 1823–1864). Dramatist and poet. The son of a Portuguese father and a Brazilian mother of black and indigenous ancestry, Gonçalves Dias was born in Maranhão and traveled to Coimbra to study law, where he also extensively read Portuguese and European classics and wrote his first poems. He became associated with "medievalist" writers who published in the **journals** *Gazeta Literária* and *O Trovador*, who cultivated patriotic nostalgia, as evidenced in his historical plays, *Beatriz Cenci* (1844; Beatriz Cenci), *Patkull* (1844; Patkull), and *Leonor de Mendonça* (1847; Leonor of Mendoza), and in his Portuguese medieval ballad, "Sextilhas de Frei Antão" (1848; Sextilles of Friar Antão). But his main literary reputation was established with the publication of *Primeiros Cantos* (1846; First Songs), inspired by patriotic feelings and the figure of the Brazilian Indian. Gonçalves Dias's **romanticism** and **indianism** are also evident in the subsequent poetry collections *Segundos Cantos* (1848; Second Songs) and *Últimos Cantos* (1851; Last Songs), in his unfinished **epic poem** *Os Timbiras* (1857; The Timbiras), and in his ballad *I-Juca Pirama* (1851; I-Juca Pirama).

Back in Brazil, Gonçalves Dias moved around, working as a professor and journalist, and was also officially commissioned to undertake historical, ethnographic, and linguistic research in the north of Brazil and in Europe, material he later used to produce *Dicionário da Língua Tupi* (1858; Dictionary of the Tupi Language), published in Leipzig. The other great theme of Gonçalves Dias's work was romantic love, partly inspired by his real-life passion for Ana Amélia Ferreira Vale, whom he was unable to marry because of her family's racial prejudice. On a return trip from Europe, where he had gone to seek cures for his ailing health, he was killed in a shipwreck, the only victim to die. At the time of his death, Gonçalves Dias was considered Brazil's greatest poet. Several stanzas of his famous poem "Canção do Exílio" ("Song of Exile") are included in the Brazilian national anthem. *See also* THEATER.

DÍAZ, GRÉGOR (Peru, 1933–). Dramatist. As an advocate of the proletariat, his plays focus principally on the lives of the poorest sectors of urban society. *La huelga* (1971; The Strike) established his place in Peruvian **theater** and was the first work in Peru to bring labor issues to the stage. Later works include *Los cercadores* (1974; The Oppressors) and *Los cercados* (1974; The Oppressed), *Con los pies en el agua* (1974; With the Feet in the Water), *Cuento del hombre que vendía globos* (1978; Tale of the Man Who Sold Balloons), and *Los del 4* (1981; Those of the Fourth).

DÍAZ, JORGE (Chile, 1930–). Dramatist. He made his name with *El cepillo de dientes* (1961; The Toothbrush), a play in the style of the **theater of the absurd**, whose two characters, named He and She, engage in bizarre games to alleviate the boredom of daily life. Several other plays followed, including *Requiém por un girasol* (1961; Requiem for a Sunflower) and *El lugar donde mueren los mamíferos* (1963; *The Place Where the Mammals Die*), which also highlight the problems of communication and the stifling conditions of bourgeois society. In 1965, Díaz moved to Spain, where he has lived ever since, and had a long, productive career in **theater**. Experimentation in a variety of themes and styles is a feature of his drama, which is characterized by word games, linguistic innovation, black humor, violence, social commentary, and political satire. Among his notable compositions are the erotic drama *La orgástula* (1970; The Orgastulum); *Mear contra en viento* (1974; Pissing in the Wind), about U.S. involvement in the overthrow of Salvador Allende's government in Chile in 1973; *La puñeta* (1977; Up the Creek), based on poems by **Nicanor Parra**; and *Desde la sangre y el silencio, o Fulgor y muerte de Pablo Neruda* (1984; From Blood and Silence, or Death and Glory of Pablo Neruda), on the last days of **Pablo Neruda**. Díaz has also contributed to **children's literature** with plays written for young audiences.

DÍAZ DE GUZMÁN, RUY (Paraguay, c. 1558–1629). Chronicler. He was the author of the **chronicle** *Historia argentina del descubrimiento, población y conquista de las provincias del Río de la Plata* (Argentinean History of the Discovery, Settlement, and Conquest of the River Plate Provinces), likely written to support his pretensions for an administrative position in the colonial government but not published until 1835. It is popularly known as *La Argentina* and has been shown to suffer from partisan errors. As the title suggests, it covers not only the early history of **Argentina**, but also the regions occupied today by **Uruguay** and Paraguay.

DÍAZ DEL CASTILLO, BERNAL (Mexico, 1496–1584). Chronicler. A conquistador and member of the force led by **Hernán Cortés** to Mexico, his **chronicle** *Historia verdadera de la conquista de la Nueva España* (written 1555?–1584, published 1632; *The Discovery and Conquest of Mexico: 1517–1521*) is an eyewitness account of the expedition and an invaluable historical resource. He wrote his version of the conquest long after the events, motivated in part by the desire to represent the role played by the members of **Hernán Cortés**'s expedition in contrast to accounts, notably that by **Francisco López de Gómara**, which tended to highlight the actions of Cortés to the detriment of his companions.

DÍAZ MIRÓN, SALVADOR (Mexico, 1853–1928). Poet. He was an unconventional figure in his life and writings. In his younger days, he fought duels with pistols, some with lethal results. His support for the governments of Porfirio Díaz (1876–1880, 1884–1911) and Victoriano Huerta (1913–1914) led to a period of exile after the latter was ousted during the Mexican Revolution. In his writing, Díaz Mirón turned his attention to the form and aesthetics of poetry, notably in the collection *Lascas* (1901; Stone Chips), which made him a precursor of **modernismo** and an influence on **Rubén Darío**.

DÍAZ RODRÍGUEZ, MANUEL (Venezuela, 1871–1927). Novelist and essayist. He wrote a critical appreciation of **modernismo** in an essay published in *Camino de la perfección* (1908; The Way of Perfection) and is considered one of Spanish America's foremost modernist prose writers. His best-known novels are *Ídolos rotos* (1901; Broken Idols) and *Sangre patricia* (1902; Patrician Blood). The former, considered a critique of **arielismo**, tells about a sculptor, schooled in Europe, who struggles against conservative narrow-mindedness in his native Venezuela.

DÍAZ SÁNCHEZ, RAMÓN (Venezuela, 1903–1968). Novelist and essayist. In his novels *Mené* (1936; *Mene*), *Cumboto* (1950; *Cumboto*), *Casandra* (1957; Casandra), and *Borburata* (1960; Borburata) he wrote about problems in the oilfields and the cocoa plantations, with a focus on racial conflicts and the African population of Venezuela. His essays are concerned mainly with the history of Venezuela and Venezuelan literature, including a book on the author **Teresa de la Parra**.

DÍAZ VARGAS, HENRY (Colombia, 1948–). Dramatist. Author of plays about the history and contemporary life of Colombia. *Más* *allá de la ejecución* (1984; Beyond the Execution) is set in the conquest period, and *Josef Antonio Galán o de cómo se sublevó el común* (Josef Antonio Galán or How the Commune Revolted) (1981) is a story from 1781. *Las puertas* (1984; The Doors); *El cumpleaños de Alicia* (1985; Alice's Birthday), about two lesbian lovers; and *La sangre más transparente* (1992; The Clearest Blood), concerned with adolescent crime and drugs in a Medellín *barrio*, all portray marginalized characters in the modern city and show the impact of Antonin Artaud (1896–1948) and the **theater of cruelty**. *See also* THEATER.

DICTATOR NOVEL. Although the dictator novel might be traced to **Domingo Faustino Sarmiento**'s 19th-century *Civilización y barbarie: vida de Juan Facundo Quiroga, y aspecto físico, costumbres, y hábitos de la República Argentina* (1845; *Facundo: Civilization and Barbarism*), it is a predominantly 20th-century literary phenomenon. The dictators whose regimes are represented come from many different countries, from the near present to the more distant past, and include both historical and fictional figures, although the latter are commonly based on persons from history. Thus, *El señor presidente* (1946; *The President*) by **Miguel Ángel Asturias** draws on the regime of Manuel Estrada Cabrera (1898–1920) in **Guatemala**; *Yo, el supremo* (1974; *I, the Supreme*) by **Augusto Roa Bastos** is an account of the rule of **José Gaspar Rodríguez de Francia** (1814–1840) in **Paraguay**; and *La fiesta del chivo* (2000; *The Feast of the Goat*) by **Mario Vargas Llosa** is based on the life of the Dominican strongman Rafael Leónidas Trujillo (1930–1961). By contrast, the protagonist of **Gabriel García Márquez**'s *El otoño del patriarca* (1975; *The Autumn of the Patriarch*) is a fictional character, even if there is much to be found in him that has a precedent in real-life Latin American dictators. *See also* AGUILERA MALTA, DEMETRIO; ARÉVALO MARTÍNEZ, RAFAEL; IBARGÜENGOITIA, JORGE; LAFOURCADE, ENRIQUE; and ZALAMEA, JORGE.

DIEZ-CANSECO, JOSÉ (Peru, 1904–1949). Novelist and short story writer. He is known for two works: *Estampas mulatas* (1930; Mulatto Scenes), a collection of short narratives about Afro-Peruvian urban life, and *Duque* (1934; Duke), a novel about the Peruvian oligarchy that caused quite a stir when it first appeared and has since been compared with *Un mundo para Julius* by **Alfredo Bryce Echenique**.

DISCÉPOLO, ARMANDO (Argentina, 1887–1971). Dramatist. He was popular between 1910 and 1934 and wrote more than 30 plays during that time. With his *Mateo* (1923; Matthew), he is said to have initiated the *grotesco criollo* in Argentina. Other *grotescos* include *Stéfano* (1928; Stephen), *Cremona* (1932; Cremona), and *Relojero* (The Watchmaker). In these and in plays such as *Babilonia* (1925; Babylon), he put the language of immigrants to Buenos Aires onstage and wrote about the gulf between reality and their expectations in a combination of drama and comedy that showed the influence of Luigi Pirandello (1867–1936). *See also* THEATER.

DONOSO, JOSÉ (Chile, 1924–1996). Novelist and short story writer. One of Latin America's most significant 20th-century novelists and a member of the **boom** generation, about which he wrote in *Historia personal del "boom"* (1972; *The Boom in Spanish American Literature*). His fiction shows the depth of his cultural formation in works that combine the themes of psychology and sexuality with an analysis of Chilean social and political structures. His first publication was *Veraneo y otros cuentos* (1955; Summer Vacation and Other Tales), a collection of stories later included in translation in *Charleston and Other Stories*. His first novel was *Coronación* (1958; *Coronation*), a realistic representation of the upper middle class that also shaped *Este domingo* (1966; *This Sunday*) and *Lugar sin límites* (1967; *Hell Hath No Limits*), although these works already showed the breakdown of the realist code in Donoso's work.

By this time, he was already living in Spain, where he enjoyed one of the most productive periods of his life and wrote his most ambitious work, *El obsceno pájaro de la noche* (1970; *The Obscene Bird of Night*), a novel he had worked on for several years before it was published. It is a complex, labyrinthine representation of Chile that leaves behind the trends in **realism** present in Donoso's earlier fiction. With a narrator who is both a character in the story and a witness to it, the novel also confronts the nature of writing. It embodies the myth of Oedipus and the indigenous myth of the *imbunche*, a deformed figure created by closing all the openings in the body, such that the monstruous takes over, in a novel set in a decaying mansion in Santiago, inhabited by nuns and the children of upper-class families in their charge. In *Casa de campo* (1978; *A House in the Country*), a historical allegory reflecting Chile under the rise and fall of Salvador Allende, Donoso also produced a long, complex work that examines both the nature of his country and the act of writing about it. By contrast, Donoso's next two novels are quite short and, in some ways, more conventional. *La misteriosa desaparición de la marquesita de Loria* (1980; The Mysterious Disappearance of the Marchioness of Loria) is an erotic farce, and *El jardín de al lado* (1981; *The Garden Next Door*) is a story of the Latin American intellectual in exile.

After returning to Chile in 1981, Donoso wrote *La desesperanza* (1986; *Curfew*), a novel about Chile under dictatorship. Other works from the last period of his life include *Taratuta; naturaleza muerta con cachimba* (1990; *Taratula; Still Life with Pipe*), *El mocho* (1992; The One-armed Man), *Donde van a morir los elefantes* (1995; Where Elephants Go to Die), and a volume of memoirs, *Conjeturas sobre la memoria de mi tribu* (1996; Conjectures About the Memory of My Tribe).

DORFMAN, ARIEL (Chile, 1942–). Novelist, dramatist, and essayist. Although born in **Argentina**, he adopted Chilean citizenship and as a member of Salvador Allende's administration in Chile was forced into exile in 1973 after the president's overthrow. He eventually settled in the United States after a period in Europe. Dorfman's writing is esentially political. Among his earlier essays are *Imaginación y violencia en América Latina* (1970; Imagination and Violence in Latin America) and *Para leer al Pato Donald* (1971; *How to Read Donald Duck: Imperialist Ideology in the Disney Comic*). The second of these, written with Armand Mattelart, is an important text of cultural analysis. Later essays include *Hacia la liberación del lector latinoamericano* (1984; *Some Write to the Future: Essays on Contemporary Latin American Fiction*) and several books in English: *Chile from Within, 1873–1990* (1990), with **Marco Antonio de la Parra**, a volume of memoirs; *Looking South, Heading North: A Bilingual Journey* (1998); and *Exorcising Terror: The Incredible Unending Trial of Augusto Pinochet* (2002).

Dorfman's novels are complex works. *Moros en la costa* (1973; *Hard Rain*), on the theme of revolution, is constructed as a collage and has some similarity to novels by **Julio Cortázar**. *Viudas* (1981; *Widows*) deals with the 1973 coup by Augusto Pinochet in Chile and the exile that followed for many. It was recast as a play in 1988. *La última canción de Manuel Sendero* (1982; *The Last Song of Manuel Sendero*) is a novel with a layered plot and multiple voices dealing with Chile under Pinochet (1973–1990). *Máscaras* (1988; *Mascara*), a difficult work on betrayal, deception, and alienation, has been compared with works by Franz Kafka (1883–1924) and George Orwell (1903–1950). *Konfidenz* (1995; Confiding) is about an anti-Nazi conspiracy in 1939 Germany.

Among Dorfman's works for the **theater**, the most celebrated is *La muerte y la doncella* (1990; *Death and the Maiden*), about a woman who recognizes and kidnaps the man she believes was her torturer. The play has been widely performed internationally and was made into a highly successful film in English.

DOURADO, VALDOMIRO AUTRAN (Brazil, 1926–). Novelist and short story writer. Attempting a renovation of Brazilian narrative, despite apparently traditional themes, Dourado's award-winning work combines lyricism, humor, and psychological insight. In the short stories of *Nove Histórias em Grupos de Três* (1957; Nine Stories in Sets of Three), augmented and republished as *Solidão Solitude* (1972; Solitude Solitude), he created an imaginary Faulknerian city called Duas Pontes. His best-known novel is *Ópera dos Mortos* (1967; Opera of the Dead). His novella *Uma Vida em Segredo* (1964; A Secret Life) was adapted for the screen.

DRAGÚN, OSVALDO (Argentina, 1929–1999). Dramatist. He was part of a generation that, in the 1950s, represented a movement in Argentina away from the facile comedies and **costumbrismo** of the past to incorporate more recent developments in European **theater**. Dragún's first successes were historical dramas, including *Tupac Amaru* (1957; Tupac Amaru), the retelling of a 1780 rebellion in colonial **Peru** against the Spanish. In plays that followed, under the general title of *Historias para ser contadas* (1957; Stories to Be Told), he wrote socially committed **Brechtian theater** that developed the aesthetic of the grotesque associated with the *grotesco* *criollo*. The best known of these, perhaps Dragún's most celebrated play, is *Historia del hombre que se convirtió en perro* (1957; *The Man Who Turned into a Dog*), about a man who applies for a job as a watchdog and turns into one. It has been successfully staged in several countries and reflects a concern for people caught in desperate situations. Dragún returned periodically to the formula used in his *historias*, such as *Historias con cárcel* (1972; Jail Stories), in which the metaphor of imprisonment is used to represent restrictions on freedom in Argentina. He also wrote for television and films and, in 1981, became part of **Teatro Abierto**, an attempt to revitalize the stage in Argentina at a time when artistic expression of all kinds was politically constrained.

DROGUETT, CARLOS (Chile, 1915–1996). Novelist. The author of psychological, introspective novels, often about violence and socially marginalized characters, written in a very fragmented style. His first collection of narratives, *Los asesinos del Seguro Obrero* (1940; Killers at the Seguro Obrero Building), became the source of his first novel, *Sesenta muertos en la escalera* (1954; Sixty Dead on the Stairway), based on the historical events of a student massacre in 1935. His next novel, *Eloy* (1959; Eloy), was his most successful work. Also derived from historical events, it describes the last hours of a celebrated bandit who, mainly through interior monologue, remembers events from his past as he is hunted down by the police. Other novels by Droguett fall into two groups. *Cien gotas de sangre y doscientas de sudor* (1961; One Hundred Drops of Blood and Two Hundred of Sweat), *Supay el cristiano* (1967; Supay the Christian), and *El hombre que trasladaba las ciudades* (1973; The Man Who Moved Cities) deal with historical subjects. The second group is about the lives of troubled, isolated individuals, characterized by difference, whose dilemmas are described through interior recollections. It includes *Patas de perro* (1965; Dog Legs), *El compadre* (1967; The Godfather), *El hombre que había olvidado* (1968; The Man Who Had Forgotten), and *Todas esas muertes* (1971; All Those Deaths).

DUARTE DE PERÓN, EVA (1919–1952). Popularly known as Evita. The circumstances of the rise of María Eva Duarte from poverty and social marginality to a position of wealth and influence through her marriage to Argentinean president **Juan Domingo Perón** made her one of the most controversial women of 20th-century Latin America. Her impact on politics and civil society in Argentina was significant, and her premature death from cancer at the age of 33, at the height of her popularity, only served to enhance the controversy and the myths surrounding her as a public figure. Her life and death continue to be a source of reference and narrative for writers in Argentina such as **Tomás Eloy Martínez**, **Abel Posse**, and **Mario Szichman**. See also ROA BASTOS, AUGUSTO.

DUNCAN, QUINCE (Costa Rica, 1940–). Novelist and short story writer. Considered the first successful black Costa Rican writer in Spanish, he focuses principally on working-class African Americans in Puerto Limón. His most ambitious novel is *La paz del pueblo* (1978; The Peace of the People), set in the context of a 1934 strike against the United Fruit Company in Costa Rica.

DURÃO, JOSÉ DE SANTA RITA (Brazil, 1722–1784). Poet. Born in Brazil, Santa Rita Durão studied at Coimbra, and later, fleeing from trouble with the Church, led a scholarly existence in Italy for a number of years. Returning to Portugal in 1777, he dictated his Camonian **epic poem** *Caramuru* (1779; Caramuru), on the discovery of Bahia, to the Portuguese poet José Agostinho de Macedo. Written at a time when **arcadianism** was already beginning to take hold, Santa Rita Durão's poem was not received with enthusiasm because of its perceived archaic form.

DUVAL, ADALBERTO GUERRA (Brazil, 1872–1947). Poet. A career diplomat who served in several countries, Guerra is remembered for his Portuguese- and Belgian-inspired symbolist *Palavras que o Vento Leva. . .* (1900; Words Gone with the Wind), which introduced free verse into Brazilian poetry.

– **E** –

ECHEVERRÍA, AQUILEO J. (Costa Rica, 1866–1909). Poet. Known as "the poet of Costa Rica," a title given to him by **Rubén**

Darío, he wrote mainly popular verses, *romances*, or ballads, and *concherías*, referring to a saying or action spoken or performed by a *concho* or *tico*, an inhabitant of the Costa Rican coast. His verses describe the drama and humor of everyday situations, featuring recognizable social types and colloquial language. During his lifetime, *Romances* (1903; Ballads) and *Concherías* (1905; Costa Ricanisms) were published. However, many collections or different compilations of his work have appeared since his death and have established his reputation as one of the primary verse exponents of Costa Rican **costumbrismo**.

ECHEVERRÍA, ESTEBAN (Argentina, 1805–1851). Poet and short story writer. He was deeply influenced by European **romanticism**, although his poem *Elvira, o la novia del Plata* (1832; Elvira, or the Bride of the River Plate), one of the earliest examples of romantic writing in Latin America, was greeted with indifference when it first appeared. Echeverría was also a significant contributor to formulations of Argentinean nationalism after independence from Spain. His main contributions to the literary canon in Argentina are "El matadero" (written in about 1839; published in 1871; "The Slaughter House") and *La cautiva* (1837; The Captive), both classics of Latin American literature and examples of the preoccupation with **civilization and barbarism**. The former is a short story that represents violence under the dictatorship of **Juan Manuel Rosas** (1793–1877) as an allegory of carnage, and the latter is a narrative poem in the style of **indianismo**, about a white woman captured by Indians. *See also* AIRA, CÉSAR.

ECUADOR. Although Ecuador produced no widely recognized literary figures during the colonial period, the writer whose verse caught the spirit of the war of independence in Spanish America and sang the praises of the liberator **Simón Bolívar** was the Ecuadorian **José Joaquín Olmedo**. Three writers stand out in the 19th century for their contributions to the formation of an image of Ecuador: **Juan Montalvo** sniped at the country's dictatorial rulers in his political writing; **José Fermín Cevallos** was the country's first historian; and **Juan León Mera**, Ecuador's principal representative of **romanticism**, was the author of *Cumandá* (1879), a classic of Spanish American **indianismo**.

A turn toward **realism** in the early 20th century figures variously in Ecuador in the different regions of the country. The southern coastal region is represented by the **Grupo Guayaquil**, which included **José de la Cuadra, Joaquín Gallegos Lara, Enrique Gil Gilbert, Alfredo Pareja Diezcanseco**, and **Demetrio Aguilera Malta**, the last of whom is the most widely known of the group as one of Ecuador's most significant novelists and an important figure of Latin American **magic realism** and **indigenismo**. The high sierra region and the harsh reality of indigenous life are represented by **Jorge Icaza** and his novel *Huasipungo* (1934), although a somewhat gentler account may be found in the fiction of **Ángel Felicísimo Rojas**. Another marginalized group, African Ecuadorians in the northern coastal regions of Esmeraldas, is described by **Adalberto Ortiz** and **Nelson Estupiñán Bass**.

During the 1930s, **avant-garde** ideas and manifestos circulated without deterring the continuation of other trends, such as the realist narrative mentioned above, the lyric verse of **Jorge Carrera Andrade**, or the very idiosyncratic prose of **Pablo Palacio**. Ecuador's principal avant-garde writer, both in verse and prose, was **Jorge Enrique Adoum**, whose writing also reflected his Marxist outlook. Since the mid-20th century, literature in Ecuador has become as diverse as in other countries of Latin America. The country's authors have focused on political events; government oppression; **women**'s issues; **gay** and lesbian rights; and elements of life, language, and culture that have a particularly Ecuadorian value. Among the representatives of this trend, and one of the few writers from the country whose reputation is also firmly established beyond the country's borders, is **Alicia Yáñez Cossío**.

The earliest records of **theater** in Guayaquil and Quito, Ecuador's two main cites, are of performances of religious *autos* in the 16th century. Commercial theaters were not established there, however, until the Teatro de Guayaquil in 1857 and the Teatro Nacional Sucre in Quito in 1880. In the intervening centuries, the theater of Spain, performed mainly for the ruling class, predominated. Juan Montalvo, with his political themes, figured among dramatists of the 19th century, but a move toward **costumbrismo** and the comedy of manners was more pronounced in Francisco Aguirre Guarderas and **Víctor Manuel Rendón**. **Realism** was also a feature of the plays of **Carlos**

Arturo León, whose emphasis on national life and character would lead to a social theater to which Jorge Icaza, **Enrique Avellán Ferrés**, and **Pedro Jorge Vera** contributed.

The flourishing of the Teatro Íntimo between 1954 and 1956, with which both Vera and Aguilera Malta collaborated, ushered in a period of experimentation during the 1960s as the avant-garde took root in Ecuadorian theater. Among the prominent dramatists of this development were **Francisco Tobar García** and Jorge Enrique Adoum. Their work would open the door to the diversity of the contemporary stage in Ecuador, which has all the variety of most Latin American countries, even if it has yet to make a broad impact in the region. *See also* ANTIPOETRY; ARIELISMO; CHILDREN'S LITERATURE; JOURNALS; NEO-CLASSICISM; NEW NOVEL; WOMEN.

EDWARDS, JORGE (Chile, 1931–). Novelist, short story writer, and essayist. His first collections of short stories, *El patio* (1952; The Backyard) and *Gente de la ciudad* (1961; People of the City), with their emphasis on the middle class and an urban environment, represented a break from the established trend of **criollismo** in Chilean fiction. In his first novel, *El peso de la noche* (1965; The Burden of the Night), a biting critique of the Chilean middle class, Edwards developed the same group of themes as in his stories. Before returning to fiction, he published a widely read memoir *Persona non grata* (1973; *Persona Non grata: An Envoy in Castro's Cuba*) that records his disenchantment, as a diplomat and writer, with the Cuban Revolution. His critical stance resulted in his expulsion from Cuba (1971) and earned him the approbium of many Latin American intellectuals.

Edwards has published several novels since this controversial work. *Los convidados de piedra* (1978; The Stone Guests) and *El museo de cera* (1981; The Wax Museum) are both reflections on the condition of Chile under the dictatorship of Augusto Pinochet (1973–1990), and in *La mujer imaginaria* (1985; *The Imaginary Woman*), the story of the liberation of a female, upper-class, middle-aged artist anticipates the political liberation of Chile from that regime. *El anfitrión* (1988; The Host) is a reworking of the Faust legend. In *El origen del mundo* (1996; The Origin of the World) and *El sueño de la historia* (2000; The Dream of History), Edwards turned to historical themes. His two most recent novels are *El inútil de la familia*

(2004; The Useless One of the Family) and *La casa de Dostoievsky* (2008; Dostoievsky's House). He has also contributed to newspapers in Latin America (notably *El Mercurio* in Chile) and Europe, and many of his articles have been collected in *El whisky de los poetas* (1997; The Poets' Whiskey) and *Diálogos en un tejado* (2003; Conversations on a Rooftop). In *Adiós poeta* (1990; Farewell, Poet), he presented reminiscences of **Pablo Neruda**, with whom he worked as a diplomat in Paris between 1971 and 1973. Edwards received the **Miguel de Cervantes Prize for Literature** in 1999.

EDWARDS BELLO, JOAQUÍN (Chile, 1887–1968). Novelist and journalist. His first novel, *El inútil* (1912; The Loser), is a satire of the upper class to which the author, a member of the influential Edwards family in Chile, belonged. In a later work, *El roto* (1920; The Down-and-Out), he turned to the other end of the social spectrum. The novel, one of Edwards Bello's most popular, belongs to the tradition of **naturalism** and introduces Esmeraldo, a character born in a brothel who figures in other novels by the same author. Subsequent works of fiction appeared in fairly quick succession: *El chileno en Madrid* (1928; The Chilean in Madrid), whose protagonists, like Edwards Bello, are wealthy expatriates; *Cap Polonio* (1929; Cape Polonio), about a transatlantic journey from Buenos Aires aboard a luxury liner; *Valparaíso, la ciudad del viento* (1931; Valparaíso, the Windy City), set in a time before the devastating earthquake of 1906; *Criollos en París* (1933; Creoles in Paris), another novel of Chilean expatriates, set in the gambling dens of the French capital before World War I; and *La chica del Crillón* (1935; The Girl from the Crillon), a story with lesbian themes on the downfall of a girl from a good family. After the last of these novels, Edwards Bello published no new works of fiction, although he revised and republished some of his earlier ones. By the 1920s, he had also established a career as a journalist and written many **chronicles** of everyday life, many of which were gathered and published in several collections.

EGURÉN, JOSÉ MARÍA (Peru, 1874–1942). Poet. For his musicality, language, and themes, he is associated with **modernismo**, but his verse also anticipated the **avant-garde**. Although a marginal figure during his lifetime, when he was criticized for his difficulty, he is now considered Peru's principal representative of **symbolism**. He published three collections of verse. *Simbólicas* (1911; Symbolicals) and *La canción de las figuras* (1916; The Song of the Figures) are rich in references to the exotic and the fantastic. His last collection, *Poesías* (1929; Poems), is a reissue of some of his earlier verse along with poems from collections titled *Sombra* (Shadow) and *Rondinelas* (Rondinos), parts of which had already been published in magazines. Eguren was also an accomplished watercolorist and photographer. His interest in music is reflected in his verse, and late in life he began to write short prose notes, which were collected and published post-humously as *Motivos estéticos* (1959; Aesthetic Motifs).

EICHELBAUM, SAMUEL (Argentina, 1894–1967). Dramatist. His first success, *La mala sed* (1920; Bad Thirst), anticipated the psychological themes and moral issues presented in many of his later plays, in which he stretched the conventions of **naturalism** and **costumbrismo** of his day and contributed to modernizing the **theater** in Argentina with the kinds of social and character analysis that had already begun in Europe. In several of his works from the 1920s, such as *La hermana terca* (1924; The Stubborn Sister) and *Nadie la conoció nunca* (1926; No-one Ever Knew Her), he explored the psychology of **women** through his female characters. As the author of more than 20 published plays, he remained a productive and successful writer throughout his career. In later dramas, he turned to a dissection of realist conventions to analyze established social stereotypes. *Un guapo del 900* (1940; A Gallant for 1900) is a late example of **gaucho literature** in the theater that parodies the gaucho, and in *Un tal Servando Gómez* (1942; A Man Called Servando Gómez), he dramatizes the absurdity of macho jealousy. He also published three collections of short stories: *Un monstruo en libertad* (1925; A Monster at Large), *Tormenta de Dios* (1929; A Storm from God), and *El viajero inmóvil* (1933; The Stationary Traveler).

***EL GÜEGÜENSE* (Nicaragua).** One of the oldest theatrical traditions in Latin America, *El güegüense* grew out of a popular **theater** in Nahuatl and Spanish in **Nicaragua** that thrived in the colonial period between the mid-16th and mid-18th centuries. The name for the central character, *el güegüense*, is derived from the Nahuatl *huehue*, meaning an old or wise man. He is a merchant who attempts to deceive the colonial authorities intent on enforcing the tax law. As such, his antics continue to be relevant in contemporary times. *See also* THEATER IN QUECHUA.

EL SALVADOR. As in other Latin American countries, especially in Central America, the direction taken by literature in El Salvador has responded as much to the tides of conflicts within the country as to broader aesthetic and literary movements. Although the newly independent country had its share of minor contributors to **neo-classicism** and **romanticism**, its national literature is considered as having been founded by **Francisco Gavidia**, who introduced **modernismo** to the country in both poetry and prose. The **costumbrismo, realism**, and **naturalism** of the end of the 19th and early 20th centuries are represented by **Arturo Ambrogi** and **José María Peralta Lagos**.

Of all the civil conflicts that have afflicted the country, the peasant uprising led in 1932 by Augustín Farabundo Martí (1893–1932) and brutally suppressed by the dictator Maximiliano Hernández Martínez (1931–1944) indelibly marked the 20th century and was the inspiration for later uprisings. It became known as *La Matanza* and was also the background against which the work of **Salarrué**, **Claudia Lars**, the country's first major lyric voice, and **Hugo Lindo** was written and published. These events and their continuations were also the context of the poetry and **testimonio** of **Roque Dalton**, the fiction of **Manlio Argueta**, and the varied writings of **Claribel Alegría**. Like them, Salvadoran writers have continued since the end of the civil war in 1992 to document and interpret the conflicted history of their country.

Popular **theater** was enjoyed in colonial El Salvador, especially in the form of dances performed in imitation of animals. The first decades of independence brought foreign touring companies to the country and saw the construction of theaters. Then, with the beginnings of a Salvadoran national literature in the early 20th century, more theater was written locally, notably by Francisco Gavidia and José María Peralta Lagos. However, the theater in El Salvador has stuttered between progress and setbacks during much of the last century. Economic depression and dictatorship hampered its growth in the 1930s and 1940s. Nevertheless, the opening of a theater by the national university preceded a more productive period during the 1960s, when classical and modern foreign plays were staged and a group of Salvadoran dramatists began to emerge, but this activity was curtailed in the 1970s as the country moved once more toward civil war. Since the ending of the last conflict in 1992, theater has once more begun to progress and has received state support, but El Salvador has still to achieve the same levels of productivity and recognition it has obtained in poetry and prose. *See also* CASA DE LAS AMÉRICAS; CHILDREN'S LITERATURE; CRIOLLISMO; MAGIC REALISM; WOMEN.

ELIZONDO, SALVADOR (Mexico, 1932–2006). Novelist. His fiction has little social context and not much in terms of plot. It is essentially about writing and incorporates several other forms of discourse, such as dialogue, letters, and essays. The use of language and treatment of time are highly experimental, having some affinity with the **new novel**, and he presents a somewhat sadistic view of human relations. *Farabeuf o la crónica de un instante* (1965; *Farabeuf or the Chronicle of an Instant*) is about a moment of lovemaking and is highly reminiscent of the experimentalism of the French new novel by authors such as Alain Robbe-Grillet (1922–2008). *El hipogeo secreto* (1968; The Secret Cellar) is about a man writing a novel called "The Secret Cellar." Other fiction includes *Narda, o el verano* (1966; Narda, or the Summer), *El retrato de Zoe y otras mentiras* (1969; Portrait of Zoe and Other Falsehoods), and *El grafógrafo* (1972; The Graphographer). Elizondo also wrote verse, **theater**, criticism, and journalism, although the overlapping of genres in his work sometimes makes it diffcult to categorize them.

ELTIT, DIAMELA (Chile, 1949–). Novelist. She belongs to the post-coup (1973) generation in Chile. Her writing is challenging and transgressive with respect to both language and content. She often presents herself as her narrator, but linear plots are not typical of her fiction. Ludic language; use of artistic, cinematic, and video effects; and evocation of the body are features of her works that give them the character of performance texts. *Lumpérica* (1983; *E. Iluminata*) is a highly fragmented novel that offers a vision of the contemporary urban scene from the perspective of the city's most economically marginalized. In *Por la patria* (1986; For the Fatherland), the protagonist Coya-Coca and other **women** are interrogated and tortured in prison after the military invasion of a shantytown. *El cuarto mundo* (1988; *The Fourth World*), narrated in various voices belonging to characters of different genders, has incest between twins at its core. *El padre mío* (1989; Father of Mine) is a monologue spoken by a schizophrenic from a Santiago slum that mocks national mythologies. *Vaca sagrada* (1991; *Sacred Cow*), set in the city under repression, presents the narrator's reflections on the oppression of women and her own sexuality and desires. *Los vigilantes* (1994; *Custody of the Eyes*) is also a study of life under dictatorship. More recent works include *Mano de obra* (2002; Labor), *Puño y letra* (2005; Handwriting), and *Jamás el fuego nunca* (2007; No More Fire Ever Again). *See also* ZURITA, RAÚL.

ENTREMÉS. A short, comic, or farcical play or interlude, usually in one act, that originated in Spain in the 16th century. *Entremeses* were initially intended to entertain an audience during the interval between two acts of a longer play, although they eventually came to be performed independently also. They were often based on practical jokes played on ordinary people and commonly included music and dancing. Brought to the Americas by the Spanish, they became part of the repertoire of the colonial **theater**, for example in the work of **Fernán González de Eslava (Mexico)** and **Pedro de Peralta y Barnuevo (Peru)**. *See also* SAINETE.

EPIC POETRY. The drama of the history of the conquest and settlement of the Americas provided ample scope for epic narratives in verse, a genre that had been revived in Renaissance Europe and enjoyed considerable popularity at the same time that Europeans encountered the New World and were establishing the first colonies. **Juan de Castellanos (Colombia)** wrote a verse history of the Indies. **Alonso de Ercilla y Zúñiga** turned his experience with **Pedro de Valdivia**'s military campaign in **Chile** into an epic poem and had several imitators and continuators, of whom **Pedro de Oña** was one. **Gabriel Lobo Lasso de la Vega** wrote two verse narratives celebrating the deeds of **Hernán Cortés** in **Mexico**. **Bernardo de Balbuena** wrote on Mexico City and **Pedro de Peralta y Barnuevo**

on the founding and history of Lima. By contrast, on different topics, but in keeping with the traditional range of epic poetry, the narrative of the passion and death of Christ by **Diego de Hojeda (Peru)** was the New World's first religous epic. Verse narratives also featured in the 19th century and **romanticism** (*see* ACUÑA DE FIGUEROA, FRANCISCO; ECHEVERRÍA, ESTEBAN; HERNÁNDEZ, JOSÉ; ZORILLA DE SAN MARTÍN; JUAN) as well as in the 20th century (see ADOUM, JORGE ENRIQUE).

In **Brazil**, *The Lusiads* by the Portuguese poet Luís de Camões (1524–1580) provided the model for neo-classical epic poems of exploration, settlement, and battle by **José de Anchieta, José Basílio da Gama, Cláudio Manuel da Costa**, and **José de Santa Rita Durão**. Epic poetry was revived in the 19th century with the rise of nationalism in Brazil, albeit not unpolemically, by **Domingos José Gonçalves de Magalhães, José de Alencar**, and **Antônio Gonçalves Dias**. With lesser ambition, 20th-century poets like **Olavo Bilac, Cassiano Ricardo Leite, Jorge de Lima**, and even **Haroldo de Campos** borrowed from this tradition. *See also* SOUSÂNDRADE, JOAQUIM DE.

ERCILLA Y ZÚÑIGA, ALONSO DE (Chile, 1533–1594). Poet. He was a member of the Spanish court and part of the expeditionary force led by **Pedro de Valdivia** sent to Chile in 1557 to quell a rebellion by Araucanian Indians. He wrote about the wars in Chile in *La Araucana* (in three parts: 1569, 1578, 1589; *The Araucaniad*), a narrative poem that not only is of interest to historians because of its account of the early history of Chile, but is sympathetic to the Araucanian Indians and was a paradigm for **epic poetry** in the 17th century. *See also* GÓNGORA DE MARMOLEJO, ALONSO DE; OÑA, PEDRO DE.

ESPÍNOLA, FRANCISCO (Uruguay, 1901–1973). Short story writer. He was a drama critic who tried his hand at writing for the **theater** in *La fuga en el espejo* (1957; Escape into the Mirror). He also wrote *Sombras sobre la tierra* (1933; Shadows over the Land), a novel, but is best known for short stories that focus on isolated individuals from suburban Buenos Aires. His collections include *Raza ciega* (1926; Blind Race) and *El rapto y otros cuentos* (1950; The Abduction and Other Stories).

ESPINOSA MEDRANO, JUAN DE ("EL LUNAREJO") (Peru, 1629?–1688). Dramatist, critic, and sermon writer. A celebrated orator and prominent figure of the **baroque** known for his defense of the style of the Spanish poet Luis de Góngora (1561–1627) in *Apologético en favor de Don Luis de Góngora príncipe de los poetas líricos de España* (1662; Apology in Support of Don Luis de Góngora, Prince of Lyric Poets in Spain). His sermons were published posthumously in a volume titled *La novena maravilla* (1699; The Ninth Wonder), and he was the author of a biblical drama, *Amar su propia muerte* (Love Your Own Death), as well as two *autos*, of unknown date, written in Quechua: *El hijo pródigo* (The Prodigal Son) and *El rapto de Proserpina y sueño de Endimión* (The Abduction of Persephone and the Dream of Endymion). *See also* THEATER.

ESQUIVEL, LAURA (Mexico, 1949–). Novelist. Her fiction often includes several overlaying elements. She is best known for the novel *Como agua para chocolate* (1989; *Like Water for Chocolate*), a historical romance with elements of **magic realism** set partly during the Mexican Revolution. It is framed as a cookery book and narrates a story of unfulfilled love in which the emotions of the protagonist are transferred to the food she prepares and are felt by those who eat her cooking. The movie version of the novel, itself an international **best seller**, became one of the largest grossing foreign films ever released in the United States. Esquivel's second novel, *La ley del amor* (1995; *The Law of Love*), is also a romance. It is set in Mexico in the year 2200 and concerns a psychoanalyst whose patients' problems arise from events in previous lives. The novel was marketed with a CD of romantic music. Other works by Esquivel include *Íntimas suculencias* (1998; Intimate Succulence), *Estrellita marinera* (1999; Little Star of the Sea), *El libro de las emociones* (2000; The Book of Emotions), *Tan veloz como el deseo* (2001; *Swift as Desire*), and *Malinche* (2006; *Malinche*). The last of these is about the interpreter and mistress of the Spanish conqueror of Mexico, **Hernán Cortés**. It explores the cultural heritage of the protagonist, and the novel includes an Aztec codex that serves as her diary. *See also* WOMEN.

ESTRIDENTISMO. One of the first **avant-garde** movements in **Mexico** (1921–1927), of which the principal literary figure was

Manuel Maples Arce; its literary **journals** were *Irradiador* (1923) and *Horizonte* (1926–1927). Its supporters (*estridentistas*) included writers and artists who called on Mexican intellectuals to unite against the academicism and **symbolism** of the past in favor of an aesthetic reflecting the modern transformation of the world. It was strongly influenced by Italian futurism and **ultraísmo**. Other members included the poet **Germán List Arzubide** and the prose writers Salvador Gallardo (1893–1981) and Arqueles Vela (1899–1977).

ESTUPIÑÁN BASS, NELSON (Ecuador, 1912–2002). Poet and novelist. His native province of Esmeraldas is a significant source of reference in his work. His poems, *Canto negro por la luz* (1956; Black Song for the Night), *Las tres carabelas* (1963; The Three Caravelles), and *Las huellas digitales* (1971; Finger Prints), celebrate negritude, among other themes, and show a consciousness of the relation between race and social class. Similar themes appear in his fiction, often characterized by a discontinuous narrative, although the best known, *El último río* (1966; *Pastrana's Last River*), about the career of a provincial governor, has a more conventional structure. His fiction includes *Cuando los guayacanes florecían* (1954; When the Guayacanas Flowered), a novel about a black worker's revolt against the government in 1913–1916; *El paraíso* (1958; Paradise); *Senderos brillantes* (1974; Shining Paths); *Las puertas del verano* (1978; The Gates of Summer); *Toque de queda* (1978; Curfew Bell); *Bajo el cielo nublado* (1981; Under the Cloudy Sky), a novel of **magic realism**; and the thriller *El crepúsculo* (1992; Twilight).

EXISTENTIALISM. Although this train of thought may be traced to philosophers such as Søren Kierkegaard (1813–1855), Friedrich Nietzsche (1844–1900), and Martin Heidegger (1889–1976), its influence in Latin America was also felt through the literary work of Fyodor Dostoyevsky (1821–1881), Franz Kafka (1883–1924), Jean Paul Sartre (1905–1980), and Alberta Camus (1913–1960) and had its greatest impact in literature on the novel. At the core of existentialism is the notion that individuals give meaning to their own lives. Although this makes them free and responsible, it also highlights the potential meaninglessness and absurdity of existence that results in confusion and produces individuals at odds with themselves and society. This condition is amply reflected in the main characters of novels by **Juan Carlos Onetti** and **Ernesto Sábato** and figures also in the short stories of **Juan José Arreola** and in the **theater** of **Carlos Solórzano**, as well as in the work of a number of other authors. *See also* LISPECTOR, CLARICE; MALLEA, EDUARDO; MONTEFORTE TOLEDO, MARIO; OROZCO, OLGA; SOLOGUREN, JAVIER; VARGAS VILA, JOSÉ MARÍA.

– F –

FALLAS, CARLOS LUIS (Costa Rica, 1909–1966). Novelist. After working for the United Fruit Company, he became a militant union and political activist against it. His experiences are represented in his best-known novel, *Mamita Yunai* (1941; Mama Yunai), a title that refers to United Fruit. The same political stance is maintained in other works, including *Gentes y gentecillas* (1947; People and Plebs), *Marcos Ramírez* (1952; Marcos Ramírez), and *Mi madrina* (1954; My Godmother), but without the same success as in *Mamita Yunai*.

FANTASTIC LITERATURE. The genre originated in 19th-century Europe and was popularized in North America by Edgar Allan Poe (1809–1849). It is based on the narration of events whose ambiguity cannot be entirely resolved, either through a rational explanation or through a clear attribution to the paranormal or supernatural. Belonging mainly, but not exclusively, to the realm of the short story, one of its earliest successful exponents in Latin America was the Uruguayan **Horacio Quiroga**, who was heavily influenced by Poe. Although authors from other countries, such as **Salarrué** in **El Salvador, Juan José Arreola** and **Carlos Fuentes** in **Mexico, Teresa de la Parra** in **Venezuela**, and **Manuel Antônio Álvares de Azevedo, Murilo Rubião**, and **Moacyr Scliar** in **Brazil**, have also contributed to it, the genre was especially attractive to writers in the River Plate countries of **Uruguay** and **Argentina**. It was promoted there by **Adolfo Bioy Casares, Jorge Luis Borges**, and **Silvina Ocampo** in an anthology of stories published in 1940. Then, in the 1960s and after, their fellow Argentinean **Julio Cortázar** is said to have revived and renewed the genre in what is known as the "neo-fantastic" by emphasizing the emergence of the traditional ambiguity in the context of everyday life. *See also* ANDERSEN IMBERT, ENRIQUE; FERNÁNDEZ, MACEDONIO; GARMENDÍA, JULIO; HERNÁNDEZ, FELISBERTO; LUGONES, LEOPOLDO; PERI ROSI, CRISTINA; PEYROU, MANUEL; QUEIRÓS, DINAH SILVEIRA DE.

FARIA, OTÁVIO DE (Brazil, 1908–1980). Essayist and novelist. Trained in law, de Faria is one of the main exponents of the generation that followed **Brazilian modernism.** He wrote political essays reflecting a conservative position, including *Maquiavel e o Brasil* (1931; Machiavelli and Brazil), *Destino do Socialismo* (1933; The Future of Socialism), and *Cristo e César* (1937; Christ and Caesar). He is better known, however, for an uneven 13-volume cycle of novels, *Tragédia Burguesa* (1937–1971; Bourgeois Tragedy), which portrays characters plagued by spiritual and ethical conflicts. *See also* MORAES, VINÍCIUS DE.

FAUSTINO, MÁRIO (Brazil, 1930–1962). Poet. Born in Teresina, Piauí, Faustino studied in Belém, then at Pomona College in California. On his return to Brazil he went to Rio, where he taught and wrote for the newspaper *Jornal do Brasil*. Between 1953 and 1958, his criticism column "Poesía Experiencia" was fundamental in introducing many modern poets into the Brazilian context through his translations and commentary. Faustino, who died in a plane crash that had been predicted by a seer, published only one book in his life: *O Homem e Sua Hora* (1955; Man and His Hour). His poetics, employing traditional forms, were a mix of **symbolism** and **surrealism,** influenced by French poets and also **Jorge de Lima.** Later on he became interested in Ezra Pound (1885–1972) and e.e. cummings (1894–1962). Faustino is seen as a brilliant poet who anticipated **concrete poetry,** whose premature death kept him from finishing a projected long autobiographical and cosmic poem based on the ideogrammic method. His posthumous volume *Poesias* (1966; Poems) gathers uncollected poems.

FEINMANN, JOSÉ PABLO (Argentina, 1943–). Novelist and essayist. A philosopher whose television presentations have won him wide recognition in Argentina, Feinmann's writing in general is characterized by its philosophical underpinnings. He has also written for the cinema as well as television and often resorts to the forms of popular culture in his work. In his novels, he makes ample and innovative use of the conventions of **crime fiction** as a means to explore contemporary society. His novels include *Últimos días de la víctima* (1979; Last Days of the Victim), *Ni el tiro del final* (1981; Not Even the Final Shot), *El ejército de ceniza* (1994; Army of Ash), *Los crímenes de van Gogh* (1994; The Crimes of Van Gogh), *El mandato* (2000; The Mandate), *La astucia de la razón* (2001; The Astuteness of Reason), *El cadáver imposible* (2003; The Impossible Corpse), *La crítica de las armas* (2003; The Critique of Arms), and *La sombra de Heidegger* (2005; Heidegger's Ghost). As an essayist, Feinmann has written on cinema in *Pasiones de celuloide* (2000; Celluloid Passions) and *El cine por asalto* (2006; Cinema by Assault) and on philosophy in *La filosofía y el barro de la historia* (2008; Philosophy and the Clay of History), and in *La sangre derramada: ensayo sobre la violencia política* (2003; Spilt Blood: An Essay on Political Violence) he has undertaken an anlysis of the history of political violence in Argentina.

FERNANDES, MILLÔR (Brazil, 1924–). Humorist, novelist, and dramatist. An award-winning cartoon artist, Fernandes (who signs his name as Millôr) is also known for his successful cosmopolitan comedies, among which is *Liberdade, Liberdade* (1965, Freedom, Freedom), written in collaboration with Flávio Rangel. *See also* THEATER.

FERNÁNDEZ, MACEDONIO (Argentina, 1874–1952). Novelist. An **avant-garde** writer whose work is sometimes associated with **fantastic literature**, but is not easily classified. He was an eccentric who became increasingly reclusive and uninterested in his own writing, to the extent that it was published mainly thanks to the initiative of friends and admirers. In works such as *Papeles de recienvenido* (1929; Papers of a New Arrival) and the posthumously published *Museo de la novela de la eterna* (1967; Museum of the Novel of the Eternal Woman), he challenges conventional fiction and the literary enterprise, proposing that readers should become authors. He was an important influence in Argentina, especially on **Jorge Luis Borges**

and **Julio Cortázar**, whose novel *Rayuela* embodies the principle of reader engagement. *See also* PIGLIA, RICARDO.

FERNÁNDEZ DE LIZARDI, JOSÉ JOAQUÍN (Mexico, 1776–1827). Novelist and journalist. He was a prolific journalist and pamphleteer whose writing often attracted the attention of the censors and led to periods of imprisonment. He founded the periodical *El Pensador Mexicano* (1812–1814; The Mexican Thinker) in support of the fledgling independence movement in Mexico and adopted its title as his pseudonym. Shortly after, he turned to fiction as a means to criticize colonial society and the status quo. His *El periquillo sarniento* (1816; *The Mangy Parrot*) is considered the first truly Spanish American novel and a classic of Mexican literature. Adapting the European tradition of the **picaresque novel**, his hero's wanderings serve to offer a critical panorama of colonial society. His second novel, *Noches tristes y día alegre* (1818; Sad Nights and Happy Day), a didactic work on marriage, is less of an adventure novel and more reflective. *La Quijotita y su prima* (1819; Little Quixote and Her Cousin) is concerned with the education of women, and in *Vida y hechos del famoso caballero don Catrín de la Fachenda* (written 1820; published 1832; The Life and Deeds of the Celebrated Knight Don Catrín de la Fachenda) he returned to the picaresque genre to tell the story of an unreformed social parasite. Lizardi also wrote several short pieces for the **theater**, one of the genres to which he turned after his journalism was curtailed by the censor. His plays include *El fuego de Prometeo* (The Fire of Prometheus), *Auto mariano* (A Marian Auto), *La noche más venturosa* (The Happiest Night), and *Todos contra el payo* (All Against the Fool). *See also* PAYNO, MANUEL.

FERNÁNDEZ DE OVIEDO, GONZALO (Spain, 1478–1557). Chronicler. His *Sumario de la natural historia de las Indias* (1526; *Natural History of the West Indies*) was the first natural history of the New World and anticipated the author's longer *Historia general y natural de las Indias* (1535; General and Natural History of the Indies). This ambitious **chronicle** sets out to describe the natural world and tell the story of the discovery, conquest, and colonization of the Americas. Although the first part appeared in 1535, the complete work was not published till 1851–1855. Parts of it, such as the story of the shipwreck and wanderings of **Alvar Núñez Cabeza de Vaca**, have been published separately in English translation.

FERRAZ, HEITOR (Brazil, 1964–). Poet. In his early works, such as *Resumo do Dia* (1996; Summary of the Day) and *A Mesma Noite* (1997; The Same Night), Ferraz appears as an heir to **Manuel Bandeira**'s poetry of the everyday. His later collections, such as *Goethe nos Olhos do Lagarto* (2001; Goethe in the Eyes of the Lizard) and *Hoje Como Ontem ao Meio-Dia* (2002; Today Like Yesterday at Midday), evidence a more ironic perspective and clearer existential concerns.

FILHO, ADONIAS (Brazil, 1915–1990). Journalist, novelist, and publisher. His Faulknerian trilogy *Os Servos da Morte* (1946; The Servants of Death), *Memórias de Lázaro* (1952; *Memories of Lazarus*), and *Corpo Vivo* (1962; Live Body), set in the cacao-growing region of Bahia, exposes the violence and fatalism associated with the third phase of Northeastern **Brazilian modernism**. *O forte* (1965; The Strong One) explores existential drama, and *Luanda, Beira, Bahia* (1971; Luanda, Beira, Bahia) depicts the saga of Portuguese colonization in Angola, Mozambique, and Brazil.

FILHO, ARMANDO FREITAS (Brazil, 1940–). Poet. Initially attracted to **concrete poetry**, Freitas Filho then joined **Mário Chamie**'s dissident "praxis poetry" with titles such as *Dual* (1966; Dual) and *Marca Registrada* (1970; *Trademark*). Influenced by poets such as **Ferreira Gullar**, he then evolved into an antirhetorical poetry that joins **avant-garde** concerns to the body in works such as *De Corpo Presente* (1975; Present Body), *Longa Vida* (1982; Long Life), *De Cor* (1988; By Heart), *Cabeça de Homem* (1991; Man's Head), *Duplo Cego* (1997; Double Blind), *Fio Terra* (2000; Ground Wire), and *Raro Mar* (2006; Strange Sea). His book *3X4* (1985; 3X4) won the **Jabuti Prize**.

FILLOY, JUAN (Argentina, 1894–2000). He was something of a literary curiosity. Although he was a prolific author in a wide variety of genres, much of his work remained unpublished. Several books appeared in the 1930s in private editions, including *Periplo* (1931;

Journey), *¡Estafen!* (1932 and 1968; Swindle!), *La potra* (1973; Filly), and *La purga* (1992; The Purge), then nothing until many years later, when he became a celebrity, although he was already known to some writers, **Julio Cortázar** among them. His work is characterized by humor and irony. His titles all tend to have seven letters and to begin with a different letter of the alphabet. He was a great collector and writer of palindrones, claiming to have amassed over 6,000 of them, and he was one of Latin America's longest-lived writers, dying at the age of 107.

FOGWILL, RODOLFO ENRIQUE (Argentina, 1941–). Poet, short story writer, and novelist. Customarily known only by his last name, Fogwill was a sociologist and businessman who turned to writing full time after winning a prize for his short story "Muchacha punk" (Punk Girl) in 1980. Since then, he has become one of Argentina's established contemporary writers, and his work is frequently anthologized. His poetry includes *El efecto de realidad* (1979; The Effect of Reality), *Las horas de citas* (1980; Times of Appointments), *Partes del todo* (1991; Parts of the Whole), *Lo dado* (2001; The Given), and *Últimos momentos* (2004; Last Moments). Among his collections of short stories are *Mis muertos punk* (1980; My Punk Dead), *Música japonesa* (1982; Japanese Music), *Ejércitos imaginarios* (1983; Imaginary Armies), *Pájaros de la cabeza* (1985; Birds of the Head), *Muchacha punk* (1992; Punk Girl), *Restos diurnos* (1993; Remains of the Day), and *Cantos de marineros en las pampas* (1998; Songs of Pampas Sailors).

Fogwill's first novel, *Los pichiciegos* (1983; *Malvinas Requiem*), also one of his most widely read novels, was one of the first works of fiction in Argentina to deal with the Malvinas/Falklands War against Great Britain (1982). His more recent novels have dealt with the society emerging in Argentina in the post-dictatorship period after 1983, reflecting new technologies and a new economy, changes in mass culture, and a sense of disorientation as the country reestablishes itself in the context of a new reality and memories of the recent past. *Vivir Afuera* (1998; Living Outside) is one of the most representative novels in this respect, a loosely structured narrative presenting six disparate, somewhat alienated characters, whose lives intersect briefly in Buenos Aires for a few hours during one night and early morning. Other novels by Fogwill include *La buena nueva de los libros del caminante* (1990; The Good News of the Books of the Wanderer), set in the period between 1955 and 1970; *Una pálida historia de amor* (1991; A Pale Love Story); *La experiencia sensible* (2001; The Notable Experience); *En otro orden de cosas* (2001, On the Other Hand); *Urbana* (2003; Urban); and *Runa* (2003; Rune).

FONSECA, RUBEM (Brazil, 1925–). Novelist and short story writer. Born in Minas Gerais, Fonseca has lived in Rio since the age of eight, however, and in his literary work has become a true representative of the urban fiction of that city, an heir to **Joaquim Maria Machado de Assis, Afonso Henriques de Lima Barreto**, and **Marques Rebelo**. Fonseca first became known for short **crime fiction** that portrays, in a crude style of realism, violence and lawlessness across all segments of Rio society, especially the southern part of the city. Having served in the police force in the 1950s, Fonseca had firsthand knowledge of his subject matter. Some of his most celebrated collections of short stories are *Feliz Ano Novo* (1975; Happy New Year) and *O Cobrador* (1979; *The Taker and Other Stories*). In "Feliz Ano Novo," a gang invades a private New Year's party, killing and raping the guests. "O Cobrador" is a first person account by a serial killer. Other short story collections include *Os Prisioneiros* (1963; The Prisoners), *A Coleira do Cão* (1965; The Dog's Leash), *Lúcia McCartney* (1967; Lúcia McCartney), and *O Homem de Fevereiro ou Março* (1973; The Man from February or March). Although these tales could be seen as overly violent and lurid, as a whole, they represent a critical view of Brazilian society at the turn of the century.

In the 1980s, Fonseca began to write novels instead of short stories, many of which became **best sellers**. *A Grande Arte* (1983; *High Art*) features Mandrake, a lawyer looking to unmask a serial killer of women. In *Bufo & Spallanzani* (1986; *Bufo & Spallanzani*), a police officer investigates the murder of a socialite and her involvement with a writer. *Vastas Emoções e Pensamentos Imperfeitos* (1988; *Vast Emotions and Imperfect Thoughts*) tells the story of a filmmaker, battling a creative and personal crisis, who finds inspiration for his work again in a famous jewel and the tales of Isaak Babel (1894–1940). *Agosto* (1990; August) tells of the violent circumstances that led to the suicide of Brazilian president Getúlio Vargas in 1954. *Histórias*

de Amor (1997; Love Stories) unsentimentally portrays the consequences of misguided passions. The influence of cinema is evident
in Fonseca's fiction, some of which has been adapted for the screen,
and he has been recognized as one of Brazil's key writers of the 20th
century by such important prizes as the **Jabuti** and the Camões. *See
also* BONASSI, FERNANDO.

FRANÇA JR., JOAQUIM JOSÉ DA (Brazil, 1838–1890). Journalist
and dramatist. França Jr.'s **chronicles** portrayed Rio society during
the Second Empire, ridiculing the rising bourgeoisie's corrupt politics and morals. As a dramatist, he is noted as a precursor of light
comedy. His plays include *Meia Hora de Cinismo* (1861; Half an
Hour of Cynicism), *A República Modelo* (1861; The Model Republic), and *Amor com Amor se Paga* (1882; Love Breeds Love). His
best comedy, *As Doutoras* (written 1889; published 1932; The Lady
Doctors), features the theme of feminism. *See also* THEATER.

FRANCOVICH, GUILLERMO (Bolivia, 1901–1990). Dramatist. He
was best known as a philosopher and critic and the author of books
about Bolivia and the national character, such as *La filosofía en
Bolivia* (1945; Philosophy in Bolivia), *El pensamiento boliviano en
el siglo XX* (1956; Bolivian Thought in the Twentieth Century), and
Los mitos profundos de Bolivia (1980; Profound Myths of Bolivia).
In the 1970s, however, he turned to drama as a way of expressing his
thoughts and wrote more than 20 plays, some of them one-act plays.
They are all collected in the two volumes of his complete **theater**
(1985) and include *Soledad y tiempo* (Time and Solitude), *Reencuentro* (Re-encounter), *El monje de Potosí* (The Monk from Potosí),
Monseñor y los poetas (Monseigneur and the Poets), and *Como los
gansos* (Like Geese).

FRESÁN, RODRIGO (Argentina, 1963–). Novelist and short story
writer. He has published several collections of short stories: *Historia
argentina* (1991; History of Argentina), *Vidas de santos* (1993; Lives
of the Saints), and *La velocidad de las cosas* (1998; The Speed of
Things). His novels include *Esperanto* (1995; Esperanto), *Mantra*
(2001; Mantra), and *Jardines de Kensington* (2003; *Kensington
Gardens*). He is a **post-boom** writer and inveterate storyteller whose

fiction often focuses self-reflexively on the process of literary production. International mass culture is a constant source of reference in his work, and he frequently adopts an iconoclastic attitude with respect to literary and cultural traditions.

FREYRE, GILBERTO DE MELO (Brazil, 1900–1984). Sociologist and essayist. Born into a wealthy landowning family from Pernambuco, Freyre attended a Baptist school and then traveled to Baylor University in Texas for his undergraduate degree. In 1923, he received a master's degree in anthropology from Columbia University with a thesis entitled "Social Life in Brazil in the Middle of the 19th Century." After extended travels in Europe, he returned to Brazil, where he began writing for newspapers and gathered a group of intellectuals around the concept of **regionalism,** aiming at promoting local values. He organized the First Brazilian Congress of Regionalism in 1926, at which the *Manifesto regionalista* (1952; Regionalist Manifesto) was first read. His *Guia Prático, Histórico e Sentimental da Cidade do Recife* (1934; Practical, Historical, and Sentimental Guide of the City of Recife) is a practical guide but also a poetic text extolling Freyre's native city. As a result of his political troubles in the Revolution of 1930, he exiled himself in Portugal, where he worked as a journalist and translator and began to draft his best-known work, *Casa-Grande e Senzala* (1933; *The Masters and the Slaves*), published upon his return to Brazil.

Casa-Grande e Senzala is a theory of the formation of Brazilian society from the patriarchal structures of the sugar mill economy. Freyre argues that the labor and culture of African slaves are central to Brazilian identity. He was the first intellectual of stature to draw attention to the contribution of Afro-Brazilians and organized the Congress of Afro-Brazilian Studies. Freyre's insistence on regional and local values had a wide and lasting influence on a number of writers and artists, notably **José Lins do Rego Cavalcanti**, **Jorge de Lima**, and **Manuel Bandeira**. Freyre continued developing his ideas on miscegenation (or racial mixing), which in his mind made Brazil a "racial democracy," in the sequel to *Casa-Grande e Senzala, Sobrados e Mocambos* (1936; *The Mansions and the Shanties*).

In *O Mundo Que o Português Criou* (1940; The World the Portuguese Created), Freyre advanced the notion of "lusotropicalism," or the ability of the Portuguese to settle and thrive in the tropics. Other reflections on Brazilian culture include *Brazil: An Interpretation* (1945), *Ordem e Progresso* (1959; *Order and Progress: Brazil from Monarchy to Republic*), and *New World in the Tropics: The Culture of Modern Brazil* (1959). In addition to his groundbreaking ideas on race and the formation of Brazilian society and culture, Freyre was also innovative in his research methods, paying attention to documents such as newspaper ads and personal diaries, popular clubs, and interviews with former slaves and masters. A highly influential and somewhat controversial figure, Freyre remains one of Brazil's key cultural interpreters. *See also* HOLANDA, SÉRGIO BUARQUE DE; RIBEIRO, DARCY; RIBEIRO, JOÃO UBALDO; ROMERO, SÍLVIO.

FRÍAS, HERIBERTO (Mexico, 1870–1925). Novelist. His first novel, *Tomochic* (1906; Tomochic), also his most successful, was based on an uprising in Chihuahua witnessed by the author as a lieutenant in the force sent to repress it. His earliest version of the events was written as a report for an opposition newspaper, for which he was imprisoned and came close to being executed. Frías was an admirer of Emile Zola (1840–1902) and adopted the philosophy of **naturalism** in *Tomochic*, which is also considered a precursor of the **novel of the Mexican Revolution**. His other novels include *El naufragio* (1895; The Shipwreck), *El amor de las sirenas* (1908; The Sirens' Love), *El último duelo* (1896; The Last Duel), *El triunfo de Sancho Panza* (1911; Sancho Panza's Triumph), *Las miserias de México* (1916; Mexico's Miseries), and *¿Águila o sol?* (1923; Heads or Tails?).

FUENTES, CARLOS (Mexico, 1928–). Novelist, short story writer, and essayist. He is one of Mexico's major literary figures and among those who have achieved most international recognition. Having spent significant periods of his life outside Mexico, Fuentes is a cosmopolitan writer, although his work is still very much concerned with Mexico, albeit written by one who has had the benefit of seeing it from an external perspective. In *Los días enmascarados* (1954; The

Masked Days), his first work of fiction, notably in the story "Chac Mool," he used the mode of **fantastic literature** as a way to evoke the persistence of Mexico's mythic past in the present, a theme on which he often dwells.

His first three novels, with a focus on Mexican society after the revolution, continue the process, already begun by **Agustín Yáñez** and **Juan Rulfo**, of moving fiction in Mexico further away from the traditional **novel of the Mexican Revolution.** *Las buenas conciencias* (1959; *The Good Conscience*), set in Guanajuata, is framed as a conventional coming-of-age novel showing the loss of idealism of the revolution in a provincial bourgeois family, exemplified through the novel's young protagonist. In *La región más transparente* (1958; *Where the Air Is Clear*), influenced by John Dos Passos (1896–1970), Fuentes turned to Mexico City to offer a broad view of the capital's social classes and analyze the pragmatic capitalism of the country in the 1940s and 1950s. In his third novel, *La muerte de Artemio Cruz* (1962; *The Death of Artemio Cruz*), the revolution is again placed in a longer historical context through the narration of the life of Artemio Cruz, told from his deathbed in the first, second, and third persons, representing, respectively, his present, future, and past. This is likely the author's best-known novel. With a content and narrative technique that show traces of the work of William Faulkner (1897–1962), it located him among the **boom** writers and marked him as one of the most significant Latin American novelists of his generation.

Since the appearance of *La muerte de Artemio Cruz*, Carlos Fuentes has published more than 20 works of fiction. Although their content varies, Mexican history and mythology, the relation between the past and the present, and the psychological development of themes and characters are dominant features. *Aura* (1962; *Aura*) is a short novel written in the future tense that belongs to the genre of fantastic literature. *Cambio de Piel* (1967; *A Change of Skin*) and *Zona sagrada* (1967; *Holy Place*) are both fragmented narratives embodying, respectively, elements of Mexican and Greek mythology. The former deals with themes of violence and evil in Mexico and Europe; the latter has the lives of the Mexican movie star María Félix (1914–2002) and her son as its central motifs.

Terra Nostra (1975; *Terra Nostra*), recipient of the 1977 **Rómulo Gallegos Prize**, has perhaps been Fuentes's most ambitious narrative project. At close to 800 pages, it is his longest work of fiction. It deals with the historical relations between Europe and Latin America. Part of the narrative is set in the Escorial in the time of Philip II of Spain (1556–1598), and it includes such archetypal figures of Spanish literature as Celestina, Don Juan, and Don Quixote. *La cabeza de la hidra* (1978; *The Hydra Head*) is a novel of intrigue about the petroleum industry in Mexico. *Una familia lejana* (1980; *A Distant Family*), set in France, is a novel with a Proustian flavor. *Gringo viejo* (1987; *Old Gringo*), based on the disappearance in Mexico of U.S. writer Ambrose Bierce (1842–1914?) at the time of the revolution, shows Fuentes's affinity with **post-boom** writers and the emerging Latin American **new historical novel**. The novel provided the basis of a successful commercial movie. In *Cristóbal Nonato* (1987; *Christopher Unborn*), he again explores the persistence of the mythic past in the present, portraying an apocalyptic vision of Mexico City. More recent titles include *El naranjo* (1993; *The Orange Tree*) *La frontera de cristal: una novela en nueve cuentos* (1995; The Crystal Frontier: A Novel in Nine Stories), *Los años con Laura Díaz* (1999; *The Years with Laura Díaz*), and *Todas las familias felices* (2006; *Happy Families: Stories*).

Carlos Fuentes's work for the **theater** includes *Todos los gatos son pardos* (1970; All Cats Are Grey), *El tuerto es rey* (1970; The One-eyed Man Is King), *Los reinos originarios* (1971; The Kingdoms of Origin), *Orquídeas a la luz de la luna: comedia mexicana* (1982; Orchids by Moonlight: A Mexican Comedy), and *Ceremonias del alba* (1990; Dawn Ceremonies). He is also a prominent public intellectual in Mexico who has written and spoken widely on Latin American literature, politics, culture, and social issues. Among his published essays are *La nueva novela hispanoamericana* (1969; The New Spanish American Novel), *Cervantes o la crítica de la lectura* (1976; Cervantes or the Critique of Reading), *Tiempo mexicano* (1971; Time in Mexico), *El Espejo Enterrado* (1992; *The Buried Mirror: Reflections on Spain and the New World*), and *Contra Bush* (2004; Against Bush).

FUTORANSKY, LUISA (Argentina, 1939–). Novelist and poet. She is the author of more than 15 volumes of poetry, the first of which were *Trago fuerte* (1963; Strong Drink), *El corazón de los* *lugares* (1964; The Heart of Places), and *Babel Babel* (1968; Babel Babel). Her fiction, noteworthy for her sardonic humor and settings in France and the Far East, where the author has lived, includes *Son cuentos chinos* (1983; Chinese Tales), *De Pe a Pa* (1986; From Beginning to End), and *Urracas* (1992; Magpies). Her themes include exile and language, identity and **Jewishness**. *See also* WOMEN.

– G –

GALEANO, EDUARDO (Uruguay, 1940–). Journalist, essayist, and historian. He is a very widely read and translated author on the social, cultural, and political history of Latin America. *Las venas abiertas de América Latina* (1971; *The Open Veins of Latin America*) is a collection of essays on the economic exploitation of Latin America through the mining of natural resources and plantation economies. In *Memoria del fuego* (3 vols., 1982–1986; *Memory of Fire*), he draws on the work of many writers to give a broad view of Latin American history through scores of short sketches. In this book, and in *El libro de los abrazos* (1989; *The Book of Embraces*), Galeano focuses on the significance of people, places, and events in short chapters or poetically evocative fragments (sometimes in verse) rather than through the extended narrative perspective of a conventional academic historian. In *Las palabras andantes* (1993; *Walking Words*) he brings together a collection of oral narratives in texts and images to give voice to the voiceless. Other more recent titles include *El fútbol a sol y sombra* (1995; *Football in Sun and Shadow*), *Patas arriba: la escuela del mundo al revés* (1998; *Upside Down: A Primer for the Looking-Glass World*), and *Bocas del Tiempo* (2004; *Voices of Time: A Life in Stories*). Some of his journalism has been collected in *Nosotros decimos no: crónicas, 1963–1988* (1989; *We Say No, 1963–1991*) and *Ser como ellos y otros artículos* (1992; To Be Like Them and Other Articles).

GALICH, MANUEL (Guatemala, 1915–1984). Dramatist. Like many other Guatemalan writers and members of opposition groups, he spent much of his life in exile and died in Cuba. His first works for the **theater**, *El retorno* (1938; The Return) and *El señor Gukup-*

Kakix (1939; Mr. Sunbird), the latter based on an episode from the *Popol Vuh*, were written for schools. In 1949, he wrote a group of historical dramas: *Carta a su ilustrísimo* (Letter to His Grace), set in the 17th century; *Belem, 1813* (Belem, 1813); and *15 de septiembre* (15 September), on the independence movement in Guatemala. At the same time, he had also begun to write plays that were more socially and politically critical, including *M'hijo el bachiller* (1939; My Boy the Graduate) on the education system; *De lo vivo a lo pintado* (1947; From the Living to the Painted), a critique of the legal system and the status of **women**; *El tren amarillo* (1954; The Yellow Train), about the banana companies; *Entre cuatro paredes* (1964; Between Four Walls), a comedy of manners satirizing the middle class; and *El último cargo* (1974; The Last Charge), on the guerrilla war.

GALINDO, SERGIO (Mexico, 1926–1993). Novelist and short story writer. His books of short stories include *La máquina vacía* (1951; The Empty Machine), *Oh, hermoso mundo* (1975; Oh, Beautiful World), *El hombre de los hongos* (1976; The Mushroom Man), *Este laberinto de hombres* (1979; This Labyrinth of Men), and *Terciopelo violeta* (1985; Violet Velvet). His first novel, *Polvos de arroz* (1958; Rice Powder), conveys the tedium of provincial life through the memories of a spinster. *La justicia de enero* (1959; January Justice) is about the life of migrants to Mexico City. *El Bordo* (1960; *The Precipice*), his best-known work, returns to the provinces, to a family living in a country house in Las Vigas, Veracruz, where reverberations from the revolution are still felt. *La comparsa* (1964; Carnival) is a story of the freedom felt at carnival time. *Nudo* (1970; Knot), another of the author's widely read works, has been compared to *Under the Volcano* (1947) by Malcolm Lowry (1909–1957). Galindo's late novels include *Los dos ángeles* (1984; The Two Angels), *Declive* (1985; Decline), and *Otilia Rauda* (1986; Otilia's Body).

GALLARDO, SARA (Argentina, 1931–1988). Novelist. The central theme of her writing is alienation in its various forms (social, environmental, spiritual, economic, and personal). *Enero* (1958; January) is a story set in the country about an adolescent who is raped and becomes pregnant. Both *Pantalones azules* (1963; Blue Pants) and *Los galgos, los galgos* (1968; The Greyhounds, the Greyhounds) are novels about rebellion by members of the social elite against the conventions imposed on them. *Eisejuaz* (1971; Eisejuaz) narrates the conflict of a Chaco Indian between the world and the spirit. *La rosa en el viento* (1979; The Rose in the Wind), set in Patagonia, conveys the stories of immigrants seeking to establish themselves in a new land. Gallardo has also written **children's literature** and published a collection of short stories, *El país del humo* (1977; The Smoke Country). *See also* WOMEN.

GALLEGOS, RÓMULO (Venezuela, 1884–1969). Novelist. His first two novels, *El último Solar* (1920; The Last Solar), later published as *Reinaldo Solar* (1930), and *La trepadora* (1925; The Creeper), introduce the author's concern for the formation of Venezuela as a modern state, one of the central concerns of both his literary work and his life in politics. His greatest literary success came with *Doña Bárbara* (1929; *Doña Bárbara*), a novel that has become one of Latin America's standard works of fiction. It is a **novel of the land** set on the plains in Venezuela and tells a story of struggle against authoritariansm in terms of the conflict between **civilization and barbarism**. These themes are continued in *Cantaclaro* (1934; Cantaclaro), also set on the plains, and *Canaima* (1935; *Canaima*), set in the jungle. In later novels—*Pobre negro* (1937; Poor Black), a **historical novel** about a slave uprising in the 1860s; *El forastero* (1942; The Outsider), also about rebellion against oppression; and *Sobre la misma tierra* (1943; On the Same Land)—Gallegos was unable to reach the levels of his earlier novels of the land. In 1948, he served as president of Venezuela for eight months and wrote his last two novels, *La brizna de paja en el viento* (1952; The Blade of Straw in the Wind) and *La tierra bajo los pies* (1971; The Ground Beneath the Feet), while living in exile (1948–1958) after being forced from office by a military coup. The former novel is set in Cuba, the latter in Mexico. The **Rómulo Gallegos Prize** was established in his honor in 1964. See also LISCANO, JUAN.

GALLEGOS LARA, JOAQUÍN (Ecuador, 1911–1947). Novelist and short story writer. He was one of the prime movers of the **Grupo de Guayaquil** and coauthor, with **Demetrio Aguilera Malta** and **Enrique Gil Gilbert**, of the collection of short stories *Los que se* *van* (1930; Those Who Leave), but published little on his own. He advocated socially committed writing, to which he adhered in *Las cruces sobre el agua* (1946; Crosses on the Water), a novel based on a 1922 workers' massacre in Guayaquil, and in *La última erranza* (1947; The Last Wandering), a collection of short stories.

GALVÃO, PATRÍCIA a.k.a. **PAGÚ (Brazil, 1910–1962).** Journalist and novelist. Born in São Paulo, Galvão attended teachers college and wrote for newspapers. In 1928, she joined the **antropofagia** group, associating especially with **Raúl Bopp**, who suggested she use the literary name "Pagú," and **Oswald de Andrade**, whom she married in 1930. In 1931, Galvão and Andrade founded the **journal** *O Homem do Povo* (The Man of the People), for which Galvão wrote the feminist section "A Mulher do Povo" ("The Woman of the People"). They also joined the Communist Party and were political activists. Under the pseudonym Mara Lobo, Galvão published the proletarian novel *Parque Industrial* (1933; *Industrial Park*), a tale of class oppression in São Paulo influenced linguistically by **Brazilian modernism.** In the years that followed, Galvão traveled extensively in Europe and Asia, also visiting the Soviet Union, where she became disillusioned with Communism when she witnessed the reigning inequality. Due to her political involvement, she was deported back to Brazil, where she was imprisoned. Upon her release in 1940, she broke with the Communist Party and married Geraldo Ferraz, with whom she authored her second novel, *A Famosa Revista* (1945; The Famous Review), a critique of the ills of the Communist Party. She also wrote a book of criticism, *Vanguarda Socialista* (1945–1946; Socialist Vanguard), and in the 1950s became involved in **theater,** writing reviews for numerous newspapers. *See also* WOMEN.

GÁLVEZ, MANUEL (Argentina, 1882–1962). Novelist and biographer. He wrote some 20 novels on a wide range of subjects, covering both contemporary society and history. He was a Catholic traditionalist who often reflected a stern moral position in his fiction and wrote in the manner of **realism** and **naturalism.** His first novel, *La maestra normal* (1914; The Normal School Teacher), is a portrayal of life in a provincial town. In *Nacha Regules* (1919; *Nacha Regules*), the story of a prostitute, and *Historia de arrabal* (1922; Suburban Story), set in the sordid industrial world of Buenos Aires, he presents the unsuccessful struggle of **women** against heredity and a hostile social environment. Gálvez's **historical novels** include a trilogy on the war with Paraguay (1865–1870)—*Los caminos de la muerte* (1928; The Roads of Death), *Humaitá* (1929; Humaitá), and *Jornadas de agonía* (1929; Marches of Agony)—and a seven-volume series, *Escenas de la época de Rosas* (Scenes from the Age of Rosas), on the life and times of the dictator **Juan Manuel Rosas**. His biographies include the lives of a number of distinguished Argentineans, including Juan Manuel Rosas (1793–1877) and Hipólito Yrigoyen (1852–1933), **Domingo Faustino Sarmiento** (1811–1888), and **José Hernández** (1834–1886).

GAMA, JOSÉ BASÍLIO DA (Brazil, 1741–1795). Poet. Educated in Brazil by the Jesuits until their expulsion in 1773, da Gama later traveled to Portugal and Italy, where he assimilated **arcadianism** from other poets. After a short period in Brazil, he went back to Portugal, where he was accused of being a Jesuit and sent to prison in Angola. In prison, he wrote a poem in honor of the daughter of a powerful Portuguese nobleman, the Marquis of Pombal (1699–1782), which earned him his freedom. His main work is the short epic poem *O Uraguai* (1769; Uruguay), which narrates the battles fought by the Portuguese and Spanish against the natives and the Jesuits in the mission settlements of Uruguay. The poem, in five cantos and blank verse, uses various meters, making it more of a narrative-lyrical poem that attempted to distinguish itself from the celebrated Portuguese **epic poetry** of Luís de Camões (1524–1580). Other works include *Declamação Trágica, Poema Dedicado às Belas-Artes* (1772; Tragic Declamation, Poem Dedicated to the Fine Arts) and *Quitúbia* (1791; Quitúbia). *See also* PEIXOTO, INÁCIO JOSÉ DE ALVARENGA.

GAMBARO, GRISELDA (Argentina, 1928–). Dramatist, novelist, and short story writer. She is best known for her **theater** and is one of Latin America's most significant **women** dramatists. She participated in influential theater groups in Argentina, including **Teatro Abierto**. Her early plays, such as *El desatino* (1965; The Absurdity), *Las paredes* (1966; The Walls), *Los siameses* (1967; Siamese Twins), and *El campo* (1967; *The Camp*), show the characteristics of the **theater of**

cruelty and the **theater of the absurd** and are allegories of socio-political conditions in Argentina. Their themes of imprisonment and sadism are common to much of her later drama and fiction, although *Lo impenetrable* (1984; *The Impenetrable Madam X*), a parody of an exotic novel, is a notable exception.

Gambaro's novel *Ganarse la muerte* (1977; Earning Death) was banned by the military under conditions that prompted her to leave Argentina for three years. As a result, her theater sometimes works through analogy. In *La malasangre* (1982; *Bad Blood*), set during the dictatorship of **Juan Manuel Rosas**, and *Del sol naciente* (1984; From the Rising Sun), set in Japan, for example, she used historical or foreign locations to represent contemporary situations and therefore avoid censorship. At the same time, however, the dramatization of a situation analogous to that prevailing in her own country is a way of drawing out the universal implications of national politics. Such is the case in *Antígona furiosa* (1988; Antigone's Fury), in which the Greek myth serves as a basis for examining the terror of repressive regimes everywhere.

Her work is also experimental. In *Información para extranjeros* (1987; *Information for Foreigners*), she used the techniques of **total theater** to dissolve the barriers between reality and performance and draw audiences into the themes of her drama. Her more recent work for the theater includes *Penas sin importancia* (1991; Insignificant Troubles), *Atando cabos* (1991; Tying Loose Ends), *La casa sin sosiego* (1991; House Without Peace), and *Es necesario entender un poco* (1994; It's Necessary to Understand a Little). Many of her plays have been published in numbered volumes. The first of these, *Teatro 1* (Theater 1), appeared in 1984. The most recent, *Teatro 7* (Theater 7), was published in 2004. Gambaro has also written **children's literature**.

GAMBOA, FEDERICO (Mexico, 1864–1939). Novelist. Affiliation with the regime of Porfirio Díaz (1876–1880, 1884–1911) and the counterrevolutionary government of Victoriano Huerta (1913) affected his reputation and led to six years in exile in Cuba (1913–1919). As a novelist, he successfully accommodated European **naturalism** to Mexican **positivism** in works such as *La ley suprema* (1896; The Supreme Law) and *Santa* (1903; Santa), the story of a country girl who turned to prostitution in the city after being seduced and abandoned. Gamboa also wrote for the **theater**, and *Santa*, which was an extraordinarily popular novel, was the source of the screenplay for Mexico's first commercial sound movie in 1932. In his last novels, *Reconquista* (1908; Reconquest) and *La llaga* (1913; The Wound), Gamboa turned away from his earlier attraction to naturalism. *See also* MAGAÑA, SERGIO.

GAMERO, LUCILA (Honduras, 1873–1964). Novelist. Considered the initiator of the novel in her country, her fiction is a derivative of **romanticism**. Her best-known novel, *Blanca Olmedo* (1903; Blanca Olmedo), drew attention for its criticism of the clergy. Other titles include *Adriana y Margarita* (1897; Adriana and Margarita), *Páginas del corazón* (1897; Pages of the Heart), *Aída* (1932; Aida), *Betina* (1941; Betina), *Amor exótico* (1954; Exotic Love), *La secretaria* (1954; The Secretary), and *El dolor de amar* (1955; The Pain of Love). See also WOMEN.

GÂNDAVO, PERO DE MAGALHÃES (Portugal, 16th century). Historian and chronicler. A Portuguese of Flemish origin, Gândavo was a professor of Latin and a friend of the poet Luís de Camões (1524–1580). He is the first systematic chronicler and historian of Brazil. Never published during his lifetime, his *Tratado da Terra do Brasil* (1827; Treatise on the Land of Brazil) was written around 1570. Better known is his *História da Província Santa Cruz a que Vulgarmente Chamamos Brasil* (1576; History of the Province of Santa Cruz Which Is Commonly Called Brazil). Both works, written from a Catholic humanist perspective, narrate the discovery and settlement of Brazil, but more important, praise the beauty and resources of the land destined to be a successful Portuguese colony. Although some of the hyperbolic descriptions are influenced by medieval myths of El Dorado and the Garden of Eden, he also left descriptions of the Brazilian natives and their way of life, always framed by an apology for the Jesuit missionary efforts. (See CHRONICLE.)

GARCÍA, SANTIAGO (Colombia, 1928–). Dramatist. As director of the **theater** collective La Candelaria, founded in Bogotá in 1966, he was, with **Enrique Buenaventura**, one of the key figures in the renovation of theater in Colombia. La Candelaria would become an important theatrical institution in Colombia and win an international reputation. Its early successes included *La ciudad dorada* (1972; The Golden City), on migration to urban centers, and *Guadalupe, años sin cuenta* (1975; Guadalupe, Countless Years), on the life of Guadalupe Salcedo Unda, a 1950s revolutionary leader during **la violencia** in Colombia. García's own writing for the theater includes *Corre, corre Carigüeta* (1987; Run, Run, Carigüeta), *El diálogo de rebusque* (1987; Conversation on the Side), *Maravilla Estar* (1991; Marvelous Star), *El paso* (1991; The Passage), and *La trifulca* (1992; The Squabble).

GARCÍA CALDERÓN, VENTURA (Peru, 1887–1959). Short story writer. Born in France and having spent most of his life there, he wrote in both French and Spanish with equal facility. *Dolorosa y desnuda realidad* (1914; Bare and Painful Reality) has the flavor of European modernism, but later collections, *La venganza del cóndor* (1924; *The White Llama*) and *Cuentos peruanos* (1952; Peruvian Tales), are more distinctly Peruvian. He also wrote **chronicles** about Peru and Europe.

GARCÍA MÁRQUEZ, GABRIEL (Colombia, 1927–). Novelist, short story writer, and journalist. He was the 1982 recipient of the **Nobel Prize for Literature**, is the best known of the **boom** writers, and is one of Latin America's most celebrated authors of all times. García Márquez's vision of Colombia goes back to his rural childhood and the world of history and legend he derived from the grandparents who raised him. His specific creation of the fictional world of Macondo, the mythical country that stands in for Colombia, began in early short narratives of the 1950s and 1960s. *La hojarasca* (1954; *Leaf Storm*) is an account of the arrival of a foreign-owned banana company. *El coronel no tiene quien le escriba* (1958; *No One Writes to the Colonel*), set in the time of Colombia's civil wars and **la violencia**, tells the story of a colonel waiting for news of the pension he expects in exchange for his service to his country. *Funerales de la Mamá Grande* (1962; The Funeral of Mama Grande) is a mocking view of social authority, and *La mala hora* (1962; *In Evil Hour*) is a story of the corrupting effects of power.

The novel that grew out of these novellas and short stories was García Márquez's masterpiece *Cien años de soledad* (1967; *One Hundred Years of Solitude*), a work that for its narrative power and storytelling is sometimes considered as important for Latin America as *Don Quixote* is for Spain. It received the 1972 **Rómulo Gallegos Prize**. The story told in the novel is an allegory of Colombian history and a central work of **magic realism**, with which much of García Márquez's work is associated. A series of short texts followed the author's landmark novel, including *La increíble y triste historia de la cándida Eréndira y su abuela* (1972; *Innocent Eréndira and Other Stories*), which prefigured in part the style of his second novel, *El otoño del patriarca* (1975; *The Autumn of the Patriarch*), a **dictator novel** about a fictional Caribbean tyrant, written in a breathless style without paragraphs and periods.

A series of works of fiction have appeared since the early 1980s, all of them marked by García Márquez's indomitable capacity as a storyteller. *Crónica de una muerte anunciada* (1981; *Chronicle of a Death Foretold*), taken from true-life events in Colombia, unfolds with the inevitability of Greek tragedy. *El amor en los tiempos del cólera* (1985; *Love in the Time of Cholera*) is a love story, exemplifying the themes of decline and renewal, loosely based on the experiences of the author's parents. *El general en su laberinto* (1989; *The General in His Labyrinth*) is a **new historical novel** that offers a revisionist version of the life and last journey of the Liberator of South America, **Simón Bolívar**. *Doce cuentos peregrinos* (1992; *Strange Pilgrims: Twelve Stories*), in which García Márquez appears as himself, is a varied collection of narratives about the experiences of Latin Americans in Europe. *Del amor y otros demonios* (1994; *Of Love and Other Demons*) is a story of love, demonic possession, and miracles set in 18th-century Colombia. *Memoria de mis putas tristes* (2004; *Memories of My Melancholy Whores*) is a novella about an old man's memories and his affair with an adolescent girl.

In addition to writing fiction, García Márquez worked in journalism for much of his life and earned his living at it in his early years. His newspaper writings of the 1950s are collected in *Cuando era féliz e indocumentado* (1973; *When I Was Happy and Unknown*), and a larger collection has appeared as *Obra periodística* (6 vols., 1981–1984; Journalistic Work). He has also written several books with a basis in reporting and journalism. These include *Relato de un náufrago* (1970; *The Story of a Ship-Wrecked Sailor*), based on a series of newspaper articles first published by the author in 1955; *La aventura de Miguel Littín clandestino en Chile* (1986; *Clandestine in Chile: The Adventures of Miguel Littín*), a report on the Chilean film director; and *Noticia de un secuestro* (1997; *News of a Kidnapping*) about events in the drug wars in Colombia.

García Márquez has also had a lifelong interest in cinema. Some of his works have a cinematic quality. He has written screenplays and has held positions in institutes and foundations for the promotion and development of cinema in Latin America. He has talked about himself and his work in conversation with Plinio Apuleyo Mendoza in *El olor de la guayaba* (1982; *The Fragrance of Guava*) and has published the first volume of his memoirs, *Vivir para contarla* (2002; *Living to Tell the Tale*). *See also* ALLENDE, ISABEL; COBO BORDA, JUAN GUSTAVO; QUIROGA, HORACIO; SABINO, FERNANDO; SCORZA, MANUEL; VARGAS LLOSA, MARIO.

GARCÍA MONGE, JOAQUÍN (Costa Rica, 1881–1958). Novelist. He figured significantly throughout his life as an editor and was notable for his association with the Costa Rican cultural **journal** *Repertorio americano*, which he founded in 1919 and remained with until his death. The novels he wrote early in life contributed to the introduction of **realism** and the realist novel in Costa Rica. *El moto* (1900; The Orphaned Calf) is a rural romance, and *Las hijas del campo* (1900; Daughters of the Countryside) is an urban novel that shows the influence of **naturalism**.

GARCÍA PONCE, JUAN (Mexico, 1932–2003). Novelist, short story writer, and essayist. He began his literary career writing for the **theater** but is better known for his fiction. His fictional worlds focus on the everyday through an exploration of the erotic in themes related to voyeurism, love triangles, encounters and separations, overlapping identities, and the demonic side of life. His novels include *Figura de paja* (1964; Straw Man), *La casa en la playa* (1966; The House on the Beach), *La presencia lejana* (1968; The Distant Presence), *La cabaña* (1969; The Cabin), *La vida perdurable* (1970; Everlasting Life), *El nombre olvidado* (1970; The Forgotten Name),

La invitación (1972; The Invitation), and *Inmaculada, o los placeres de la inocencia* (1989; Inmaculada, or the Pleasures of Innocence). His most ambitious novel was *Crónica de la intervención* (1982; Chronicle of Intervention), a two-volume work about middle-class Mexico set in the context of the **Tlatelolco massacre**. García Ponce's short stories have the same themes as his novels and include *Imagen primera* (1963; First Image), *La noche* (1963; The Night), and *Encuentros* (1972; Encounters). As an essayist, he has published books on painting and literature, including: *Rufino Tamayo* (1967; Rufino Tamayo), *Nueve pintores mexicanos* (1968; Nine Mexican Painters), *Entrada en materia* (1968; Entry Into Matter: Modern Literature and Reality), and *La errancia sin fin: Musil, Borges, Klossowsky* (1981; Endless Wandering: Musil, Borges, Klossowsky).

GARCILASO DE LA VEGA, EL INCA (Peru, c. 1539–1616). Chronicler. He was the illegitimate child of a Spanish aristocrat and an Inca princess who moved to Spain in 1560. He is customarily styled "El Inca" to distinguish him from the Spanish poet Garcilaso de la Vega. In Spain he wrote his *Comentarios reales de los Incas* (in 2 parts, 1609, 1617; *Royal Commentaries of the Incas*), a **chronicle** of the dynastic history of the Incas accompanied by a narrative of the Spanish conquest of Peru (both written from an Incan point of view) and an important source of Peruvian history. His other works include *La Florida del Inca* (1605; *The Florida of the Inca*), a narrative of the expedition (1538–1542) led by Hernando de Soto (ca. 1496/1497–1542) to Florida, and *Diálogos de amor* (1590; Dialogues of Love), a translation from Italian into Spanish of the celebrated debate by León Hebreo (ca. 1465–c. 1523). *See also* CISNEROS, ANTONIO.

GARMENDÍA, JULIO (Venezuela, 1898–1977). Short story writer. Although credited with having brought the **avant-garde** to Venezuela, in his lifetime he only published two books, which were two collections of short stories, each containing eight stories: *La tienda de muñecos* (1927; The Puppet Store) and *La tuna de oro* (1957; The Golden Players). The title stories of both collections, with elements of the **fantastic** and escape from reality, are especially celebrated. A further 10 stories by Garmendía were published posthumously in *La* *hoja que no había caído en su otoño* (1979; The Leaf That Hadn't Fallen in Autumn).

GARMENDÍA, SALVADOR (Venezuela, 1928–2001). Novelist and short story writer. He wrote novels about the **existential** angst of the urban bourgeoisie with characters who experienced alienation, isolation, hallucinations, and fear of madness. His main works are *Los pequeños seres* (1959; Small Beings), *Día de cenizas* (1964; Ash Wednesday), *Los habitantes* (1968; The Inhabitants), and *La mala vida* (1968; The Bad Life). His short stories include *El brujo hípico y otros relatos* (1979; The Horse Racing Wizard and Other Tales), *El único lugar posible* (1981; The Only Place Possible), *El capitán Kid* (1988; Captain Kid), and *La vida buena* (1995; The Good Life). Garmendía was also the scriptwriter of popular television soaps.

GARRO, ELENA (Mexico, 1920–1998). Novelist, short story writer, and dramatist. Her reputation did not initially stand as high as it does now, when she is considered one of Mexico's finest **women** writers. Her first novel, *Los recuerdos del porvenir* (1963; *Recollection of Things to Come*) was completed in the 1950s but not published until several years later, a delay characteristic of a number of her works. The novel, set in Ixtepec during the time of civil unrest in Mexico known as the Cristero War (1926–1929), draws on the author's memories of her childhood in Iguala, in the state of Guerrero. It is about a tragic love, but also introduces themes that figure in the author's later work. These include the persecution and violence perpetrated against women and marginalized groups in society; the importance of memory, the circularity of time, and the experience of multiple chronologies, as in the coexistence of the present with a mythical time; and the **magic realism** with which many of the events narrated in her fiction are told. *La semana de colores* (1964; Week of Colors) was also written in the 1950s and includes one of her best-known stories, "La culpa es de los tlaxcaltecas" ("The Tlaxcalans Are to Blame").

Garro's later works were in some ways affected by two factors: her marriage to **Octavio Paz** and her implication in events surrounding the **Tlatelolco massacre**. Allegations that she was complicit in the student demonstrations and that she had betrayed fellow intellectuals when she was held in prison led to her taking refuge in France in 1972, where she remained for 20 years.

Andamos huyendo Lola (1980; Let's Flee, Lola) is a set of 11 interconnected stories tracing the flight of two women through Mexico, New York, and Spain away from a malevolent force that is reminiscent of the author's own flight into exile. *Testimonios sobre Mariana* (1981; Testimonies About Mariana) consists of the memories about Mariana of three different people. It has been read as a thinly disguised portrait of the author's former husband. *Reencuentro de personajes* (1982; A Reunion of Characters) is the story of a masochistic relationship, and *La casa junto al río* (1983; The House Beside the River) tells of a woman who is murdered when she goes in search of her relatives in her father's hometown in Spain. *Y Matarazo no llamó* (1989; And Matarazo Did Not Call) reexamines some of the events of Tlatelolco, and *Inés* (1995; Inés) is another story of female persecution.

Garro earned a solid reputation for her work for the **theater**, although her writing in this area belongs mainly to the 1950s and 1960s. Her plays have themes similar to her works of fiction, including her inclination toward representation of a magical reality. *Felipe Ángeles* (published 1979; Felipe Ángeles) takes its title from the name of the revolutionary hero whose story is dramatized. The title of *La dama boba* (1963; The Foolish Lady) comes from a play of the same name by the Spanish dramatist Lope de Vega (1562–1535) and is an example of theater within theater used to confront issues in rural life in Mexico. A collection of one-act plays, published in *Un hogar sólido* (1958 and 1983; A Solid Family), conveys a good idea of the range of issues and styles of Garro's writing for the stage.

GAUCHO LITERATURE. Representations of the life and culture of the gaucho occur in all literary genres. The gaucho and his way of life, often compared to that of the North American cowboy, evolved during the colonial period in the pampas regions of **Argentina** and **Uruguay** and had an impact on the independence movements and postindependence politics of both countries. As he appears in literature, the gaucho is a strong, independent individual, often living close to nature and on the margins of society. His songs, language, quick wit, and personality were captured in the early 19th-century work of

Bartolomé Hidalgo and were developed further by later authors such as **Hilario Ascasubi, Estanislao del Campo,** and **José Hernández,** who gave shape to an icon representing the rural origins of the national character of Argentina and Uruguay at the same time that they established an appetite for literature featuring this regional type. In the theater, verse, and prose fiction, the gaucho became a literary staple of the late 19th and early 20th centuries in both those countries. *See also* AMORIM, ENRIQUE; CIVILIZATION AND BARBARISM; EICHELBAUM, SAMUEL; GÜIRALDES, RICARDO; GUTIÉRREZ, EDUARDO; LARRETA, ENRIQUE; LUGONES, LEOPOLDO; LUSSICH, ANTONIO DIONISIO; MADARIAGA, FRANCISCIO; PAYRÓ, ROBERTO JORGE; REYLES, CARLOS; *SAINETE*; TREJO, NEMESIO; VIANA, JAVIER DE.

GAVIDIA, FRANCISCO (El Salvador, 1863–1955). Poet, short story writer, and dramatist. His pursuits were eclectic, and he wrote in several different literary forms. In poetry, he published *Libro de los azahares* (1885; Book of Blossoms). His interest in the French alexandrine verse led him to suggest it to **Rubén Darío,** who used it with celebrated effect. His short stories have the exoticism of **modernismo** and were collected in *Cuentos y narraciones* (1931; Tales and Narratives) and *Cuentos de marinos* (1947; Seamen's Tales). As a dramatist, he contributed to the first surge in **theater** in El Salvador at the beginning of the 20th century. His best-known work is *Júpiter* (1895; Jupiter), about Salvadoran independence. Other plays include *Los aeronautas* (1909; The Aeronauts), *Héspero* (1931; Hesperos), *Los juramentos* (1943; The Oaths), and *La torre de marfil* (1949; The Ivory Tower).

GAY AND LESBIAN WRITERS AND WRITING. Representations of gender and sexuality that challenged an established order remained relatively taboo until well into the 20th century, although some writers, such as **Adolfo Caminha** and **Qorpo-Santo** in **Brazil,** provoked scandal by venturing into the topic in the 19th century. By contrast, contemporary gay and lesbian writers openly declare their sexuality, and contemporary literature is open to homosexual themes as an integral element of the literary description and analysis of human life and society. Among the most prominent authors in this respect are **Caio Fernando Abreu, Glauco Mattoso**, and **João do Rio (Brazil), Fernando Vallejo (Colombia), Cristina Peri Rossi (Uruguay), Manuel Puig (Argentina)**, and **Pedro Lemebel (Chile)**. *See also* BAYLY, JAIME; BRUNET, MARTA; COSTA, HORÁCIO; D'HALMAR, AUGUSTO; DÍAZ VARGAS, HENRY; ECUADOR; EDWARDS BELLO, JOAQUÍN; HILST, HILDA; MORO, CÉSAR; NOVO, SALVADOR; PERLONGHER, NÉSTOR; RODRIGUES, NELSON; ROFFÉ, REINA; SANTIAGO, SILVIANO; WOMEN.

GELMAN, JUAN (Argentina, 1930–). Poet. He is one of Argentina's most prestigious 20th-century poets and the author of more than 20 books. He is also a journalist and political commentator. His involvement in politics and the Montoneros urban guerrillas led to 12 years of exile in 1976 after the coup that brought the regime of Jorge Videla (1976–1981) to power. Politics and social reality are reflected in his writing, which addresses a wide range of themes, including the sufferings endured by himself and his family, exile, his **Jewish** heritage, the Cuban revolution, popular culture, and the tango. Languages and the language of painting are a significant dimension of his work, but he has established his own poetics without drawing on classical traditions or the work of his contemporaries, laying out his project as a poet in his first four books: *Violín y otras cuestiones* (1958; Violin and Other Matters), *El juego en que andamos* (1959; The Game We Are Playing), *Velorio del solo* (1961; Solo Vigil), and *Gotán* (1962; Tango). Later books include *Los poemas de Sidney West* (1969; The Poems of Sidney West), *Fábulas* (1971; Fables), *Citas y comentarios* (1982; Quotes and Commentaries), *Cartas a mi madre* (1989; Letters to My Mother), and *Dibaxu* (1994; Below). He was awarded the **Miguel de Cervantes Prize** for literature in 2007.

GENERATION OF '45. The postwar period in **Brazil** ushered in important changes, including the end of Getúlio Vargas's first presidency (1930–1945) and the redemocratization of Brazil. Parallel to those changes, debates about the development of Brazilian literature sought to chart **Brazilian modernism** in three stages: 1922 (modernism), 1930 (postmodernism), and 1945 (neomodernism), which also became known as "Geração de 45" or Generation of '45. This new generation sought to abandon both the combative spirit of 1922 and the regional concerns of 1930 and instead espouse a more timeless and universal approach to literature. Although some see novelists such as **Clarice Lispector** and **João Guimarães Rosa** as portraying this new ethos, the actual debate itself took place more in the realm of poetry. Representatives of this tendency include **Geir Campos, Ledo Ivo, João Cabral de Melo Neto**, Péricles Eugênio da Silva Ramos (1919–1992), and Darci Damasceno (1922–1988). *See also* GULLAR, FERREIRA; PIGNATARI, DÉCIO.

GERBASI, VICENTE (Venezuela, 1913–1992). Poet. A member of the Grupo Viernes, he developed into one of Venezuela's most prominent 20th-century poets. He published steadily throughout his life, although his early affinity for **surrealism** and the work of the German Rainer Maria Rilke (1875–1926), evident in *Vigilia del Náufrago* (1937; The Castaway's Vigil), *Bosque Doliente* (1940; Sorrowful Forest), and *Liras* (1943; Lyres), became more attenuated in later collections when his own voice had matured. His long poem *Mi padre, el inmigrante* (1945; My Father the Immigrant), one of the central pieces of his oeuvre, traces the cycle of life and death. In *Espacios cálidos* (1952; Warm Spaces), he evokes memories of childhood in Venezuela and his father's hometown in Italy. *Olivos de eternidad* (1961; Eternal Olive Trees) recalls a journey to Jerusalem. *Tirano de sombra y fuego* (1955; Tyrant of Shadow and Fire), a more historical work, is about the Spanish conquistador rebel Lope de Aguirre (ca. 1510–1561). Other collections include *Poemas de la noche y de la tierra* (1943; Poems of the Night and the Land), *Tres nocturnos* (1947; Three Nocturns), *Círculos del trueno* (1953; Thunder Circles), *La rama del relámpago* (1953; Branch Lightning), *Por arte del sol* (1958; Through the Art of the Sun), *Edades perdidas* (1981; Lost Ages), *Los colores ocultos* (1985; Hidden Colors), *Un día muy distante* (1987; A Very Distant Day), and *El solitario viento de las hojas* (1990; The Lonely Wind of the Leaves).

GERCHUNOFF, ALBERTO (Argentina, 1889–1950). Novelist, short story writer, and journalist. Born in the Ukraine, he grew up in the province of Entre Ríos and became fully acculturated to Argentina while retaining his own cultural heritage. For 40 years, he worked for the daily newspaper *La Nación*. In addition to eight works of fiction, Gerchunoff also wrote a number of books on literature and life and culture in Argentina, including *Nuestro señor don Quijote* (1913; Our Lord Don Quixote), *El problema judío* (1945; The Jewish Problem), and most notably, *Los gauchos judíos* (1910; *The Jewish Gauchos of the Pampas*), a significant contribution to **gaucho literature** and **Jewish writing** in Argentina.

GIARDINELLI, MEMPO (Argentina, 1947–). Novelist and journalist. Although he is a widely published journalist and commentator, he is best known for his novels. He left Argentina in 1976 after his novel *Toño tuerto, rey de ciegos* (One-eyed Tony, King of the Blind) was destroyed by his publisher for political reasons, and his early work was completed while living in exile in **Mexico**. Giardinelli is a **post-boom** writer known for his referencing of other texts and genres in his work. This is especially so in two of his most successful works, *Luna caliente* (1983; *Sultry Moon*) and *Qué solos se quedan los muertos* (1985; How Lonely Are the Dead), in which the tradition of hard-boiled **crime fiction** figures prominently, both as a parody of the genre and as a way to examine social violence. Other novels include *La revolución en bicicleta* (1980; Revolution on a Bicycle); *¿Por qué prohibieron el circo?* (1983; Why Was the Circus Banned?); *Santo oficio de la memoria* (1991; Holy Office of Memory), which received the 1993 **Rómulo Gallegos Prize**; and *Imposible equilibrio* (1995; Impossible Balance).

GIL GILBERT, ENRIQUE (Ecuador, 1912–1973). Short story writer and novelist. He was a member of the **Grupo de Guayaquil** and coauthor, with **Demetrio Aguilera Malta** and **Joaquín Gallegos Lara**, of the short story collection *Los que se van* (1930; Those Who Leave). He also published several collections of his own: *Yunga* (1933; Yunga), *Relatos de Emmanuel* (1939; Tales of Emmanuel), and *La cabeza de un niño en un tacho de basura* (1967; The Head of a Child in a Garbage Can). Political militancy is a feature of his writing, notably in *Nuestro pan* (1942; *Our Daily Bread*), a novel of social protest about conditions in the countryside and the rice fields in Ecuador that placed second, behind *El mundo es ancho y ajeno* by **Ciro Alegría**, in a competition sponsored by the U.S. publisher Farrar & Rinehart.

GIRONDO, OLIVERIO (Argentina, 1891–1957). Poet. His work went through several stages, at times reflecting the ongoing changes in aesthetics and the broader literary environment. After writing for literary **journals** in Buenos Aires, he was drawn into the circle of **ultraísmo** and **Jorge Luis Borges**, and was linked with the **avant-garde** from his earliest collections. He was one of the moving forces behind the avant-garde journal *Martín Fierro* and wrote its manifesto in 1924. *Veinte poemas para ser leídos en el tranvía* (1922; Twenty Poems to Be Read on a Trolley) is a mock-serious collection that includes verses, prose poems, and drawings representing the author's travels through cities in Europe and America. *Calcomanías* (1925; Decals) is concerned with Spain. Later collections, beginning with *Espantapájaros* (1932; *Scarecrow*), introduce a more interior world. Then, in collections such as *Interlunio* (1937; Intermoonlude) and *Persuasión de los días* (1942; The Days' Persuasion), he began to produce a poetry based on wordplay, leading to *En la masmédula* (1954; Moremarrow), his best-known work, in which he sought to create a new vocabulary and break with established syntax. See also LANGE, NORAH; MADARIAGA, FRANCISCO; MOLINA, ENRIQUE.

GIRRI, ALBERTO (Argentina, 1919–1991). Poet. He was a prolific writer, with over 30 collections of poetry to his credit. As a member of a group that began to publish in the 1940s, which included **Olga Orozco** and **Enrique Molina**, he belonged to a generation representing a post-**avant-garde** trend in literature and a return to a more traditional style. Like others of his generation, he was strongly influenced by poetry in English, by both North American and British writers, and habitually appended a selection of translations from English to his own collections. His early books include *Playa sola* (1946; Lonely Beach), *Coronación de la espera* (1947; The Coronation of Hope), *La penitencia y el mérito* (1957; Penitence and Worth), *Propiedades de la magia* (1959; The Properties of Magic), and *El ojo* (1963; The Eye).

Girri developed and refined his writing with each collection; his best work began with *Valores diarios* (1970; Daily Values) and was sustained in subsequent volumes, among which are *Poesía de observación* (1973; Observation Poetry), *El motivo es el poema* (1976;

The Motive Is the Poem), *Homenaje a W.C. Williams* (1981; Homage to W.C. Williams), and *Monodías* (1985; Monodies). He often made poetry and artistic creation the subject of his writing, and at the same time that he published one of his collections, *En la letra, ambigua selva* (1972; Within the Writing, Ambiguous Jungle), he also published *Diario de un libro* (1972; Diary of a Book), containing the notes written while composing the poems. In *Notas sobre la experiencia poética* (1883; Notes on the Poetic Experience), he published an account of his poetics. Girri contributed to a number of the prominent literary **journals** of his time, including *Sur*, and also wrote two novels, *Crónica del héroe* (1946; The Hero's Chronicle) and *Un brazo de Dios* (1966; An Arm of God).

GLANTZ, MARGO (Mexico, 1930–). Novelist, critic, and essayist. She is the author or editor of more than 30 books. Her fiction includes *Las mil y una calorías: novela dietética* (1978; A Thousand and One Calories: A Dietetic Novel), *Zona de derrumbe* (2001; Slide Area), and *El rastro* (2002; *The Wake*). Her criticism and essays cover a wide range of themes and include five books on **Sor Juana Inés de la Cruz**, essays on **la onda** and on **Alvar Núñez Cabeza de Vaca**, and a study of mysticism and nuns during the colonial period. Among her best-known publications is *Las genealogías* (1981; *Family Tree*), an autobiography that traces the history of an intellectual **Jewish** family, Jewish cultural history, and the Mexicanization of Jewish culture. *See also* WOMEN.

GOIC, CEDOMIL (Chile, 1928–). Critic. As a teacher, writer, and editor, Goic's work has had a profound impact in Chile and throughout Spanish America. He has written many essays of literary criticism; his major books include *La poesía de Vicente Huidobro* (1956; The Poetry of Vicente Huidobro), *La novela chilena* (1968; The Chilean Novel), *Historia de la novela hispanoamericana* (1972; History of the Spanish American Novel), and *La novela de la Revolución Mexicana* (1983; The Novel of the Mexican Revolution).

GOLDEMBERG, ISAAC (Peru, 1945–). Novelist and poet. He is the author of books on **Jewish** themes and is best known for his novel

La vida a plazos de don Jacobo Lerner (1978; *The Fragmented Life of Don Jacobo Lerner*). He has lived in the United States since 1964.

GOMES, ALFREDO DIAS (Brazil, 1922–1999). Dramatist. Born in Bahia, Dias Gomes won a playwriting contest at age 15, and at age 20, his plays were already being staged in Rio and São Paulo. He gained recognition for the comedies *Pé-de-Cabra* (1942; Crowbar), followed by *Doutor Ninguém* (Doctor Nobody), *Amanhã será outro dia* (Tomorrow Will Be Another Day), and *Zeca Diabo* (Joe Devil). In the 1950s, he had to leave the stage for political reasons and began writing plays for the radio. His best-known play is *O Pagador de Promessas* (1960; The Keeper of Promises). Set in rural Bahia and featuring aspects of popular religiosity, this tale of a simple man intent on keeping a religious vow was adapted for the screen, becoming the first Brazilian production to win a major prize at the Cannes Film Festival. After the 1964 military coup, Dias Gomes was banned from radio and turned successfully to writing scripts for soap operas, one of which was based on his play *Doutor Getúlio, sua Vida e sua Gloria* (1968; Doctor Getúlio, His Life and His Glory), a portrait of the populist leader Getúlio Vargas written in collaboration with **Ferreira Gullar**. Dias Gomes was killed in an accident one night while returning home from the **theater** in a taxi.

GÓMEZ CARRILLO, ENRIQUE (Guatemala, 1873–1927). Novelist, essayist, and journalist. After traveling to Europe at an early age, he established himself in Paris, where he led a somewhat bohemian existence and figured in the European literary scenes of his time. His output was prodigious, amounting to more than 50 books and a vast amount of journalism; his **chronicles** appeared in major newspapers in Spain, **Mexico**, **Argentina**, and **Chile** and were widely read. The aesthetics of **modernismo** and contemporary tastes are reflected in his fiction, such as *El evangelio de amor* (1922; The Gospel of Love), his most popular novel, combining paganism and Christianity and set in the 14th century. His fiction never attained the popularity of his newspaper columns or even the books on his travels throughout the world and those he wrote about World War I. He was an inveterate Francophile and commentator on developments in French literature and culture who remained in the public eye for more than 25 years. A significant part of his work was ephemeral, however, and remains uncollected in the columns of newspapers and magazines where it first appeared.

GÓMEZ VALDERRAMA, PEDRO (Colombia, 1923–1995). Poet, short story writer, and novelist. His poetry, *Normas para el efímero, 1938–1942* (1943; Norms for the Ephemeral) and *Biografía de la campana* (1946; Biography of the Bell), belongs to his youth. He produced several collections of short stories: *¡Tierra!* (1960; Land Ho!), with a title story about the sighting of land during the first voyage of **Christopher Columbus**; *El retablo de Maese Pedro* (1967; Maese Pedro's Tableau); *La procesión de los ardientes* (1975; The Procession of the Fervid); and *La nave de los locos y otros relatos* (1984; The Ship of Fools and Other Tales). However, he wrote only one novel, *La otra raya del tigre* (1977; The Tiger's Other Stripe), the story of a German immigrant in 19th-century Colombia. His essays were mainly on literature and education.

GÓNGORA DE MARMOLEJO, ALONSO DE (Chile, 1523–1575). Chronicler. Born in Spain, he wrote an eyewitness **chronicle** of the conquest of Chile, *Historia de todas las cosas que han acaecido en el Reino de Chile y de los que lo han gobernado, 1536–1575* (History of Everything That Has Happened in the Kingdom of Chile and of Those Who Have Governed It, 1536–1575). Góngora de Marmolejo is thought to have been inspired by **Alonso de Ercilla y Zúñiga** and is considered one of the more reliable historical sources of the period. His chronicle was not published until 1862.

GONZAGA, TOMÁS ANTÔNIO (Brazil, 1744–1810?). Poet. Born in Portugal of Brazilian parents, Gonzaga received his early education in Brazil before attending university in Portugal. He taught in Portugal for a while and then held public office in Brazil. In Vila Rica, where he was a magistrate and solicitor, he wrote *Cartas Chilenas* (1957; Chilean Letters), a series of satirical letters in verse supposedly written by a Chilean named Critilo to a friend in Madrid, ridiculing Fanfarrão Minésio, a disguise for the governor of Minas, Gonzaga's political enemy. While in Bahia as a public official, he met and courted Maria Joaquina Dorotéia das Seixas, a young woman who inspired his poem cycle, *Marília de Dirceu* (1792–1812; Marília of Dirceu). In 1789, he was denounced as the head of the Minas Gerais conspiracy and sent to prison for three years in Ilha das Cobras. He wrote some of his best poems during his imprisonment. He was then sentenced to life in prison in Angola, but his sentence was reduced to 10 years in Mozambique, where he married the daughter of a wealthy slave trader. He was promoted to customs judge in 1809 but died shortly thereafter.

Gonzaga's main work, *Marília*, is a cycle of short poems known as *liras* in the style of **arcadianism**, in which Dirceu, the shepherd lover, sings of his platonic love for Marília, an ideal woman, in a bucolic setting. The poems, however, escape the conventions of the genre to reflect the circumstances of Gonzaga's life. His *Obras Completas de Tomás Antônio Gonzaga* (1957; Complete Works of Tomás Antônio Gonzaga) also contains *Tratado de Direito Natural* (Treatise of Natural Law), which he wrote as a student, and *Carta Sobre a Usura* (Letter on Usury). *See also* PEIXOTO, INÁCIO JOSÉ DE ALVARENGA.

GONZÁLEZ DE ESLAVA, FERNÁN (Mexico, 1534–1601?). Dramatist and poet. His place in Mexican literature is based mainly on a collection of 16 short dramatic pieces known as *coloquios* (colloquies). They are written mainly in verse with some prose and share some of the characteristics of the traditional *auto*, but they also introduce topics of interest to the local Mexican population within the religious themes. Their structure is similar to that of plays of the early Spanish **theater** of the 16th century and incorporates dramatic forms such as the *loa* and *entremés*.

GONZÁLEZ LANUZA, EDUARDO (Argentina, 1900–1984). Poet. As an adherent to the aesthetics of **ultraísmo**, he collaborated with **Jorge Luis Borges** in the production of the literary journals *Prisma* and *Proa* and contributed to *Martín Fierro* in the 1920s. During this period he published two collections of poetry, *Prismas* (1924; Prisms) and *Treinta y tantos poemas* (1932; Thirty or So Poems), as well as *Aquelarre* (1927; Witches' Sabbath), a collection of short stories, although González Lanuza is not known for fiction. His later poetry became rather conventional in both its content and form. He also published essays on travel and literature.

GONZÁLEZ LEÓN, ADRIANO (Venezuela, 1933–2008). Novelist, short story writer, and poet. His reputation was made with the novel *País portátil* (1968; Portable Country), dealing with rural and urban violence. Through the narrative of its protagonist, a student carrying a suitcase across Caracas for delivery to a group of *guerrilleros*, without knowing what the suitcase contained, the novel introduced the theme of urban guerrilla conflict to Latin American fiction. González León published another novel, *Viejo* (1994; Old), long after the appearance of his more successful work, and he is the author of several collections of short stories: *Las hogueras más altas* (1957; The Tallest Fires), *El hombre que daba sed* (1967; The Man Who Made People Thirsty), *Linaje de árboles* (1988; Lineage of Trees), and *Crónicas del rayo y de la lluvia* (1998; Chronicles of Rain and Lightning). His poetry, somewhat in the style of **César Vallejo**, includes *Hueso de mis huesos* (1997; Bone of My Bones), *De ramas y secretos* (1980; Of Branches and Secrets), and *Damas* (1998; Checkers).

GONZÁLEZ MARTÍNEZ, ENRIQUE (Mexico, 1871–1952). Poet. His work is marked by a movement away from **modernismo** and an exploration of the theme of the hidden meanings of the universe. He is best known as the author of the poem "Tuércele el cuello al cisne . . ." ("Wring the swan's neck . . ."), in which he suggests doing away with the swan, one of the images symbolic of modernismo, in favor of the owl. He published more than 15 books of poetry. Those from his early period include *Preludios* (1903; Preludes), *Lirismos* (1911; Lyricisms), *La muerte del cisne* (1915; Death of the Swan), *La hora inútil* (1915; The Empty Hour), *Parábolas y otros poemas* (1918; Parables and Other Poems), and *La palabra del viento* (1921; The Word of the Wind). Later works include *Segundo despertar* (1945; Second Awakening) and *El nuevo Narciso* (1952; The New Narcissus).

GONZÁLEZ PRADA, MANUEL (Peru, 1944–1918). Poet and essayist. His collections of verses *Minúsculas* (1901; Miniatures) and *Exóticas* (1916; Exotica) show the characteristics of **modernismo,**

but he is better known for his polemical writings, such as *Páginas libres* (1894; *Free Pages*), calling for social reform. He was an important figure in the development of **indigenismo** in Peru and an influence on other writers, including **Clorinda Matto de Turner**, **César Vallejo**, and **José Carlos Mariátegui**. *See also* CABELLO DE CARBONERA, MERCEDES.

GONZÁLEZ TUÑÓN, RAÚL (Argentina, 1905–1974). Poet. He published his first poem at the age of 17 and continued to write and publish throughout his life. In the 1920s, he was affiliated with **ultraísmo** and contributed to other **avant-garde journals** of the time, including *Martín Fierro*. His first books, *El violín del diablo* (1926; The Devil's Violin) and *Miércoles de ceniza* (1928; Ash Wednesday), depict the suburbs of Buenos Aires during a period of rapid transformation. His next work, *La calle del agujero en media* (1930; The Street with a Hole in the Middle), is a collection of sketches of Paris written after a visit to France. González Tuñón was also a journalist, and his poetry became more militant after joining the Communist Party and experiencing the Spanish Civil War (1936–1939) as a war correspondent. His poetry from that period includes *La rosa blindada* (1936; The Armored Rose), *Las puertas del fuego* (1938; The Doors of the Fire), *La muerte en Madrid* (1939; Death in Madrid), *Canciones del tercer frente* (1941; Songs from the Third Front), and *Himno de pólvora* (1943; Gunpowder Hymn). Other collections followed, including a cycle of poems from his alter ego, Juancito Caminador.

GONZÁLEZ ZELEDÓN, MANUEL (Costa Rica, 1864–1936). Journalist. Writing under the pseudonym "Magón," González Zeledón became a popular **costumbrismo** author. He published his first costumbrista article in 1885 and continued to contribute to Costa Rican newspapers thereafter, even though he was living in exile in the United States from 1901 until shortly before his death in 1936. His articles, consisting of short sketches, brief narratives, and commentaries, usually drawn from personal experience, have been anthologized in various compilations. He produced only one longer work, a novella, *La propia* (1909; His Wife), a tragic tale, although it still has many of the lighter touches of his shorter pieces.

GORODISCHER, ANGÉLICA (Argentina, 1928–). Novelist and short story writer. She has written more than 15 books and is celebrated for her science fiction and fantasy writing. Gender and language, the domestic world of **women**, and their relation to men figure prominently in her work and have earned her a significant place among contemporary women writers in Argentina. Her novels include *Floreros de alabastro, alfombras de Bokhara* (1985; *Vases of Alabaster, Carpets from Bokhara*), *Fábula de la virgen y el bombero* (1993; Fable of the Virgin and the Fireman), *Prodigios* (1994; Prodigies), and *La noche del inocente* (1996; The Night of the Innocent). Among her collections of short stories are *Opus dos* (1967; Opus Two), *Bajo las jubeas en flor* (1973; Under the Yubayas in Bloom), and *Casta luna electrónica* (1977; Chaste Electronic Moon). The two volumes of tales about an imaginary empire, *Kalpa Imperial* (1983–1984; *Kalpa Imperial: The Greatest Empire That Never Was*), in particular have brought her international recognition.

GOROSTIZA, CARLOS (Argentina, 1920–). Dramatist. He began his career in the **theater** as a puppeteer, and his plays for children included *La clave encantada* (1942; The Enchanted Clavichord) and *Nuevos títeres de la clave encantada* (1949; New Puppets from the Enchanted Clavichord). His first play for the commercial theater, *El puente* (1949; The Bridge), on class conflict, was very successful and is noted for technical innovations in its use of performance space. Later works, generally on the themes of identity and human relationships, include *El pan de la locura* (1958; The Bread of Madness), *Los prójimos* (1966; Neighbors), *Los hermanos queridos* (1978; The Beloved Brothers), and *Aeroplanos* (1990; Airplanes). Gorostiza participated in the **teatro abierto** project. Although his work was generally realist, it also had elements of the **theater of the absurd** and the *grotesco criollo*. His play *El acompañamiento* (1981; The Accompaniment) was the basis of a successful 1991 musical film in Argentina. He also wrote several novels.

GOROSTIZA, CELESTINO (Mexico, 1904–1967). Dramatist. He participated in experimental theater groups in the 1920s, and his plays of this period include *El nuevo paraíso* (1930; The New Paradise), *Ser o no ser* (1934; To Be or Not to Be), and *Escombros del* *sueño* (1939; Remains of the Dream). During the 1940s, he wrote mainly for the cinema, but returned to the theater in the 1950s. The plays from this period include *La leña está verde* (1958; The Firewood Is Green), a historical drama about the relationship between **Hernán Cortés** and Doña Marina, his Native American mistress, and dramas on social issues of the day, such as *El color de nuestra piel* (1952; The Color of Our Skin), about racial prejudice, one of Gorostiza's best-known works.

GOROSTIZA, JOSÉ (Mexico, 1901–1979). Poet. He was a member of **Los Contemporáneos** and published two main collections of poetry. The first, *Canciones para cantar en las barcas* (1925; Songs to Sing in Ships), is mostly a series of poems about the sea, as its title suggests. The second, *Muerte sin fin* (1939; *Death Without End*), has been hailed as one of the most important works of poetry of the **avant-garde**, as significant as T. S. Eliot's *The Waste Land* (1922) or *Four Quartets* (1945). It is a long, philosophical poem on death with the idea at its core that death is fundamental to the possibility of life. He was a descendant of the dramatist **Manuel Eduardo de Gorostiza**. *See also* TORRES BODET, JAIME.

GOROSTIZA, MANUEL EDUARDO DE (Mexico, 1789–1851). Dramatist. Although he was born in Mexico, he lived in Spain and England between 1794 and 1833. He wrote light, gently moralizing domestic comedies somewhat in the style of **neo-classicism**, and most of his surviving six plays were first performed in Spain. His best works are *Indulgencia para todos* (1818; Tolerance for All), *Don Dieguito* (1820; Little Don Diego), and *Contigo pan y cebolla* (1833; Through Thick and Thin). *See also* GOROSTIZA, JOSÉ; THEATER.

GORRITI, JUANA MANUELA (Argentina, 1818–1892). Novelist, short story writer, and essayist. She was one of South America's most important 19th-century **women** writers. Although she was born in Argentina, the politics of the postindependence era drove her family into exile in 1831. She eventually returned to Argentina in 1875, after living in both **Bolivia** and **Peru**, and her later life was spent between Buenos Aires, Lima, and La Paz. In Bolivia, she attained social and political prominence through her marriage to Manuel Isidoro Belzú, who became president of Bolivia (1848–1855), albeit after their separation. In Peru, she was known for her literary and cultural salon, whose members included such notable figures as **Ricardo Palma**, **Clorinda Matto de Turner**, and **Mercedes Cabello de Carbonera**.

Gorriti's writing reflects her travels, knowledge of history, and experience of the social and political conflicts of the countries she lived in, often presented through her fictional female protagonists. Her short novels, short stories, and essays were published mainly in several compilations. The first of these, in two volumes, was *Sueños y realidades* (1865; Dreams and Realities). Among the many texts included are *La quena* (The Flute), a story of doomed loved in colonial times; *El guante negro* (The Black Glove), about two women vying for the love of the same man, set in the time of the conflict between Unitarians and Federalists in Argentina; and *Gubi Amaya: historia de un salteador* (Gubi Amaya: Story of a Bandit), the adventures of a woman dressed as a man. A second collection, *Panoramas de la vida* (1876; Panoramas of Life), was published 10 years later. It is also in two volumes and, as its subtitle promises, is a "collection of novels, fantasies, legends and descriptions of America." *Misceláneas* (1878; Miscellany) has a similar subtitle and content. *El mundo de los recuerdos* (1886; The World of Memories) is a mix of fiction and autobiography. A final volume of memoirs, *Lo íntimo de Juana Manuela Gorriti* (1893; The Personal Story of Juana Manuela Gorriti), was published posthumously. More recently, **Martha Mercader** has written a fictionalized biography drawing on Gorriti's life and writings as her sources.

GREIFF, LEÓN DE (Colombia, 1895–). Poet. Although his poetry addresses some standard themes, such as nature, love, death, solitude, poetry, and art, it is also very idiosyncratic. León de Greiff was quite eccentric and followed his own paths. His poetry is full of Nordic characters, fantasies, and his own mythologies. It is collected mainly in eight "hefty volumes," from *Tergiversaciones: primer mamotreto* (1925; Distortions: First Hefty Volume) to *Nova et vetera: octavo mamotreto* (1973; New and Old: Hefty Volume Number Eight).

GREZ, VICENTE (Chile, 1847–1909). Novelist. He worked as a journalist and produced several books on Chilean history before turning to fiction. As a novelist, he followed in the footsteps of **Alberto Blest Gana** and wrote in the tradition of European **realism**. His novels, *Emilia Reynals* (1883; Emilia Reynals), *La dote de una joven* (1884; A Young Woman's Dowry), *Marianita* (1881; Marianita), and *El ideal de una esposa* (1887; A Wife's Ideal), unfold in domestic interiors and feature passionate characters.

GRIFFERO, RAMÓN (Chile, 1954–). Dramatist. He has written about dictatorship and postdictatorship Chile, notably in the trilogy *Historias de un galpón abandonado* (1984; Stories from an Abandoned Warehouse), *Cinema-Utoppia* (1985; Cinema Utoppia), and *La morgue* (1987; The Morgue), using the **theater** and its space strategically as a way to circumvent textual censorship. Later works, such as *Río abajo* (1995; Downstream), about life in a Santiago tenement, are also centered on social conditions.

GROTESCO CRIOLLO. "Grotesque" in this context alludes to a predominantly pessimistic view of life reflecting the defeated social aspirations of immigrants to **Argentina** that pervaded urban life and culture in the early decades of the 20th century. The *grotesco criollo* refers in particular to the dramatic form through which this condition was represented in the **theater**. Derived from the 19th-century *sainete*, the *grotesco criollo* makes use of the comic, the absurd, and the dramatic to convey the stories of a wide range of social characters and types. The dramatists who contributed to the genre include **Francisco Defilippis Novoa**, **Armando Discépolo**, **Osvaldo Dragún**, **Carlos Gorostiza**, **Carlos Maggi**, and **Ricardo Talesnik**.

GROUSSAC, PAUL (Argentina, 1848–1929). Essayist. Although born in France, he lived in Buenos Aires from the age of 18 and became a prominent figure in Argentinean literary circles through essays on literary history and criticism published in literary **journals** and through the auspices of the national library, of which he became director. His posthumous reputation owes much to **Jorge Luis Borges**, who prepared an anthology of his work and alluded to him in his own writing.

GRUPO DE BOEDO. Boedo is the name of a street in working-class Buenos Aires attached to a literary group in 1920s **Argentina**, associated with the periodical *Claridad*, which espoused social **realism** in its writing. The Grupo de Boedo contrasted with the **Grupo de Florida**, which represented the **avant-garde**, and the conflict between the two became a matter of public record as well as a symbol of the cultural and economic divide in 1920s Argentina. It ended in reconciliation in 1930, although some writers, such as **Roberto Arlt**, had already contributed to the publications of both groups. See also KORDON, BERNARDO.

GRUPO DE FLORIDA. Named for one of the most elegant streets in Buenos Aires, members of the group were adherents of the literary **avant-garde** in **Argentina** in the 1920s and contrasted with the **Grupo de Boedo**, which espoused social **realism**. The Florida group's **journals** were *Martín Fierro* and *Proa,* whose contributors included **Jorge Luis Borges, Oliverio Girondo, Raúl González Tuñón, Ricardo Güiraldes, Norah Lange, Leopoldo Marechal,** and **Conrado Nalé Roxlo.**

GRUPO DE GUAYAQUIL. A group of writers of the 1930s in **Ecuador** whose social **realism**, **indigenismo**, and interest in popular culture ran contrary to the predominant **avant-garde** style of the day. The collection of short stories *Los que que se van* (1930; Those Who Leave), by **Demetrio Aguilera Malta, Joaquín Gallegos Lara**, and **Enrique Gil Gilbert**, became their manifesto. **José de la Cuadra** and **Alfredo Pareja Diezcanseco** were also members of the group. *See also* ICAZA, JORGE.

GUAMAN POMA DE AYALA, FELIPE (Peru, ca. 1550–post 1616). An indigenous Peruvian whose *El primer nueva corónica y buen gobierno* (First New Chronicle and Good Government) is a unique **chronicle** of colonial life, written from an indigenous perspective, that exposes the harshness of colonial rule in a manuscript of more than 1,200 pages with almost 400 illustrations. Although written between 1612 and 1615, it was not widely available until a facsimile edition appeared in 1936, and a transcription was published in 1980 under the title *Nueva crónica y buen gobierno* (New Chronicle and Good Government).

GUARNIERI, GIANFRANCESCO (Brazil, 1934–2006). Dramatist. Born in Italy, Guarnieri arrived in Brazil as a small child with his parents, who were fleeing Italian fascism. He received his education in São Paulo. His first and most famous play, *Eles Não Usam Black Tie* (1958; They Don't Use Black Ties), is the story of a factory worker who comes into conflict with his father, the leader of a strike, when his girlfriend becomes pregnant and he must choose financial stability over the workers' struggle. This play was staged in the famed Teatro Arena, where Guarnieri also worked with **Augusto Boal**, and was adapted for the screen. Guarnieri's social and political drama displays Marxist and **Brechtian theater** influences. Other plays include *Gimba, o Presidente dos Valentes* (1959; Gimba, or the President of the Brave), a musical on life in the Rio shantytowns; *A Semente* (1961; The Seed), a piece criticizing the political methods of both the Right and the Left; *Um Grito Parado no Ar* (1973; A Cry Suspended in Mid-Air), about the difficulties of artists; and *Ponto de Partida* (1976; Point of Departure), a play about censorship and repression. His last play was *A Luta Secreta da Maria Encarnação* (2001; Maria Encarnação's Secret Struggle). *See also* BOAL, AUGUSTO; THEATER.

GUATEMALA. Pre-Columbian Guatemala, **indigenous traditions**, and the hybrid culture that began to evolve soon after the conquest are represented in the *Annals of the Cakchiquel*, the *Books of Chilam Balam*, and the *Popol Vuh* (the last discovered and transcribed by **Francisco Ximénez** in the early 18th century). As literature in Spanish began to establish a national tradition after independence in the early 19th century, the most significant lyric poet was **José Batres Montúfar**, whose verse narratives in the mold of Spanish **romanticism** anticipated the *tradiciones* of the Peruvian **Ricardo Palma**. However, prose has in general inclined to be more dominant than verse in Guatemalan literature. **José Milla y Vidaure** introduced **costumbrismo** to Guatemala, and his **historical novels** made him a pioneer in fiction. During the heyday of **modernismo**, **Enrique**

Gómez Carrillo was one of the most widely influential writers in Latin America, and his younger contemporary **Rafael Arévalo Martínez**, although not so widely read in his time, anticipated some of the later trends in Latin American fiction.

The first half of the 20th century in Guatemala was dominated politically by two dictators, Manuel Estrada Cabrera (1898–1920) and Jorge Ubico (1931–1944), and in economics by foreign fruit companies. The early part of this period is represented in fiction in the **criollismo** of **Carlos Wyld Ospina**, the costumbrismo of **César Brañas**, and the **indigenismo** of the novels by **Flavio Herrera**. However, the two giants of Guatemalan literature in the first half of the 20th century are **Luis Cardoza y Aragón** and the **Nobel Prize** winner **Miguel Ángel Asturias**, whose fiction connected with the indigenous traditions of Guatemala, the contemporary political travails of the country, and the European **avant-garde**. They were followed by two other significant writers, both belonging to the post-Ubico era: the novelist **Mario Monteforte Toledo** and the short story writer **Augusto Monterroso**.

The post-1944 history of Guatemala is one of failed presidencies, military coups, interventionism, dictatorships, and revolutionary movements that endured until a peace agreement ended the last civil war in 1996. Asturias, Monteforte Toledo, and Monterroso remained the dominant figures for much of the second half of the 20th century. New writers appeared, including a significant group of **women** poets, but the oppressiveness of the times made it difficult for them to rise above their sociopolitical circumstances. Among the revolutionary poets, the work of **Otto René Castillo** stands out, and in prose the **testimonio** of the 1992 winner of the Nobel Peace Prize, **Rigoberta Menchu**, provides a vision of those conflictive times, notwithstanding the controversy surrounding it about its authenticity.

Guatemalan **theater** also traces its origins to preconquest times, notably to the dance-drama *Rabinal Achí*. Theater was part of formal culture in the 19th century, but the history of the genre in the country has been one of alternating activity and decline, with few dramatists establishing anything more than a local reputation. The period between 1954 and 1974, although politically troubled, was one of the most notable in the history of the theater. It was marked by the presence of several significant contributors to the stage, including the novelist Miguel Ángel Asturias; **Manuel Galich**; **Hugo Carrillo**, whose 1974 stage adaptation of Asturias's novel *El señor presidente* was a highlight of the period; and **Carlos Solórzano**, although he has lived mostly in Mexico and has a high profile in Mexican theater. In more recent decades, after an initial decline, the theater has begun to grow again thanks to a rise in public interest and an increase in the number of commercial theaters, touring companies, and institutions such as café-theaters. *See also* CHOCANO, JOSÉ SANTOS; CHRONICLE; CIVILIZATION AND BARBARISM; DICTATOR NOVEL; MAGIC REALISM; MOLINA, JUAN RAMÓN; NEO-INDIGENISMO; ODIO, EUNICE; OREAMUNO, YOLANDA; THEATER IN QUECHUA.

GUIDO, BEATRIZ (Argentina, 1925–1988). Novelist and short story writer. Her novels are about contemporary politics and tell stories of **women** struggling for independence and self-realization, such as *La casa del ángel* (1954; *The House of the Angel*), *La caída* (1956; The Fall), and *La mano en la trampa* (1961; The Hand in the Trap). Her short stories, which include the collections *Los insomnes* (1974; The Insomniacs) and *Piedra libre* (1976; Free Stone), are notable for the inventiveness of their plots. Several of her novels and stories have been adapted for the cinema in films directed by her husband, Leopoldo Torre Nilsson, and Guido wrote the screenplay for the 1973 film version of *Los siete locos* (The Seven Madmen) by **Roberto Arlt**.

GUIMARAENS, ALPHONSUS DE, pseudonym of **AFONSO HEN-RIQUES DA COSTA GUIMARÃES (Brazil, 1870–1921).** Poet. Born in Minas Gerais to a family related to the writer **Bernardo Guimarães**, Alphonsus de Guimaraens studied law in São Paulo and Belo Horizonte. After a short trip to Rio to meet the poet **João Cruz e Sousa**, he returned to the interior of Minas Gerais, where he worked as a judge, settling in Mariana. For the rest of his life, he left the town only once, to attend an homage his friends organized for him in the capital. From the mountains where he lived, he sent his poems to the newspapers and literary **journals** in which they were published. His relative isolation did not allow him to achieve much recognition in his lifetime, but he was hailed as one of the most important voices of **symbolism** in Brazil after his death. His poetry was noted for its musical qualities and its invented and archaic vocabulary, as reflected in the archaic spelling he used for his name. The recurrent theme in Guimaraens's poetry is the death of the beloved, perhaps inspired by the real-life death of his teenage fiancée, Constança. There are numerous references to nature, art, and mysticism in works such as *Setenário das Dores de Nossa Senhora* (1899; Septenary of the Sorrows of Our Lady), *Câmara Ardente* (1899; Burning Chamber), and *Dona Mística* (1899; Mystical Lady). *Kyriale* (1902; Kyriale) portrays death through funeral rites. A disciple of the French poets Stéphane Mallarmé (1842–1898) and Paul Verlaine (1844–1896), he published *Pauvre Lyre* (1921, Poor Lyre) in French. His works published posthumously include *Pastoral aos Crentes do Amor e da Morte* (1923; Pastoral of the Believers and of Death), *Poesias* (1938, Poems), and *Obra Completa* (1960; Complete Works).

GUIMARÃES, BERNARDO JOAQUIM DA SILVA (Brazil, 1825–1884). Uncle of the poet **Alphonsus de Guimaraens**, Bernardo Guimarães studied in Minas Gerais and then in São Paulo, where he met, among others, **Manuel Antônio Alvares de Azevedo**, and founded the literary circle Epicurean Society. During this period, he produced humorous nonsense poems known as "bestialógicos." Although he was a prolific writer in many genres, he is best remembered for his narratives centered on national subjects and specific social issues. *O Seminarista* (1872; The Seminarist) is a tragic story portraying the problem of celibacy in the clergy. *O Índio Afonso* (1873; Afonso the Indian) presents indigenous characters but not as the "noble savage" stereotype of **indianismo**. Celebrated as the Brazilian *Uncle Tom's Cabin* (1852), the antislavery novel *A Escrava Isaura* (1875, The Slave Isaura) denounces the abuses of slave owners but not without romantic idealization. These works have earned him a place as one of the founders of the Brazilian novel in the period of **romanticism**. Guimarães was also noted for his **regionalism**, or the portrayal of regional ambiances and popular speech, particularly of the central plateau and backlands, as seen in *O Ermitão de Muquém* (1864; The Hermit of Muquém). **Manuel Bandeira** admired his preromantic *Poesias* (1865; Poems), with their mythological allusions and meditations on the landscape.

GUIMARÃES, JÚLIO CASTAÑON (Brazil, 1951–). Poet. Castañon Guimarães began his career with *Vertentes* (1975; Currents), poems influenced by **concrete poetry** and the work of Fernando Pessoa (1888–1934), **Carlos Drummond de Andrade**, and **Murilo Mendes**, about whom he wrote the essay *Territorios/Conjunções* (1993; Territories/Conjunctions). Castañon Guimarães writes a self-reflexive poetry that explores relationships between meaning and sound. Other works include *17 Peças* (1983; 17 pieces), *Inscrições* (1992; Inscriptions), *Dois Poemas Estrangeiros* (1995; Two Foreign Poems), and *Matéria e Paisagem e Poemas Anteriores* (1998; Matter and Landscape, and Other Poems). Recent titles include *Práticas de Extravio* (2003; Loss Practices) and *Poemas, 1975–2005* (2006; Poems, 1975–2005).

GÜIRALDES, RICARDO (Argentina, 1886–1927). Novelist. He is best known for *Don Segundo Sombra* (1926; *Mr Second Shadow*), a classic of Spanish American literature, although he had already published other books before it appeared toward the end of his life. His first book, *El cencerro de cristal* (1915; The Crystal Cowbell), is a miscellaneous collection of short pieces in descriptive and poetic prose. It was followed promptly by a volume of short stories, *Cuentos de muerte y de sangre* (1915; Tales of Death and Blood), some taken from oral tradition. These were followed by *Raucho: momentos de una juventud contemporánea* (1917; Raucho: Moments of a Contemporary Youth), a partly autobiographical work on the adventures at home and abroad of a young well-to-do Argentinean; *Rosaura* (1922; Rosaura), a tragic story of a young woman who dreams of escaping a small town on the pampas; and *Xaimaca* (1923; Xaimaca), a tale of travel and romance in the Caribbean, a product of the author's own voyage in 1916–1917. *Don Segundo Sombra* is a wistful coming-of-age **novel of the land** set against the traditions of life on the pampas and **gaucho literature**. Its success is due in no small measure to how it captured the rural dimension of the Argentinean national psyche.

GULLAR, FERREIRA, pseudonym of **JOSÉ RIBAMAR FERREIRA (Brazil, 1930–).** Poet and dramatist. Born in São Luís, Maranhão, in northern Brazil, Ferreira Gullar studied in the local schools and then worked as journalist and radio host. Upon winning a literary contest in 1950, he moved to Rio, where he met important writers, such as **Oswald de Andrade**. In this period he began writing *A Luta Corporal* (1954; The Bodily Struggle), a book of prose poems that signaled a new poetic diction different from that of **Brazilian modernism** and the **Generation of '45**. From 1955 to 1957, Ferreira Gullar joined **Augusto de Campos** and **Haroldo de Campos** in the **concrete poetry** movement. Finding the paradigms of concrete poetry too restrictive, he broke with that movement—and in 1959 founded the neo-concrete movement and published his essay *Teoria do Não-Objeto* (1959; Theory of the Non-Object).

Throughout the 1960s, Ferreira Gullar was active in cultural politics and cowrote plays with dramatists such as **Alfredo Dias Gomes**. In 1968, he was jailed for his political activism, along with other artists and musicians such as **Caetano Veloso**. Due to his run-ins with the military regime of Brazil, he lived in exile from 1971 to 1976, residing first in Paris and then in **Chile**, where he wrote *Dentro da Noite Veloz* (1975; Inside the Fast Night) and *Poema Sujo* (1976; Dirty Poem), perhaps his best-known work. In this 2,000-verse poem, Ferreira Gullar denounces political persecution and also reminisces about his childhood and youth in Maranhão. On his 50th birthday, he published *Na Vertigem do Dia* (1980; In the Vertigo of the Day). Other books of poems include *Barulhos* (1987; Noises) and *Muitas Vozes* (1999; Many Voices), all included in *Toda Poesia* (2000; Complete Poetry). *See also* FILHO, ARMANDO FREITAS; GOMES, ALFREDO DIAS; THEATER.

GUSMÁN, LUIS (Argentina, 1944–). Novelist and short story writer. His first novel, *El frasquito* (1973; The Small Flask), the story of a twin accused of murdering his brother, was critically acclaimed, although it was banned in 1977 by the military dictatorship. Several other novels have also now appeared: *Brillo* (1975; Shine); *Cuerpo velado* (1978; The Body Watched Over), which received a **Casa de las Américas** prize; *En el corazón de junio* (1983; In the Heart of June); *La música de Frankie* (1993; Frankie's Music); *Tennessee* (1997; Tennessee); and *Ni muerto has perdido tu nombre* (2000; Even Death Hasn't Taken Your Name). His collections of short stories include *La muerte prometida* (1986; Promise of Death), *Lo más* *oscuro del río* (1990; The Darkest Part of the River), and *De dobles y bastardos* (2000; Of Doubles and Bastards). Gusmán's professional interest in psychology and psychoanalysis is reflected in his writing, which is often quite dark, incorporates elements of **crime fiction** in the situations narrated, and presents characters who confront their memories or re-encounter their past.

GUTIÉRREZ, EDUARDO (Argentina, 1851–1889). Novelist. He was one of Argentina's most popular authors of serialized novels (*folletines*), of which he published more than 30. They include gaucho novels, **historical novels**, and **crime fiction**. Among his contributions to **gaucho literature** are several fictionalized biographies of well-known 19th-century characters, such as *Juan Moreira* (1879; Juan Moreira) and *Santos Vega* (n.d.; Santos Vega). In the novel *Hormiga negra* (n.d.; Black Ant), he showed the violence of gaucho life. His novel about Juan Moreira was based on real events and became the source from which **José J. Podestá** introduced the gaucho to the **theater** of the River Plate region. Gutiérrez's historical fiction includes several works set in the time of **Juan Manuel Rosas**, such as *La mazorca* (n.d.; The Secret Police), *Viva la Santa Federación* (n.d.; Long Live the Holy Federation), and *El puñal del tirano* (n.d.; The Tyrant's Dagger). His crime fiction, with titles like *Un capitán de ladrones en Buenos Aires* (1879; A Captain of Thieves in Buenos Aires), *Infamias de una madre* (n.d.; A Mother's Infamy), and *Los enterrados vivos* (n.d.; Buried Alive), is often inspired by the most bloodthirsty cases in police files. His novels had long, complicated plots, and his perspective on nationalism and the history of Argentina corresponded more with conventional popular views than with those of the governing class.

GUTIÉRREZ, JUAN MARÍA (Argentina, 1809–1878). Essayist. Literature was one among his several interests, which included history, science, and ethnography. He was one of Argentina's earliest literary historians. *América poética* (1848; Poetic America), compiled by Gutiérrez, was the first continentwide anthology of poetry in Spanish America, and in essays such as *Estudios bibliográficos y críticos sobre algunos poetas sud-americanos anteriores al siglo XIX* (Bibliographical and Critical Studies of South American Poets Prior to the Nineteenth Century), he encouraged a rediscovery of the literature of the colonial period. In 1876, he was at the center of a heated debate after he declined membership in the Spanish Royal Academy because he refused to accept the primacy of peninsular Spanish.

GUTIÉRREZ NÁJERA, MANUEL (Mexico, 1859–1895). Poet and journalist. His verse, collected and published posthumously in *Poesías* (1896; Poems) by **Justo Sierra**, represents a significant stage in the early development of **modernismo**. Death and the anguish of existence predominate in his poetry, which clearly reflects his reading of French 19th-century authors. Although his poetry is more accessible, his prose works are more numerous, a consequence of his life as a journalist. He signed himself with a variety of picturesque pseudonyms ("El Duque Job" was the best known), in part to avoid censorship, in part so that he could publish variations of the same text in different places. He wrote about art, literature, politics, culture, and the issues of the day, accommodating the **chronicle** to the newspaper in Mexico by fictionalizing and subjectivizing historical events in imitation of practices already found in European literary journalism.

GUZMÁN, AUGUSTO (Bolivia, 1903–1994). Novelist and historian. He wrote biographies of prominent figures from Bolivian history and several books concerned with the history of Bolivian literature. His fiction includes *La sima fecunda* (1933; The Fruitful Abyss), set in his native Cochabamba, and *Prisionero de guerra* (1937; Prisoner of War), a novel of the Chaco War (1932–1935) between Bolivia and Paraguay, based on personal experiences.

GUZMÁN, MARTÍN LUIS (Mexico, 1887–1976). Novelist and journalist. Guzmán's major contribution to the **novel of the Mexican Revolution** is *El águila y la serpiente* (1928; *The Eagle and the Serpent*), a title derived from elements of the Mexican national flag. It is an episodic narrative that benefits from the author's training as a journalist and his personal experience of the revolution under the command of **Francisco "Pancho" Villa**, whose biography he later wrote, *Memorias de Pancho Villa* (1936–1951, 5 vols.; *Memoirs of Pancho Villa*). Guzmán also wrote *La sombra del caudillo* (1929;

The Shadow of the Caudillo), a novel that successfully captures the intrigue and violence of politics during the revolutionary period in Mexico by following the career of one particular strongman, or *caudillo*.

– H –

HALLEY MORA, MARIO (Paraguay, 1927–2003). Dramatist and novelist. He was one of Paraguay's most prolific writers of the 20th century and obtained recognition in both **theater** and fiction. His work for the theater includes scripts for more than 50 different performances, including some written in Yopará, the local mix of Spanish and Guaraní, and the libretto for musical plays. One of his best-known works was *El juego del tiempo* (1986; The Play of Time), and his other works for the stage include *Se necesita un hombre para cosa urgente* (Man Needed for Something Urgent), *El dinero del cielo* (Money from Heaven), *El último cuadillo* (The Last Chief), *Magdalena Servín* (Magdalena Servín), *Nada más que uno* (No More Than One), *Memorias de una pobre diabla* (Memories of a Wretched Devil), *Despedida de soltero* (Bachelor's Farewell), *La mano del hombre* (The Man's Hand), and *Testigo falso* (False Witness).

As a narrative author, Halley Mora's novels and short stories are published in two dozen books, and he is credited with having created the urban novel in Paraguay. *La quema de Judas* (1965; The Burning of Judas) is one of the first novels about Asunción. *Los hombres de Celina* (1981; Men of Celina) is a coming-of-age novel about a boy who leaves the country to find his fortune in the city, and *Memoria adentro* (1989; Memory Within) is a detective novel that incorporates the story of the capital of Paraguay. Early in his literary career, Halley Mora also published a book of poems, *Piel adentro* (1967; Skin Inside).

HATOUM, MILTON (Brazil, 1952–). Novelist. He was born to Lebanese parents in Manaus, the largest city in the Amazon. Hatoum's fiction has been noted for its portrayal of the ethnic and cultural variety of peoples who came together in that part of the world, from Arab immigrants working as traders, to the native Indians, to the descendants of the Portuguese. Though recognition came slowly, his four novels to date have sold thousands of copies. *Relato de um Certo Oriente* (1989; *The Tree of the Seventh Heaven*, also translated as *Tale of a Certain Orient*), which tells the story of a Lebanese immigrant family in Manaus and their struggle to adapt to a new cultural environment, won the **Jabuti Prize**. His subsequent works, *Dois Irmãos* (2000; *Two Brothers*) and *Cinzas do Norte* (2005; *Ashes of the Amazon*), contain veiled critiques of Brazil's military government.

HAYA DE LA TORRE, VÍCTOR RAÚL (Peru, 1895–1979). Essayist. As the founder of the Alianza Popular Revolucionaria Americana (APRA; American Popular Revolutionary Alliance), he was a significant 20th-century political figure and several times an unsuccessful candidate for the presidency of Peru. His advocacy of the link between workers and intellectuals had an impact on literature, particularly **indigenismo**. He was an active writer whose ideas were first gathered in *El antimperialismo y el APRA* (1927; Anti-Imperialism and APRA) and later in publications such as *Espacio-tiempo histórico* (1948; Historical Space-Time) and *Treinta años de aprismo* (1956; Thirty Years of Aprismo). *See also* ALEGRÍA, CIRO; MARIÁTEGUI, JOSÉ CARLOS; PORTAL, MAGDA.

HEIREMANS, LUIS ALBERTO (Chile, 1928–1964). Dramatist and short story writer. His first publications were collections of short stories, *Los niños extraños* (1950; Strange Children) and *Los demás* (1952; The Others), but he is best known for his writings for the **theater**. Some of his early plays, including *Noche de equinoccio* (1951; Night of the Equinox), *La hora robada* (1952; The Stolen Hour), *La jaula en el árbol* (1957; *The Cage in the Tree*), and *El palomar a oscuras* (1962; Dovecot in the Dark), present variations of the conflict between desires and reality, similar to the themes developed in his fiction, and reflect the influence of the French dramatists Jean Anouilh (1910–1987) and Jean Giraudoux (1882–1944). In the last few years before his death, however, his drama took a different turn and showed more maturity and independence, influenced by Chilean folklore and a desire to offer a Christian view of the world. With some of the character of a Christmas *auto*, *Versos de ciego* (1961; A Blindman's Poems) presents the three Magi, who follow the Star of Bethlehem as a group of wandering musicians and are joined by others on their journey. In *El abanderado* (1962; The Man with a Kerchief), he combines the biblical story of the crucifixion with local legends to tell the tale of a human Christ who approaches death through guilt and fear. Heiremans's last play, *El tony chico* (1964; The Littlest Clown), first performed a few days after he died, is the story of a man who identifies with his past as he confronts his death and the afterlife.

HERNÁNDEZ, FELISBERTO (Uruguay, 1902–1964). Short story writer. His literary production went largely unrecognized during his lifetime, perhaps because of the unconventionality of its themes and the social and economic marginality of his life. He gained some following in the later part of his life, and his influence has since been acknowledged by writers such as **Julio Cortázar** for stories written in the vein of **fantastic literature** and their affinity with the **avant-garde**.

Hernández's early collections were *Fulano de tal* (1925; So-and-so), *Libro sin tapas* (1928; Book Without Covers), *La cara de Ana* (1930; Ana's Face), and *La envenenada* (1931; The Poisoned Woman). Humor and unusual points of view are characteristics of these stories. "Historia de un cigarrrillo," for example, is the story of a cigarette. "El balcón" ("The Balcony") is a tale about a woman who becomes enamoured of the balcony on her house. Several other books appeared after a lapse of 10 years: *Por los tiempos de Clemente Colling* (1942; In the Time of Clemente Colling), a novella; and *El caballo perdido* (1943; The Lost Horse), *Nadie enciende las lámparas* (1947; No-one Lights the Lamps), *Las Hortensias* (1949; The Hortenses), and *La casa inundada* (1960; The Flooded House), all further collections of stories, the last three of which were included in English translation in *Piano Stories* (1993). These later collections contain a number of narratives about childhood and adolescence and themes of eroticism and infantilism. The title story in *Las Hortensias*, for example, is about a man who replaces his wife with dolls.

HERNÁNDEZ, JOSÉ (Argentina, 1834–1886). Poet. The author was virtually unknown before the publication of *El gaucho Martín Fierro* (1872; The Gaucho Martín Fierro). He drew on the travails of his own life when writing his narrative poem: his situation as an orphan, his experience of poverty and war, life on the Argentinean pampas, and his lack of a permanent home. His work is a landmark of Latin American **romanticism**, a defense of rural life and values, and perhaps the most important contribution to **gaucho literature**, being the one that gave canonical literary status to verse narratives of gaucho life. The story of Martin Fierro, set at the time of the frontier wars in Argentina, when the traditional life of the gaucho was already disappearing under the advance of modernity, exalts the virtues of manliness and self-reliance and is one of the foundational texts of Argentinean identity. In *La vuelta de Martín Fierro* (1878; The Return of Martín Fierro), Hernández continued the story, reflecting some of the changes that had occurred in his own life, but also reasserting the virtues that had figured in the first part of the poem. *See also* ASCASUBI, HILARIO; LUSSICH, ANTONIO DIONISIO; MARTÍNEZ ESTRADA, EZEQUIEL.

HERNÁNDEZ, LUISA JOSEFINA (Mexico, 1928–). Dramatist and novelist. She was a student of **Rodolfo Usigli** and has been a successful writer for the **theater** since the age of 21. She has written in a variety of styles and on different historical and fictional themes. Her output amounts to more than 30 plays, including *Los sordomudos* (1950; Deaf Mutes), *Aguardiente de caña* (1951; Rum), *La corona del ángel* (1951; The Angel's Crown), *Los frutos caídos* (1957; Fallen Fruit), *La fiesta del mulato* (1970; The Mulatto's Orgy), *La paz ficticia* (1974; False Peace), *Caprichos y disparates de Francisco Goya* (1979; Francisco Goya's Caprices and Follies), *En una noche como ésta* (1988; On a Night Like This), and *Las bodas* (1992; The Wedding). She professes no particular ideology, although she is one of Mexico's prominent **women** writers and is often considered a feminist, notwithstanding her disclaimers about being classified as such.

Women, as victims, but also as strong, assertive characters intent on self-realization and self-identity, are at the core of her dramas. Marginalization, justice, marriage, and divorce figure significantly among the social themes she has tackled. Similar themes also appear in Hernández's novels, of which she has published more than a dozen, although she is better known for her theater. Among her novels are *La noche exquisita* (1965; The Exquisite Night), *Nostalgia de Troya* (1970; Nostalgia for Troy), and *Apostasía* (1978; Apostasy). She has also translated work by authors such as Christopher Fry (1907–2005) and Dylan Thomas (1914–1953) from English into Spanish. *See also* MAGAÑA, SERGIO.

HERRERA, DARÍO (Panama, 1883–1914). Poet. He was a friend of **Rubén Darío**, whom he met in Buenos Aires in 1898, and is Panama's best-known poet of **modernismo**. However, he published only one book during his lifetime, *Horas lejanas* (1903; Distant Hours), a collection of poems about love and the landscape, in which he experimented with versification.

HERRERA, ERNESTO (Uruguay, 1889–1917). Dramatist. A prominent figure at the beginning of the 20th century during the period when the **theater** in Uruguay first flourished, he wrote a number of plays on Uruguayan themes, which reflect his political commitment to anarchism. *La moral de Misia Paca* (Dame Paca's Morality), *El pan nuestro* (1914; Our Daily Bread), and *La bella Pinguito* (1916; Beautiful Pinguito) were set in the city. *El estanque* (1910; The Pond), *Mala laya* (1911; Bad Kind), *El león ciego* (1911; The Blind Lion), and *El caballo de comisario* (1915; The Policeman's Horse) all have rural themes. He also published a collection of short stories, *Su majestad el hambre* (1910; Her Majesty Hunger).

HERRERA, FLAVIO (Guatemala, 1895–1968). Novelist and poet. He is noted in particular for *El tigre* (1932; The Tiger), *La tempestad* (1938; The Storm), and *Caos* (1949; Chaos), novels about native America, concerned with the theme of civilization in the tropics, that fall between the tendencies of **indianismo** and **indigenismo**.

HERRERA LUQUE, FRANCISCO (Venezuela, 1927–1990). Novelist and essayist. His early essays, beginning with *Los viajeros de Indias* (1961; Travelers in the Indies), were psychological studies of Venezuela that grew out of his training as a psychiatrist. He later turned to fiction and wrote a very popular series of **historical novels** covering the history of Venezuela. These include *La luna de Fausto* (1983; Fausto's Moon) and *Los amos del valle* (1979; Masters of the Valley), concerned with the colonial period; *Boves el Urogallo*

(1972; Boves the Urogallo) and *Manuel Piar, caudillo de dos colores* (1987; Manuel Piar, Two-Faced Chieftain), located during the wars of independence; and *En la casa del pez que escupe el agua* (1975; In the House of the Fish That Spits Water), a family saga from republican times.

HERRERA Y REISSIG, JULIO (Uruguay, 1875–1910). Poet. Although he gathered his poetry in various collections, such as *La éxtasis de la montaña* (The Ecstasy of the Mountain) and *Los parques abandonados* (The Abandoned Parks), he prepared only one volume of verse for publication, *Los peregrinos de piedra* (1910; The Pilgrims of Stone), which appeared posthumously the year he died. The excesses of his language and daring images are often seen in light of his experiments with narcotics, prescribed for him for a heart condition. *Los parques abandonados* was inspired by *Los crepúsculos del jardín* by **Leopoldo Lugones**, but Herrera y Reissig's images of the grotesque and sadomasochism take him much further than his source. Similarly, the sonnets in *La éxtasis de la montaña* represent a darker side of the pastoral tradition. In these respects, his style made him a bridge between **modernismo** and the **avant-garde**, and his importance has been acknowledged by later poets such as **César Vallejo**, **Vicente Huidobro**, and **Pablo Neruda**. *See also* VAZ FERREIRA, MARÍA EUGENIA; VILARIÑO, IDEA; VITALE, IDA.

HIDALGO, ALBERTO (Peru, 1893–1967). Poet. He published two early volumes of poetry in Peru, *Arenga lírica* (1916; Lyric Declamation) and *Panoplia lírica* (1917; Lyrical Panoply), but lived mainly in **Argentina** after 1918 and was a prominent figure of the **avant-garde**. In Buenos Aires, he produced several collections arising from his association with **ultraísmo**: *Muertos, heridos y contusos* (1920; Dead, Wounded, and Bruised), *Tu libro* (1923; Your Book), *Química del espíritu* (1923; Chemistry of the Spirit), and *Simplismo* (1926; Simplism). The last of these became his manifesto for a poetry reduced to metaphor as its primary essential element. His later publications included *Descripción del cielo* (1928; Description of the Sky), *Actitud de los años* (1933; Attitude of the Years), *Edad de corazón* (1940; The Age of the Heart), *Oda a Stalin* (1945; Ode to Stalin), *Patria completa: canto a Macchu Picchu* (1960; Complete

Fatherland: Song to Macchu Picchu), and *Árbol genealógico* (1963; Genealogical Tree).

HIDALGO, BARTOLOMÉ (Uruguay, 1788–1822). Poet. Although born in Montevideo, he fled to **Argentina** in 1818 and wrote much of the work for which he is best known while living in Buenos Aires. Nevertheless, he is still acclaimed as one of Uruguay's major poets. In 1820 he published *Cielitos*, a collection of songs traditionally known by that name, with patriotic themes and written in the language of the gaucho. He subsequently wrote *Diálogos patrióticos, o Diálogos de Chano y Contreras* (1822; Patriotic Dialogues, or Dialogues Between Chano and Contreras), conversations in verse between two men from the country in their own language, which are now seen as one of the main points of departure of **gaucho literature.**

HILST, HILDA (Brazil, 1930–2004). Dramatist, short story writer, and poet. Only daughter of a landowning couple, Hilst was young when her parents separated and was deeply affected as a teenager by her father's schizophrenia. A free-spirited, unconventional young **woman,** after briefly practicing law she led a bohemian life in São Paulo in the 1950s. She traveled widely in Europe and had numerous liaisons with actors and writers, among whom were the American actor Dean Martin and **Vinícius de Moraes.** In the 1960s, she abandoned her life as a socialite to dedicate herself to literature, living in semi-isolation on an estate she built near Campinas (state of São Paulo), which she called Casa do Sol. There she hosted many writers, especially during the period of the military dictatorship in Brazil (1964–1984). She was a close friend of the writer **Lygia Fagundes Telles.**

Hilst's oeuvre is a mix of poetry, **chronicle,** and fiction. Going from one extreme to another, her poetry revisits the religious vein of authors such as **Jorge de Lima** and **Murilo Mendes** and also the medieval tradition of the troubadors. Her first publications were poetry collections, among which are *Sete Cantos do Poeta para o Anjo* (1962; Seven Songs of the Poet for the Angel) and *Cantos de Perda e Predileção* (1984; Songs of Loss and Preference), but she is better known for her narratives and plays.

Her early fiction, *Fluxo-Poema* (1970; Flux-Poem) and *Quadós* (1973), republished in 2002 as *Kadosh* (Kadosh), is a reflective prose with hardly a narrative. *A Obscena Senhora D* (1982; The Obscene Mrs. D) tells the story of a woman who goes to live in a building stairwell after her lover dies, continuing to mourn her lost love despite being harassed by neighbors. Some of her work is explicitly sexual and deliberately obscene or pornographic, at times focusing on **lesbian** relationships. In this vein, she wrote the trilogy that includes *O Caderno Rose de Lory Lambi* (1990; The Rose Notebook of Lory Lambi), *Contos d'Escárnio/Textos Grotescos* (1990; Stories of Mockery/Grotesque Texts), and *Cartas de um Sedutor* (1991; Songs of a Seducer), which also makes use of metalinguistic devices and parody.

Hilst received major literary prizes, including the **Jabuti Prize.** Her theater, much of which was performed but not published, was influenced by her poetic work and reflects the environment of São Paulo, such as in *Rato no Muro* (Mouse in the Wall) and *A Possessa* (The Possessed Woman). A somewhat eccentric personality, toward the end of her life Hilst was preoccupied by questions of immortality and often affirmed she had contact with beings from another world. *See also* ABREU, CAIO FERNANDO.

HISTORICAL NOVEL. Introduced to Latin America from Europe in the 19th century, the popularity of the historical novel is attested by the frequent serialization in **newspapers** and magazines, even in the 20th century, of works by authors, such as Walter Scott (1771–1832) and Alexandre Dumas, father (1802–1870) and son (1824–1995). Contributors to the genre, whether through single volumes or through series in which the history of a country is represented in fiction, include **Eligio Ancona, Ignacio Manuel Altamirano, Julio Jiménez Rueda, Fernando del Paso, Manuel Payno, Vicente Riva Palacio, Justo Sierra O'Reilly, Manuel Payno,** and **Artemio de Valle Arizpe** in **Mexico; José Milla y Vidaure** in **Guatemala; Tomás Carrasquilla** and **William Ospina** in **Colombia; Rómulo Gallegos, Francisco Herrera Luque, Miguel Otero Silva,** and **Arturo Uslar Pietri** in **Venezuela; José de Alencar, Moacyr Scliar,** and **Dinah Silveira de Queirós** in **Brazil; Néstor Taboada Terán** in **Bolivia; Enrique López Albújar** in **Peru; Manuel Gálvez, Eduardo Gutiérrez, Sylvia Iparraguirre, Enrique Larreta, Vicente Fidel López, Manuel Mujica Láinez,** and **Roberto Payró** in **Argentina;**

Eduardo Acevedo Díaz in **Uruguay**; **Daniel Barros Grez, Aberto Blest Gana, Magdalena Petit,** and **Benjamín Subercaseaux** in **Chile.**

In Mexico, the historical novel, introduced in the 19th century, is often referred to as the **colonial novel.** Both in Mexico and other countries, however, historical novels may be set in more recent times as well as in the colonial period that tended to be favored by novels written in the mold of 19th-century **romanticism.** Since the 1970s, a new version of the historical novel, known as the **new historical novel,** has developed in Latin America, departing from the conventions of the traditional genre by focusing on the nature of historical discourse and historiography.

HOJEDA, DIEGO DE (Peru, ca. 1571–1615). Poet. Hojeda was a Dominican friar whose *La Christiada* (1611; The Christiad), based on the passion and death of Christ, was the first important New World religious epic and a notable contribution to 17th-century **epic poetry** in Spanish America.

HOLANDA, SÉRGIO BUARQUE DE (Brazil, 1902–1982). Essayist and historian. Father of **Chico Buarque,** Buarque de Holanda was an early participant in **Brazilian modernism,** cofounding the **avant-garde journal** *Estética* (1924–1925) and writing criticism under the influence of futurism and other European trends. Later on, his interests alternated between history and literature seen from a sociological perspective, particularly influenced by Max Weber (1864–1920). Along with the essayists Arthur Ramos (1903–1949) and **Gilberto Freyre,** among others, he is one of a number of celebrated "interpreters of Brazil" who, beginning in the 1930s, attempted to systematically define the Brazilian national character on the basis of anthropological research.

Buarque de Holanda's most famous works are *Raízes do Brasil* (1936; Roots of Brazil) and *Visão do paraíso: Os Motivos Edênicos no Descobrimento e Colonização do Brasil* (1959; Vision of Paradise: Edenic Motifs in the Discovery and Colonization of Brazil). The former is a historical interpretation of the role of Portuguese colonization in the formation of Brazilian society, including adaptation processes, and the latter offers an analysis of the myth of the

Garden of Paradise in conquest and colonization narratives from the 15th to the 18th centuries.

HOMOSEXUALITY. *See* GAY AND LESBIAN WRITERS AND WRITING.

HONDURAS. Although a small country, Honduras has had many notable writers. However, few of them are part of the Latin American literary canon. The two most significant figures of the 19th century were **José Cecilio del Valle** and **José Trinidad Reyes**, both of whom contributed to several cultural domains and had considerable influence on the formation of the literary culture of Honduras. A similar role was played by **Rafael Heliodoro Valle** in the 20th century. Two poets stand above others as having achieved recognition beyond the borders of Honduras. **Juan Ramón Molina** is a well-known figure in Latin American **modernismo**, and **Roberto Sosa**, in more recent times, has been widely read and translated. In the field of narrative, the first novelist was **Lucila Gamero de Medina**, who wrote in a romantic vein. After her, the narrative of the first half of the 20th century was dominated by **costumbrismo** and **criollismo**. Since then, more recent writers of fiction have developed a more socially committed writing. They have also explored trends in Latin American fiction, such as **magic realism**, as well as focusing on economic and political conditions in Honduras and the country's language and culture.

In spite of several attempts, the formation of a firmly established national **theater** in Honduras is yet to be achieved. Among those who have contributed to its development, however, the names of José Trinidad Reyes and **Andrés Morris** stand out, the former for the 19th century, the latter for the mid-20th. See also CASA DE LAS AMÉRICAS; MONTERROSO, AUGUSTO; THEATER OF THE ABSURD.

HUERTA, EFRAÍN (Mexico, 1914–1982). Poet. His first collection of verse, *Absoluto amor* (1935; Absolute Love), evokes the many forms taken by love, but his later books range more widely. His themes include Mexico City and everyday life on its streets, as well as his place in the cosmos. His poetry is often militantly political, a reflection of his sympathies for the downtrodden. Later books include *Línea del alba* (1936; Line of Dawn), *Poemas de guerra y esperanza* (1943; Poems of War and Hope), *La rosa primitiva* (1950; The Primitive Rose), *Estrella en alto* (1956; Star on High), and *Circuito interior* (1977; Interior Circuit). **Pablo Neruda** was the greatest influence on his work.

HUIDOBRO, VICENTE (Chile, 1893–1948). Poet. A key figure of the Latin American **avant-garde** whose work contributed to the break with **modernismo**. Even before he traveled to Paris in 1916, he had published the literary manifesto *Non serviam* (1914; I Will Not Serve) and begun to develop the poetics that would become known as **creacionismo**. Several collections of poetry had also appeared, notably *El espejo de agua* (1916; Water Mirror), which already indicated the direction his work would take. In Paris, he associated with leading figures of the French avant-garde and published both in French and Spanish. The themes of his poetry of this period, which includes *Poemas árcticos* (1918; Arctic Poems), stress the idea of fragmentation, and the format of his verses and the disposition of the text on the page break with all conventions. Huidobro also traveled frequently between Paris and Madrid, where he was one of the founders of **ultraísmo**. He returned to Chile in 1925 and published two major works several years later, *Temblor de cielo* (1931; Skyquake) and the work that is acknowledged as his masterpiece, *Altazor, o el viaje en paracaídas* (1931; *Altazor, or A Voyage in a Parachute*). This is a poem in seven cantos, deploying the techniques and poetics of the avant-garde, which uses the image of a fall to describe the discontinuity and disintegration of modern life and the creative drive of the poet in exploring the limits of expression. Huidobro also carried his theory of poetics into other genres and wrote several works of fiction as well as two plays. *See also* HERRERA Y REISSIG, JULIO; MORO, CÉSAR; OQUENDO DE AMAT, CARLOS; PARRA, NICANOR; TEITELBOIM, VOLODIA; THEATER.

– I –

IBÁÑEZ, ROBERTO (Uruguay, 1907–1978). Poet. Some of the universal themes of human existence, such as lost youth, love, death, and solitude, figured in his early work, although he later turned to more social themes. His collection *La frontera* (1961; The Frontier) received the first **Casa de las Américas** poetry prize. His other collections include *Olas* (1925; Waves), *La danza de los horizontes* (1927; Dance of the Horizons), and *Mitología de la sangre* (1939; Blood Mythology). He was a notable literary critic and one of the first in Uruguay to adopt a scholarly approach to literary commentary. He was married to **Sara de Ibáñez**.

IBÁÑEZ, SARA DE (Uruguay, 1909–1971). Poet. She wrote on nationalistic, patriotic themes taken from Uruguayan history as well as on war and apocalypse, death, nature, and love. Her publications include *Canto* (1940; Song), with a prologue by **Pablo Neruda**; *Canto a Montevideo* (1943; Song for Montevideo); *Artigas* (1952; Artigas); *La batalla* (1967, The Battle); and *Apocalipsis XX* (1970; Apocalypse XX). She was married to **Roberto Ibáñez**.

IBARBOUROU, JUANA DE (Uruguay, 1892–1979). Poet. Her poetry represents a move toward a simpler style after **modernismo**. She was a feminist writer who questioned the conservative middle class from within. Her work obtained wide popularity and earned her a number of national and international awards, including the title "Juana de América," granted in Montevideo in 1929. Nature and a sensually erotic lyricism predominate in her first book, *Las lenguas de diamante* (1919; Diamond Tongues), and a pantheistic attitude toward nature is sustained in her next two books, the first, *El cántaro fresco* (1920; The Refreshing Pitcher), in prose, the second, *Raíz salvaje* (1922; Wild Root), in verse. Between these two books and her later publications there is a gap of some 20 years, during which her poetry became more reflective, giving greater prominence to death, nostalgia, the passage of time, and biblical imagery, as in *Perdida* (1950; Lost), *Azor* (1953; Falcon), *Oro y tormenta* (1956; Gold and Tempest), and *Elegía* (1967; Elegy). Ibarbourou's other prose works also include *Estampas de la Biblia* (1934; Scenes from the Bible) and autobiographical sketches in *Chico Carlo* (1944; Young Carlo). *See also* VAZ FERREIRA, MARÍA EUGENIA.

IBARGÜENGOITIA, JORGE (Mexico, 1928–1983). Dramatist, novelist, short story writer, and journalist. He was a popular satirical writer whose literary career began in the **theater**. His early notable plays include *Susana y los jóvenes* (1954; Susana and the Youths) and *Clotilde en su casa* (1955; Clotilde at Home), both irreverent glimpses into the daily life of middle-class Mexico. Later dramas included *Antes varias esfinges* (1959; Before Various Sphinxes), *El tesoro perdido* (1960; The Lost Treasure), and *El atentado* (1964; The Assassination). *El atentado* deals with the 1928 assassination of Mexican president Álvaro Obregón (1920–1924), but it was not performed until 1974 because of its political content.

The same play was also the source of Ibargüengoitia's best-known novel, *Los relámpagos de agosto* (1964; *Lightning in August*), a spoof of the myths of the Mexican Revolution that won the author a **Casa de las Américas** prize. In this work, as in some of his other novels, he took historical events and transformed them into literature, treating them with humor, irony, and sarcasm, but often with a dark undertone. His other narratives in this vein include *Maten al león* (1969; Kill the Lion), a **dictator novel** written as a farce; *Estas ruinas que ves* (1975; The Ruins You See), an autobiographical satire on academic life in Guanajuato; *Las muertas* (1977; *The Dead Girls*), based on a celebrated real-life case about two brothel-keepers who were also serial killers; *Dos crímenes* (*Two Crimes*), another thriller; and *Los pasos de López* (1982; López's Steps), a novel developed from *La conspiración vendida* (1965; The Sold Out Conspiracy), another of the author's plays, a critique of revolutions led from above set at the beginning of the Mexican War of Independence.

Ibargüengoitia published several collections of short stories, of which *La ley de Herodes* (1967; Herod's Law), narratives about daily life in Mexico City, is the best known. His regular journalistic contributions to publications such as the Mexican **journal** *Vuelta* and the Mexican daily *Excelsior* have been collected and published in volumes such as *Viajes en la América ignota* (1972; Journeys Through Unknown America) and *Sálvese quien pueda* (1975; Every Man for Himself). Ibargüengoitia died in the **Madrid air disaster**.

ICAZA, JORGE (Ecuador, 1906–1978). Novelist. Although not a member of the **Grupo de Gayaquil**, his fiction was contemporary with theirs and he shared their objectives. He is best known for the novel *Huaspipungo* (1934; *Huasipungo: The Villagers*), a story of the frustrated attempts of an Indian community to retain possession of ancestral lands. It is a significant **indigenista** novel, albeit a deterministic and pessimistic portrayal of Native Americans in the social realist style of **naturalism**. The origins of the novel may be found in *Barro de la sierra* (1933; Clay of the Mountain), a collection of stories by Icaza that appeared the year before *Huasipungo*. In later novels, including *El chulla Romero y Flores* (1958; The Upstart Romero y Flores) and *Atrapados* (1973; Trapped), Icaza attempted to give a broader view of Ecuadorian culture and society, with particular attention to the figure of the *mestizo*. He also wrote for the **theater** and completed several plays before he turned to fiction, among them *Flagelo* (1932; Scourge), a drama that anticipates the content of the novel *Huasipungo*.

INCLÁN, LUIS G. (Mexico, 1816–1875). Novelist. He is known for his only work of fiction, *Astucia, el jefe de los hermanos de la hoja o los charros contrabandistas de la rama* (1965; Astucia, Chief of the Brotherhood of the Leaf or the Smuggler Horsemen of the Branch), about the adventures of a band of 19th-century tobacco smugglers in rural Mexico, told with an attention to detail characteristic of **costumbrismo**.

INDIANISMO. The word is used to refer to the conventions of representation of Latin American native peoples and their cultures by non-Indians in terms that subordinate Indians to preconceptions derived from the cultural perspective of the viewer. As such, the Indian is made a source of exoticism or nostalgia or becomes the projection of a cultural other. Indianismo has its origins in the earliest documents, or **chronicles**, of the conquest and colonization, which set the framework for how indigenous peoples were viewed during the colonial period and for a long time thereafter. The term is used in particular to designate the trends prevailing in literary works of 19th-century **romanticism** that idealized, exoticized, and demonized Indians following the influence of concepts such as primitivism and the "noble savage" and the writings of authors such as François-René de Chateaubriand (1768–1848), whose indianist novels *Atala* (1801) and *René* (1802) were widely read in Latin Amerca. Prominent indianista authors in Spanish America include **Esteban Echeverría (Argentina)**, **Juan León Mera (Ecuador)**, and **Juan Zorrilla de**

San Martín (**Uruguay**), whose works also embodied elements of the incipient nationalism of the 19th century.

Indianismo began in **Brazil** with **arcadianism** and poets such as **Basílio da Gama** and **Santa Rita Durão**, who saw native Brazilians only through the Enlightenment lens of the "noble savage" or the Christian perspective of heathens to be converted. Indianism became truly prominent during romanticism, which promoted the creation of national literature, culture, and identity following Brazil's independence from Portugal, achieved between 1808 and 1822. Most point to "Nênia" by Firmino Rodrigues Silva (1816–1879) as the first truly Indianist poem, followed by important figures such as the poets **Domingos José Gonçalves de Magalhães** and **Antônio Gonçalves Dias** and the novelist **José de Alencar**. Romantic indianism came under attack in the modernist period by **Oswald de Andrade**, who countered the romanticized "noble savage" with the figure of the cannibal in his "Manifesto Antropófago." **Mário de Andrade** and **Raul Bopp** also explored native motifs from a modernist, primitivist perspective. *See also* GUIMARÃES, BERNARDO JOAQUIM DA SILVA; HERRERA, FLAVIO; INDIGENISMO; NEO-INDIGENISMO.

INDIGENISMO. In contrast to 19th-century **indianismo**, which exoticized the native people and cultures of Latin America, indigenismo (derived from *indígena*, meaning "indigenous") highlighted their marginalized condition and the centuries of subjugation and exploitation endured by native populations. It belongs in particular to the first half of the 20th century and developed in Spanish America in the context of the rise of political philosophies that challenged the status quo and advocated more egalitarian societies.

The movement was strongest in the Andean region, where the indigenous population is demographically dominant. **Clorinda Matto de Turner** was a literary precursor, and the theory of indigenismo owed much to her fellow Peruvians **Manuel González Prada** and **José Carlos Mariátegui**. The principal indigenista novelists of the region were **Ciro Alegría (Peru)**, **Alcides Arguedas (Bolivia)**, and **Jorge Icaza (Ecuador)**. In **Mexico** the indigenista novel is often associated with the **novel of the Mexican Revolution**, in which a movement for social change is also documented, such as in the work of **Mariano Azuela, Gregorio López y Fuentes,** and **Mauricio Magdalena.** Other authors whose work has elements of indigenismo include **Flavio Herrera** and **Mario Monteforte Toledo (Guatemala), Miguel N. Lira** (Mexico), **Enrique López Albújar** (Peru), **Jesús Lara** (Bolivia), **Augusto Roa Bastos (Paraguay), Ángel Felicísimo Rojas** and members of the **Grupo de Gayaquil** (Ecuador), and **Patricio Manns (Chile).**

Although they promoted political change, most of these authors were not themselves indigenous and tended to write in manners that originated with 19th-century **costumbrismo, realism,** and **naturalism.** Some of this, at least with respect to approaches to indigenous questions and the style in which indigenista literature was written, would begin to change in the 1950s with **neo-indigenismo.** See also ARGUEDAS, JOSÉ MARÍA; HAYA DE LA TORRE, VÍCTOR RAÚL; PALACIO, PABLO.

INDIGENOUS TRADITIONS. Although the myths and legends of pre-Columbian times were expressed through oral traditions, ritual practices, and the monuments of preconquest America, they were not written down until European writing made this possible. Following the arrival of the Europeans, many of the stories were transcribed. The **chronicles,** especially those by mestizo authors, such as **Fernando de Alva Ixlilxochitl** in **Mexico** and **El Inca Garcilaso de la Vega** in **Peru,** are important sources. Other stories are preserved in dramatic form, such as *El güegüense* (**Nicaragua**), *Rabinal Achí* (**Guatemala**), and *Ollantay* (Peru), and some texts, such as the *Popol Vuh* and the *Books of Chilam Balam*, both from Guatemala, have important religious and historical significance. Although the Indian has figured as a topic of Brazilian literature in **romanticism** and **indianismo,** in **Brazilian modernism,** and especially **antropofagia,** indigenous cultures have only been thematized in fiction by writers such as **Darcy Ribeiro.** The oral traditions of indigenous peoples have had little impact on mainstream Brazilian literature. *See also* INDIGENISMO.

INGENIEROS, JOSÉ (Argentina, 1877–1925). Essayist. A psychiatrist by profession, he wrote a number of books related to his professional activities and was also one of the most significant voices of **positivism** in Argentina. His pertinent contributions in this area include *Sociología argentina* (1918; Argentinean Sociology) and *La evolución de las ideas argentinas* (1920; The Evolution of Argentinean Ideas).

IPARRAGUIRRE, SYLVIA (Argentina, 1947–). Novelist. She is best known for her **new historical novel** *Tierra del Fuego* (2000; *Tierra del Fuego: A Biography from the End of the World*), the story of Jemmy Button (ca. 1815–1864), a Fuegian taken to England by Robert FitzRoy, captain of the HMS *Beagle*, on which Charles Darwin made his momentous voyage to South America, and later returned to his homeland. The same story is the subject of a **historical novel** by **Benjamín Subercaseaux.** Iparraguirre's other works include *En el invierno de las ciudades* (1988; In the Winter of the Cities), *Probables lluvias por la noche* (1993; Probable Rain at Night), *El parque* (1996; The Park), and *El muchacho de los senos de goma* (2007; Boy with Rubber Breasts). Iparraguirre has also published essays on literature and painting.

ISAACS, JORGE (Colombia, 1837–1895). Novelist. Although he produced a small body of poetry, published in *Poesías* (1864; Poems), his reputation rests on the novel *María* (1867; *María: A South American Romance*). This is a significant work of Spanish American **romanticism** and was the most widely read Spanish American novel of the 19th century. Within the convention of a story of love thwarted by separation and tragic death, borrowed in many respects from French sources, the novel also explores the relationships connecting humanity both to the natural world and to the worlds of religion, politics, and the social order.

IVO, LEDO (Brazil, 1924–). Essayist, journalist, short story writer, and poet. Born in the Northeast but residing most of his life in Rio, Ivo is primarily known as an editor of the **journal** *Orfeu* during the polemical neomodernist wave known as the **Generation of '45.** His main poetry books, which revive traditional forms such as the sonnet, include *Ode e Elegia* (1945; Ode and Elegy) and *Antologia Poética* (1991; Selected Poetry). Among his narrative works are *Ninho de Cobras: Uma História Mal Contada* (1973; *Snake's Nest or A Tale*

Badly Told), which recalls life in the author's native state of Alagoas, and the short-story collection *O Flautim e Outras Histórias Cariocas* (1966; The Piccolo and Other Tales from Rio de Janeiro). He has also produced the essays *A Morte do Brasil* (1984; The Death of Brazil) and *A Experiência da Imaginação* (1991; The Experience of Imagination).

IXTLILXOCHITL, FERNANDO DE ALVA (Mexico, 1568–1648). Chronicler. He was a mestizo, a descendant of the emperors of Mexico and the lords of Texcoco, who wrote two **chronicles**, the *Relación histórica de la nación tulteca* (1600–1608; Historical Narrative of the Toltec Nation) and the *Historia chichimeca* (1610–1640; History of the Chichimecas), both of which drew significantly on **indigenous traditions** for the pre-Columbian part of their narrative.

– J –

JABUTI PRIZE. Founded in 1958 by Edgard Cavalheiro, the Prêmio Jabuti (literally "Tortoise Prize") is one of **Brazil**'s most prestigious book awards. The jabuti, a kind of tortoise native to Brazil, was picked as a symbol to honor book authors and publishers because in Brazilian folklore it represents patience and tenacity in overcoming obstacles. There are 20 categories, including the major literary genres, **children's literature**, and other areas in the sciences and humanities. Winners for the short story include **Caio Fernando Abreu**, **Marçal Aquino**, **Hilda Hilst**, **Rubem Fonseca**, and **Lygia Fagundes Telles**; for poetry, **Francisco Alvim**, **Affonso Ávila**, **Carlito Azevedo**, **Haroldo de Campos**, **Armando Freitas Filho**, **Sebastião Uchoa Leite**, **Adélia Prado**, **Bruno Tolentino**; and for the novel, Rubem Fonseca, **Milton Hatoum**, and **Silviano Santiago**.

JAIMES FREYRE, RICARDO (Bolivia, 1863–1933). Poet. He was born in **Peru** and spent a significant part of his early life in **Argentina**, where he collaborated with **Rubén Darío** and **Leopoldo Lugones** and became an important contributor to **modernismo**. Although he wrote short stories and other works in prose, he is best known for two collections of verse, both influenced by European symbolism and **parnassianism**. The first, and most celebrated, of these collections is *Castalia bárbara* (1899; Barbarous Castalia), set in Nordic mythology and landscape, on the theme of death and the conflict between pagan and Christian values. Death also figures in his second collection, *Los sueños son vida* (1917; Dreams Are Life), but is approached from a more universal point of view, without the Nordic associations of his earlier verse. Jaimes Freyre was one of the first practitioners of free verse in Spanish and a theorist who expressed his thoughts on poetic practice in *Leyes de la versificación castellana* (1912; Rules for Spanish Versification). He also wrote some fiction and several historical works, notably on Tucumán (Argentina), as well as several dramas. These included *Los conquistadores* (The Conquerors), on the Spanish conquest, and the biblical drama *La hija de Jefthé* (1889; Jephtha's Daughter), both written in verse and in the style of Spanish romantic **theater**.

JARAMILLO LEVI, ENRIQUE (Panama, 1940–). Short story writer. Collections of his stories include *Duplicaciones* (1973; Duplications and Other Stories), *La voz despalabrada* (1986; Voice Without Words), *El fabricante de máscaras* (1992; The Mask Maker), *Tocar fondo* (1996; Touch Bottom), *En un abrir y cerrar de ojos* (2002; In a Twinkling of an Eye), *Híbridos* (2004; Hybrids), and *Para más señas* (2005; To Be More Precise). Jaramillo Levi has also edited a large number of collections of short stories by other authors.

JAURETCHE, ARTURO (Argentina, 1904–1974). Essayist. He was a prominent conservative intellectual and cofounder of Fuerza de Orientación Radical de la Joven Argentina (FORJA; Force for the Radical Orientation of Young Argentina). He found favor in the first government of **Juan Domingo Perón**. He turned to writing more fully after a fall from grace in 1951 and produced a number of commentaries on Argentinean culture and society, including *El medio pelo de la sociedad argentina* (1966; The Middle Brow in Argentinean Society) and *Manual de zonceras argentinas* (1968; Guide to Argentinean Follies).

JESÚS MARTÍNEZ, JOSÉ DE (Panama, 1929–1991). Dramatist, essayist, and poet. Although born in **Nicaragua**, he was Panamanian by adoption and taught mathematics at the Universidad de Panamá. His biography *Mi general Torrijos* (1987; General Torrijos) of the Panamanian dictator Omar Torrijos (1929–1981), written after serving as his adviser, received a **Casa de las Américas** prize. He also wrote more than a dozen plays exploring themes related to his background in philosophy and mathematics, such as the nature of being and religion, the soul and solitude, death, communication, and time and space. His most successful plays included *La mentira* (1954; The Lie), *Caifás* (1961; Caiphas), *El juicio final* (1962; The Last Judgement), and *Segundo asalto* (1968; Second Assault). *See also* THEATER.

JEWISH WRITING. Writers whose work displays an awareness of their Jewish heritage commonly approach their identity by examining the combination of Jewishness with the life and culture embodied in particular Latin American nationalities. One of the earliest examples is **Alberto Gerchunoff**'s *Los gauchos judíos* (1910; *The Jewish Gauchos of the Pampas*). The same trend is apparent in more recent authors, where it may also be combined with a search for roots, such as in work by **Margo Glantz** (**Mexico**) or **Luisa Futoransky** (**Argentina**). See also ARIDJIS, HOMERO; BRAZIL; GELMAN, JUAN; GOLDEMBERG, ISAAC; PERU; PORZECANSKI, TERESA; SCLIAR, MOACYR; SZICHMAN, MARIO; URUGUAY.

JIMÉNEZ RUEDA, JULIO (Mexico, 1896–1960). Dramatist, novelist, and essayist. As a dramatist, he wrote in a variety of styles. *Tempestad en las costumbres* (1922; An Upset in Customs) is a comedy of manners; *La silueta de humo* (1927; The Smoke Silhouette) is a farce; *Toque de diana* (1928; Reveille) is a drama about the Mexican Revolution; and *Miramar* (1943; Miramar) is a historical play about the Empress Carlota of Mexico (1864–1867). He is perhaps better known for his **historical novels**, set mainly in the colonial period. These include *Sor Adoración del Divino Verbo* (1923; Sister Adoration of the Divine Word), *Moisén* (1924; Moses), and *Novelas coloniales* (1949; Colonial Novels). As an essayist, Jiménez Rueda is known primarily as a critic of Mexican literature, including studies of the **theater** of **Juan Ruiz de Alarcón**.

JOURNALS, MAGAZINES, NEWSPAPERS, AND PERIODI-CALS. Although books are the form most commonly associated with the production and distribution of literature, other print media have also had important, long-standing connections. Since at least the beginning of the 19th century in Latin America, literature has figured significantly in the diverse world of printing and publication under the heading of journals, magazines, newspapers, and periodicals, an eclectic collection of different types of publications that often overlap with respect to their function and form.

Literary journals have had an important role as a focal point for writers with interests in common and have served to give a voice to particular literary groups or movements. As vehicles for the dissemination of information relating to literature, they are specifically dedicated to the publication of literary texts, book reviews, manifestos and theory, commentary, and criticism. Although many of them have been short-lived, others have proven to be more durable. Cultural and news magazines and periodicals, with broader mandates governing their content, have also considered literature within their purview, and their impact has been no less than that of newspapers since the advent of the mass circulation press in the late 19th century. Not only have newspapers contributed to the circulation of creative and critical writing, both in their daily columns and through the publication of literary supplements, but the steady source of income they gave to writers advanced the professionalization of writing in a way that might not otherwise have been possible.

Brazil's first periodical, *As Variedades ou Ensaios de Literatura* (Varieties or Essays on Literature), was an ephemeral publication that appeared in Bahia in 1812. The first major literary journal was *Niterói: Revista Brasiliense* (1836; Niteroi: Brazilian Review), founded by **Domingos José Gonçalves de Magalhães**, which helped officially introduce the ideas of **romanticism** into the country. In Spanish America, periodic publications were associated with the movements for political independence and counted a number of significant literary figures among their founders and contributors. One of the most celebrated was **José Joaquín Fernández de Lizardi**, also known as El Pensador Mexicano (The Mexican Thinker), a pen name he took from the title of one of his periodicals. During the 19th century **costumbrismo**, which promoted a greater taste for **realism** in writing, was a feature of newspapers and periodicals and is associated with authors such as **José Álvarez (Argentina)**, **Manuel González Zeledón (Costa Rica)**, **Guillermo Prieto (Mexico)**, and **José Joaquín Vallejo (Chile)**, who wrote regularly for the press. In the 20th century it was replaced in due course by the **chronicle**, a daily column of commentary and narrative that has enhanced the reputation of many authors ever since, including **Jorge Ibargüengoitia**, **Ramón López Velarde**, and **Carlos Monsiváis** in Mexico; **Manuel Bandeira**, **João do Rio**, and **Fernando Sabino** in Brazil; **Enrique Bernardo Núñez** in **Venezuela**; **Clemente Palma** in **Peru**; **Elena María Walsh** in Argentina, and **Joaquín Edwards Bello** in Chile. For all these writers, whether costumbristas or chroniclers, the narratives and commentaries that first appeared in the columns of the press were subsequently collected and published as books.

Both in Brazil and Spanish America, literary journals are especially associated with the various **avant-garde** movements in literature that emerged in the early decades of the 20th century. One of the signature movements of **Brazilian modernism, antropofagia**, gave rise to the *Revista de Antropofagia* (1928–1929; Cannibal Review), cofounded by **Oswald de Andrade**, **Raul Bopp**, and **António de Alcântara Machado**, to which **Murilo Mendes** also contributed. Other journals of the same era include *Klaxon* (1922–1923; Klaxon), in which Oswald de Andrade also published, as did **Sérgio Milliet da Costa e Silva**; *Estética* (1924–1925; Aesthetics), of which **Sérgio Buarque de Holanda** was a cofounder; *A Revista* (1925; The Review), founded by **Carlos Drummond de Andrade**; and *Festa* (1927; Feast), cofounded by **Cecília Meireles**. Later developments of Brazilian modernism, such as **concrete poetry**, also had their journals, such as the poetry review *Noigandres* (founded in 1952), which published work by **Pedro Xisto** and was edited by **Augusto de Campos, Haroldo de Campos**, and **Décio Pignatari**. The journal *Invenção*, with **Paulo Leminski** as a contributor, was also founded by this group, and **Glauco Mattoso** conceived the parodic *Jornal Dobrabil, 1977–1981* (2001; *Foldable News*), a mimeographed newspaper.

In avant-garde **Mexico, Los Contemporáneos** and **estridentismo** were both represented by journals. *Contemporáneos* (1928–1931; Contemporaries), the voice of the former, was edited by **Bernardo**

Ortiz de Montellano. The estridentistas published in *Irradiador* (1923; Radiator) and *Horizonte* (1926–1927; Horizon), under the direction of **Manuel Maples Arce** and **Germán List Arzubide.** *Martín Fierro* and *Proa* (Prow), both founded in 1924, under the auspices of **ultraísmo** in **Argentina,** included writings by **Jorge Luis Borges, Oliverio Girondo, Eduardo González Lanuza, Raúl González Tuñón,** and **Conrado Nalé Roxlo,** among many others.

Since the 1920s and 1930s, a number of magazines and periodicals, appealing to a wider audience than journals having a somewhat narrowly defined literary purpose, have flourished in Latin America and are among some of the continent's most significant undertakings in publishing. In Mexico, *Plural* (1971–1976) and *Vuelta* (founded 1976; Returned), both founded by **Nobel Prize** winner **Octavio Paz,** have attracted wide attention. The reputation of *Repertorio Americano* became well established beyond the borders of Costa Rica, where it was founded in 1919 by **Joaquín García Monge; Yolanda Oreamuno** contributed to it. *Zona Franca,* founded in 1964 by **Juan Liscano** and edited by him for almost 20 years, was a prominent journal in **Venezuela.** *Amauta* (1926–1930), established by **José Carlos Mariátegui** in Lima, **Peru,** was an important cultural and political journal in its time. *Marcha,* in Montevideo, **Uruguay,** fulfilled a similar role and featured such notable figures as **Ángel Rama** and **Emir Rodríguez Monegal** among its writers. One of the most prestigious long-running periodicals in South America of importance for literature was *Sur,* founded by **Victoria Ocampo** in 1931 and published in Argentina. In addition to Jorge Luis Borges, its contributors included **Alberto Girri, Eduardo Mallea,** and **Héctor A. Murena.** The tradition established by *Sur* is maintained today by *Punto de Vista,* one of Argentina's major cultural periodicals, founded in 1978 by **Beatriz Sarlo** and still edited by her. In Brazil, *Revista do Brasil,* founded in 1916, is a long-standing publication with a nationalist focus and has had many notable contributors, including **Dinah Silveira de Queirós** and **José Bento Monteiro Lobato.**

Daily newspapers in Latin America, as in other countries of the world, are often prominent social institutions with significant roles in political and cultural life. Their journalists, correspondents, and reporters include many who have also made a name in literature. In Mexico, **Vicente Leñero** wrote for *Excélsior* and **Rafael F. Muñoz** for *El Universal*. In Brazil, **Guilherme de Almeida, Moacir Amân-cio,** and **João Ubaldo Ribeiro** wrote for *O Estado do São Paulo*, and **Nelson Ascher** and **Bernardo Carvalho** for *Folha de São Paulo*. **Marco Denevi** and **Alberto Gerchunoff** published in the Buenos Aires daily *La Nación*. In Chile, **Jorge Edwards** contributed to *El Mercurio*. Indeed, the number of literary authors who have written for newspapers or have had extended careers in journalism is legion and includes major figures such as **Roberto Arlt** (Argentina), **Joaquim Maria Machado de Assis** (Brazil), **Rosario Castellanos** (Mexico), **Euclides da Cunha** (Brazil), **Gabriel García Márquez (Colombia), Clarice Lispector** (Brazil), **Tomás Eloy Martínez** (Argentina), **Gabriela Mistral** (Chile), **Elena Poniatowska** (Mexico), and **Mario Vargas Llosa** (Peru).

The connection of literature with newspapers is also maintained through the literary supplements, often published weekly, such as the one published with *Minas Gerais* in Brazil, or *La cultura en México*, a supplement of the newspaper *Siempre!*, with which Carlos Monsiváis was associated for a number of years. Through their supplements and their daily columns, the newspapers also publish poetry and fiction. Many of the short stories of **Horacio Quiroga** (Uruguay), **Benito Lynch** (Argentina), and **Baldomero Lillo** (Chile) first appeared in newspapers. And through serial publication, the novels of authors such as **Manuel Antônio Almeida** (Brazil), **José Milla y Vidaurre** (Guatemala), and **Mariano Azuela, Manuel Payno,** and **Justo Sierra** (Mexico), as well as many European authors, first found their way to readers through the pages of the daily press. It is a tradition still maintained today. *See also* ACOSTA DE SAMPER, SOLEDAD; ALMEIDA, JÚLIA LOPES DE; ÁLVAREZ GARDEAZÁBAL, GUSTAVO; CABELLO DE CARBONERA, MERCEDES; CARBALLIDO, EMILIO; CORTÁZAR, JULIO; DIAS, ANTÔNIO GONÇALVES; EGUREN, JOSÉ MARÍA; FREYRE, GILBERTO DE MELO; FRÍAS, HERIBERTO; GALVÃO, PATRÍCIA; GROUSSAC, PAUL; GRUPO DE FLORIDA; GUIMARAENS, ALPHONSUS DE; IVO, LEDO; KILKERRY, PEDRO; LEITE, SEBASTIÃO UCHOA; MACHADO, DUDA; MAGGI, CARLOS; MOLINA, ENRIQUE; MONTALVO, JUAN; MUJICA LÁINEZ, MANUEL; ODIO, EUNICE; PARDO Y ALIAGA, FELIPE; RAMOS, GRACILIANO; RAMOS SUCRE,

JOSÉ ANTONIO; REBOLLEDO, EFRÉN; REGO CAVALCANTI, JOSÉ LINS DO; SCHMIDT, AUGUSTO FREDERICO; SOCA, SUSANA; SOLOGUREN, JAVIER; SORIANO, OSVALDO; SOUSÂNDRADE, JOAQUIM DE; TEITELBOIM, VOLODIA; TIMERMAN, JACOBO; USLAR PIETRI, ARTURO; VALLE, RAFAEL HELIODORO; VERÍSSIMO DIAS DE MATOS, JOSÉ; ZAPIOLA, JOSÉ.

JUANA INÉS DE LA CRUZ, SOR (Mexico, 1651–1695). Poet, dramatist, and prose writer. She is one of the major figures of Mexican and Latin American colonial literature and one of Latin America's most significant **women** writers. She was a precocious child and had already established her literary reputation at the viceregal court in Mexico before she resolved to enter a convent in 1667 to pursue her intellectual vocation. As a woman in a man's world, however, her success was made a source of conflict among both secular and religious authorities, and she eventually felt compelled to abandon her writing. As a poet of the colonial **baroque**, Sor Juana's highly intellectual verse stands alongside the work of the great Spanish poets of the 16th and 17th centuries. In her sonnets and *Primero sueño* (1692; First Dream), she pursues the themes of the inevitability of death and the transience of human life, but she also wrote songs (*villancicos*), ballads (*romances*), and other verse in a lighter vein.

Sor Juana's writing for the **theater** has a similar wide range and includes both religious and secular dramas. *El divino Narciso* (1690; *The Divine Narcissus*) is an allegorical *auto* based on the classical story of Echo and Narcissus as a vehicle for dramatizing Catholic teachings. By contrast, *Los empeños de una casa* (1683; Family Obligations) and *Amor es más laberinto* (1689; Love the Greatest Labyrinth) are plays that present traditional love intrigues in the style of those performed in the Spanish court of the late 17th century. Among Sor Juana's prose writings, her *Respuesta a Sor Filotea de la Cruz* (1691; *Answer to Sister Filotea de la Cruz*) is viewed today as an important early-modern feminist essay. It is a declaration of her religious faith and her commitment to an intellectual life, which is all the more remarkable for having been written in the late 17th century by a woman and a member of a religous order. Her life and work have been the subject of several movies, and the bibliography of interpretations of her life is extensive, including books by **Octavio Paz** and **Isabel Allende**. *See also* GLANTZ, MARGO; NERVO, AMADO; REIN, MERCEDES.

JUARROZ, ROBERTO (Argentina, 1925–1995). Poet. He published 14 collections between 1958 and 1997, each titled *Poesía vertical* (Vertical Poetry) and numbered consecutively, the last being *Décimocuarta poesía vertical* (Vertical Poetry Number Fourteen). The poems are an exploration of the uses of language and are often quite abstract, although the impact of their originality diminishes in the later volumes. Juárroz has been highly praised by **Octavio Paz** and **Julio Cortázar**.

– K –

KILKERRY, PEDRO (Brazil, 1885–1917). Poet. The son of an Irishman and a Brazilian mestizo woman, Kilkerry was born in Bahia. One of the main exponents of **symbolism** in Brazil, he studied law, but led a penniless bohemian life, suffering from tuberculosis and writing poetry, a veritable *poète maudit* who died during a windpipe operation. Kilkerry translated Tristan Corbière (1845–1875) and developed a distinct "colloquial-ironic" style in the manner inaugurated by Jules Laforgue (1860–1887). He is the most radical and modern symbolist poet of Brazil, eliciting comparisons with Arthur Rimbaud (1854–1891) and Stéphane Mallarmé (1842–1898). Thanks to his poetic explorations of the unconscious and the world of dreams, he has been seen as a precursor of **surrealism**. His poetry also has a mystical and intellectual vein despite its apparent sentimentalism. He died without having published any books, although he had contributed to the periodicals *Os Anais*, *A Voz do Povo*, and *Nova Cruzada*. Largely ignored for years, his poems were collected in 1970 by **Augusto de Campos** in *Revisão de Kilkerry* (1970; Revision of Kilkerry). Other works can be found in Jackson de Figueiredo, *Humilhados e Luminosos* (1921; Humiliated and Luminous) and Andrade Murici, *Panorama do Movimento Simbolista Brasileiro* (1952; Panorama of the Brazilian Symbolist Movement).

KORDON, BERNARDO (Argentina, 1915–2002). Novelist and short story writer. He inherited the brand of social realism commonly associated with the **Grupo de Boedo** and wrote about working-class Buenos Aires with humor and authenticity, using a colloquial language that successfully captures the reality of daily life. His fiction includes *La vuelta de Rocha* (1936; The Bend in the Rocha), *Un horizonte de cemento* (1940; Cement Horizon), *Reina del Plata* (1946; Queen of the River Plate), *Hacele bien a la gente* (1968; Do Good to People), and *Adiós pampa mía* (1978; Farewell My Pampa). Several of Kordon's stories have been turned into films. Kordon was also the only Argentinean whose interest in China's communist revolution was followed by a visit to the country and the publication of several books about it, one based on an interview with Mao Tse-tung.

– L –

LA ONDA. Meaning "on the same wave-length" or "in the groove," the term was coined by **Margo Glantz**, who used it to refer to a tendency in narrative in **Mexico** of the 1960s and 1970s. It principal exponents were **José Agustín** and **Gustavo Sainz**, whose fiction, both in its language and content, represents the changes in Mexico City society brought on by new forms of popular culture, the sexual revolution, and new patterns in the use of drugs reflected in the lifestyle of middle-class adolescents.

LA VIOLENCIA. The term is used in **Colombia** to refer to a period of civil conflict between 1948 and 1965. Although it had roots in the long-standing animosity between Liberals and Conservatives and was preceded by an intensification of the hostility between them, it was sparked by the 9 April 1948 assassination of the liberal leader Jorge Eliécer Gaitán and the three days of rioting in Bogotá that followed and became known as *el bogotazo*. This period of conflict is represented most notably in the fiction of **Gabriel García Márquez** and in the work of the Colombians **Gustavo Álvarez Gardeazábal**, **Eduardo Caballero Calderón**, **Manuel Mejía Vallejo**, and **Manuel Zapata Olivella**.

LAFOURCADE, ENRIQUE (Chile, 1927–). Novelist. He is a popular novelist who has written on a wide variety of themes. *La fiesta del rey Acab* (1959; *King Acab's Feast*) is a satirical **dictator novel** based on the life of the Dominican Rafael Leónidas Trujillo (1930–1938, 1942–1952). *Palomita blanca* (1971; Little White Dove), about class differences, was a **best seller** in Chile, and *El Gran Taimado* (1984; The Great Deceiver), an anti-Augusto Pinochet novel that got the author into trouble with the regime, was also very widely read. Other novels include *Frecuencia modulada* (1968; Modulated Frequency); *Hoy está solo mi corazón* (1990; Today My Heart Is Lonely); and, more recently, *El inesperado* (2004; Unexpected), about the life in Africa of the French poet Arthur Rimbaud (1854–1891). Lafourcade also contributes editorials and **chronicles** regularly to the Santiago daily *El Mercurio* and frequently appears on Chilean television.

LAMBORGHINI, OSVALDO (Argentina, 1940–1985). Novelist and poet. Although his work has been variously associated with the **neo-baroque** and the late **avant-garde** of the 1960s and 1970s, it is difficult to classify. His writing appears as a collage of fragments that makes all sense of narrative impossible and goes against all conventions in its obscenity and representation of violence. Only three of his books were published during his lifetime: *El fiord* (1969; The Fjord), a novel about politics in 1960s Argentina; *Sobregondi retrocede* (1973; Sobregondi Retires), a long prose poem; and *Poemas* (1980; Poems). Other volumes have appeared since his death, notably *Novelas y cuentos* (1988; Novels and Tales), compiled and introduced by **César Aira**.

LANDA, DIEGO DE (Mexico, 1524–1579). Chronicler. He was a Franciscan friar and among the first missionaries sent to the Yucatán, a province of which he would eventually be appointed bishop (1571). His **chronicle** *Relación de las cosas de Yucatán* (ca. 1566; *Yucatan Before and After the Conquest*) is an account of the language, writing, religion, and culture of the Maya. Although the *Relación* is an important document for understanding the Maya at the time of the conquest, Landa also contributed to the destruction of their culture through his zealous pursuit of the objectives of the Spanish conquest and the conversion of indigenous people to Christianity.

LANGE, NORAH (Argentina, 1906–1972). Poet, novelist, and autobiographer. As a poet and **avant-garde** writer, she was associated with **ultraísmo** and the circle of **Jorge Luis Borges** and **Oliverio Girondo**, whom she married in 1946. Their home became a hub for artists and intellectuals, repeating the situation in her parents' home when she was a child. Her collections of verse include *La calle de la tarde* (1925; The Street in the Evening) and *Los días y las noches* (1927; Days and Nights), both exemplifying the aesthetics of ultraísmo. Among her early novels were *Voz de la vida* (1927; Voice of Life), an epistolary novel about female passion and adultery, and *45 días y 30 marineros* (1933; 45 Days and 30 Sailors), the story of a **woman** on board a ship bound for Oslo from Buenos Aires. In *Personas en la sala* (1950; People in the Room) and *Los dos retratos* (1956; Two Portraits), she wrote stories about the self, the enclosed female world, and the realization of identity through literary creation. Her published work also includes *Discursos* (1942; Speeches) and *Estimados congéneres* (1968; Dear Friends), collections of addresses given at the salons held at her home, and a notable autobiography, *Cuadernos de infancia* (1937; Childhood Notebooks), narrated anonymously, but drawn from her own life, which became standard reading in Argentinean schools for several decades.

LARA, JESÚS (Bolivia, 1898–1980). Novelist. A militantly political writer, one of his first books was a memoir of the Chaco War (1932–1935), *Repete, diario de un hombre que fue a la guerra del Chaco* (1938; Repete, Diary of a Man Who Fought in the Chaco War). He then wrote a series of novels in the mode of **indigenismo** in defense of Bolivian Indians: *Suruni* (1943), *Yanakuna* (1952), *Yawarninchij: nuestra sangre* (1959; Yawarninchij: Our Blood), *Sinchikay* (1962), *Llalliypacha: tiempo de vencer* (1965; Llalliypacha: Time to Triumph), and *Sujnapura* (1965). His writing on this theme extended to essays about indigenous culture and the compilation of literature in Quechua. In a collection of short stories, *Ñancahuazú* (1969), he also wrote about the death of Ernesto "Che" Guevara (1967) in Bolivia.

LARRETA, ENRIQUE (Argentina, 1873–1961). Novelist. He is best known for *La gloria de don Ramiro* (1908; *The Glory of Don Ramiro*), a **historical novel** set in the Spanish city of Ávila in the time of Felipe II (1556–1598), in which the protagonist is caught between his Christian and Moorish heritage, the aesthetic life of religion and the call of love and adventure. The description of exotic objects and the sensuality of some of its scenes have made the novel one of the most significant examples of **modernismo** in prose. Larreta's second novel, *Zogoibi* (1926; Zogoibi), published almost 20 years later, is a story of the Argentinean pampas in the tradition of **gaucho literature** that praises the virtues of the author's homeland, contrasting the ways of the upper class with the simple life of country folk. His subsequent writing, including four more novels, a collection of verse, and several works for the **theater**, developed both contemporary and historical themes from Spain and Argentina, but without repeating the success of his first novel.

LARS, CLAUDIA (El Salvador, 1899–1974). Poet. Although born Carmen Brannon Beers, she wrote under her pseudonym. In the course of several volumes of poetry, her thematic interests developed from the personal, intimate experiences of her own life to more universal philosophical issues and social questions. In *Estrellas en el pozo* (1934; Stars in the Well), she writes about poetry itself and about motherhood. *Canción redonda* (1937; Rounded Song), her second book of verse, is about romantic love. In *Romances de norte y sur* (1946; Ballads of North and South), she adopts a greater sense of social consciousness, particularly in her acknowledgment of her Native American heritage. Later collections, *Sonetos* (1947; Sonnets), *Donde llegan los pasos* (1953; Where the Steps Lead), and *Sobre el ángel y el hombre* (1962; About the Angel and the Man), are representative of a spiritual quest through the exploration of love and religion. Lars also contributed to the development of **children's literature** through a number of books of verse for children, including *La casa de vidrio* (1942; The Glass House), *Escuela de pájaros* (1955; School for Birds), *Canciones* (1960; Songs), and *Girasol* (1962; Sunflower), an anthology that includes poems for children by her and other well-known writers.

LAS CASAS, BARTOLOMÉ DE (Spain, 1484–1566). Chronicler. He first traveled to the Americas in 1502, where he witnessed some of the early stages of the conquest and colonization. In 1522 he joined the Dominican Order; by that time, he had already begun to express sympathy for the suffering of indigeous populations. In due course, he became their most prominent defender and an advocate for reform, a point of view documented in his **chronicles**. His *Brevísima relación de la destrucción de las Indias* (written 1542; published 1552; *A Brief Account of the Destruction of the Indies*) was widely read and frequently cited to criticize the conduct of the Spanish in the Americas in what became known as the "black legend" of the conquest. In a longer work, *Historia general de las Indias* (written 1527–1562; published 1875; *History of the Indies*), Las Casas covers the years 1492–1520 in three volumes, giving most attention to the time of Columbus and the period of which Las Casas was himself a witness. The diary of the first voyage (1492) of **Christopher Columbus** has survived, in effect, only through the edited transcription Las Casas included in his chronicle.

LASSO DE LA VEGA, GABRIEL LOBO (Spain, ca. 1558–1615). Poet. Although he does not appear to have ever traveled to the Americas, his work figures among the **chronicles** and **epic poetry** of the New World thanks to two verse narratives of the exploits of Hernán Cortés, *Cortés valeroso* (written 1582–1584; Stout Cortés) and *Mexicana* (1594; Mexicana). Lasso de la Vega also figures in the history of **theater** in Spain for the tragedies he wrote in a classical style.

LASTARRIA, JOSÉ VICTORINO (Chile, 1817–1888). Essayist and short story writer. He is known as Chile's first fiction writer for his short story "El mendigo" ("The Beggar"). He was also a prominent intellectual in 19th-century Chile and an advocate of **positivism**. His writings that are read most today are *Miscelánea literaria* (1855; Literary Miscellany), for his short stories, and *Recuerdos literarios* (1878; *Literary Memoirs*), for the insights into intellectual life in Chile of the mid-1800s, written by one who was a disciple of **Andrés Bello** in his youth and a friend of **Rubén Darío** when he was much older.

LEITE, SEBASTIÃO UCHOA (Brazil, 1935–2003). Poet, essayist, and translator. A contemporary poet who incorporated modernist techniques into his poetry without major innovations, Uchoa Leite won the **Jabuti Prize** for his book *Antilogia* (1979; Antilogy). He also was partly responsible for editing the eclectic poetry **journal** *José* in the 1970s and translated the work of Lewis Carroll (1832–1898), Julio Cortázar (1914–1984), Octavio Paz (1914–1998), and Stendhal (1783–1842), among others. Other books of poetry include *A Uma Incógnita* (1991; To an Unknown), *A Ficção Vida* (1993; The Fiction Life), *A Espreita* (2000; Spying), and *A Regra Secreta* (2002; The Secret Rule).

LEMEBEL, PEDRO (Chile, 1952–). Novelist and essayist. Both as a writer and a performance artist, he addresses reality from a **homosexual** perspective. His first book of fiction, *Incontables* (1986; Untellable Tales), presents writing as a form of transvestism with which to deal with homosexual desire. Lemebel's first novel, *Tengo miedo torero* (2001; *My Tender Matador*), which has made his name more widely known outside Chile, is set in Santiago in 1986. It is the story of a gay male known only as La Loca del Frente (The Queen of the Corner), who comes under the sway of a student revolutionary plotting against President Augusto Pinochet (1974–1990).

Lemebel is also well known for his humourously critical **chronicles** of life in Santiago, of which he has published several volumes. *La esquina es mi corazón: crónica urbana* (1995; The Corner Is My Heart: Urban Chronicle) focuses on marginalization and poverty in the neoliberal city, where gays from the poor suburbs are seen as symbols of waste and injustice. In *Loco afán: crónicas del sidario* (1996; Queer Desire: AIDS Chronicles), he writes about victims of AIDS in Chile, and in *Adiós, Mariquita Linda* (2004; Farewell, Pretty Mary), he presents 30 autobiographical chronicles of queer life in the city.

LEMINSKI, PAULO (Brazil, 1944–1989). Poet, essayist, and translator. Born in Curitiba of Polish and Afro-Brazilian ancestry, Leminski became an important cultural icon of the bohemian and rebellious generation of the 1970s and 1980s in Brazil. He was a popular musician and a black belt judo instructor as well as a poet. His poetic career began under the sign of **concrete poetry**, publishing texts influenced by the visual in the **journal** *Invenção*. Later he broke with this tendency, turning toward a more colloquial poetry that also dialogued with popular culture, a trend known as **poesia marginal**. Leminski's irony, however, distanced him from any particular tendency and allowed him to follow a unique path. His early works, mostly published by a self-run small press, are gathered under the titles *Caprichos e Relaxos* (1983; Capricious and Relaxed) and *Distraídos Venceremos* (1987; Distracted We Shall Prevail). His attention to sound and conciseness in poetry is indebted to his involvement with popular music and the Japanese poetic form haiku, which he studied and favored in his writing. Besides Japanese, Leminski knew English and French and translated writers such as Alfred Jarry (1873–1907), James Joyce (1882–1941), Samuel Beckett (1906–1989), and Yukio Mishima (1925–1970).

Leminski's erudition and intellectual acumen were legendary, only matched by his inventiveness, as seen in his "biography essays": *Matsuó Bashô* (1983; Matsuo Basho), *Jesus a. C.* (1984; Jesus BC), and *Cruz e Sousa* (1983; Cruz e Sousa), about **João da Cruz e Sousa**. Perhaps his most daring work is *Catatau* (1975; Catatau), an exuberant, **avant-garde** narrative about a fictitious visit of René Descartes (1596–1651) to Brazil in a style influenced by the **baroque**. Leminski was a prolific author, yet many of his works were out of print for a long time before being republished. His native city, Curitiba, hosts a yearly event in his honor called "Perhappiness" (from one of his one-word poems). A bohemian and laborious intellectual who often experimented with drugs and alcohol, which undermined his health, Leminski died before his time.

LEÑERO, VICENTE (Mexico, 1933–). Novelist, dramatist, and journalist. He often plays with different genres and styles in his novels. His first success was *Los albañiles* (1963; The Bricklayers), a suspense novel about the killing of a night watchman. This was followed by *Estudio Q* (1965; Studio Q), which explores the relationship between reality and performance for television, and *El garabato* (1967; The Scrawl), a narrative framed as the story of a critic who is reading a novel. In other novels, fiction and nonfiction sometimes overlap: *Los periodistas* (1978; The Journalists) is partly drawn from his own experiences as one of several writers ousted from the newspaper *Excélsior*; *El evangelio según Lucas Gavilán* (1979; The Gospel According to Lucas Gavilán) is a rewriting of Saint Luke's gospel from the perspective of liberation theology; and *La gota de agua* (1983; The Drop of Water) is a comic domestic **chronicle** about water shortages in Mexico City.

As a dramatist, Leñero was one of the first exponents of documentary drama in Mexico, in works such as *Pueblo rechazado* (1968; Rejected People); *El juicio* (1972; The Trial), about the trial of those accused of the assassination of president-elect Álvaro Obregón in 1928; and *Los hijos de Sánchez* (1972; The Children of Sánchez), a dramatization of the well-known Óscar Lewis (1914–1970) study in urban anthropology. Leñero has also been a very successful screenwriter and journalist, having contributed to the Mexican daily *Excélsior* and the periodicals *Proceso* and *Claudia*, of which he was editor (1969–1972). *See also* THEATER.

LEÓN, CARLOS ARTURO (Ecuador, 1886–1967). Dramatist. His plays, with their emphasis on everyday lives, the national character, and satire of social customs, contributed to the development of a social **theater** in Ecuador. The play that had the most impact was *El recluta* (1918; The Recruit), which created a stir that ended with the abolition of military conscription. Other titles include *Reparación* (1914; Reparation), *La huérfana* (1928; The Orphan Girl), *La mujer de tu prójimo* (1936; Thy Neighbor's Wife), and *En pos de felicidad* (1927; Pursuit of Happiness).

LESBIAN WRITERS AND WRITING. *See* GAY AND LESBIAN WRITERS AND WRITING.

LIERA, ÓSCAR (Mexico, 1946–1990). Dramatist. He began writing in 1979 and by 1985 had already written 30 of his 36 plays. Notwithstanding the humor in his writing, his plays are known for their biting criticism of the Church and state. *Cúcara y Mácara* (1980; Eeny Meeny Miny Moe), for example, was the source of public outcry because of its criticism of the Church. He is also known for his innovative staging, such as *El gordo* (1980; The Big One), in which the actors transform the stage to represent their illusions about winning the lottery. His other plays include *El lazarillo* (1979; The Guide), *La fuerza del hombre* (1982; The Man's Force), *Los camaleones* (1980; The Chameleons), *La verdadera revolución* (1982; The True

Revolution), *El crescencio* (1979; The Crescence), *Aquí no pasa nada* (1979; Nothing Happening Here), *La pesadilla de una noche de verano* (1982; Nightmare of a Summer Night), *Soy el hombre* (1982; I Am the Man), *El oro de la revolución mexicana* (1984; The Gold of the Mexican Revolution), and *Repaso de indulgencias* (1990; Review of Indulgences). *See also* THEATER.

LIHN, ENRIQUE (Chile, 1929–1988). Poet, novelist, essayist, and dramatist. Best known as a poet, he followed first in the wake of **Pablo Neruda**, but soon began to develop his own, more radical voice. In some of his earlier collections, such as *La musiquilla de las pobres esferas* (1969; The Little Music of the Poor Spheres) and *Escrito en Cuba* (1969; Written in Cuba), he explores the nature of poetic creation and, in common with his compatriot **Nicanor Parra**, pursues the notion of **antipoetry** in search of new directions. Among themes that recur in his work are the sensual and the erotic. In *La pieza oscura* (1963; *The Dark Room and Other Poems*), also an early collection, they surface in the context of childhood, memory, and sexual awakening, and the erotic figures in his mature verse, in *Al bello aparecer de este lucero* (1983; At the Beautiful Appearance of This Bright Star), a relatively late publication. Travel is another of Lihn's recurring themes and figures in *Estación de los desamparados* (1973; Station for the Forsaken), *París, situación irregular* (1977; Paris, Situation Irregular), and *A partir de Manhattan* (1979; From Manhattan).

Toward the end of his life, darker elements began to appear in Lihn's poetry. In *El paseo ahumado* (1983; The Smokey Stroll), he writes of his sense of internal exile in Chile under dictatorship and, in *Diario de muerte* (1989; Death's Diary), published posthumously, there are anticipations of his end. Lihn's three novels are all caricatures of the genre. The first, *Batman en Chile; o, El ocaso de un ídolo; o, Solo contra el desierto* (1973; Batman in Chile; or, the Decline of an Idol; or, Alone Against the Desert), is a political satire. His second novel, *La orquesta de cristal* (1976; The Glass Orchestra), as the title suggests, is a history of an orchestra equipped with glass instruments, and his third, *El arte de la palabra* (1980; The Art of the Word), is a burlesque of writers and writing. In addition to his novels, Lihn also published two collections of short stories and used drawing as another form of self-expression.

LILLO, BALDOMERO (Chile, 1867–1923). Short story writer. With his first collection of stories, *Sub terra* (1904; Below Ground), Baldomero acquired a reputation as one of Latin America's most significant representatives of **naturalism**. Like the French novel *Germinal* (1885) by Emile Zola (1840–1902), with which they are compared, the Chilean's stories tell of the inhuman conditions endured by underground mine workers. One of his narratives most frequently anthologized is "La compuerta número 12" ("Hatch No. 12"), the tragedy of an eight-year-old boy forced to work in the mine. The author's second book of stories, *Sub sole* (1907; Under the Sun), is a more eclectic collection, however. It still represents aspects of a harsh, unforgiving reality, but its themes are more varied, and it has touches of **modernismo** in stories with a more aesthetically oriented style. Baldomero wrote many other stories for publication in newspapers and magazines, and a number have since been collected and published in several volumes: *Relatos populares* (1942; Popular Tales), *El hallazgo y otros cuentos del mar* (1956; The Discovery and Other Sea Stories), and *Pesquisa trágica* (1963; Tragic Inquiry).

LIMA, JORGE DE (Brazil, 1893–1953). Poet. Born in Alagoas, Jorge de Lima studied medicine in Salvador and Rio de Janeiro, during which time he began to write poetry in the style of **parnassianism**. He became known for his sonnet "O Acendedor de Lampiões" (Lamplighter), part of his collection *Quatorze Alexandrinos* (1914; Fourteen Alexandrines). After his studies, de Lima set up a medical practice in Maceió, where he published *O Mundo do Menino Impossível* (1925; The World of the Impossible Boy), his first truly personal poetry. He then abandoned the worn out parnassian forms for the nascent style of **Brazilian modernism**, particularly the substyle of **regionalism**, which is evident in his *Poemas* (1927; Poems) and in one of his best-known works, *Essa Negra Fulô* (1928; That Black Woman Fulô), a collection on the topic of slavery.

Following the 1930 revolution, de Lima moved to Rio de Janeiro, where he practiced medicine and participated in intellectual life. His subsequent collections, *Novos Poemas* (1929; New Poems) and *Poemas Escolhidos* (1932; Selected Poems), evoke childhood scenes and explore regional and Afro-Brazilian themes. A new phase, this time of religious inspiration under the motto "Let us restore the poetry in Christ," began with *Tempo e Eternidade* (1935; Time and Eternity), written in collaboration with **Murilo Mendes**. *A Túnica Inconsútil* (1938; The Seamless Tunic) was inspired by the Old Testament and continues this line of religious poetry; *Poemas Negros* (1947; Black Poems) revisits the Afro-Brazilian theme he had previously explored.

De Lima's last creative phase is marked by the influence of **surrealism** in novels such as *O Anjo* (1934; The Angel). Though returning to meter in *Livro de Sonetos* (1949; Book of Sonnets), de Lima's poetic expression became more obscure, culminating in *Obra Poética* (1950; Poetic Works), edited by Otto Maria Carpeaux, which contains *Anunciação e Encontro de Mira-Celi* (Annunciation and Meeting at Mira-Celi) and *Invenção de Orfeu* (1952; Invention of Orpheus), an original poem based on quotes from classic authors and one of his best-known works.

De Lima also published a few novels: *Salomão e as Mulheres* (1927; Solomon and the Women), *Calunga* (1935; Calunga), and *A Mulher Obscura* (1939; The Obscure Woman). He taught literature at various higher education institutions and published *Dois Ensaios: Proust e Todos Cantam a Sua Terra* (1929; Two Essays: Proust and Everyone Sings His Own Land), a fine piece of literary criticism. Despite the variety of his subject matter, de Lima is constant in his lyrical approach to poetry and is noted for his versatility and for having been one of the few Brazilian poets of the period to combine his engagement in black poetics with surrealism. *See also* FAUSTINO, MÁRIO; FREYRE, GILBERTO DE MELO; HILST, HILDA.

LIMA BARRETO, AFONSO HENRIQUES DE (Brazil, 1881–1922). Novelist and short story writer. Although not much recognized in his day, Lima Barreto today is considered one of Brazil's best fiction writers in the style of **realism**. He was born to a family of mixed racial background and lost his mother at a young age. His relatively short life was plagued by mental illness and economic struggles. Although he received a good education, paid for by a family friend, he had to interrupt an engineering career to take care of his father, who became mentally ill. He nevertheless read avidly and acquired a good library. Employed as a secretary in the Ministry of War, he also began to write regularly for the press.

Lima Barreto's semiautobiographical novel *Recordações do Escrivão Isaías Caminha* (1909; Memoirs of the Secretary Isaías Caminha) contains elements of satire in the portrayal of various urban types. This satirical vein is continued in his best-known novel, *Triste Fim de Policarpo Quaresma* (1915; *The Patriot*), whose protagonist, Major Policarpo, an honest and quixotic man, is often ridiculed by his peers for his patriotic projects. This novel, like his *Vida e Morte de M. J. Gonzaga de Sá* (1919; Life and Death of M.J. Gonzaga de Sá), chronicles and criticizes urban life in post-abolition Rio de Janeiro. Racial inequalities and class conflicts inspired his unfinished novel, *Clara dos Anjos* (1948; Clara dos Anjos).

Lima Barreto's political preoccupations mirror the racial and social contradictions of late 19th- and early 20th-century Brazil, brought on by abolition and modernization, as pictured in the social satire of *Os Bruzundangas* (1922; The Bruzundangas) and *Coisas do Reino de Jambon* (1952; Things of the Kingdom of Jambon). Some of Lima Barreto's best nonfiction was also inspired by his own struggles with alcohol and mental illness, as witnessed by his posthumous *Diário Íntimo* (1953; Personal Diary), which contains the memoir of his stay in a psychiatric institution, and *O Cemitério dos Vivos* (1953; Cemetery of the Living). Other works include the novel *Numa e a Ninfa* (1915; Numa and the Nymph), the collection of short stories *Histórias e Sonhos* (1920; Stories and Dreams), and the nonfiction *Bagatelas* (1923; Bagatelles) and *Vida Urbana* (1956; Urban Life). De Lima died at age 41 from a heart attack. *See also* FONSECA, RUBEM; REBELO, MARQUES.

LINDO, HUGO (El Salvador, 1917–1985). Poet, novelist, and short story writer. Less political than others of his generation, he was a Catholic intellectual who wrote in a refined style and was highly appreciated in his own country. Among more than 20 books of poetry, the most representative are *Poema eucarístico y otros* (1943; Eucharistic Poem and Others), *El libro de las horas* (1948; The Book of Hours), and *Sinfonía del límite* (1963; Symphony of the Limit). His collections of short stories include *Guaro y champaña* (1957; Moonshine and Champagne), *Aquí se cuentan cuentos* (1959; Tales Told Here), and *Espejos paralelos* (1974; Parallel Mirrors). Of his four novels *¡Justicia, señor Gobernador!* (1960; Justice, Mr. Governor!), a story of suspense about a judge charged with bringing down a verdict in a brutal murder case, is the most widely read. The others are *El anzuelo de Dios* (1943; God's Bait), *Cada día tiene su afán* (1965; Each Day Brings Its Desire), and *Yo soy la memoria* (1983; I Am Memory).

LINS, OSMAN (Brazil, 1924–1978). Novelist, dramatist, and short story writer. Born in the Northeast, Lins studied economics and worked for the Bank of Brazil in São Paulo for many years. His first novel, *O Visitante* (1955; The Visitor), already revealed the innovative style he would become known for. Likewise, the short stories in *Os Gestos* (1957; The Gestures) feature an introspective style and characters faced with difficult moral choices. *O Fiel e a Pedra* (1961; The Scale Pointer and the Stone) is a novel set in the Northeast, featuring a man who heroically defends his honesty in a corrupt environment. The stories in *Nove, Novena: Narrativas* (1966; Nine, Novena: Narratives) include characters who overlap from one story to the next, an innovative structure partly inspired by the **baroque** and medieval religious literature. *Avalovara* (1973; *Avalovara*), whose title is derived from one of the avatars of Buddha, is a radically creative allegorical novel with mysterious, fluid characters. This novel, like *A Rainha dos Cárceres da Grécia* (1976; The Queen of the Prisons of Greece), also presents the reader with a variety of reading options, much like **Julio Cortázar**'s novel *Rayuela* (1963; *Hopscotch*). Lins also had a successful career as a dramatist, and his plays *Lisbela e o Prisioneiro* (1964; Lisbela and the Prisoner), *Guerra do "Cansa Cavalo"* (1967; War of the "Cansa Cavalo"), *"Capa Verde" e o Natal* (1967; "Green Cape" and Christmas), and *Santa, Automóvel e Soldado* (1975; Saint, Car and Soldier), social dramas in the style of **regionalism**, were staged in Rio and São Paulo. *See also* THEATER.

LINS, PAULO (Brazil, 1958–). Novelist. Born in Rio de Janeiro, Lins lived as a young boy in the low-income housing project known as Cidade de Deus. His personal experience as well as anthropological research in this poverty-stricken and gang-plagued district inspired his acclaimed novel *Cidade de Deus* (1997; *City of God*), which was turned into an Oscar-nominated movie of the same name in 2004.

The novel portrays a world dominated by drug deals and violence through the eyes of the young photographer Busca-pé.

LIRA, MIGUEL N. (Mexico, 1905–1961). Novelist. Although he made his entry into literature through poetry and **theater**, Lira is remembered mainly for his novels. In the manner of **indigenismo**, *Donde crecen los tepozanes* (1947; Where the Tepozan Grows) focuses on the survival of native beliefs and practices in spite of modernization and conversion to Christianity. By contrast, *La escondida* (1947; The Hidden Woman) is a **novel of the Mexican Revolution** that traces the sentimental journey of a female protagonist as the wife of a federalist general and then as the lover of a revolutionary leader. Other narratives by Lira are an epistolary novel, *Una mujer en soledad* (1956; A Woman in Solitude), and *Mientras la muerte llega* (1958; As Death Approaches), a story also set against the background of the revolution.

LISBOA, HENRIQUETA (Brazil, 1904–1985). Poet. Born in Minas Gerais, Lisboa was trained as an educator. Her early poetry books *Fogo Fâtuo* (1925; St. Elmo's Fire) and *Enternecimento* (1929; Tenderness) were influenced by **symbolism**, but she soon evolved into a modern diction in *Velário* (1936; Velarium). Among her didactic and **children's** poetry are *Prisioneira da Noite* (1941; Prisoner of the Night) and *O Menino Poeta* (1943; The Child Poet), respectively. Other important works in an introspective and historical vein are *Madrinha Lua* (1952; Godmother Moon) and *Azul Profundo* (1956; Deep Blue). *Lírica* (1958; Lyric Poetry) is a collection of works selected by the author herself. Among her metaphysical and meditative texts are *A Face Lívida* (1945; The Sallow Face), *Flor da Morte* (1949; Flower of Death), *Além da Imagem* (1963; Beyond the Image), *O Alvo Humano* (1973; The Human Goal), *Miradouro e Outros Poemas* (1976; Belvedere and Other Poems), and *Reverberações* (1976; Reverberations). She is considered an important lyric voice in **Brazilian modernism** of the 1930s and received many literary awards. *See also* WOMEN.

LISCANO, JUAN (Venezuela, 1915–2001). Poet and essayist. He was an influential figure in the literary and intellectual life of Venezuela in the 20th century. Among other ventures, he founded the **journal** *Zona Franca* and was its editor for almost 20 years (1964–1983), and he served as director of the state-owned publishing company Monte Ávila. The themes of Venezuela and the Americas figure significantly in his poetry, which also draws on his extensive folklore research. Among his collections are *8 poemas* (1937; 8 Poems), *Nuevo mundo Orinoco* (1959; New Orinoco World), *Cármenes* (1966; Songs), and *Fundaciones* (1981; Foundations). As an essayist, he wrote on Venezuelan literature in *Panorama de la literatura venezolana actual* (1973; Panorama of Contemporary Venezuelan Literature) and on the work of **Rómulo Gallegos** in *Rómulo Gallegos y su tiempo* (1961; Rómulo Gallegos and His Time), *Rómulo Gallegos, vida y obra* (1968; Life and Work of Rómulo Gallegos), and *La geografía venezolana en la obra de Rómulo Gallegos* (1970; The Geography of Venezuela in the Work of Rómulo Gallegos).

LISPECTOR, CLARICE (Brazil, 1925–1977). Novelist, short prose writer, and journalist. One of Brazil's most gifted prose writers of the 20th century and a major representative of the last phase of **Brazilian modernism**, Lispector was born in Ukraine but emigrated to Brazil as a young child. Growing up in Recife, Northeastern Brazil, she moved to Rio as a teenager and attended law school there. She married a career diplomat at a young age and, due to her husband's job, spent several decades of her life abroad. As a law student, Lispector began to publish in periodicals. Her first novel, *Perto do Coração Selvagem* (1944; *Near to the Wild Heart*), an introspective young **woman**'s coming-of-age story told in an innovative style, was a critical success. Along similar lines, *O Lustre* (1946; The Chandelier) and *A Cidade Sitiada* (1949; The Besieged City) also depict female characters in fragmented narratives that explore psychological states. A novel with a more developed plot, *A Maçã no Escuro* (1961; *The Apple in the Dark*), tells the story of Martim, a man who seeks refuge on a farm after committing a crime he is not punished for. One of her most celebrated novels, *A Paixão Segundo G.H.* (1964; *The Passion According to G.H.*), portrays a woman who, confined to a room, extensively reflects on the fragility of life and love after killing a cockroach.

Lispector also excelled as a writer of short stories in her collections *Laços de Família* (1960; *Family Ties*), *A Legião Estrangeira*

(1964; The Foreign Legion), *Uma Aprendizagem ou o Livro dos Prazeres* (1969; An Apprenticeship or the Book of Pleasures), *Felicidade Clandestina: Contos* (1971; Secret Joy: Short Stories), *Onde Estivestes de Noite* (1974; Where You Were Last Night), and *A Via Crucis do Corpo* (1974; *Soulstorm: Stories*). Her unconventional tales often portray introspective situations linked to **existentialism**. Some of her last novels, such as *Água Viva* (1973; Stream of Life) and *Um Sopro de Vida* (1978; A Breath of Life), adopt a more poetic than narrative form. *A Bela e a Fera* (1979; Beauty and the Beast) is a posthumously published collection of stories written in the 1940s and 1970s.

Although she was often accused of not being Brazilian and of not referring to Brazil in her works, her last novel, *A Hora da Estrela* (1977; *The Hour of the Star*), is the sympathetic yet tragic tale of an impoverished young woman from Northeastern Brazil seeking a better life in the South. It mirrors the life of many internal migrant workers and was adapted for the screen. Lispector's contributions to **children's literature** include *O Mistério do Coelhinho Pensante* (1967; The Mystery of the Thinking Bunny) and *A Mulher Que Matou os Peixes* (1968; The Woman Who Killed the Fish). Her contributions to the **chronicle** were in the form of extensive columns for newspapers that were gathered under the titles *Visão do Esplendor: Impressões Leves* (1975; Vision of Splendor: Fleeting Impressions), *De Corpo Inteiro* (1975; Full-Length), and *A Descoberta do Mundo* (1984; The Discovery of the World). *See also* PRADO, ADÉLIA.

LIST ARZUBIDE, GERMÁN (Mexico, 1898–1998). Poet. He was a combatant in the Mexican Revolution under the leadership of **Emiliano Zapata** and wrote his first poems on revolutionary themes. After the war, he became associated with the **avant-garde** movement **estridentismo**. He contributed to the group's manifesto, edited the **journal** *Horizonte* (1926–1927), and produced an account of the movement, written in both verse and prose, *El movimiento estridentista* (1926; The Strident Movement). In his own poetry of that period, in *Esquina* (1923; Corner) and *El viajero en el vértice* (1926; The Traveler at the Apex), he writes about the modern world and its technological progress.

LOA. Originally a dramatic prologue that preceded a one-act or full-length play, it was often a poem written in praise of a patron or to extol the virtues of the play and its themes. The *loa* was brought to Spanish America from Spain and figures in the work of colonial writers such as **Fernán González de Eslava, Sor Juana Inés de la Cruz,** and **Pedro de Peralta y Barnuevo.**

LOBATO, JOSÉ BENTO MONTEIRO (Brazil, 1882–1948). Journalist, essayist, and short story writer. A man of many talents, Monteiro Lobato is remembered today mostly for his didactic and **children's literature.** He published more than a dozen children's books, later adapted for television, mostly set in the imaginary *Sítio do Picapau Amarelo* ("Yellow Woodpecker Ranch"), populated by invented characters with educational roles. Monteiro Lobato was also a nationalist and progressive thinker who played a key role in supporting the **Week of Modern Art.** Among his other books are the collections of short stories, *Urupês* (1918; Urupês), *Cidades Mortas* (1919; Dead Cities), and *Negrinha* (1920; Little Black Girl), and the novel *O Choque das Raças ou o Presidente Negro* (1926; The Black President). *Urupês,* the best known, portrays the hard life in the rural interior of Brazil and features his character Jeca Tatu, a personification of Brazilian mixed-race peasants riddled by ignorance, illness, and poverty, also further explored in *Idéias de Jeca Tatu* (1919; Ideas of Jeca Tatu). An admirer of modern civilization, Monteiro Lobato lived for some time in the United States as a commercial attaché, an experience that inspired his books of essays and memoirs, *Mr. Slang e o Brasil* (1929; Mr. Slang and Brazil) and *América* (1932; America). As an editor and publisher, Monteiro Lobato directed the **journal** *Revista do Brasil* (1918–1944) and founded several publishing houses.

LÓPEZ, LUIS CARLOS (Colombia, 1879–1950). Poet. He wrote four books of verse: *De mi villorio* (1908; From My Old Town), *Posturas difíciles* (1919; Difficult Positions), *Por el atajo* (1920; By the Short Cut), and *Versos* (1946; Verses), as well as collaborating on a fifth, *Varios a varios* (1910; Various to Various). With irony and humor, he wrote mainly about the people and events of his hometown,

Cartagena, where he spent most of his life. Nevertheless, his poetry traveled considerably and was widely influential, much like that of the Mexican **Ramón López Velarde**, which also occupied a pivotal position between **modernismo** and the **avant-garde**.

LÓPEZ, VICENTE FIDEL (Argentina, 1815–1903). Novelist. Primarily the author of histories of Argentina and one of the precursors of modern Argentinean historiography, he also produced two works of fiction, both written while living in exile in **Chile** to escape the regime of **Juan Manuel Rosas**. One of these, a novella, *La loca de la guardia* (1848; The Mad Woman of the Guard), about a woman who accompanies the army of José de San Martín (1778–1850) across the Andes in South America's War of Independence, has had little resonance. The other, *La novia del hereje, o La inquisición en Lima* (1846; The Heretic's Bride, or The Inquisition in Lima), has fared better, however. A **historical novel**, set in 1578 Lima, it is the story of two ill-fated lovers, a criollo girl and a seaman from one of the ships of Sir Francis Drake (1540–1595), told in the manner of full-blown **romanticism**.

LÓPEZ ALBÚJAR, ENRIQUE (Peru, 1872–1966). Novelist and short story writer. He was a follower of **Manuel González Prada**, and his fiction brought racial issues into Peruvian literature. The stories in *Cuentos andinos* (1920; Andean Tales) had considerable impact because of their representation of the gross ill-treatment of Indians. They are thought to have influenced **Ciro Alegría** and the direction taken by **indigenismo** in Peru. A second collection, *Nuevos cuentos andinos* (1937; New Andean Tales), appeared almost two decades later and, in *Las caridades de la señora Tardoya* (1955; Señora Tardoya's Charitable Deeds), López Albújar published a book of stories in the style of **naturalism**. He also wrote two novels. The better known is the **historical novel** *Matalaché* (1928; Matalaché), a tale of sexual freedom, based on the true story of a love affair between a mulatto and an aristocratic landowner in 1816 in Piura, set against the background of a slave-owning society on the eve of independence. His other novel, *El hechizo de Tomayquichua* (1943; The Spell of Tomayquichua), has a similar erotic theme.

LÓPEZ DE GÓMARA, FRANCISCO (Spain, 1511?–1566?). Chronicler. Although he never traveled to the Americas, he wrote a **chronicle**, *Historia de las Indias y la conquista de México* (1552; *Cortés: The Life of the Conqueror by His Secretary*), relying on eyewitness accounts and written documents. Its first part is a general history of the Americas, showing little sympathy for native peoples and their culture. The second part is a history of the conquest of Mexico told as a biography of the conqueror **Hernán Cortés**. *See also* DÍAZ DEL CASTILLO, BERNAL.

LÓPEZ PORTILLO Y ROJAS, JOSÉ (Mexico, 1850–1923). Novelist and short story writer. His first collection of narratives appeared in *Seis leyendas* (1883; Six Legends) and was followed by several others: *Novelas cortas* (1900; Short Novels), *Sucesos y novelas cortas* (1903; Events and Short Novels), and *Historias, historietas y cuentecillos* (1918; Stories, Fables, and Little Tales). They are mainly tales of rural life, but López Portillo's success in this genre has been largely overshadowed by the success of his first novel, *La parcela* (1898; The Parcel of Land), a **regional** novel of rural Mexico and one of the best among those of his generation who were influenced by Spanish **realism** and, in his case in particular, by the Spanish regionalist writer José María de Pereda (1833–1906). Two later novels by López Portillo, *Los precursores* (1909; The Precursors) and *Fuertes y débiles* (1919; The Strong and the Weak), were less well received.

LÓPEZ VELARDE, RAMÓN (Mexico, 1988–1921). Poet. The themes of nostalgia and the opposition between metropolitan and provincial values characterize his verse, which belongs aesthetically between **modernismo** and the **avant-garde** and is therefore at an important juncture in the history of poetry in Mexico. In the two books of verse published during his lifetime, he worked his themes around a central preoccupation with love. In *La sangre devota* (1915; Devout Blood), this is a romantic, unfulfilled, even platonic sentiment, thought to be inspired by Josefa de los Ríos, known as "Fuensanta," although there are underpinnings of eroticism. The verses in *Zozobra* (1919; Anguish), marked by experiences in the city and the poet's relationship with Magarita Quijano, are, as the title suggests, more intense and express a sensual love felt more physically. Finally, in the posthumously published *El son del corazón* (1932; The Sound of the Heart), there is a return to the poet's earlier, less anguished, reflection on love and a use of more conventional verse forms. Although López Velarde's writings have little to say about the politics of the revolution, his preoccupation with Mexico and his poem "Suave patria" ("Gentle Fatherland"), published in *El son de corazón*, have given him the status of national poet. His prose **chronicles**, written for the newspapers *El minutero* (1923; The Minute Hand) and *El don de febrero* (1952; The Gift of February), were collected and published posthumously. See also LÓPEZ, LUIS CARLOS; REBOLLEDO, EFRÉN.

LÓPEZ Y FUENTES, GREGORIO (Mexico, 1897–1967). Novelist. His sympathy for the lower classes, rural Mexicans, and Indians is already apparent in his first novels, *El vagabundo* (1922; The Vagabond) and *El alma del poblacho* (1924; Soul of the Hick Town). *Campamento* (1931; Encampment), *Tierra* (1932; Land), and *¡Mi general!* (1934; My General!) are all considered **novels of the Mexican Revolution**. All three are episodically constructed: *Campamento* consists of scenes in a military encampment; *Tierra* is an account of **Emiliano Zapata**'s campaign; and *¡Mi general!* is the story of a revolutionary general or *caudillo*, which shows considerable disenchantment with the revolution and subsequent political processes in Mexico.

López y Fuentes's best-known work is *El indio* (1935; El indio), a novel of **indigenismo** that may be read as an allegory of the history of Mexican Indians since the Spanish conquest, presented through the lens of **naturalism** and against the background of the revolution. Later fiction by this author includes *Arrieros* (1937; Mule Drivers), a political novel; *Huasteca* (1939; Huasteca), about the petroleum industry; *Acomodaticio* (1943; Accommodating), a second look at themes first developed in *¡Mi general!*; *Los peregrinos inmóviles* (1948; Immobile Pilgrims); *Entresuelo* (1948; Between Floors); and *Milpa, potrero and monte* (1951; Cornfield, Pasture, and Mountain).

LOS CONTEMPORÁNEOS. Sharing the same name as the **journal** to which they contributed, *Contemporáneos* (1928–1931), members of this **avant-garde** group of writers in **Mexico** advocated a modern country connected both to its origins and to developments taking place in the world at large. Its members included **Jorge Cuesta, José Gorostiza, Bernardo Ortiz de Montellano, Salvador Novo, Gilberto Owen, Carlos Pellicer, Jaime Torres Bodet,** and **Xavier Villaurrutia.**

LOYOLA BRANDÃO, IGNÁCIO DE (Brazil, 1936–). Novelist and short story writer. Loyola Brandão began his writing career as a journalist. His first novel, *Bebel Que a Cidade Comeu* (1968; Bebel Who Was Eaten by the City), was adapted for the screen, as were some of his short stories. His second and best-known novel, *Zero* (1975; Zero), influenced by the cinema of Federico Fellini (1920–1993) and banned for some time in Brazil, is an honest portrait of a common man living in a violent city during a period of dictatorship. Among other novels and short story collections he has published are *Dentes ao Sol* (1976; Teeth in the Sun), *Cadeiras Proibidas* (1976; Illegal Chairs), *Não Verás País Nenhum* (1981; You Will Not See Any Country), and *O Anônimo Célebre* (2002; The Famous Anonymous Man).

LUCO CRUCHAGA, GERMÁN (Chile, 1894–1936). Dramatist. Although his oeuvre is not extensive, he was a significant figure in the revival of **theater** in Chile in the early 20th century. He used traditional structures and wrote realist plays that embodied the then new theories of Sigmund Freud. *Amo y señor* (1926; Lord and Master) is a critique of bourgeois corruption, and *La viuda de Apablaza* (1928; The Widow of Aplabaza) is a retelling of the Phaedra myth transferred to a rural setting in Chile.

LUGONES, LEOPOLDO (Argentina, 1874–1938). Poet, essayist, and short story writer. His work covers a wide range of genres, moods, and styles, a reflection of his shifting interests and loyalties. Although an ardent socialist in his youth, he was later equally fervent in his support of fascism. Lugones's early volumes of poetry, *Las montañas de oro* (1897; Mountains of Gold), *Los crepúsculos del jardín* (1905; The Garden Twilights), and *Lunario sentimental* (1909; Sentimental Moon), show European influence but are innovative representatives of **modernismo** that made him one of the most important South American exponents of this trend and very influential. *Lunario sentimental*, for example, is a miscellany of pieces, in prose and verse, on the theme of the moon and represents a shift toward the **avant-garde**. Later collections, in which Argentinean themes figured prominently, were less experimental. These included *Odas seculares* (1910; Secular Odes), written as part of the nation's centenary celebrations; *Romancero* (1924; Ballads); *Poemas solariegos* (1928; Ancestral Poems); and *Romance del Río Seco* (1938; The Ballad of Rio Seco), which reveal a more traditional aesthetic affiliated to more conventional verse forms, the Argentine landscape, and its customs and people.

Lugones's fiction includes *La guerra gaucha* (1904; Gaucho War), a series of episodes about the exploits of a 19th-century gaucho, which along with elements of the author's verse, such as *Odas seculares*, locates his work in the tradition of **gaucho literature**. In an entirely different vein, *Las fuerzas extrañas* (1906; *Strange Forces*) is a collection of short stories that demonstrates his originality in the area of **fantastic literature**. His essays, amounting to almost 20 published volumes, covered a wide range of subjects, including education, history, politics, and literary criticism. Among his books that have had most impact are *La patria fuerte* (1930; The Strong Fatherland), written in defense of the pro-military stance he took over the military coup of 1930, and *El payador* (1916; The Troubador), a study of **José Hernández**'s *Martín Fierro*. Lugones committed suicide at the age of 63. *See also* HERRERA Y REISSIG, JULIO; JAIMES FREYRE, RICARDO.

LUSSICH, ANTONIO DIONISIO (Uruguay, 1848–1928). Poet. He followed in the tradition of **gaucho literature** established by Bartolomé Hidalgo and owes his celebrity in part to the notion that his *Los tres gauchos orientales* (1872; Three Uruguayan Gauchos) was once considered the inspiration for *Martín Fierro* by **José Hernández**. Other works he wrote in the same tradition are *El matrero Luciano Santos* (1873; The Oulaw Luciano Santos) and *Diálogo entre los paisanos Cantalicio Quirós y Miterio Castro en un baile del club Paraguay* (1883; Dialogue Between the Compatriots Cantalicio Quirós and Miterio Castro at a Dance at the Paraguay Club).

LYNCH, BENITO (Argentina, 1880–1951). Novelist and short story writer. He wrote nine novels and many short stories, predominantly in the vein of **naturalism**. His fiction deals mainly with rural life of the late 19th and early 20th centuries, reminiscent of **criollismo**, and has not generally transcended his own time. Few of his novels have been republished, and many of his short stories remain uncollected in newspapers and magazines. *El inglés de los güesos* (1924; The Englishman with the Bones), Lynch's best-known novel, is the story of the conflicts arising in a rural community when a young woman falls for an English paleontologist, whose presence is an example of the many English people who visited or settled in Argentina between the late 1800s and 1930.

LYNCH, MARTA (Argentina, 1929–1985). Novelist, short story writer, and journalist. She was a popular and public figure, recognized for the success of her fiction and journalism, her involvement in politics, and her television appearances. She committed suicide, perhaps in response to a fear of aging and loss of public attention, at a time when her popularity was greatest. The themes that dominate her fiction are love, female desire, and politics, but the outcomes are rarely positive. Lynch's first published novel was *La alfombra roja* (1962; The Red Carpet), written as a series of monologues spoken by characters who accompany a politician on his rise to becoming president, based on the presidential campaign of Arturo Frondizi (1958–1962). *Al vencedor* (1965; To the Victor), her second novel, is a bleak look at two military draftees whose experiences anticipate the violence that would overcome the country in the 1970s. Her third novel, also her most popular, was *La señora Ordóñez* (1967; Mrs. Ordóñez), whose female protagonist, the bored wife of a doctor, has been considered by many to be an autobiographical representation of the author. Her later novels—*Un árbol lleno de manzanas* (1974; A Tree Full of Apples), *La penúltima versión de Colorada Villanueva* (1978; The Penultimate Version of Colorada Villanueva), and *Informe bajo llave* (1983; Report Under Wraps)—all intertwine love and politics and show the darker side of existence, reflecting events in Argentina. Lynch's collections of short stories, with their variations on loneliness, sex, and politics, present the same themes as her longer fiction and include *Crónicas de la burguesía* (1965;

Chronicles of the Bourgeosie), *Los cuentos tristes* (1967; Sad Tales), *Los dedos de la mano* (1976; The Fingers of the Hand), *Los años de fuego* (1980; Years of Fire), and *No te duermas, no me dejes* (1985; Don't Sleep, Don't Leave Me). *See also* WOMEN.

LYRA, CARMEN (Costa Rica, 1888–1949). Short story writer. Born María Isabela Carvajal, Lyra was a noted educator, a politically militant figure, and Costa Rica's first major **woman** writer. She published one novel, *En una silla de ruedas* (1918; In a Wheelchair), a view of Costa Rican life and customs represented through a sentimental story and the eyes of a young handicapped artist. Her collection of stories, *Los cuentos de mi tía Panchita* (1920; Tales from My Aunt Fanny), containing traditional European fairy tales as well as tales from folklore, all told in the voice of the same female narrator, is her most celebrated book and a notable contribution to **children's literature**. A similar strategy of stories all told by the same narrator was also used two years previously in *Las fantasías de Juan Silvestre* (1918; Juan Silvestre's Fantasies). Lyra's other collections of stories, *Siluetas de la maternal* (1929; Maternal Silhouettes) and *Bananos y hombres* (1931; Bananas and Men), have a more political content and reflect the author's use of literature for social protest. She was, in effect, one of the earliest authors in Central America to protest the dominance of transnational fruit companies. Lyra also wrote for the stage, including theater for children.

– M –

MACEDO, JOAQUIM MANUEL DE (Brazil, 1820–1882). Novelist and dramatist. Although Macedo studied medicine, he followed a career in teaching and politics. His doctoral thesis, a study of nostalgia, was published in the same year as his first novel *A Moreninha* (1844; The Dark Girl), which was also the first novel in Brazil in the style of **romanticism** influenced by European models such as Sir Walter Scott (1771–1832) and Alexandre Dumas (1802–1870). This tale of fidelity to childhood love is Macedo's best-known work. Considered the father of the sentimental novel in Brazil, Macedo employed a number of plot formulas, including mistaken identities, conflicts between duty and passion, and humorous situations involving secondary characters, and was responsible for introducing vernacular speech in literature. He wrote a total of 17 novels, attempting, like Honoré de Balzac (1799–1850), a broad portrait of 19th-century urban (in this case Brazilian) society. His novels include *Rosa* (1849; Rosa), *Vicentina* (1853; Vicentina), *O Forasteiro* (1855; The Foreigner), *Romances da Semana* (1861; Romances of the Week), *O Culto do Dever* (1865; The Cult of Duty), *As Vítimas Algozes* (1869; The Victim Executioners), *O Rio do Quarto* (1869; Rio from the Bedroom), *A Namoradeira* (1870; The Flighty Girl), *Um Noivo e Duas Noivas* (1871; One Groom and Two Brides), *Os Quatro Pontos Cardeias* (1872; The Four Cardinal Points), *A Misteriosa* (1872; The Mysterious Woman), *A Baronesa do Amor* (1876; The Baroness of Love), and *O Moço Loiro* (1845; The Blonde Boy). Macedo also wrote satirical dramas with less success, though *O Primo da Califórnia* (1858; The Cousin from California) is still staged occasionally. *See also* THEATER.

MACHADO, ANÍBAL (Brazil, 1894–1964). Short story writer and novelist. Born in Minas Gerais, where he studied law and wrote for the newspapers alongside **Carlos Drummond de Andrade** and other members of **Brazilian modernism**, Machado is mostly known for short narratives that he first published in newspapers and then gathered in the volumes *Vida Feliz* (1944; Happy Life) and *Histórias Reunidas* (1959; Collected Short Stories), among which "Viagem aos Seios de Duília" ("Voyage to Duília's Breasts"), "Tati, a Garota" ("Tati, the Girl"), and "A Morte da Porta-Estandarte" ("The Death of the Standardbearer") are well-known and are often anthologized. In a succinct and ironic style, often psychologically introspective, Machado commented on the daily life of obscure characters, much in the style of Franz Kafka, whom he translated. His "poem/essay" *Cadernos de João* (1957; John's Notebooks) is a collection of lyrical meditations inspired by Paul Valéry (1871–1941) and prose poems in the style of **surrealism**. *João Ternura* (1965; John Tenderness) is a posthumously published, semiautobiographical narrative and set of personal reflections. Linked also to **regionalism**, he wrote *Brandão Entre o Mar e o Amor* (1942; Brandão Between the Sea and Love) collectively with **José Lins do Rêgo, Raquel de Queirós, Jorge**

Amado, and **Graciliano Ramos**. Among other things, Machado belonged to **theater** groups, wrote movie scripts based on his short stories, and was a soccer player with Clube Atlético Mineiro.

MACHADO, ANTÓNIO DE ALCÂNTARA (Brazil, 1901–1935). Journalist, novelist, and short story writer. Born in São Paulo, Alcântara Machado studied law, but soon turned to journalism, working for *Jornal do Comércio*. In 1925, he published a series of humorous travel chronicles, which he later brought out as the volume *Pathé-Baby* (1926; Pathé Baby). These texts were influenced in style and content by the new medium of cinema, as seen in the title of the collection, taken from the name of a popular film camera. Alcântara Machado soon joined the ranks of **Brazilian modernism** by frequenting artists gathered around the **Week of Modern Art**, especially **Oswald de Andrade**, with whom he collaborated on the **journals** *Terra Roxa e Outras Terras* and *Revista de Antropofagia*. Notably, Alcântara Machado also portrayed the life of Italian immigrants in São Paulo in his collections of short stories, *Brás, Bexiga e Barra Funda* (1927; Brás, Bexiga and Barra Funda), named after three well-known working-class districts in São Paulo, and *Laranja da China* (1928; Mandarin Orange). As chronicler of music and culture, Alcântara Machado left the important volume, *Cavaquinho e Saxofone* (1940; Cavaquinho and Saxophone), containing mostly pieces published in periodicals. Machado died prematurely from complications after an appendectomy.

MACHADO, DIONÉLIO (Brazil, 1895–1986). Novelist. Born in Rio Grande do Sul, Machado studied psychiatry and later worked as a journalist. Following his first book of short stories, *Um Pobre Homem* (1927; A Poor Man), his first novel, *Os Ratos* (1935; The Rats), earned him almost instant fame. The novel describes one day in the life of a low-level bureaucrat who is desperately looking for money to pay the milkman, focusing on his psyche and the stress and frustrations of daily life, in the style of **realism**. Machado's next novel, *O Louco de Cati* (1942; The Madman from Cati), was written entirely by dictation and makes much use of the oral. Although he attempted to use similar plots and techniques in his following novels, *Desolação* (1944; Desolation), *Passos Perdidos* (n.d.; Lost Steps), and *Os Deuses Econômicos* (1966; The Economic Gods), he was less successful. Machado was in jail at the same time as **Graciliano Ramos** during Getúlio Vargas's Estado Novo (1930–1945).

MACHADO, DUDA, a.k.a. CARLOS EDUARDO LIMA MACHADO (Brazil, 1944–). Poet and translator. Born in Salvador, Machado was linked to the Tropicália movement, writing song lyrics with fellow poet **Waly Salomão**. He studied social sciences and literature in São Paulo and today is a university professor in Minas Gerais. He has also translated works by Gustave Flaubert (1821–1880), Ford Madox Ford (1873–1939), and Marcel Schwob (1867–1905). Machado's poetry emerges from the lessons of the **concrete poetry** movement moving through the impact of popular culture from Tropicália. His early poems evince a concern with the visual and with language as a topic, but evolve toward more awareness of the political. The title of Machado's first book *Zil* (1977; Zil) is not a word, but rather a fragment whose sound suggests a number of possibilities, including the word "Brazil" and "fuzil," setting the stage for a poetry of indeterminacy and verbal play. For years Machado did not publish another book and gathered all his uncollected poems published in **journals** in the volume *Crescente* (1990; Crescent) and his unpublished book *Um Outro* (1990; An Other). Other titles by Machado include *Margem de Uma Onda* (1997; Edge of a Wave) and *Histórias com Poesia, Alguns Bichos & Cia.* (1997; Stories with Poetry, Some Animals, & Co.), a work of **children's literature**.

MACHADO, GILKA (Brazil, 1893–1980). Poet. Born in Rio, Machado married a fellow poet and had two children. Her first poetry book was *Cristais Partidos* (1915; Broken Crystals), soon followed by *Estados d'Alma* (1917; States of the Soul). Her poetry, written in the styles of **parnassianism** and **symbolism,** was considered scandalous because of its open eroticism. Machado, hailed as the greatest female poet of Brazil in 1933, was gradually forgotten, but has been recently rediscovered by scholars of writing by **women**. Other works by Machado include *Mulher Nua* (1922; Nude Woman), *Meu Glorioso Pecado* (1928; My Glorious Sin), and *Sublimação* (1938; Sublimation).

MADARIAGA, FRANCISCO (Argentina, 1927–2000). Poet. The province of Corrientes, where he was born and grew up, figures significantly in his work, which evokes the landscape, the contrast between the urban and the rural, and the coexistence of Spanish and Guaraní. As a member of the group founded by **Aldo Pellegrini,** **surrealism** was a fundamental part of his aesthetic vision, although his writing also shows the influence of the **baroque, gaucho literature,** and the writers **Oliverio Girondo** and **Pablo Neruda.** He published more than a dozen books of poetry, including *El pequeño patíbulo* (1954; The Small Scaffold), *Las jaulas del sol* (1960; Cages of the Sun), *Los terrores de la suerte* (1967; The Terrors of Luck), *Tembladerales de oro* (1973; Golden Quicksands), *Una acuarela móvil* (1985; A Moving Watercolor), and *Aroma de apariciones* (1998; Scent of Apparitions). Collected editions of his poetry have appeared in *La balsa mariposa* (1982; Butterfly Raft) and *El tren casi fluvial* (1988; The Almost Riverine Train).

MADRID AIR DISASTER. This was a plane crash on 27 November 1983, at Barajas Airport, which claimed the lives of 180 passengers and crew, including the Latin American writers **Jorge Ibargüengoitia, Ángel Rama, Manuel Scorza,** and **Marta Traba,** who had all been in Spain to attend a congress.

MAGALHÃES, DOMINGOS JOSÉ GONÇALVES DE (Brazil, 1811–1882). Poet and dramatist. Trained as a painter, Gonçalves de Magalhaes also received a degree in medicine in 1832, the year he published his *Poesias* (Poems). He traveled to Europe to further his studies in medicine, and during his stay there became acquainted with French and Italian romantic authors. In 1836, he published the poetry volume *Suspiros Poéticos e Saudades* (1836; Poetic Sighs and Nostalgia) in Paris, which officially introduced **romanticism** to Brazil. In that year also, with Francisco Sales Torres-Homem (1812–1876) and Manuel de Araújo Porto Alegre (1806–1879), he founded the **journal** *Niterói: Revista Brasiliense* (1836; Niterói: Brazilian Magazine), in which they theorized and promoted the romantic nationalist and religious ideal and rejected foreign classical models.

Gonçalves de Magalhães also attempted to reform the **theater** with his play *Antônio José ou o Poeta e a Inquisição* (1838; Antônio

José or the Poet and the Inquisition), the first Brazilian tragedy on a national subject, which still employed an antiquated verse form. This too is the case with his contribution to **epic poetry**, *A Confederação dos Tamoios* (1856; The Confederation of the Tamoio Indians), which deals with Brazilian native themes but was rejected as backward-looking by other romantics such as **José de Alencar** and sparked a debate on the role of **indianismo** in Brazilian literature. Gonçalves de Magalhães, however, was defended by writers and by the emperor Pedro II (1821–1891), in whose cultural enterprises he collaborated and who named him baron and viscount. Gonçalves de Magalhães's *Ensaio Sobre a História da Literatura do Brasil* (1834; Essay on the History of Literature in Brazil), a lecture he delivered at the Institut Historique de France, presents and develops reflections on Brazilian cultural history by scholars such as Ferdinand Denis (1798–1890) and Almeida Garrett (1799–1854). *See also* PENA, LUÍS CARLOS MARTINS.

MAGAÑA, SERGIO (Mexico, 1924–1990). Dramatist. Although he wrote novels and short stories at the beginning of his career, Magaña soon turned to the **theater**, where he established his reputation. His early mentors were **Salvador Novo** and **Rodolfo Usigli**, and he was later associated with **Luisa Josefina Hernández** and **Emilio Carballido**. Much of his work is in a realist vein, but he has written in many modes and on a wide variety of themes, including the revolution, nationalism, pre-Hispanic history, love and incest, suicide and death, and diverse aspects of urban life. Among his urban plays, *Los signos del Zodíaco* (1951; Signs of the Zodiac), about a neighborhood afflicted by adversity, is one of his best-known dramas. *El pequeño caso de Jorge Lívido* (1958; The Small Case of Jorge Lívido), a critique of the justice system and methods used to obtain confessions, and *Los motivos del lobo* (1965; The Wolf's Motives), about a man who shuts his family in to protect it from the world outside, are both set in urban environments. Magaña's historical drama includes *Moctezuma I* (1953; Montezuma I), in which the Aztec emperor is destroyed by his gods amid premonitions of religious conflict, and *Los argonautas* (1967; The Argonauts), about Hernán Cortés and his native mistress, La Malinche.

Children's literature finds a place in the dramatist's work with *El viaje de Nocresida* (1952; Nocresida's Journey), written in collaboration with Emilio Carballido, and *El anillo de oro* (1960; The Golden Ring), the story of some mice and a cat that come to the aid of a mother and child. Magaña's musical dramas, to which he contributed music and lyrics, include a dig at landlords and civil servants in *Rentas congeladas* (1960; Frozen Rents); an *auto*, *El mundo que tú heredas* (1970; The World You Inherit); and *Santísima* (1980; Santísima), a musical play based on **Federico Gamboa**'s best-known novel. Magaña also wrote a number of plays taken from literary sources: *El reloj y la cuna* (1952; The Clock and the Cradle), about a woman who is seduced and betrayed, murders her son, and falls into madness, based on the Greek tragedy *Medea* (431 BCE) by Euripides (480–403 BCE); *La dama de las camelias* (1979; The Lady of the Camellias), inspired by a work by the younger Alexandre Dumas (1824–1895); and *Ensayando a Molière* (1966; Rehearsing Molière), an interview with the celebrated French comic dramatist.

MAGAZINES. *See* JOURNALS, MAGAZINES, NEWSPAPERS, AND PERIODICALS.

MAGDALENO, MAURICIO (Mexico, 1906–1986). Novelist. Commonly associated with the **novel of the Mexican Revolution**, his work does not deal directly with the revolution, which tends rather to form the background to his narratives. His early novels were *El compadre Mendoza* (1934; The Godfather Mendoza), *Campo Celis* (1935; Campo Celis), and *Concha Bretón* (1936; Concha Bretón). These were followed by *El resplandor* (1937; Sunburst), his most celebrated novel, which pits an Indian community afflicted by drought against the rich and powerful. Elements of **indigenismo** and the rural setting also figure in his later fiction: *Sonata* (1941; Sonata), *Cabello de elote* (1949; Corn Silk), and *La tierra grande* (1949; The Big Land). His best short stories were published in *La ardiente verano* (1954; Burning Summer). Magdaleno was also a highly successful screenwriter, who wrote the screenplays for a number of classic Mexican films of the 1930s, 1940s, and 1950s, beginning with the adaptation of his own novel, *El compadre Mendoza*.

MAGGI, CARLOS (Uruguay, 1922–). Dramatist and essayist. Fiction appears among Maggi's works, notably the short story collections *Cuentos de humoramor* (1967; Tales of Humorlove) and *El libro de buen humor* (1985; The Book of Good Humor), but is not where he has made his most significant mark. He is known as the author of ironically humorous essays on Uruguayan society, including *Polvo enamorado* (1951; Enamored Dust), *El Uruguay y su gente* (1961; Uruguay and Its People), *Gardel, Onetti y algo más* (1964; Gardel, Onetti, and Something Else), and *Los militares, la televisión y otros razones de uso interno* (1986; The Military, Television and Other Reasons for Internal Use). Above all, his reputation as a dramatist is well established. His first works for the **theater**, *La trastienda* (1958; The Back Room) and *La biblioteca* (1961; The Library), the latter a Kafkaesque encounter with bureaucracy during the building of a library, were realistic, written in the tradition of the River Plate **sainete** and **grotesco criollo**. In later works, with which he had considerable critical and commercial success, he turned to a more impressionistic style akin to the **theater of the absurd**, such as *La noche de los ángeles inciertos* (1962; The Night of Uncertain Angels) and *Esperando a Rodó* (1968; Waiting for Rodó). Maggi has also written for newspapers, radio, and the cinema.

MAGIC REALISM. This term is used to refer to one of the most characteristic trends in Latin American literature, especially fiction, of the second half of the 20th century. It is commonly associated with the **boom**, largely on the strength of **Gabriel García Márquez**'s *Cien años de soledad* (1967; One Hundred Years of Solitude). Magic realism is not easily defined, and there has been disagreement about the kinds of works to which it applies virtually since critics first began to use the term. The most common application is to narratives in which elements of myth, religion, magic, or superstition are represented as if they were part of everyday reality. This style therefore challenges the rational conventions of modernity and proposes a more syncretic reality in which the primitive or premodern coexists alongside the modern, a condition that was taken to be representative of Latin America itself. Although García Márquez's groundbreaking novel is considered one of magic realism's paradigms, elements of the trend are also found in the work of many authors, including **Laura Esquivel, Elena Garro,** and **Juan Rulfo (Mexico); Rafael Arévalo Martínez (Guatemala); Manlio Argueta** and **Salarrué (El Salvador); Rogelio Sinán (Panama); Arturo Uslar Pietri (Venezuela); Demetrio Aguilera Malta** and **Nelson Estupiñán Bass (Ecuador); Augusto Roa Bastos (Paraguay); César Aira** and **Haroldo Conti (Argentina);** and **Isabel Allende (Chile).** *See also* CUADRA, JOSÉ DE LA; HONDURAS; WOMEN.

MALLEA, EDUARDO (Argentina, 1903–1982). Novelist, short story writer, and essayist. He was a prolific writer, editor (1931–1955) of the literary supplement of the Buenos Aires daily *La Nación*, and a longtime contributor to the literary **journal** *Sur*. His book-length essay on Argentina in the 1930s, *Historia de una pasión argentina* (1935; *History of an Argentine Passion*), won him considerable notoriety and provided what is often considered the theoretical underpinning of his fiction. Indeed, several of his "thesis" novels are thought to be essay-like. With elements in common with European **existentialism**, his fiction explores the internal worlds of characters searching for authenticity in an Argentinean culture that has exhausted itself. This tendency appeared in *La ciudad junto al río inmóvil* (1936; The City Beside the Stagnant River), a collection of short stories depicting the anguish and alienation of life in Buenos Aires.

Mallea's first novel, *Fiesta en noviembre* (1938; *Fiesta in November*), sets the tone for much of his later work. Telling the story of a lavish party into which an account of the murder of a young idealist is interleafed, it was written against the background of Fascist violence in Europe and the execution of the Spanish poet Federico García Lorca in 1936 at the beginning of the Spanish Civil War (1936–1939). The novel *Bahía de silencio* (1940; *The Bay of Silence*) is the autobiography of a writer, Martín Tregua, struggling to realize his hopes and aspirations. *Todo verdor perecerá* (1941; *All Green Shall Perish*), often considered the author's best work, develops similar themes of isolation, silence, and alienation from reality through the story of a female character, Ágata Cruz. Other novels by Mallea include *Chaves* (1953; *Chaves*), *Los enemigos del alma* (1950; Enemies of the Soul), *Triste piel del universo* (1971; Sad Skin of the Universe), and *En la creciente oscuridad* (1973; In the

Growing Dark). He published several collections of short narratives, including *La sala de espera* (1953; The Waiting Room), *La barca de hielo* (1967; The Ice Ship), and *La penúltima puerta* (1969; The Last Door But One). *See also* OCAMPO, VICTORIA.

MANCISIDOR, JOSÉ (Mexico, 1894–1956). Novelist, short story writer, and essayist. Mancisidor fought in the revolutionary army and obtained the rank of lieutenant colonel of artillery before ending his military career in 1920. He also became a militant communist whose novels, customarily included in the **novel of the Mexican Revolution**, sought to convey a socialist perspective. His first novel was *La asonada* (1931; The Coup), followed by *La ciudad roja* (1932; The Red City), described as a "proletarian novel." *En la rosa de los vientos* (1941; At the Mercy of the Wind) and *Frontera junto al mar* (1953; Frontier by the Sea) are both narratives of the revolution, the latter set in Veracruz in 1914 at the time of the occupation of the port by U.S. marines. Mancisidor's short stories were collected in several books: *Cómo cayeron los héroes* (1930; How the Heroes Fell), *120 días* (1937; 120 Days), *El juramento* (1947; The Oath), *El destino* (1947; Destiny), *La primera piedra* (1950; The First Stone), and *Me lo dijo María Kaimlova* (1955; María Kaimlova Told Me). As an essayist, he wrote books on Karl Marx (1818–1883), Vladimir Ilych Lenin (1870–1924), and Joseph Stalin (1878–1953) and on French and Russian literature.

MANNS, PATRICIO (Chile, 1937–). Novelist, essayist, poet, and musician. As a singer-songwriter, Manns has had a successful musical career, both before and after leaving Chile for exile in 1973. He is a politically committed writer and performer who campaigned for Salvador Allende in 1964 and 1970 and whose musical style extends from the Chilean new song of the 1960s to more recent styles. As a writer, he has published a number of novels, including *Buenas noches los pastores* (1973; Goodnight Shepherds); *Actas de Marusia* (1974; Acts of Marusia), the basis of a highly successful film from the Chilean director Miguel Littín (1942–); *El corazón a contraluz* (1996; The Heart in Silhouette); and *La vida privada de Emile Dubois* (2004; The Private Life of Emile Dubois). His published poetry includes *Memorial de Bonampak* (1995; Bonampak Memorial), a work of **indigenismo** that speaks for the oppressed Maya. He is also the author of a biography of the Chilean singer-songwriter and folklorist **Violeta Parra** and has written for the stage and screen.

MANSILLA, LUCIO V. (Argentina, 1831–1913). Essayist. Although he wrote a number of books, he is remembered as a writer mainly for his memoir, *Una excursión a los indios ranqueles* (1870; *An Expedition to the Ranquel Indians*), an account of his journey into the province of Córdoba to negotiate a treaty with the Ranquel Indians that became a significant text in the debate on **civilization and barbarism** in Argentina.

MAPLES ARCE, MANUEL (Mexico, 1900–1985). Poet. He was the leading voice of the **avant-garde** movement **estridentismo** and editor of several of its publications, including the broadsheet *Actual* (1921) and the **journals** *Irradiador* (1923) and *Horizontes* (1926–1927). His own poetry from the time of his involvement with estridentismo was published in *Andamios interiores* (1922; Interior Scaffolds); *Urbe* (1924; Metropolis), focused on the modern city; and *Poemas interdictos* (1927; Forbidden Poems). His later poetry was collected in *Memorial de la sangre* (1947; Blood Memorial) and *La semilla de tiempo* (1971; Seed of Time). As a prose writer, Maples Arce also produced three volumes of memoirs and numerous essays on a wide range of topics, including Mexican art and literature.

MARECHAL, LEOPOLDO (Argentina, 1900–1970). Poet, novelist, and dramatist. As a Peronist intellectual, he held government positions in education, but lapsed into relative obscurity after the fall of **Juan Domingo Perón** in 1955. His writing is shaped by two main factors: his position as a writer of the **avant-garde** and his unequivocal Catholicism. Marechal was a metaphysician who also recognized the place of science. His first two significant collections of poetry, *Días como flechas* (1926; Days Like Arrows) and *Odas para el hombre y la mujer* (1929; Odes for Man and Woman), explore aspects of his daily life and show his affiliation with **ultraísmo**. His next collections, *Laberinto de amor* (1935; Labyrinth of Love), *Cinco poemas australes* (1937; Five Southern Poems), *El centauro* (1940; The Centaur), and *Sonetos a Sophía y otros poemas* (1940; Sonnets for Sophia and Other Poems), are more clearly religious. They show the development of his work from Spanish mysticism and the presence of symbols derived from religious sources. These elements are further pursued in the author's later, mature poetry: *El heptamerón* (1966; The Heptameron), *El poema de Robot* (1966; Robot's Poem), and *Poemas de la creación* (1979; Poems of Creation).

Marechal is better known for his three novels, which repeat each other thematically to some extent and explore concepts similar to those developed in his poetry. Nevertheless, each of the novels is a separate work, with its own structure and fictional world. The first to appear was *Adán Buenosayres* (1948; Adam Buenosayres), an allegory of the soul's passage to a superior reality that traces the metaphysical quest of the hero through the city. At the same time, the novel is notable for its attention to daily life, humor, autobiographical content, and poetic and colloquial language. With its introduction of mythology, it represents a new phase in the Argentinean novel reminiscent of *Ulysses* (1922) by James Joyce (1881–1941). Although the best known of the three novels, *Adán Buenosayres*, passed almost unnoticed when first published, it is now considered a seminal work of Argentinean narrative and was acclaimed by writers such as **Julio Cortázar** and **Ricardo Piglia**. Marechal's other two novels are *El banquete de Severo Arcángelo* (1966; Severo Arcángelo's Banquet) and *Megafón, o la guerra* (1970; Megafón, or War), which both explore the inner self and the human struggle in history.

In addition to poetry and narrative, he also wrote five plays, among which are *Antígona Vélez* (1965; Antígona Vélez), a reworking of Sophocles's drama on the theme of destiny, and *Don Juan* (1978; Don Juan), a version of the story of the Spanish dramatic protagonist that provides a further opportunity to explore questions of metaphysics. Marechal's work for the **theater** benefits from being viewed in the light of his poetry and fiction.

MARIÁTEGUI, JOSÉ CARLOS (Peru, 1894–1930). Essayist and journalist. He also wrote short stories, poetry, and plays, but is known principally for his political activities and writings. He was a political associate of **Víctor Raúl Haya de la Torre**, although the two went different ways after 1927. Mariátegui founded the Peruvian Socialist Party and the **journal** *Amauta*, which became an important vehicle of expression for the political Left. He also published many volumes of essays. His *Siete ensayos de interpretación de la realidad peruana* (1928; *Seven Interpretive Essays on Peruvian Reality*) is a classic of political writing and continues to be read. It was a highly influential text in its advocacy of a Peruvian socialism and an important political underpinning of **indigenismo**. *See also* ALEGRÍA, CIRO; GONZÁLEZ PRADA, MANUEL.

MARÍN CAÑAS, JOSÉ (Costa Rica, 1904–1980). Novelist and journalist. He first drew attention with the novel *Lágrimas de acero* (1929; Tears of Steel), based on his student days in Spain, and *Los bígardos del ron* (1929; The Drunken Beggars), a collection of short pieces about socially marginalized characters in Costa Rica. He became more widely known later, however, through two additional novels. *El infierno verde* (1935; Green Inferno) is a story of the Chaco War (1932–1935) between **Bolivia** and **Paraguay**, told in a first person account by a Paraguyan soldier. Although Marín had no experience of the war and had never been to either of the two countries involved, the work was first serialized in the newspaper *La Hora* in Costa Rica, where it passed successfully as a factual account. By contrast, *Pedro Arnáez* (1942; Pedro Arnáez) is closer to home. It is set in Central America during the social and political turmoil of the period between the two world wars and is the life story of a simple man, reconstructed by a doctor who met him during three moments of crisis. Marín Cañas also wrote for the **theater**, including the plays *Como tú* (1929; Like You), *En busca de un candidato* (1935; In Search of a Candidate), and *Una tragedia de ocho cilindros* (1938; A Tragedy in Eight Cylinders). After his literary activity of the 1920s and 1930s, however, he did not return to literature, but published only a number of journalistic books in the second half of his life, in which he collected essays, **chronicles**, articles, and impressions from his travels, especially in Spain.

MÁRMOL, JOSÉ (Argentina, 1817–1871). Novelist, poet, and journalist. He was politically active in opposition to the dictator **Juan Manuel Rosas** and suffered imprisonment and exile as a consequence, experiences that marked much of his writing. His novel *Amalia* (1851; *Amalia*), the work for which he is most remembered, one of the most popular novels of Spanish American **romanticism**, was written in exile in Montevideo and is an anti-Rosas narrative that prompted similar works by other authors. The novel displays a manichean view of Argentina, presented in the terms of a conflict between **civilization and barbarism**. It was adapted for the cinema in 1914 and became the source of Argentina's first full-length feature film. Mármol's poetry includes an autobiographical narrative called *El peregrino* (1847; The Pilgrim), an account of a sea voyage from Brazil to Montevideo, written in the manner of *Childe Harold's Pilgrimage* by Lord Byron (1788–1824), and a collection of lyric verse titled *Armonías* (1851; Harmonies), which express the poet's feelings for nature and social justice.

MARTÍNEZ, TOMÁS ELOY (Argentina, 1934–2010). Novelist, journalist, and short story writer. Part of the **post-boom** generation, Martínez's rise to prominence came through two novels, *La novela de Perón* (1985; *The Peron Novel*) and *Santa Evita* (1995; *Santa Evita*), both **new historical novels** and the latter an international **best seller**. He was a prolific journalist in his early years and wrote for numerous periodicals, including *Primera Plana* and *La Opinión*, both founded by **Jacobo Timerman**, and the Buenos Aires daily *La Nación*. His first major book, *La pasión según Trelew* (1973; The Passion According to Trelew), was also a product of journalism. It is a documentary analysis of atrocities committed by the military in the southern Argentinean town of Trelew. The compilation of multiple narratives and points of view in the book is a strategy to which he would return later. Inevitably, *La pasión según Trelew* met with the displeasure of the authorities: the book was banned and Martínez went into exile under death threats. He continued his work as a journalist in Venezuela and published two books of essays there: *Los testigos de afuera* (1978; Outside Witnesses) and *Retrato de un artista enmascarado* (1979; Portrait of a Masked Artist), as well as *Lugar común de la muerte* (1979; The Commonplace of Death), a volume of short stories.

Although Martínez had already published *Sagrado* (1969; Sacred), a novel of the fantastic, he did not gain wide attention until *La novela de Perón* appeared in 1985, by which time he had begun to establish himself in the United States. *La novela de Perón* takes the figure of **Juan Domingo Perón** in exile (1955–1973) as its subject. Based in part on extensive interviews the author conducted with the former president, he narrates the many different versions of Perón's story, including those that the president tells about himself, as if the protagonist were writing his own novel. Martínez would return to the Peronist period in Argentinean history, but not before publishing the novel *La mano del amo* (1991; The Hand of the Master), an allegory of attempted escape from authority represented through a protagonist striving to become his own person against an overpowering mother.

When he returned to Peronism in 1995, it was to publish a novel, *Santa Evita*, about the second wife of the president, **Eva Duarte de Perón**. *Santa Evita* examines the mythology of Evita. It has a basic linear momentum, but is also a novel within a novel, the story of how Martínez wrote it by assembling a collage of narratives from Evita's life and the memories that others retained of her, including those of her hairdresser. Using the story of what happened to Evita's body after her death and embalmment, the novel traces the movement of her corpse from place to place and the incidents it provokes, until it is finally interred in La Recoleta cemetery in Buenos Aires. After completing this novel, Martínez continued to publish other works, including the novels *El vuelo del la reina* (2002; The Flight of the Queen) and *El cantor de tango* (2004; *The Tango Singer*).

MARTÍNEZ ESTRADA, EZEQUIEL (Argentina, 1895–1964). Poet, short story writer, essayist, and literary critic. He was a prolific writer, who wrote poetry in his younger days and short stories throughout his life, collecting them in *La inundación* (1944; The Flood), *Marta Riquelme: ensayo sin conciencia* (1956; Marta Riquelme: Essay Without a Conscience), and *La tos y otros acontecimientos* (1957; The Cough and Other Events). He is recognized mainly, however, for sociohistorical studies of the psychology of Argentina, such as *Radiografía de la pampa* (1933; *X-ray of the Pampa*), a critique of **Domingo Faustino Sarmiento**'s notion of **civilization and barbarism**; *La cabeza de Goliat* (1940; Goliath's Head), on the impact of Buenos Aires on the history of Argentina; and *Muerte y transfiguración de Martín Fierro* (1948; Death and Transfiguration of Martín Fierro), a commentary on **José Hernández**'s narrative poem that expands aspects of *Radiografía de la pampa*. Martínez

Estrada's other works on politics and literature include *Sarmiento* (1946; Sarmiento), *El mundo maravilloso de Guillermo Enrique Hudson* (1951; The Marvelous World of William Henry Hudson), and *Martí revolucionario* (1957; Martí the Revolutionary). *See also* MURENA, HÉCTOR A.

MARTÍNEZ MORENO, CARLOS (Uruguay, 1917–1986). Novelist and short story writer. The political content of his writing is a reflection of his own militancy. In 1972, his home was bombed in retaliation for having published a series of articles critical of the government and for having served as legal representative of political detainees. He went into exile in 1977, eventually moving to **Mexico**, where he spent the last years of his life. *El paredón* (1963; The Wall), his first novel, caused a stir when it was published because of its treatment of the Cuban Revolution (1959). In *La otra mitad* (1966; The Other Half), he presents the figure of **Delmira Agustini** as a key to understanding contemporary reality. *Con las primeras luces* (1966; At First Light) is a novel about an upper-class family. *Coca* (1970; Cocaine) is a story of trafficking and addiction and *Tierra en la boca* (1974; Dirt in the Mouth) portrays lives of petty crime and violence. Martínez Moreno's last novel, *El color que el infierno me escondiera* (1981; *Inferno*), with a title borrowed from Dante, brings together stories of the civil strife in Uruguay of the 1960s and 1970s and the experiences of his work as a lawyer in the years before he went into exile. His short stories were published in the following volumes: *Los días por vivir* (1960; Days to Live), *Cordelia* (1961; Cordelia), *Los aborígenes* (1964; *Native People*), *Los prados de la conciencia* (1968; Fields of Conscience), and *De vida o muerte* (1971; Of Life and Death). He also wrote essays on literary topics.

MÁRTIR DE ANGLERÍA, PEDRO (Spain, 1457–1526). Chronicler. He was the author of *Décadas del Nuevo Mundo* (written 1493–1525; *De orbe novo. The Eight Decades of Peter Marty d'Anghera*), a **chronicle** written in Latin as a series of reports or letters and published as he completed them. He wrote in the florid style of literary humanism characteristic of the age and without the benefit of firsthand experience, because he never visited the New World and was not involved in any of the events about which he wrote.

MASTRETTA, ÁNGELES (Mexico, 1949–). Novelist, short story writer, and journalist. Her first novel, *Arráncame la vida* (1985; *Tear This Heart Out*), was a **best seller** in Mexico and abroad and established her reputation for strong female characters. Using the Mexican bolero among its motifs, it tells the story of the wife of a revolutionary general turned politician who rejects a submissive role beside her husband and follows her own path. Her second novel, *Mal de amores* (1996; *Lovesick*), was equally well received and won her the 1997 **Rómulo Gallegos Prize**, the first time this prestigious award had been given to a **woman**. It covers 50 years in the history of 20th-century Mexico through the life of Emilia Sauri, who is in love with two men, one a revolutionary, the other a doctor. Between these two novels, Mastretta published *Mujeres de ojos grandes* (1990; Women with Big Eyes), a collection of 38 short pieces, each about a woman who defies social convention. Her most recent works of fiction are *Ninguna eternidad como la mía* (1999; No Eternity Like Mine), a novel set in early postrevolutionary Mexico about a young immigrant woman who studies dancing and is determined to retain her independence, and a further collection of short stories, *Maridos* (2007; Husbands). Mastretta has also published two anthologies of essays from her work as a journalist: *Puerto libre* (1993; Free Port) and *El mundo iluminado* (1998; The Enlightened World).

MATTO DE TURNER, CLORINDA (Peru, 1852–1909). Novelist. Some of her earliest writings were "traditions," written in the style of **Ricardo Palma** and collected in her first book *Tradiciones cuzqueñas* (1884; Traditions from Cuzco). In her three novels, *Aves sin nido* (1889; *Torn from the Nest*), *Índole* (1891; Human Nature), and *Herencia* (1895; Heredity), however, her writing took a turn toward **naturalism** and the representation of contemporary reality. *Aves sin nido* is the best known of the three. Its denunciation of the treatment of native people made it a controversial novel in its day and one of the earliest works of **indigenismo**. *Índole*, with some of the anticlericalism also appearing in *Aves sin nido*, presents two contrasting families in an Andean village, a newlywed Indian couple and a criollo couple whose relationship is falling apart. In contrast to these two novels, *Herencia* is set in Lima and is a story of social segregation. In addition to her treatment of racial issues, Matto de

Turner's fiction also has an undercurrent of feminism evident in her portrayal of female characters who resist the confinement of their lives to the domestic sphere, although this aspect of her work is more apparent in her journalism and in her ventures in publishing undertaken to promote writing by **women**. *See also* CABELLO DE CARBONERA, MERCEDES; GONZÁLEZ PRADA, MANUEL; GORRITI, JUANA MANUELA.

MATTOS, TOMÁS DE (Uruguay, 1947–). Novelist and short story writer. He has published two collections of short stories, *Libros y perros* (1975; Books and Dogs) and *Trampas de barro* (1983; Clay Traps), as well as the novels *La fragata de las máscaras* (1996; Frigate of Masks) and *La puerta de la Misericordia* (2002; The Door to Mercy). His best-known work, however, is *¡Bernabé, Bernabé!* (1988; Bernabé, Bernabé!), a **new historical novel** that reexamines the foundation of Tacuarembó in Uruguay by Colonel Bernabé Rivera. The novel revisits the massacre of the Charrúa Indians in 1831, the construction of a sense of national identity that silences minorities, and the long-standing debate about **civilization and barbarism**.

MATTOS E GUERRA, GREGÓRIO DE (Brazil, 1636–1695). Perhaps Brazil's most noted **baroque** satirist and poet, de Mattos (also spelled de Matos) was born in Salvador (Bahia) into a rich and distinguished family. After initial studies with the Jesuits in Salvador, he traveled to Coimbra, Portugal, where he obtained a degree in canonical law. He also became acquainted at the time with Spanish and baroque poetry, especially Luis de Góngora (1561–1827), Francisco de Quevedo (1580–1645), and Luís de Camões (1524–1580). De Mattos held public positions and practiced law in Portugal and only returned to Brazil when he was in his fifties. Settling back in Salvador, he became a virulent critic of Bahian society, a practice that earned him the sobriquet "Boca do Inferno" (Hell's Mouth) and deportation to Angola, whence he returned to Brazil only one year before his death in Recife.

Although he is best known for his satirical poetry, de Mattos was accomplished as a religious poet and a love poet in the Petrarchan tradition. In his religious poetry, he exemplified the Counter-Reformation concerns of man's relationship with God, and his love poetry features the idealization of the beloved and the poet's dissatisfaction with unfulfilled passion. Other poems also mix the erotic with the grotesque. The variety and contrast of his writings reflect similar contradictions in a society apparently ruled by strict religious codes yet riddled with ambition for pleasure and riches. De Mattos's works circulated mostly in manuscript during his lifetime and were only published for the first time in the 19th century, a fact that has made the study of his work problematic. Among the editions of his work are the six-volume *Obras* (1923–1933; Works), edited by **Afrânio Peixoto**; the seven-volume *Obras Completas* (1968; Complete Works), edited by James Amado; and *Poemas Escolhidos* (1976; Selected Poems), edited and with an introduction and notes by José Miguel Wisnik. *See also* MATTOSO, GLAUCO; OLIVEIRA, MANUEL BOTELHO DE; RIBEIRO, JOÃO UBALDO.

MATTOSO, GLAUCO, pseudonym of PEDRO JOSÉ FERREIRA DA SILVA (Brazil, 1951–). Poet. An heir to the satirical tradition of the Portuguese medieval songs of mockery and to the Brazilian poet **Gregório de Mattos**, Glauco Mattoso is one of the few poets of the 1970s countercultural movements such as **poesia marginal** who continue to write effectively in that vein. Initially attracted to **concrete poetry** and visual poems, Mattoso, whose pseudonym derives from the congenital glaucoma he suffers from, had to abandon that mode when he lost his sight completely, returning to metered forms such as the sonnet and song lyrics. Early works such as *Jornal Dobrabil, 1977–1981* (2001; *Foldable News*), a newspaper distributed by mimeograph whose title puns on the daily *Jornal do Brasil*, reflect the time when artists sought alternative modes of distribution to avoid censorship under the Brazilian dictatorship. His work also makes explicit reference to **gay and lesbian writers and writing** in works such as *Manual do Pedólatra Amador* (1986; Manual of the Amateur Pedolatrist). In his so-called blind period, Mattoso continued his satirical vein in sonnets that explore polemical and transgressive topics, such as *Centipéia: Sonetos Nojentos & Quejandos* (1999; Centipede: Disgusting and Similar Sonnets), *Paulisséia Ilhada: Sonetos Tópicos* (1999; Paulicéa Ilhada: Topical Sonnets), *Geléia de Rococó: Sonetos Barrocos* (1999; Rococo Jelly: Baroque Sonnets), and *Panacéia: Sonetos Colaterais* (2000; Panacea: Collateral Sonnets).

MAYA, RAFAEL (Colombia, 1897–1980). Poet. Rather than adopting any precise influences from the past or subscribing to any contemporary movements, he followed his own inclinations derived from Catholicism and nationalism and his conservative view of the world. His books of poetry include *La vida en la sombra* (1925; Life in the Shadow), *Coros del mediodía* (1928; Midday Choruses), *Después del silencio* (1938; After the Silence), and *Navegación nocturna* (1959; Nocturnal Navigation). He also published short stories and wrote essays on literature and nationalism.

MEIRELES, CECÍLIA (Brazil, 1901–1964). Poet. Orphaned at a young age, Meireles was raised by her grandmother from the Azores. She attended school in her native Rio, earning honors and a medal conferred by the district school inspector and poet **Olavo Bilac**. She graduated from teachers college in 1917 and followed a teaching career. Two years later, she published her first book of poetry, *Espectros* (1919; Specters), written under the influence of **parnassianism**. *Nunca Mais . . . e Poema dos Poemas* (1923; Nevermore . . . and Poems of Poems) and *Baladas para El-Rei* (1925; Ballads for the King) were her next collections in this early phase in the style of **symbolism** and displayed an interest in the mystical and the supernatural. In this period, Meireles also associated with other writers who professed a Catholic faith and with them founded the **journal** *Festa* in 1927, to which she also contributed poems. In 1934 Meireles founded the first children's library of Brazil and visited Portugal, lecturing at various universities.

In the next few years, Meireles suffered the loss of her grandmother and her husband, and was left with three young daughters to raise. She published little for some 14 years. Her next volume to appear, *Viagem* (1939; Voyage), written in meter, displayed existential concerns, often hermetic and despondent. *Viagem* was awarded the Brazilian Academy of Letters Prize for 1939, although her conservative poetics was the subject of controversy.

Meireles wrote in a different modern style that did not follow the **Week of Modern Art**, but evolved individually from symbolism. Her deeply personal lyricism is present in *Vaga Música* (1942; Vague Music), *Mar Absoluto e Outros Poemas* (1945; Absolute Sea and Other Poems), and *Retrato Natural* (1949; Portrait from Life), in which she also begins to reflect on external realities. *Amor em Leonoreta* (1951; Love in Leonoreta) and *Doze Noturnos da Holanda e O Aeronauta* (1952; Twelve Nocturnes from Holland and the Aeronaut) are inspired by her travels and experiences of flying. Meireles was an avid traveler and visited **Mexico**, India, and Portugal for long periods. In one of her best-known works, *Romanceiro da Inconfidência* (1953; Inconfidência Ballads), she employs the Iberian ballad tradition to recount the tragic fate of the poets who rebelled against the Portuguese crown in the 18th century in the prosperous mining region of Minas Gerais. *Pequeno Oratório de Santa Clara* (1955; Little Oratorio for St. Clair), written for the 700th anniversary of the saint, retells her life in verse. Other works include *Pistóia* (1955; Pistóia), *Canções* (1956; Songs), *Romance de Santa Cecília* (1957; Romance of St. Cecilia), *A Rosa* (1957; The Rose), *Metal Rosicler* (1960; Pyrite Rock), *Poemas Escritos na Índia* (1962; India Poems), *Solombra* (1963; Sun and Shadow), and *Ou Isto ou Aquilo* (1964; This or That).

Besides poetry, Meireles also wrote **chronicles** and prose, including *Evocação Lírica de Lisboa* (1948; Lyrical Remembrances of Lisbon). She lectured widely on literature and was a folklore expert. At the time of her death from cancer, she was considered Brazil's greatest **woman** poet and a major figure in **Brazilian modernism**.

MEJÍA VALLEJO, MANUEL (Colombia, 1923–1998). Novelist and short story writer. Much of Mejía Vallejo's fiction is set in rural Antioquía, where he was born, and deals with history and the theme of **la violencia** in Colombia. His first novel, *La tierra éramos nosotros* (1945; We Were the Land), was a traditional evocation of rural life and customs in the manner of **regionalism**, but in the two that followed, *Al pie de la ciudad* (1958; At the Foot of the City) and *El día señalado* (1964; The Appointed Day), he applied more modern techniques. *El día señalado* in particular won him recognition both within and beyond Colombia and gave new life and form to both the novel of Antioquía and the Colombian novel of violence. The mature novels that followed include *Los negociantes* (1965; The Businessmen); *Aire de tango* (1973; Tango Melody), set in Medellín, about a man who was born on the day (24 June, 1935) that Carlos Gardel died in that city and who believes himself to be a reincarnation of the great singer; *Las muertes ajenas* (1979; The Deaths of Others), also set in Medellín; *La casa de las dos palmas* (1989; The House with Two Palms), which won its author further wide recognition as recipient of the 1989 **Rómulo Gallegos Prize** and was filmed for Colombian television; and *Memoria del olvido* (1990; Memory of Forgetfulness). His books of short stories are *Tiempo de sequía* (1957; Time of Drought), *Cielo cerrado* (1963; Closed Sky), *Cuentos de zona tórrida* (1967; Tales from the Torrid Zone), *Las noches de las vigilias* (1975; Nights on Watch), *Otras historias de Balandú* (1990; Other Stories of Balandú), *Sombras contra el muro* (1993; Shadows on the Wall), and *La venganza y otros relatos* (1995; Revenge and Other Stories).

MELO NETO, JOÃO CABRAL DE (Brazil, 1920–1999). Poet. One of the most influential Brazilian poets of the 20th century, Cabral was born in Recife but grew up on the family's plantation in the rural interior. Contact with the popular narrative poems known as *literatura de cordel* would later shape his poetics, firmly rooted in the arid landscapes of the Northeastern backland and hard life of its inhabitants. In 1930, Cabral moved with his family to Recife, whose river, the Capibaribe, features in his poems. Although he had no formal studies, Cabral came from a literary family and was an avid reader who soon acquainted himself with French, English, and Spanish authors. In 1942, he moved to Rio and published his first book of poetry, *Pedra do Sono* (1942; Stone of Sleep), a collection influenced by **surrealism** and word association, that already anticipates his later poetry in its use of stark images and concise language. Cabral joined the diplomatic corps in 1945, married in 1946, and resided abroad for many years of his life, serving in the Brazilian consulates of Asunción, Barcelona, and Dakar.

In his next two books of poetry, *O Engenheiro* (1945; The Engineer) and *Psicologia da Composição* (1947; Psychology of Composition), Cabral abandoned the surrealist mode and the sentimental and irrational aspects of poetry in favor of an antilyrical and constructivist "ars poetica." Many of these poems deal thematically with the mechanics of a concise and precise poetry. This return to an attention to form originally aligned him with the poets of the **Generation of '45**, but eventually Cabral would follow his own path. His concern with form was complemented by social concern in his later works, *O Cão sem Plumas* (1950; *The Dog without Feathers*), an allegory of the Capibaribe River and its impoverished denizens, and *O Rio* (1954; The River).

This dual nature in his poetry was reflected in the title of the volume *Duas Águas* (1956; Two Waters), which included *Morte e Vida Severina* (*Death and Life of a Severino*), *Paisagens com Figuras* (*Landscapes with Figures*), and *Uma Faca só Lâmina* (*A Knife All Blade*). *Morte e Vida Severina*, a long dramatic/narrative poem in a vernacular vein that recounts the trials and tribulations of impoverished migrant sugarcane workers of Northeastern Brazil, was later staged in France, subtitled "Auto de Natal Pernambucano" (A Pernambuco Nativity Play), earning Cabral prizes and international recognition. The poetry from this period, written while Cabral resided in Spain, also evidences Cabral's awareness of the arid Castilian plains and its medieval poetry. *Paisagens com Figuras* and *Uma Faca Só Lâmina* focus on the hardness of landscapes and figures expressed in a nominal and stonelike language, and *Quaderna* (1960; *Four Spot*) also incorporates the use of the Spanish *cuaderna vía* or medieval quatrain form. *Serial* (1961; Serial) eliminates the lyrical "I" and hints at the **avant-garde** musical experiments of the period. *Dois Parlamentos* (1961; Two Voices) returns to the topic of the life of the impoverished sugarcane workers. *A Educação pela Pedra* (1966; *Education by Stone*), one of Cabral's fundamental books, focuses on a poetics inspired by the hardness of the stone in the Northeastern backlands, yet devoid of all sentimentalism and marked by a rigor of construction. *Museu de Tudo* (1975; Museum of Everything) collects stylistically varied poems on a wide variety of subjects and set in different places.

A Escola das Facas (1980; The School of Knives) returns to the topic of the Northeastern backlands and sugar plantations of Cabral's childhood, this time in a memoirlike mode. Similarly, *Agrestes* (1985; Rough and Rude) includes poems about Cabral's memories of Pernambuco and the poet's own death. *Crime na Calle Relator* (1987; Crime in Calle Relator) contains personal memoir poems set in both Pernambuco and Spain, where the hardness of the early poems is less apparent. *Auto do Frade* (1983; The Friar) a narrative poem later adapted for the stage, recounts the life of Frei Caneca, a friar sentenced to death for his involvement in the Pernambuco revolution in the 19th century.

Among Cabral's essayistic prose works are *Considerações Sobre o Poeta Dormindo* (1941; Remarks on the Poet Sleeping), *Joan Miró* (1950; Joan Miró), and *Da Função Moderna da Poesia* (1957; Of the Modern Function of Poetry). Cabral received two important literary prizes: the Camões Prize in 1990 and the Neustadt Prize in 1992. In his last years, Cabral began to lose his eyesight and stopped writing because he said he could not dissociate the literary from the visual. He died in Rio, where he had resided during the last years of his life.

MENCHÚ, RIGOBERTA (Guatemala, 1959–). Political activist. She received the 1992 Nobel Peace Prize and was the subject of a celebrated **testimonio**, *Me llamo Rigoberta Menchú y así me nació la conciencia* (1982; *I, Rigoberta Menchú: An Indian Woman in Guatemala*), by Elisabeth Burgos-Debray, which was the source of a heated controversy when its historical authenticity was questioned. *See also* WOMEN.

MENDES, MURILO (Brazil, 1901–1975). Poet. Born in Minas Gerais, Mendes began his studies there, but soon moved to Rio. At age nine, he was inspired to become a poet after seeing the passage of Halley's comet. He was also fascinated by the dancer Vaslav Nijinsky (1890–1950) and escaped from boarding school in 1917 to attend a performance by him. Mendes began writing for the literary **journals** *Verde* and *Revista de Antropofagia* and joined the ranks of **Brazilian modernism**. His first book, *Poemas* (1930; Poems), already reveals a dreamlike quality that some associate with **surrealism**. It was followed by *Bumba-meu-Poeta* (1930; Dance of the Poet and the Ox), and *História do Brasil* (1932; History of Brazil), a satire of the events of Brazilian history. Mendes met and befriended the painter Ismael Nery, who influenced him and was responsible for Mendes's conversion to Catholicism. After the painter's death in 1934 due to tuberculosis, Mendes fell into depression.

Written in collaboration with **Jorge de Lima**, *Tempo e Eternidade* (1935; Time and Eternity) employs the confessional mode to solemnly address the Muse. *A Poesia em Pânico* (1938; Poetry in a Panic) is a record of the poet's struggle with his obligation to God and to the Muse, which the Muse eventually wins, leaving the poet in distress. *O Visionário* (1941; The Visionary) again recalls the dream states of his early poetry. *As Metamorfoses* (1944; The Metamorphoses) was written in the midst of World War II and evidences pessimism in the face of destruction, a mood somewhat tempered by love in his next volume, *Mundo Enigma* (1945; Enigma World). In *Poesia Liberdade* (1947; Poetry Freedom), published the year he married, Mendes again explores a pessimistic outlook.

In private life, Mendes worked in various government jobs and traveled in Europe in 1953–1954 before settling in Italy in 1957 as a teacher of Brazilian literature. Other works by Mendes include *Tempo Espanhol* (1950; Spanish Time), in which he mixes observations about Spain with Brazil; *Contemplação de Ouro Preto* (1954; Thoughts on Ouro Preto), introspective meditations on old cities from Minas Gerais; *Siciliana* (1954–1955; Sicilian) and *A Idade do Serrote* (1968; The Age of the Serrote), poems about personal memories; *Convergência* (1970; Convergence); *Poliedro* (1972; Polyhedron); a volume in Italian *Ipotesi* (1977; Hypotheses); and his *Poesias (1925–1955)* (1955: Poems), which includes the unpublished *Sonetos Brancos* (1946–1948; Blank Sonnets) and *Parábola* (1946–1952; Parabola). Mendes also wrote the short stories in *O Discípulo de Emaús* (1944; The Disciple from Emaus) and *Retratos-Relâmpago* (1973; Flash Portraits). See also GUIMARÃES, JÚLIO CASTAÑON; HILST, HILDA.

MENDOZA, MARÍA LUISA (Mexico, 1938–). Novelist and journalist. Her career as a journalist has resulted in a wide and varied contribution to print and broadcast media as a political commentator, drama critic, and writer about her own and **women**'s experiences. Several collections of her **chronicles** have been published, including *Crónica de Chile* (1972; Chilean Chronicle), on political and cultural topics, and *Las cosas* (1976; Things), a memoir of daily life during her childhood. As a novelist and one of Mexico's prominent women writers, her writing has a clear autobiographical voice and a significant focus on the world of women. Her first novel, *Con él, conmigo, con nosotros tres* (1971; With Him, with Me, with We Three), written as a monologue, is concerned with the events of the **Tlatelolco massacre**. *De Ausencia* (1974; About Ausencia) challenges conventional proprieties through the narrative of the erotic life of its 19th-century female protagonist, Ausencia Bautista Lumbre. *El perro de la escribana o las Piedecasas* (1982; The Scrivener's Dog, or the Piedecasas Women) is also a biographical novel, based on the memories of Leona Piedecasas and the different houses where she has lived. Mendoza has also written **children's literature**, and one of her most recent books is the novel *De amor y lujo* (2003; Of Love and Luxury).

MENESES, GUILLERMO (Venezuela, 1911–1978). Novelist and short story writer. Notable for treatment of Afro-Venezuelan themes, such as the novel *Canción de negros* (1934; Song of Blacks), the novella *La balandra Isabel llegó esta tarde* (1934; The Sloop Isabel Arrived This Afternoon), a classic of Venezuelan literature, and the stories in *Campeones* (1939; Champions). *El mestizo José Vargas* (1942; José Vargas the Mestizo), a story of fishermen, is also set against the background of racial issues, but is concerned with Venezuelans of indigenous rather than African background. Meneses's best novel is perhaps *El falso cuaderno de Narciso Espejo* (1952; Narciso Espejo's Fake Journal), a complex novel within a novel in which the notions of fiction and reality are played off against each other. A similar interplay is also at the core of the author's last novel, *La misa de Arlequín* (1962; Harlequin's Mass).

MERA, JUAN LEÓN (Ecuador, 1832–1894). Poet, novelist, journalist, and critic. Beginning his literary career as a poet, Mera wrote on the themes of family, patriotism, and religion in *Poesías* (1858; Poems); *La virgen del sol* (1861; Virgin of the Sun), an Indian legend written in verse; and *Poesías devotas y nuevo mes de María* (1867; Devotional Verse: A New Month for Mary). He was a conservative thinker, who remained faithful to the Spanish classics in his writing. At the same time, he brought nativist elements into his work, reflecting them in aspects of indigenous folklore, evocations of the natural world, historical anecdotes, and the description of local customs. His politics identified him with the two-time president and strongman Gabriel García Moreno (1859–1865, 1869–1875), about whom he wrote in *La dictadura y la restauración* (written 1884; published 1932; The Dictatorship and the Restoration). Juan León Mera's best-known literary work is the novel *Cumandá, o un drama entre salvajes* (1879; Cumandá, or a Drama Among Savages), a novel of tragic love in the manner of **indianismo** and **romanticism**, heavily influenced by the French novel of the early 19th century, in which the author sought to examine the role of religion in society and to offer a model based on former Jesuit enterprises in South America for an alliance between Church and state. One of his poems is the source of Ecuador's national anthem.

MERCADER, MARTHA (Argentina, 1927–). Novelist and short story writer. Her best-known novel is *Juanamanuela mucha mujer* (1980; Juanamanuela, a Lot of Woman), based on the life of **Juana Manuela Gorriti**. Like her more recent *Belisario en son de guerra* (1984; Belisario Ready For War) and *Vos sabrás* (2001; You'll Know), it is also considered a **new historical novel**. Other works by Mercader include her collections of short stories, *Octubre en el espejo* (1966; October in the Mirror) and *El hambre de mi corazón* (1989; The Hunger in My Heart). *See also* WOMEN.

MERCADO, TUNUNA (Argentina, 1939–). Novelist and short story writer. Mercado's autobiographical novel *En estado de memoria* (1990; *State of Memory*) is a narrative of exile and return that echoes the author's own experiences. Her other work includes the collections of short stories *Celebrar a la mujer como la pascua* (1967; Celebrate Woman Like a Holiday) and *Canon de alcoba* (1988; Bedroom Lore), the novels *Narrar después* (2003; Relate Later) and *Yo nunca te prometí la eternidad* (2005; I Never Promised You Eternity), and her memoir, *La madriguera* (1996; The Lair). *See also* WOMEN.

MEXICO. Of all national literary histories of Latin America, Mexico's is one of the longest and fullest. Its pre-Columbian traditions are preserved in its architectural heritage, its oral traditions, and in the codices and narratives compiled both in the pre-Hispanic era and by native and mestizo Mexicans after the conquest. Literature in Spanish begins with the **chronicles**, the record of the conquest and colonization. Accounts are preserved in the writings of participants, such as the letters of **Hernán Cortés** and the narrative of **Bernal Díaz del Castillo**, and in the work of historians such as **Francisco López de**

Gómara and the verse chronicler **Gabriel Lobo Lasso de la Vega**, neither of whom ever traveled to Mexico from their native Spain. The view of events from the conquered Indians is told by mestizo chroniclers such as **Hernando Alvarado Tezozomoc** and **Fernando de Alva Ixtlilxóchitl**, whereas the history of the christianization of the native population and a description of their culture at the time of the conquest has been recorded by a number of missionary priests and friars, including **Bernardino de Sahagún**, **Diego de Landa**, and **Toribio de Benavente (Motolinía)**.

During the colonial period, a popular culture began to take shape from the combination of elements of both local and European traditions, whereas the more formal aspects of cultural life were centered at the viceregal court in the capital. In poetry and prose, the **baroque** 16th and 17th centuries produced works by three notable figures: the **epic poetry** and lyric eulogy of Mexico City by **Bernardo de Balbuena**; the lyric verse and religious writings of **Sor Juana Inés de la Cruz**; and the varied scientific writings, poetry, and novel of **Carlos de Sigüenza y Góngora**. The pre-independence period of the late 18th century and the early years of independence are represented by another significant figure, **José Joaquín Fernández de Lizardi**, whose critique of colonial society in his fiction and journalism captures the intellectual climate surrounding the break with Spain.

After Lizardi's work, the first important 19th-century novel was an anonymous **historical novel** called *Xicoténcatl* (1826), set in the conquest period, but the first significant novelist was **Manuel Payno**, whose fiction shows elements of **romanticism**, **costumbrismo**, and the historical novel, sometimes known as the **colonial novel** in Mexico. After him, the same combination of characteristics are found in the fiction of **Justo Sierra O'Reilly**, **Luis G. Inclán**, **Vicente Riva Palacios**, **Eligio Ancona**, **José Tomás de Cuéllar**, and **Ignacio Manuel Altamirano**, the most influential of them all. In the 20th century, the colonial novel found a popular exponent in **Artemio de Valle Arizpe**. Costumbrismo led to **realism** and to more of a focus on contemporary society toward the close of the 19th and the beginning of the 20th centuries, in writers such as **Ángel de Campo**, **Rafael Delgado**, **Emilio Rabasa**, and **José López Portillo y Rojas**. It would be followed by the more deterministic view of reality represented by a Mexican version of **naturalism**, a trend found in novels by **Federico Gamboa** and **Heriberto Frías**.

Mexico's most significant 19th-century poet was **Guillermo Prieto**, a highly popular figure sometimes considered the founder of the national literary tradition. Among others of his generation were Vicente Riva Palacio and Ignacio Manuel Altamirano. It was initially through **modernismo**, centered on the literary **journals** *Revista azul* and *Revista moderna*, that Mexican poetry really began to flourish in the first two decades of the century, however. **Manuel José Othón, Efrén Rebolledo, Luis G. Urbina,** and **Salvador Díaz Mirón** were among the premodernists who adopted the new aesthetics in due course. The modernists themselves included **Manuel Gutiérrez Nájera, Amado Nervo, Enrique González Martínez, Alfonso Reyes**, and the early **Juan José Tablada.**

Although modernismo had a strong presence in Mexico, it yielded in due course to the **avant-garde**. Bridging the two movements is the poetry of **Ramón López Velarde,** who also achieved recognition as a national poet. The Mexican avant-garde itself is represented mainly by **estridentismo** and a group known as **Los Contemporáneos**, also the title of the journal founded in 1928 in which they published their philosophy and poetry. The *estridentistas* were the smaller group, led by **Manuel Maples Arce** and including **Germán List Arzubide.** Los Contemporáneos included **Salvador Novo, Xavier Villaurrutia, José Gorostiza, Jorge Cuesta, Bernardo Ortiz de Montellano, Jaime Torres Bodet, Gilberto Owen,** and **Carlos Pellicer.**

After the avant-garde of the 1920s and 1930s, writers have been more inclined to follow personal interests and aesthetics and have tended less to associate in literary movements. Poetry of the second half of the 20th century was dominated by Mexico's **Nobel Prize** winner **Octavio Paz**, although there have also been other very notable figures. Those who have achieved most recognition are **José Emilio Pacheco** and **Jaime Sabines**, but a list of acknowledged 20th-century Mexican poets would also include **Alí Chumacero, Efraín Huerta, Rosario Castellanos,** and **Homero Aridjis.**

Modernismo also influenced prose writing, such as Amado Nervo's fiction, but prose writing and much else in Mexico was more strongly affected by the armed conflict known as the Mexican Revolution (1910–1920). It resulted in one-party rule for over 70 years, not ended until 2000. The revolution also provided a context for reflection about national identity and culture. This had already begun with writers such as **Servando Teresa de Mier** and **Justo Sierra** in the 19th century. Prominent authors of the 20th century who have also concerned themselves with these questions include **José Vasconcelos**, Octavio Paz, and **Carlos Fuentes**. More recently, in chronicles on life and culture in Mexico, **Carlos Monsiváis** examined the significance of 20th-century mass culture on national identity. In fiction, the immediate product of the military conflict was the **novel of the Mexican Revolution**. The first cycle of novels, begun in 1915 by **Mariano Azuela**, including works by **Nellie Campobello, Martín Luis Guzmán, Miguel Lira, Gregorio López y Fuentes, Mauricio Magdaleno, José Mancisidor, Rafael F. Muñoz, José Rubén Romero, Francisco L. Urquizo,** and **José Vasconcelos**, consisted primarily of narratives of the military campaigns, often based on the authors' personal experiences. A second cycle, initiated by **Agustín Yáñez** in 1947 and continued in the work of **Juan Rulfo**, Carlos Fuentes, **José Revueltas, Sergio Galindo**, and Rosario Castellanos, took a broader view of the war and its contexts, focusing on its place in social history and the continuing impact of its consequences. Throughout the remainder of the 20th century, the revolution and its aftermath were frequent sources of reference, often subject to new interpretations, as in novels by **Ángeles Mastretta** and **Laura Esquivel**, both of whom have written popular works from a feminist perspective.

In terms of both the range and quality of his writing, Mexico's most important 20th-century novelist is undoubtedly Carlos Fuentes, who also figures among Latin America's **boom** writers. However, the second half of the 20th century produced a significant body of prose writers and a range of fictional works covering a wide variety of topics and styles. The experiments of **Julieta Campos, Salvador Elizondo, Vicente Leñero**, and **Sergio Pitol** in the 1960s and 1970s had some of the characteristics of the **new novel**. The killing of student demonstrators in 1968 that has come to be known as the **Tlatelolco massacre** became a focal point for examining the social and political life of the times and was the source of novels by **Luis Spota, Juan García Ponce, María Luis Puga**, and **Elena Poniatowska**. After the massacre, a movement known as **la onda** focused on youth countercultures and the continuing modernization of Mexico, produced two notable novelists, **José Agustín** and **Gustavo Sainz**. The number of **women** writers increased as the century progressed, including, in addition to those already mentioned above, **Elena Garro**, **Margo Glantz**, **María Luisa Mendoza**, and **Carmen Boullosa**. Writers who contributed to the **new historical novel** included **Fernando del Paso** and Homero Aridjis. Other genres with notable representatives are the **fantastic** short stories of **Juan José Arreola** and the popular narratives of **Bruno Traven**, both belonging to the mid-20th century; the **crime fiction** of **Paco Ignacio Taibo II**; and the **testimonios** of Elena Poniatowska, which cover several events in 20th-century Mexican history.

The **theater** in Mexico had its origins in religious plays, *autos* written in either Spanish or native languages and intended both to entertain and instruct. The theater was also a medium for the Jesuits, who took classical models in Latin as the basis of exercises in rhetoric. By the second half of the 16th century, the secular theater had also become established, making Mexico one of the Latin American countries with the oldest commercial theaters. Although the plays performed were not necessarily by local dramatists, writers like **Fernán González de Eslava** became known for their *entremeses*, *sainetes*, and *coloquios*, short comic pieces usually performed between the acts of a longer play.

The 17th century in Mexico produced two notable contributors to the theater: **Juan Ruiz de Alarcón,** who also became known in Spain, and Sor Juana Inés de la Cruz, whose work for the stage includes the beginnings of musical theater. The 18th century was marked by the continued rise of the secular theater and the increase in writing on local themes, but produced no outstanding figures save for, perhaps, **Eusebio Vela**. José Joaquín Fernández de Lizardi wrote a few short pieces for the stage at the begining of the 19th century, but the more notable dramatists were **Manuel Eduardo de Gorostiza** during the first half of the century and Manuel José Othón during the second half. During this period, writing for the stage was dominated by romantic plays, historical dramas, and comedies of manners modeled principally on the European sources. By this time, although most theaters were in the capital, there were also others established in cities such as Guadalajara and San Luis Potosí.

Mexican theater of the 20th century began in the 1920s with the avant-garde, the establishment of institutionalized support under the auspices of José Vasconcelos and others, and the founding of a sequence of theater enterprises. The Teatro Ulises, founded in 1928, provided a stage for the work of Xavier Villaurrutia, Salvador Novo, Gilberto Owen, **Julio Jiménez Rueda**, and **Celestino Gorostiza**, who would go on to set up the Teatro Orientación and contribute to the introduction of mainstream world theater to Mexico. More Mexican themes and writing were featured by 1932 in the Teatro de Ahora and the Teatro de Media Noche, under the tutelage of Mauricio Magdaleno and **Rodolfo Usigli**, respectively. To these dominant figures of the 1930s were then added several others from Spain, notably Max Aub (1903–1972), who took refuge in Mexico from civil war in their own country.

During the 1940s, the pursuit of new directions was sustained by Miguel N. Lira and **María Luisa Ocampo**, while **Sergio Magaña** and **Emilio Carballido** represented two important additions to the world of theater. At the same time, in 1947, the theater section of the Instituto Nacional de Bellas Artes (INBA; National Institute of Fine Arts) was established, consolidating the continuation of institutionalized support for the theater in Mexico. By the 1950s, several of Usigli's students, including **Luisa Josefina Fernández** and **Jorge Ibargüengoitia**, began to have an impact, and **Luis G. Basurto** registered his early successes. The 1950s and 1960s were, in effect, a golden age for Mexican theater, not just on account of the work of dramatists already mentioned, but through the addition of further writers for the stage such as as Elkena Garro, Vicente Leñero, and **Maruxa Vilalta**.

In contrast to the preceding decades, the 1970s represented a decline in the performance of work by Mexican dramatists. By the 1980s and 1990s, however, a new generation of writers, including **Óscar Lieras** and **Sabina Berman**, brought renewed vigor to the stage. With a cohort of established dramatists, strong institutions, and revivals of plays from the Mexican repertoire, theater in Mexico is one of the strongest in Latin America. Its national success is also complemented by an international presence, not just through frequent performance of Mexican plays in the Southwestern United States, but through performances in other countries and continents as well. *See also* ACOSTA, JOSÉ DE; BEST SELLER; CARDOZA Y ARAGÓN, LUIS; CIVILIZATION AND BARBARISM; COSTA, HORÁCIO; GIARDINELLI, MEMPO; GÓMEZ CARRILLO, ENRIQUE; INDIGENISMO; INDIGENOUS TRADITIONS; MAGIC REALISM; MARTÍNEZ MORENO, CARLOS; MEIRELES, CECÍLIA; MIGUEL DE CERVANTES PRIZE; MONTEFORTE TOLEDO, MARIO; MONTERROSO, AUGUSTO; MORO, CÉSAR; MUTIS, ÁLVARO; NEO-BAROQUE; NEO-CLASSICISM; NEO-INDIGENISMO; ODIO, EUNICE; OREAMUNO, YOLANDA; SELVA, SALOMÓN DE LA; VITALE, IDA.

MEYER, AUGUSTO, JR. (Brazil, 1903–1970). Poet and critic. Born in Rio Grande do Sul, Meyer is linked to **Brazilian modernism** in its regional variant. His poetry explores provincial life, expressing optimism tempered by irony. Among his poetry books are *A Ilusão Querida* (1923; The Dear Illusion), *Coração Verde* (1926; Green Heart), *Poemas de Bilu* (1929; Bilu's Poems), *Sorriso Interior* (1930; Inner Smile), *Folhas Arrancadas* (1940–1944; Torn Pages), and *Últimos Poemas* (1950–1955). As a critic, Meyer also wrote reviews and essays for the press and published books of literary criticism: *Machado de Assis* (1935; Machado de Assis) and *Camões o Bruxo e Outros Ensaios* (1958; Camões the Wizard and Other Essays).

MICROTALES. Microtales are miniature short stories, not much more than a paragraph or two, or barely a page, in length. The first accomplished writer to produce them was **Jorge Luis Borges (Argentina)**, some of whose microtales are celebrated examples of the genre. Other authors who have written them include **Augusto Monterroso (Guatemala)**, **Nuno Ramos (Brazil)**, **Marco Denevi** (Argentina), and **Pía Barros (Chile)**.

MIER, SERVANDO TERESA DE (Mexico, 1763–1827). Essayist, sermonist, and memorialist. A Catholic priest, his opinions on religion and government brought him into conflict with both ecclesiastical and civil authorities in Mexico and Spain, resulting in several periods of exile and imprisonment, from which he invariably managed to escape. His principal writings include *Cartas de un ameri-*

cano, 1811–1812 (Letters from an American) and his autobiography, *Memorias* (1819; *The Memoirs of Fray Teresa Servando de Mier*).

MIGUEL DE CERVANTES PRIZE. Considered the **Nobel Prize for Literature** of the Spanish-speaking world, this prize, first awarded in 1976, is given annually to acknowledge the lifetime achievement of a writer in Spanish. Latin American recipients have been **Juan Gelman** (2007; **Argentina**), **Sergio Pitol** (2005; **Mexico**), **Gonzalo Rojas** (2003; **Chile**), **Álvaro Mutis** (2001; **Colombia**), **Jorge Edwards** (1999; **Chile**), **Mario Vargas Llosa** (1994; **Peru**), **Adolfo Bioy Casares** (1990; Argentina), **Augusto Roa Bastos** (1989; **Paraguay**), **Carlos Fuentes** (1987; Mexico), **Ernesto Sábato** (1984; Argentina), **Octavio Paz** (1981; Mexico), **Juan Carlos Onetti** (1980; **Uruguay**), and **Jorge Luis Borges** (1979; Argentina).

MILLA Y VIDAURRE, JOSÉ (Guatemala, 1822–1882). Novelist. Writing under the pseudonym "Salomé Gil" and publishing in serial form in newspapers, he was one of Guatemala's first significant fiction writers. His novels, in the style of **costumbrismo** and the **historical novel**, were very popular and have all the characteristics of the 19th-century serialized novel, with its meandering, melodramatic plot. His most significant works were *La hija del Adelantado* (1866; The Governor's Daughter), *Los nazarenos* (1867; The Nazarenes), *El visitador* (1867; The Inspector), *Historia de un Pepe* (1872; Story of a Nobody), and *Memorias de un abogado* (1876; Memoirs of a Lawyer). *El esclavo de don Dinero* (1881; Slave to Money), his last novel, reflects a shift in his work toward social criticism, in contrast to his earlier work, which is rigidly conservative. In *Un viaje a otro mundo, pasando por otras partes, 1871–1874* (1875; Journey to Another World by Way of Other Places), a fictionalized account of a period of exile endured for political reasons, Milla y Vidaure introduced the popular figure Juan Chapín, who has acquired the status of the stereotypical Guatemalan.

MILLIET DA COSTA E SILVA, SÉRGIO (Brazil, 1898–1966). Poet and critic. Born in São Paulo, Milliet studied social sciences in Geneva and began his career as a poet writing in French. Among his early poetry books are *Par le Sentier* (1917; Along the Road), *Le Départ sous la Pluie* (1919; The Departure in the Rain), and *L'œil de Bœuf* (1923; The Bull's Eye). Milliet joined **Brazilian modernism**, participating in the **Week of Modern Art**. From that point on, he collaborated with **journals** such as *Klaxon* and *Terra Roxa e Outras Terras*. In his early books of poetry in Portuguese, such as *Poemas Análogos* (1927; Analogous Poems), he employed a technique where images are joined by analogy. His later books, such as *Poemas* (1937; Poems), *Oh Valsa Latejante* (1943; Oh Palpitating Waltz), *Poesias* (1946; Poems), *Poema do Trigésimo Dia* (1950; Poem of the Thirtieth Day), *Alguns Poemas Entre Muitos* (1957; Some Poems Among Many), and *Cartas à Dançarina* (1959; Letters to the Dancer), explore the theme of love, but with a sense of ennui and pessimism.

Milliet became better known for his essays and criticism, in which he displayed his vast erudition and explored the nature of the Brazilian national character. His books of essays include *Terminus Seco e Outros Cocktails* (1932; Dry Terminus and Other Cocktails), *Marcha à Ré* (1936; Backing Up), *Ensaios* (1938; Essays), *Roteiro de Café* (1938; Coffee Itinerary), *O Sal da Heresia* (1940; The Salt of Heresy), and *Fora de Forma* (1942; Out of Shape). He left a *Panorama da Poesia Moderna Brasileira* (1955; Panorama of Modern Brazilian Poetry) and, as director of the Museum of Modern Art, also wrote *Pintores e Pintura* (1940; Painters and Painting), *A Marginalidade da Pintura Moderna* (1942; The Marginality of Modern Painting), and *Pintura Quase Sempre* (1943; Painting Almost Always). His *Diário Crítico* (1944–1959; Critical Diary) spans 10 volumes.

MIRÓ, RICARDO (Panama, 1883–1940). Poet. Recognized for his patriotic verses as one of his country's national poets, he wrote mainly under the influence of **modernismo**, and **Rubén Darío** was instrumental in the publication of his first book of poems, *Preludios* (1908; Preludes). His later collections were *Segundos preludios* (1916; Second Preludes), *La leyenda de Pacífico* (1919; Legend of the Pacific), *Versos patrióticos y recitaciones escolares* (1925; Patriotic Verses and Student Recitations), *Caminos silenciosos* (1929; Silent Paths), and *El poema de la reencarnación* (1929; The Poem of Reincarnation). He also wrote two novels, *Las noches de Babel*

(1913; Babel Nights) and *Flor de María* (1922; Mary's Flower), and a volume of his short stories was published posthumously in 1957.

MISTRAL, GABRIELA (Chile, 1889–1957). Poet. Born Lucila Godoy Alcayaga, she is universally known by her pen name, Gabriela Mistral. Highly respected as a teacher, she was a prominent figure in education and diplomacy, and a prolific contributor to newspapers and magazines in the Spanish-speaking world. She achieved immense popularity during her lifetime, both in Chile and beyond, and was the recipient of many honors and awards, including the 1945 **Nobel Prize for Literature**, the first Latin American author to be so honored. She traveled widely and after 1926 returned to Chile only briefly, on two occasions.

Gabriela Mistral's poetry is contained mainly in five collections. The first three, *Desolación* (1922; Desolation), *Ternura* (1924; Tenderness), and *Tala* (1938; Tree Felling), underwent several revisions and re-editions. The fourth collection was *Lagar* (1954; Wine Press), and the last, *Poema de Chile* (1967; Poem of Chile), was published posthumously. Her poetry is aesthetically independent, and the simplicity of her verse is said to reflect the reaction of her generation to **modernismo**. An identification with ordinary people; a concern for peace, education, children's rights, and social justice for the dispossessed; and respect for the land figure significantly among her themes. Although she also wrote of maternity, frustrated love, and death, much of her poetry was also intended for children, giving her a very visible place among writers of **children's literature**. *See also* ALEGRÍA, CIRO; DALTON, ROQUE; PARRA, NICANOR; TEITELBOIM, VOLODIA; VAZ FERREIRA, MARÍA EUGENIA.

MODERNISMO. Unlike European or **Brazilian modernism**, which refers to different forms of **avant-garde** artistic expression, and with which it is not to be confused, Spanish American modernismo was a predominantly literary phenomenon that began to coalesce in the 1890s and maintained its influence until the 1920s, when it began to wane before the advance of the avant-garde. It was not a movement as such, having no manifestos or the following of a coherent group of members committed to a set of principles. Nevertheless, it was characterized by certain distinguishable trends and had focal points in various countries, represented by the work of particular authors. Modernism was "modern" in that it entailed a break from the prevailing styles of the past, especially the sentimentality of **romanticism** and certain types of **realism** such as **costumbrismo**. Drawing on French **parnassianism** and **symbolism**, it endeavored to renew poetic imagery, language, and form and to place Latin American writing in an international cultural context, exploiting the exotic and valuing both the object of art and the artist for their own sake.

The impact of modernismo was felt throughout Spanish America on all literary genres, although its greatest effect was on poetry. Its principal exponent was the Nicaraguan **Rubén Darío**, whose work transcended the borders of his own country, being read throughout the continent and having some influence in Europe. Other significant poets whose work reflects the characteristics of modernismo include **Manuel Gutiérrez Nájera**, **Ramón López Velarde**, and **Amado Nervo (Mexico)**; **Juan Ramón Molina** and **Rafael Heliodoro Valle (Honduras)**; **Guillermo Valencia (Colombia)**; **Ricardo Jaimes Freyre** and **Franz Tamayo (Bolivia)**; **José Santos Chocano** and **José María Egurén (Peru)**; **Delmira Agustini** and **Julio Herrera y Reissig (Uruguay)**; and **Leopoldo Lugones (Argentina)**.

The effects on prose were less extensive, but quite diverse. In fiction, the characteristics of modernismo seemed to lend themselves best to the short story in writers such as **Francisco Gavidia (El Salvador)** or the Argentinean Leopoldo Lugones. With respect to the novel, a modernist style is evident in **José María Vargas Vila (Colombia)**, **Manuel Díaz Rodríguez (Venezuela)**, and **Enrique Larreta (Argentina)**. The emergence of modernismo also coincided with an advance in the professionalization of the writer, due in part to a growth in literacy and the spread of mass circulation newspapers. The **chronicle** became a feature of the daily press, with contributors such as Rubén Darío, the Mexican Manuel Gutiérrez Nájera, and, above all, the Guatemalan **Enrique Gómez Carrillo**. Notable critics of modernismo include **Rufino Blanco Fombona** (Venezuela) and **Angel Rama** (Uruguay).

See also AMBROGI, ARTURO; ARÉVALO MARTÍNEZ, RAFAEL; CHILE; CORREA, JULIO; CUADRA, PABLO ANTONIO; D'HALMAR, AUGUSTO; DÍAZ MIRÓN, SALVADOR;

GONZÁLEZ MARTÍNEZ, ENRIQUE; GONZÁLEZ PRADA, MANUEL; HERRERA, DARÍO; HUIDOBRO, VICENTE; IBARBOUROU, JUANA DE; LILLO, BALDOMERO; LÓPEZ, LUIS CARLOS; MIRÓ, RICARDO; MISTRAL, GABRIELA; MOLINA, JUAN RAMÓN; MUNDONOVISMO; NERUDA, PABLO; NICARAGUA; NÚÑEZ, RAFAEL; OTHÓN, MANUEL JOSÉ; PERU; PRADO, PEDRO; QUIROGA, HORACIO; RIVERA, JOSÉ EUSTASIO; RODÓ, JOSÉ ENRIQUE; SABAT ERCASTY, CARLOS; SELVA, SALOMÓN DE LA; SILVA, JOSÉ ASUNCIÓN; STORNI, ALFONSINA; TABLADA, JOSÉ JUAN; TORRESRIOSECO, ARTURO; ULTRAÍSMO; URBINA, LUIS G.; USLAR PIETRI, ARTURO; WOMEN.

MOLINA, ENRIQUE (Argentina, 1910–1997). Poet. Formed under the influence of **Aldo Pellegrini** and the tutelage of **Oliverio Girondo**, Molina became one of Argentina's most steadfast adherents of **surrealism**. He was part of a group of poets known in Argentina as the Generation of 1940, which included **Olga Orozco** and **Alberto Girri**. He edited the literary **journal** *A partir de cero* (Begining at Zero) from 1952 until 1956. In his poetry he frequently revisited the dreams of childhood with a sense of adventure and undying optimism, and he sought the traces of human history in domestic objects. His books are *Las cosas y el delirio* (1941; Things and Delerium), *Pasiones terrestres* (1946; Terrestrial Passions), *Costumbres errantes o la redondez de la tierra* (1951; Wandering Customs or the Roundness of the Earth), *Amantes antípodas* (1961; Polar Lovers), *Fuego libre* (1962; Free Fire), *Los últimos soles* (1980; The Last Suns), *El ala de la gaviota* (1989; The Seagull's Wing), *Hacia una isla incierta* (1992; Towards an Uncertain Island), and *El adiós* (1997; The Farewell). He also published a novel, *Una sombra donde sueña Camila O'Gorman* (1973; A Shade Where Camila O'Gorman Dreams), a version of the historical tragic love story of Camila O'Gorman and Ladislao Gutiérrez narrated as a series of surreal images set in 19th-century Argentina under **Juan Manuel Rosas**.

MOLINA, JUAN RAMÓN (Honduras, 1875–1908). Poet. He spent his life between Honduras, **Nicaragua**, and **Guatemala**, affected by the changing political scene in Central America. Much of his writing is gathered in a single volume, *Tierras, mares y cielos* (1911; Lands, Seas and Skies), published postumously in Honduras after he had succumbed to the consequences of drug and alcohol addiction. This volume has been reedited several times and has brought the author considerable recognition in Central America. It contains some prose works, including short stories, but his reputation has come mainly from his poetry, which he used to exorcise his personal anguish. He wrote in traditional forms (almost half his poems were sonnets), but also belonged aesthetically to **modernismo**.

MOLINARI, RICARDO E. (Argentina, 1898–1996). Poet. From the publication of his first collection, *El imaginero* (1927; The Image Maker), Molinari established his credentials with the Argentinean **avant-garde** and a position among prominent Argentinean writers of the 20th century through a style of writing informed by **ultraísmo**, **surrealism**, and the classical tradition of Spain. He would go on to publish more than 50 books, some illustrated and many private or presentation editions of just a few pages prepared for friends. Molinari remained out of the public eye, however, and spent his entire working life in the civil service. His themes were concerned with the landscape, the human condition and its metaphysical dimensions, escape to the inexpressible and intangible, loneliness, melancholy, and the elegiac. His poems were collected in two anthologies during his lifetime: *Un día, el tiempo, las nubes* (1964; One Day, Time, the Clouds) and *Las sombras del pájaro tostado: obra poética, 1923–1973* (1975; The Shadows of the Brown Bird: Poetic Works, 1923–1973).

MONSIVÁIS, CARLOS (Mexico, 1938–2010). Essayist and journalist. Monsiváis was the most prominent commentator on Mexican culture of his generation. For 15 years (1972–1987), he served as editor of *La cultura en México*, a supplement of the newspaper *Siempre!*, but also contributed to all of Mexico City's major newspapers and magazines and appeared regularly on television. Although a public figure, who taught at various universities, he was an independent writer with no fixed institutional affiliation. As a cultural commentator, he has written on Mexican national culture, especially mass culture and the sense of identification established between people and cultural forms. His **chronicles** cover politics, personalities, literature, popular music, art, film, religion, and sport and gave particular attention to Mexico City, especially to the urban chaos arising from its size and its struggles to survive the crises that have afflicted it, such as the **Tlatelolco massacre** and the 1985 earthquake.

Monsiváis was an acerbic critic, who wrote with considerable humor and irony. His published books include *Días de guardar* (1970; Red Letter Days), *Amor perdido* (1977; Lost Love), *Historias para temblar: 19 de septiembre de 1985* (1988; Stories for Quaking: 19 September, 1985), *Los rituales del caos* (1995; The Rituals of Chaos), *Aires de familia: cultura y sociedad en América Latina* (1995; Family Resemblances: Culture and Society in Latin America), *Las tradiciones en la imagen: notas sobre poesía mexicana* (2001; Traditions in the Image: Notes on Mexican Poetry), and *Las alusiones perdidas* (2007; Lost Allusions). An anthology of his chronicles has been published in English translation under the title *Mexican Postcards* (1997).

MONTALVO, JUAN (Ecuador, 1832–1889). Essayist. He is considered one of Ecuador's greatest stylists. Parts of his life were spent in exile, the result of his opposition to two Ecuadorian presidents, Gabriel García Moreno (1859–1865, 1869–1875) and Ignacio de Veintemilla (1876–1883). His best-known and most frequently published work is *Las Catilinarias* (1880–1882; Speeches Against Cataline), a series of 12 pamphlets, all written against the dictatorship of Veintemilla, in which the insult is raised to a fine art. Montalvo founded and edited several **journals**, published a number of essays on moral philosophy, and left *Capítulos que se le olvidaron a Cervantes* (Chapters Cervantes Forgot), a sequel to *Don Quixote*, unpublished at his death. He also contributed to 19th-century **theater** in Ecuador with plays on political themes, although they were intended to be read rather than performed. They include *La leprosa* (1872; The Leprous Woman); *El dictador* (1873; The Dictator), written in opposition to García Moreno; and *Granja* (1873; Farm).

MONTEFORTE TOLEDO, MARIO (Guatemala, 1911–2003). Novelist. Politics played an important role in the first half of his life. He opposed the government of Jorge Ubico (1931–1944) and subsequently had roles in the administrations of Juan José Arévalo (1945–1951) and Jacobo Arbenz (1951–1954), serving as Arévalo's vice president. He lived in exile in **Mexico** between 1954 and 1987. In keeping with his public life, Monteforte Toledo's early fiction has a significant political content and is characterized by social realism. His first novel, *Anaité* (1948; Anaité), follows in the tradition of the theme of **civilization and barbarism**. His second, *Entre la piedra y la cruz* (1948; Between the Stone and the Cross), is thematically more akin to **indigenismo** and documents abuses committed against Guatemalan Indians. By contrast, his later novels, *Donde acaban los caminos* (1953; Where the Roads End), *Una manera de morir* (1957; A Way to Die), and *Llegaron al mar* (1966; They Reached the Sea), are more psychologically oriented and have some of the characteristics of **existentialism**. *La cueva sin quietud* (1949; The Cave Without Calm) and *Cuentos de derrota y esperanza* (1962; Tales of Defeat and Hope) are collections of short stories. His complete works also include several essays and pieces for the **theater**.

MONTERROSO, AUGUSTO (Guatemala, 1921–2003). Short story writer. Although born in **Honduras**, Monterroso has become fully associated with Guatemala and is considered one of that country's most significant writers. Political involvement led to periods of exile in **Chile** and **Mexico**, and in 1956 he took up permanent residence in Mexico. It is sometimes difficult to classify his writing, to determine in which genre he is writing, or to separate fiction from reality. He is commonly thought of as a writer of short texts or **microtales** such as the following, one of his most celebrated: "When he awoke, the dinosaur was still there." His work is a constant engagement with the world of literature and a search for novelty, characteristics that have often led to comparisons with **Jorge Luis Borges**. Monterroso's first book has the ironic title *Obras completas y otros cuentos* (1959; Complete Works and Other Stories), but his second book, *La oveja negra y demás fábulas* (1969; The Black Sheep and Other Fables), examines the short story genre more explicitly through a series of humorous animal fables. *Movimiento perpetuo* (1972; Perpetual Motion) is a collection of brief texts, part essay and part narrative. By contrast, *Lo demás es silencio: la vida y obra de Eduardo Torres*

(1978; The Rest Is Silence: The Life and Work of Eduardo Torres) is a more unified text than Monterroso's earlier books and purports to be the biography of a real writer told from several different points of view. *La palabra mágica* (1983; The Magic Word) is a collection of essays, notes, and brief narratives, mainly about literature. *Los buscadores de oro* (1993; The Gold Seekers) and *La vaca* (1998; The Cow) both have a more autobiographical orientation as a collection of confessional, humorous texts tinged with some of the melancholy of old age and approaching death. Finally, in *Viaje al centro de la fábula* (1981; Journey to the Center of the Story), there is a collection of interviews given by the author during the course of his life.

MOOCK, ARMANDO (Chile, 1894–1942). Dramatist. As the author of more than 50 plays, many never published, he was one of Chile's most significant dramatists of the first half of the 20th century. His success also extended to **Argentina**, where he lived for more than 20 years and where his biggest commercial success, *La serpiente* (The Serpent), was first performed in 1920. Moock's preferred style was the bourgeois comedy of manners characterized by the creation of popular social types, somewhat in the traditions of **costumbrismo** and **naturalism**, but he also explored other styles and wrote *sainetes*, dramas, and **theater** for puppets. His most successful works include *Los demonios* (1917; The Demons), *M. Ferdinand Pontac* (1922; M. Ferdinand Pontac), *Mocosita, o La luna en el pago* (1929; Mocosita, or Moon over the Homestead), and *Algo triste que llaman amor* (Something Sad They Call Love). He also wrote plays for the radio. As a writer of fiction, he had short stories published in literary **journals** and produced the novels *¡Pobrecitas!* (1916; Poor Things!), *Sol de amor* (1924; Sun of Love), and *Vida y milagos de un primer actor* (1926; The Life and Miracles of a Leading Actor), an autobiographical work.

MORAES, VINÍCIUS DE (Brazil, 1913–1980). Poet, dramatist, and lyricist. Born into a musical family, his father was a guitarist and his mother a pianist, Vinícius de Moraes began to compose music and write lyrics and poetry at an early age. He grew up in Rio, between the suburb Gávea and Governor's Island. While a law student, he met and befriended the conservative writer **Otávio de Faria**, who influenced his first two collections of poetry in the style of **symbolism**, *O*

Caminho para a Distância (1933; The Road to Distance) and *Forma e Exegese* (1935; Form and Exegesis). In those early books and in the following three, *Ariana, a Mulher* (1936; Ariana, the Woman), *Novos Poemas* (1938; New Poems), and *Cinco Elegias* (1943; Five Elegies), Moraes explored transcendental and mystical themes, using long lines of blank and free verse. During the 1930s and 1940s, Moraes worked as a film critic and censor and studied English literature at Oxford. In 1943, he entered the Brazilian diplomatic corps and served in the United States, South America, and Europe.

In his poetic production, *Poemas, Sonetos e Baladas* (1946; Poems, Sonnets, and Ballads) marks a transition into a new phase when Moraes experimented with metrical forms such as the sonnet and the ballad. In this new phase, he wrote *Pátria Minha* (1949; My Country), *Livro de Sonetos* (1957; Book of Sonnets), *Novos Poemas II* (1959; New Poems II), and *Para Viver Um Grande Amor* (1962; To Live a Great Love), a book of poems and chronicles. In this period also Moraes went thematically from a mystical symbolism to more carnal and material topics and came to be considered by many one of Brazil's best erotic poets. He also wrote many lyrics for the bossa nova movement in the 1950s, and his play *Orfeu da Conceição* (1956; Orfeu da Conceição), a retelling of the myth of Orpheus in Brazil during carnival time, was turned into the blockbuster *Black Orpheus*. His **chronicles** are gathered in *Para uma Menina com uma Flor* (1966; For a Girl with a Flower). His poetry is collected in *Obra Poética* (1968; Poetry Works). *See also* HILST, HILDA; SABINO, FERNANDO.

MORO, CÉSAR (Peru, 1903–1956). Poet and painter. Born Alfredo Quíspez Asín in Lima, Moro spent significant periods of his life outside Peru, notably in France and **Mexico**. In Paris, he was drawn to **surrealism** and was an active member of the movement headed by André Breton (1896–1966). He also adopted French as his preferred language of expression, making his poetry less accessible among Spanish-speaking readers. In 1935, he organized an exhibition of surrealist art in Lima, the first on the continent, which also sealed his reputation as an *enfant terrible* on account of his aesthetic preferences, his homosexuality, and his outspoken opinions. The catalog to the exhibition appeared under the heading of a quotation from the painter Francis Picabia (1879–1953), "Art is a pharmaceutical product for imbeciles," and included a vitriolic attack against **Vicente Huidobro**, who later responded in kind. Moro's poetry in Spanish has been collected in *La tortuga ecuestre y otros poemas, 1924–1949* (1956; The Equestrian Tortoise and Other Poems), and his prose in Spanish in *Los anteojos de azufre* (1958; The Sulfur Tinted Spectacles).

MORRIS, ANDRÉS (Honduras, 1928–). Dramatist. Although born in Spain, he settled in Tegucigalpa in 1961, where he had considerable impact on **theater**. He collaborated in the founding of a national theater, which began producing both foreign and local plays, including some of his own, although it was not long-lived. Morris's plays are socially conscious works that dramatize the triumphs and problems of everyday life in the context of a country dominated by external economic forces. Among his best-known works is a trilogy of plays called the *Trilogía ístmica* (Isthmus Trilogy), written in the style of the **theater of the absurd**, on the theme of underdevelopment. It consists of a rural play, *El Guarizama* (1967; Guarizama); *La miel de abejorro* (1968; Bumblebee Honey), on land and technical development; and *Oficio de hombres* (1969; Men's Work), about employment in an urban context. Other titles include *La tormenta* (1955; The Storm) and *Los ecos dormidos* (1957; Dormant Echoes).

MOYANO, DANIEL (Argentina, 1930–1992). Novelist and short story writer. In 1976, he left Argentina for exile in Spain, where he spent the rest of his life. He writes about poverty, marginalization in the city, childhood, and the mysterious side of life. Franz Kafka (1883–1924) and Cesare Pavese (1908–1950) figure significantly among writers who influenced him, and his own fiction often inclines to the allegorical. His novels include *Una luz muy lejana* (1966; A Very Distant Light), *El oscuro* (1967; The Dark One), *El trino del diablo* (1974; *The Devil's Trill*), *El vuelo del tigre* (1981; *Flight of the Tiger*), and *Libro de navíos y borrascas* (1983; Book of Ships and Squalls). Among his books of short stories, *Artista de variedades* (1960; Vaudeville Artist), *La lombriz* (1964; The Earthworm), *El fuego interrumpido* (1967; Interrupted Fire), *Mi música es para esta gente* (1970; My Music Is for These People), and *El estuche de cocodrilo* (1974; The Crocodile Skin Case) are worthy of note.

MUJICA LÁINEZ, MANUEL (Argentina, 1910–1984). Novelist and short story writer. He was born into an aristocratic, but no longer wealthy, Argentinean family and worked as a journalist for much of his life for the daily *La Nación*. Unlike others of his generation, he formed no affiliation with the literary groups or **journals** of his day, and his classical tastes separated him from the **avant-garde**. However, he was a popular writer, the author of more than 20 books, a number of which continue to be re-edited and read. Buenos Aires and the history of the city figure prominently in much of his work. His first novel, *Don Galaz de Buenos Aires* (1938; Don Galaz from Buenos Aires), is a **picaresque** tale set in colonial times. *Canto a Buenos Aires* (1943; Song to Buenos Aires), his only known poem, was written in praise of the city, and *Misteriosa Buenos Aires* (1950; Mysterious Buenos Aires) is a series of episodes covering its history from the 16th to the 20th centuries. The core of his fiction, representing the work of his early maturity, is a series of novels about the Argentinean upper class: *Los ídolos* (1952; The Idols), *La casa* (1954; The House), *Los viajeros* (1955; The Travelers), and *Invitados en El Paraíso* (1957; Guests at El Paraíso). Of these, the most celebrated is *La casa*, the story of a mansion and its inhabitants on Calle Florida in Buenos Aires, told by the building itself as it faces demolition. Mujica returned to the theme of the Argentinean upper class in *El gran teatro* (1979; The Great Theater).

The **historical novel** also holds a significant place in Mujica Láinez's work. *Bomarzo* (1962; Bomarzo) is a broad excursion into the world of Renaissance Europe. It was also the source of an opera by the Argentinean composer Alberto Ginastera (1916–1983), for which Mujica Láinez wrote the libretto. *Unicornio* (1965; Unicorn) is set in medieval France and the time of the Crusades. *El laberinto* (1974; The Labyrinth) is the story of a Spanish adventurer at large during the conquest of America, and *El escarabajo* (1981; The Scarab), the author's last novel, follows the history of a piece of jewelry, beginning with its origin in antiquity. In several works, Mujica Láinez combines history and fantasy. Thus, *Crónicas reales* (1967; Royal Chronicles) is a collection of humorous stories about the kings of an imaginary eastern European country; *De milagros y melancolías* (1968; Of Miracles and Melancholy) is the history of an imagined American city; and *El viaje de los siete demonios* (1974;

The Journey of the Seven Devils) is a volume of stories about the seven deadly sins, ranging in time and place from Pompei in the first century to Siberia in the future. Fantasy is also the dominant mode of the short stories published in *El brazalete y otros cuentos* (1978; The Bracelet and other Stories). Mujica Láinez's other publications include biographies of **Hilario Ascasubi** (1943) and **Estanislao del Campo** (1947), *Cecil* (1972; Cecil), a chronicle of part of his own life told by his dog, and a posthumously published volume of short stories, *Un novelista en el Museo del Prado* (1984; A Novelist in the Prado Museum).

MUNDONOVISMO. The term was originally coined to designate a trend in early 20th-century Spanish American literature that focused on life and its contexts in the New World, in contrast to the aestheticism represented by **modernismo**. More recently, it has come to refer to the **novel of the land** and narratives that evoke rural life and the landscape. It is synonymous with **criollismo** and **regionalism**. *See also* CHILE.

MUÑOZ, RAFAEL F. (Mexico, 1899–1974). Novelist and short story writer. He earned his living as a journalist and wrote about the Mexican Revolution in his fiction, drawing on memories of the conflict from his youth and inspired in part by an encounter with **Francisco Villa**. His short stories about the war were first published in the daily newspaper *El Universal* and were subsequently collected in *El feroz cabecilla* (1928; The Fierce Leader), *El hombre malo* (1930; The Evil Man), and *Si me han de matar mañana* (1934; If I Am to Die Tomorrow), which were all published posthumously in a single volume, *Relatos de la Revolución* (1976; Tales of the Revolution). Muñoz is remembered most, however, for two **novels of the Mexican Revolution**, *¡Vámonos con Pancho Villa!* (1931; Let's Join Up with Pancho Villa) and *Se llevaron el cañón para Bachimba* (1941; They Took the Cannon to Bachimba). The first of these is an episodic narrative of six comrades who are drawn to Pancho Villa and enlist in his army. It became the source of a classic of Mexican cinema. The second is the autobiographical story of a youth who becomes a man through the revolution, a narrative that is thought to represent the aspirations of the author when young.

MURENA, HÉCTOR A. (Argentina, 1923–1975). Essayist, novelist, poet, and short story writer. He was the author of more than 20 books and contributed regularly to the literary **journal** *Sur* and the cultural section of the daily newspaper *La Nación*, although he remained independent of any schools or movements. His published poetry includes *La vida nueva* (1951; The New Life), *El círculo de los paraísos* (1958; The Circle of Paradises), *El escándalo y el fuego* (1959; The Scandal and the Fire), *El demonio de la armonía* (1964; The Devil of Harmony), and *El águila que desaparece* (1975; The Disappearing Eagle). His novels were written in two cycles, the first of which consists of narratives of a single event seen from different perspectives: *La fatalidad de los cuerpos* (1955; The Fatality of the Bodies), *Las leyes de la noche* (1958; *The Laws of the Night*), and *Los herederos de la promesa* (1965; The Inheritors of the Promise). In *Epitalámica* (1969; Epithalamic), *Polipuercón* (1970; Polipuercón), *Caína muere* (1972; Caína Dies), and *Folisofía* (1976; Pholisophy), the novels of his second cycle, he presents a pessimistic world bereft of human communication.

As an essayist, Murena first followed in the steps of **Ezequiel Martínez Estrada** in his analysis of the American condition in *El pecado original de América* (1954; America's Original Sin), a commentary on immigration, uprootedness, and the effects of geography. In later essays, he showed his disdain for a consumer society. *Homo atomicus* (1961; Atomic Man) is a critique of nihilism, and in *La metáfora y lo sagrado* (1973; The Metaphor and the Sacred), he undertook a search for the sacred through religion. His other essays are *Ensayos sobre la subversión* (1962; Essays on Subversion) and *El hombre secreto* (1969; The Secret Man). His short stories were collected in *El centro del infierno* (1956; The Center of Hell) and *El coronel de caballería y otros cuentos* (1971; The Cavalry Colonel and Other Stories). Murena also translated Walter Benjamin (1892–1940) and Theodor Adorno (1903–1969) into Spanish.

MUTIS, ÁLVARO (Colombia, 1923–). Poet and novelist. Part of his childhood and adolescence was spent in Belgium, where his father was a diplomat, and he has lived in **Mexico** since 1956. In the 1950s he spent 15 months in a Mexican jail, a consequence of charges of fraud leveled against him while working for Standard Oil in Colombia. Since then Mutis has traveled widely and worked as sales manager for Twentieth Century Fox and Columbia Pictures. He first made his mark in literature as a poet and received the support of **Octavio Paz** for his early work.

His published books of poetry include *Los elementos del desastre* (1953; The Elements of the Disaster), *Los trabajos perdidos* (1964; The Lost Works), *Crónica regia y alabanza del reino* (1985; Royal Chronicle and Praise of the Kingdom), and *Reseña de los hospitales de ultramar* (1986; Review of the Hospitals Overseas). Although these established his reputation in poetry, his wider fame is more firmly based on fiction. His early prose includes *Diario de Lecumberri* (1960; Lecumberri Prison Diary), an account of his imprisonment in Mexico; *La mansión de Araucaíma* (1973; The Mansion), a gothic thriller set in the tropics; and *La verdadera historia del flautista de Hammelin* (1982; The True Story of the Piper of Hammelin), a reworking of the children's story.

In the 1980s, Mutis began a series of novellas featuring his literary alter ego, an adventurer and wanderer called Maqroll el Gaviero (Maqroll the Lookout), who had first appeared in his poetry. The first of the novellas was *La nieve del almirante* (1986; The Snow of the Admiral), followed by *Ilona llega con la lluvia* (1987; Ilona Comes with the Rain), *La última escala del Tramp Steamer* (1988; The Tramp Steamer's Last Port of Call), *Un bel morir* (1989; A Beautiful Way to Die), *Amirbar* (1990; Amirbar), *Abdul Bashur, soñador de navíos* (1991; Abdul Bashur, Dreamer of Ships), and *Tríptico de mar y tierra* (1993; Triptych on Sea and Land). The English translations appear in *The Adventures and Misadventures of Maqroll* (2002). In 2001, Mutis was awarded the **Miguel de Cervantes Prize**.

– N –

NABUCO, JOAQUIM (Brazil, 1849–1910). Statesman, historian, and essayist. Nabuco was born into an affluent family in Recife, studied law, and became involved in politics after extended travels in Europe. One of Brazil's most fervent abolitionists, he published *O Abolicionismo* (1884; Abolitionism), the most important work on the subject in Portuguese. He also served as a diplomat abroad for many years and was known for his negotiation and social skills. Nabuco left behind a vast oeuvre in many genres (poetry, criticism, historiography, and political writings), but he is best remembered for his autobiography, *Minha Formação* (1900; My Education), a work noted for its style and the rich content of his life experience. He also wrote *Um Estadista do Império* (1899; A Statesman of the Empire), a four-volume biography of his father, Nabuco de Araújo (1813–1878). *See also* ALVES, ANTÔNIO FREDERICO DE CASTRO.

NALÉ ROXLO, CONRADO (Argentina, 1898–1971). Short story writer, poet, and dramatist. Although he first won recognition for a collection of poems, *El grillo* (1923; The Cricket), Nalé Roxlo published only two further books of poetry: *Claro desvelo* (1937; Clear Insomnia) and *De otro cielo* (1956; From Another Sky). His verse has a melancholy tone and is aesthetically related more to 19th-century traditions than to 20th-century innovation. As a dramatist, he wrote imaginative, poetic plays for the **theater** that contrasted with the realism of his day. *La cola de la sirena* (1941; The Mermaid's Tail) is about a man who falls for a mermaid; *El pacto de Cristina* (1945; Cristina's Pact) is a retelling of the Faust legend, and *Judith y las rosas* (1956; Judith and the Roses) is a farse based on the biblical story of Judith and Holophernes. He is remembered most for the short, humorous pieces he published in newspapers and magazines, including the **journal** *Martín Fierro*, under a variety of pseudonyms, of which "Chamico" was the most celebrated. These pieces have been collected in a number of volumes: *Cuentos de Chamico* (1941; Tales by Chamico), *El muerto profesional* (1943; The Professional Corpse), *Cuentos de cabecera* (1946; Bedside Stories), *La medicina vista de reojo* (1952; A Sideways Look at Medicine), *Mi pueblo* (1953; My Home Town), *Libro de quejas* (1953; Book of Complaints), *El humor de los humores* (1953; The Humor of Humors), *Sumarios policiales* (1955; Police Reports), and *El ingenioso hidalgo* (1965; The Ingenious Knight).

NARANJO, CARMEN (Costa Rica, 1928–). Novelist, poet, and short story writer. In addition to being Costa Rica's most important female writer, she has had a successful career in public administration and was the first woman in Costa Rica to hold high office in a number of significant institutions. Her first publications were verse, and her volumes of poetry include *América* (1961; America), *Canción de la ternura* (1964; Song of Tenderness), *Misa a oscuras* (1964; Mass Under Darkness), *Hacia tu isla* (1966; Towards Your Island), *Homenaje a don Nadie* (1981; Homage to Mr. Nobody), and *En esta tierra redonda y plana* (2001; On This Round Flat Earth). She is better known for her fiction, in which she often draws on her knowledge of bureaucratic institutions and portrays the plight of lonely, alienated characters. Her first novel was *Los perros no ladraron* (1966; The Dogs Didn't Bark), about a bureaucrat trapped in the system in which he works. *Memorias de un hombre palabra* (1968; Memoirs of a Word-Man) is the story of a man who overcomes his social marginality when he encounters others like him. *Diario de una multitud* (1974; Diary of a Crowd) has a similarly alienated protagonist, and the novelist uses dialogue to convey the narration, a technique with which she also experimented in earlier novels. *Sobrepunto* (1985; Overpoint), Naranjo's first novel with a female protagonist, explores the roles traditionally given to **women** in a predominantly patriarchal society. Her more recent novels include *Más allá de Parismina* (2004; Beyond Parismina). Among Naranjo's collections of short stories are *Hoy es un largo día* (1974; Today Is a Long Day), *Nunca hubo alguna vez* (1984; There Never Was a Once Upon a Time), *Ondina* (1985; Ondina), and *Otro rumbo para la rumba* (1989; Another Route for the Rumba). She has written essays, including *Cinco temas en busca de un pensador* (1977; Five Themes in Search of a Thinker), on negative aspects of human development. She has also written for the stage.

NASCIMENTO, ABDIAS DO (Brazil, 1914–). Dramatist. A scholar and political activist, do Nascimento's contributions to the **theater**, including the 1944 founding of the *Teatro Experimental do Negro* (Black Experimental Theater) to promote awareness of Afro-Brazilian culture and values. He also published the anthology *Dramas para Negros e um Prólogo para Brancos* (1961; Plays for Blacks and a Prologue for Whites). His play *Sortilege* (1978; *Black Mystery*) features elements of Candomblé, an Afro-Brazilian religion.

NASSAR, RADUAN (Brazil, 1935–). Novelist. Born into a Lebanese immigrant family, Nassar studied law and philosophy in São Paulo. His first novel, *Lavoura Arcaica* (1975; *To the Left of the Father*), based on conflict in a rural family, earned him many prizes. His next novel, *Um Copo de Cólera* (1978; A Glass of Wrath), also met with great critical success. In the 1980s, however, Nassar quit writing and retired to a farm, devoting his time to raising animals. His book of stories, *Menina a Caminho* (Girl on the Road), appeared in 1997, although it was written decades before. In 2001, *Lavoura Arcaica* was adapted for the screen.

NATURALISM. This late 19th- and early 20th-century movement grew out of **realism** and was represented especially in the work of the French novelist Emile Zola (1840–1902). It entailed a focus on the underbelly of society, especially on the consequences of increased industrialization and urbanization. It also reflected a Darwinian determinism arising from heredity and the social environment, although its deterministic elements in Latin America were sometimes attenuated by the Christian concept of free will. Its characteristics are apparent in a number of trends in fiction: the **novel of the Mexican Revolution** of **Mariano Azuela** and **Gregorio López y Fuentes**; the **indigenismo** of **Jorge Icaza** and **Clorinda Matto de Turner (Peru)** and **Alcides Arguedas (Bolivia)**; the urban novels of **Federico Gamboa (Mexico)** and **Manuel Gálvez** and **Eugenio Cambaceres (Argentina)**; and the theater in dramatists such as **Samuel Eichelbaum** (Argentina) and **Armando Moock** (Chile). Other Spanish American authors whose work shows the influence of naturalism include **Heriberto Frías** (Mexico), **Joaquín García Monge (Costa Rica)**; **Enrique López Albújar** (Peru); **Benito Lynch** and **Manuel T. Podestá (Argentina)**, **Carlos Reyles (Uruguay)**, and **Joaquín Edwards Bello**, **Marta Brunet**, **Augusto D'Halmar**, and **Baldomero Lillo (Chile)**.

In **Brazil**, naturalism is clearly tied to realism, but there are few works that embody only Zola's model, among them the novels of **Adolfo Caminha**. After the publication of **Aluísio Azevedo**'s *O Mulato* (1881; Mulatto), naturalism became established as a new fashion through writers such as **José Veríssimo**, but it was soon followed by authors who are today considered more under the heading of realism, including some of Brazil's most notable 19th-century fiction and nonfiction writers such as **Manuel Antônio de Almeida, Joaquim Maria Machado de Assis, Henrique Maximiano Coelho Neto, Euclides da Cunha, Afonso Henriques de Lima Barreto,** and **Raúl d'Ávila Pompéia.** *See also* AMBROGI, ARTURO; EL SALVADOR; PERALTA LAGOS, JOSÉ MARÍA; RAMOS, GRACILIANO; REGIONALISM; SYMBOLISM; TAUNAY, ALFREDO D'ESCRAGNOLLE, VISCONDE DE; WOMEN.

NEO-BAROQUE. The term refers to a 20th-century revival of the **baroque** style in literature of the 17th century in Spain and colonial Spanish America that entailed complex metaphors and allusions, a tortuous syntax, and an elaborate vocabulary. Although more commonly associated with Cuba, it also appeared elsewhere in the work of writers such as **Osvaldo Lamborghini** and **Néstor Perlongher (Argentina), Augusto Roa Bastos (Paraguay),** and **Gustavo Sainz (Mexico).**

NEO-CLASSICISM. The term refers to a new revival of the literary styles, content, and form associated with classical Greek and Roman cultures popularized in Europe in the Renaissance of the 15th and 16th centuries. Although neo-classicism in Europe was a predominantly 18th-century phenomenon, it appeared in Latin America mainly in the first half of the 19th. Among its exponents were **Manuel Eduardo de Gorostiza (Mexico)** and **Manuel Ascensio Segura (Peru)** in **theater** and **Andrés Bello (Venezuela), Cláudio Manuel da Costa (Brazil),** and **José Joaquín Olmedo (Ecuador)** in poetry. *See also* CHILE; EL SALVADOR.

NEO-INDIGENISMO. Although sharing the same objective as **indigenismo** of representing the plight of native Americans as marginalized and exploited subjects, neo-indigenismo offers a more complex image than was possible in the first half of the 20th century. Neo-indigenismo is more anthropologically grounded than its predecessor. It recognizes the existence of mestizo populations and draws them into consideration, and it abandons the different forms of **realism** inherited from the 19th century in favor of the more innovative forms of the modern novel and its aesthetics, sometimes drawing on avant-garde trends. Neo-indigenismo begins with the work of **José María Arguedas (Peru)** and includes authors such as **Miguel Ángel Asturias (Guatemala), Rosario Castellanos (Mexico)**, and **Manuel Scorza (Peru)**.

NERUDA, PABLO (Chile, 1904–1973). Poet. He was born Neftalí Ricardo Reyes Basoalto in Parral, Chile, but is universally known by the pseudonym he adopted in 1920. A prolific writer, who published more than 40 volumes of poetry, he is one of Latin America's great poets. His work has been translated into many languages and is widely read. His poetry, produced over a period of 50 years, has a protean quality, constantly evolving to reflect changes in literary styles as well as the events of both his own life and the world at large. *Crepusculario* (1923; Twilight Poems), his first volume of published poems, still showed the thematic and stylistic influences of **modernismo**. In *Veinte poemas de amor y una canción desesperada* (1924; *Twenty Love Poems and a Song of Despair*), Neruda's first major work, a more personal style began to emerge. His poetic evocation of sexual encounters and the landscape won him immediate recognition and has proven to be of enduring value.

Between 1927 and 1939, Neruda held a series of consular appointments in Asia, Europe, and Latin America. Even before his departure for the first of these in Burma, Ceylon, and Java, his writing had taken a turn toward the **avant-garde**. *Residencia en la tierra* (1933; *Residence on Earth*), a cycle of poems expanded in 1935 and 1947, belongs mainly to this period and represents the sense of alienation and despair he felt about his existence while living in the Far East. By contrast, the time he spent in Spain (1933–1937) brought him more success and friendships. It also impacted him ideologically and converted him to the political Left, a position he would maintain for the rest of his life. Among his writings from this period, *España en el corazón* (1937; Spain in My Heart) expressed his sympathy for the Republican cause during the Spanish Civil War (1936–1939).

Neruda formally entered Chilean politics in 1945, when he was elected to the Senate. Shortly after, he joined the Chilean Communist Party. In 1947, after criticizing President González Videla's repression of striking miners, he was forced to live in hiding, and then in 1949 he went into exile. While in exile he published his *Canto General* (1950; *General Song*) in Mexico, a collection of some 250 poems he had begun in 1938 and continued to write while in hiding in Chile. This epic work on the natural and human history of Latin America, focused on struggles against tyranny, is the centerpiece of Neruda's output. It was published clandestinely in Chile and translated into several other languages. Some sections of the collection, particularly "Las alturas de Macchu Picchu" (*The Heights of Macchu Picchu*) are well known independently of their original context.

When Neruda returned to Chile in 1952, he was a national cultural icon, the most prominent literary spokesperson for the Left, and an international celebrity. He continued to write prolifically. *Los versos del capitán* (1952; *The Captain's Verses*) celebrated his love for his third wife, Matilde Urrutia. *Las uvas y el viento* (1954; *The Grapes and the Wind*) covered recent political journeys. In the *Odas elementales* (*Odes to Common Things*), the first volumes of which began to appear in 1954, Neruda wrote of everyday objects in simple terms, repudiating the more opaque poetry of his earlier *Residencias*. *Estravagaria* (*Extravagaria*) appeared in 1958; *Cien sonetos de amor* (*100 Love Sonnets*) in 1960, also inspired by Matilde Urrutia; *Memorial de Isla Negra* (*Memoir from Isla Negra*), a five-volume poetic biography, in 1964; *Fin del mundo* (*The End of the World*) and *Aún* (*Still Another Day*), both in 1969; and *La rosa separada* (*The Separate Rose*), about a journey to Easter Island, in 1973.

In 1970, after declining to run for president, Neruda campaigned for Salvador Allende, and became Chilean ambassador to France after Allende's victory. He was awarded the **Nobel Prize for Literature** in 1971. In 1972, he returned to Chile, already seriously ill, and died in September 1973, not long after the military coup that overthrew Allende. *Confieso que he vivido: memorias* (1974; *Pablo Neruda: Memoirs*), a prose autobiography, appeared posthumously, compiled and edited by Matilde Urrutia. *See also* CARDENAL, ERNESTO; DÍAZ, JORGE; EDWARDS, JORGE; HERRERA Y REISSIG, JULIO; HUERTA, EFRAÍN; IBÁÑEZ, SARA DE; LIHN, ENRIQUE; MADARIAGA, FRANCISCO; OROZCO, OLGA; PARRA, NICANOR; RODRÍGUEZ MONEGAL, EMIR; ROKHA, PABLO DE; SABAT ERCASTY, CARLOS; TEITELBOIM, VOLODIA.

NERVO, AMADO (Mexico, 1870–1919). Poet, novelist, and short story writer. In both his poetry and prose, Nervo's writing shows the characteristics of **modernismo** and the influence of European **symbolism** and **parnassianism**. He was especially drawn to the spiritual dimensions of existence and explored the potential of different beliefs and religions as a way of transcending the material world, especially the pragmatic materialism of 19th-century **positivism**. The novels *El bachiller* (1895; The Bachelor) and *El domador de almas* (1897; The Soul Breaker), as well as the short story collections *Almas que pasan* (1906; Passing Souls) and *El diablo desinteresado* (1916; The Disinterested Devil), are noteworthy examples of his prose. He also wrote *Juana de Asbaje* (1910; Juana de Asbaje), a biography of **Sor Juana Inés de la Cruz**.

Nervo's poetry seems unaffected by the social upheavals of his time, notably the Mexican Revolution. In his early collections of verse, *Místicas* (1898; Mystiques) and *Perlas negras* (1898; Black Pearls), he explores feelings of eroticism and religious doubt. In *Los jardines interiores* (1905; Interior Gardens) and *En voz baja* (1909; In a Soft Voice), he examines his place in the material world. *La amada inmóvil: versos a una muerta* (written 1912; published 1920; The Immobile Beloved: Verses for a Dead Woman) was written on the occasion of his wife's death. In his last collections, *Serenidad* (1914; Serenity), *Elevación* (1917; Elevation), and *El estanque de los lotos* (1919; The Lotus Pool), he seeks the consolation of religion and philosophy.

NEW HISTORICAL NOVEL. Unlike the **historical novel**, which conventionally tells a fictional story set in a previous time in history, new historical novels are concerned with the examination and problematization of history itself and how the past has been represented and understood. The events narrated and the characters they involve are usually taken from history. They often entail iconic elements of national identity, but are told from perspectives that challenge traditional interpretations. At the same time, by making writing and written documents part of the structure of the text, the new historical novel questions the nature of historical discourse and historiography. This approach to history was heightened in the context of the commemoration in 1992 of the 500th anniversary of the arrival of Europeans in the New World and the focus this gave to five centuries of Latin American history. But it also occurred in the wake of the authoritarian regimes of the 1970s and 1980s, which produced a sense of disillusion with how national stories had been written and interpreted and coincided with a postmodern distrust of traditional narratives of interpretation. Among those who have written new historical novels, some of the most prominent are **Homero Aridjis, Carlos Fuentes,** and **Fernando del Paso (Mexico); Gabriel García Márquez (Colombia); Sylvia Iparraguirre, Tomás Eloy Martínez, Martha Mercader, Abel Posse, Andrés Rivera,** and **Juan José Saer (Argentina); Napoleón Baccino Ponce de León** and **Tomás de Mattos (Uruguay);** and **Augusto Roa Bastos (Paraguay).** *See also* POST-BOOM.

NEW NOVEL. The term is a translation of *nouveau roman,* a style in fiction that flourished between the 1950s and 1970s among a group of French authors that includes Alain Robbe-Grillet (1922–2008), Marguerite Duras (1914–1996), Nathalie Sarraute (1900–1999), and Michel Butor (1926–). New novels sought to subordinate the conventional elements of the novel, such as plot, chronological narrative, and character, to the subjective experience of objects. Hence they appear disjointed, repetitive, focused on detail, and having a circular structure. Latin American novelists whose work incorporates elements of the new novel include **Salvador Elizondo** and **José Emilio Pacheco (Mexico), Julio Cortázar** and **Juan José Saer (Argentina),** and **Jorge Enrique Adoum (Ecuador).** *See also* PERU.

NEWSPAPERS. *See* JOURNALS, MAGAZINES, NEWSPAPERS, AND PERIODICALS.

NICARAGUA. There was little major literary production during the colonial period and much of the 19th century. Literature in Nicaragua came to life with **Rubén Darío,** the leader of Spanish American **modernismo.** Although he lived much of his life outside the country, he still had considerable influence and was the first of a series of poets whose work has resonated widely. **Salomón de la Selva** bridges the gap between modernist poetry and the **avant-garde,** which itself includes figures such as **José Coronel Urtecho, Pablo**

Antonio Cuadra, and **Joaquín Pasos**. As the 20th century advanced, the continuing conflicts that shook the country during the Somoza dynasty (1936–1979), ending eventually in the triumph of the Sandinista Revolution, affected the direction taken by literature. In addition to other preoccupations expressed by it authors, poetry became politically more committed, as in the work of **Ernesto Cardenal** and **women** writers such as **Gioconda Belli** and **Daisy Zamora**. Prose writing and the novel also reflected the moment and, for the first time, several prominent prose writers became part of the literary scene. Gioconda Belli is a respected novelist as well as a poet, although the dominant figure is **Sergio Ramírez**. At the same time, the guerrilla war and the Sandinista Revolution were propitious contexts for the **testimonio**, for which the most representative author in Nicaragua is **Omar Cabezas**.

The **theater** in colonial Nicaragua, with its popular religious festivals, was built in part on the traditions of ritual performance of pre-Columbian times. Its most notable result was the development of a theater in Nahuatl and Spanish that flourished between the mid-16th and mid-18th centuries and left the legacy of *El güegüense,* a comic piece in which a popular character outwits government tax officials, which continues to be performed today. A more formal theater in Nicaragua took somewhat longer to develop, however. During the 19th century, stages were dominated by foreign plays and visiting companies, with local dramatists not becoming more numerous and productive until the 20th century. **Hernán Robledo**, who was the first major figure, introduced **costumbrismo** to the theater, and the avant-garde writers José Coronel Urtecho and Pablo Antonio Cuadra both wrote successfully for the stage. The theater grew between the 1950s and 1970s, during an economic boom that saw the founding of several companies, including the Teatro Experimental de Managua. Of the dramatists whose work was staged during this period, **Rolando Steiner** stands out. However, the situation changed with the triumph of the Sandinista Revolution in 1979, and in the 1980s greater emphasis was placed on forms of popular theater, including collective creation, associated with a different cultural climate. *See also* ALEGRÍA, CLARIBEL; BEST SELLER; BRECHTIAN THEATER; CASA DE LA AMÉRICAS; CRIME FICTION; INDIGENOUS TRADITIONS; JESÚS MARTÍNEZ, JOSÉ DE; MO-

LINA, JUAN RAMÓN; SOLÓRZANO, CARLOS; THEATER IN QUECHUA; THEATER OF THE ABSURD.

NOBEL PRIZE FOR LITERATURE. The Nobel laureates from Latin America are **Gabriela Mistral** (1945; **Chile**), **Miguel Ángel Asturias** (1967; **Guatemala**), **Pablo Neruda** (1971; Chile), **Gabriel García Márquez** (1982; **Colombia**), and **Octavio Paz** (1990; **Mexico**), and **Mario Vargs Llosa** (2010; **Peru**).

NÓBREGA, MANUEL DA (Brazil, 1517–1570). Historian and chronicler. A Portuguese priest, Nóbrega headed the first Jesuit mission in the Americas. His *Cartas do Brasil* (1886; Letters from Brazil), written as reports to his superiors in Portugal, are important early **chronicles** of Brazil. He was particularly concerned with the issue of conversion, as shown in his *Diálogo Sobre a Conversão do Gentio* (1556; Dialogue on the Conversion of the People).

NOVEL OF THE LAND. The term refers to novels, mainly from the early 20th century, that focus on the landscape and the ways of life it has fostered. They are sometimes referred to under the terms **mundonovismo** and **criollismo** and include works such as *La vorágine* (1942; *The Vortex*) by **José Eustasio Rivera (Colombia)**, *Doña Bárbara* (1929; *Doña Bárbara*) by **Rómulo Gallegos (Venezuela)**, and *Don Segundo Sombra* (1926; *Mr. Second Shadow*) by **Ricardo Güiraldes (Argentina)**. *See also* REGIONALISM; YÁÑEZ, AGUSTÍN.

NOVEL OF THE MEXICAN REVOLUTION. Although the first novel of the Mexican Revolution, **Mariano Azuela**'s *Los de abajo*, was published in 1915 in serialized form in a Texas **newspaper**, it did not attract attention until it appeared as a book a decade later. Other novels about the conflict began to appear by the late 1920s, establishing a trend in fiction that would continue until the early 1940s. The novels published during these two decades were narratives of events, often chronicling the campaigns of revolutionary leaders such as **Francisco ("Pancho") Villa** and **Emiliano Zapata** and presenting a fictionalized version of the authors' own experiences. The novelists of this period include **Nellie Campobello** (the only **woman** to be included in the canon), **Martín Luis Guzmán, Miguel N. Lira, Gregorio López y Fuentes, Mauricio Magdaleno, José Mancisidor, Rafael F. Muñoz, José Rubén Romero, Francisco L. Urquizo,** and **José Vasconcelos.** In the late 1940s and after, beginning with **Agustín Yáñez**'s *Al filo del agua* (1947; *The Edge of the Storm*), the novel of the revolution gave less attention to the events of the war and was more concerned with the social causes and conditions from which it emerged and the kind of society it came to produce. In addition to Yáñez, other authors whose fiction reflects this development include **Carlos Fuentes, Juan Rulfo,** and **José Revueltas.** *See also* FRÍAS, HERIBERTO; NATURALISM.

NOVO, SALVADOR (MEXICO, 1904–1974). Poet, chronicler, and dramatist. In his early life, Novo was affiliated with **Los Contemporáneos** in Mexico. His poetry of that time, in collections such as *xx poemas* (1925; xx poems) and *Poemas proletarios* (1934; Proletarian Poems), associate him with the **avant-garde** and modernity. Another collection of that period, *Espejo* (1933; Mirror), is a poetic autobiography written as a series of lyric and humorous verses. In *Nuevo amor* (1933; New Love), he explored the themes of love and solitude. Urban themes also figure in his poetry, although he wrote about the city more fully as official chronicler of Mexico City. Among his **chronicles** are a series of volumes, edited by **José Emilio Pacheco,** about life in the capital during the term of a number of Mexican presidents. Other prose works include *Continente vacío* (1935; Empty Continent), about a trip to South America, with illustrations by the Spanish poet Federico García Lorca (1898–1936), whom he met in Buenos Aires; *Nueva grandeza mexicana* (1951; New Grandeur of Mexico), a gloss on the poem by **Bernardo de Balbuena**; and *La estatua de sal* (1998; The Salt Statue), an account of his early life that was not published until long after his death because of the frank revelations it contains about his contemporaries. Salvador Novo was a flamboyant public figure, one of the first of some eminence in Mexican cultural institutions to be open about his **homosexuality** yet retain the patronage of the state. In 1968, he adopted a progovernment stance with respect to the **Tlatelolco massacre.** *See also* MAGAÑA, SERGIO.

NUEVO GRUPO. Formed by **José Ignacio Cabrujas, Román Chalbaud,** and **Isaac Chocrón,** and inspired by **César Rengifo,** Nuevo Grupo, or New Group, fostered the introduction of **avant-garde** forms to the **theater** in **Venezuela,** such as the **theater of the absurd** and **total theater,** and contributed to the renaissance in the country's stage that had begun in the 1950s. The group's first success was Chocrón's *Tric-trac* (1967; Tick-Tock).

NÚÑEZ, ENRIQUE BERNARDO (Venezuela, 1895–1964). Novelist and journalist. After two early novels, *Sol interior* (1918; Interior Sun) and *Después de Ayacucho* (1929; After Ayacucho), he published *Cubagua* (1931; Cubagua), his best-known novel, a fantasy work that foreshadows trends in fiction of the 1960s. His fourth and last novel was *La galera de Tiberio* (1938; Tiberius' Galley). As a journalist, he contributed to many Caracas newspapers and was first named official chronicler of the Venezuelan capital in 1945. At about this time, his interests became more attached to history than to literature, and he wrote many **chronicles** of Caracas as well as books on the history of Venezuela. One of his most popular books was *La ciudad de los techos rojos* (1947; The Red Roof City).

NÚÑEZ, RAFAEL (Colombia, 1825–1894). Poet, journalist, and essayist. A notable politician, he served twice as president of Colombia (1887–1892 and 1892–1894). He is best known for his journalism on culture and literature as well as essays such as *Reforma política en Colombia* (1885; Political Reform in Colombia). As a poet, his early work was quite exploratory, but later became more conservative and inclined to the traditions of **romanticism,** although he was also a patron of **Rubén Darío** and **modernismo.** His verse, initially published in newspapers in Europe and the Americas, was collected in *Poesías* (1889; Poems) and published in Paris. Although important in his day, Núñez is remembered as a poet mainly for having written the lyrics of the Colombian national anthem.

NÚÑEZ CABEZA DE VACA, ALVAR (1490?–1559?) Chronicler. He was a member of a disastrous Spanish expedition to Florida led by Pánfilo de Narváez (1470–1528) in 1528 that was shipwrecked on the Gulf of Mexico. In his **chronicle**, in the form of a report presented to the Spanish crown, commonly known as *Los Naufragios* (1542; *The Narrative of Cabeza de Vaca*), Cabeza de Vaca gave an account of his captivity among native people and his wanderings across southwestern North America, from present-day Texas to California and northern Mexico, in the company of three other survivors of the expedition. After returning to Spain, he was sent in 1540 to be governor of the region of Río de la Plata in South America and wrote of his experiences in his *Comentarios* (1555; *The Commentaries of Alvar Núñez Cabeza de Vaca*). *See also* FERNÁNDEZ DE OVIEDO, GONZALO; GLANTZ, MARGO; POSSE, ABEL.

NÚÑEZ DE PINEDA DE BASCUÑÁN, FRANCISCO (Chile, 1607–1680). Chronicler. Captured in 1629 during an expedition to defeat the Mapuche in Chile, he was held captive for seven months. Years later, in 1673, after a successful military career, he wrote about his experiences in the **chronicle** *El cautiverio feliz, o razón de las guerras dilatadas de Chile* (*The Happy Captive*). His book is both a memoir and an analysis of the protracted conflict between the Spanish and the Mapuche.

– O –

OCAMPO, MARÍA LUISA (Mexico, 1905–1974). Dramatist. She first made her name on the stage with her play *Cosas de la vida* (1923; Things of Life) and was a member of a significant group of writers who gave new life to Mexican **theater** in the 1920s and beyond. Her works include *La quimera* (1923; The Illusion), *La hoguera* (1924; The Bonfire), *La jauría* (1925; The Pack of Hounds), *Puedes irte* (1926; You May Leave), *Las máscaras* (1926; The Masks), *La sed en el desierto* (1927; Thirst in the Desert), *Más allá de los hombres* (1929; Beyond Men), *El corrido de Juan Saavedra* (1929; The Ballad of Juan Saavedra), *Castillos en el aire* (1931; Castles in Spain), *La casa en ruinas* (1936; The House in Ruins), and *Una vida de mujer* (1938; A Woman's Life). *See also* WOMEN.

OCAMPO, SILVINA (Argentina, 1906–1993). Short story writer and poet. She was the sister of **Victoria Ocampo** and was married to **Adolfo Bioy Casares**. Her reputation rests principally on her short stories. Recollections of childhood in *Viaje olvidado* (1937; Forgotten Journey) provided the basis for her first collection. This was followed by *La furia* (1959; Fury) and *Las invitadas* (1961; The Guests), which established her as the author of stories characterized by horror, violence, and strange, contradictory events, a reputation to some extent consolidated in two further collections, *Y así sucesivamente* (1987; And So On) and *Cornelia frente al espejo* (1988; Cornelia in the Mirror), although the degree of violence in both of them is more subdued. An English translation of her stories has appeared as *Fantasies of the Feminine: The Short Stories of Silvina Ocampo*.

In contrast to her fiction, Ocampo's poetry is relatively conventional and includes *Los sonetos del jardín* (1946; Sonnets from the Garden), *Poemas de amor deseperado* (1949; Poems of Despairing Love), *Lo amargo por dulce* (1962; Bitter Sweet); *Amarillo celeste* (1972; Sky-blue Yellow), and *Breve santoral* (1984; A Small Book of Saints). In collaboration with Adolfo Bioy Casares, Ocampo wrote a detective novel, *Los que aman odian* (1946; Those Who Love Hate), and she joined with Bioy Casares and **Jorge Luis Borges** to edit two celebrated anthologies, *Antología de la literatura fantástica* (1946; The Book of Fantasy) and *Antología poética argentina* (1941; Anthology of Argentinean Poetry). In the 1970s, she wrote several books of **children's literature**, including *El cofre volante* (1974; The Flying Trunk), *El tobogán* (1975; The Toboggan), *El caballo alado* (1976; The Winged Horse), and *La naranja maravillosa* (1977; The Magic Orange). Among her translations of poetry are the complete poems of Emily Dickinson (1830–1886). *See also* WOMEN.

OCAMPO, VICTORIA (Argentina, 1890–1979). Essayist and translator. She came from an influential family and was the eldest of six daughters. **Silvina Ocampo** was her sister. At a time in Argentina when **women** faced discrimination in public and there were few of any prominence in the field of letters, Victoria Ocampo was a notable exception. She published numerous translations into Spanish and more than 20 volumes of essays on a wide range of cultural topics. Her books include a series of 10 *Testimonios* (1935–1977; Testimonies) on life and literature; *De Francesca a Beatrice* (1924; From Francesca to Beatrice), on Dante; *Lawrence de Arabia y otros ensayos* (1951; Lawrence of Arabia and Other Essays); *Virginia Woolf en su diario* (1954; Virginia Woolf in Her Diary); *Juan Sebastián Bach, el hombre* (1964; Johann Sebastian Bach, the Man); *La bella y sus enamorados* (1964; Beauty and Her Lovers); and, in collaboration with **Jorge Luis Borges** and **Eduardo Mallea**, *Diálogos* (1969; Dialogues). In 1931, she founded the literary **journal** *Sur*, which became an important vehicle for writers of her generation, a source of contact with writers outside Argentina, and one of the most prestigious periodicals of its kind in the Spanish-speaking world. In 1975, she was made a member of the Argentinean Academy of Letters, the first woman to be so honored. Her autobiography is a notable example of the genre and was published posthumously (1979–1984) in six volumes.

ODIO, EUNICE (Costa Rica, 1922–1974). Poet. She was a rather solitary figure, in part the consequence of her own polemical temperament both in literature and politics. Her work remained virtually unknown until the 1980s in her own country, which she left in 1947 for **Guatemala** and then settled in **Mexico** in 1955, where she died alone and in poverty. Although Odio's work had already been recognized earlier through publication in literary magazines, her first volume of poetry was *Los elementos terrestres* (1948; Terrestrial Elements), a series of eight long poems in free verse with themes of mystic eroticism, echoes of the Bible, and a cosmic view of reality. Her second collection, *Zona en territorio del alba* (1953; Zone in the Land of Dawn), establishes her adoption of an **avant-garde** aesthetic, notably through her adherence to **creacionismo**. *El tránsito de fuego* (1957; Passage of Fire), an extensive poem of more than 400 pages on the central themes of creation and exile, represents the culmination of her literary work. *See also* OREAMUNO, YOLANDA; WOMEN.

OLIVEIRA, ALBERTO DE (Brazil, 1857–1937). Poet. One of the major representatives of **parnassianism** in Brazil, Oliveira studied pharmacy but worked as a civil servant and educator. He was one of the founders of the Brazilian Academy of Letters (*see* ACA-

DEMIAS). His *Canções românticas* (1878; Romantic Songs) contain parnassian motifs but are still in the style of **romanticism**. In *Meridionais* (1884; Southerners) and *Sonetos e poemas* (1885; Sonnets and Poems), he achieved the impassibility and "cult of form" that parnassianism preached. However, later volumes such as *Livro de Ema* (1900; Emma's Book), *Por amor de uma lágrima* (1912; For the Love of a Tear), and *Alma Livre* (1905; Free Soul) evidence the influence of **symbolism** in their portrayal of sentimental and sensual love. Oliveira was also noted for his lyrical portrayal of nature. He was crowned King of Poets in 1924. *See also* CORREIA, RAIMUNDO.

OLIVEIRA, MANUEL BOTELHO DE (Brazil, 1636–1711). Poet and dramatist. Born into a privileged family from Bahia, Botelho de Oliveira studied law in Coimbra, where he met **Gregório de Mattos** and came into contact with the Spanish and Portuguese literary **baroque**. Back in Brazil, he practiced law and held public office. He was a virtuoso poet who had mastered all the baroque devices used by poets such as Luis de Góngora (1561–1627) and could write poetry in Portuguese, Spanish, Italian, and Latin. He was also the first Brazilian-born poet to see his work in print, namely the volume *Música do Parnaso* (1705; Music of Parnassus), which included poems and his comedies written in Spanish, *Hay amigo para amigo* (There Is a Friend for a Friend), and *Amor, engaños y celos* (Love, Deceit, and Jealousy). *See also* THEATER.

OLLANTAY. An anonymous 18th-century Peruvian drama written in Quechua and set in Incan times that tells a story of love and rebellion and effectively combines elements from both the Hispanic and indigenous dramatic traditions. *See also* TABOADA TERÁN, NÉSTOR; THEATER IN QUECHUA.

OLLÉ, CARMEN (Peru, 1947–). Poet and novelist. After the appearance of her first book of poems, *Noche de adrenalina* (1981; Nights of Adrenaline), Carmen Ollé was soon established as one of Peru's prominent contemporary **women** writers. Her second book was a collection of verse and prose, *Todo orgullo humea la noche* (1988; The Night Turns All Pride Smokey). Since then she has published several narrative works, including *¿Por qué hacen tanto ruido?* (1992; Why

Are They So Noisy?), *Las dos caras del deseo* (1994; The Two Faces of Desire), *Pista falsa* (1999; False Trail), and *Una muchacha bajo su paraguas* (2002; A Girl Beneath Her Umbrella).

OLMEDO, JOSÉ JOAQUÍN (Ecuador, 1780–1847). Poet. A prominent politician, he served his country as both vice president and president. He is known principally for two poems, both written in the style of **neo-classicism**. The first of these is *La victoria de Junín, canto a Bolívar* (1825), written to honor the victory of **Simón Bolívar** at the Battle of Junín (6 August 1824), which turned the tide against the Spanish. It made Olmedo the most renowned poet of the war of independence in South America. His second celebrated poem, *Al general Flores, vencedor de Miñarica* (1835), was also written to honor a battle and its victor, Juan José Flores, who served as Ecuador's first president after the breakup in 1830 of the union of Colombia, Venezuela, and Panama known as Gran Colombia.

OÑA, PEDRO DE (Chile, 1570–1643?). Poet. Although he was Chile's first native-born poet of note, he left his homeland at the age of 20 and lived in **Peru**. He is best remembered for *Arauco domado* (1596; Arauco Tamed), a narrative poem in the cycle of **epic poetry** initiated by **Alonso de Ercilla y Zúñiga** concerning the conquest and colonization of Chile. In his version of history, Oña sought to honor his patron, the Viceroy of Lima, García Hurtado de Mendoza (1589–1596), who had been attributed no more than a secondary role in Ercilla's narrative.

ONETTI, JUAN CARLOS (Uruguay, 1909–1994). Novelist and short story writer. Through the device of stories within stories, much of Onetti's fiction is about the nature of literature. It also reflects his desire for a new way of writing, which he endeavored to exemplify in his own work, in which he broke with a tradition of writing on rural themes in favor of the city. His short novel *El pozo* (*The Pit*) appeared in 1939, and his other major works of fiction before 1970, but Onetti did not obtain broad critical recognition until he moved to Madrid in 1975, after being imprisoned in Uruguay by the military government. *El pozo* had already introduced many of the features of his later fiction. His poetic view is Faulknerian and his characters are sombre, introspective figures, trapped in Kafkaesque predicaments and afflicted by a Sartrean **existentialism**, representations, perhaps, of his own reclusive existence. They are given to imagining alternative lives, so that Onetti's stories often unfold on several levels at the same time.

Alternative narratives figure in the life of Brausen in *La vida breve* (1950; *A Brief Life*), in which the author introduced the fictional town of Santa María, located on the River Plate, the setting for much of his later fiction. *Una tumba sin nombre* (1959; *A Grave With no Name*) tells conflicting versions of the life of Rita, a maid exploited as a prostitute whose funeral takes place in Santa María. *El astillero* (1961; *The Shipyard*) is the story of Larsen, who attempts to redeem himself by throwing himself into the impossible task of restoring a ruined shipyard. *Juntacadáveres* (1964; *Body Snatcher*) contains two interconnected stories, both of which entail the pursuit of impossible dreams: Larsen's fantasy of a perfect brothel and Julita's attempt to establish a perfect relationship after the death of her husband. Although published after *El astillero*, *Juntacadáveres* narrates events that are chronologically earlier. In *Dejemos hablar al viento* (1979; *Let the Wind Speak*), Onetti ended his Santa María saga by referring to his own earlier work, as if rounding out his literary activity, and by narrating the burning of the town. He published two more short novels, however: *Cuando entonces* (1987; When Then) and *Cuando ya no importe* (1993; When It No Longer Matters). Among his short stories are the collections *Un sueño realizado* (1951; A Dream Come True), *El infierno tan temido* (1962; The Hell So Fearful), and *Jacob y el otro y otros cuentos* (1965; Jacob and the Other and Other Stories). Onetti was awarded the **Miguel de Cervantes Prize** for Literature in 1980. *See also* ARLT, ROBERTO; BENEDETTI, MARIO; SAER, JUAN JOSÉ; VILARIÑO, IDEA.

OQUENDO DE AMAT, CARLOS (Peru, 1905–1936). Poet. He was a political activist and member of the Communist Party, which he joined in 1930, although little is known about his life. After leaving Peru he eventually reached Europe and died of tuberculosis in a hospital in Spain shortly after the outbreak of the Spanish Civil War. His published literary output consists of one collection of poetry, *5 metros de poemas* (1927; 5 Meters of Poems), a folding book that measures five meters when unfolded, in which he marries the **avant-garde** to indigenous themes in the manner of **Vicente Huidobro's creacionismo**.

OREAMUNO, YOLANDA (Costa Rica, 1916–1956). Novelist and short story writer. Like her compatriot **Eunice Odio**, with whom she had a long and close friendship, she renounced her homeland and lived much of the latter part of her life in **Guatemala** and **Mexico**. She wrote a number of short stories, which were published in the Costa Rican cultural periodical *Repertorio americano* and eventually collected in *A lo largo del corto camino* (1961; Along the Short Road), together with much of the author's other published work. Although there were references to several novels, only one was ever published, *La ruta de su evasión* (1950; Their Escape Route), which explores the story of a family, both in the present and the past, through its female members. It is an important work, one of the first in the region to introduce narrative techniques already established by the likes of Marcel Proust (1871–1922), Thomas Mann (1875–1955), Virginia Woolf (1882–1941), and, above all, James Joyce (1882–1941). *See also* WOMEN.

OROZCO, OLGA (Argentina, 1920–1999). Poet. Born Olga Noemí Gugliotta, she grew up in La Pampa province and felt the influence of its geography, which had a lasting effect on her writing. She wrote two books of stories about childhood, *La oscuridad es otro sol* (1967; Darkness Is Another Sun) and *La luz también es un abismo* (1975; Light Is Also an Abyss), which are often taken to be autobiographical and used as a source for interpreting her poetry. In total she published nine books of verse: *Desde lejos* (1946; From Afar), *Las muertes* (1952; Deaths), *Los juegos peligrosos* (1962; Dangerous Games), *Museo salvaje* (1974; Savage Museum), *Cantos a Berenice* (1977; Songs for Berenice), *Mutaciones de la realidad* (1979; Mutations of Reality), *La noche a la deriva* (1984; Night Adrift), *En el revés del cielo* (1987; On the Back of the Sky), and *Con esta boca, en este mundo* (1994; With This Mouth, in This World). She was a member of a group of poets known in Argentina as the Generation of 1940, which included **Enrique Molina** and **Alberto Girri** among others, a group of neo-romantics preoccupied with death, love, and the anguish of human life. Among the influences on her work were **Pablo Neruda**, Rainer Maria Rilke (1875–1926), the surrealist André Breton (1896–1966), and the **existentialist** writers Jean-Paul Sartre (1905–1980) and Albert Camus (1913–1960). *See also* PIZARNIK, ALEJANDRA; WOMEN.

ORREGO LUCO, LUIS (Chile, 1866–1948). Novelist. Although trained as a lawyer, he made his living from his journalism and diplomatic appointments as a representative for Chile in Europe and several Latin American countries. Like his compatriot, **Alberto Blest Gana**, whose success he never equaled, however, Orrego Luco was drawn to the **realism** of the French novelist Honoré de Balzac (1799–1850). His principal novels were *Un idilio nuevo* (1900; A New Idyll), concerned with middle-class incomes and conflicts very much in the manner of Balzac; *Memorias de un voluntario de la Patria Vieja* (1905; Memoirs of a Volunteer for the Old Country), set in the early 19th century; *Casa grande* (1908; The Big House), his most celebrated work, which offers a portrait of aristocratic Santiago; *Al través de la tempestad* (1914; Across the Storm), about a period of civil conflict in 1891 Chile in which the author was himself caught up; and *Playa negra* (1947; Black Beach), dealing with the times of the author's childhood.

ORTEGA, JULIO (Peru, 1942–). Poet, dramatist, novelist, and essayist. Although he has written a number of works of creative literature and first obtained recognition as a poet, he is best known for his critical work on Latin American literature. His books include *La contemplación y la fiesta* (1968; Contemplation and Feast), *Figuración de la persona* (1971; Figuration of the Person), *Acto subversivo* (1984; Subversive Act), *Ayacucho Goodbye* (1994; Goodbye Ayacucho), *El combate de los ángeles: literatura, género, diferencia* (1999; The Fight of the Angels: Literature, Gender, Difference), and *Caja de herramientas: prácticas culturales para el nuevo siglo chileno* (2000; Box of Tools: Cultural Practices for the New Chilean Century).

Ortega's writing for the **theater** amounts to over a dozen plays that gave him some prominence on the Peruvian stage in the 1960s and 1970s. A number of his pieces, including *El intruso* (The Intruder),

Sociedad anónima (Limited Company), *Como cruzar la calle* (How to Cross the Street), and *Moros en la costa* (Someone's Listening), were published together in 1965. Among his later plays are *Varios rostros de verano* (1968; Several Faces of Summer), *Mesa pelada* (1971; Bare Table), and *Infierno peruano* (1980; Peruvian Inferno). Ortega has also edited works by many other writers and compiled a number of literary anthologies. He has lived in the United States since 1969.

ORTIZ, ADALBERTO (Ecuador, 1914–2003). Novelist, poet, and short story writer. Much of his writing represents and explores the world of the black minority in Ecuador in the northeast area of the country, especially in Esmeraldas, where the author was born. As a novelist, his most successful work was *Juyungo* (1943; *Juyungo*), which tells the life story of its hero through a combination of history and folklore and shows the influence of the American writers John Dos Passos (1896–1970) and John Steinbeck (1902–1968). Other narrative works include the novels *El espejo y la ventana* (1967; The Mirror and the Window) and *La envoltura del sueño* (1974; Dream Wrapping) and collections of short stories: *Los contrabandistas* (1945; The Smugglers), *La mala espalda* (1971; Bad Back), and *La entundada* (1971; The Bewitched Woman). Ortiz's first book of poetry, *Tierra, son y tambor* (1945; Land, Song and Drum), on the music and traditions of the place where he was born, gave him an early widespread reputation as a writer on black themes. A later collection of his poetry, *El animal herido* (1961; The Wounded Animal), has some of the characteristics of **antipoetry**. Ortiz published several anthologies of Ecuadorian and Spanish American short stories, and he was also a painter known for the naïf style he cultivated.

ORTIZ, JUAN L. (Argentina, 1896–1976). Poet. He worked in the government records office and spent much of his life in Gualeguay in the province of Entre Ríos. This retired life is echoed in his poetry, which expresses his feelings of withdrawal and is a representation of familiar riverine landscapes. His first four books—*El agua y la noche* (1933; Water and Night), *El alba sube* (1937; Dawn Arises), *El ángel inclinado* (1938; The Bowing Angel), and *La rama hacia el este* (1940; The Eastward Branch)—serve to establish the terrain, its people, and its atmosphere. In *El aire conmovido* (1949; The Emotional Aire), Ortiz emphasized his poetic language. He continued to explore the same riverside world in five additional books: *La mano infinita* (1951; The Infinite Hand), *El alma y las colinas* (1956; The Soul and the Hills), *De las raíces del cielo* (1958; From the Roots of the Sky), *La orilla que se abisma* (1970; The Plunging Shore), and *El Gualeguay* (1970; The Gualeguay). In *En el aura del sauce* (3 vols., 1970–1970; In the Aura of the Willow), Ortiz collected much of his previous work, including some earlier limited editions and unpublished poems.

ORTIZ DE MONTELLANO, BERNARDO (Mexico, 1899–1949). Poet. A member of **Los Contemporáneos**, he was editor of the group's periodical. His own poetry includes the collections *Avidez* (1921; Eagerness), *El trompo de siete colores* (1925; The Seven-Colored Top), *Red* (1928; Net), *Sueños* (1933; Dreams), and *Muerte de cielo azul* (1937; Blue Sky Death). Dream is the central motif of his poetry, although he inclines to a more traditional approach than that pursued by **surrealism**. Ortiz de Montellano also wrote plays, short stories, and literary criticism. *See also* TORRES BODET, JAIME.

OSPINA, WILLIAM (Colombia, 1954–). Poet, novelist, and essayist. When already established as a poet, he published his first novel, *Ursúa* (2005; Ursúa), a **historical novel** about the Spanish conquistador Pedro de Ursúa (1526–1561). However, he is better known for his essays on Latin America and Colombia. Among these are *Los amores de sangre: Juan de Castellanos y el descubrimiento poético de América* (1998; Love from Blood: Juan de Castellanos and the Poetic Discovery of America), *América mestiza: el país del futuro* (2000; *Mestizo América: The Country of the Future*), *La decadencia de los dragones* (2001; The Decline of the Dragons), and *Érase una vez Colombia* (2006; Once Upon a Time There Was Colombia). His most recent novel, *El país de la canela* (2008; The Country of Cinnamon), is set in the time of the conquest and was the 2009 winner of the **Rómulo Gallegos Prize**.

OTERO SILVA, MIGUEL (Venezuela, 1908–1980). Poet and novelist. This author's first novel, *Fiebre* (1939; Fever), was his most autobiographical and also his most conventional in terms of narrative structure. It deals with the struggle in Venezuela against the military ruler Juan Vicente Gómez (1908–1935), which forced Otera Silva into exile. His later novels were more experimental, especially with respect to his handling of chronology. *Casas muertas* (1955; Dead Houses) and *Oficina no. 1* (1961; Office Number 1) are thematically linked through their treatment of the decline of the agriculture-based economy in Venezuela and the rise of the petroleum industry. *La muerte de Honorio* (1963; Honorio's Death) is a narrative of political militancy told through five interconnected stories. *Cuando quiero llorar no lloro* (1970; When I Want to Weep I Don't), set in the 1960s, has the complicated structure of the lives of three young men, each called Victorino, told in alternating chapters, which culminate in the deaths of all three.

Lope de Aguirre, príncipe de la libertad (1979; Lope de Aguirre, Prince of Freedom) is a **historical novel** based on the rebellion of Lope de Aguirre (ca. 1510–1561), told through a complex narrative structure in a way that foreshadows independence in the Americas. The same historical materials were used by **Abel Posse** and **Arturo Uslar Pietri** and were the subject of the film *Aguirre: The Wrath of God* (1972), directed by Werner Herzog (1942–). Otero Silva's last novel was a fictionalized life of Christ, *La piedra que era Cristo* (1984; The Rock That Was Christ). His collections of poetry include *Agua y cauce* (1937; Water and Channel), *25 poemas* (1942; 25 Poems), *Elegía coral a Andrés Eloy Blanco* (1958; Choral Elegy for Andrés Eloy Blanco), *La mar que es el morir* (1965; The Sea That Is Death), *Umbral* (1966; Threshold), and *Un morrocoy en el cielo* (1972; A Tortoise in the Sky). He was also an essayist and wrote some humorous plays for the **theater**.

OTHÓN, MANUEL JOSÉ (Mexico, 1858–1906). Poet and dramatist. He was a poet in the traditional manner whose verse tended toward the style of **romanticism**. He later disowned his early collection *Poemas* (1880; Poems), and only one other collection, *Poemas rústicos* (1902; Rustic Poems), appeared during his lifetime. This was mainly descriptive compositions, but included verses on which his reputation as a poet is principally founded: "Himno de los bosques" (1891; "Hymn to the Woods"), on the countryside at dawn, and a set of elegiac sonnets, "Noche rústica de Walpurgis" (1897; "Rustic

Walpurgis Night"). Although written in a relatively austere style, they are not without some touches of **modernismo**, notwithstanding the author's energetic repudiation of it. He also wrote several short plays and monologues for the **theater**.

OTT, GUSTAVO (Venezuela, 1963–). Dramatist. His plays are quite eclectic in both style and content and have been widely performed and translated. Notable among them are *Los peces crecen con la luna* (1983; Fish Grow with the Moon), *El siglo de las luces* (1986; The Enlightenment), *Passport* (1988; Passport), *Divorciadas, evangélicas y vegetarianas* (1989; *Divorcées, Evangelists and Vegetarians*), *80 dientes, 4 metros, 200 kilos* (1996; 80 Teeth, 4 Meters, 200 Kilos), *Dos amores y un bicho* (2001; Two Loves and a Bug), *Tu ternura Molotov* (2004; *Your Molotov Kisses*), and *120 vidas x minuto* (2007; *120 Lives a Minute*). See also THEATER.

OVIEDO Y BAÑOS, JOSÉ AGUSTÍN (Venezuela, 1671–1738). Historian. He is considered the founder of Venezuelan historiography for his **chronicle** *Historia de la conquista y población de la provincia de Venezuela* (1723; History of the Conquest and Settlement of Venezuela).

OWEN, GILBERTO (Mexico, 1905–1952). Poet and novelist. He was a member of the group **Los Contemporáneos**. While part of that group he wrote a lyrical novel, *La llama fría* (1925; The Cold Flame), and an experimental novel, *Novela como nube* (1928; Novel Like a Cloud). His production as a poet includes a collection of prose poems, *Línea* (1930; Line), published in Buenos Aires; *El libro de Ruth* (1944; The Book of Ruth); and what is considered his best work, *Perseo vencido* (1952; Perseus Conquered), published in Lima. Like others in his group, he was profoundly influenced by English poets, notably T. S. Eliot (1888–1965).

– P –

PACHECO, JOSÉ EMILIO (Mexico, 1939–). Poet, novelist, and short story writer. A prolific and versatile writer, Pacheco is one of Mexico's notable contemporary public intellectuals, whose work has been recognized by many awards. He has written in several literary genres, worked as a literary journalist and translator, and collaborated on projects with visual artists. Influenced initially by **Octavio Paz**, he is the most important poet of his generation. His early collections include *Los elementos de la noche* (1963; The Elements of the Night), *El reposo del fuego* (1966; Fire at Rest), and *No me preguntes cómo pasa el tiempo: poemas 1964–1968* (1969; Don't Ask Me How Time Goes By: Poems 1964–1968). These already showed his predilection for everyday language and the use of set phrases and quotations, practices that also reflect his awareness of 20th-century Mexican history and a cultural knowledge that stretches far beyond his own country. Subsequent collections of verse include *Islas a la deriva* (1976; Islands Adrift); *Ayer es nunca jamás* (1978; Yesterday Is Never Again); *Desde entonces: poemas 1975–1978* (1980; Since Then: Poems 1975–1978); *Tarde o temprano* (1980; Sooner or Later), which includes translations of poems by other authors; *Los trabajos del mar* (1983; Toils of the Sea); *Fin de siglo y otros poemas* (1984; End of the Century and Other Poems) and *Album de zoología* (1985; *An Ark for the Next Millenium*), both concerned with human–animal relations; *Alta traición* (1985; High Treason); *Miro la tierra: poemas 1985–1986* (1986; I Look at the Land: Poems 1985–1986); *Ciudad de la memoria: poemas 1986–1989* (1989; City of Memory: Poems 1986–1989); and *Silencio de la luna: poemas 1985–1993* (1994; Silence of the Moon).

Pacheco is also well known as an anthologist and critic of Mexican and Latin American literature and, as a writer of prose fiction, is the author of several collections of short narratives, some of which show the influence of **Jorge Luis Borges**. The title story in *Las batallas en el desierto* (1981; *Battles in the Desert and Other Stories*) is a novella, a coming-of-age narrative set during the social and economic changes experienced by Mexico City in the 1940s. Other collections of short stories include *El viento distante y otros relatos* (1963; Distant Wind and Other Stories), *El principio del placer* (1972; The Beginning of Pleasure), and *La sangre de Medusa y otros cuentos* (1988; Medusa's Blood and Other Stories). Pacheco is also the author of a significant novel, *Morirás lejos* (1967; You Will Die Far Away), written in the style of the French author Alain Robbe-Grillet (1922–2008) and the **new novel**. Dwelling on the theme of Nazism, the novel presents a series of recurring scenes understood to be the immediate before and after of a particular event. *See also* NOVO, SALVADOR.

PAIXÃO, FERNANDO (Brazil, 1955–). Poet. Born in Portugal, Paixão moved to Brazil at an early age. His collection *Fogo dos Rios* (1989; Fire of the Rivers) is a lyrical meditation on the *Fragments* of Heraclitus (ca. 535–ca. 475 BCE). His volumes *25 Azulejos* (1994; 25 Tiles) and *Poeira* (2001; Dust) display a concise, image-based poetics.

PALACIO, PABLO (Ecuador, 1906–1947). Short story writer and novelist. Although the predominant trends in fiction during his time emphasized **indigenismo** and social realism, Palacio followed his own inclinations and wrote fiction that has received more attention recently than during his lifetime. He was afflicted with syphilis and suffered the gradual loss of reason in the last years of his life, which ended with his confinement and suicide. His literary work was not extensive and belongs to his early life. A play, *Comedia inmortal* (1926; Immortal Comedy), appeared first, then a collection of short stories, *Un hombre muerto a puntapiés* (1927; A Man Kicked to Death), and a short novel *Débora* (1927; Deborah). Several years later, *Vida del ahorcado* (1932; Life of the Hanged Man), also a short novel, appeared. Palacio's short stories are based on a series of unusual characters, just as his two novels are based on usual situations. *Débora* tells of a man who waits for something to happen in order to begin his story, but nothing ever happens. *Vida del ahorcado* is the story of a crime committed by a man who has hanged himself in his cell and narrates events from within his consciousness.

PALMA, CLEMENTE (Peru, 1872–1946). Novelist and short story writer. He was the son of **Ricardo Palma**, but wrote in a style quite different from that of his more famous father. His collections of short stories *Cuentos malévolos* (1904; Malevolent Tales) and *Historietas malignas* (1924; Evil Tales) were written in the style of the French author Villiers de l'Isle-Adam (1838–1889), with pathologically affected characters, dark humor, and eccentric content. His short novels *Mors ex vita* (1923; Death from Life) and *XYZ* (1935) are along the same lines. Palma was also a journalist and collected some of his newspaper writings in *Crónicas político-doméstico-taurinas de Juan Apapucio Corrales* (Politico-Domestic Bull-Fighting Chronicles by Juan Apapucio Corrales). "Corrales" was his pseudonym.

PALMA, RICARDO (Peru, 1833–1919). Chronicler. Although he tried his hand at poetry and drama, Ricardo Palma is known mainly for his *Tradiciones peruanas* (*Peruvian Traditions*). His "traditions," a genre he invented, are **chronicles** or historical variants of the sketches of contemporary customs and manners associated with **costumbrismo**. They are short historical anecdotes, set mainly in colonial Peru, covering the full social spectrum, from low to upper class, are frequently humorous, with digressive commentaries, and are often derived from oral sources. Palma published his first series of traditions in 1872, and subsequent series continued to appear until 1911. See also BATRES MONTÚFAR, JOSÉ; GORRITI, JUANA MANUELA; MATTO DE TURNER, CLORINDA; PALMA, CLEMENTE; SEGURA, MANUEL ASCENSIO; TABOADA TERÁN, NÉSTOR; VALLE ARIZPE, ARTEMIO DE.

PALOMARES, RAMÓN (Venezuela, 1935–). Poet. Along with others of his generation, he was initially drawn to **surrealism**. His work is distinguished, however, by the presence of nature and his homeland, his narrative inventiveness, his use of archaic language, and references to myth and legend. He first came into the public eye with *El reino* (1958; The Kingdom) and has published a number of collections since then, including *Al ahogado* (1964; To the Drowned Man), *Paisano* (1964; Countryman), *Honras fúnebres* (1965; Funeral Rites), *Santiago de León de Caracas* (1967; Santiago de León of Caracas), *El vientecito suave del amanecer con los primeros aromas* (1969; The Gentle Breeze of Dawn with the First Scents), *Adiós Escuque* (1974; Farewell Escuque), *Elegía 1830* (1980; Elegy 1830), *Mérida, elogio de sus ríos* (1984; Merida, in Praise of Its Rivers), *Alegres provincias* (1988; Happy Provinces), and *Lobos y halcones* (1997; Wolves and Falcons).

PANAMA. Known more for its canal than its literature, few of the country's writers have transcended its borders. The first notable figures were two poets of **modernismo, Darío Herrera** and **Ricardo Miró**. The recurring themes of nationalism, coinciding in the latter with the independence newly won from **Colombia** in 1903, have made him one of Panama's national poets. Panama's most recognized writer, however, is **Rogelio Sinán**, who also introduced the **avant-garde** to the country and had a considerable impact both on poetry and prose. He was followed by a number of avant-garde and post-avant-garde poets. Among short story writers, **Enrique Jaramillo Levi** is a representative figure, but the novel has grown slowly. Themes such as independence, the building of the canal, the treaty with the United States, Panamanian society and politics, and the U.S. invasion of 1989 have provided many subjects, and the number of novelists has increased. Among a group of contemporary authors in the genre, **Rosa María Britton** is one of the most productive and widely known.

Theater in Panama before the 1930s was mainly for the upper classes and represented by touring companies, among which was one that brought Sarah Bernhardt (1844–1923) to perform for executives of the Panama Canal Company. The homegrown theater has been less successful and has yet to produce any major dramatists. A list of writers who have contributed to the Panamanian stage, however, would include Rogelio Sinán, **José de Jesús Martínez**, and Rosa María Britton. *See also* CASA DE LAS AMÉRICAS; MAGIC REALISM.

PARAGUAY. Although Spanish remains the language of power and authority, a full account of Paraguayan literature would also entail an account of literary expression in Guaraní, the language of the majority of the population. Moreover, any history of the development of a literary culture in either language in Paraguay must necessarily acknowledge the numerous obstacles it has had to face. Asunción had some strategic and commercial significance in colonial times, but was culturally subordinated to Lima and Buenos Aires. Since independence, the country has been embroiled in two major wars with its neighbors, the War of the Triple Alliance (1864–1870) against **Brazil, Argentina**, and **Uruguay**, which decimated the Paraguayan population, and the Chaco War (1932–1935) against **Bolivia**. It has also endured long periods of authoritarian rule, notably under José

Gaspar Rodríguez de Francia (1814–1840) and Alfredo Stroessner (1954–1989), which entailed tight censorship and hampered the growth of a literary culture.

Paraguayan literature begins with the Asunción-born **Ruy Díaz de Guzmán**'s **chronicle** of 16th-century Spanish settlements in the River Plate region. History is also one of the main topics of prose writing in the late 19th and early 20th centuries, as writers retold the myths of national formation, influenced by the late arrival of **romanticism**. It was only after the Chaco War that fiction began to develop and to offer a more realistic interpretation of reality. The 1950s saw the emergence of a group of writers that included **Augusto Roa Bastos**, Paraguay's most recognized author, **Gabriel Casaccia**, and **Rubén Bareira Saguier**. Although they opened the door through which others have since passed, none has yet to achieve a similar recognition, especially that obtained by Roa Bastos. Like its fiction, much of Paraguay's poetry has been written in exile, as writers took refuge from dictatorial regimes at home. The major poets are **Josefina Pla**, **Hérib Campos Cervera**, **Elvio Romero**, and **Hugo Rodríguez Alcalá**, and the last of these, along with Josefina Pla, is one of the country's most significant cultural historians. Since the end of the Stroessner dictatorship, a number of other poets have also made their mark, **Delfina Acosta** among them, one of several prominent **women** writers in both poetry and prose.

The **theater** is the weakest of the literary genres in Paraguay. Its development has been affected by political conditions and prolonged periods of censorship, as well as the country's predominantly agrarian status, without the urban population, economy, and infrastructure needed to support it. Although theater was present in the ritual performances practiced in pre-Columbian times and was used in colonial times as part of the process of Christianization, with the traditional *autos* and *loas* often translated into Guaraní, few writers emerged to develop a local tradition until the second half of the 20th century. The founding of the Ateneo Paraguayo and the Escuela de Arte Escénica de Asunción in 1948 became a source of continuing support, and several writers have had a significant impact. Of these, the most important are **Julio Correa**, Josefina Pla, and **Mario Halley Mora**. Some further strides have been made during the last 25 years, with several active theaters in Asunción and participation by national companies in international festivals, but the contemporary theater scene has yet to produce the dramatists needed to engage the public or obtain an international profile. *See also* ACUÑA DE FIGUEROA, FRANCISCO; CASA DE LAS AMÉRICAS; DICTATOR NOVEL; INDIGENISMO; MAGIC REALISM; MARÍN CAÑAS, JOSÉ; MIGUEL DE CERVANTES PRIZE; NEO-BAROQUE; NEW HISTORICAL NOVEL; TABOADA TERÁN, NÉSTOR; TAUNAY, ALFREDO D'ESCRAGNOLLE, VISCONDE DE.

PARDO Y ALIAGA, FELIPE (Peru, 1806–1868). Poet, journalist, and dramatist. Although born in Lima, he was educated in Spain and returned to Peru after the country had won its independence. A member of the conservative faction of the ruling class, he wrote satirical verse and essays on Peruvian life and customs for newspaper publication. His place in Peruvian literature is secured mainly, however, by several plays, including *El espejo de mi tierra* (1840; Mirror of My Land), which made him one of the country's first postindependence dramatists. His earliest work for the stage was *Frutos de la educación* (1829; Benefits of Education), a comedy of manners that uses the convention of generational conflicts over marriage as a device for commenting on social attitudes and presenting scenes of **costumbrismo**. Two other plays, *La huérfana de Chorrillos* (1833; The Orphan from Chorrillos) and *Don Leocadio y el aniversario de Ayacucho* (1834; Don Leocadio and the Anniversary of Ayacucho), are also moralizing comedies of manners. *See also* THEATER.

PAREJA DIEZCANSECO, ALFREDO (Ecuador, 1908–1993). Novelist. He was one of the most productive members of the **Grupo de Guayaquil**. *El muelle* (1933; The Pier), perhaps his best work, was the novel that first drew attention to him. It was followed by *La Beldaca* (1935; Beldaca), *Baldomera* (1938; Baldomera), *Hechos y hazañas de don Balón de Baba y su amigo don Inocente Cruz* (1939; Life and Deeds of Don Balón de Baba and His Friend Don Inocente Cruz), *Hombres sin tiempo* (1941; Men Without Time), and *Las tres ratas* (1944; Three Rats). In 1956, under the title *Los nuevos años* (The New Years), he began to write a series of novels intended to tell the story of Ecuador in the 20th century, although, within the historical framework, the novels became progressively more psychological and existential. They include *La advertencia* (1956; The Warning), *El aire y los recuerdos* (1959; Air and Recollections), *Los poderes omnímodos* (1964; Absolute Powers), *Las pequeñas estaturas* (1970; Small Statures), and *La mantícora* (1975; The Manticore). In addition to his fiction, Pareja Diezcanseco wrote biographies, a study of the German novelist Thomas Mann (1875–1955), and books on the history of Ecuador.

PARNASSIANISM. This was the name of a movement in French poetry of the 1860s and 1870s that took its name from Mount Parnassus, the home of the muses in Greek mythology. It was formed in response to the sentimental excesses of **romanticism** and gave particular importance to the notion of "art for art's sake." Charles Leconte de Lisle (1818–1894), Stephane Mallarmé (1842–1898), and Paul Verlaine (1844–1896) were among the major figures in French parnassianism. In Spanish America it had a significant influence on the work of **Rubén Darío** and the emergence of **modernismo**. In **Brazil**, both "scientific poetry" and realist poetry, which were also reactions to romantic excess, had been practiced since 1870. Beginning in 1886, they were called "parnassianism" for their similarity to the French movement of the same name. The emphasis was on the perfection of poetic form, particularly the sonnet, and the avoidance of sentimentalism, although not sentiment. The main exponents of parnassianism were **Alberto de Oliveira**, **Raimundo Correia**, Vicente de Carvalho (1866–1924), and **Olavo Bilac**. *See also* ALMEIDA, GUILHERME DE; ANJOS, AUGUSTO DOS; CARVALHO, RONALD DE; JAIMES FREYRE, RICARDO; LIMA, JORGE DE; MACHADO, GILKA; MEIRELES, CECÍLIA; NERVO, AMADO; PICCHIA, PAULO MENOTTI DEL; POMPÉIA, RAUL D'ÁVILA; REALISM; REBOLLEDO, EFRÉN; RICARDO LEITE, CASSIANO; SOUSA, JOÃO CRUZ E; SYMBOLISM; VALENCIA, GUILLERMO.

PARRA, MARCO ANTONIO DE LA (Chile, 1952–). Dramatist. In addition to his literary work, he is a practicing psychiatrist. His **theater** is characterized by its uninhibited language and use of popular culture, treatment of taboo themes, and demystification of national myths, especially the corrupting influence of power. His early plays include *Quiebrespejos* (1974; Cracked Mirrors) and *Brisca* (1974; Whist). In *Lo crudo, lo cocido, lo podrido* (1978; The Raw, the Cooked, and the Rotten), he takes on Chilean national institutions. *Matatangos* (1978; Tango Killer) is concerned with the life of the celebrated singer Carlos Gardel (1887/1890–1935), and in *La secreta obscenidad de cada día* (1984; The Secret Obscenity of Every Day) he presents Karl Marx (1818–1883) and Sigmund Freud (1856–1939) in a verbal conflict drawn from their own theories and related to the state of Chile under Augusto Pinochet (1973–1990). This play and others, such as *King Kong Palace* (1990; King Kong Palace), have made the author a significant commentator on the Pinochet dictatorship and the postdictatorship period in Chile. Other titles include *El deseo de toda ciudadana* (1987; Every Woman's Desire), *La noche de los volantines* (1989; Night of the Kites), *Límites* (1991; Limits), and *El padre muerto* (1991; The Dead Father). Marco Antonio de la Parra has also written novels, among which are *La secreta guerra santa de Santiago de Chile* (1985; *The Secret Holy War of Santiago de Chile*) and *El año de la ballena* (2001; *The Year of the Whale*). *See also* DORFMAN, ARIEL.

PARRA, NICANOR (1914–). Poet. The brother of the folk singer-songwriter **Violeta Parra**, he is a physicist by profession and one of Chile's most significant 20th-century poets. His first book of poetry, *Cancionero sin nombre* (1937; Songbook Without a Name), was a collection of mainly conventional verse, which the author has since disowned. His second volume, published 17 years later, was quite different. *Poemas y antipoemas* (1954; *Poems and Antipoems*), written under the rubric of **antipoetry,** was an iconoclastic work that marked a new turn in Chilean poetry, away from the more complex verse of **Gabriela Mistral, Vicente Huidobro,** and the **Pablo Neruda** of the *Residencias* toward a simpler style represented by a more colloquial language. It also represented a search for a poetic voice that was not bound by tradition but embodied the author's own irreverent view of the world and black sense of humor. The same attitude has been sustained in much of Parra's later work, which includes *La cueca larga* (1958; The Long Cueca); *Versos de salón* (1962; Salon Verses); *Discursos* (1962; Discourses), written in collaboration with Pablo Neruda; *Manifiesto* (1963; Manifesto); *Canciones* *rusas* (1967; Russian Songs); *Los profesores* (1971; The Teachers); *Artefactos* (1972; Artefacts), reflecting his skepticism of the Popular Unity government in Chile (1970–1970); *Sermones y prédicas del Cristo de Elqui* (1977; *Sermons and Homilies of the Christ of Elqui*); and *Chistes para desorientar a la policía* (1983; Jokes for Misleading the Police), a critique of the government of Augusto Pinochet (1973–1990). *See also* DÍAZ, JORGE; RULFO, JUAN.

PARRA, TERESA DE LA (Venezuela, 1890–1936). Novelist. Although much of her life was spent outside Venezuela, she is considered the country's first major female writer. Some of her earliest literary endeavors were short stories in the vein of **fantastic literature**, published in journals. She is known mainly, however, for two novels, both of which reflect on conflicts arising from the encounter between modernization and tradition and on questions of gender and female identity. *Ifigenia: diario de una señorita que escribía porque se fastidiaba* (1924; *Ifigenia: The Diary of a Young Lady Who Wrote Because She Was Bored*) is the story of a young woman with progressive ideas who returns to Caracas after a European upbringing and engages in a futile struggle against the assimilation of **women** into the conventional world prescribed by a patriarchal society. *Las memorias de Mamá Blanca* (1929; *Mama Blanca's Souvenirs*), her second novel, is set initially in rural Venezuela and is subsequently relocated in the city. It deals with the education of a young girl, particularly the heritage received from her mother. *See also* DÍAZ SÁNCHEZ, RAMÓN.

PARRA, VIOLETA (Chile, 1917–1967). Poet and songwriter. She came from a talented, artistic family and was the sister of **Nicanor Parra**. As a singer-songwriter, folklorist, collector of traditional songs, and prominent figure in the New Song movement of the 1950s and 1960s, she was an icon of popular culture. More recently, however, she has also been recognized for her writing, not just song lyrics, but also her verse autobiography. At the same time that this is a narrative of 40 years of history, *Las décimas: autobiografía en versos chilenos* (1970; Décimas: Autobiography in Chilean Verses) is also the story of her own journey through Chilean society. An anthology of her writings and interviews is presented in *Toda Violeta Parra* (1974; All Violeta Parra), and her biography has been written by **Patricio Manns**. *See also* WOMEN.

PASO, FERNANDO DEL (Mexico, 1935–). Novelist. The three novels for which Fernando del Paso is principally known are gargantuan works, ranging in length from 500 to over 1,200 pages each. Although each has a story of sorts, they do not have a linear structure, but rather a series of apparently disconnected narratives in a seemingly arbitrary content characterized by all kinds of linguistic games. They are also **historical novels**, in that they explore facets of Mexican history. *José Trigo* (1966; José Trigo) is concerned with the railway workers' movement that figured prominently in 1958–1959. *Palinuro de México* (1977; *Palinurus of Mexico*), recipient of the 1982 **Rómulo Gallegos Prize**, covers a wide swath of history, from pre-Columbian times to the **Tlatelolco massacre** in 1968, in which the protagonist dies. *Noticias del Imperio* (1987; *News from the Empire*) is based on the reign of Maximilian and Carlota (1864–1867) and, as a work that reconstructs history through multiple points of view, has some of the characteristics of the **new historical novel**. Fernando del Paso has also published a volume of poetry, *Sonetos del amor y de lo diario* (1958; Sonnets of Love and the Everyday), and the novel *Linda 67: historia de un crimen* (1995; Linda 67: The Story of a Crime).

PASOS, JOAQUÍN (Nicaragua, 1914–1947). Poet. He was an important figure in the **avant-garde** movement in Nicaragua, although some of his most significant work did not appear until after his death. His poetry is humorous, playful, and imaginative. He wrote about the indigenous people of Nicaragua and also about foreign countries and travel, without ever having left his homeland. The devastation of two world wars is also reflected in his verse, and one of his best-known pieces, "Canto de la guerra de las cosas" (1943; "Song of the War on Things"), is often compared to *The Waste Land* (1922) by T. S. Eliot (1888–1965). His writing for the **theater** includes his collaboration with **José Coronel Urtecho** on *La chinfonía burguesa* (1939; The Bourgeois Chinphony).

PAVLOVSKY, EDUARDO (Argentina, 1933–). Dramatist. Trained as a doctor and psychiatrist, he began writing for the **theater** in the 1960s. He was one of the first in Latin America to write psychodramas and became a significant contributor to the **avant-garde** theater in Argentina of the 1960s and 1970s. He has published extensively on psychodramas, psychoanalysis and the theater, and psychotherapy for children. His work for the stage includes *La espera trágica* (1962; The Tragic Wait), *Somos* (1962; We Are), *Camellos sin anteojos* (1963; Camels Without Glasses), *El robot* (1966; The Robot), *La cacería* (1969; The Hunt), *La mueca* (1970; The Grimace), *Último match* (1971; Last Match), *El señor Galíndez* (1973; Mr. Galindez), *Telarañas* (1976; Spider Webs), *El señor Laforgue* (1983; Mr. Laforgue), *Potestad* (1985; Authority), *Pablo* (1987; Paul), *Voces* (1990; Voices), and *La muerte de Marguerite Durás* (2000; The Death of Marguerite Duras).

PAYNO, MANUEL (Mexico, 1810–1894). Novelist. After **José Joaquín Fernández de Lizardi**, he was the first major Mexican novelist of the 19th century. His fiction shows some of the characteristics of **romanticism**, **costumbrismo**, and the **historical novel** and was published in serial form in literary magazines, a trend he initiated in Mexico. His three principal works are *El fistol del diablo* (1845–1846; The Devil's Tiepin), a fantastic adventure story; *El hombre de la situación* (1861; The Man of the Moment), a historical tale set in colonial times; and *Los bandidos del Río Frío* (1889–1891; The Bandits from Rio Frio), a long, rambling work set in the first half of the 19th century. Payno also published a collection of short stories, *Tardes nubladas* (1871; Overcast Afternoons).

PAYRÓ, ROBERTO JORGE (Argentina, 1867–1928). Novelist, short story writer, dramatist, and journalist. Payró's writing embraces a wide range of subjects and genres. He produced accounts of his travels and **historical novels** (part of a project to tell national history through fiction) and was an influential writer for the **theater** in his day who contributed to the popularity of the *sainete* through his comic writing. He is most remembered, however, for three works in a **picaresque** vein. *El casamiento de Laucho* (1906; Laucha's Marriage) is the story of a character whose unscrupulous marriage and journey through society is used to convey the ills of turn-of-the-century Argentina. *Pago Chico* (1908; Pago Chico) is a collection of stories about rogues in a rural setting that reveals the corruption and pecadilloes of the inhabitants of a small town. Finally, in *Divertidas aventuras del nieto de Juan Moreira* (1910; The Amusing Adventures of Juan Moreira's Grandson), the picaresque is linked to **gaucho literature** to argue the need for a progressive Argentina to move on from its past. *See also* ANDERSON IMBERT, ENRIQUE.

PAZ, OCTAVIO (Mexico, 1914–1998). Poet and essayist. A prolific writer and one of Mexico's most influential 20th-century voices, whose contributions to literature were recognized by the **Miguel de Cervantes Prize** in 1981 and the **Nobel Prize for Literature** in 1990. Octavio Paz was associated with numerous literary **journals** throughout his life, including *Taller* (founded 1938), *Plural* (1971–1976), and *Vuelta* (founded 1976), some of them important vehicles of expression for his generation and later. Paz's collections of essays have ranged widely. In *Laberinto de la soledad* (1950; *The Labyrinth of Solitude*), he addressed the question of Mexicanness, to which he returned in *Posdata* (1970; *The Other Mexico: Critique of the Pyramid*). Although some of his ideas are now somewhat outdated, *Laberinto* has been highly influential and is a classic text.

He first developed his approach to poetry and poetics in *El arco y la lira: el poema, la revelación poética, poesía e historia* (1956; *The Bow and the Lyre: The Poem, Poetic Revelation, Poetry and History*) and took up these themes again in later publications, notably *Las peras del olmo* (1958; Pears from the Elm Tree), *Cuadrivio* (1965; Quadrivium), *Los signos en rotación* (1965; Signs in Rotation), *Corriente alterna* (1967; Alternating Current), and *Los hijos del limo: del romanticismo a la vanguardia* (1974; *Children of the Mire: Modern Poetry from Romanticism to the Avant-Garde*). Paz has also written on anthropology in *Claude Lévi-Strauss o el nuevo festín de Esopo* (1967; *Claude Lévi-Strauss: An Introduction*) and on art in *Marcel Duchamp o el castillo de la pureza* (1968; *Marcel Duchamp or the Castle of Purity*). Among his later major publications was *Sor Juana Inés de la Cruz o las trampos de la fe* (1982; *Sor Juana Inés de la Cruz or the Traps of Faith*).

Octavio Paz's first two books of poetry, *Luna silvestre* (1933; Wild Moon) and *Raíz del hombre* (1937; The Root of Man), already showed his intellectual rigor and lyrical abilities. His writing matured during the 1940s in the context of travel and periods of residence away from home: in the Yucatán (1937), at the Second International Congress of Antifascist Writers in Spain (1937), in the United States (1943–1945), and in Paris after he joined the Mexican diplomatic service in 1945. His first major collection of poetry, *Libertad bajo palabra* (Freedom on Parole), was published in 1949 and would appear again later in several revised editions (1960, 1968, 1975, 1988). This collection shows the influence of English and French poetry and also Paz's emerging interest in history and Mexicanness, which found its first significant expression in 1950 in *El laberinto de la soledad*. Such themes are explored poetically with more intensity in the prose poems of *¿Aguila o sol?* (1951; *Eagle or Sun*) and, above all, in *Piedra de sol* (1957; *Sun Stone*), a meditation on time and history framed in relation to the celebrated Aztec stone calendar now on display in the National Museum of Anthropology in Mexico City.

Shortly after the publication of *Piedra de sol*, Paz was named Mexican ambassador to India, where he remained until he resigned in 1968 to protest the **Tlatelolco massacre**. His encounters with Asia are represented in the collection *Ladera este* (1969; *East Slope*), which shows his absorption with the East and his fascination with otherness and the differences between Eastern and Western cultures. At about the same time, he published *Blanco* (1967; *Blanco*) and *Discos visuales* (1968; Visual Disks), both explorations of systems of rotating signs in life, nature, and culture obtained in part by the form of publication. *Blanco* was printed on a single scroll that could be folded and unfolded to create a single or several poems. *Discos visuales* consisted of four poems printed on four paper disks, with artwork by Vicente Rojo (1932–). These publications were trends Paz continued in his later verse, often working with other authors, such as in *Renga* (1972; *Renga: A Chain of Poems*) and *Hijos del aire/Airborn* (1979), a Spanish/English collaboration with the British poet Charles Tomlinson. *See also* GARRO, ELENA; JUARROZ, ROBERTO; MUTIS, ÁLVARO; PACHECO, JOSÉ EMILIO.

PEIXOTO, AFRÂNIO (Brazil, 1876–1947). Novelist and short story writer. Trained in medicine, Peixoto had a career in politics and education. In Leipzig, he published *Rosa Mística* (1900; Mystical Rose), a poetic drama in the style of **symbolism**. In the years that followed, he traveled to Europe and concentrated on medicine, returning to literature after a trip to Egypt, when he wrote his first novel *Esfinge* (1911; Sphynx), which met with great success. *Maria Bonita* (1914; Mary the Lovely) was followed by his best-known novel, *Fruta de Mato* (1920; Fruit of the Forest), set in the backlands and based on folkloric motifs. Less successful were novels such as *Uma Mulher Como as Outras* (1928; A Woman Like the Others), set in an urban environment. Peixoto, who knew and studied the work of Sigmund Freud (1856–1939), wrote psychological novels that explored mostly female characters. Embracing the values of the land and **regionalism**, he strongly opposed the budding **Brazilian modernism**, and for that reason he was ignored by the critics. Other novels and collections of short stories include *Sinhazinha* (1929; Little Mistress), *Parábolas* (1920; Parabolas), and *Amor Sagrado e Amor Profano* (1942; Sacred Love and Profane Love). Peixoto was also a philologist and literary critic, publishing essays on Luís de Camões (ca. 1524–1580) and histories of literature such as *Panorama da Literatura Brasileira* (1940; Panorama of Brazilian Literature). *See also* MATTOS E GUERRA, GREGÓRIO DE.

PEIXOTO, INÁCIO JOSÉ DE ALVARENGA (Brazil, 1744?– 1793). Poet. After initial studies in Brazil, Alvarenga Peixoto traveled to Portugal and obtained a degree in law from the University of Coimbra, where he met and befriended the poet **Basílio da Gama**. Back in Brazil, he married the poet Barbara Heliodora (1758–1819) and held a number of public posts, including judge and senator. After retiring from public office, Alvarenga Peixoto went into agriculture and mining. His poetry based on love themes is considered one of the best examples of **arcadianism**, as seen in his *Obras Poéticas* (1865; Poetic Works). Along with other landowners, some of whom were poets, such as **Cláudio Manoel da Costa** and **Tomás Antônio Gonzaga**, he participated in the 1789 political insurrection against the Portuguese crown known as the Inconfidência Mineira (Minas

Conspiracy) and was arrested, tried, and condemned to hard labor in a prison in Angola, where he died.

PELLEGRINI, ALDO (Argentina, 1903–1973). Poet. In 1926, he was one of the first to introduce **surrealism** to Argentina, just two years after the first *Surrealist Manifesto* appeared in Paris. His poetry included *El muro secreto* (1949; The Secret Wall), *La valija de fuego* (1952; Suitcase of Fire), *Construcción de la desconstrucción* (1957; Construction from Deconstruction), and *Distribución del silencio* (1966; Distribution of Silence). Pellegrini was also an art critic and wrote for the **theater**. His *Antología de la poesía surrealista* (1961; Anthology of Surrealist Poetry) was a significant text for the dissemination of **avant-garde** poetry in Latin America. *See also* MADARIAGA, FRANCISCO; MOLINA, ENRIQUE.

PELLICER, CARLOS (Mexico, 1899–1977). Poet. Although linked to **Los Contemporáneos**, his association with the group was minimal, and he had much wider connections. He was primarily a visual poet, who was drawn to art and wrote a number of poems to painters. He was head of the government's Department of Fine Arts and Museums for a term. The landscape figures significantly in his work, although with a certain tropical flare, the result of his travels in the Far East and South America. He also wrote on pre-Columbian and religious themes and was a fervent Catholic, while also adhering to a left-wing philosophy in politics. His collections of poetry were *Colores en el mar y otros poemas* (1921; Colors in the Sea and Other Poems), *Piedra de sacrificios* (1924; Sacrificial Stone), *6, 7 poemas* (1924; 6, 7 Poems), *Hora y 20* (1927; An Hour and 20), *Camino* (1929; Pathway), *Hora de junio* (1937; June Time), *Exágonos* (1941; Hexagons), *Recinto y otras imágenes* (1941; Enclosure and Other Images), *Subordinaciones* (1949; Subordinations), *Práctica de vuelo* (1956; Flying Practice), *Cuerdas, percusión y aliento* (1976; Strings, Percussion and Wind), *Reincidencias* (1978; Re-occurrences), and *Cosillas para el nacimiento* (1977; Little Pieces for the Christmas Creche). *See also* TORRES BODET, JAIME.

PENA, LUÍS CARLOS MARTINS (Brazil, 1815–1848). Chronicler and dramatist. Born in Rio to family of humble means, Martins Pena was orphaned at a young age. He went on to study commerce and also attended the Academy of Fine Arts, studying drawing, music, and **theater**. He taught himself French and Italian and began to write for the stage at a young age. In 1838, *O Juiz de Paz na Roça* (1842; The Justice of the Peace in the Country), a **picaresque** comedy that chastised the venality of priests, judges, and society in general, was performed by the theater company of João Caetano (1808–1863), the most famous actor and impresario of his time. The play's success earned Martins Pena the support of Caetano and **Domingos Gonçalves de Magalhães**, who were trying to create a Brazilian national theater. That same year, Martins Pena also obtained a government position, and in 1847 he was named attaché to the Brazilian embassy in London. However, he contracted tuberculosis there and died in Lisbon on his way back to Brazil.

Martins Pena is credited with introducing the comedy of manners into Brazilian theater with great success, satirizing both country and urban types in plays such as *Os Três Médicos* (1845; The Three Physicians), *O Diletante* (1845; The Dilettante), *O Judas em Sábado de Aleluia* (1846; Judas on Easter Saturday), *Os Irmãos das Almas* (1847; The Alms Brothers), and *O Noviço* (1853; The Novice), some of which are still performed. Although later he attempted more serious dramatic pieces, he was less successful than in the satirical and farcical genres. He was also an active **chronicler** of theater life in the period. Martins Pena has been hailed as the Brazilian Molière, and his talent for precise observation of social types and situations, particularly for recreating popular speech, secured him an important place in Brazilian theater. His reviews and chronicles are gathered in *Folhetins: A Semana Lírica* (1965; Feuilletons: The Lyrical Week). In total, he wrote 28 plays, which are all included in the two-volume *Teatro de Martins Pena* (1956; Theater of Martins Pena). See also AZEVEDO, ARTUR NABANTINO GONÇALVES.

PERALTA LAGOS, JOSÉ MARÍA (El Salvador, 1873–1944). Novelist and dramatist. Writing in the realist trends of **costumbrismo** and **naturalismo**, his prose works contributed to the emergence of a Salvadoran national literature at the beginning of the 20th century. The books *Burla burlando* (1923; Mocking the Mocker) and *Brochazos* (1925; Brushstrokes) are both collections of sketches of

Salvadoran life and people. *Doctor Gonorreitigorrea* (1933; Doctor Gonorreitigorrea) is a short novel that takes a satirical look at Salvadoran society, and *La muerte de la tórtola* (1933; Death of the Turtledove) is a costumbrista novel. His contribution to the **theater** is represented by *Candidato* (1931; Candidate), a satirical representation of the 1930–1931 presidential campaign that would have such disastrous consequences for the country.

PERALTA Y BARNUEVO, PEDRO DE (Peru, 1663–1743). Poet and dramatist. He was a luminary of colonial Peru, proficient in several languages, adept at the sciences, and the author of more than 50 books. As a poet, he is remembered mainly for his contribution to the **epic poetry** of colonial Latin America, *Lima fundada, o conquista del Perú* (1732; The Foundation of Lima, or the Conquest of Peru), an erudite composition that exalts the virtues of the Spanish conquistador Francisco Pizarro (ca. 1471 or 1476–1541). He wrote the dramas *Triunfos de amor y poder* (1711; Triumphs of Love and Power), *Afectos vencen finezas* (1720; Affectation Conquers Courtesy), and *La Rodoguna* (date unknown; Rodogune), as well as several short pieces (*loas* and *entremeses*) to accompany them. *La Rodoguna* was adapted from a work by the French dramatist Pierre Corneille (1606–1684). Other influences were the French author of comedies Molière (1622–1673) and the Spanish dramatist Pedro Calderón de la Barca (1600–1681). *See also* THEATER.

PEREDA VALDÉS, ILDEFONSO (Uruguay, 1899–1996). Poet. His first two collections were *La casa iluminada* (1929; The Illuminated House) and *El libro de la colegiala* (1921; The Schoolgirl's Book). In two subsequent collections, *La guitarra de los negros* (1926; Black Guitar) and *Raza negra* (1929; Black Race), he turned to themes drawn from black history and culture, which dominated his writing thereafter in a series of books on folklore and history, among them *El negro rioplatense y otros ensayos* (1937; Black River Plate and Other Essays), *Línea de color* (1938; Color Line), *Negros esclavos y negros libres* (1941; Black Slaves and Free Blacks), *El cancionero popular uruguayo* (1947; The Uruguayan Popular Songbook), and *El negro en el Uruguay, pasado y presente* (1965; Blacks in Uruguay, Past and Present).

PÉREZ ROSALES, VICENTE (Chile, 1807–1886). Autobiographer. Although he also wrote in other genres, Pérez Rosales is remembered mainly for his *Recuerdos del pasado* (1882; Recollections of the Past), an autobiography that still retains a readership. It is a rich work of **costumbrismo**, focused primarily on the author himself and the life he encountered on his many travels and adventures, including periods of time he lived in Europe and California.

PERI ROSSI, CRISTINA (Uruguay, 1941–). Novelist, poet, and short story writer. She is one of Latin America's most significant **women** writers. With two early collections of short stories, *Viviendo* (1963; Living) and *Los museos abandonados* (1968; The Abandoned Museums), Peri Rossi already began to explore some of themes that would become important to her work, including gender and **lesbianism**, the enclosed and oppressive world of women, cultural decline, revolution, and **fantastic literature**. Her first novel, *El libro de mis primos* (1969; My Cousins' Book), is an experimental novel, with many shifts in voices, perspectives, and forms, which offers an acute satire of economic, social, and political intitutions. Like *Indicios pánicos* (1970; *Panic Signs*), a miscellaneous collection of short pieces that followed, it also foreshadows the collapse of Uruguayan society and the military dictatorship that began in 1973. Her first volume of poetry, *Evohé* (1971; *Evohe: Erotic Poems*), caused a considerable stir for its celebration of the female body.

In 1972, Peri Rossi moved to Spain to escape political persecution. She has continued to publish regularly and is the author of more than 37 books. The problems of living in exile appeared in *Descripción de un naufragio* (1975; Description of a Shipwreck) and *Diáspora* (1976; Diaspora) and are a recurring theme of much of her subsequent writing. In two collections of short stories, *La tarde del dinosaurio* (1976; Afternoon of the Dinosaur) and *La rebelión de los niños* (1980; Revolt of the Children), she contrasts the attitudes and perspectives of children and adults. In 1983, she published *El museo de los esfuerzos inútiles* (The Museum of Useless Efforts), a collection, like *Indicios pánicos*, of miscellaneous short pieces, some of them with a journalistic flavor. *Una pasión prohibida* (1986; A Forbidden Passion) has a similar content.

One of Peri Rossi's best-known works is her novel *La nave de los locos* (1984; *Ship of Fools*), a highly experimental text that sustains her earlier focus on themes such as authoritarianism, gender, and different sexualities. The novel presents many of the elements to which she returns in her subsequent fiction, albeit without the same degree of experimentation, such as in the novels *Solitario de amor* (1988; *Solitaire of Love*), *La última noche de Dostoievski* (1992; *Dostoevsky's Last Night*), and *El amor es una droga dura* (1999; *Love Is an Addiction*) and in the short story collections *Cosmoagonías* (1994; Cosmic Agonies), *Desastres íntimas* (1997; Intimate Disasters), *Te adoro y otros relatos* (1999; I Adore You and Other Stories), and *Por fin solos* (1994; Alone at Last). Among her more recent books of poetry are *Estado de exilio* (2003; State of Exile) and *Mi casa es la escritura* (2006; Writing Is My Home).

PERIODICALS. *See* JOURNALS, MAGAZINES, NEWSPAPERS, AND PERIODICALS.

PERLONGHER, NÉSTOR (Argentina, 1949–1992). Poet. He was a student activist and one of the founders of the movement for recognition of rights for **homosexuals** in Argentina. His poetry is **neo-baroque**, characterized by excess, although he used the term *neobarroso* by which, with a play on words, he wished to refer to a style newly muddied (*barroso*) by the River Plate, at the mouth of which Buenos Aires is located. He published six books of poetry: *Austria-Hungría* (1980; Austria-Hungary), *Alambres* (1980; Fences), *Hule* (1989; Rubber), *Parque Lezama* (1990; Lezama Park), *Aguas aéreas* (1992; Aerial Waters), and *El chorreo de las iluminaciones* (1992; The Gushing of the Lights). In 1982, he went to São Paulo, **Brazil**, where he worked as an anthropologist, teaching and researching in the field of sexuality.

PERÓN, JUAN DOMINGO (1895–1974). A colonel in the army, he was elected president of **Argentina** on three occasions, for two consecutive terms between 1946 and 1955, before being ousted and going into exile, and for part of a third term between 1973 and 1974, which ended with his death from illness. His populism had a lasting impact on the politics of Argentina and contributed to some of the divisions that plagued the country during the second half of the 20th century. Both his life and the political doctrine of Peronism have left their mark on Argentinean literature in the work of authors such as **Julio Cortázar, Tomás Eloy Martínez,** and **David Viñas.** See also COSSA, ROBERTO; DUARTE DE PERÓN, EVA; JAURETCHE, ARTURO; MARECHAL, LEOPOLDO; PEYROU, MANUEL.

PERU. Although the Incas had a system of knotted strings, known as a *quipu,* used both to tally numbers and as a mnemonic aid to historical narrative, writing was not introduced to the country until the conquest. The story of the conquest and the early years of colonization, and an account of Spanish perceptions of the land and the life and customs of the people who inhabited it, are recorded in the **chronicles** of **Pedro de Cieza de León** and **Agustín de Zarate.** The history of preconquest Peru and the plight of its peoples after subjugation to the Spanish are told by a mestizo, the Inca **Garcilaso de la Vega,** and the Indian **Felipe Guaman Poma de Ayala.**

As the capital of the Viceroyalty of Peru, Lima was also the political and cultural center of Spanish South America for much of the colonial period and had a thriving literature, especially in drama, **epic poetry,** and **baroque** verse. **Diego de Hojeda, Juan de Espinosa Medrano, Juan del Valle y Caviedes,** and **Pedro de Peralta y Barnuevo** were its luminaries. The brilliance of literary viceregal Lima did not continue into the 19th century after independence, however. A glimpse into life in the postindependence period is given by the traveler **Flora Tristán. Costumbrismo** was introduced to Peru with **Felipe Pardo y Aliaga**'s 1840 *El espejo de mi tierra* (Mirror of My Land), but the most acclaimed prose writer of the 19th century was **Ricardo Palma,** who gave a historical turn to costumbrismo with his *tradiciones* on colonial life. A more serious tone began to appear in prose after the disastrous loss of territory to **Chile** in the War of the Pacific (1879–1883). Its political implications are reflected in the essays of **Manual González Prada** and, in fiction, in the turn to **realism** of the later novels of **Mercedes Cabello de Carbonera** and one of the first examples of Peruvian **indigenismo, Clorinda Matto de Turner**'s *Aves sin nido* (1889; *Torn from the Nest*).

Although **neo-classicism** and **romanticism** in poetry are represented respectively by Felipe Pardo y Aliaga and Manuel González Prada, major figures in Peruvian poetry did not appear until the advent of **modernismo** and the work of **José Santos Chocano** and **José María Egurén**. Early in the new century, however, there were further aesthetic and political changes that heralded the advent of some of Peru's most important writers. **Abraham Valdelomar, Ventura García Calderón, Clemente Palma**, and **Enrique López Albújar** were transitional writers, but by the 1920s the literary **avant-garde** and political challenges from the Left were already in the wind. The political writings of **Víctor Raúl Haya de la Torre** and **José Carlos Mariátegui**, and the founding of the Alianza Popular Revolucionaria Americana (APRA; American Popular Revolutionary Alliance) and the Peruvian Communist Party, with which they were associated, respectively, resonated throughout the 20th century. The politics of the time are reflected in some of the writings of **Magda Portal**, and the full impact of the avant-garde is represented by a group of notable poets: **Alberto Hidalgo, Emilio Adolfo Westphalen, Carlos Oquendo de Amat, César Moro**, and **César Vallejo**, the last considered a major figure in Latin American poetry in general. By the 1940s and 1950s, the work of **Martín Adán, Javier Sologuren, Carlos Germán Belli**, and **Blanca Varela**, one of Peru's most significant **women** poets, had begun to appear and to sustain the level of achievement obtained by the preceding generation. In the second half of the 20th century other accomplished poets, such as **Antonio Cisneros** and **Carmen Ollé**, emerged, continuing the tradition.

In fiction, the first half of the 20th century was marked by social criticism and regionalism in **Enrique López Albújar** and **José Diez Canseco** and, above all, by indigenismo in **Ciro Alegría**'s landmark novel *El mundo es ancho y ajeno* (1941; *Broad and Alien Is the World*) and the early fiction of **José María Arguedas**. In the later work of Arguedas and the stories of **Julio Ramón Ribeyro**, there is already an anticipation of the **new novel** and **boom**, which reached fruition in Peru in **Mario Vargas Llosa**, the country's most widely recognized author and recipient of the **2010 Nobel Prize for Literature. Manuel Scorza** and **Alfredo Bryce Echenique** are of the same generation. They also represent the same divide in Peru that separates José María Arguedas from Mario Vargas Llosa, the former focused internally on the majority mestizo and indigenous cultures, the latter turned more toward Europe and the Europeanized cultures of middle- and upper-class Peru. In addition to these fiction writers, there is a cluster of others who have contributed to broadening the range of the recent novel: **Isaac Goldemberg** has written about the Perevian **Jewish** community, the work of **Carlos Reynoso** has focused on the urban cultures of Lima, and **Jaime Bayly**'s novels deal with questions of sexuality and gender.

Peru has produced several distinguished essayists and literary critics, among whom two of the most prominent are **Luis Alberto Sánchez** and **Julio Ortega**. As most historians recognize, however, Peruvian **theater**, notwithstanding its long history, has not achieved the same heights or had the same consistency as the country's 20th-century poetry and prose. The evidence from chroniclers such as the Inca Garcilaso de la Vega suggests that theater figured in Incan culture, a point endorsed in some discussions by the existence of the Quechuan drama *Ollantay*. Whatever the case, Spanish theater took root quickly in Peru, and the performance of *autos* to celebrate both religious and secular occasions was soon established. The first theater was built in Lima in 1594, and the city became a center for the performing arts in colonial times rivaled in the New World only by Mexico City. The plays performed were mainly in the European tradition, some written by Peruvian dramatists, of which the most celebrated was Pedro de Peralta y Barnuevo. A more Peruvian theater did not emerge until the mid-19th century, when costumbrismo was introduced to the stage by Felipe Pardo y Aliaga, and romanticism was the dominant feature of plays by Ricardo Palma. The title of founder of the Peruvian theater is usually given, however, to **Manuel Ascensio Segura**, who wrote 13 plays, mainly about middle-class Peru.

After Segura's death in 1871, the theater went into decline. Performances of comedies of manners dominated the stage for several decades. There were a number of dramatists and several prominent writers, such as Clorinda Matto de Turner and José Santos Chocano, wrote for the stage, but the next dramatist of consequence, **Sebastián Salazar Bondy**, did not emerge until the 1940s. At the same time, the theater began to receive government support for the funding of companies and national prizes. Yet Salazar Bondy was in some ways unique, both for the quality and number of his plays. Other dramatists, such as **Enrique Solari Swayne**, although they wrote successful plays, were far from prolific, and the theater continued to suffer from a lack of writers dedicated to the genre.

By the 1970s, the theater had become more stable, and among the predominant writers were **Grégor Díaz**, **Julio Ortega**, and **Alonso Alegría**. Moreover, during the 1980s and 1990s two new phenomena emerged: collective theater and *teatro de guerrilla* (guerrilla theater). The former, also called "third theater," dispensed with traditional formal structures in favor of an alternative way of approaching audiences. The language of performance might be Quechua, Aymara, or Spanish. Performances were in public spaces and addressed issues of social concern of particular interest to the collectives who presented them. One of the most succesful among many collectives is Cuatrotablas, first formed in the mid-1970s. Guerrilla theater was similarly organized. It featured song, dance, and mime, and was developed especially by militant radical groups such as Sendero Luminoso (Shining Path) as a form of propaganda. Thus, in a country where traditional forms of modern theater had often struggled to survive, new models have taken shape to replace them. *See also* ACOSTA, JOSÉ DE; ARIELISMO; CASA DE LAS AMÉRICAS; CREACIONISMO; DRAGÚN, OSVALDO; *ENTREMÉS*; GORRITI, JUANA MANUELA; INDIGENOUS TRADITIONS; JAIMES FREYRE, RICARDO; JOURNALS; MAGIC REALISM; MARÍN CAÑAS, JOSÉ; MEXICO; MIGUEL DE CERVANTES PRIZE; NEO-BAROQUE; OÑA, PERDO DE; THEATER OF THE ABSURD; WOMEN.

PETIT, MAGDALENA (Chile, 1903–1968). Novelist. She wrote biographical-**historical novels**: *Don Diego de Portales* (1938; Don Diego de Portales), *Los Picheira* (1939; The Picheiras), *Caleuche* (1946; Caleuche), and *Un hombre en el Universo* (1951; A Man in the Universe). Her most successful work, however, was *La Quintrala* (1932; La Quintrala), a novelized biography of Catalina de los Ríos y Lísperguer (1604–1665), whose treatment of her tenants and lovers in colonial Chile made her notorious as an enduring symbol of female cruelty. Petit also wrote literary criticism and **theater** for children.

PEYROU, MANUEL (Argentina, 1902–1974). Novelist and short story writer. He is celebrated most for his contributions both to **crime**

fiction in the cerebral English tradition and to **fantastic literature** in novels and short stories. His novels include *El estruendo de las rosas* (1948; *Thunder of Roses: A Detective Novel*) and *El Hijo Rechazado* (1969; The Rejected Son), and among his collections of short stories are *La espada dormida* (1944; The Sleeping Sword), *La noche repetida* (1953; The Repeated Night), *El árbol de Judas* (1961; The Judas Tree), and *Marea de fervor* (1967; Tide of Fervor). He also wrote an anti-**Peronist** trilogy: *Las leyes de juegos* (1960; Rules of the Game), *Acto y ceniza* (1963; Act and Ashes), and *Se vuelven contra nosotros* (1966; They Turned Against Us).

PICARESQUE NOVEL. The genre originated in 16th-century Spain and conventionally features the humorous story of a low-class rogue who relies on his wits to survive in society and whose eventful journey through life is a source of social satire and criticism. **José Joaquín Fernández de Lizardi**'s 1816 *El periquillo sarniento* (*The Mangy Parrot*), written on the eve of Mexican independence, is Spanish America's most celebrated picaresque novel. Other colonial authors whose work has picaresque elements include **Alonso Carrió de la Vandera (Colombia)** and **Carlos de Sigüenza y Góngora (Mexico)**. More recent writers who have returned to the genre include **Manuel Antônio de Almeida, Fernando Sabino, Luís Carlos Martins Pena**, and **Ariano Vilar Suassuna (Brazil), José Rubén Romero** (Mexico), **Manuel Mujica Láinez** and **Roberto Jorge Payró (Argentina)**, and **Daniel Barros Grez** and **Manuel Rojas (Chile)**.

PICCHIA, PAULO MENOTTI DEL (Brazil, 1892–1988). Poet and novelist. A major voice in **Brazilian modernism**, Menotti del Picchia studied and practiced law while he also turned to poetry. His first book, *Poemas do Vício e da Virtude* (1913; Poems of Vice and Virtue), was influenced by **parnassianism**. *Juca Mulato* (1917; Joe Mulatto), a book of poems based on the backland and Afro-Brazilian motifs and written in a vivid, straightforward language with romantic overtones, met with considerable success. He used a similar style in *Moisés, Poema Bíblico* (1917; Moses, Biblical Poem), *As Máscaras* (1917; The Masks), and *A Angústia de D. João* (1925; The Anguish of Don Juan). After Del Picchia met **Mário de Andrade** and **Oswald**

de Andrade, he enthusiastically participated in the **Week of Modern Art** and became one of the staunchest supporters of modernist tendencies. Later on, together with **Plínio Salgado** and **Cassiano Ricardo,** he founded the more nationalist modernist tendency known as "verdeamarelismo" (green-yellowism) and wrote the manifesto "O Curupira e o Carão" (1927; "The Curupira Being and the Big-Faced Monster"). He also collaborated on the "Manifesto do Verdeamarelismo ou da Escola da Anta" (1929; "Green-Yellow Manifesto or of the School of the Tapir"). In this period, he published the free verse rhapsody *República dos Estados Unidos do Brasil* (1928; Republic of the United States of Brazil). Menotti del Picchia was criticized for his colorful, witty language, which appeared to be too popular for the taste of some modernists, but his later *Poemas Transitorios* (1947; Transitory Poems) display a more personal voice. He also wrote the science fiction novels *A República 3000* (1930; The 3000 Republic), *Kalum, O Sangrento* (1936; Kalum, the Bloody), and *Kamunká* (1938; Kamunka), and the erotic novel *Salomé* (1940; Salomé). Menotti del Picchia outlived most of his fellow modernists and received many prizes and honors. *See also* RICARDO LEITE, CASSIANO.

PICÓN SALAS, MARIANO (Venezuela, 1901–1965). Essayist and cultural critic. After spending much of his younger life in exile in **Chile** during the dictatorship in Venezuela of Juan Vicente Gómez (1908–1935), he became an important figure in the foundation of Venezuelan cultural institutions, and his writings on literature and culture, both in Venezuela and Spanish America at large, were widely read in his day. His writings show the influence of **arielismo**. *De la conquista a la independencia: tres siglos de historia cultural hispanoamericana* (1944; *A Cultural History of Spanish America: From Conquest to Independence*) is particularly noteworthy. He also wrote biographies of notable Venezuelans and the autobiographical books *Viaje al amanecer* (1943; Journey to the Dawn), *Regreso de tres mundos* (1959; Return from Three Worlds), and *Las nieves de antaño: pequeña añoranza de Mérida* (1958; The Snows of Yesteryear: A Little Longing for Mérida), as well as several novels: *Buscando el camino* (1920; Looking for the Road), *Odisea en tierra firme* (1931;

Odyssey on the Mainland), *Registro de huéspedes* (1934; Hotel Register), and *Los tratos de noche* (1955; Dealings at Night).

PIGLIA, RICARDO (Argentina, 1941–). Novelist, short story writer, and critic. Writing literature about literature and combining literary and critical practices in the same text, his work belongs in the tradition of **Jorge Luis Borges**. Piglia first won wide attention with *Respiración artificial* (1980; *Artificial Respiration*), a novel written in Argentina during the 1976–1983 dictatorship that uses coded writing to reflect the contemporary situation and deflect official attention. It combines elements of philosophy, the literary and cultural history of Argentina, and crime and political writing. His next novel, *La ciudad ausente* (1992; *The Absent City*), based on aspects of the life and work of **Macedonio Fernández**, gives an apocalyptic view of Buenos Aires. It served as the basis for an opera by Gerardo Gandini (Argentina 1936–) with a libretto by Piglia. *Plata quemada* (1997; *Money to Burn*), the novel that followed, is the story of a botched bank robbery, representing a new direction in Piglia's fiction, although he already had a history as an editor of **crime fiction** of the hard-boiled variety. The novel was made into a film with the same title in 2000.

Piglia's first collection of short stories, *La invasión* (1967; The Invasion), received a **Casa de las Américas** prize under the title *Jaulario* (Cages) and introduced many of the themes developed in his later fiction, including his literary alter ego Emilio Renzi, who has figured in several subsequent works. Among his other collections of short stories are *Nombre falso* (1975; *Assumed Name*), *Prisión perpetua* (1988; Perpetual Prison), and *Cuentos morales* (1995; Moral Tales). His critical essays include *Formas breves* (1999; Brief Forms), *Diccionario de la novela de Macedonio Fernández* (2000; Dictionary of the Novel of Macedonio Fernández), and *El último lector* (2005; The Last Reader). *See also* MARECHAL, LEOPOLDO.

PIGNATARI, DÉCIO (Brazil, 1927–). Poet, essayist, and translator. Born in the state of São Paulo of Italian descent, Pignatari published his first poems in *Revista Brasileira de Poesia* (Brazilian Poetry Review), associated with the **Generation of '45**. His first book of poetry was *O Carrosel* (1950; The Carrousel). In 1952, he joined the brothers **Augusto de Campos** and **Haroldo de Campos** as editors of the **journal** *Noigandres*, in which they began publishing Brazilian **concrete poetry** for the first time. Pignatari is considered, with the de Campos brothers, one of the founders of this **avant-garde** trend, theorized in the book *Teoria da Poesia Concreta* (1965; Theory of Concrete Poetry), coauthored by all three. In 1954, after receiving his law degree, Pignatari left for Europe, where he came into contact with a number of avant-garde artists and poets, among whom were Pierre Boulez (1925–), John Cage (1912–1922), and Eugen Gomringer (1925–). He remained in Europe until 1956, and his literary and intellectual exchanges were crucial for the development of concrete poetry.

In the years that followed, Pignatari devoted himself to promoting and defending concrete poetry through exhibitions, lectures, and the poems he published in a variety of journals. Much of his work was inspired not only by the materiality of language, but also by a dialogue with the mass media—he read and translated Marshall McLuhan (1911–1980)—and was published first in a variety of journals. Pignatari explored more the communication and technological aspect of poems, perhaps due to his own work in advertising and communications as a professor and designer. He also became involved in politics, wrote a soccer column for a national daily, became an academic, and even starred in a film. His poems, scattered in journals, were published eventually as *Poesia Pois É Poesia 1950/1975* (1977; Poetry, That's It, Poetry), *Poesia Pois É Poesia e Po&tc 1976/1986* (1986; Poetry, That's It, Poetry and Po&tc). Other works include *O Rosto da Memória* (1986; The Face of Memory), *Panteros* (1992; Panteros), *Errâncias* (2000; Wanderings), and *Céu de Lona* (2003; Canvas Sky).

PIÑON, NÉLIDA (Brazil, 1937–). Novelist. The child of Galician immigrants to Brazil, Piñon was born in Rio and grew up amid Portuguese, Spanish, and Galician immigrants. When she was 10, her family moved back to the countryside, where she became fascinated with the rural way of life, particularly traditional storytellers, which would influence her own narrative works. Piñon studied journalism and was the first **woman** to be elected president of the Brazilian Academy of Letters (*see* ACADEMIAS). In her first novel, *Guia-Mapa de Gabriel Arcanjo* (1961; Map/Guide of Gabriel Archangel), the protagonist discusses such topics as sin, love, and religious doctrine. During the years of the Brazilian military regime (1964–1984), Piñon became famous for her erotic novels such as *A Casa de Paixão* (1972; The House of Passion) and *Força do Destino* (1977; The Force of Destiny). However, she has been acclaimed worldwide for *A República dos Sonhos* (1984; *The Republic of Dreams*), an epic narrative about the travails of a family from Galicia that emigrates to Brazil. This 700-page novel, which Piñon struggled to finish in time to celebrate the arrival of democracy in Brazil, takes the form of a conversation between a grandfather and a granddaughter attempting to preserve their memory and is largely based on Piñon's own family story. Piñon has received numerous national and international awards, including the prestigious **Juan Rulfo** (Mexico) and Príncipe de Asturias (Spain) prizes. Her other works include *Tempo das Frutas* (1966; The Time of Fruits), *Fundador* (1969; Founder), *Sala de Armas* (1973; Armory), *Tebas do Meu Coração* (1974; Thebes of My Heart), *O Calor das Coisas* (1980; The Heat of Things), and *A Doce Canção de Caetana* (1987; Caetana's Sweet Song). *See also* PRADO, ADÉLIA.

PITOL, SERGIO (Mexico, 1933–). Novelist and short story writer. He is somewhat more cosmopolitan than other Mexican authors, with less emphasis on Mexico in his work, a consequence perhaps of his travels and periods of residence abroad. He has translated extensively from Polish and English, including the work of Witold Gombrowicz (1904–1969), Joseph Conrad (1857–1924), and Henry James (1843–1916). The publication of his own work began with short stories: *Tiempo cercado* (1959; Time Surrounded), *El infierno de todos* (1964; Hell for All), and *Los climas* (1966; The Climates). His first novel was *El tañido de una flauta* (1972; The Sound of a Flute), followed by *Juegos florales* (1983; Floral Games). His third novel, *El desfile del amor* (1984; Love Parade), is set in 1973, but tells a story from 1942, when Mexico entered World War II on the side of the Allies. The novel is the first of a triptych which is central to Pitol's work and features some of the prominent features of his fiction: monstrous female characters, bizarre plots, and embedded narratives. *Domar a la divina garza* (1988; Taming the Peacock), the second of the sequence, features stories within stories: a novelist in contemporary Mexico writes about a demented man, who tells a family whose home he has invaded about his meeting in Istanbul 25 years earlier with a crazy female anthropologist, who narrates a fecal propitiation ceremony practised by a group of Mexican Indians. The third part of the triptych is *La vida conyugal* (1991; Conjugal Life), the story of a woman's affairs and the attempts by her lovers, which repeatedly misfire, to murder her unfaithful husband. Other works of fiction include *Asimetría* (1980; Asymmetry), *Cementerio de todos* (1982; Cemetery for Everyone), *La casa de la tribu* (1989; Tribal House), *Cuerpo presente* (1990; Present and Correct), *El relato veneciano de Billie Upward* (1992; The Venetian Story of Billie Upward), *El viaje* (2000; The Journey), and *El mago de Viena* (2005; The Magician of Vienna). Pitol is also the author of *El arte de la fuga* (1996; The Art of the Fugue), a book about travels, friendships, and other experiences, and *Pasión por la trama* (1998; Passion for the Plot), in which he has collected some of his essays on literature. In 2005 he received the **Miguel de Cervantes Prize**.

PIZARNIK, ALEJANDRA (Argentina, 1936–1972). Poet. She emphasizes the importance and substantiality of words in poetry and often disregards standard verse arrangements and punctuation. Since her suicide in 1972, much of her writing has been read in relation to her death, one of her constant themes. She published seven books of poetry. The first, *La tierra más ajena* (1955; The Most Alien Land), already showed the influence of **surrealism** that is apparent in much of her work. This was followed by two collections, *La última inocencia* (1956; The Last Innocence), in which poetry appears as a form of escape, and *Las aventuras perdidas* (1958; Lost Adventures), about the attractions of childhood. Images of night and death figure in both books.

For four years (1960–1964), she lived in France, where she produced a number of translations from French, among them works by Yves Bonnefoy (1923–) and Marguerite Duras (1914–1996). From her time in France there also came three more books of poetry: *Árbol de Diana* (1962; Diana's Tree), *Los trabajos y las noches* (1965; Travails and Nights), and *Extracción de la piedra de locura* (1968; Extraction from the Stone of Madness), as well as *La condesa sangrienta* (1971; The Bloody Countess), a book inspired by the story of the infamous Hungarian countess Elizabeth Bathory (1560–1614), who was reputed to have tortured and murdered hundreds of young **women**. Pizarnik's last volume of poetry was *El infierno musical* (1971; Musical Hell). A number of years after she died, her unpublished writings were collected and edited by **Olga Orozco** and Ana Becciú in *Textos de sombra y últimos poemas* (1982; Texts from the Shadows and Last Poems), which included a play and a short novel.

PLA, JOSEFINA (Paraguay, 1909–1999). Poet, dramatist, short story writer, and cultural critic. Although born in the Canary Islands, she adopted Paraguay through marriage and became a prominent figure in Paraguayan culture, whose influence was felt by younger generations. She is considered to have been a mentor to the country's most important 20th-cenury writer, **Augusto Roa Bastos**. Her first volume of poetry was *El precio de los sueños* (1935; The Price of Dreams), a collection of mainly romantic love poems, which, like much of her early work in general, shows the influence of Spanish literature. After her first collection of verse, several others followed in which the survival of love after the death of a beloved is a prominent theme, an effect of the loss of her husband in 1937: *La raíz y la aurora* (1960; The Root and the Dawn), *Rostros en el agua* (1963; Faces in the Water), *Invención de la muerte* (1965; Invention of Death), *El polvo enamorado* (1968; Enamored Dust), *Antología poética* (1978; Poetic Anthology), *Follaje del tiempo* (1981; Foliage of Time), and *Tiempo y tiniebla* (1892; Time and Darkness). Her meditations on death also extend to deaths suffered in time of war, such as her elegy *Los treinta mil ausentes* (1985; Thirty Thousand Absentees), for those who died in the Chaco War (1932–1935), and *Alguien muere en San Onofre de Cuaramí* (1984; Someone Is Dying in San Ofre de Cuaramí), a novel written in collaboration with Ángel Pérez Pardella, set at the time of Paraguay's war with **Brazil**, **Argentina**, and **Uruguay** (1865–1870).

Pla's short stories include the collections *La mano en la tierra* (1963; The Hand in the Earth), *El espejo en el canasto* (1981; The Mirror in the Basket), and *La pierna de Severina* (1983; Severina's Leg) and feature strong **women**, tragedy, and extensive use of regional Pararguayan dialects. Her **theater** was written mainly in collaboration with others. Among her most successful plays are *Aquí no pasa nada* (1942; Nothing Happening Here), a comedy of manners;

Historia de un número (1948; Story of a Number), the biography of a prisoner; and *Fiesta en el río* (1977; Celebration in the River), the story of an unmarried mother in a medieval town and the punishment that awaits her. Aside from her literary writing, Josefina Pla has also produced a large number of books on a wide variety of topics relating to Paraguayan history and culture, including *El grabado en el Paraguay* (1962; The Engraving in Paraguay), *Arte moderno en el Paraguay* (1962; Modern Art in Paraguay), *Cuatro siglos de teatro en el Paraguay* (1966; Four Centuries of Theater in Paraguay), *Historia de la cultura paraguaya* (1968; History of Paraguayan Culture), and *El barroco hispano guaraní* (1975; Hispano-Guaraní Baroque).

PODESTÁ, JOSÉ J. (Uruguay, 1858–1936). A comic actor whose adaptation of **Eduardo Gutiérrez**'s novel *Juan Moreira* first brought the figure of the gaucho to the stage in Argentina. See also GAUCHO LITERATURE; THEATER.

PODESTÁ, MANUEL T. (Argentina, 1853–1920). Novelist. He was an admirer of the French novelist Emile Zola (1840–1902) and followed the social determinism of **naturalism**. His best-known work was *Irresponsable* (1889; Irresponsible).

POESIA MARGINAL. Portuguese for "marginal poetry," this term refers in a wide sense to the series of poetic and artistic practices that accompanied the counterculture Tropicália movement in **Brazil** of the 1960s and 1970s, led by the pop musicians **Caetano Veloso** and Gilberto Gil (1942–). Among the attitudes and practices of this trend are the interaction with popular music and media; the use of alternative channels of publication and distribution (such as the sale of mimeographed books by the authors themselves in bars and cafés); the depiction of the vulgar or physical aspects of life with an eye to provocation; and, on the part of **women**, the frank exploration of sexuality. Among the poets associated with this trend are **Glauco Mattoso**, Leila Miccolis (1947–), **Ana Cristina César**, **Paulo Leminski**, and **Francisco Alvim**. *See also* AZEVEDO, CARLITO.

POLETTI, SYRIA (Argentina, 1921–1991). Short story writer and novelist. Born in Italy, Poletti emigrated to Argentina in 1943. Her collections of short stories include *Línea de fuego* (1964; Line of Fire) and *Historias en rojo* (1967; Sensational Tales), published at the same time that her short stories were beginning to appear in anthologies along with those by celebrated Argentinean writers. Poletti's two novels are *Gente conmigo* (1962; People with Me) and *Extraño oficio* (1971; Strange Profession). Among the constants of her writing are a concern for the plight of Italian immigrants in Argentina, the representation of a child's point of view, the presence of an older **woman** or grandmother figure, and the need to overcome a physical handicap, characteristics that might all be considered autobiographical. In addition to her writing for adults, Poletti also produced works of **children's literature**, and her books in this field include *El rey que prohibió los globos* (1966; The King Who Banned Balloons), *Reportajes supersónicos* (1972; Supersonic Reports), *El juguete misterioso* (1977; The Mysterious Toy), *El misterio de las valijas verdes* (1978; The Mystery of the Green Suitcases), *Marionetas de aserrín* (1980; Sawdust Puppets), and *El monito Bam-Bin* (1981; Bam-Bin the Little Monkey).

POMPÉIA, RAUL D'ÁVILA (Brazil, 1863–1895). Novelist. Born near Rio, Pompéia attended school in Rio and later studied law in São Paulo, where he was politically involved in republican and abolitionist causes. He held a variety of positions, from mythology professor to director of the National Library. Pompéia's first novel, *Uma Tragédia no Amazonas* (1880; A Tragedy in the Amazon), is a tale of lawlessness and violence in that remote region of Brazil, revealing the restless personality that led Pompéia into literary conflicts with other poets such as **Olavo Bilac** and eventually to his suicide. While still a student, he frequented bohemian circles and published the prose poems *Canções sem Metro* (1881; Songs Without Meter), influenced by **parnassianism** and **symbolism**. His best-known work is *O Ateneu* (1888; The Atheneum), a coming-of-age novel inspired by his own negative experiences in an all-boys boarding school. *O Ateneu* has been noted both for its psychological exploration of teenage feelings and its artistic writing. For this he has been linked with **naturalism**, but tinted by specifically Brazilian traits such as social pessimism, explicit sexuality, and social determinism.

PONIATOWSKA, ELENA (Mexico, 1932–). Novelist and journalist. She is descended from Polish and Mexican aristocracy, a prolific writer, and one of Mexico and Latin America's foremost **women** writers. As a prominent political activist and public intellectual, she intervenes often on questions relating to the status of women and indigenous peoples, the handicapped, dissidents, and the poor in Mexico. One of the most prestigious awards she has received is the National Prize for Journalism, given to her in 1979. It not only affirmed her status as a journalist, the first woman in Mexico to be so honored, but also acknowledged that much of her literary work has its origin in her journalism or in her application of the methods of journalism. One of her earliest books was a collection of interviews, *Palabras cruzadas* (1961; Crossed Words), undertaken for newspaper publication. Subsequent interviews have appeared in other books under the title *Todo México* (All Mexico), the first in 1990, and several of Poniatowska's more literary books owe much to methodologies acquired as a journalist.

The book that first gave her literary prominence was *Hasta no verte, Jesús mío* (1969; *Here's To You, Jesusa!*), the life of the farm worker Jesusa Palancares. It is set in part against the background of the Mexican Revolution and based on taped interviews, and was the first of several historical accounts derived from reportage that established her reputation as a significant contributor to the **testimonio**. *La noche de Tlatelolco* (1971; *Massacre in Mexico*) is a narrative of the **Tlatelolco massacre**, similarly drawn from oral and documentary accounts. It won her the prestigious **Xavier Villaurrutia** Prize, which she declined in protest against the government. *Nada, nadie: las voces del temblor* (1988; *Nothing, Nobody: The Voices of the Mexico City Earthquake*) is a collective testimonial account of the earthquake that struck Mexico City in 1985. Other historical accounts include *Luz y luna, las lunitas* (1994; Light and Moon, Little Moons), a collection of five texts mainly about women; *Las soldaderas* (1999; Female Soldiers), about women who were camp followers or fought in the Mexican Revolution; and *Amanecer en el Zócalo: los 50 días que confrontaron a México* (2007; Dawn in the Zocalo: 50 Days Confronted by Mexico), about the 2006 elections in Mexico.

Poniatowska's earliest fiction was *Lilus Kikus* (1967; *Likus Kikus and Other Stories*) and *De noche vienes* (1989; You Come at Night), two overlapping collections of short stories, some autobiographical. *La Flor de Lis* (1988; Flower of the Lily) also has autobiographical elements. Other novels include *Querido Diego* (1978; *Dear Diego*), an epistolary novella consisting of fictional letters written to the Mexican painter Diego Rivera by his former lover, a Russian painter named Angelina Beloff; *Tinísima* (1991; *Tinisima*), based on the life of the celebrated Italian photographer Tina Modotti; *La piel del cielo* (2001; *The Skin of the Sky*), the story of a man searching for answers in science; and *El tren pasa primero* (2006; The Train Passes First), which won the 2007 **Rómulo Gallegos Prize**, about a Mexican railway worker and his struggle for justice, set against the Mexican railway strikes of 1958 and 1959. As in Poniatowska's other books, there is a combination in these of testimonial and fictionalized biography.

POPOL VUH. An important repository of pre-Columbian traditions of the Quiché Maya in **Guatemala**, this document contains stories from the mythic period of creation to the time of the Spanish conquest. It was first written down in an alphabetic version between 1554 and 1558 and survived through a copy and translation into Spanish made by the Dominican friar **Francisco Ximénez** between 1701 and 1703. See also GALICH, MANUEL.

PORTAL, MAGDA (Peru, 1903–1989). Poet. She was a political activist and one of the founding members of the Peruvian branch of the Alianza Popular Revolucionaria Americana (APRA; American Popular Revolutionary Alliance) under **Víctor Raúl Haya de la Torre**. She wrote and published very widely in Latin America on political issues, especially **women**'s rights. Her first published collection of poetry was *Una esperanza i el mar* (1927; A Hope and the Sea), a sombre collection about solitude and images of the sea. The sea has an equally strong presence in her next collection, *Costa sur* (1945; South Coast), but also contains a section derived directly from her political militancy. In *Constancia del ser* (1965; Proof of Being), she republished a selection of her earlier poems along with some new compositions, which are a testimony to her experiences and to having lived. Her fiction amounts to a collection of short stories, *El derecho de matar* (1926; The Right to Kill), cowritten with her partner, the poet Serafín Delmar, and a novel, *La trampa* (1965). The former is a rather bleak series of narratives of violence and poverty set mainly outside Peru; the latter is a semiautobiographical narrative and an attempted vindication of a political colleague imprisoned for murder.

PORZECANSKI, TERESA (Uruguay, 1945–). Novelist and short story writer. A teacher and researcher in anthropology and social work, she has published a number of books in her field. Several of her literary works were written during the 1973–1985 miliary regime in Uruguay and reflect the atmosphere of those times. She often represents the mix of cultures in Montevideo in her fiction, notably the **Jewish** experience, but the urban world described is dark and sombre. Her collections of short stories include *El acertijo y otros cuentos* (1967; The Riddle and Other Stories), *Construcciones* (1979; Constructions), *Ciudad impune* (1986; Invulnerable City), and *La respiración es una fragua* (1989; Breathing Is a Forge). Her novels are *Invención de los soles* (1982; Invention of the Suns), *Mesías en Montevideo* (1989; Messiah in Montevideo), *Perfumes de Cartago* (1994; Perfumes of Carthage), *La piel del alma* (1996, The Skin of the Soul), and *Una novela erótica* (2000; An Erotic Novel). Porzecanski has also published one book of poems, *Intacto el corazón* (1976; The Heart Intact).

POSITIVISM. The term was coined by French philosopher Auguste Comte (1798–1857) to designate a belief that knowledge derives from what the senses experience and that metaphysical speculation is ineffective. Adherence to this line of thought in Latin America led to an advocacy of the social benefits of science and technology and the emergence of regimes in the late 19th and early 20th centuries founded on the concepts of order and progress. Writers who reflect these beliefs include **Federico Gamboa** in **Mexico, Augusto dos Anjos, Tobias Barreto de Meneses,** and **Sílvio Romero** in **Brazil, Mercedes Cabello de Carbonera** and **José Ingenieros** in **Argentina,** and **José Victorino Lastarria** in **Chile. Arielismo** represented a contrary point of view by positing the spiritual nature of Latin American culture. *See also* NERVO, AMADO; REYES, ALFONSO; TAMAYO, FRANZ; VERÍSSIMO DIAS DE MATOS, JOSÉ.

POSSE, ABEL (Argentina, 1934–). Novelist. A diplomat by profession, he has received considerable criticism both for continuing to represent Argentina during the 1976–1983 military regime and for his apparent fascination with Nazism. His first two novels are about Latin Americans living abroad. *Los bogavantes* (1970; The Crew) is set in 1960s Paris, and *La boca del tigre* (1971; Mouth of the Tiger) in the former Soviet Union. Three of his subsequent novels are historical works in the manner of the **new historical novel**: *Daimón* (1978; *Daimon*) follows the Spanish colonial project across the centuries, based on the story of the colonial rebel Lope de Aguirre, a narrative also taken up by **Miguel Otera Silva** and **Arturo Uslar Pietri**; *Los perros del paraíso* (1983; The Dogs of Paradise) is a recipient of the 1987 **Rómulo Gallegos Prize**, set in the time of **Christopher Columbus,** but with ample use of anachronism and the collapsing of different events into one; and *El largo atardecer del caminante* (1992; The Long Twilight of the Wanderer) is a creative retelling of the experiences of **Alvar Núñez Cabeza de Vaca.** Other novels are set in Argentina: *Momento de morir* (1979; Moment of Dying) and *Reina de la Plata* (1988; Queen of the River Plate) take place in Buenos Aires; *Los demonios ocultos* (1987; The Hidden Demons) and *El viajero de Agartha* (1989; Traveler from Agartha) are both concerned with Nazism and its presence in Argentina; *La pasión según Eva* (1994; The Passion According to Eva) is a biographical novel of **Eva Duarte de Perón** told from the perspective of the time shortly before her death; and *El inquietante día de la vida* (2001; The Disturbing Day of Life) represents a return to Argentina in the 19th century. Finally, *Los cuadernos Praga* (1998; The Prague Journals) is a story based on the life of Ernest "Che" Guevara (1928–1967).

POST-BOOM. As the prefix suggests, post-boom refers to both the writers and the trends in fiction that followed the **boom,** beginning in the mid-1970s. There was not a sudden shift, but rather a transition from one to the other that also encompassed the major boom authors, whose productive years were far from over. In contrast to earlier trends, post-boom writing is inclined to focus more on immediate political and social realities. It was formally less experimental, and its authors often made connections with elements of mass culture such as music, film, and popular literature. History also figured significantly, a factor that contributed to the emergence of the **new historical novel**. Among its prominent authors were **Isabel Allende** and **Antonio Skármeta (Chile)**; **Rodrigo Fresán, Mempo Giardinelli, Tomás Eloy Martínez, Osvaldo Soriano**, and **Luisa Valenzuela (Argentina)**; and **Carlos Fuentes, Elena Poniatowska**, and **Gustavo Sainz (Mexico)**, a group that includes several important **women** writers.

PRADO, ADÉLIA (Brazil, 1935–). Poet and novelist. Prado began to write poetry as a result of her mother's death when she was 15. After attending teachers college in her native Minas Gerais, Prado worked as a teacher, married a bank employee, and had five children. She later returned to university and received a degree in philosophy. She came into the literary limelight when her then-unpublished book *Bagagem* (1976; Baggage) was enthusiastically read by **Carlos Drummond de Andrade**, who recommended its publication, even though it contained a poem, "Com Licença Poética" ("With Poetic License"), that parodied Drummond's famous "Poem of Seven Faces." Numerous literary figures, including Carlos Drummond de Andrade, **Clarice Lispector**, and **Nélida Piñon**, attended the launch of *Bagagem*. Prado's next poetry book, *O Coração Disparado* (1978; The Shot Heart), received the **Jabuti Prize**. *Soltem os Cachorros* (1979: Let the Dogs Loose) was her first prose effort.

Her poetry, following the example of **Manuel Bandeira**, deals with the joys and sorrows of everyday life; her connection with the small town of Divinópolis, a city of 200,000, where she grew up and continues to live; and her Catholic faith. Among the themes she explores from a religious perspective are death, love, sex, jealousy, and the body. Prado's literary success forced her to abandon her teaching career. She then attended conferences and gave readings in Brazil and abroad. Other later poetry books by Prado are *Terra de Santa Cruz* (1981; Land of Santa Cruz), *O Pelicano* (1987; The Pelican), and *A Faca no Peito* (1988; The Knife in the Chest). She then suffered writer's block for several years, until she published *O Homem da Mano Seca* (1994; The Man with the Dry Hand). Many of her texts have been adapted for the stage. Recent works include *Oráculos* *de Maio* (1999; Oracles of May), and her fiction is collected in the volume *Prosa Reunida* (1999; Collected Prose). *See also* WOMEN.

PRADO, PAULO (Brazil, 1869–1943). Essayist. Born into a well-to-do family in São Paulo, Prado received a law degree and spent many years living and studying in Europe. Back in Brazil, he generously and enthusiastically supported the **Week of Modern Art** in 1922. Prado is remembered mainly for his important essay *Retrato do Brasil* (1934; Portrait of Brazil), which attempts to define the Brazilian national character. This pessimistic and influential essay, subtitled "Essay on Brazilian Sadness," presents lust, greed, and sadness as the defining traits of the three races (Amerindian, African, and European) that constituted Brazil.

PRADO, PEDRO (Chile, 1886–1951). Novelist and poet. His aesthetic sensibilities made him one of the most significant prose writers of **modernismo**. His earliest publications were poetry written in free verse, such as *Flores de cardo* (1908; Flowers of the Thistle), and poetic prose, including *La casa abandonada* (1912; The Abandoned House), *El llamado del mundo* (1913; Called from the World), and *Los pájaros errantes* (1915; The Wandering Birds). His first novel, *La reina de Rapa Nui* (1914; The Queen of Rapa Nui), is a fictional tour de force based on the history of Easter Island, a place never visited by the author. *Alsino* (1920; Alsino), likely his best novel, is an allegorical retelling of the myth of Icarus, with links to José Enrique Rodó and **arielismo**, focused on rural poverty in Chile. *Un juez rural* (1924; *Country Judge: A Novel of Chile*), the story of a man who becomes a judge without the benefit of having studied the law, is thought to have been inspired by the author's own experiences. In poetry, Prado represents a movement away from modernismo. This tendency, and some of his best verses, particularly his sonnets, may be found in *Viejos poemas inéditos* (1949; Old Unpublished Poems).

PRIETO, GUILLERMO (Mexico, 1818–1897). Poet, essayist, and dramatist. A popular writer in his day, he was hailed as "the national poet" and is considered one of the founders of Mexican national literature. His *Musa callejera* (1883; Street Muse) is a collection of humorous verses in the manner of **costumbrismo**, and in his *Romancero* *nacional* (1885; National Ballads) he wrote verse stories from popular history and the time of the war of independence. More of his poetry is collected in *Poesías escogidas* (1877; Selected Poems) and *Versos inéditos* (1879; Unpublished Verses). He also wrote several pieces for the **theater**, and his prose works include books on his travels and an anthology of his newspaper writings on everyday life in the city.

PUGA, MARÍA LUISA (Mexico, 1944–2004). Novelist and short story writer. She published 10 novels and four collections of short stories, as well as essays, **chronicles**, collected interviews, and works of **children's literature**. Among the books for which she is best known are the novel *Las posibilidades del odio* (1978; The Possibilities of Hatred), set in Kenya, where the author had traveled, and *Pánico o peligro* (1987; Panic or Danger), a coming-of-age story set at the time of the **Tlatelolco massacre**. *See also* WOMEN.

PUIG, MANUEL (Argentina, 1932–1990). Novelist. He is customarily associated with the **post-boom** generation of Latin American writers. From an early age he was an enthusiastic lover of cinema, which had considerable effect on his life and work. His writing is characterized by an ability to create the different registers of the spoken language, such as voices on the telephone, dialogue, colloquial speech, and interior monologues, and to include different kinds of writing in his narratives, such as personal diaries, letters, formal reports, or newspaper clippings, often without the benefit of mediation by a narrative voice. Popular culture, in the form of soap operas, films, song lyrics, and pulp fiction, figures significantly in his work both as a structural resource and as the sources on which characters model their feelings and expectations. Some of his major themes are male and female stereotypes, sexual identity, the cultural psychology of individuals, and national politics. Many of these elements already appeared in Puig's first two novels and were developed further in subsequent works.

La traición de Rita Hayworth (1968; *Betrayed by Rita Hayworth*) deals with the interaction of the worlds of fiction and reality, and *Boquitas pintadas* (1969; *Heartbreak Tango*) also portrays popular culture as a source of escapism from the stultifying environment of everyday life. *The Buenos Aires Affair* (1973; *The Buenos Aires Af-*

fair) is a story of frustrated love, modeled on a detective story, that also shows Puig's extraordinary use of language. *El beso de la mujer araña* (1976; *Kiss of the Spider Woman*), perhaps Puig's best-known novel, is the story of a revolutionary and a **homosexual** who share a cell in a Buenos Aires prison. Much of the narrative is developed through dialogue into which accounts of several films are intercut. Film also figures in Puig's last novel, *Cae la noche tropical* (1988; *Tropical Night Falling*), a novel about two elderly Argentinean women who have retired to Rio de Janeiro but remain fascinated by the life going on around them. Other novels are *Pubis angelical* (1979; Angelic Pubis), *Maldición eterna a quien lea estas páginas* (1980; *Eternal Curse on the Reader of These Pages*), and *Sangre de amor correspondido* (1982; *Blood of Requited Love*), all intensely psychological narratives. Puig also wrote for the **theater** and the cinema. He adapted *El beso de la mujer araña* for the stage in 1983 and later turned it into a screenplay, from which a highly successful film was made by Héctor Babenco in 1985. The same novel was also the source of a Broadway musical in 1993. *See also* SABINO, FERNANDO.

– Q –

QORPO-SANTO, pseudonym of JOSÉ JOAQUIM DE CAMPOS LEÃO (Brazil, 1829–1883). Dramatist. A teacher and commercial agent in the south of Brazil, de Campos Leão adopted the pseudonym Qorpo-Santo, a capricious spelling of "corpo santo" (holy body), because he believed himself to be a saint. Although he wrote poetry that anticipates **Brazilian modernism**, his main contributions were his unconventional plays, which have been seen as forerunners of the **theater of the absurd** for their use of space, mixture of reality and illusion, and satirical intent. There is controversy over his alleged mental illness; he was deemed insane, but this diagnosis was later questioned. He founded a print shop in Porto Alegre to aid in the distribution of his works, including *Enciclopédia* (1877; Encyclopedia), which includes the texts of his plays *Mateus, Mateusa* (1866; Mateus, Mateusa), *As Relações Naturais* (1866; Natural Relations), and *Eu sou Vida, Eu Não sou Morte* (1866; I Am Life, I Am Not Death).

Qorpo-Santo's plays were not staged in his lifetime, and he was long forgotten after his death, until his rediscovery by **theater** critics in 1966. He was the first Brazilian dramatist to portray **homosexuals**.

QUEIRÓS, DINAH SILVEIRA DE (Brazil, 1911–1982). Journalist, novelist, and short story writer. Born in São Paulo, Silveira de Queirós published her first short story, "Pecado" (1938; "Sin") at age 17, and in 1939 the novel *Floradas na Serra* (Blossomings on the Hill), to this day a **best seller**. The novel, set in the sanatoriums for tuberculosis patients in Campos do Jordão (São Paulo), deals with issues of health and illness, hope and disillusion. Her novella *A Sereia Verde* (1941; The Green Mermaid) was published for the first time in *Revista do Brasil* (Review of Brazil). Her novel *Margarita La Rocque: A Ilha dos Demônios* (1949; Margarida La Rocque: The Island of Demons) is based on autobiographical experiences, and thanks to its powerful style brought her much recognition as a forerunner of **fantastic literature**. Silveira de Queirós also wrote **crime fiction**, **children's literature**, and newspaper columns, as well as **historical novels** such as *A Muralha* (1954; The Wall), set in colonial Brazil. *See also* ROSA, JOÃO GUIMARÃES; WOMEN.

QUEIRÓS, RAQUEL DE (Brazil, 1910–2003). Novelist, dramatist, translator, and short prose writer. The first **woman** admitted to the Brazilian Academy of Letters (*see* ACADEMIAS), Raquel de Queirós (formerly spelled Rachel de Queiroz) is considered by some to be Brazil's greatest female writer. Born and raised in the Northeast, her work remains deeply rooted in the plight of the inhabitants of that region and its traditions. After publishing short prose pieces in local papers (*see* CHRONICLE), her first novel, *O Quinze* (1930; Nineteen Fifteen), a story of love and survival in the Northeast during the 1915 drought, made her famous throughout Brazil. Queirós joined the Communist Party and was a militant Trotskyite, for which she was arrested. During this period, she also published *João Miguel* (1932; João Miguel), *Caminho de Pedras* (1937; Stone Path), and *As Três Marias* (1939; The Three Marys), novels of social criticism set against political polarizations of the Estado Novo of Getúlio Vargas (1882–1954) and influenced by the popular speech style of *A Bagaceira* (1928; The Sugar Cane Worker) by José Américo de Almeida

(1887–1980). In the next three decades, while living in Rio's Ilha do Governador, Queirós focused mostly on journalism and published short prose pieces based on life in the Northeast. Her political leanings also went from leftist libertarianism to a traditional conservatism, and she embarked on a defense of local values, for which she is seen as a representative of **regionalism**.

Works from this period include *A Donzela e a Moura Torta* (1948; The Damsel and the Cross-Eyed Moorish Woman), *100 Crônicas Escolhidas* (1958; One Hundred Selected Chronicles), *O Brasileiro Perplexo* (1963; The Perplexed Brazilian), *O Caçador de Tatu* (1967; The Armadillo Hunter), and *As Menininhas e Outras Crônicas* (1976; The Little Girls and Other Chronicles). She published two more novels, *Dôra, Doralina* (1975; Dôra, Doralina), a psychological portrait with elements of the Northeast, and *O Galo de Ouro* (1985; The Golden Cock), a working-class tale of Afro-Brazilian types set in Rio, published originally in 1950 as a serial, but completely rewritten for the book edition. Her plays, *Lampião* (1953; Lampião) and *A Beata Maria do Egito* (1958; Saint Mary of Egypt), and the novel *Memorial de Maria Moura* (1992), later turned into a TV series, feature strong female characters in stories of banditry and fanaticism set in the Northeast. Queirós was also an active translator, with more than 40 translated books to her credit. *See also* AMADO, JORGE; MACHADO, ANÍBAL; RIBEIRO, JOÃO UBALDO; THEATER.

QUINTANA, MÁRIO (Brazil, 1906–1994). Poet. Born in Alegrete (Rio Grande do Sul), Quintana established himself in Porto Alegre as a journalist and translated Marcel Proust (1871–1922), Virginia Woolf (1882–1941), Voltaire (1694–1778), and Charles Morgan (1894–1958), among others. His poetic debut came relatively late, with *Rua dos Cata-Ventos* (1940; Street of the Weathervanes), followed by *Canções* (1946; Songs) and *Sapato Florido* (1948; Flowery Shoe). His poetry does not follow the paths opened by **Brazilian modernism**, leaning instead toward a more traditional and nostalgic idiom. Perhaps for this reason he has been ignored by some critics. His themes focus on the simple aspects of everyday life, introspection, existential issues, and self-analysis. Many poems are reflections on his own life in Porto Alegre. *Espelho Mágico* (1948; Magic Mirror) and *O Aprendiz de Feiticeiro* (1950; The Magician's Apprentice) are volumes of prose poems. Other works include *Apontamentos de História Sobrenatural* (1976; Notes on Supernatural History) and the volumes of short prose pieces, *A Vaca e o Hipogrifo* (1977; The Cow and the Hippogryph) and *Caderno H* (1973; Notebook H). Among his last books are *Nova Antologia Poética* (1981; New Selected Poems), containing a number of unpublished poems; *Batalhão das Letras* (1997; The Army of Letters), a poem for children based on the alphabet; and *Água* (2001; *Water*), a trilingual (Portuguese/Spanish/ English) collection of texts on the subject of water, inspired by the Brazilian landscape.

QUIROGA, HORACIO (Uruguay, 1878–1937). Short story writer. He is credited with having laid the foundation for the modern short story in Latin America. His life was notoriously tragic and ended in suicide when he learned he had cancer. Much of his adult life was spent in **Argentina**, part of it in the remote Chaco region and Misiones, where his stories are often set. Although associated early with **modernismo**, he developed a more realistic, spare style of writing that shows the influence of Edgar Allan Poe (1809–1849). His stories are in the vein of **fantastic literature**, with themes that include the confrontation with death and the struggle for survival against nature. He wrote more than 200 stories, most published in newspapers or magazines before they were collected in books. Among the best-known collections are *Cuentos de amor, de locura y de muerte* (1917; *The Decapitated Chicken and Other Stories*), *Cuentos de la selva* (1918; *South American Jungle Tales*), *El salvaje* (1920; The Savage), *Anaconda* (1921; Anaconda), *El desierto* (1924; The Desert), and *Los desterrados* (1925; *The Exiles and Other Stories*). Quiroga was widely read and admired by later writers such as **Julio Cortázar** and **Gabriel García Márquez**. *See also* RODRÍGUEZ MONEGAL, EMIR; STORNI, ALFONSINA; VAZ FERREIRA, MARÍA EUGENIA.

– R –

RABASA, EMILIO (Mexico, 1856–1930). Novelist. An eminent legal expert, he wrote a number of significant books on Mexico, constitutional law, and history, and devoted only a few years of his life to literature. His four novels, in the style of 19th-century **realism**, form a cycle based on contemporary social and political life represented through the experiences of a single protagonist, Juanito Quiñones. In *La bola* (1887; The Revolution), he participates in an uprising after experiencing disappointment in love. *La gran ciencia* (1887; The Great Science) draws him into the world of politics. *El cuarto poder* (1888; The Fourth Estate) sees him in the capital and involved in journalism. Finally, in *Moneda falsa* (1888; Counterfeit Coin), disillusioned by the falsehood of life in the capital, Quiñones returns to the country.

RABINAL ACHÍ (*THE DANCE OF THE TRUMPET*). A preconquest dance-drama from **Guatemala** written in Quiché, telling the story of the sacrifice of a Quiché lord. The first version in Spanish was completed by **Luis Cardoza y Aragón** in 1930 from a version in French. *See also* THEATER IN QUECHUA.

RADRIGÁN, JUAN (Chile, 1937–). Dramatist. Writing in a manner that has often been compared with the styles of Samuel Beckett (1906–1989) and Arthur Miller (1915–2005), Radrigán's **theater** has remained focused on social marginality in the context of dictatorship Chile (1973–1990) ever since his first play, *Testimonio de las muertes de Sabina* (1979; Witness to Sabina's Deaths). His characters are often prostitutes, the destitute and homeless, and the proletariat. Among his best-received plays are *Hechos consumados* (1981; Accomplished Facts) and *El toro por las astas* (1982; The Bull by the Horns). Other works include *Los olvidados* (1982; The Forgotten), *La felicidad de los García* (1983; The Happiness of the Garcias), *La contienda humana* (1988; The Human Struggle), *Isabel desenterrada en Isabel* (1989; Isabel Disenterred in Isabel), *Islas de porfiado amor* (1993; Islands of Stubborn Love), *El loco y la triste* (1993; The Madman and the Sad Woman), and *El encuentramiento* (1996; The Encounter).

RAMA, ÁNGEL (Uruguay, 1926–1983). Critic and essayist. He was a prominent writer whose work contributed significantly to the development of ideas about the formation of literature and culture in

Latin America since the 19th century. Although he began his career as a writer in fiction, he soon turned to journalism and was active in the Uruguayan periodical *Marcha*. He was forced into exile by the 1973 military coup in Uruguay and subsequently lived in Venezuela, the United States, and Europe. He died in the **Madrid air disaster**.

Among Rama's early works are two studies on **modernismo** and **Rubén Darío**, *Los poetas modernistas en el mercado económico* (1968; Modernist Poets in the Economic Market) and *Rubén Darío y el modernismo: circunstancia socioeconómica de un arte americano* (1970; Rubén Darío and Modernism: The Socioeconomic Circumstance of an American Art). In these he considered literature in its broad social context, a trend he continued to develop in subsequent writings: *Las máscaras democráticas del modernismo* (1973; The Democratic Masks of Modernism), *Los gauchipolíticos rioplatenses* (1976; Gaucho Politicians of the River Plate), and *Transculturación narrativa en América Latina* (1982; Narrative Transculturation in Latin America). Of two further books that appeared posthumously, *Literatura y clase social* (1984; Literature and Social Class) and *La ciudad letrada* (1984; *The Lettered City*), the latter, a study of the role of discourse and the lettered class in the foundation and growth of Latin American cities, has been particularly influential. *See also* TRABA, MARTA.

RAMÍREZ, SERGIO (Nicaragua, 1942–). Novelist, short story writer, and essayist. He is Nicaragua's most important prose writer. As a member of a group of 12 prominent Nicaraguan civilians, in 1977 he endorsed the Sandinista bid to overthrow Anastasio Somoza (1967–1979). He was part of the 1979 Government of National Reconstruction and served as vice president of Nicaragua, 1985–1990. His early works of fiction, such as the stories in *Charles Atlas también muere* (1976; Charles Atlas Also Dies); *¿Te dio miedo la sangre?* (1983; *To Bury Our Fathers*), a novel that tells the history of Nicaragua under Somoza; or *Castigo divino* (1988; Divine Punishment), a novel representing the hypocrisy of bourgeois life in the 1930s city of León in Nicaragua, are concerned with the history and politics of Nicaraguan society. Without abandoning this focus, he has broadened it in subsequent works.

One of his most recent novels, *El cielo llora por mí* (2008; Heaven Weeps for Me), for example, is a work of **crime fiction**. Ramírez's other novels include *Tiempo de fulgor* (1970; Time of Brightness), *Un baile de máscara* (1995; Masked Ball), *Margarita, está linda la mar* (1998; *Margarita, How Beautiful the Sea*), *Sombra nada más* (2002; Nothing But Shadow), and *Mil y una muertes* (2004; A Thousand and One Deaths). His other collections of short stories are *Catalina y Catalina* (2001; Catalina and Catalina); *El reino animal* (2006; The Animal Kingdom), which takes some unusual looks at the world of animals; and *Juego perfecto* (2008; Perfect Game), which draws on sport motifs. He has published two testimonios: *La marca del zorro* (1989; Mark of Zorro), a conversation with a comandante in the Sandinista army, and *Adiós muchachos* (1999; Farewell, Boys), a retrospective on the revolution 20 years later. He is also an active journalist and has published more than a dozen books of essays, among which one of the most significant is *El pensamiernto vivo de Sandino* (1984; The Living Thought of Sandino).

RAMOS, GRACILIANO (Brazil, 1892–1953). Novelist and short story writer. In his memoir *Infância* (1945; Childhood), Ramos recalls a somewhat unhappy childhood spent in his native Alagoas and Pernambuco, Northeastern Brazil. His father was a stern, hard-working cattle rancher who eventually purchased a store in Palmeira dos Índios, where the family settled. A self-educated man, Ramos decided to move to Rio to work as a journalist, but returned to Palmeira dos Índios when he learned that bubonic plague had killed several family members. Ramos prospered in business there, got married, and was elected mayor in 1927. During this period, he also taught languages and contributed to newspapers, while working on his first novel, *Caetés* (1933; The Caeté Indians), written in the style of **naturalism**.

While convalescing from an illness, Ramos finished his novel *São Bernardo* (1934; *São Bernardo*), the first person narrative of a rough landowner, Paulo Honório, which secured Ramos a reputation as one of Brazil's most important novelists. Two more novels, *Angústia* (1936; Anguish) and *Vidas Secas* (1938; *Barren Lives*), complete a trilogy that recounts the plight of the poverty-stricken inhabitants of Northeastern Brazil. *Barren Lives* was adapted for the screen in 1963. From 1930 to 1936, when Ramos lived in Maceió working as a public servant, he met and befriended important writers in the style of **regionalism**, such as **José Lins do Rego, Raquel de Queirós, Jorge Amado**, and **Aníbal Machado**, with whom he collectively wrote the book *Brandão Entre o Mar e o Amor* (1942; Brandão Between the Sea and Love).

In 1936, facing vague political accusations, Ramos was arrested and jailed, suffering physical abuse and humiliations, as retold in his four-volume *Memórias do Cárcere* (1953; Prison Memoirs), which go beyond a personal narrative to constitute a true denunciation of the evils of the Estado Novo (1937–1945). Released in 1937, Ramos settled in Rio de Janeiro, where he continued publishing novels, **children's** books, and short stories, among which are *Dois Dedos* (1945; Two Fingers), *Histórias Incompletas* (1946; Incomplete Stories), *Insônia* (1947; Insomnia), *A Terra dos Meninos Pelados* (1939; The Land of the Hairless Children), and *Histórias de Alexandre* (1944; Stories by Alexander). In 1945, Ramos joined the Communist Party, and he traveled to Soviet bloc countries in 1952 as president of the Brazilian Writers' Association, a trip remembered in his book *Viagem* (1954; Voyage). Upon his return, he became very ill, was operated on, and died less than a year later. Other nonfiction books include *Linhas Tortas* (1962; Crooked Lines) and *Viventes das Alagoas* (1962; Inhabitants of Alagoas). After Machado de Assis, Ramos was considered Brazil's greatest novelist due to the regional themes he adopted and the objective and unadorned style that became his signature. *See also* RIBEIRO, JOÃO UBALDO; SANTIAGO, SILVIANO.

RAMOS, NUNO (Brazil, 1960–). Short prose and short story writer. Before turning to writing, Ramos had a successful career as a visual artist. He became known as one of Brazil's most creative contemporary prose writers with the publication of *Cujo* (1993; Whose) and *Pão do Corvo* (2001; Crow Bread), the first a book of aphorisms or short reflections and second consisting of mini-stories, or **microtales**. Both works focus on objects and are written in an abstract style.

RAMOS SUCRE, JOSÉ ANTONIO (Venezuela, 1890–1930). Poet. An erudite figure, competent in several languages, and teacher of history, geography, and classical languages. He suffered from mental illnesses and took his own life after several earlier unsuccessful attempts. His entire work consists of collections of prose and prose poems, some of which were first published in newspapers and periodicals: *Trizas de papel* (1921; Shreds of Paper), *Sobre las huellas de Humboldt* (1923; In the Footsteps of Humboldt), *La torre de Timón* (1925; The Tower of Timón), *Las formas del fuego* (1929; Forms of Fire), and *El cielo de esmalte* (1929; The Enamel Sky). His writing has been considered a foreshadowing of **Jorge Luis Borges** and of **surrealism** in Latin America.

RAZNOVICH, DIANA (Argentina, 1945–). Dramatist. Her plays present reality from unexpected angles and have elements of the **theater of the absurd.** Four of her plays have been published in bilingual editions: *Defiant Acts/Actos desafiantes* (2002): *Desconcierto* (1981; *Disconcerted*), *Jardín de otoño* (1983; *Inner Garden*), *Casa Matrix* (1991; *MaTRIX, Inc.*), and *De atrás para adelante* (1995; *Rear Entry*). *See also* THEATER; WOMEN.

REALISM. In contrast to romanticism, which offered a view of the world mediated by the senses, advocates of realism sought a more objective description of everyday life and focused in particular on the newly emerging middle class. Realism was established in Europe in the first half of the 19th century, notably through the work of the French novelist Honoré de Balzac (1799–1850), but did not gain ground in Latin America until after 1850. In the late 19th and early 20th centuries, it coincided with other forms of realism such as **costumbrismo, naturalism,** and **criollismo.** The major realist novelists in Spanish America include **Rafael Delgado** and **Emilio Rabasa** in **Mexico; Joaquín García Monge** in **Costa Rica; Soledad Acosta de Samper** and **Tomás Carrasquilla** in **Colombia; Enrique Amorin** and **Eduardo Acevedo Díaz** in **Uruguay; Roberto Arlt** in **Argentina;** and **Alberto Blest Gana, Marta Brunet, Vicente Grez, Luis Orrego Luco,** and **Manuel Rojas** in **Chile.** Realism in the theater is associated with a number of dramatists, including **Mauricio**

Rosencof and **Florencio Sánchez** (Uruguay) and **Carlos Somgigliana** (Argentina).

Realism in **Brazil** flourished approximately between 1870 and 1900, influenced philosophically and aesthetically by social and scientific notions of progress in vogue at the time. In poetry, it assumed the form of **parnassianism** and **symbolism**, whereas in prose it found expression in naturalism. Prominent authors include **Júlia Lopes de Almeida**, **Manuel Antônio de Almeida**, and **Afonso Henriques de Lima Barreta** in the novel and **Nelson Rodrigues** in theater. *See also* ASSIS, JOAQUIM MARIA MACHADO DE; AZUELA, MARIANO; CAMPO, ÁNGEL DE; CASTELLANOS, ROSARIO; COELHO NETO, HENRIQUE MAXIMIANO; DONOSO, JOSÉ; ECUADOR; EL SALVADOR; GÁLVEZ, MANUEL; GRUPO DE BOEDO; GRUPO DE FLORIDA; GRUPO DE GUAYAQUIL; INDIGENISMO; MACHADO, DIONÉLIO; NEO-INDIGENISMO; PORTILLO Y ROJAS, JOSÉ; REGIONALISM; WOMEN.

REBELO, MARQUES, pseudonym of EDI DIAS DA CRUZ (Brazil, 1907–1973). Novelist and short story writer. Although Marques Rebelo began as a poet, he soon switched to fiction, portraying his experience in the army in his book of short stories, *Óscarina* (1931; Óscarina), which he wrote while convalescing from a military injury. Through the use of both irony and empathy, Marques Rebelo depicted the social and psychological drama of working-class people on the north side of Rio de Janeiro: adventurous **women**, lower echelon bureaucrats, drifters, samba musicians, and city dwellers. He denounced inequality and representing colloquial speech, for example in *Marafa* (1935; A Rake's Life). Rebelo continues a tradition of urban narrative begun by **Manuel Antônio de Almeida** and continued by **Afonso Henriques de Lima Barreto**. Some of his introspective work, including *Três Caminhos* (1933; Three Roads) and *Estela Me Abriu a Porta* (1942; Estela Answered the Door), is also based on the author's childhood memories. The world of radio stations inspired *A Estrela Sobe* (1938; The Star Rises). The trilogy *O Espelho Partido* (The Broken Mirror), encompassing *O Trapicheiro* (1959; The Sugar Mill Worker), *A Mudança* (1962; The Move), and *A Guerra Está em Nós* (1968; War Is Within Us), portrays life during Getúlio Vargas's

Estado Novo (1937–1945) through the diary of a fictitional writer from Rio. *See also* FONSECA, RUBEM.

REBOLLEDO, EFRÉN (Mexico, 1877–1929). Poet. He was an active member of groups formed around the publication of literary journals, notably *Revista Moderna* and *Pegaso*, which he founded in 1917 in collaboration with **Ramón López Velarde** and others. His poetry reflects the fin de siècle in its **parnassianism** and the eroticism of some of his verses. It also benefited from his travels in Europe and a seven-year residence in Japan. His poetry collections include *Cuarzos* (1902; Quartzes), *Hilo de corales* (1904; Thread of Coral), *Estela* (1907; Wake), *Joyeles* (1907; Jewels), *Rimas japonesas* (1907 and 1917; Japanese Rhymes), and *Libro de loco amor* (1919; Book of Mad Love). *Caro Victrix* (1916; Flesh Triumphant), a late collection of erotic poetry, is the book on which much of Rebolledo's reputation depends. He also wrote several prose books, including impressions of his travels and his life in Japan.

REGIONALISM. Regionalism in Brazilian literature is reflected in the influence that the language and culture of the various regions of the country have exerted on the literature. It is apparent specifically in the representation of particularities of the spoken language and local habits and customs that resulted from populating **Brazil**'s large and varied territory at different stages of the country's history and the isolation in which in some regions remained, favoring the development of typical regional traits. Critics trace the origins of literary regionalism to **romanticism** in writers like **José de Alencar**, whose novel *O Guarani* (1857; The Guarani) depicted the life of the backlands man as more authentically Brazilian than the life and customs of the Europeanized court in Rio de Janeiro. Other romantic authors in this vein include **Bernardo de Guimarães** and **Alfredo d'Escragnolle, Visconde de Taunay**, who wrote works with typically romantic plots, but against the backdrop of a particular region. In the late 19th and early 20th centuries, the folklorist Valdomiro Silveira (1873–1941) authored short stories that reflected the customs and language of the state of São Paulo.

In the 20th century, the focus shifted to regional language and portrayal of regional motifs as constitutive elements of the literary text, with a radical transformation to more universalized concerns under the artistry of writers such as **João Guimarães Rosa, Henrique Maximiano Coelho Neto, Gilberto Freyre** (who organized the First Regionalist Congress in 1926 and published a Regionalist Manifesto in 1952), **Jorge de Lima, Osman Lins, Aníbal Machado, Afrânio Peixoto, Raquel de Ramos Queirós, Graciliano Ramos, José Lins do Rego Cavalcanti, Erico Veríssimo,** and **João Ubaldo Ribeiro.**

Regionalism in Spanish America has characteristics similar to those in the work of Brazilian regionalists, but was not a formally constituted movement. It includes writers such as **José López Portillo y Rojas (Mexico), Tomás Carrasquilla** and **Manuel Mejía Vallejo** (Colombia), and **Volodia Teitelboim** (Chile), whose narratives generally represented the life and traditions of rural regions. Regionalism is also associated in Spanish America with **criollismo, mundonovismo, naturalism, realism,** and the **novel of the land.**

REGO CAVALCANTI, JOSÉ LINS DO (Brazil, 1901–1957). Novelist. Born on his grandfather's sugar plantation in Paraíba, José Lins do Rego attended local boarding schools and then enrolled in law school in Recife. There he also began writing for newspapers and magazines and met some of the major intellectuals associated with **regionalism**, in particular **Gilberto Freyre**, who greatly encouraged his literary efforts in that vein. During a period in Maceió, he also befriended **Jorge de Lima** and **Graciliano Ramos**, and in 1935, he moved to Rio de Janeiro, where he led an active literary life.

Menino de Engenho (1932, *Plantation Boy*) was Lins do Rego's first and widely acclaimed novel, based on his childhood experience of growing up on a plantation. It was followed by several others that came to form his "Sugar Cane Cycle." Together they recount a saga that begins with Carlos de Mello's childhood in *Plantation Boy*, continues with his school days in *Doidinho* (1933; *Doidinho*), and ends with his early adulthood between the city and the sugar plantation in *Bangüê* (1934; *Bangüê*). *O Moleque Ricardo* (1935; Black Boy Richard) and *Usina* (1936; The Sugar Refinery) portray the fate of less fortunate companions of Carlos's childhood and the periodic droughts that plague the region. *Fogo Morto* (1943; Dead Fire), Lins do Rego's masterpiece, depicts the waning of the economy and way of life of the plantations. Many details in these novels were drawn from life, as his memoir *Meus Verdes Anos* (1956, My Tender Years) later confirmed.

Lins do Rego claimed that his writing was spontaneous and instinctive and was inspired by the itinerant singers and storytellers of the Northeast, where he set his next cycle of novels. *Pedra Bonita* (1938; Wondrous Rock) is a tragic tale of religious fanaticism, and *Cangaceiros* (1953; The Bandits) depicts the phenomenon of rural banditry that plagued that region in the early 20th century. Other works include *Pureza* (1937; *Pureza*), *Riacho Doce* (1939; Freshwater Creek), *Água-Mãe* (1941; The Water Mother), and *Eurídice* (1947; Eurydice). Although not all of these are set in the Northeast or in the past, the composition still exploits the techniques of the memoir and uses other oral devices that recall Lins do Rego's earlier novels. In collaboration with **Jorge Amado**, Graciliano Ramos, **Aníbal Machado**, and **Raquel de Queirós**, he also contributed to the second part of *Brandão Entre o Mar e o Amor* (1942; Brandão Between the Sea and Love).

REIN, MERCEDES (Uruguay, 1931–2007). Dramatist, novelist, short story writer, and critic. Her most successful play, written with Jorge Curi, was *El herrero y la muerte* (1981; *Ballad of the Blacksmith*), based on the legend of a **gaucho** and his encounter with Death. Other work for the **theater** includes *Entre gallos y mediasnoches* (1987; Between the Roosters and Midnights) and *Juana de Asbaje* (1993; Juana de Asbaje), the latter on the life of **Sor Juana Inés de la Cruz**. Among her works of fiction are *Zoologismos* (1967; Zoologisms), *Casa vacía* (1984; Empty House), and *Marea negra* (1996; Black Tide). The first two contain elements of fantasy and magic. The third is the last in a trilogy concerned with the economic decline of Uruguay since the 1960s. *See also* WOMEN.

RENDÓN, VÍCTOR MANUEL (Ecuador, 1859–1940). Dramatist. Although he lived much of his life in France and wrote some of his work in French, he is nonetheless credited with having renovated Ecuadorian **theater** by steering it away from **romanticism** toward a more realistic view of society and by revising how the *sainete* had hitherto been known in Ecuador. His plays were published together in 1937. The best known of these is *Salus populi* (Health of the

People), about the 19th-century president of Ecuador Gabriel García Moreno (1861–1865, 1869–1875). Other titles include *Cuadro heroico* (Heroic Picture), *Madrinas de guerra* (Godmothers of War), *Hoy, ayer y mañana* (Today, Yesterday and Tomorrow), *El ausentismo* (Absenteeism), *Almas hermosas* (Beautiful Souls), and *Las tres Victorias* (The Three Victorias).

RENGIFO, CÉSAR (Venezuela, 1905–1985). Dramatist. He is considered the founder of modern **theater** in Venezuela and was the author of a large number of prize-winning plays, among them *Por qué canta el pueblo* (1938; Why the People Sing), *La sonata del alba* (1948; Dawn Sonata), *Harapos de esta noche* (1948; Shreds of Tonight), *El vendaval amarillo* (1952; The Yellow Storm), *Un tal Ezequiel Zamora* (1956; A Certain Ezequiel Zamora), *La fiesta de los moribundos* (1966; The Feast of the Dying), *El raudal de los muertos cansados* (1969; The Flood of Tired Dead), *Las torres y el viento* (1969; The Towers and the Wind), and *Volcanes sobre el Mapocho* (1974; Volcanoes on the Mapocho). Rengifo's plays cover a wide range of topics, but often focus on history and politics, social issues, and class, especially the plight of the underdog. He was also a celebrated painter and among the influences on his work, some of which surface in his drama, was the work of the Mexican muralist Diego Rivera (1886–1957).

REVUELTAS, JOSÉ (Mexico, 1914–1976). Novelist and essayist. As a member of the Mexican Communist Party, he was active in a number of Marxist-Leninist groups. However, he often found himself in difficulties because he was not always able to tow the party line. Moreover, his lifelong political activism resulted in imprisonment, including detention for the "intellectual authorship" of the student movement suppressed by the **Tlatelolco massacre** in 1968. His political writings include *Ensayo sobre un proletariado sin cabeza* (1962; Essay on a Leaderless Proletariat), and some of his best pieces are collected in *México 68: juventud y revolución* (1978; Mexico 68: Youth and Revolution). His politics are also a significant source of his literary work.

Revueltas was very drawn to the **theater** and wrote five plays, as well as several screenplays. He is known mainly for his fiction, however. His first collection of short stories, *Dios en la tierra* (1944; God on Earth), is framed by two stories about the religious uprising in Mexico known as the Cristero War (1927–1929) and shows its brutality. The content of the two collections that followed, *Dormir en tierra* (1960; To Sleep on the Ground) and *Material de sueños* (1974; The Stuff of Dreams), is repetitive, in that both include some of the same stories, but the two books are thematically different. The former deals with civil strife in Mexico; the latter is more concerned with identifying what lies beneath the surface of appearances and seeing into the darkness below.

Revueltas's novels, on which his literary reputation principally stands, are better known than his short stories. They depart from the social realism that preceded him and are sombre works. *Los muros de agua* (1941; Walls of Water) shows the influence of Russian realism and is concerned with the time he spent in prison at Islas Marías. *El luto humano* (1943; *The Stone Knife*), the author's best-known work, is a peasant novel dealing with 20th-century Mexican history and has some of the characteristics of the **novel of the Mexican Revolution**. This was followed by *Los días terrenales* (1949; Days on Earth), about internal conflicts within the Communist Party. Then came *En algún valle de lágrimas* (1956; In Some Vale of Tears), a critique of bourgeois materialism represented through the figure of a cruel and inhuman landowner. The next novel, *Los motivos de Caín* (1957; Cain's Motives), a critique of American imperialism set in part during the Korean War (1950–1953), is one of the author's most politically orthodox novels. In *Los errores* (1964; Errors), however, he returned to his difficulties with the political Left and the problems of dogmatism. Finally, in *El apando* (1969; The Isolation Cell), the theme of imprisonment resurfaced as Revueltas fictionalized the time he spent in the prison of Lecumberri.

REYES, ALFONSO (Mexico, 1889–1959). Essayist and poet. A prolific and very prominent literary figure in his day, much admired for his erudition, stylistic grace, and contributions to cultural life in Mexico. His work has since attracted considerable critical attention, although little popular following, perhaps on account of his erudition. As a member of the Mexican diplomatic service, he also acquired some prominence in the literary circles of the countries to which he was appointed, notably France, Spain, and **Argentina**. In general, he held a humanist's perspective on the world and an exalted view of culture that associated him with **arielismo** rather than with 19th-century **positivism**.

Reyes's essays were collected in books on theory and criticism of classical, European, and Mexican literatures, including *Cuestiones estéticas* (1911; Questions of Aesthetics), *El paisaje en la poesía mexicana del siglo XIX* (1911; The Landscape in 19th-Century Mexican Poetry), and *Influencia artúrica en la literatura castellana* (1938; Arthurian Influence in Spanish Literature). In his essays he often advocated the location of Mexico and its traditions within universal culture, and one of his most frequently cited books is *Visión de Anahuac* (1917; Vision of Anahuac), an evocation of preconquest Mexico. As a translator, he produced versions from both English and French authors, but achieved his greatest success with *Ilíada* (1951), a translation of Homer's *Iliad*. Reyes's creative work includes both prose and poetry, but he has not obtained a lasting reputation in either genre. Of the 20 or so books of poetry he published during his life, the best known is *Ifigenia cruel* (1924; Cruel Iphigenia), a dramatic retelling of the classical story of Iphigenia.

REYES, JOSÉ TRINIDAD (Honduras, 1797–1855). Writer and composer. A Franciscan friar and prominent cultural figure in the first half of the 19th century, he is credited with having promoted the cultural development of Honduras during the period after independence. He wrote school textbooks, poetry, and music and is considered the country's first dramatist on account of his series of *pastorelas*, or Nativity plays, for which he also wrote the music. *See also* THEATER; VALLE, JOSÉ CECILIO DEL.

REYLES, CARLOS (Uruguay, 1868–1938). Novelist. Although he came from a wealthy landowning family, he spent his fortune by 1929 on high living and agricultural enterprises and lived his last years in poverty. He produced novels, short stories, and essays throughout his life, but is remembered mainly as a novelist, the first Uruguayan to become widely recognized as such. His first attempt, *Por la vida* (1888; For Life), was not very successful and was greatly surpassed by *Beba* (1894; Beba), a novel about Uruguayan ranch life that, like several of the author's later works, adhered to **naturalism**. *La raza de Caín* (1900; Cain's Race) gave full expression to his anti-intellectualism and the use of unsympathetic characters as his main device. In later novels, Reyles maintained his readership, but rarely changed his narrative strategies. In *El terruño* (1916; Plot of Land), he took up the theme of ranch life again, and in *El embrujo de Sevilla* (1922; *Castanets*), he drew upon his earlier life for inspiration. One of his best novels, also one of his last, was *El gaucho Florido* (1932; The Gaucho Florido), a story of the changing world of the **gaucho**.

RIBEIRO, DARCY (Brazil, 1922–1997). Novelist and essayist. Born in Minas Gerais, Ribeiro studied social sciences and had a passion for ethnography. He spent 10 years living in indigenous villages, married an Indian woman, and published studies on native Brazilians. He was involved in education and politics, and the 1964 military coup forced him to flee to **Uruguay**. In exile, Ribeiro wrote a study of unequal social development in the Americas, *As Américas e a Civilização* (1970; The Americas and Civilization), and an essay on national identity, *Os Brasileiros: Teoria do Brasil* (1972; The Brazilians: Theory of Brazil), which were both later gathered under the general title *Antropologia da Civilização* (1970–1997; Anthropology of Civilization).

During the same period, he also wrote the novels *Maíra, Romance* (1976; *Maíra*) and *O Mulo* (1981; The Mule), which are deeply influenced by anthropology. *Maíra*, for instance, highlights the irreconcilable cultural differences that set the Mairun people apart and the unfortunate consequences of their contact with "civilization." *O Mulo* depicts the exploitative relationship between landowners and peasants. The allegorical novel *Utopia Selvagem* (1982; Savage Utopia) is a parodic, playful fable about Brazil and Latin America. The fictional autobiography *Migo* (1988; My-Self), written in a self-mocking confessional mode, reveals Ribeiro's personal and intellectual life.

Ribeiro's writing style, particularly in his books of essays such as *Sobre o Óbvio: Ensaios Insólitos* (1979; On the Obvious: Unlikely Essays) and *Aos Trancos e Barrancos: Como o Brasil Deu no que Deu* (1985; In Fits and Starts: How Brazil Came to Be), a historical overview of Brazil from 1900 to 1980, is exuberant, sarcastic, and passionate, mirroring his flamboyant personality. His model was **Gilberto Freyre**, who achieved both literary and persuasive qualities in his important essays on Brazilian culture. In 1976, Ribeiro returned to Brazil and was again involved in politics. Having survived a tumor years before, Ribeiro fell victim to cancer again in the 1990s, but he left the hospital to finish *O povo brasileiro* (1995; *The Brazilian People*), his final study on the anthropology of civilization.

RIBEIRO, JOÃO UBALDO (Brazil, 1941–). Novelist and short story writer. One of Brazil's most innovative prose writers, João Ubaldo Ribeiro was born on the island of Itaparica, Bahia, and grew up in Aracajú (Sergipe) and Salvador (Bahia). A voracious reader, as a child he would spend hours locked up in the family library. Ribeiro began writing for the newspapers while studying law. His first book of short stories was *Reunião* (1961; Gathering). In 1962–1964, Ribeiro lived in the United States studying public administration, but he gave up on an academic career and returned to journalism.

Encouraged by his filmmaker friend, Glauber Rocha (1939–1981), and **Jorge Amado**, Ribeiro published his first novel, *Setembro Não Tem Sentido* (1968; September Makes No Sense). Two important Brazilian narrative traditions converge in his next novel, *Sargento Getúlio* (1971; Sergeant Getúlio): the traditional **regionalism** of authors such as **Graciliano Ramos** and **Raquel de Queirós** and the more universal **Brazilian modernism** set in the metaphysical backlands represented by **João Guimarães Rosa**. The protagonist of this novel, the rough-and-tumble police sergeant Getúlio Santos Bezerra, a man with 20 deaths to his name, is hired by a powerful politician to capture and deliver a dangerous prisoner. During a journey that takes them across miles of backlands in an old car, Getúlio narrates his life story in a stream-of-consciousness style. Ironically, after he receives word that the prisoner should be released, Getúlio is unable to give up the mission and becomes an insurgent himself. Besides elaborating on Guimarães Rosa's figure of the rural hoodlum who philosophizes in the midst of the arid backlands, Ribeiro also critiques the corruption and violence of the social system and contrasts the rural and the urban, the archaic and the modern ways of life.

Ribeiro has also been acclaimed for *Viva o Povo Brasileiro* (1984; *An Invincible Memory*), which the author himself translated into

English, an account of Brazilian history from the Dutch colonization of Rio de Janeiro in the 16th century to Getúlio Vargas's Estado Novo (1937–1945). The narrative, whose Portuguese title translates literally as "Long Live the Brazilian People," places the lowly and oppressed people as protagonists in a saga about the formation of Brazilian identity, hinting at the concept of miscegenation espoused by **Gilberto Freyre**. Its literary style is influenced by two classical authors from Bahia, the satirical poet **Gregório de Mattos** and the Jesuit preacher **Antônio Vieira**.

Invited to create a novel portraying lust as a capital sin, Ribeiro wrote *A Casa dos Budas Ditosos* (1999, The House of the Joyful Buddhas), the tale, at times funny, at times shocking, of an elderly woman on the brink of death, who reminisces about the infinite sexual adventures of her life. The author claimed this was a true story he took from an anonymous manuscript that was delivered to his doorstep. Other books by Ribeiro include *Vencecavalo e o Outro Povo* (1974; Vencecavalo and the Other People), *Livro de Histórias* (1981; Book of Stories), *O Sorriso do Lagarto* (1989; The Smile of the Lizard), *O Feitiço da Ilha do Pavão* (1997; The Charm of the Island of the Peacock), and *Diário do Farol* (2002; Diary of the Lamppost).

RIBEYRO, JULIO RAMÓN (Peru, 1929–1994). Short story writer and novelist. Ribeyro left for Europe in 1952 and eventually settled in Paris, where he remained, save for two short visits to Peru. In the history of Peruvian literature, he represents the generation that preceded **Mario Vargas Llosa** and **Alfredo Bryce Echenique**. He wrote three novels. *Crónica de San Gabriel* (1960; *Chronicle of San Gabriel*), the best known of the three, is the story of an adolescent who witnesses the decline of a landowning family. *Los geniecillos dominicales* (1965; The Little Weekend Geniuses) is about a group of dissolute middle-class urban youths, and *Cambio de guardia* (1976; Changing of the Guard) is concerned with a coup d'état in Peru.

Although his novels are eminently readable, Ribeyro's reputation rests firmly on his short stories, of which he wrote more than 80 and which earned him a considerable following, almost in spite of himself. His stories show changes in Peru of the 1940s and 1950s and their effects on the middle class, especially in urban settings. His collections include *Los gallinazos sin plumas* (1955; Vultures

Without Feathers), *Cuentos de circunstancias* (1958; Tales of Circumstances), *Las botellas y los hombres* (1964; Bottles and Men), and *Tres historias sublevantes* (1964; Three Rebellious Stories). His *Cuentos completos* (Complete Short Stories) were published in 1992. He also published a miscellaneous collection of essays, *Prosas apátridas* (1975; Unpatriotic Writings) and wrote eight plays. *See also* THEATER; VALDELOMAR, ABRAHAM.

RICARDO LEITE, CASSIANO (Brazil, 1895–1974). Poet. The evolution of Cassiano Ricardo's poetry mirrors the transformations of Brazilian poetry in the 20th century. Born in the interior of São Paulo, he received a law degree but worked as a journalist and held public office. Somewhat belatedly, he adhered to the trend of **Brazilian modernism** he had once opposed. Ricardo's early work began as late **symbolism**, with *Dentro da Noite* (1915; Inside the Night), and adapted the style of **parnassianism** in *Evangelho de Pã* (1917; Pan's Gospel), *Jardim das Hespérides* (1920; The Garden of the Hesperiads), *Atalanta: A Mentirosa de Olhos Verdes* (1923; Atalanta: The Green-Eyed Liar), and *A Frauta de Pã* (1925; Pan's Flute), volumes written in fixed forms with regular meter and rife with references to classical mythology.

Borrões de Verde e Amarelo (1926; Green and Yellow Drafts) and *Vamos Caçar Papagaios* (1926; Let's Go Parrot Hunting) were Ricardo's first modernist volumes that also embraced the nationalist ideals he would develop with **Plínio Salgado** and **Menotti del Picchia** in the "Manifesto do Verdeamarelismo ou de Escola da Anta" (1929; Manifesto of the Green-Yellow Movement of the School of the Tapir). The goal of this nationalist trend was to construct a modern cultural identity for Brazil based on its Amerindian elements and culminating in a contemporary multiracial and multicultural society as a result of miscegenation. Hence, Ricardo's most ambitious poem, *Martim Cererê* (1928; Martim Cererê), resembles similar attempts by **Mário de Andrade** in *Macunaíma* and **Raúl Bopp**'s *Cobra Norato*. But unlike the pan-Brazilian impulse of these works, which focused on different regions of Brazil, Ricardo's work centered more and more on the region of São Paulo, creating a narrative that went from the early Indian settlements to the urban coffee affluence of São Paulo.

Abandoning the nationalist and picturesque mode, the postwar period inspired in Ricardo poems with a more universal appeal and a more inner reflection. Among them are *Um Dia Depois do Outro* (1947; One Day After Another), *O Sangue das Horas* (1943; The Blood of the Days), and *A Face Perdida* (1950; The Lost Face), which are lyrical meditations on modern daily life. *O Arranha-Céu de Vidro* (1956; The Glass Skyscraper), *Montanha Russa* (1960; Rollercoaster), *A Difícil Manhã* (1960; The Difficult Dawn), *Jeremias sem Chorar* (1964; Jeremiah Without Crying), and *Os Sobreviventes* (1971; The Survivors) focus on the Cold War atomic age and universal concerns. Ricardo also continued his quest for innovation by experimenting with **avant-garde** trends such as **concrete poetry**. *See also* VERDEAMARELISMO.

RÍO, ANA MARÍA DEL (Chile, 1948). Novelist and short story writer. One of Chile's prominent contemporary **women** writers, Del Río's first works of fiction appeared toward the end of the regime of Augusto Pinochet (1974–1990). Her writing is often subversive, touching on subjects that remain unspoken, such as autoeroticism and the female discovery of the body. Her collections of short stories include *Entreparéntesis* (1983; Between Parentheses) and *Gato por liebre* (1995; Conned). She has published two novellas, *Óxido de Cármen* (1986; Carmen's Rust) and *Siete días de la señora K* (1993; Señora K's Seven Days), and the novels *De golpe, Amalia en el umbral* (1990; Suddenly, Amalia at the Door), *Tiempo que ladra* (1991; Barking Time), *A tango abierto* (1996; With an Open Tango), and *La esfera media del aire* (1998; The Middle Sphere of the Air).

RIO, JOÃO DO, pseudonym of PAULO BARRETO (Brazil 1881–1921). Journalist, chronicler, short story writer, and dramatist. The son of a math professor and a mulatto woman, Barreto was educated by his father and began writing young. An openly **gay** man, influenced by the decadent French writer Jean Lorrain (1855–1906) and Óscar Wilde (1854–1900), some of his short stories in collections such as *Dentro da Noite* (1910; Inside the Night), *A Mulher e os Espelhos* (1911; The Woman and the Mirrors), *Rosário de Ilusão* (n.d.; Rosary of Illusion), and *A Correspondência de uma Estação de Cura* (1918; Correspondence from a Sanatorium) deal with gay and sexual themes that were taboo in his time. His cosmopolitan and refined demeanor and his writing also reflect the aesthetics of decadence and dandyism in vogue at the time. Barreto chose "João do Rio" as his pen name following the example of Jean de Paris, a columnist from the French newspaper *Le Figaro*. He had a number of other pseudonyms, including Godofredo de Alencar, who, in *Crônicas e Frases de Godofredo de Alencar* (1916; Chronicles and Phrases of Godofredo de Alencar), had a fictional biography of his own, much like the heteronyms of the Portuguese writer Fernando Pessoa (1888–1935).

João do Rio was the first writer to seriously engage in social **chronicle** writing for **journals** such as *Cidade do Rio*, *Gazeta de Notícias*, *O País*, *Rio-Jornal*, *Revista Atlântica*, and *A Pátria*, the last two of which he cofounded. Some of these texts were gathered in *O Momento Literário* (n.d.; The Literary Moment). With greater literary ambitions and written in an original and agile style, *As Religiões do Rio* (1906; The Religions of Rio), investigative journalism about Afro-Brazilian religions, and *A Alma Encantadora das Ruas* (1918; The Charming Soul of the Streets), reports on street culture, also have value as documents charting the modernization of Rio de Janeiro and its changing life. As a writer for the **theater**, Barreto staged *A Bela Madame Vargas* (n.d.; The Beautiful Madame Vargas) in 1912 with great success. He also founded the Brazilian Society for Theater Authors.

His frankness about sexual taboos and ironic style earned him many enemies and explain the controversy surrounding his death. Some claim he died of a heart attack in a taxi when leaving the newspaper office where he worked. Others think he died as a result of injuries he had received earlier from a group of sailors, probably hired by one of his enemies. His funeral was attended by more than 100,000 people. Recently he has inspired documentary films and literary soirées in the city he helped immortalize in his chronicles.

RIVA PALACIO, VICENTE (Mexico, 1832–1896). Novelist. Although he trained as a lawyer, he enlisted in the war against the French intervention (1862–1867) and rose to the rank of general. He tried his hand at **theater** and poetry, but found his forte in the novel. His first was *Calvario y Tabor* (1868; Calvary and Tabor), based on his military experiences. Thereafter, he turned to the **historical novel**, becoming one of the first in Mexico to write in the genre, sometimes known as the **colonial novel** in Mexico. For the most part, he located his stories in the colonial period, but not without taking some liberties, notwithstanding his generally careful documentation. In the space of three years he wrote five more novels: *Martín Garatuza* (1868; Martin Garatuza), *Monja y casada, virgen y mártir* (1886; Nun and Wife, Virgin and Martyr), *Las dos emparedadas* (1869; Two Walled Up Women), *Los piratas del Golfo* (1869; Pirates of the Gulf), *La vuelta de los muertos* (1870; Return of the Dead), and *Memorias de un impostor, D. Guillén de Lampart, rey de México* (1872; Memoirs of an Imposter, Don Guillen de Lampart, King of Mexico), which is considered to be one of the sources of the fictional character Zorro. During the same period he also wrote a series of short stories noted for their humor, published posthumously as *Cuentos del general* (Tales by the General). His other writings include a collection of poems, *Flores del alma* (1875; Flowers of the Soul), published under the pseudonym Rosa Espino, and a history of Mexico.

RIVERA, ANDRÉS (Argentina, 1928–). Novelist. Born Marcos Ribak, the son of immigrant parents, he was once a textile worker. His first novels, *El precio* (1957; The Price), *Los que no mueren* (1959; Those Who Don't Die), *Sol de sábado* (1962; Saturday's Sun), and *Cita* (1965; Appointment), were written within the context of his membership of the Argentinean Communist Party, which he joined in 1945 and from which he was expelled in 1964, and are highly political. In 1972, he published a collection of short stories, *Ajustes de cuentas* (Settling the Score), in the tradition of **crime fiction**, based on works by the Americans Dashiell Hammett (1894–1961) and Raymond Chandler (1888–1959). He then published nothing for 10 years, until the appearance of the novel *Una lectura de la historia* (1982; A Reading of History), in which he revealed a style free of the political didacticism that had characterized his earlier work.

Rivera's subsequent work has gained enormously in popularity, with the publication of a string of novels, among which are *La revolución es un sueño eterno* (1987; Revolution Is an Eternal Dream), *Los vencedores no dudan* (1989; Winners Have No Doubts), *El amigo de Baudelaire* (1991; Baudelaire's Friend), *La sierva* (1992;

The Servant), *El verdugo en el umbral* (1994; Executioner on the Threshold), *El profundo sur* (1999; Deep South), *Tierra de exilio* (2000; Land of Exile), *Hay que matar* (2001; A Need to Kill), *El manco Paz* (2003; One-Armed Paz), *Cría de asesinos* (2004; Brood of Assassins), and *Esto por ahora* (2005; No More for Now). Several of his novels are historical, exhibiting some of the elements of the **new historical novel**, notably *El farmer* (1996; The Farmer), Rivera's most popular work, which describes the former dictator **Juan Manuel Rosas** living in exile in England. Like some of his compatriots, Rivera turns to the past as a way to draw attention to the violence of his own time.

RIVERA, JOSÉ EUSTASIO (Colombia, 1888–1928). Novelist. He would initially have liked to have made his name as a poet and published *Tierra de promisión* (1921; Promised Land), a collection of 55 sonnets, with some touches of **modernismo** about them, describing the different regions of Colombia. He is remembered, however, for his second book, the novel *La vorágine* (1924; The Vortex), one of the classics of Latin American literature. Although the work may be read as a denunciation of the treatment of rubber workers, it is, above all, a landmark **novel of the land** in which previous romantic representations are set aside and the jungle is shown to be a force of nature.

ROA BASTOS, AUGUSTO (Paraguay, 1917–2005). Novelist and short story writer. Although he lived much of his life in exile, he was Paraguay's most important writer of the 20th century and is a significant figure of Latin American literature. He had begun his literary career as a dramatist, but turned to fiction after 1947 when he first left Paraguay, remaining in exile thereafter to escape the regime of Alfredo Stroessner (1954–1989). His first collection of short stories was *El trueno entre las hojas* (1953; Thunder Among the Leaves), in which he covered 100 years of Paraguayan history and addressed the social concerns that are central to his work as a whole. Other collections appeared at intervals throughout his life. Notable among them are *El baldío* (1966; The Vacant Lot), *Madera quemada* (1967; Burnt Wood), and *Morencia* (1971; Dying). Roa Bastos is best known, however, for two **dictator novels**, *Hijo de hombre*

(1960; *Son of Man*) and *Yo, el supremo* (1974; *I, the Supreme*), both concerned with Paraguayan history. The former is centered on resistance to dictatorship from the mid-19th century to the conflict with **Bolivia** known as the Chaco War (1932–1935), which the author experienced in his youth. The theme of resistance relates the novel to **indigenismo**, and the style of writing has some of the characteristics of **magic realism**.

Yo, el supremo, one of the major works of 20th-century Latin American fiction, focuses on the life of José Gaspar Rodríguez de Francia (1766–1840), who ruled Paraguay from 1814 until 1840. The novel has a particularly complex narrative structure. It appears as a compilation of a large amount of historical documents, sometimes presented in the manner of modern history, including footnotes and clarifications. Much of the text is ostensibly dictated by Francia himself to his secretary Patiño, who also intervenes in the presentation of materials, such that the true version of events is obscured and the exact nature of Francia's rule and the history of Paraguay remains ambiguous. The **neo-baroque** style of the novel thus serves the purpose of exemplifying the constant rewriting of history and the difficulty of obtaining an objective view of it, characteristics it has in common with the Latin American **new historical novel**. After this major work, Roa Bastos published several other novels, including *Vigilia del admirante* (1992; The Admiral's Vigil), about **Christopher Columbus;** *El fiscal* (1993; The Prosecutor); *Contravida* (1994; Counterlife); and *Madama Sui* (1995; Madam Sui), the story of a Japanese admirer of **Eva Duarte de Perón**. He was unable to reach the same heights achieved in his more celebrated novel, however. *See also* PLA, JOSEFINA.

ROBLEDO, HERNÁN (Nicaragua, 1892–1969). Novelist and dramatist. Of his dozen novels, the first two, *Sangre en el trópico* (1930; Blood in the Tropics) and *Los estrangulados* (1933; Strangulated), both about American intervention in Nicaragua, were the most successful. He also wrote two narratives of the Mexican Revolution: *La mascota de Pancho Villa* (1934; Pancho Villa's Mascot) and *Obregón, Toral y la madre Conchita* (1935; Obregón, Toral, and Mother Conchita). As a dramatist, he introduced **costumbrismo** to the **theater** in Nicaragua, *La rosa del paraíso* (1920; The Rose of

Paradise) being his most acclaimed work in that vein. He also wrote political dramas, such as *Pájaros del norte* (1982; Birds from the North), about the U.S. intervention. Other plays include *El milagro* (1921; The Miracle), *La señorita que arrojó el antifaz* (1928; The Woman Who Tore off the Mask), and a set of three dramas, all from 1946: *La cruz de ceniza* (Cross of Ashes), *La niña soledad* (Solitude Child), and *Muñecos de barro* (Mud Puppets).

RODÓ, JOSÉ ENRIQUE (Uruguay, 1871–1917). Essayist. He was also a journalist, university professor, and politician who was twice elected to Congress in Uruguay. He was widely known in his time, and his writings, which are frequently republished, continue to attract readers and critics. This is especially true of two of his earliest essays: *Rubén Darío* (1899; Rubén Darío) and *Ariel* (1900; *Ariel*). The first is a critique of *Prosas profanas* by the Nicaraguan poet **Rubén Darío**, which influenced the direction taken by both the poet's future work and **modernismo**. *Ariel*, however, has obtained a wider and more enduring continental recognition. Borrowing from Shakespeare's *The Tempest*, Rodó represents Prospero as a professor lecturing to his students about the nature of America. He identifies Latin America with values represented by the spirit Ariel from Shakespeare's play and Mediterranean cultural traditions, in contrast to North American utilitarianism and materialism. Rodó's essay, the source of **arielismo**, has continued to resonate in discussions of the development of Latin American cultural identity, although the figure of Ariel has in some contexts been displaced by Caliban as a more representative symbol of the continent. Other essays by Rodó include the collections *Motivos de Proteo* (1909; *The Motives of Proteus*), a discussion of change and the evolution of the human personality, and *El mirador de Próspero* (1913; Prospero's Observatory), essays on historical and literary topics. *See also* BOTELHO GONSÁLVEZ, RAÚL; RODRÍGUEZ MONEGAL, EMIR; VAZ FERREIRA, MARÍA EUGENIA; ZORRILLA DE SAN MARTÍN, JUAN.

RODRIGUES, NELSON (Brazil, 1912–1980). Dramatist and journalist. Considered the most prominent Brazilian playwright of the 20th century, Rodrigues was born in Recife, where his father was a journalist. Due to political problems, the family moved to Rio when Rodrigues was young, eventually relocating from the lower-middle-class Zona Norte to the more affluent Zona Sul when Rodrigues was a teenager. His experience growing up in these neighborhoods would be crucial for the characters he developed later in his plays. Rodrigues began writing with success in the family newspaper when he was 14, but in 1929 his brother, a graphic artist, was shot by a woman whose divorce was exposed in the paper, and his father died shortly after as a result of the shock. Rodrigues was then forced to take on a number of different jobs and was diagnosed with tuberculosis, a disease he fought on and off for the rest of his life.

His first play, *A Mulher sem Pecado* (1948; The Woman Without Sin), received mixed reviews when performed in 1939, but his second and perhaps most famous piece, *Vestido de Noiva* (1944; The Wedding Dress), was a resounding success when it was staged in 1943. In this play, considered by many a watershed in Brazilian **theater**, the author explored the psychology of a car accident victim by dividing the stage into three parts that represented the character's memories, the actual events, and the delusions she suffered while on the operating table. Rodrigues's next play, *Album de Família* (1946; Family Album), a story of incest, rape, and murder plaguing a family, was banned from the stage for some 20 years. Nelson Rodrigues wrote a total of 17 plays, which critics have divided into psychological plays, mythical plays, and Rio tragedies. *Anjo Negro* (1948; Black Angel) and *A Senhora dos Afogados* (1956; The Lady of the Drowned), a tale of incest and murder by drowning, belong to the second category. *A Falecida* (1956; The Deceased Woman), *Boca de Ouro* (1960; Gold Mouth), *O Beijo no Asfalto* (1961; The Kiss on the Asphalt), *Bonitinha, mas Ordinária* (1965; Pretty But Vulgar), and *Toda Nudez Será Castigada* (1966; All Nudity Will Be Punished) are all Rio tragedies, and some were adapted for the screen. Rodrigues's theater insistently explores sexual taboos such as adultery, incest, and homosexuality, and he deliberately saw himself as exposing the darker side of human nature in the style of **realism**, although his narratives are often nonlinear. He also introduced the use of the vernacular on the stage and focused on the lives of the ordinary, lower-middle-class people of Rio, elevating their obsessions to tragic heights.

His unabashed treatment of moral degradation alienated Rodrigues from bourgeois conservatives. Ironically, critics see him as a conservative who, longing for a past order, supported the military regime that took power in 1964 and vehemently fought communism while still protesting against censorship and maintaining contacts with left-wing intellectuals. After his death, commemorative stagings of his plays and the publication of his *Teatro Completo* (1981–1989; Complete Theater) in four volumes helped seal his reputation as one of Brazil's greatest dramatists.

RODRÍGUEZ ALCALÁ, HUGO (Paraguay, 1917– 2007). Critic. Among his more than 50 books there is some poetry, including the collections *Estampas de la guerra* (1937; Scenes from the War), based on his experiences in the Chaco War (1932–1935); *La dicha apenas dicha* (1968; Happiness Hardly Spoken); and *El canto del aljibe* (1973; Song of the Well), as well as at least two volumes of stories: *Relatos del norte y del sur* (1983; Tales from the North and the South) and *El ojo del bosque* (1985; Eye of the Forest). After teaching for 40 years in North American universities, however, he is best known for his books on literature and culture, among which are *El arte de Juan Rulfo* (1965; The Art of Juan Rulfo), *Historia de la literatura paraguaya* (1970; History of Paraguayan Literature), *La incógnita de Paraguay y otros ensayos* (1987; The Mystery of Paraguay and Other Essays), and *Poetas y prosistas pararuayos y otros breves ensayos* (1988; Paraguayan Poets and Prose Writers and Other Short Essays).

RODRÍGUEZ FREYLE, JUAN (Colombia, ca. 1566–ca. 1640). Chronicler. He was the author of a **chronicle** known as *El Carnero*, a book that according to its original (very long) title purports to be a history of the founding of Colombia (formerly known as New Granada) and the foundation of its capital, Santa Fe de Bogotá. However, with the exception of its opening chapters, rather than being a history of conquest and colonization, it is a collection of stories about the social and bureaucratic life of the city. The unlikely title *El Carnero*, of which the meaning is uncertain, possibly comes from the author's nickname. The book was probably written between 1636 and 1638, but was not published until 1859.

RODRÍGUEZ MONEGAL, EMIR (Uruguay, 1921–1985). Critic. He was among the 20th-century's most notable critics and promoters of Latin American literature and a prolific writer. His involvement in literary and cultural **journals** included the Uruguayan publication *Marcha*, to which he contributed for almost 15 years. More important, he founded *Mundo Nuevo*, a journal he also edited for two years in Paris (1966–1968) and made into a significant vehicle for the dissemination and publicizing of the **boom** writers, a term he is said to have coined. As a critic, he wrote on **Pablo Neruda, Jorge Luis Borges, Eduardo Acevedo Díaz, Andrés Bello, Enrique Rodó, Mário de Andrade,** and **Horacio Quiroga,** among others. His major books include *José Enrique Rodó en el novecientos* (1950; Enrique Rodó in the 1900s), *Las raíces de Horacio Quiroga* (1961; Horacio Quiroga's Roots), *Eduardo Acevedo Díaz, dos versiones de un mismo tema* (1963; Eduardo Acevedo Díaz: Two Versions of a Single Theme), *Literatura uruguaya de medio siglo* (1966; Uruguayan Literature at Mid-Century), *El otro Andrés Bello* (1969; The Other Andrés Bello), and *Jorge Luis Borges: A Literary Biography* (1978).

ROFFÉ, REINA (Argentina, 1951–). Novelist. Writing from a feminist perspective, the themes of **lesbianism** and female sexuality, **women** in society, and the politics of Argentina figure prominently in her novels. The first of these was *Llamado al Puf* (1973; Called to Puf), followed by *Monte de Venus* (1976; Mount of Venus), which was banned by the military government; *La rompiente* (1987; The Breaker); and *El cielo dividido* (1996; The Divided Sky), which narrates the endeavors of a woman to reestablish her life in Buenos Aires after a period of exile in the United States. She has written a book on **Juan Rulfo,** *Juan Rulfo: autobiografía armada* (1973; Juan Rulfo: An Assembled Autobiography), and one of her more recent works of fiction is a collection of short stories, *Aves exóticas: cinco cuentos con mujeres raras* (2004; Exotic Birds: Five Stories with Rare Women), in which she continues to explore the condition of women in a patriarchal society.

ROJAS, ÁNGEL FELICÍSIMO (Ecuador, 1909–2003). Novelist. His fiction is set mainly in southern Ecuador and may be associated with **indigenismo** because of his treatment of Native American themes, albeit without the episodes of violence characteristic of much of the writing in that trend. His first novel was *Banca* (1938; Bench), the autobiographical tale of a young student learning about life. It was followed by *Un idilio bobo* (1948; A Foolish Idyll), a collection of short stories, several of which have indigenous themes. His most significant work of fiction, however, was *El éxodo de Yangana* (1949; Exodus from Yangana), a story of the migration of an entire community into the jungle after the death of a white man. Rojas also wrote many essays on Ecuadorian literature and culture, notably *La novela ecuatoriana* (1948; The Ecuadorian Novel).

ROJAS, GONZALO (Chile, 1917–). Poet. He is a prolific writer, the author of about 60 books, and one of Chile's most significant contemporary poets. After a flirtation with **surrealism** during the period 1938–1943, he adopted a more independent position, although that trend has continued to figure in his aesthetics. His first book, *La miseria del hombre* (1948; The Miseries of Man), was an austere collection, marked by the author's political militancy. *Contra la muerte* (1965; Against Death), his second volume, did not appear until almost 20 years later. By that time, he had begun to move in literary and university circles and to represent Chile diplomatically. His association with the government of Salvador Allende (1970–1973) forced him into exile in 1973, however. Denied the possibility of holding a university appointment in Chile, Rojas taught at universities in Europe, Venezuela, and the United States, before returning to his own country in 1994. By then he was an established literary personality.

Rojas's reputation and firm following were first acquired with *Oscuro* (1977; Dark), and he has published steadily ever since. He also adopted the practice of making each new book he published a combination of old and new poems, a process he saw as a gradual movement toward unity in his work. At the same time, he ordered the poems into three main categories, the spiritual, love and sexuality, and the world around him, although these divisions are not observed absolutely. Of the many books of poetry that Rojas has published in the last 30 years, the following are some of the most representative: *Del relámpago* (1981; Lightning), *50 poemas* (1982; 50 Poems), *El alumbrado* (1986; Lighting), *Materia de testamento* (1988; Testamentary Matter), *Esquizotexto y otros poemas* (1988; Schizotext and Other Poems), *Desocupado lector* (1990; Idle Reader), *Las hermosas: poesías de amor* (1992; The Beautiful: Love Poems), *Cinco Visiones* (1992; Five Visions), *Diálogo con Ovidio* (1999; Dialogue with Ovid), *¿Qué se ama cuando se ama?* (2000; What Is Loved When You Love?), *Velocities of the Possible* (2000), and *Requiem de la mariposa* (2001; Requiem for a Butterfly).

ROJAS, MANUEL (Chile, 1896–1973). Novelist and short story writer. He was born in Buenos Aires and spent his early life between **Argentina** and Chile. In his youth he was drawn to the anarchist politics of the day and earned his living at jobs that led him to travel widely in Argentina and Chile and to become familiar with working-class life. Although his first literary successes were in poetry, he is best known for his fiction, for which he drew on his own life experiences, writing in a style that made him a significant figure in Latin American **realism**. His first works of fiction were three collections of short stories: *Hombres del sur* (1926; Men from the South), *El delincuente* (1929; The Delinquent), and *Travesía* (1934; Crossing), which consisted mainly of versions of his own experiences or stories he had heard.

Although Rojas republished his stories in various anthologies along with a few new texts, he then abandoned the genre in favor of the novel. *Lanchas en la bahía* (1932; Barges in the Bay), a short coming-of-age narrative set in Valparaíso, was his first. *La ciudad de los Césares* (1938; City of the Caesars), a longer work, came next. Rojas's best-known work, *Hijo de ladrón* (1951; Born Guilty), appeared over 10 years later. In this novel he began a cycle of works in the manner of the **picaresque** tradition, centered on the autobiography of Aniceto Hevía, the author's literary alter ego. The cycle includes *Mejor que el vino* (1958; Better Than Wine), *Punta de rieles* (1960; Railway Points), *Sombras contra el muro* (1964; Shadows Against the Wall), and *La vida oscura radiante* (1971; The Dark Shining Life). It features a large cast of characters and is set in the working world of the 1920s.

ROJAS, RICARDO (Argentina, 1882–1957). Essayist, poet, and dramatist. Although he contributed to several genres, his greatest impact came from his essays, which made him a prominent public intellectual during the first half of the 20th century. In volumes such as *El alma española* (1908; The Spanish Soul), *La restauración nacionalista* (1909; The Nationalist Restoration), and *La argentinidad: ensayo histórico sobre nuestra conciencia nacional en la gesta de la emancipación 1810–1816* (1910; Argentineanness: Historical Essay on Our National Consciousness During the Movement for Freedom, 1810–1816), he proposed an idea of the nation that incorporated Argentina's indigenous people and the country's colonial past. His advocacy of national values is also expressed in biographies of prominent Argentineans, notably his life of the liberator José de San Martín (1778–1850), *El santo de la espada* (1933; *San Martín, Knight of the Andes*), and his life of **Domingo Faustino Sarmiento**, *El profeta de la pampa* (1945; Prophet of the Pampas). Rojas also wrote on literature, and his works include *La literatura argentina: ensayo filosófico sobre la evolución de la cultura en la Plata* (4 vols., 1917–1922; Argentinean Literature: Philosophical Essay on the Evolution of Culture on the River Plate), one of the first attempts at a systematic history of literature in Argentina.

ROKHA, PABLO DE (Chile, 1894–1968). Poet. Born Carlos Ignacio Díaz Loyola, he was a controversial, not to say eccentric, figure, whose relationship with cultural institutions was generally problematic and who maintained an ongoing feud with several of his contemporaries. Of these, the most celebrated was **Pablo Neruda**, whom Rokha accused of plagiarism and excoriated on various occasions, most notably in the two-volume *Neruda y yo* (1955; Neruda and Me). Rokha's first book, *Versos de infancia* (1916; Childhood Verses), still showed some of the characteristics of **romanticism**, but also some of the author's anarchist leanings. His first major work was *Los gemidos* (1922; Moans), a long prose poem that showed him to be one of the first Latin American authors to have assimilated the **avant-garde** and **surrealism**. It represented a break with tradition and was not well received, perhaps for that reason, although Rokha would go on to write more than 30 more books of poetry. He wrote mainly in response to what was happening in his own life and the world around him, and most of his poetry was self-published and distributed.

Cosmogonía (1925; Cosmogony), a book about the author's personal dilemmas, was followed by others that had a more political outlook. Rokha joined the Communist Party in 1932 and remained a member until he was expelled in 1940. *Escritura de Raimundo Contreras* (1929; Writing by Raimundo Contreras) is about the life of a peasant. *Jesucristo* (1933; Jesus Christ) and *Moisés* (1937; Moses) focus on the epic hero and social compromise. *Imprecación a la bestia fascista* (1937; Curse on the Fascist Beast) and *Cinco cantos rojos* (1938; Five Red Songs) are both works of socialist realism, the second in praise of prominent figures from the Soviet Union. Several books are a response to World War II. *Morfología del espanto* (1942; Morphology of Terror) is a search for a way out from the violence of war and history; *Canto al ejército rojo* (1944; Song for the Red Army) was written in praise of Soviet resistance to the German invasion; and *Los poemas continentales* (1945; Continental Poems) is dedicated to the American fight against the Axis powers. Rokha's remaining books of poetry include *Fuego negro* (1951; Black Fire), written on the occasion of the death of his wife, and *Canto de fuego a China Popular* (1963; Song of Fire to the People's Republic of China) and *China roja* (1964; Red China), both written after a visit to China in 1962–1963.

In addition to his poetry, Rokha also published several prose works, among which were a book of travels, *Carta magna del continente* (1949; Continental Magna Carta) and others on life and culture: *Idioma del mundo* (1958; Language of the World), *Genio del pueblo* (1960; Genius of the People), *Estilo de masas* (1965; Style of the Masses), and *Epopeya de las bebidas y comidas de Chile* (1965; Epic of Chilean Food and Drink). He died by his own hand a few months after one of his sons also committed suicide.

ROMANTICISM. Although a complex aesthetic and political movement in its origins in Europe, romanticism became established in Latin America in a somewhat diluted form through French and Spanish influence toward the end of the first half of the 19th century, by which time the movement had already declined in Europe. Romanticism in Latin America endured well into the second half of the century and coincided while still at its height with the early stages of **realism**. The debates about literary form, which marked some of romanticism's early passage in Europe, were of lesser significance in Latin America, where an increased sensibility toward nature and human relations and an awakening sense of nationalism in the newly independent republics were among the principal characteristics.

The sentimental novel, modeled on European counterparts, became an especially appropriate vehicle through which to convey both a romantic sensibility and the problems experienced by the fledgling societies of the continent. Its most prominent examples include *Amalia* (1851; *Amalia*), by **José Mármol** from Argentina; *María* (1867; *María: A South American Romance*) by **Jorge Isaacs** from **Colombia**; *Iracema* (1865; Iracema), by **José de Alencar**; *A Escrava Isaura* (1875; The Slave Isaura), by **Bernardo Joaquim de Silva Guimarães**, and *A Moreninha* (1844; The Dark Girl), by **Joaquim Manuel de Macedo**, from **Brazil**; Clemencia (1869; *Clemencia*), by the **Mexican Ignacio Manuel Altamirano**; and *Cumandá* (1879; Cumandá), by the **Ecuadorian Juan León Mera**. The emergence of a sense of nation was also fostered by a recourse to history, such as in the *tradiciones* of **Ricardo Palma** (**Peru**), the history of Brazil by **Francisco Adolfo de Varnhagen**, and the **historical novel** by **Vicente López Fidel** (Argentina). Similar objectives were expressed through confrontations with the primitive worlds of nature and the native peoples of the Americas in verse narratives such as *El gaucho Martín Fierro* (1872; *The Gaucho Martín Fierro*), by the Argentinean **José Hernández**; the indianist epics *Os Timbiras* (1857; The Timbiras) and *I-Juca Pirama* (1851; I-Juca Pirama), by the Brazilian **Antônio Gonçalves Dias**; and *Tabaré* (1888; *Tabaré: An Indian Legend of Uruguay*), by the **Uruguayan Juan Zorilla de San Martín**, which are among some of Latin America's foundational texts. Although romantic lyric verse had some notable exponents, such as **Manuel José Othón** (Mexico), **José Batres Montúfar (Guatemala), Casimiro José Marques de Abreu, Manuel Antônio Álvares de Azevedo, Domingos José Gonçalves de Magalhães** (Brazil), and **Esteban Echeverría** (Argentina), the lyric had less impact. A more profound revolution in poetry would come later, first through **modernismo** and then through the **avant-garde** in Spanish America and through **parnassianism, symbolism**, and **Brazilian modernism** in Brazil. *See also* ACEVEDO DÍAZ, EDUARDO; ACUÑA DE FI-

GUEROA, FRANCISCO; ASSIS, JOAQUIM MARIA MACHADO DE; AZEVEDO, ALUÍSIO; CABELLO DE CARBONERA, MERCEDES; CHILE; CHOCANO, JOSÉ SANTOS; CORREIA, RAIMUNDO; DARÍO, RUBÉN; EL SALVADOR; EPIC POETRY; GAMERO, LUCILA; INDIGENOUS TRADITIONS; NÚÑEZ, RAFAEL; OLIVEIRA, ALBERTO DE; PARAGUAY; PAYNO, MANUEL; REGIONALISM; RENDÓN, VÍCTOR MANUEL; ROKHA, PABLO DE; ROMERO, SÍLVIO; SILVA, JOSÉ ASUNCIÓN; SOUSA, JOÃO DA CRUZ E; SOUSÂNDRADE, JOAQUIM DE; URBINA, LUIS G.; WOMEN.

ROMERO, ELVIO (Paraguay, 1926–2004). Poet. Political conditions in Paraguay forced him into exile in 1947. He lived in **Argentina** for the rest of his life, although he remained spiritually attached to his native land and is considered one of his country's most important 20th-century poets. His early works, *Días roturados* (1948; Plowed Days), *Resoles áridos* (1950; Dry Heat Hazes), and *El sol bajo las raíces* (1956; The Sun Beneath the Roots), showed his social and political militancy. *De cara al corazón* (1961; Facing the Heart) and *Un relámpago herido* (1967; A Wounded Streak of Lightning) are both about love. In *El libro de la migración* (1966; Book of Migration) and *Los valles imaginarios* (1985; Imaginary Valleys), he narrated popular Guaraní legends. Later books include *Esta guitarra dura* (1967; This Hard Guitar), *Los innombrables* (1970; The Unmentionable), and *Destierro y atardecer* (1975; Exile and Evening). *El poeta y sus encrucijadas* (1991; The Poet and His Dilemmas), one of his last books, received Paraguay's National Prize for Literature the year the prize was inaugurated.

ROMERO, JOSÉ RUBÉN (Mexico, 1890–1952). Novelist. He was an unsuccessful poet who turned to fiction in later life. His first prose work, *Apuntes de un lugareño* (1932; *Notes of a Villager*), was prompted by nostalgia while serving as Mexican consul in Barcelona. On his return to Mexico he published *El pueblo inocente* (1934; The Innocent Town) and *Desbandada* (1934; Route), both set in rural Mexico against the background of the Mexican Revolution. In his next novel, *Mi caballo, mi perro y mi rifle* (1936; My Horse, My Dog, and My Rifle), the autobiographical dimension of his writing is associated more fully with the **picaresque** and the **novel of the Mexican Revolution** through the story of a soldier whose experiences follow the rise and fall of the revolutionary movement. The picaresque tradition is also a feature of Romero's best-known novel, *La vida inútil de Pito Pérez* (1938; *The Futile Life of Pito Pérez*), based on a real-life person whose antics serve to expose the foibles of a small town and its inhabitants. Other novels include *Anticipación de la muerte* (1939; Anticipation of Death), a humorous view of death, and *Rosenda* (1946; Rosenda). Romero also penned a commentary on his own writing, *Breve historia de mis libros* (1942; Short History of My Books).

ROMERO, MARIELA (Venezuela, 1949–). Dramatist. She is one among a group of **women** writing for the **theater** who have contributed to maintaining the vitality of the contemporary genre in Venezuela. Her first play was *Algo alrededor del espejo* (1966; Something Around the Mirror). Since then she has written *El juego* (1978; The Game), a feminist work with two female characters, Ana I and Ana II, two manifestations, perhaps, of the same person; *El inevitable destino de Rosa de la noche* (1980; The Inevitable Fate of Rosa of the Night), about prostitution and street people; *El vendedor* (1981; The Salesman), a play on games; *Esperando al italiano* (1988; Waiting for the Italian), on male–female relationships; and *Las risas de nuestras medusas* (1992; The Smiles of Our Medusas). Romero also writes for television.

ROMERO, SÍLVIO (Brazil, 1851–1914). Critic, essayist, and poet. Born in Sergipe, Romero studied law in Recife, where he came in contact with **Tobias Barreto** and his positivist School of Recife. His first book of poetry, *Cantos do Fim do Século* (1878; Songs of the End of the Century), was an infelicitous attempt at producing a "scientific poetry" in accordance with the principles of **positivism** he espoused. With respect to criticism, he attacked romantic poetry through a series of articles that were later gathered in *A Literatura Brasileira e a Crítica Moderna* (1880; Brazilian Literature and Modern Criticism). After receiving his degree, he became a federal representative and eventually moved to Rio, where he taught and wrote extensively, especially for the press, engaging in famous debates in which he always defended the superiority of Barreto and his positivist tendencies. Although criticized nowadays for his dismissive views of authors such as **Castro Alves** and **Machado de Assis**, expressed in *Machado de Assis* (1897; Machado de Assis), Romero had the merit of attempting to apply objective and "logical" methods to literary study, as seen in *Da Crítica e Sua Exata Definição* (1909; Of Criticism and Its Exact Definition). He produced a number of important and original studies on various aspects of Brazilian culture: *A Filosofia no Brasil* (1878; Philosophy in Brazil), *Estudos Sobre a Poesia Popular do Brasil* (1888; Studies on the Popular Poetry of Brazil), and *Etnografia Brasileira* (1888; Brazilian Ethnography).

These studies all anticipated Romero's best-known work, the two-volume *História da Literatura Brasileira* (1888; History of Brazilian Literature), in which, unlike previous authors, he consciously adopted a nationalist and positivist lens and attempted to explain the evolution of literature through extraliterary sociological factors, particularly miscegenation, foreshadowing the work of intellectuals such as **Gilberto Freyre**. Romero was also one of the founding members of the Brazilian Academy of Letters (*see* ACADEMIAS). Though critics now fault Romero for his excessive commitment to the positivist ideology and his lack of appreciation of style and aesthetics, he remains a key figure in understanding the transition from **romanticism** to 20th-century Brazilian culture. *See also* VERÍSSIMO DIAS DE MATOS, JOSÉ.

RÓMULO GALLEGOS PRIZE. First awarded in 1967, this prize was named for **Rómulo Gallegos**, one of Venezuela's most celebrated novelists and a former president of the country. It was first open to novels written in Spanish by Latin Americans, but may now be awarded to any novel written in Spanish regardless of the place of origin of the author. Latin American recipients include **Mario Vargas Llosa** (1967), **Gabriel García Márquez** (1972), **Carlos Fuentes** (1977), **Fernando del Paso** (1982), **Abel Posse** (1987), **Manuel Mejía Vallejo** (1989), **Arturo Uslar Pietri** (1991), **Mempo Giardinelli** (1993), **Ángeles Mastretta** (1997), **Fernando Vallejo** (2003), **Elena Poniatowska** (2007), and **William Ospina** (2009).

ROSA, JOÃO GUIMARÃES (Brazil, 1908–1967). Novelist and short story writer. Guimarães Rosa was born and raised in a small town in the rural interior of Minas Gerais, a region of cowboys and storytellers that inspired many of his literary works. He studied medicine in Belo Horizonte, and after receiving his degree in 1930 worked as a physician in rural areas of Minas Gerais. At this time he had already begun to write and publish short stories, for which he won prizes. Guimarães Rosa had a penchant for languages from an early age, and he taught himself Russian and German. In 1934, he applied for the Brazilian Foreign Service and became a career diplomat. He won a prize in 1936 for *Magma* (Magma), a poetry volume he never published, and he began writing his collection of stories *Sagarana* (1946; Sagarana), based on childhood memories of life on the cattle ranches of Minas Gerais. Posted to Hamburg in 1938, he was captured and sent to prison in Baden-Baden in 1942. He was liberated a few months later with other diplomats. Upon his return to South America, he completely rewrote *Sagarana*, which he then published in 1946, with great success. Nevertheless, Guimarães Rosa did not become well known in the literary world until later. In the following years he served as a diplomat in South America and Europe.

   Com o Vaqueiro Mariano (1952; With the Cowboy Mariano), a poetic account of his encounter with a cowboy from the Pantanal region, anticipates the idiosyncratic prose of Guimarães Rosa's novellas *Corpo de Baile* (1956; Corps de Ballet)—later divided into *Manuelzão e Miguilim* (1964; Big Manuel and Little Manuel), *No Urubuquaquá, no Pinhém* (1965; In Urubuquaquá, in Pinhém), and *Noites do Sertão* (1965; Nights in the Backlands)—and of his only but greatly acclaimed novel, *Grande Sertão: Veredas* (1956; *The Devil to Pay in the Backlands*). These two works, published within months of each other, attracted great critical attention and forever secured his literary reputation. In the seven novellas of *Corpo de Baile*, Guimarães Rosa introduces characters and literary language that he would later refine in *Grande Sertão: Veredas*. The characters of *Corpo de Baile*, inspired by typical inhabitants of the backlands, cross from one novella to another like dancers in a ballet; hence the title of the collection. Guimarães Rosa also created a unique, innovative language inspired by the folk speech of the Brazilian backlands, but using literary devices such as rhyme, onomatopoeia, alliteration,

metaphor, and metonymy, and, among other innovations, he introduced magical events and narratives within narratives.

Grande Sertão: Veredas, considered Guimarães Rosa's masterpiece and one of the most important books of Brazilian literature, has
been compared by some to Joyce's *Finnegans Wake* for its peculiar
and inventive use of language and its mythical and poetic qualities.
It is a metaphysical tale of the fight between good and evil as embodied in the character of Riobaldo, a hoodlum cowboy who roams
the backlands trying to deny the existence of the devil, with whom
he made a pact when he attempted to kill another man. His memories
and reflections assume metaphysical levels and the form of an existential drama when he declares, for instance, that the backlands are
the size of the world and a place where everything is simultaneously
certain and uncertain.

Along the same lines and in the language created for *Grande
Sertão: Veredas*, *Primeiras Estórias* (1962; First Stories) is a collection of short stories in which spatio-temporal limits are transgressed.
The characters in this collection (children, madmen, and simple
folk) are involved in miraculous events that defy logic. Among
other works, *Tutaméia (Terceiras Estórias)* (1967; Tutaméia) is a
collection of very short enigmatic tales, and *O Mistério dos M M M*
(1962, The Mystery of the M M M) was written in collaboration with
Viriato Correia and **Dinah Silveira de Queirós**. Guimarães Rosa,
considered one of the icons of **Brazilian modernism**, died of a heart
attack three days after he was admitted into the Brazilian Academy of
Letters (*see* ACADEMIAS). *See also* RIBEIRO, JOÃO UBALDO.

ROSAS, JUAN MANUEL (1793–1877). An Argentinean *caudillo*,
or strongman, he ruled postindependence **Argentina** as governor of
Buenos Aires province between 1829 until 1852. He was a populist
dictator who ruled from a position of strength and intimidation and
by the elimination of his opponents. He left an enduring mark on the
country, and his life and times have become the subject of numerous
works of literature by authors such as **Esteban Echeverría, Manuel Gálvez, Griselda Gambaro, Eduardo Gutiérrez, Domingo
Faustino Sarmiento,** and **Andrés Rivera**. *See also* CIVILIZA-
TION AND BARBARISM; LÓPEZ, VICENTE FIDEL; MÁRMOL,
JOSÉ; MOLINA, ENRIQUE.

ROSENCOF, MAURICIO (Uruguay, 1933–). Dramatist and novelist. One of the most significant dramatists to emerge in Uruguay since **Florencio Sánchez**, he broke with established trends in **realism** and **naturalism**. His theater dramatized socially marginalized settings and he combined elements of dream and reality in the development of themes of self-deception and evasion. *El gran Tuleque* (1961; The Great Tuleque) was one of the first dramatizations of *la murga*, a popular form of musical theater in Uruguay associated with carnival. *Las ranas* (1962; The Frogs) is about life in a shanty town; *La calesita rebelde* (1964; The Rebellious Carousel) is a play for **children**; and *Los caballos* (1966; The Horses) is concerned with sugarcane workers in northern Uruguay.

Rosencof's involvement with the Tupamaros urban guerrillas led to his arrest in 1972 and imprisonment; he was released in 1985 under a general amnesty after the collapse of the dictatorship. While in prison, Rosencof wrote a number of plays, including *El combate en el estable* (1985; Fight in the Stable), *El saco de Antonio* (1985; Antonio's Jacket), *Y nuestros caballos serán blancos* (1985; And Our Horses Will Be White), *El gran bonete* (1986; The Big Cap), and *El hijo que espera* (1986; The Waiting Son). The first play he wrote after his release was *El regreso del gran Tuleque* (1987; Return of the Great Tuleque). Since then, he has also turned to fiction. He has written an account of his time in prison, *Memorias del calabozo* (1990; Memories of the Dungeon), and several novels that draw in part on his experience of prison and torture. They include *El bataraz* (1999; The Rooster), *Las cartas que no llegaron* (2000; The Letters That Never Came), *El enviado del fuego* (2004; Sent from the Fire), *El barrio era una fiesta* (2005; The Barrio Was a Holiday), and *Una góndola ancló en la esquina* (2007; A Gondola Tied up at the Corner).

ROZENMACHER, GERMÁN (Argentina, 1936–1970). Dramatist and short story writer. His writing springs in part from feelings of discrimination as a **Jew** and the consequences of his affiliation with Peronism. He published two collections of short stories: *Cabecita negra* (1962; Black Head) and *Los ojos del tigre* (1967; The Tiger's Eyes). His work for the **theater** includes the plays *Réquiem para un viernes a la noche* (1964; Requiem for a Friday Night); *Lazarillo* *de Tormes* (1971; Lazarillo de Tormes), an adaptation for the stage of the 16th-century Spanish novel of the same title; *El caballero de Indias* (1982; Knight of the Indies); and *El avión negro* (1970; The Black Plane), written in collaboration with **Roberto Cossa, Carlos Somigliana,** and **Ricardo Talesnik.**

RUBIÃO, MURILO (Brazil, 1916–1991). Short story writer. Born in Minas Gerais, where he lived most of his life, Rubião received a degree in law, but devoted himself to journalism. In 1966, he founded the well-known literary **journal** *Suplemento Literário do Minas Gerais,* which he directed until 1969. Rubião is known for his painstaking approach to writing: in every place the *mot juste* and precise turn of phrase combine with the plot to produce the **fantastic** and the unusual that characterize his work. Rubião is also a painstaking revisionist, often changing major aspects of his works before republishing them. His collections of short stories include *O Ex-Mágico* (1947; The Ex Magician), *A Estrela Vermelha* (1953; The Red Star), *Os Dragões e Outros Contos* (1965; Dragons and Other Stories), *O Pirotécnico Zacarias* (1974; The Pyrotechnician Zachary), and *O Convidado* (1974; The Guest). An uncommon writer in Brazilian literature, Rubião's fantastic fiction, in which the absurd is inserted into "normal" reality, also exhibits a political concern for the massification of contemporary life. His texts therefore always work on a literal and a larger allegorical level.

RUIZ DE ALARCÓN, JUAN (Mexico, 1581?–1639). Dramatist. He was born in colonial Mexico but emigrated to Spain in 1600. Although successful and one of a group of popular playwrights in his day, he was always considered a foreigner and was the butt of his contemporaries' humor on account of his physical deformity. His plays were published in two volumes, eight plays in 1628 and twelve in 1634. However, they were all written some time before they were published, because he abandoned the **theater** after receiving a court appointment in 1626. His theater contains frequent reference to his native land, but is commonly read in the context of 17th-century Spanish drama, whose dramatic conventions and themes he generally adopted. The distinctive feature of his plays is their satirical or moralistic content, presented through a character afflicted with a particular moral flaw. His most celebrated play is *La verdad sospechosa* (1594; *Truth Can't Be Trusted, or the Liar*), about the misadventures of a habitual liar. Other well-known titles are *Las paredes oyen* (Walls Have Ears) and *La cueva de Salamanca* (The Cave in Salamanca). He is also celebrated for his influence on later French and Spanish dramatists. *See also* JIMÉNEZ RUEDA, JULIO.

RULFO, JUAN (Mexico, 1917–1986). Novelist and short story writer. Although he ranks among the most highly acclaimed writers of the 20th century in Latin America, Rulfo's reputation rests on the two works that amount to almost his entire literary output, a collection of short stories, *El llano en llamas* (1953; *The Burning Plain and Other Stories*), and the novel *Pedro Páramo* (1955; *Pedro Páramo*). The novel and several of the short stories are set in the mythical town of Comala against the background of the Mexican Revolution and other civil conflicts of the first half of the 20th century, which suffices to locate Rulfo's writing in the general context of the **novel of the Mexican Revolution**, although his writing focuses much more on the cultural and social contexts and the psychology of the characters than on a narrative of military or political events. Comala is a cruel, infernal place of violence and corruption, whose inhabitants struggle to survive in an oppressive world controlled by landowners and political bosses. *Pedro Páramo* is told by Juan Preciado, sent back to Comala by his dying mother to discover the paradise of her youth, but the town to which he returns is the world of the dead, from whom he learns the story of its past. Rulfo's two books were highly innovative works for the time, and the mythic dimensions of his novel foreshadow **magic realism**. Rulfo was also an accomplished photographer, whose images of rural, indigenous Mexico often complement the world represented in his fiction. The Juan Rulfo Prize for literature was created in his honor in 1991, and the first recipient was **Nicanor Parra (Chile)**. *See also* FUENTES, CARLOS; ROFFÉ, REINA.

– S –

SABAT ERCASTY, CARLOS (Uruguay, 1887–1982). Poet. During a period of over 60 years, between 1917 and 1982, he published more than 60 books. Although the influence of **modernismo** is apparent in his early work, he subsequently followed his own path, but was particularly influenced by the European world of the classics, the Orient, and Hinduism. He is said to have had some influence on **Pablo Neruda**, but did not achieve the latter's success. Among his many books are several eulogies of notable persons, including *Vidas* (1923; Lives), *Himno a Rodó y oda a Martí* (1938; Hymn to Rodó and Ode to Martí), *Oda a Luis Salguero* (1940; Ode to Luis Salguero), *Himno universal a Roosevelt* (1946; Universal Hymn to Roosevelt), *Himno a Artigas* (1946; Hymn to Artigas), *Oda a Eduardo Fabini* (1947; Ode to Eduardo Fabini), and *Libro de José Martí* (1953; Book of José Martí).

SÁBATO, ERNESTO (Argentina, 1911–). Essayist and novelist. Sábato was trained as a scientist and earned a doctorate in physics before becoming disillusioned with science. Both his essays and novels dwell on the conflicts of reason and logic with intuition and the irrational. Although he has not developed a philosophical system of his own, his work shows the influence of European **existentialism**. In collections of essays such as *Uno y el universo* (1945; One and the Universe) and *Hombres y engranajes* (1951; Men and Gears), he has written on topics that reflect humanity's decline through dependence on science and technology. He has also written about Argentina in *El otro rostro del peronismo* (1956; The Other Face Peronism), *Tango: discusión y clave* (1963; Tango: Discussion and Key), and *La cultura en la encrucijada nacional* (1973; Culture at the National Crossroads). In *El escritor y sus fantasmas* (1963; The Writer and His Ghosts), he considered the art and ethics of writing. After the 1976–1983 military dictatorship in Argentina, Sábato headed the commission charged with investigating atrocities committed by the regime. The commission's report, *Nunca más* (Never Again), appeared in 1984.

Sábato's three novels are intense and at times perplexing psychological studies, explorations of the self undertaken through the representation of characters who find themselves in intensely stressful conditions. The first, *El túnel* (1948; *The Tunnel*), is a confessional novel in the tradition of *Notes from Underground* (1864) by the Russian author Fyodor Dostoyevsky (1821–1881) and novels by the French existentialist writers Jean Paul Sartre (1905–1980) and Albert Camus (1913–1960). It is the memoir of a man who narrates the events that led him to murder the woman he loved. *Sobre héroes y tumbas* (1961; *On Heroes and Tombs*), Sábato's second novel, also has at its center a perplexing tale of love, set in the context of the decline of an Argentinean family, the social unrest of the 1950s, and a world of irrational violence. *Abbadón el exterminador* (1974; *The Angel of Darkness*), Sábato's third novel, is an equally unconventional work, fragmented by all manner of extended discussions on different topics, that conveys a disturbing vision of the present. It has no clear plot, unless it is the attempt of a writer, Sábato himself, to write in spite of the distraction from the voices that surround him, including those of characters from his previous work.

SABINES, JAIME (Mexico, 1926–1999). Poet. A writer who had little association with the literary circles of his day, he nevertheless gained an extraordinary following by becoming known primarily through the open and approachable style of his poetry. For the most part, he wrote on everyday themes: a walk along a street or across a park; family ties; a scene in a bar; and common feelings such as a fear of death, frustration at illness, or the expression of love. His books include *Horal* (1950; Hourly), *La señal* (1951; The Signal), *Adán y Eva* (1952; Adam and Eve), Tarumba (1956; *Tarumba: The Selected Poems of Jaime Sabines*), *Diario semanario y poemas en prosa* (1961; Weekly Diary and Prose Poems), *Maltiempo* (1972; Bad Times), and *Algo sobre la muerte del mayor Sabines* (1973; Something About the Death of Major Sabines).

SABINO, FERNANDO (Brazil, 1923–2004). Novelist and chronicler. An extremely prolific writer, Sabino attended school in his native Minas Gerais and began writing for newspapers while he studied law. He published his first book of short stories, *Os Grilos Não Cantam Mais* (1941; Crickets No Longer Sing), encouraged by writers such as **Mário de Andrade**, whom he later befriended. Sabino valued his friendships with other writers, such as **Carlos Drummond de Andrade**, **Vinícius de Moraes**, and especially **Clarice Lispector**. In 1946, he moved to New York and began to send columns to dailies and magazines in Brazil, a practice he continued when he returned home in 1948. Some of these texts relating his experiences in the United States were published in *A Cidade Vazia* (1950; The Empty City). Other books of **chronicles** include *O Homem Nu* (1960; The Naked Man), *A Companheira de Viagem* (1965; The Female Travel Companion), *A Inglesa Deslumbrada* (1967; The Dazzled English-woman), *Gente I e Gente II* (1975; People I and People II), *A Mulher do Vizinho* (1975; The Neighbor's Wife), *Deixa o Alfredo Falar!* (1976; Let Alfredo Speak!), and *O Encontro das Águas* (1977; The Meeting of the Waters).

While in New York, he also began work on passages that would become his best-known novel, *O Encontro Marcado* (1956; *A Time To Meet*), a semiautobiographical coming-of-age novel that reflected the existential drama of Sabino's generation. This novel was a break-through for its portrayal of urban life, in contrast with a tradition of literature inspired by rural settings. Sabino also published the no-vella collections *A Marca* (1944; The Mark) and *A Vida Real* (1952; The Real Life); according to the author, the latter was inspired by "emotions lived in dreams." Other notable books include *O Grande Mentecapto* (1979; The Great Fool), a **picaresque novel** based on a simple character called Viramundo, and *A Faca de Dois Gumes* (1985; The Double-Edged Sword), a trilogy of novellas that revisit classic themes and genres, which became required reading in schools.

With **Rubem Braga**, Sabino founded several publishing houses that were instrumental in disseminating the work of contemporary authors from Brazil and Latin America, including **Manuel Puig**, **Mario Vargas Llosa**, and **Gabriel García Márquez**. He was also active in film as producer, director, and reviewer. Sabino, who died of cancer, requested the following inscription for his grave: "Here lies Fernando Sabino, who was born a man and died a child."

SAÉNZ, JAIME (Bolivia, 1921–1986). Poet and novelist. Alcoholism, public scandals, his open bisexuality, and sympathy for Nazism made him a figure of considerable notoriety. He wrote in a very individual, often hermetic style, in a manner close to **surrealism**, such that his metaphors are not always easy to penetrate. His poetry includes *El escalpelo* (1955; The Scalpel), *Muerte por el tacto* (1957; Death by Touch), *Aniversario de una visión* (1960; Anniversary of a Vision), *Visitante profundo* (1964; Profound Visitor), *El frío* (1967; The

Cold), *Recorrer esta distancia* (1973; Covering this Distance), and *Bruchner: las tinieblas* (1978; Bruchner: Darkness). In two of his last books, *La noche* (1984; The Night) and *La piedra imán* (1989; Lodestone), the latter published posthumously, he described the terrifying world of an alcoholic crisis. As a novelist, he produced two successful works: *Felipe Delgado* (1979; Felipe Delgado), the memoirs of an alcoholic set in the social underbelly of La Paz, and *Los cuartos* (1985; Rooms), the story of an old woman's search for a place to live in the poor districts of the Bolivian capital. Another work of fiction by Saénz, a volume of short stories, *Vidas y muertes* (1986; Lives and Deaths), was published posthumously.

SAER, JUAN JOSÉ (Argentina, 1957–2005). Novelist and short story writer. Although he lived in France after 1968, where he worked as a university professor, he is considered one of Argentina's most important 20th-century prose writers. His fiction is characterized by its predominant focus on a single area of Argentina, the littoral of the Paraná River in the Province of Santa Fe. *En la zona* (1960; In the Zone), a collection of short stories, in which he introduced some of the narrative strategies and many of the characters who would figure later in his writing, is thus the point of departure for a fictional world developed in subsequent collections of short stories and novels. In this respect, his fiction is comparable to that of **Juan Carlos Onetti** or the American William Faulkner (1897–1962). Another significant influence was the French **new novel**, notably by Alain Robbe-Grillet (1922–2008) and Nathalie Sarraute (1900–1999), from whom he drew elements such as chronological fragmentation, a focus on the untellability of stories, and a questioning of the reality of events. He often narrates events in parallel time-space dimensions, allowing him to combine different narratives about the same characters in the same text, a technique that echoes aspects of the writing of earlier Argentineans such as **Jorge Luis Borges** and **Julio Cortázar**.

Other collections of short stories include *Palo y hueso* (1965; Stick and Bone); *Unidad de lugar* (1967; Unity of Place); *Cicatrices* (1969; Scars), a set of four stories connected by a single crime, which first drew major critical attention to Saer's work; *La mayor* (1976; "A" Major); and *Lugar* (2000; Place). The author of a dozen novels, he often took a particular genre, such as **crime fiction**, or the work of a particular author, such as Marcel Proust (1871–1922) or James Joyce (1882–1941), as a point of departure for his own writing. His novels include *Responso* (1964; Prayer for the Dead); *La vuelta completa* (1966; Complete Turn); *El limonero real* (1974; The Royal Lemon Tree), about the cyclical return of events during a day in the life of the main character; *Nadie nada nunca* (1980; *Nobody Nothing Never*); *Glosa* (1986; Gloss); *La ocasión* (1988; *The Event*), set in the pampas; *Lo imborrable* (1993; Indelible); *La pesquisa* (1994; *The Investigation*), a crime novel; *Las nubes* (1997; The Clouds); and *La grande* (2005; The Great One). His best-known work of fiction is the **new historical novel** *El entenado* (1983; *The Witness*), an old man's recollections of a period of captivity as a boy during the early colonial period, when he witnessed the ritual cannibalism of his captors. It has several of the hallmarks of Saer's fiction, notably the ambiguous role of literature and narrative as the means of preserving a disappeared reality.

Although fiction is the main source of Saer's literary reputation, he also wrote poetry and published two collections of verse, both under the same ironic title, *El arte de narrar* (1977 and 2000; The Art of Narrating), containing, respectively, work for 1960–1975 and 1960–1987. Saer's essays about literature in general, writing, and his own work were published as *Juan José Saer por Juan José Saer* (1986; Juan José Saer by Juan José Saer), *Una literatura sin atributos* (1986; A Literature Without Attributes), *El río sin orillas* (1991; The River Without Banks), and *El concepto de ficción* (1997; The Concept of Fiction).

SAHAGÚN, BERNARDINO DE (Mexico, 1499–1590). Chronicler. He was a Franciscan friar who was sent as a missionary to Mexico in 1529 and remained there for the rest of his life. He wrote in Spanish and Nahuatl, the language of the Aztecs, and was the author of a number of religious texts, linguistic works, and a history of the Franciscan Order in Mexico. He is most celebrated, however, for his **chronicle** *Historia general de las cosas de Nueva España* (*General History of the Things of New Spain*), also known as the *Florentine Codex*. First completed in Nahuatl in 1569 and later prepared in a Nahuatl/Spanish version, it is one of the richest sources on life in Aztec Mexico.

SAINETE. A short, one-act play, originating in Spain in the mid-18th century. Like the ***entremés***, which it replaced, a *sainete* was a comic or farcical presentation of scenes from low-life and often performed between the acts or at the end of another, longer play. In **Argentina**, where it evolved into the ***grotesco criollo*** and was also known as the *sainete orillero* (river-bank *sainete*, referring to the location of Buenos Aires on the River Plate), it became an important part of popular **theater** of the late 19th and 20th centuries, which featured scenes from the life of the **gaucho** and the lives of immigrants and the urban poor by playwrights such as **Francisco Defilippis Novoa, Carlos Maggi, Roberto Payró, Florencio Sanchez, Nemesio Trejo**, and **Alberto Vacarezza**. In **Ecuador, Víctor Manuel Rendón** also adapted the *sainete* to stage a realistic view of the world. *See also* MOOCK, ARMANDO; VENEZUELA.

SAINZ, GUSTAVO (Mexico, 1940–). Novelist. He is one of Mexico's most prominent contemporary novelists. He is commonly related to the **post-boom** and has published 18 novels to date. His early fiction is associated with the literary movement in Mexico known as **la onda**. *Gazapo* (1965; *Gazapo*), his first novel, uses the tape recorder as a narrative device to alter perceptions of time and space. It is concerned with youth counterculture in Mexico City, was very popular, and has been widely translated. Culture and language are also significant elements of later works, including *Obsesivos días circulares* (1969; Obsessive Circular Days), about young urban intellectuals, set in a private high school owned by a gangster. Several of his subsequent novels often combine different perspectives or different social worlds. *La princesa del Palacio de Hierro* (1974; *The Princess of the Iron Palace*) is a story of the collision between generations that sets tradition and the modern urban world against each other and is told through the experiences of a department store salesclerk who represents the urban middle class. *Compadre Lobo* (1977; Bubby Lobo) is a coming-of-age novel set in a working-class neighborhood that contrasts the world of art with the real world through the experiences of a young man who aspires to become a painter.

Fantasmas aztecas (1982; Aztec Ghosts) is a more historical work, set during the excavation of the Great Temple in the center of Mexico City, that juxtaposes different times and cultures. *Paseo en trapecio* (1985; Ride on a Trapeze) describes the changing feelings of its narrator on a journey from New Mexico to Mexico City. *Muchacho en llamas* (1988; Boy in Flames) is an account of a year in the life of a young writer at work on his first novel. *A la salud de la serpiente* (1991; To the Serpent's Health) takes the **Tlatelolco massacre** as its main event and tells it from a double perspective, that of a participant and that of a distant observer. *Retablo de inmoderaciones y heresiarcas* (1992; Altarpiece of Immoderation and Heretics) uses elements of the **neo-baroque** to reconsider colonial Mexico and tells the story of a young man accused of heresy. Sainz's more recent works include *A troche y moche* (2002; Helter-Skelter) and *El juego de las sensaciones elementales* (2006; The Play of Elementary Sensations).

SALARRUÉ (El Salvador, 1899–1975). Novelist and short story writer. Although born Salvador Arrué Salazar, he is generally known by the pseudonym Salarrué. His first novel, *El Cristo negro* (1926; The Black Christ), is set in colonial times and draws on the legend of the Black Christ of Esquipulas, a figure still venerated in Central America. Salarrué uses the icon to explore the nature of good and evil, a theme to which he frequently returned, often to invert conventional standards. Other novels followed, but his first is likely his best. In *El señor de la burbuja* (1927; Lord of the Bubble), the author presented his religious beliefs. *La sed de Sling Bader* (1971; Sling Baber's Thirst) is an adventure story for children, and *Catleya Luna* (1974; Catleya Luna) examines the occult.

His novels aside, Salarrué's reputation also owes much to his short stories, in which he pursued two quite different tendencies. In some of his collections, *O'Yarkandal* (1929; O'Yarkandal), *Retomando el Uluán* (1932; Returning to Uluán), and *Eso y más* (1940; That and More), he wrote about alternative worlds and the **fantastic** in a style that anticipates aspects of **magic realism**, although it likely derives from his lifelong belief in theosophy. In other collections of stories, notably *Cuentos de barro* (1933; Tales of Clay); *Cuentos de cipotes* (1945; Kids' Tales), which are notable for their representation of the language and situation of children; *Trasmallo* (1954; Net); and *La espada y otras narraciones* (1960; The Sword and Other Tales), he wrote about the lives of people from the region of El Salvador he knew best, in a style more associated with **criollismo** and **costumbrismo**.

SALAZAR BONDY, SEBASTIÁN (Peru, 1924–1965). Poet, dramatist, short story writer, and essayist. His short life and his interest in several genres are perhaps among the reasons that his work is not more widely celebrated, although his importance in Peru has been acknowledged by compatriots such as **Mario Vargas Llosa**. Salazar Bondy's poetry is generally simple and direct, an unruffled exploration of the people and places of his own world. His first books of poetry—*Rótulo de la esfinge* (1943; Sign of the Sphinx), *Voz desde la vigilia* (1944; A Voice from the Vigil), and *Cuaderno de la persona oscura* (1946; The Dark Person's Notebook)—are from the period before he left for **Argentina** in 1947. *Máscara del que duerme* (1949; Mask of the Sleeper), *Tres confesiones* (1950; Three Confessions), *Pantomimas* (1950; Pantomimes), and *Los ojos del pródigo* (1951; Eyes of the Prodigal) are from his time in Buenos Aires. Several more collections of poetry were published during the few years before his death: *Confidencia en voz alta* (1960; A Secret Spoken Aloud), *Vida de Ximena* (1960; Life of Ximena), *Conducta sentimental* (1963; Sentimental Behavior), *Cuadernillo de Oriente* (1963; Little Notebook from the Orient), and *El tacto de la araña* (1965; The Spider's Touch).

Although Salazar Bondy had already written at least one play for the **theater** before he left for Argentina, a political allegorical farce, *Amor, gran laberinto* (1947; Love the Great Labyrinth), his activities in relation to the stage were more intense after his return in 1952, and he was a significant figure in the rebirth of Peruvian theater at mid-century. His writing for the stage includes two historical dramas, *Rodil* (1952; Rodil), on the battle for independence in Peru, and *Flora Tristán* (1959; Flora Tristán), about the Peruvian writer of that name. He also wrote several realist plays—*No hay isla feliz* (1954; There's No Happy Island), *En el cielo no hay petróleo* (1956; There's No Petroleum in Heaven), *Un cierto tic tac* (1956; A Certain Ticking), and *Algo que quiere morir* (1957; Something Wanting to Die)—and comedies of manners: *Dos viejas van por la calle* (1959; Two Old Women Go Down the Street), *Ifigenia en el mercado* (1963; Iphigenia at the Market), and *El fabricante de deudas* (1964;

The Debt Maker). His last play, *El rabdomante* (1965; The Diviner), represented a return to political allegory, with which his career in the theater had begun.

The author's short stories were collected in *Náufragos y sobrevivientes* (1954; Shipwrecks and Survivors), on the monotony of life in the lower middle class; *Dios en el cafetín* (1954; God in the Café); and *Pobre gente de París* (1958; Poor People of Paris), about the bohemian life of Latin American students in Paris. Of all his writings in prose, however, the one that has had most impact is *Lima la horrible* (1964; Lima the Horrid), an essay that dissects the state of the Peruvian capital and criticizes its backwardness, the result of control by an oligarchy that perpetuates the conditions of colonial times.

SALGADO, PLÍNIO (Brazil, 1895–1975). Novelist and essayist. Salgado's first novels, *O Estrangeiro* (1931; The Stranger), *O Esperado* (1931; The Expected One), and *O Cavaleiro de Itararé* (1932; The Gentleman of Itararé), present sociopolitical situations and social types related to the urban life and history of São Paulo in the 1930s. Salgado was initially influenced by the **Week of Modern Art**, but eventually he rejected **avant-garde** tendencies and embraced nationalism instead. With **Cassiano Ricardo** and **Menotti del Picchia**, he signed the manifesto "O Curupira e o Carão" (1927; "The Curupira Being and the Big-Faced Monster"). He also collaborated on "Manifesto do Verdeamarelismo ou de Escola da Anta" (1929; "Green-Yellow Manifesto or of the School of the Tapir"). This nationalist tendency, named *Integralismo*, despite its enthusiasm for natural forces, its appeal to indigenous civilizations, and its purported democratic aims, degenerated into a racist, exclusionary ideology. Other works by Salgado include *Discurso às Estrelas* (1927: Address to the Stars), *Literatura e Política* (1927; Literature and Politics), *O Que é o Integralismo* (1933; Integralism), and *Psicologia da Revolução* (1933; Psychology of Revolution).

SALOMÃO, WALY (Brazil, 1944–2003). Poet and lyricist. The child of a Syrian father and a Brazilian mother, Salomão was an important figure in the 1960s and 1970s counterculture movement known as Tropicália. He wrote lyrics for a number of singers and musicians, including **Caetano Veloso**. His first book of poetry, *Me Segura que*

Eu Vou Dar um Troço (1972; Hold Me Because I'm Going to Have a Fit), written while the author was in prison, is seen as the first post-Tropicalist work. His later poetry found its roots in the **baroque**, **Brazilian modernism**, and the Dionysiac. He also published the following collections: *Algaravias: Câmara de Ecos* (1996; Gibberish: Echo Chamber), *Lábia* (1998; Labia), *Tarifa de Embarque* (2000; Boarding Fee), and *Mel do Melhor* (2001; Honey from the Best). *See also* MACHADO, DUDA.

SALVADOR, VICENTE DO (Brazil, 1564–1636?). Historian. Born in Brazil of Portuguese ancestry, Salvador studied in Coimbra and was an ordained priest. He held several important offices, before resigning them to join the order of Saint Francis. In Portugal, he began drafting his **chronicle** *História do Brasil* (1889; History of Brazil). Finished in 1627, but not published during do Salvador's lifetime, it is the first systematic attempt to record the history of Brazil, transcending a mere personal narrative to include many sources, including oral traditions.

SÁNCHEZ, FLORENCIO (Uruguay, 1875–1910). Dramatist. His successes occurred in **Argentina**, where, as the author of musical plays, *sainetes*, and social dramas, he figured importantly in the development of a national **theater**. A political shift from the conservatism of his roots in his native Uruguay to sympathy with the anarchist movements of the early 20th century in South America also led him to dramatize situations representing the conditions of the poor and marginalized. His first triumph was *Canillita* (1902; The Newspaper Boy), a starkly realistic drama about newspaper vendors in the Argentinean city of Rosario. In the context of a rapidly modernizing society, his theater often portrays conflicts between the traditional and the new. *M'hijo el dotor* (1903; My Son the Lawyer) is about a young man who resists the morality of his parents' generation; *La gringa* (1904; The Immigrant Girl) presents a story of the change in social attitudes brought by immigrants; and *Barranco abajo* (1905; Downhill) shows the tragedy of an aging farmer in the new Argentina. By 1903, Sánchez was already ill with the tuberculosis that would eventually cost him his life, but he continued to write at a steady pace, and the titles of some of his plays are sufficient to suggest the **realism** of his work: *La gente pobre* (1904; Poor People), *En familia* (1905; In the Family), *El conventillo* (1906; The Tenement), *El desalojo* (1906; The Eviction), and *Moneda falsa* (1907; Counterfeit Coin). See also ROSENCOF, MAURICIO.

SÁNCHEZ, LUIS ALBERTO (Peru, 1900–1994). Critic and essayist. He was a distinguished educator and politician, and the author of more than 100 books on a wide range of subjects, including the literature, history, society, and culture of Peru and Latin America. Some of his writings show the influence of **arielismo**. As a literary historian, his *La literatura peruana* (1928–1936; Peruvian Literature) and *La literatura americana* (1937; American Literature) are standard works that were published in several expanded editions. He wrote a number of fictionalized biographies, including *Haya de la Torre, o el político* (1934; Haya de la Torre, or The Politician), *Garcilaso Inca de la Vega, primer criollo* (1939; Garcilaso de la Vega, the First Creole), and *Valdivia el fundador* (1941; Valdivia the Founder). Among other essays are *Lima y don Ricardo Palma* (1927; Lima and Ricardo Palma), *América, novela sin novelistas* (1933; America, a Novel Without Novelists), and *Vida y pasión de la cultura en América* (1935; The Life and Passion of Culture in America).

SANTIAGO, SILVIANO (Brazil, 1936–). Critic and novelist. Born in Minas, Santiago studied first in Brazil, then in France, and taught at various universities in the United States. Based on readings of early **chronicles**, he developed a theory of Brazilian culture as highly metaphorical. He also viewed **Brazilian modernism** as rereading tradition in the classics. His books of literary criticism include *Uma Literatura nos Trópicos* (1978; A Literature in the Tropics), *Vale Quanto Pesa* (1982; Worth Its Weight), and *Nas Malhas da Letra* (1989; In the Mesh of the Letter). As a creative writer, Santiago won the **Jabuti Prize** for the novel *Em Liberdade* (1981; In Freedom), a fictional diary of **Graciliano Ramos**, in which the author attempted a portrait of Brazil in the 1930s. His *Stella Manhattan* (1985; *Stella Manhattan*) is a story of a sex and political scandal set in New York among the Brazilian exile community and centered around a young **gay** Brazilian.

SARLO, BEATRIZ (Argentina, 1942–). Critic and essayist. One of Argentina's most prominent public intellectuals, she has written on many aspects of literature, urban life, journalism and the mass media, and cinema and mass culture. In 1978 she founded, and still edits, *Punto de Vista*, one of Argentina's major cultural periodicals. Her books include *Una modernidad periférica: Buenos Aires 1920 y 1930* (1988; A Peripheral Modernity: Buenos Aires 1920 and 1930), *Jorge Luis Borges: A Writer on the Edge (1993), Escenas de la vida posmoderna: intelectuales, arte y videocultura en la Argentina* (1994; *Scenes from Postmodern Life*), *Instantáneas: medios, ciudad y costumbres en el fin de siglo* (1996; Snapshots: Media, City, and Customs at the End of the Century), and *La máquina cultural: maestras, traductores y vanguardistas* (1998; The Culture Machine: Teachers, Translators and Members of the Avant-Garde).

SARMIENTO, DOMINGO FAUSTINO (Argentina, 1811–1888). Essayist. He was president of Argentina from 1868 until 1874 and figures among the country's most important 19th-century writers, politicians, and educators. As a liberal affiliated with the Unitarian faction, much of his early life is defined by opposition to the dictator **Juan Manuel Rosas** and his party, for which he endured extended periods of exile. Although much of this time was spent in **Chile**, he also traveled widely in Latin America, Europe, and North America and developed considerable admiration for the United States. He wrote extensively throughout his life and was the author of travelogues, memoirs, biographies, political essays, and pamphlets. His literary reputation is founded above all on *Civilización y barbarie: vida de Juan Facundo Quiroga, y aspecto físico, costumbres, y hábitos de la República Argentina* (1845; *Facundo: Civilization and Barbarism*), written during one of his periods of exile in Chile. This book, usually referred to as *Facundo*, is a complex work. At its core is a biography of the historical figure Juan Facundo Quiroga, but the story of his life also serves as an indictment of the dictator Juan Manuel Rosas and government by *caudillos*, or chieftains. It is also an account of life and customs in Argentina and a commentary on the plight of the country, examined through the lens of the opposition between **civilization and barbarism**. *See also* ANDERSON IMBERT, ENRIQUE; DICTATOR NOVEL; ROJAS, RICARDO.

SCHMIDHUBER DE LA MORA, GUILLERMO (Mexico, 1943–). Dramatist. His plays have been widely translated and performed. Many are taken from history, such as *Por las tierras de Colón* (1987; In the Lands of Columbus) or, as was *Los herederos de Segismundo* (1980; *The Heirs of Segismund*), from art or literature. He often uses metatheatrical structures such as the play within the play. Other titles include *Los héroes inútiles* (1979; *The Useless Heroes*) and *Obituario* (1993; *Obituary*). Schmidhuber is also a widely published critic of Mexican **theater**.

SCHMIDT, AUGUSTO FREDERICO (Brazil, 1906–1965). Poet. Raised in Switzerland, he abandoned his formal studies for a career in business. He also wrote for the press and served as a diplomat. Schmidt reacted negatively to the **Week of Modern Art** and the renovations it proposed. He is seen as a representative of the second phase of **Brazilian modernism**, with a poetry that explores the themes of mortality and loss. For some time he was part of the group of Catholic poets gathered around the **journal** *Festa*. His first book, *Canto do Brasileiro Augusto Frederico Schmidt* (1928; Song of the Brazilian Augusto Frederico Schmidt), rejected the folkloric nationalism of some brands of modernism in Brazil; the second one, *Cantos do Liberto A.F.S.* (1929; Song of the Liberated A.F.S.), suggests moral perspectives. After *Navio Perdido* (1929; Lost Boat), *Pássaro Cego* (1930; Blind Bird) introduced the sonnet in free verse. *Desaparição da Amada* (1931; Disappearance of the Beloved), *Cantos Iniciais* (1931; Initial Songs), and *Canto da Noite* (1934; Song of the Night) depict gloomy atmospheres and a sense of loss. Later work, despite Schmidt's repetitious and exuberant style, constitutes a return to a poetry of introspection and concern for religion, especially *Mar Desconhecido* (1942; Unknown Sea), according to some his best work. His *Poesias Completas 1928–1955* (1956; Collected Poems 1928–1955) collected all previous works, including *Novos Poemas* (New Poems) and *Meditação Sobre o Mistério da Ressurreição* (Meditation on the Mystery of Resurrection).

SCLIAR, MOACYR (Brazil, 1937–). Novelist and short story writer. Scliar was born in the south of Brazil of **Jewish** ancestry. His parents had emigrated from Russia to Brazil and settled in a tight-knit community where storytelling was a habit. Scliar grew up listening to tales of exile and immigration, all of which influenced his writing, characterized by a lightly ironic, unadorned style and noted for its use of the **fantastic** and imaginary and his exploration of Jewish themes. He studied medicine and specialized in public health. His first collection of stories, *Histórias de Médico em Formação* (1962; Stories of a Physician in Training), was based on his experiences as a medical student, and medicine has also inspired other works in different ways. Scliar's next book, *O Carnaval dos Animais* (1968; The Carnival of Animals), was a success throughout the country. Since then, he has published more than 80 books. These include *A Guerra do Bom Fim* (1972; The War of Bom Fim), *Os Deuses de Raquel* (1975; Rachel's Gods), *A Balada do Falso Messias* (1976; The Ballad of the False Messiah), *Os Mistérios de Porto Alegre* (1976; The Mysteries of Porto Alegre), *O Ciclo das Águas* (1976; The Cycle of the Waters), *Histórias de Terra Trêmula* (1977; Stories of the Trembling Earth), *Mês de Cães Danados* (1977; Month of Damned Dogs), *O Anão no Televisor* (1979; The Midget in the TV Set), *A Massagista Japonesa* (1984; The Japanese Masseuse), *O Olho Enigmático* (1986; The Enigmatic Eye), *A Orelha de Van Gogh* (1989; Van Gogh's Ear), *Sonhos Tropicais* (1992; Tropical Dreams), *A Majestade do Xingu* (1997; The Majesty of the Xingu), *A Mulher Que Escreveu a Bíblia* (1999; The Woman Who Wrote the Bible), and *Os Leopardos de Kafka* (2000; Kafka's Leopards). *O Centauro no Jardim* (1980; *The Centaur in the Garden*) is considered one of the best 100 Jewish books ever written.

SCORZA, MANUEL (Peru, 1928–1983). Novelist. His fiction is written in the vein of **neo-indigenismo**, using the narrative techniques and strategies of the **boom** generation in a style often akin to that of the **magic realism** of **Gabriel García Márquez**. His major achievement is "La guerra silenciosa" (The Silent War), a five-volume cycle about peasant resistance in the Cerro del Pasco in the Andes, which he wrote while living in Paris from 1968 to 1978. It includes the novels *Redoble por Rancas* (1970; *Drums for Rancas*), *Historia de Garabombo el invisible* (1972; History of the Invisible Garabombo), *El Cantar de Agapito Robles* (1977; The Ballad of Agapito Robles), *El jinete insomne* (1978; The Sleepless Horseman), and *La tumba del relámpago* (1979; The Tomb of the Lightning). Scorza died in the **Madrid air disaster** and left incomplete a trilogy titled "Fuego y cenizas" (Fire and Ashes), of which he had only published the first volume, *La danza inmóvil* (1983; The Static Dance).

SEGURA, MANUEL ASCENSIO (Peru, 1805–1871). Dramatist. Although he fought with the royalists, he became a prominent figure in Peruvian society after independence and one of the country's first significant dramatists. He wrote popular comedies of manners (*see* COSTUMBRISMO) in the style of **neo-classicism.** His best-known works are *El sargento Canuta* (1839; Sargeant Canuta), a satire on militarism, and *Ña Catita* (1859; Dame Catita), about a meddling old woman characterized in the tradition of the medieval Spanish bawd. Other titles include *Las tres viudas* (1862; The Three Widows) and *El santo de Panchita* (1859; Panchita's Saint), which he wrote in collaboration with **Ricardo Palma.** *See also* THEATER.

SELVA, SALOMÓN DE LA (Nicaragua, 1893–1959). Poet. Although born in Nicaragua, he spent much of his life outside his native country. He spent his youth in the United States and fought on the Western Front with the British army during World War I. Indeed, his first published poems, *Tropical Town and Other Poems* (1918) and *Soldiers' Songs* (1919), were written in English and drew in part on his war experiences, as did his first volume in Spanish, *El soldado desconocido* (1922; The Unknown Soldier). Expelled from Nicaragua for his activities as a labor union organizer, he lived first in **Costa Rica** and eventually in **Mexico,** where he held a number of political and diplomatic positions. His poetry is innovative and places him between the **avant-garde** and **modernismo,** but he never entirely freed himself from the latter, even acquiring a certain neo-classical tone in some of his writing. His major collections of verse include *Oda a la tristeza y otros poemas* (1924; Ode to Sadness and Other Poems), *Las hijas de Erechteo* (1933; The Daughters of Erechteion), *Evocación de Horacio* (1948; Evocation of Horace), *Ilustre familia* (1954; Illustrious Family), *Tres poesías a la manera de Rubén Darío* (1951; Three Poems in the Style of Rubén Darío), *Canto a la independencia nacional de México* (1955; Song for the National Independence of Mexico), *Evocación de Píndaro* (1957; Evocation of Pindar), and *Alcolmixtle Nezahualcóyotl* (1958; Alcolmixtle Nezahualcóyotl).

SERRANO, MARCELA (Chile, 1951–). Novelist. Her writing has attracted attention since the publication of her first novel, *Nosotras que nos queremos tanto* (1991; We Women Who Love Each Other So Much). As a successful author whose novels tell stories about **women**, she has become one of Chile's most prominent female writers. Her recent titles include *Para que no me olvides* (1993; So You'll Not Forget Me), *Antigua vida mía* (1995; *Antigua and My Life Before*), *El albergue de las mujeres tristes* (1997; Shelter for Sad Women), *Nuestra señora de la soledad* (1999; Our Lady of Solitude), *Lo que está en mi corazón* (2001; What Is in My Heart), and *Hasta siempre, mujercitas* (2004; For Ever, Little Women).

SIERRA, JUSTO (Mexico, 1848–1912). Poet and essayist. He was the son of **Justo Sierra O'Reilly**. His literary work was not collected until quite late. *Cuentos románticos* (1896; Romantic Tales) included narratives he had published over the years in newspapers and magazines, but his poetry was not collected for publication until 1937, 25 years after his death. His work is representative of the tastes of his time, but he is read today mainly for his historical essays and contribution to the development of the concept of Mexican nationalism and identity in texts such as *Evolución política del pueblo mexicano* (1900–1902; *The Political Evolution of the Mexican People*). *See also* GUTIÉRREZ NÁJERA, MANUEL.

SIERRA O'REILLY, JUSTO (Mexico, 1814–1861). Novelist and historian. He was the author of a number of books on the history of the state of Yucatán. As a novelist, he is best remembered for his **historical novel** *La hija del judío* (1848–1850; The Jew's Daughter). Set in 17th-century Yucatán, it tells a story of plots and counterplots involving the Inquisition and the colonial government and is written in the style of Sir Walter Scott (1771–1832). It was one of Mexico's earliest historical novels, also known as **colonial novels**, and was widely read throughout Latin America. The author's other works of fiction include the epistolary novel *Un año en el hospital de San Lázaro* (1945; A Year in Saint Lazarus's Hospital) and a pirate novel, *El filibustero* (The Buccaneer). *See also* SIERRA, JUSTO.

SIGÜENZA Y GÓNGORA, CARLOS DE (Mexico, 1645–1700).
Novelist, poet, and essayist. A mathematician and astronomer by
profession, he published a number of scientific and poetic works.
His literary reputation rests mainly on a short novel, *Infortunios de
Alonso Ramírez* (1690; *The Misadventures of Alonso Ramírez*), in
which the protagonist tells a story of journeys and mishaps between
Asia and the Americas. Sigüenza y Góngora displays his knowledge
of the lands visited by his character, and his adaptation of the autobiographical form of the **picaresque novel** also serves to offer a
critique of colonial society.

SILVA, JOSÉ ASUNCIÓN (Colombia, 1865–1896). Poet. The metrical innovations and language of Silva's poetry make him an early
representative of **modernismo**, although he disdained the affiliation. His preoccupation with the past, death, the life beyond, and the
mysterious also make him a late representative of **romanticism**. His
output was small, and much of it, including his first book, *El libro
de versos* (1928; Book of Verses), was published posthumously after
his suicide. He also wrote a novel, *De sobremesa* (1928; Around the
Table), a work in the decadent manner of Oscar Wilde (1854–1900)
that reflects his dandyism and unhappy life. *See also* VALENCIA,
GUILLERMO.

SINÁN, ROGELIO (Panama, 1902–1994). Poet, novelist, short story
writer, and dramatist. He was born Bernardo Domínguez Alba, but
is known almost exclusively by his pseudonym and is the most
prominent figure of 20th-century Panamanian literature. With his
first book of poems, *Onda* (1929; Wave), written in free verse and
characterized by unconventional forms and images, he brought the
avant-garde to Panama. Writing primarily about his native country,
he confirmed his early promise as a poet in his next books of verse:
Salonia (1933; Salonia), *Incendio* (1944; Fire), and *Semana santa
en la niebla* (1949; Holy Week in the Fog), in which he relocates
a number of biblical events to the island of Taboga, where he was
born. Sinán's first novel, *Plenilunio* (1947; Full Moon), caused some
controversy when it appeared because of its focus on the dark side of
Panama City in the 1940s. *La isla mágica* (1979; The Magic Island),

his second novel, also set in Taboga, covers a hundred years of Panamanian history written in the style of **magic realism**.

The themes and styles of his poetry and novels are typical of his short stories, which were published in collections at intervals throughout his life and have been quite influential. They include *A la orilla de las estatuas maduras* (1932; On the Shore of the Mature Statues), *Todo un conflicto de sangre* (1946; Quite a Blood Conflict), *Dos aventuras en el Lejano Oriente* (1947; Two Adventures in the Far East), *La boina roja* (1961; The Red Beret), and *El candelabro de los malos ofidios y otros cuentos* (1982; The Candelabra of Evil Snakes and Other Tales). Sinán's **theater** is also highly imaginative and includes the musical fantasy *Chiquilinga, o la gloria de ser hormiga* (1927; Chiquilinga, or the Wonder of Being an Ant) and *La cucarachita mandinga* (1937; The Little Mandinga Cockroach), a musical farce for **children**.

SKÁRMETA, ANTONIO (Chile, 1940–). Novelist and short story writer. The characteristics of Skármeta's writing associate him with the **post-boom** generation. His early reputation was established by his short stories: *El entusiasmo* (1967; Enthusiasm); *Desnudo el en tejado* (1969; Naked on the Roof), which won a **Casa de las Américas** prize; *Tiro libre* (1973; Free Kick); *El ciclista de San Cristóbal* (1973; The Cyclist of San Cristóbal); and *Novios y solitarios* (1975; Couples and Lonely People). A selection from these volumes was published in 1991 in English translation as *Watch Where the Wolf Is Going*.

Skármeta began writing novels in Berlin after leaving Chile in the wake of the fall of the government of Salvador Allende in 1973. In Germany, he wrote radio plays, worked on films, and began what would become a continuing association with the German film director Peter Lilienthal. His first novel, *Soñé que la nieve ardía* (1975; I Dreamt the Snow Was Burning), is a narrative about the years of the Salvador Allende government (1970–1973) and the coup that brought it down, told through the misadventures of a provincial soccer player who goes to Santiago to make his fortune. *No pasó nada* (1980; Nothing Happened), concerned with the problems of exile, presents the experiences of an adolescent Chilean boy in Germany. *La insurrección* (1982; The Insurrection) is a history of the Nicaraguan Revolution against the dictator Anastasio Somoza (1967–1979). *Ardiente paciencia* (1985; *Burning Patience*) was a radio play and a film before it became a novel. It has become better known under the title *El cartero de Neruda* (Neruda's Postman) and was the source of a highly successful Italian film, *Il Postino* (1994; *The Postman*). *Match Ball* (1989; Match Ball), with echoes of *Lolita* (1955) by Vladimir Nabokov (1899–1977), is about a doctor who pursues an adolescent tennis star.

Since returning to Chile in 1989, Skármeta has continued to publish fiction and has become a TV celebrity as host of *El Show de los Libros* (The Book Show). *La composición* (1998; *The Composition*) is an illustrated story about a boy confronted with the consequences of living under a dictatorial regime who tries to protect his family by changing the facts about them in a school composition. *La boda del poeta* (1999; The Poet's Wedding) and *La chica del trombón* (2001; The Girl with the Trombone) are related novels that together tell a story of immigrants to Chile in the early part of the 20th century. *El baile de la victoria* (2003; *The Dancer and the Thief*) is about two former convicts whose schemes for success go astray when they encounter a dancer named Victoria.

SOCA, SUSANA (Uruguay, 1906–1959). Poet. She published little, most of her work being contained in two collections, *En un país de la memoria* (1959; In a Country from Memory) and *Noche cerrada* (1962; Dark Night), which surfaced after her death in a plane crash. She had many international connections, was editor of the Parisian literary **journal** *La Licorne*, and was eulogized by a number of writers, including **Jorge Luis Borges**, who published a sonnet to her memory in his *El hacedor*.

SOLARI SWAYNE, ENRIQUE (Peru, 1915–1995). Dramatist. Although his output was relatively small, it had considerable impact on the Peruvian **theater** of his day. He is best known for the drama *Collacocha* (1956; Collacocha), a play that examines the conflict between human endeavor and the forces of nature in an engineering project in the high Andes. His other plays include *Pompas fúnebres* (1954; Funerals), *La mazorca* (1966; Corncob), and *Ayax Telamonio* (1969; Ajax Telamon).

SOLOGUREN, JAVIER (Peru, 1921–2004). Poet. As a publisher-editor and as editor of several literary **journals**, he played an important role in the promotion of poetic composition and its dissemination in Peru. His own work as a poet amounts to about 20 books, among which are *El morador* (1944; Inhabitant), *Dédalo dormido* (1949; Daedalus Asleep), *Bajo los ojos del amor* (1950; Beneath the Eyes of Love), *Otoño, endechas* (1959; Autumn, Laments), *Estancias* (1960; Rooms), *Recinto* (1967; Enclosure), *Surcando el aire oscuro* (1970; Plowing the Dark Air), *Folios de el Enamorado y la Muerte* (1980; Folios from the Lover and Death), *Jaikus escritos en un amanecer de otoño* (1986; Haikus Written in an Autumn Dawn), *Catorce versos dicen* (1987; Fourteen Verses Speak), and *Hojas del herbolario* (1995; Leaves from the Herbarium). He collected his poetry periodically in different editions of a volume titled *Vida continua* (1966, 1971, 1981, 1989; Continuous Life). His work is a quest for lyrical expression, for which he drew on Spanish poets of the 16th and 17th centuries, **surrealism**, and Chinese and Japanese sources. If in his earlier collections he might be considered a poet in search of beauty, in his later work he became more of an **existentialist**.

SOLÓRZANO, CARLOS (Guatemala, 1922–). Dramatist. Although born in Guatemala, he has lived mainly in **Mexico**, where many of his plays have been written and performed. As in *Los fantoches* (1958; The Puppets), one of his earlier works, in which the actors are like marionettes, unnamed and subjected to an arbitrary universe, Solórzano brought the themes of fate and **existentialism** to the Mexican stage. A preoccupation with good and evil in relation to free will and a spirit of anticlericalism are features of his writing. Among his plays are *La muerte hizo la luz* (1951; Death Made the Light); *Doña Beatriz* (1954; Doña Beatriz), about the Spanish conquest of Guatemala; *El hechicero* (1955; The Enchanter), set in a medieval town; *Las manos de Dios* (1957; The Hands of God); *El crucificado* (1958; The Crucified One), combining the Bible with Mexican folklore; *El sueño del ángel* (1960; Dream of the Angel), about a cruel woman and her guardian angel; and *El zapato* (1966; The Shoe). In addition to his own plays, Solórzano has contributed an extensive body of criticism on **theater** in Spanish America and many editions of plays by other dramatists.

SOMERS, ARMONÍA (Uruguay, 1914–1994). Novelist and short story writer. Born Armonía Etchepare, her identity and the details of her life remained obscure for many years after her first literary publications. In effect, Somers's literary career began only with the publication of her first novel in 1950 and was second to a distinguished career in education, as a teacher, administrator, and writer, from which she retired in 1971 to concentrate on her fiction. This first work, a novella, *La mujer desnuda* (1950; The Naked Woman), the story of a **woman** searching for freedom as she reaches the age of 30, caused considerable controversy for its open treatment of sexuality. Erotic themes also figure in her first collection of short stories, *El derrumbamiento* (1953; Collapse), which present characters trapped in empty lives.

A second collection of stories, *La calle del viento norte* (1963; Street of the North Wind), appeared 10 years later, followed by a second novel, *De miedo en miedo* (1965; From One Fear to Another), a chronologically fragmented narrative told by a man at midlife engaged in an extramarital relationship and attempting to make sense of his meaningless life. *Un retrato para Dickens* (1969; A Portrait for Dickens), Somers's third novel, which draws on *Oliver Twist* (1837–1839) by Charles Dickens (1812–1870), is the story of an orphaned adolescent's life in a poor tenement.

Several other collections of short narratives appeared in the last dozen years of the author's life: *Tríptico darwiniano* (1982; Darwinian Tryptich), *Viaje al corazón del día* (1986; Journey to the Heart of the Day), *La rebelión de la flor* (1988; The Flower's Rebellion), and *El hacedor de girasoles* (1994; The Sunflower Maker). Her most important work of this period, however, was the novel *Sólo los elefantes encuentran mandrágora* (1983; Only Elephants Find Mandrake). It is a complex, many-layered work, at the center of which is a woman in hospital, with a respiratory and cardiac illness, who writes memoirs that embrace not only her own life and circumstances, but also family history and a wide range of other topics. Like other characters in Somers's fictional worlds, she too searches for meaning in her life.

SOMIGLIANA, CARLOS (Argentina, 1932–1987). Dramatist. Mainly a **realist** author, he collaborated with **Germán Rozenmacher**, **Roberto Cossa**, and **Ricardo Talesnik** on *El avión negro*

(1970; The Black Plane), and was a member of the group **Teatro Abierto**, for which he wrote the manifesto and to which he contributed two plays: *El nuevo mundo* (1981; The New World), which relocates the Marquis de Sade to America, and *El oficial primero* (1982; The First Officer), a condemnation of civil rights abuses. His other plays include *Amarillo* (1959; Yellow), set in Rome before the Christian era, on justice and liberty, themes that figured predominantly in his later work; *Amor de ciudad grande* (1959; Big City Love); *La bolsa de agua caliente* (1966; The Hot Water Bottle); and *El exalumno* (1978; The Alumnus). *See also* THEATER.

SORIANO, OSVALDO (Argentina, 1943–1997). Novelist. His writing is associated with the **post-boom**, gaining popularity both in Argentina and internationally following his return to South America in 1984 after living in exile in Paris since 1976. His novels show an interest in popular culture, especially sport, cinema, and music, and the influence of hard-boiled **crime fiction** by North American writers such as Raymond Chandler (1888–1959). However, the violence characteristic of the genre, used to critique society and political authoritarianism, is tempered by exaggeration, slapstick humor, and absurdity. In his first novel, *Triste, solitario y final* (1973; Sad, Lonely and Final), Soriano introduced himself and Chandler's Philip Marlowe on a quest to discover why the celebrated comedian Stan Laurel had lost the favor of the Hollywood studios. His next two novels, *No habrá más penas ni olvido* (1979; A Funny Dirty Little War) and *Cuarteles de invierno* (1981; Winter Quarters), both written while he was living in France, are set in a claustrophobic small town in Argentina called Colonia Vela and portray the troubled times of 1970s Argentina. Both were the basis for successful films.

A sus plantas rendido un león (1988; A Lion Prostrate at Your Feet), with a title taken from a line of the Argentinean national anthem, is a satire of the Malvinas/Falklands War (1982) between Argentina and Great Britain. *Una sombra ya pronto serás* (1990; Shadows), with a title taken this time from a popular tango, was also the source of a film. It narrates a man's wanderings through the pampas and his encounters with others also traveling along life's road, a group of failed individuals who reflect their country. His last two novels were *La hora sin sombra* (1996; Time Without Shadow) and *El ojo de la patria* (1992; Eye of the Fatherland), a humorous but bitter analysis of society through the representation of cultural and historical stereotypes.

Soriano also published short stories. A collection of stories about soccer, *Memorias del Míster Peregrino Fernández y otros relatos de fútbol* (1998; Memoirs of Mr. Peregrino Fernández and Other Football Stories), was published posthumously, and some of Soriano's newspaper writings have been collected in *Artistas, locos y criminales* (1983; Artists, Madmen and Criminals) and *Cuentos de los años felices* (1987; Tales from the Happy Years).

SOSA, ROBERTO (Honduras, 1930–). Poet. Since publishing *Caligramas* (1959; Calligrams), his first book of poems, Sosa has become the country's most significant contemporary poet and one of the few whose work has become known outside it. He writes about everyday life, Honduras, social justice, and oppression, concerns that remain even in his more recent verse, He has published eight collections, including *Muros* (1966; Walls); *Un mundo para todos dividido* (1971; A World Divided for All); which received a **Casa de las Américas** prize; *Los pobres* (1979; The Difficult Days); *Secreto militar* (1985; Military Secret); and *Máscara suelta* (1994; The Common Grief: Poems). These have been collected in *Poesía total: 1959–2004* (2006; Complete Poetry), and a selection of his work appeared in English translation in *The Return of the River: The Selected Poems of Roberto Sosa* (2002).

SOUSA, GABRIEL SOARES DE (Brazil, 1540?–1591). Chronicler. Born in Portugal, Soares de Sousa was a wealthy sugar plantation owner and public official in Bahia. In his **chronicle** *Tratado Descritivo do Brasil em 1587* (1851; Descriptive Treatise of Brazil in 1587), he recorded his personal observations of nature, people (including the white, black, and indigenous populations), and the consequences of Portuguese colonization. It is considered one of the most important documents regarding life in Brazil in this period. Soares de Sousa died after an unsuccessful expedition to establish mines along the São Francisco River.

SOUSA, JOÃO DA CRUZ E (Brazil, 1861–1898). Poet. Son of a slave and a freed slave, Cruz e Sousa was raised by his parents' former owners and received a first-rate education. He began to write for the press in his native state of Santa Catarina but soon left to tour the country with a theater company. His early poetry exhibits various influences, from late **romanticism** to **parnassianism**. During this period, he wrote in collaboration with Virgílio Várzea the collection *Tropos e Fantasias* (1885; Tropes and Fantasies), a mix of sentimental and antislavery poetry. A black man in a state with a mostly white population, Cruz e Sousa suffered personally from racial discrimination. In 1890, he moved to Rio de Janeiro, where he joined in the formation of Brazil's first symbolist group. In Rio he also wrote for the press and eventually secured a modest clerical position with the Brazilian Railroads. He also married a young black woman, with whom he had four children, but who eventually proved psychologically unstable.

Cruz e Sousa's first collections of poetry in the style of **symbolism**, *Broquéis* (1893; Shields) and *Missal* (1893; Missal), rhapsodic prose poems and essays, were not very well received. These were the last books he published during his lifetime. Later posthumously published volumes include *Evocações* (1898; Evocations); the confessional volume *Faróis* (1900; Beacons); and *Últimos Sonetos* (1905; Last Sonnets), a volume in which he explores his poetic ascent to the realm of Essences. *Cruz e Sousa: Obra Completa* (Cruz e Sousa: Complete Works), edited by José Cândido de Andrade Muricy, appeared only in 1961.

Cruz e Sousa is considered one of the greatest symbolist poets of Brazil. His early work displayed a concern with social issues related to the abolition of slavery. Through parnassian aesthetics, he developed and refined his poetic craft. Symbolism provided him with some of his long-lasting themes, such as an aspiration toward truth and a search for ideal beauty. Cruz e Sousa's reputation is also due to his original exploration of language, including the use of archaic and rare words, a novel syntax, and a new and powerful hypnotic musicality. After tragic battles against poverty, lack of recognition, and family mental illness, Cruz e Sousa died at a relatively young age from tuberculosis. *See also* GUIMARAENS, ALPHONSUS DE; LEMINSKI, PAULO.

SOUSÂNDRADE (SOUSA ANDRADE), JOAQUIM DE (1833–1902). Poet. Born in the Northeastern state of Maranhão, Sousândrade grew up there, but traveled widely, especially in Europe, where he was educated, obtaining degrees in both letters and engineering in Paris. Back in Brazil, he married and began publishing his first poetry, *Harpas Selvagens* (1857; Wild Harps), in the style of a belated or second generation **romanticism**. After separating from his wife, Sousândrade traveled again, this time through South America, and eventually to New York. In order to send his daughter to a Catholic school, he settled in Manhattanville in 1871, seven miles from New York City, and collaborated with "O Novo Mundo," a Portuguese-language newspaper.

During these years, he wrote *Guesa Errante: Poema Americano* (The Wandering Guesa: American Poem), a narrative/dramatic/**epic poem** in 12 cantos, and an epilogue, which he published in several parts in 1866, 1876, 1877, and 1884. In the introduction to one of the cantos he wrote: "I have already heard twice that 'O Guesa errante' would only be read fifty years later; I was sad—the disillusion of one who writes fifty years earlier." The epic portrays the Guesa, a character from Colombian mythology, making a heroic journey along the continent that culminates in the New York Stock Exchange. "The Wall Street Inferno," as this episode in Canto X of *Guesa* is entitled, is a critique of capitalism through a parodic portrayal of New York in the Gilded Age. Sousândrade included news stories from newspapers of his time in his poem as well as events and characters from the past and present in an anarchic, polyglot montage.

Sousândrade's work never received the attention of his contemporaries, and he died impoverished, selling, or as he reported, "eating" the stones of his estate in order to survive. He was later republished by the **concrete** poets **Augusto de Campos** and **Haroldo de Campos**, who argued that Sousândrade is a great unacknowledged precursor of modern poetry in his neologisms, innovative syntax, and other verbal inventions. His literary ambitions may be seen in how he combined his two last names into one unique-sounding word having the same number of letters as Shakespeare's last name. Other editions and works by Sousândrade include *Impressos* (2 vols., 1868–1869; Writings), *Obras Poéticas* (1874; Poetic Works), *Novo Eden* (1893; New Eden), and *Inéditos* (1970; Unpublished Papers).

SPOTA, LUIS (Mexico, 1925–1985). Novelist. He was a popular writer, the author of more than 20 novels and well known for his novels on political themes dealing with contemporary topics and employing a direct, journalistic style, a reflection of his profession, perhaps. Among his most widely read works are *Murieron a mitad de río* (1948; They Died Mid-Stream), about migrants entering the United States illegally; *Las grandes aguas* (1954; The Great Waters), on the construction of a dam; *Casi el paraíso* (1956; Almost Paradise), the adventures of an Italian impostor; *Las horas violentas* (1959; The Violent Hours), concerned with labor unions and strikes; *La sangre enemiga* (1959; Enemy Blood), a severe critique of the Mexican ruling class; *La carcajada del gato* (1964; The Cat's Laughter), the true-life story of a man who imprisoned his children; *La plaza* (1971; The Plaza), on the 1968 student movement that culminated in the **Tlatelolco massacre**; *Palabras mayores* (1975; Great Words), about a president's politicking to ensure the selection of his successor; and *El primer día* (1977; The First Day), an ex-president's reaction to his loss of power at the end of his term in office. Spota was also the author of many screenplays and was involved in the production of several movies.

STEINER, ROLANDO (Nicaragua, 1936–). Dramatist. He was one of the main writers who contributed to the growth in Nicaraguan **theater** in the period between the 1950s and 1970s. Everyday life and history are among his predominant themes and are often related to biblical or classical motifs. His best-known plays are *Judit* (1957; Judith), on the disintegration of a middle-class marriage, and *La noche de Wiwilí*, about the death of the Nicaraguan revolutionary Augusto César Sandino (1895–1934). Other titles include *Antígona en el infierno* (1958; Antigone in Hell), *La pasión de Helena* (1963; Helena's Passion), *El tercer día* (1965; The Third Day), *La mujer deshabitada* (1970; The Unoccupied Woman), and *La agonía del poeta* (1977; Death of the Poet), on the death of **Rubén Darío**.

STORNI, ALFONSINA (Argentina, 1892–1938). Poet. Her simple, direct language places her in the post-**modernismo** generation of writers. She is also considered one of Latin America's first important feminist writers for her criticism of patriarchy and the social subordination of **women**. Such themes are especially evident in her first collections of poems, although her earliest work inclines to the sentimental and melodramatic: *La inquietud del rosal* (1916; The Restless Rose Garden), *El dulce daño* (1918; Sweet Harm), *Irremediablemente* (1919; Without Remedy), and *Languidez* (1920; Languor). The subjects addressed in later collections, *Ocre* (1925; Ocher) and *Mundo de siete pozos* (1934; World of Seven Wells), are broader and also show greater formal experimentation, a consequence of the impact of **ultraísmo** and her contact with the Spanish literary scene of the 1930s. Her last poems, *Mascarilla y trébol* (1938; Mask and Clover), a collection of 52 unrhymed sonnets on the cycle of disintegration, regeneration, and salvation, sustain this direction, but also anticipate her suicide, prompted by illness and occurring the year after her friend, the writer **Horacio Quiroga**, took his own life.

Although best known as a poet, Storni also wrote for the **theater**. She had some early acting experiences, and through her association with the Labardén Childrens Theater, begun in 1921, she contributed to **children's literature** by writing pieces for young performers. She also wrote several pieces for adults: *El amo del mundo* (1927; Master of the World), which was staged unsuccesfully, and *La técnica de Míster Dougall* (Mister Dougal's Technique), which she completed, but never saw staged, as well as *Dos farsas pirotécnicas* (1932; Two Pyrotechnical Farces), written after the first of her two trips to Europe. *See also* VAZ FERREIRA, MARÍA EUGENIA.

SUASSUNA, ARIANO VILAR (Brazil, 1927–). Novelist and dramatist. Suassuna was born in Paraíba, Northeastern Brazil, where his father was governor. When he was three, his father was assassinated, and the family had to move around, fleeing from further potential threats. As a result, Suassuna grew up in the backlands, where he came into contact with itinerant musicians, poets, and storytellers, whose forms of popular expression shaped his literary themes and style. In 1946, while still a law student, he cofounded the Teatro do Estudante de Pernambuco (TEP), a **theater** group inspired by the experimental and didactic traveling theater group "La Barraca," created in Spain by Federico García Lorca (1898–1936). The project also included a popular press that published some of the plays performed.

In 1948, Suassuna staged his play *Cantam as Harpas de Sião ou O Desertor de Princesa* (1948; The Harps of Sion Are Singing or the Deserter from Princesa) at the TEP and also received a theater award for *Uma Mulher Vestida de Sol* (1964; A Woman Dressed in Sun). His next two plays were *Auto de João da Cruz* (1950; Auto of John of the Cross) and *Auto da Compadecida* (1955; *The Rogue's Trial*), perhaps his most successful play and the most acclaimed Brazilian play worldwide. This comedy, harking back to the Iberian tradition of the ***auto***, recounts the story of two tricksters from the backland who, after their death, must be judged by Jesus and the Virgin Mary before being admitted to heaven.

Besides the Catholic theater tradition, including the Spanish author Calderón de la Barca (1600–1681) and medieval religious drama, Suassuna's theater blends elements from Latin comedies, the Italian *Commedia dell'Arte*, and the popular Northeastern ballads known as "literatura de cordel." In his plays, saints and religious figures like Jesus and the Virgin intermingle with real people, real life with imagination, and tradition with contemporary events to create a uniquely Brazilian theatrical form. Suassuna is a staunch defender of the culture of Northeastern Brazil, and around it he structured a cultural trend known as "Movimento Armorial," whose name alludes to coats of arms and heraldry. It gathers artists from various media to preserve and celebrate the popular culture of that region. As inspiration, Northeastern cordel ballads, in particular, embody the medieval tradition of the epic and the carnivalesque. Other notable plays by Suassuna include *O Casamento Suspeitoso* (1961; The Suspicious Marriage), *O Santo e a Porca* (1964; The Holyman and the Piggy Bank), and *A Pena e a Lei* (1971; The Sentence and the Law).

In 1971, Suassuna published his first novel, *Romance d'A Pedra do Reino e o Príncipe do Sangue do Vai-e-Volta* (1971; Ballad of the Kingdom's Stone and the Prince of the Come-and-Go Blood), and a sequel, *História d'O Rei Degolado nas Caatingas do Sertão/Ao Sol da Onça Caetana* (1977; Story of the King Who Was Beheaded in the Hills of the Backlands/Under the Sun of Caetana the Jaguar). In these works, intended as parts of a trilogy, Suassuna attempts again to combine the Iberian tradition of the epic, the novel of chivalry, and the **picaresque novel**, setting the action in Northeast Brazil. Suassuna's works have been translated into many languages, he has been the recipient of numerous prizes, and he is considered one of Brazil's foremost dramatists.

SUBERCASEAUX, BENJAMÍN (Chile, 1902–1973). Novelist. He was also a popular historian. Among his best-known works are a collection of short stories, *Y al oeste limita con el mar* (1937; And to the West Is the Sea); *Chile, una loca geografía* (1940; Chile, a Crazy Geography); and his **historical novel**, *Jemmy Button* (1951; *Jemmy Button*), about events in Tierra del Fuego in the context of Charles Darwin's voyage to South America on the British navy ship HMS *Beagle*. The same story is the subject of a novel by **Sylvia Iparraguirre**.

SURREALISM. Originating in France under the leadership of André Breton (1896–1966), the emergence of surrealism coincided with the formation of modern psychology and the exploration of the libido, dreams, and the unconscious. It spread widely and was the core of the **avant-garde**. Among its characteristics were the unusual juxtaposition of images, evocation of the marvelous, exploration of the psyche, and the representation of the world and experience in highly subjective images and language that often made the literary work seem opaque. Surrealism was manifested in various ways in Latin America and did not necessarily conform to how it was initially envisaged in France. Its greatest impact was in poetry in the work of writers such as **Mário Faustino, Pedro Kilkerry, Jorge de Lima, João Cabral de Melo Neto**, and **Murilo Mendes (Brazil); Jaime Saénz (Bolivia); César Moro (Peru); Hérib Campos Cervera (Paraguay);** and **Francisco Madariaga, Enrique Molina, Aldo Pelligrini**, and **Alejandra Pizarnik (Argentina)**. But its influence was also felt by some notable prose writers, including **Miguel Ángel Asturias (Guatemala)**, **Aníbal Machado** (Brazil), **Julio Cortázar (Argentina)**, and **María Luisa Bombal (Chile)**. *See also* CARDOZA Y ARAGÓN, LUIS; GERBASI, VICENTE; MOLINARI, RICARDO E.; ORTIZ DE MONTELLANO, BERNARDO; PALOMARES, RAMÓN; RAMOS SUCRE, JOSÉ ANTONIO; ROJAS, GONZALO; ROKHA, PABLO DE; TREJO, OSVALDO; ULTRAÍSMO; VARELA, BLANCA; WESTPHALEN, EMILIO ADOLFO; WOMEN.

SYMBOLISM. In contrast to **realism** and **naturalism**, which offered a harsh and often uncompromising view of reality, symbolism sought a more idealistic view of the world through recourse to the spiritual, the imagination, and dreams. Symbolism originated in France in 1866 with a manifesto by Jean Moréas (1856–1910) and shared some of the characteristics of **parnassianism**, which it followed, including the concept of art for art's sake. The movement had an important influence in Spanish America on **Rubén Darío** (Nicaragua) and the development of **modernismo** and on writers such as **Amado Nervo** (Mexico), **Guillermo Valencia (Colombia)**, **José María Egurén (Peru)**, and **Ricardo Jaimes Freyre** (Bolivia).

In **Brazil**, although some poetry related to French decadentism (a name also given to symbolism) appeared between 1883 and 1887, the publication of **João Cruz e Sousa**'s *Broquéis* (1893; Shields) is considered the beginning of the movement. Symbolism held sway in Brazil until the 1922 **Week of Modern Art**, and writers often cultivated parnassianism alongside it. Although there were some attempts at writing symbolist fiction, symbolism was chiefly a poetic movement. Besides Cruz e Sousa, other famous symbolists in Brazil are **Augusto dos Anjos**, **Alphonsus de Guimaraens**, and **Pedro Kilkerry**. *See also* ALMEIDA, GUILHERME DE; BANDEIRA, MANUEL; COUTO, RUI RIBEIRO; ESTRIDENTISMO; FAUSTINO, MÁRIO; LISBOA, HENRIQUETA; MACHADO, GILKA; MEIRELES, CECÍLIA; MORAES, VINÍCIUS DE; OLIVEIRA, ALBERTO DE; PEIXOTO, AFRÂNIO; POMPÉIA, RAUL D'ÁVILA; REALISM; RICARDO LEITE, CASSIANO; ROMANTICISM; TABLADA, JOSÉ JUAN; WOMEN.

SZICHMAN, MARIO (Argentina, 1945–). Novelist. Szichman is known for his contributions to **Jewish writing** in Argentina, such as the novel *A las 20:25 la señora entró a la inmortalidad* (1981; *At 8:25 Evita Became Immortal*), a title that refers to the moment when **Eva Duarte de Perón** died on 26 July 1952, and the short stories in *Los judíos del mar dulce* (1971; Jews of the Fresh Water Sea).

– T –

TABLADA, JOSÉ JUAN (Mexico, 1871–1945). Poet. His early poetic development took place in the context of the Belle Epoque, late 19th-century decadentism, and the rise of **modernismo.** The influence of French **symbolism** is evident in *El florilegio* (1899; Anthology), which also reveals his iconoclastic frame of mind and inclination to erotic exoticism, although these characteristics are present throughout his work. A second edition of *Florilegio* in 1904 also showed Tablada's growing interest in the Orient and some of the first results of a journey he is said to have made to Japan in 1900. In *Al sol y bajo la luna* (1918; In the Sun and Beneath the Moon), he consolidated his personal style and, in *Un día. . . poemas sintéticos* (1919; One Day . . . Synthetic Poems), he introduced the Japanese *haiku* to Hispanic verse. His capacity for innovation was further demonstrated in *Li-Po y otros poemas* (1920; Li-Po and Other Poems), the author's most celebrated collection. In this book, which confirms Tablada's transition from modernismo to the **avant-garde**, he included several *calligrammes*, or picture poems, verses shaped to resemble the objects described, in the style of the French poet Guillaume Apollinaire (1880–1918).

Later collections of poems include *El jarro de flores: disociaciones líricas* (1922; Vase of Flowers: Lyric Dissociations) and *La feria: poemas mexicanos* (1928; The Fair: Mexican Poems). Tablada also wrote a number of works in prose. Notable among them are his writings on painting, including *Hiroshigué: el pintor de la nieve y de la lluvia, de la noche y de la luna* (1914; Hiroshigué: Painter of the Snow and the Rain, the Night and the Moon) and *Historia del arte en México* (1927; History of Art in Mexico), an indication of a lifelong interest in art that also informed his poetry. His memoirs appeared in *La feria de la vida* (1937; Life's a Fair), the first of two projected volumes.

TABOADA TERÁN, NÉSTOR (Bolivia, 1929–). Novelist and short story writer. A Marxist whose political beliefs led to a period of exile in **Argentina** (1972–1977) and are reflected in several books about political movements in Latin America: *Cuba, paloma de vuelo* *popular* (1964; Cuba: A Dove of a Popular Flight); *Chile, con el corazón a la izquierda* (1971; Chile With Its Heart on the Left); *La revolución degollada* (1974; The Slaughtered Revolution); and *Requerimiento al rey de España* (1992; Petition to the King of Spain), a review of Spain's colonial enterprise written in the context of a visit by Pope John Paul II to the Andes. By contrast, Taboada's fiction is generally more focused on Bolivia. However, he writes from an imaginative perspective so that the **historical novel** is for him far from a conventional retelling of the past.

His first novel, *El precio de estaño* (1960; The Price of Tin), is a revisionary biography of a Bolivian tin baron. *El signo escalonada* (1975; The Sign of the Step), set in the 1930s, is concerned with the causes of the Chaco War (1932–1935) between Bolivia and **Paraguay**. The sign mentioned in the title refers both to an Indian motif and to the swastika. *Manchay Puytu, al amor que quiso ocultar Dios* (1977; Manchay Puytu, the Love God Sought to Hide), set in colonial times in the silver mining city of Potosí, deals with the mixing of cultures as a result of the conquest. Among its sources is a story that was also told by **Ricardo Palma**.

As a mestizo by birth, and knowing both Quechua and Aymara, as well as Spanish, Taboada had direct access to popular folktales. In *Angelina Yupanki, marquesa de la conquista* (1992; Angelina Yupanki, Marchioness of the Conquest), he also explored the mixing of cultures, and in *Ollantay, la guerra de los dioses* (1994; Ollantay, War of the Gods), he reworked the Quechua drama *Ollantay*, in which he introduced a relationship between the Bolivian president Mariano Melgarejo (1864–1871) and the English queen Victoria (1837–1901). Taboada's collections of short stories include *Claroscuro* (1948; Chiaroscuro), *Germen* (1950; Seed), *Mientras se oficia el escarnio* (1968; While Ridicule Rules), *Indios en rebelión* (1968; Indians in Revolt), and *Sweet and Sexy* (1977).

TAIBO II, PACO IGNACIO (Mexico, 1949–). Novelist. Although he has more than 50 books to his credit, including works of fiction, history, and social commentary, he is best known as the author of **crime fiction**. Beginning with *Días de combate* (1974; Days of Combat), he has written a lengthy series featuring the hard-boiled Mexico City detective Héctor Belascoaran, but also has novels featuring the more cerebral kind of detective and others with a female agent as their principal character.

TALESNIK, RICARDO (Argentina, 1935–). Dramatist. He arrived on the **theater** scene in Argentina with *La fiaca* (1967; Laziness), a work in the tradition of the ***grotesco criollo*** that displays the human condition through an alienated individual afflicted with indolence. Talesnik's plays are generally concerned with social or political issues or personal relationships. He collaborated with **Roberto Cossa**, **Germán Rozenmacher**, and **Carlos Somigliana** on *El avión negro* (1970; The Black Plane). His plays include *Cien veces no debo* (1970; "I Must Not . . ." One Hundred Times), *Solita y sola* (1972; Lonely and Alone), *Los japoneses no esperan* (1973; The Japanese Don't Wait), *Cómo ser una buena madre* (1977; How to Be a Good Mother), *Casi un hombre* (1979; Almost a Man), and *Yo la escribo y yo la vendo* (1979; I Write It and I Sell It).

TAMAYO, FRANZ (Bolivia, 1879–1956). Poet. He had a very successful political career that culminated in election to the presidency of Bolivia in 1935, although a coup prevented him from taking office. His poetry is highly regarded as a late aestheticized version of **modernismo**, reflecting the author's linguistic abilities and his readings in theosophy and the occult. The Hellenic orientation of his verse is clearly reflected in the titles of some of his books: *La Prometheida o las Oceánidas, tragedia lírica* (1917; The Prometheiad or the Oceanides: A Lyric Tragedy); *Nuevo Rubayat* (1927; New Rubaiyat); *Scherzos* (1932; Scherzos); *Scopas* (1939; Scopas), named for the Greek sculptor and architect; and *Epigramas griegos* (1945; Greek Epigrams). In his essay *Creación de la pedagogía nacional* (1910; Creation of the National Pedagogy), he adopted a position contrary to that of the **positivism** of his countryman **Alcides Arguedas** and argued that all Bolivia's ills, especially those afflicting its native population, were the fault of the European colonizers and their descendants.

TAUNAY, ALFREDO D'ESCRAGNOLLE, VISCONDE DE (Brazil, 1843–1899). Novelist. Born into an aristocratic family of French origin, Taunay participated in Brazil's campaign against **Paraguay**

as a military engineer and wrote a volume of war memoirs in French, *La Retraite de Laguna* (1869; The Retreat from Laguna). Although he was a prolific author in many genres and subjects, he is best remembered for his novel *Inocência* (1889; Inocência), a tragic love story set in the Northeastern backlands and belonging to the style of **regionalism**. Written at the end of the romantic period, it is also seen as a work of transition into **naturalism**.

TEATRO ABIERTO. Founded in Buenos Aires in 1981 while **Argentina** was still under a military regime, Teatro Abierto, or Open Theater, was an attempt both to revive **theater** and to confront government abuse of power through metaphorical or coded performances that addressed the issues indirectly. By giving new life to the theater and opening the way for a new generation of dramatists, it was an important achievement by an already established group of writers that included **Roberto Cossa**, **Osvaldo Dragún**, **Griselda Gambaro**, **Carlos Gorostiza**, and **Carlos Somigliana**. The group was dissolved in 1986, by which time the country had returned to democracy and its purpose had been fulfilled.

TEITELBOIM, VOLODIA (Chile, 1913–2008). Novelist, critic, and biographer. He served as leader of the Chilean Communist Party and was elected deputy and senator during the Unidad Popular government of Salvador Allende (1970–1973). He was not in Chile when the government was ousted and remained in exile throughout much of the regime of Augusto Pinochet (1974–1990), returning clandestinely in 1987, an experience about which he wrote in *En el páis prohibido: sin el permiso de Pinochet* (Inside the Forbidden Country: Without Pinochet's Permission). While living in exile he founded the **journal** *Araucaria de Chile*, which became an important link for Chilean exiles, and broadcast the radio program *Eschucha, Chile* (Listen, Chile) twice weekly from Moscow, where he was living. Teitelboim wrote two novels set in northern Chile that extend literary **regionalism** to that part of the country: *Los hijos de salitre* (1952; Children of Saltpeter) and *La semilla en la arena* (1957; Seed in the Sand). The first of these, a biographical narrative about a socialist leader, includes the massacre of nitrate workers and their families in 1906 at Santa María de Iquique, an event also commemorated in a widely performed popular cantata. As a literary critic, Teitelboim's writings include biographies of **Jorge Luis Borges, Vicente Huidobro, Gabriela Mistral,** and **Pablo Neruda.**

TELLES, LYGIA FAGUNDES (Brazil, 1923–). Novelist and short story writer. Born in São Paulo, Fagundes Telles (also spelled Lígia Fagundes Teles) published her first book of short stories, *Porão e Sobrado* (1938; Basement and Mansion), at an early age, followed by two more collections, *Praia Viva* (1944; Living Beach) and *O Cacto Vermelho* (1949; The Red Cactus). She enrolled in the law faculty and began to frequent literary circles, where she met some of the most important figures of **Brazilian modernism,** such as **Mário de Andrade** and **Oswald de Andrade,** as well as the film critic Paulo Emílio Sales Gomes (1916–1977), with whom she would later have a relationship. Fagundes Telles participated in protests against the Estado Novo (1937–1945). Her first novel was *Ciranda de Pedra* (1954; *Stone Dance Song*), a drama critical of bourgeois conventions centered on **women,** which was later adapted for television. Two more short story books, *Histórias do Desencontro* (1958; Stories of Missed Encounters) and *O Jardim Selvagem* (1965; The Wild Garden), explore themes of tragedy and human frustration. *As Meninas* (1973; *The Girl in the Photograph*), a story of friendship among three young women, told from varying perspectives and set against the backdrop of the military dictatorship, won a number of prizes, as did two more collections of stories: *Antes do Baile Verde* (1970; Before the Green Ball) and *Seminário dos Ratos* (1977; Seminary of the Rats). Her collection *Invenção e Memória* (2000; Invention and Memory) won the **Jabuti Prize.** Her most recent works include a volume of previously uncollected stories, *A Estrutura da Bola de Sabão* (1991; The Structure of the Soap Ball), and a novel, *As Horas Nuas* (1989; The Naked Hours), which uses a fragmented narrative and paradoxical language to delve into the contradictions of the human condition. *See also* HILST, HILDA.

TESTIMONIO. This term, meaning "testimony," is used to refer to documentary narratives, conventionally told in autobiographical form by a witness to or participant in the events narrated. Primarily a 20th-century phenomenon, it has come to refer to all kinds of testimonial narratives, although the term originally alluded to a certain type of documentary text resulting from a life story told by a subaltern subject but written by a journalist, literary author, or social scientist. The (auto)biography of **Rigoberta Menchú (Guatemala)** and the testimonios of **Elena Poniatowska (Mexico)** are paradigmatic examples of this kind of text, created from the interaction of the oral and the written. For the different kinds of testimonio, see **Claribel Alegría, Manlio Argueta,** and **Roque Dalton (El Salvador); Omar Cabezas (Nicaragua); Germán Castro Caycedo (Colombia); Domitila Barrios de Chungara (Bolivia);** and **Jacobo Timerman** and **Rodolfo Walsh** (Argentina).

THEATER. Although theater differs from poetry and narrative in the matter of performance, the history and social contexts of all genres in Latin America have a great deal in common. During the colonial period and a good part of the 19th century, theater in Latin America, like poetry and narrative, was very much an extension of its European counterpart, adopting the same trends already popularized on the other side of the Atlantic and often representing the same themes. It was only as a greater sense of **realism** took root in the second half of the 19th century and the early decades of the 20th, just as it was occurring in other genres, that the particular circumstances of Latin American societies were expressed more fully on the stage. This development accelerated with the arrival from Europe of **avant-garde** and post-avant-garde theater which, though prolonging the connection to external influences, also created an environment for greater innovation and experiment.

At the same time, although many of Latin America's dramatists wrote primarily for the theater and made their name through their connection with the stage, there are many writers who are known principally as authors of poetry or fiction, but who also wrote theater, sometimes, but not always, with considerable impact. This group includes such well-known figures as **Rosario Castellanos, Carlos Fuentes,** and **Elena Garro** in **Mexico; Miguel Ángel Asturias** in **Guatemala; Hilda Hilst** in **Brazil; Manuel Puig** in **Argentina; César Vallejo** and **Mario Vargas Llosa** in **Peru;** and **Vicente Huidobro** in **Chile.** Not surprisingly, therefore, given that theater and literature at large have many authors in common, there is much overlap between them with respect to their aesthetics and thematic contents.

The concept of performance was already known to Native Americans before the arrival of the Europeans and was an integral element of religious and civic rituals. Pre-Columbian performances lacked the formal structures already known as theater in Europe, but were commonplace practices of everyday life and culture, some of whose characteristics may be seen in *Rabinal Achí*, a unique dramatic text from preconquest Guatemala. Other texts with links to **indigenous traditions** include **theater in Quechua** and *El güegüense*, a popular play from **Nicaragua**. The propensity for performance in Native American cultures, when combined with the traditions of a well-developed Spanish and Portuguese religious theater, gave the missionary priests an effective tool in the Christianization of the newly colonized peoples. Thus, religious theater was well established in Latin America during the 16th century with plays written in Spanish, Portuguese, Latin, and native languages in imitation of the allegorical *autos* and biblical tales already familiar to European audiences.

After the development of religious theater in 16th-century Brazil, notably by Jesuit writers such as **José de Anchieta**, secular theater in that country grew slowly. **Manuel Botelho de Oliveira** was a notable dramatist writing in Spanish, but theater did not become more firmly established until the 19th century, when the removal of the Portuguese court from Lisbon to Rio de Janeiro (1808) and the later declaration of Brazil as an independent monarchy (1822) energized theater as a national cultural institution. Alongside the plays and operas performed by visiting troupes, there were also works by **Domingos José Gonçalves de Magalhães**, **Antônio Gonçalves Dias**, and **José de Alencar** influenced by the new trends in **romanticism**; **Luis Carlos Martins Pena** introduced the comedy of manners to Brazil in the 1840s; and **Qorpo-Santo**'s plays in the second half of the century anticipated the coming avant-garde.

In contrast with Brazil, secular theater in colonial Spanish America was somewhat more successful, although it was confined to the major cities, principally in association with the viceregal courts, where it had the patronage and infrastructural support needed for it to function. The Spanish colonies produced some original dramatists, who brought local issues and characters into their work. Notable writers included **Sor Juana Inés de la Cruz, Fernán González de Eslava,** and **Eusebio Vela** in Mexico and **Pedro de Peralta y Barnuevo** in Peru. At least one dramatist, the Mexican **Juan Ruiz de Alarcón,** also achieved success in Spain. For the most part, however, Spanish American theater of the colonial period was highly derivative. Its dramatists exploited the same genres and themes known in Spain— the familiar *autos, comedias, coloquios, entremeses,* and *loas*—and many of the plays presented were by Spanish authors, often performed by visiting companies. There were some plays written in native languages, of which the Quechuan drama *Ollantay*, from the late colonial period, is the best-known example, and in the second half of the 18th century the influence of French and Italian theater was also beginning to be felt.

Although there had been a surge in the building of theaters in the late 18th century in Spanish America, this did not translate after independence into a comparable surge in the number of plays written and produced locally. Indeed, foreign plays and productions predominated in theaters throughout the 19th century, while the form and content of works by local dramatists tended to follow fashions from Europe. Among Spanish America's most significant writers for the stage in the early and mid-19th century were writers such as the Mexican **Manuel Eduardo de Gorostiza, Luis Vargas Tejada** from **Colombia,** and the Peruvians **Felipe Pardo y Aliaga** and **Manuel Ascensio Segura,** whose comedies of manners featured middle-class, domestic crises, often centered on marriage and generational conflicts. The movement away from the heritage of **neo-classicism, romanticism,** and **costumbrismo** toward a more critical focus on political and social life in Latin America would not begin until the late 19th century and not become more fully expressed until the 20th century.

The heightened critical role undertaken by the theater in the 20th century arises in part from pressures emerging from social change, including a more developed sense of nationalism in each country of Latin America; population growth and diversification through immigration; alternation between authoritarian and liberal governments; divisions in class, political ideologies, race, and ethnicities; and the coexistence of great wealth and great poverty. At the same time, influences from outside cast theater in a new light. The avant-garde; the work of Bertolt Brecht (1898–1956), Luigi Pirandello (1867–1936), and others; and the **theater of the absurd**, the **theater of cruelty**, and **total theater** not only highlighted its social role, but drew attention to the nature of theater itself, the concept of performance, and the relationship between performers and audience. These elements were creatively assimilated by many dramatists in Latin America, who effectively gave theater a new energy in numerous centers throughout the region. To describe briefly what has taken place in theater across the continent during the last 100 years is a difficult task because of the many different points of focus and activity. However, although each national theater has its own history, briefly outlined in this dictionary in the entry for each country, there are also certain elements common to Latin American theater as a whole that serve to indicate the general directions and vitality of the stage during the last century.

Popular theater flourished in **Argentina** in the late 19th and early 20th centuries. In the expanding city of Buenos Aires, it provided both comic and serious entertainment for the new urban class of immigrants, whose life and its problems were brought to the stage in forms such as the *sainete* and the *grotesco criollo*, which drew on and transformed existing traditions in theater and other literary phenomena such as **gaucho literature**. The trend in realism and social criticism that was established endured throughout the 20th century and was embraced by many dramatists in Argentina, including **Roberto Cossa, Francisco Defilippis Novoa, Armando Discépolo, Osvaldo Dragún, Samuel Eichelbaum, Carlos Gorostiza, Carlos Maggi, Florencio Sánchez, Mauricio Rozenmacher, Ricardo Talesnik, Nemesio Trejo,** and **Alberto Vacarezza.**

Similar trends developed in other major cities as realism, politics, and social criticism also became defining elements of 20th-century theater throughout Latin America. They are represented both in drama and comedy by a roster of dramatists that includes **Luis G. Basurto** and **Jorge Ibargüengoitia** (Mexico); **Manuel Galich** (Guatemala); **Mariela Romero (Venezuela); Andrés Morris (Honduras); Artur Nabantino Gonçalves Azevedo, Alfredo Dias Gomes,** and **Gianfranceso Guarnieri** (Brazil); **Enrique Avellán Ferrés, Pedro Jorge Vera,** and **Víctor Manuel Rendón (Ecuador); Enrique Solari Swayne** (Peru); **Andrés Castillo, Ernesto Herrera,** and **Mauricio Rosencof (Uruguay);** and **Germán Luco Cruchaga** and **Juan Radrigán** (Chile).

By the 1930s, the avant-garde had appeared in Argentina and came to the theater in the work of **Roberto Arlt**. In Mexico, **Xavier Villaurrutia** became known for his experimentalism on the stage. Elsewhere, **Oswald de Andrade** wrote experimental plays in Brazil; in Nicaragua the avant-garde figured in the plays of **José Coronel Urtecho** and **Pablo Antonio Cuadra**; and in Ecuador, **Jorge Enrique Adoum** was a later representative of the avant-garde. By the 1930s in postrevolutionary Mexico, attention had also turned to questions of history and national identity, issues that were represented in the work of **Rodolfo Usigli** and **Celestino Gorostiza** and continued to resonate into the 1980s in the writing of **Sergio Magaña**, **Vicente Leñero**, and others. A similar preoccupation with identity also featured in Brazilian theater of the 1940s and 1950s, a period associated with **Nelson Rodrigues** and **Ariano Vilar Suassuna**, two of the country's foremost 20th-century dramatists.

The 1960s and 1970s were decades of cultural ferment throughout Latin America, complicated by civil conflicts in several countries and the militarization of government that would last into the 1980s. At the beginning of this time, the theater enjoyed a period of expansion. It was a moment when the avant-garde and the new waves from Europe were again felt strongly and implemented effectively, while the promise of greater stability for the theater seemed assured through support from governments and universities. Among the new ventures were Teatro Libre in Argentina; **Nuevo Grupo** in **Venezuela**, which included **José Ignacio Cabrujas**, **Román Chalbaud**, and **Isaac Chocrón**, and was inspired by their compatriot, **César Rengifo**; Rajatabla, also in Venezuela; **Enrique Buenaventura**'s successful experiment in collective theater at the Teatro Experimental de Calí in Colombia; and **Augusto Boal**'s Theater of the Oppressed in Brazil. Among several outstanding dramatists, the work by **Isidora Aguirre** and **Egon Wolff** in **Chile** and by the Argentinean **Griselda Gambaro** is particularly noteworthy for its treatment of oppression, poverty, and class divisions. Others who wrote against the dictatorial regimes and their consequences include **Chico Buarque** (Brazil), **Mario Benedetti** (Uruguay), **Rodolfo Walsh** (Argentina), and **Ariel Dorfman** and **Marco Antonio de la Parra** (Chile).

The range of particular themes addressed by all these dramatists is, of course, exceptionally wide. In addition to the many political, social, and domestic issues, questions of religion and **existential** concerns have attracted dramatists such as **Carlos Solórzano** and **Maruxa Vilalta** (Mexico), **José de Jesús Martínez (Panama)**, **Francisco Tobar García** (Ecuador), **Leopoldo Marechal** and **Eduardo Pavlovsky** (Argentina), and **Luis Alberto Heiremans** (Chile). Historical narratives figure in the works of **Rolando Steiner** (Nicaragua), **Guillermo Schmidhuber de la Mora** (Mexico), and **David Viñas** (Argentina), among many other dramatists, notably those who adopted the characteristics of **Brechtian theater**. A significant group of authors, such as **Rogelio Sinán** (Panama), **Carmen Lyra** (Costa Rica), **Enrique Avellán Ferrés** (Ecuador), **Alfonsina Storni** (Argentina), and **Magdalena Petit** (Chile), have also written theater for **children** in which the range of themes is also wide and many plays are based on fantasy worlds.

Whether by civil war in Central America or military regimes in the South, all cultural institutions in Latin America were affected in the second half of the 20th century, and theater was no exception. In some situations, as in the case of Argentina's **Teatro Abierto**, founded in 1981, new projects were undertaken both to relaunch the theater and to challenge the political status quo. As the military regimes collapsed in the 1980s and the civil wars were ended in the 1990s, however, it was not merely a matter of picking up threads that had been broken since the 1960s or 1970s. Not only had Latin American societies been changed by their recent internal conflicts, but culture itself had undergone a shift in paradigm on a global scale. While histories and narratives of the present were being shaped and told in new forms, new technologies were able to transform performances and presentations in ways that had not hitherto been possible.

For the most part, Latin American theater has responded to the challenges of the new order, and theater is thriving in the main cultural centers of the region. However, it remains true that the theater of Latin America is more vulnerable and is less known than either its poetry or its fiction. Theater requires an economy and an infrastructure that both poetry and fiction can circumvent. As a genre that thrives on public performance, it is not only more rooted to a local environment, but is also more susceptible to censorship and control. Moreover, it has had to compete throughout the 20th century with a series of alternative media—film, television, video—which in some ways are all more efficient and far-reaching means of disseminating similar content. In these respects the history of theater in Latin America has been a history of struggle, and none of its dramatists has attained the iconic cultural status of some of its poets and novelists. Nevertheless, the contemporary theater in Latin America continues to have a significant cohort of successful writers for the stage that includes **Sabina Berman** and **Carmen Boullosa** in Mexico; **Rosa María Britton** in Panama; **Fernando Bonassi** in Brazil; **Gustavo Ott** (Venezuela); and **Ramón Griffero** in Chile. Latin American theater has also traveled beyond its borders at the same time that it continues, within each country of the continent, to entertain its audiences and present them with a critical image of themselves. *See also* AGUILERA MALTA, DEEMTRIO; ALVES, ANTÔNIO FREDERICO DE CASTRO; ARREOLO, JUAN JOSÉ; BIVAR, ANTÔNIO; BOLIVIA; CALLADO, ANTÔNIO; CARRILLO, HUGO; CASA DE LAS AMÉRICAS; CASSACIO, GABRIEL; COELHO, PAULO; CORREA, JULIO; COSTA RICA; CUÉLLAR, JOSÉ TOMÁS DE; DENEVI, MARCO; EL SALVADOR; ELIZONDO, SALVADOR; ESPÍNOLA, FRANCISCO; FERNANDES, MILLÔR; FERNÁNDEZ DE LIZARDI, JOSÉ JOAQUÍN; FRANCOVICH, GUILLERMO; GALVÃO, PATRÍCIA; GARCÍA PONCE, JUAN; GAVIDIA, FRANCISCO; GULLAR, FERREIRA; GUTIÉRREZ, EDUARDO; HALLEY MORA, MARIO; ICAZA, JORGE; JAIMES FREYRE, RICARDO; JIMÉNEZ RUEDA, JULIO; LYRA, CARMEN; MACEDO, JOAQUIM MANUEL DE; MARÍN CAÑAS, JOSÉ; MONTALVO, JUAN; NALÉ ROXLO, CONRADO; NASCIMENTO, ABDIAS DO; NATURALISM; ORTEGA, JULIO; OTERO SILVA, MIGUEL; PARAGUAY; PASOS, JOAQUÍN; PELLEGRINI, ALDO; PERALTA LAGOS, JOSÉ MARÍA; PLA, JOSEFINA; PODESTÁ, JOSÉ J.; PRIETO, GUILLERMO; QUEIRÓS, RAQUEL DE; REIN, MERCEDES; REVUELTAS, JOSÉ; RIBEYRO, JULIO RAMÓN; RIO, JOÃO DO; RIVA PALACIO, VICENTE; VALLE Y CAVIEDES, JUAN DEL; WOMEN; ZALAMEA, JORGE.

THEATER IN QUECHUA. The most celebrated dramatic work written in Quechua, one of the major indigenous languages of the Andean region of South America, is *Ollantay*, an anonymous 18th-century piece from **Peru**. Two *autos* from the 17th century by **Juan de Espinosa Medrano** also survive from the colonial period, as well as the plays *El pobre más rico* (The Wealthiest Poor Man) and *Urca Paucar*, both stories set in Cuzco, Peru, about a poor Incan who sells his soul to the devil for worldly wealth but wins spiritual salvation through his devotion to the Virgin. Few of the plays written in Quechua and other native American languages, whether for entertainment or as an instrument in the Christianization of the Americas, have survived. Similar works from other regions include *El güegüense* in Nahuatl, from **Nicaragua,** and *Rabinal Achí* in Quiché, from **Guatemala.**

THEATER OF CRUELTY. This kind of **theater** is commonly associated with the style of the French dramatist Antonin Artaud (1896–1948). Although it refers to a theater characterized by the physicality of the events portrayed, sadism or the infliction of pain is not its primary objectives. The author sought to shock by removing the aesthetic from the performance and causing the audience to experience the cruelty of life. Dramatists in Latin America who were drawn to his approach include **Henry Díaz Vargas (Venezuela)** and **Griselda Gambaro (Argentina).** *See also* WOMEN.

THEATER OF THE ABSURD. Derived from a group of European dramatists that included Samuel Beckett (1906–1989), Eugène Ionesco (1909–1994), and Jean Genet (1910–1986), the theater of the absurd, like **existentialism,** focuses on life as meaningless. Its characteristics include the presentation of situations and dialogue that convey the arbitrariness of language and human relations. Latin American dramatists who explored this vein in their work include **José Coronel Urtecho (Nicaragua); Andrés Morris (Honduras); Maruxa Vilalta (Mexico); Isaac Chocrón (Venezuela); Qorpo Santo (Brazil); Carlos Maggi (Uruguay); Griselda Gambaro, Carlos Gorostiza,** and **Diana Raznovich (Argentina);** and **Jorge Díaz (Peru).** See also ARREOLO, JUAN JOSÉ; CHILE; CORONEL URTECHO, JOSÉ; NUEVO GRUPO; WOMEN.

TIMERMAN, JACOBO (Argentina, 1923–1999). Journalist. He was a respected and popular journalist who criticized violations of human rights in *La Opinión*, the **newspaper** he founded and editied. Arrested for his activities in 1977 and tortured in prison, he subsequently wrote about his experiences in *Preso sin nombre, celda sin número* (1981; Prisoner Without a Name, Cell Without a Number), a **testimonio** to what he endured. It was the basis of a 1983 film. He later wrote *Israel: la guerra más larga* (*The Longest War: Israel in Lebanon*), on the 1982 invasion of Lebanon by Israel, and *Chile: el galope muerto* (1987; *Chile: Death in the South*), a critique of life in Chile under Augusto Pinochet (1974–1990). *See also* MARTÍNEZ, TOMÁS ELOY.

TIZÓN, HÉCTOR (Argentina, 1929–). Novelist and short story writer. A lawyer and career diplomat who also made some forays into politics, Tizón also spent eight years in exile in Spain (1976–1982). His early writings derive from his life and experiences and the contexts and history of his home province of Jujuy. Since his return to Argentina from Spain, the themes of exile and separation have figured more prominently in his work. Tizón's first book was a collection of short stories, *A un costado de los rieles* (1960; On One Side of the Tracks), which has been followed by several other collections: *El jactancioso y la bella* (1972; The Braggart and the Beauty), *El traidor venerado* (1978; The Venerable Traitor), and *El gallo blanco* (1992; The White Rooster). His novels include *Fuego en Casabindo* (1969; *Fire in Casabindo*), *El cantar del profeta y el bandido* (1972; Ballad of the Prophet and the Bandit), *Sota de bastos, caballo de espadas* (1975; Jack of Clubs, Horse of Swords), *La casa y el viento* (1984; The House and the Wind), *El viaje* (1988; The Journey), *El hombre que llegó a un pueblo* (1988; *The Man who Came to a Village*), *Luz de las crueles provincias* (1995; Light from the Cruel Provinces), *La mujer de Strasser* (1997; Strasser's Wife), *Extraño y pálido fulgor* (1999; Strange, Pale Glow), *El viejo soldado* (2002; The Old Soldier), and *La belleza del mundo* (2004; The Beauty of the World). He has also published a volume of memoirs, *El resplandor de la hoguera* (2008; The Glare of the Bonfire).

TLATELOLCO MASSACRE. The Plaza de Tlatelolco in **Mexico** City, also known as the Plaza de las Tres Culturas (Square of the Three Cultures), was the site on 2 October 1968 of a student protest that was attacked by the units of the army and police acting under government orders. The attack resulted in numerous deaths, believed to be between 200 and 300. The protest was the culmination of a period of civil unrest against the policies of the administration of Gustavo Díaz Ordaz (1964–1970) and has resonated in Mexican politics and culture. It has figured both as the primary subject and as the political background to a number of literary works in Mexico by authors such as **José García Ponce, Elena Garro, María Luisa Mendoza, Carlos Monsiváis, Fernando del Paso, Elena Poniatowska, María Luisa Puga, José Revueltas, Gustavo Sainz,** and **Luis Spota.** *See also* PAZ, CARLOS.

TOBAR GARCÍA, FRANCISCO (Ecuador, 1928–1997). Poet, novelist, and dramatist. His poetry is inclined to be intellectually introspective and includes the collections *Amargo* (1951; Bitter), *Canon perpetuo* (1969; Perpetual Canon), *Ebrio de eternidad* (1992; Drunk on Eternity), and *La luz labrada* (1996; Carved Light). He wrote three novels: *Pares o nones* (1979; Odds or Evens), *La corriente era libre* (1979; The Current Was Free), and *El ocio incesante* (1994; Unending Idleness). As a dramatist, he wrote more than 20 plays, most performed at the Teatro Independiente, which he founded in Quito in 1954, where he often worked as actor and director and remained until 1970, just before his departure for Europe in search of new horizons. Belonging to a period of experimentation on the stage in 1960s Ecuador, his predominant themes were death, solitude, and the human predicament, often presented in Kafkaesque terms. His plays include *La llave del abismo* (1961; Key to the Abyss), *La res* (1962; The Beast), *Las mariposas* (1962; Butterflies), *Todo lo que brilla es oro* (1962; All That Glitters Is Gold), and *Los ojos vacíos de la gente* (1967; The Empty Eyes of the People). *See also* THEATER.

TOLENTINO, BRUNO (Brazil, 1940–2007). Poet. Born into an aristocratic family from Rio, Tolentino received a first class education and met many of the most influential intellectuals of his time. After the publication of his first book of poetry, *Anulação & Outros Reparos* (1963; Annulment & Other Objections), he left Brazil as a result of the military takeover (1964) and spent 30 years in Europe, teaching literature at various universities. Upon his return to Brazil he published the volume of poetry *As Horas de Katharina* (1994; The Hours of Katharina), which earned him the **Jabuti Prize**. He also won the same prestigious prize for *O Mundo Como Idéia* (2002; The World as Idea) and *A Imitação do Amanhecer* (2006; The Imitation of Dawn), books he considered the culmination of his poetic production and which he wrote over several decades. Even though he is the only person to win the prize three times in the same category, Tolentino's poetry is not much read and has been ignored by critics because of his rejection of modernist tenets and his embrace of traditional forms and somewhat outdated themes. As a polemicist, he had a reputation for despising the elevation of song lyrics as poetry and for dismissing popular musicians, such as **Caetano Veloso**, as serious artists. His erudition and sharp tongue also led him to engage in intellectual battles with the creators of **concrete poetry**, **Augusto de Campos** and **Haroldo de Campos**.

TORRES BODET, JAIME (Mexico, 1902–1974). Poet and novelist. He was a member of **Los Contemporáneos** in Mexico and the author of over a dozen books of poetry. One of his last, *Trébol de cuatro hojas* (1958; Four-Leaf Clover), is a tribute to four other members of the group: **José Gorostiza**, **Bernardo Ortiz de Montellano**, **Carlos Pellicer**, and **Xavier Villaurrutia**. His early collections, showing **avant-garde** influence, are represented by *Fervor* (1918; Fervor), *El corazón delirante* (1922; The Delirious Heart), *La casa* (1923; The House), and *Los días* (1923; The Days). His more mature work, in which he developed a more personal style, may be found in *Destierro* (1930; Exile), *Cripta* (1937; Crypt), and *Sonetos* (1949; Sonnets). Among his themes are the identity of the self and the other, being and nonbeing, the passage of time and the proximity of death, and the world of dreams.

The author's six novels were also written in the spirit of Los Contemporáneos and occupy a significant place in the history of 20th-century fiction in Mexico for their use of the style and techniques that were becoming more prevalent in Europe at that time. They include *Margarita de niebla* (1927; Margaret of the Mist) and *La educación sentimental* (1929; A Sentimental Education), both of which introduce elements of psychological analysis, and *Proserpina rescatada*

(1931; Proserpina Redeemed), in which both mythological and present times are combined.

In addition to a number of diplomatic and government appointments, Torres Bodet was minister of education during the presidencies of Manuel Ávila Camacho (1940–1946) and Adolfo López Mateos (1958–1964), and he was director general of UNESCO between 1948 and 1952. He also wrote on Latin American and European literature and produced a series of volumes of memoirs, of which the first was *Tiempo de arena* (1955; Time of Sand).

TORRES-RIOSECO, ARTURO (Chile, 1897–1971). Poet and critic. His volumes of poetry include *Ausencia* (1932; Absence), *Mar sin tiempo* (1935; Timeless Sea), *Canto a España viva* (1941; Song to the Living Spain), and *Elegías* (1947; Elegies), but he is remembered most as a critic, the product of his teaching career at several universities in the United States, where he immigrated in 1918. He wrote two books on **modernismo**, *Precursores del modernismo* (1925; Precursors of Modernismo) and *Rubén Darío* (1931; **Rubén Darío**), and his writings on Latin American literature in general include *Grandes novelistas de la América Latina* (2 vols., 1941–1943; Great Novelists of Latin America) and *La gran literatura iberoamericana* (1945; The Great Literature of Ibero-America).

TOTAL THEATER. A term used to refer to a kind of **theater** that endeavors to engage the audience fully and exploits a wide range of audio and visual effects. It is often associated with the work of Antonin Artaud (1896–1948) in France and, in Latin America, with **Isaac Chocrón** (**Venezuela**) and **Griselda Gambaro** (**Mexico**). *See also* NUEVO GRUPO.

TRABA, MARTA (Argentina, 1930–1984). Novelist and art critic. Although born in Argentina, she spent most of her life outside the country. She was an outspoken opponent of political oppression and denounced the abuse of human rights in both her criticism and literary writings. In **Colombia**, she established a reputation as an art critic and eventually acquired Colombian nationality after being denied a residence visa for the United States. She wrote on European and American painters, but is best known in art criticism for her publications on Latin America, which include *El museo vacío* (1958; The Empty Museum), *La pintura nueva en Latinoamérica* (1961; New Painting in Latin America), and *Dos décadas vulnerables en las artes plásticas latinoamericanas, 1950–1970* (1973; Two Vulnerable Decades in the Plastic Arts of Latin America).

Traba's literary output consists of a volume of poetry, *Historia natural de la alegría* (1951; A Natural History of Happiness); two books of short stories, *Pasó así* (1968; It Happened That Way) and *De la mañana a la noche* (1986; From Morning to Night); and seven novels. Her first novel, *Ceremonias del verano* (1966; Rites of Summer), about a **woman** who traveled from the Belgrano suburb of Buenos Aires where she grew up in search of autonomy in a male-dominated society, received a **Casa de las Américas** prize. It also introduced the themes of travel and exile, which figure in other works. In later novels, such as *Conversación al sur* (1981; *Mothers and Shadows*) and *En cualquier lugar* (1984; In Any Place), Traba wrote about fear and oppression in the countries of the Southern Cone of South America under the dictatorships of the 1970s, in a style that used flashbacks, multiple points of view, and interior monologue. Her other novels are *Los laberintos insolados* (1967; Sunburnt Labyrinths), *Homérica latina* (1979; Latin Homerica), *La jugada del sexto día* (1969; The Move on the Sixth Day), and *Casa sin fin* (1988; House Without End). Traba, who married the Uruguayan writer **Ángel Rama** in 1969, died in the **Madrid air disaster**.

TRAVEN, BRUNO (Mexico, 1882–1969). Novelist. He was a reclusive and enigmatic author who kept his private life private. Bruno Traven was one of several pseudonyms used to cover an unknown real name. He settled in Mexico in the 1920s where his eventual celebrity as a writer gave him access to the cultural elite. He wrote popular novels of social protest, originally in German, but with a wide appeal in translation. Among his best-known novels are *La rebelión de los colgados* (1936; The Rebellion of the Hanged); *El tesoro de la sierra madre* (1934; *The Treasure of the Sierra Madre*), the basis of a very successful Hollywood film (1948) directed by John Huston and starring Humphrey Bogart; and *La rosa blanca* (1961; The White

Rose), about the abuses of multinational oil companies and also the basis of a successful film.

TREJO, NEMESIO (Argentina, 1862–1916). Dramatist. Also a *payador* (gaucho troubador)**,** he was a pioneer in the popular **theater** of Buenos Aires who wrote more than 50 plays and contributed to the formation of the *sainete* in Argentina. His works include *La fiesta de don Marcos* (1890; Don Marcos's Party); *Los políticos* (1897; The Politicians); *La esquila* (1899; The Bell), his most successful piece; *Los vividores* (1902; The Freeloaders); *Los inquilinos* (1907; The Tenants); and *Las mujeres lindas* (1916; Pretty Women).

TREJO, OSVALDO (Venezuela, 1828–1996). Short story writer and novelist. His literary reputation is based mainly on several collections of short stories notable for their **surrealism** and use of the **fantastic** and the absurd: *Los cuatro pies* (1948; The Four Feet), *Cuentos de la primera esquina* (1952; First Corner Tales), *Escuchando al idiota* (1969; Listening to the Fool), *Aspasia tenía nombre de cometa* (1953; Aspasia Was Named for a Comet), and *Depósito de seres* (1965; Warehouse of Beings). His novels were also experimental, involving multiple points of view and verbal and typographical play. They include *También los hombres son ciudades* (1962; Men Are Cities Too); *Andén lejano* (1968; Distant Railway Platform), an autobiographical narrative based on the death of the author's mother in 1949; and *Textos de un texto con Teresa* (1975; Texts of a Text with Teresa).

TREVISAN, DALTON (Brazil, 1925–). Short story writer. He was born and raised in Curitiba, where he founded the literary **journal** *Joaquim*, which circulated from 1946 to 1948. There and in popular literature and ballad leaflets he first published the short stories of his collections *Sonata ao Luar* (1945; Moonlight Sonata) and *Sete Anos de Pastor* (1948; Seven Years as a Shepherd). He has excelled in this genre, being considered by some the best contemporary short story writer in Brazil. His stories, mostly set in his native Curitiba, feature compulsive individuals who struggle with frustration. Trevisan adopts a satirical attitude that castigates bourgeois obsessions.

Although he incorporates colloquial language and local color into his fiction through the use of an effective literary style, his grim depictions of life in a provincial city also have a wider universal appeal.

His works include *Novelas Nada Exemplares* (1959; Non-Exemplary Stories), *Cemitério de Elefantes* (1964; Elephant Cemetery), *A Morte na Praça* (1964; Death on the Square), *O Vampiro de Curitiba* (1965; The Vampire of Curitiba and Other Stories), *Desastres do Amor* (1968; Disasters of Love), *A Guerra Conjugal* (1969; The Marriage War), *O Rei da Terra* (1972; The King of the Earth), *O Pássaro de Cinco Asas* (1974; The Bird with Five Wings), *A Faca no Coração* (1975; The Knife in the Heart), *Abismo de Rosas* (1976; Abyss of Roses), *A Trombeta do Anjo Vingador* (1977; The Trumpet of the Avenging Angel), and the novel *A Polaquinha* (1985; The Polish Girl). Recent, more experimental titles include *Pico na Veia* (2002; A Prick in the Vein) and *Capitu Son Eu* (2003; Capitu C'est Moi). Among his writings about the city of Curitiba are *Guia Histórico de Curitiba* (1954; Historical Guide of Curitiba), *Lamentações de Curitiba* (1961; Lamentations of Curitiba), and *Minha Cidade* (1960; My City).

TRISTÁN, FLORA (Peru, 1803–1844). Diarist. She was a prominent social activist and feminist. Although born in Paris and living most of her life in France, she had aristocratic connections in Peru and spent two years in the country (1832–1834), ostensibly to claim her inheritance. While in the country she kept a diary, later published as *Peregrinaciones de una paria* (1838 in French; 1946 in Spanish; Wanderings of a Pariah), which offers an acerbic critique of Peruvian society in the immediate postcolonial period. *See also* VARGAS LLOSA, MARIO; WOMEN.

– U –

ULTRAÍSMO. This movement is associated in Latin America with **avant-garde** Buenos Aires of the 1920s. It was formed in 1918 in Madrid, where **Jorge Luis Borges** was living at the time, and also influenced the originator of **creacionismo**, **Vicente Huidobro**, when he was in Spain. Although it was a movement in poetry opposed to **modernismo**, its characteristics were somewhat less radical than **surrealism**. They included an emphasis on metaphor and the combination of images, the elimination of ornamentalism, a simpler language, the absence of rhyme, and reference to the modern world and new technologies. Borges subscribed to its precepts in *Fervor de Buenos Aires* (Fervor of Buenos Aires), published after his return to **Argentina** in 1923, and he collaborated in the founding of the **journals** *Prisma* and *Proa* as vehicles for disseminating the movement's ideas and the writing of its members. Among other Argentineans who adopted ultraísmo are **Oliverio Girondo, Eduardo González Lanuza, Raúl González Tuñón, Norah Lange, Leopoldo Marechal,** and **Alfonsina Storni**. Guillermo de Torre (1900–1971) and Ramón Gómez de la Serna (1888–1963), although from Spain, both lived in Buenos Aires and were associated with the movement. *See also* ADÁN, MARTÍN; HIDALGO, ALBERTO.

URBINA, LUIS G. (Mexico, 1864–1934). Poet, journalist, and critic. His first poems, harking back to **romanticism**, were published in *Versos* (1890; Verses) and *Ingenuas* (1902; Ingenuous). By his next collection, *Puestas del sol* (1910; Sunsets), he had entered more fully into the mode of **modernismo**, to which he also adhered in subsequent volumes: *Lámparas en agonía* (1914; Dying Lamps), *El glosario de la vida vulgar* (1916; Glossary of the Common Life), *El corazón juglar* (1920; Troubador Heart), *Los últimos pájaros* (1924; The Last Birds), and *El cancionero de la noche serena* (1941; Songs of the Clear Night). Considered overall, Urbina's poetry tends to fall between the two styles.

As a prose writer, Urbina stands out for his **chronicles** and writings on literature. His chronicles, many of them written during periods of residence outside Mexico, include *Cuentos vividos y crónicas soñadas* (1915; Lived Stories and Dreamed Chronicles), *Bajo el sol y frente al mar, impresiones de Cuba* (1916; Under the Sun and by the Sea: Impressions of Cuba), *Estampas de viaje: España en los días de la guerra* (1920; Travel Sketches: Spain During Wartime), and *Luces de España* (1924; Lights of Spain). His writings on literature provide insight into Mexico in particular and include *El teatro nacional* (1914; The National Theater), *La literatura mexicana durante la guerra de la Independencia* (1917; Mexican Literature During the

War of Independence), and *La vida literaria de México* (1917; Literary Life in Mexico).

URQUIZO, FRANCISCO L. (Mexico, 1891–1969). Novelist. A general in the Mexican army, he was active in the revolution, but left for Spain and exile after the assassination in 1920 of Venustiano Carranza, the revolutionary leader he had supported. In 1938, he was recalled to Mexico, reinstated in the army and promoted, and subsequently appointed to a number of senior positions involving the administration and development of the army. His literary career began while he was in exile, and his first novel, *Lo incognoscible* (1923; The Unknowable), was published in Madrid. His other novels include *El primer crimen* (1933; The First Crime), *Tropa vieja* (1943; Old Soldiers), and *¡Viva Madero!* (1954; Long Live Madero!). Of these the most significant is *Tropa Vieja*, which stands out among **novels of the Mexican Revolution** because it narrates the revolution from the perspective of the government through the story of a young man who had been conscripted into the federal army before the beginning of hostilities. Urquizo also published historical and biographical works, including *Don Venustiano Carranza: el hombre, el político, el caudillo* (1935; Don Venustiano Carranza: The Man, the Politician, the Leader), *Morelos, genio militar de la Independencia* (1945; Morelos, Military Genius of the Independence), and *Páginas de la Revolución* (1956; Pages from the Revolution).

URUGUAY. During colonial times, the territory now occupied by Uruguay first formed part of the Viceroyalty of Peru and then of the Viceroyalty of La Plata, with its capital in Buenos Aires. The fort where Montevideo now stands was not built until the early 18th century. Uruguayan literature therefore has few prominent antecedents before independence, and its origins are customarily traced to **Francisco Acuña de Figueroa** and **Bartolomé Hidalgo**. While the former represents the more urban side of cultural life, the latter is associated with rural life and its expression in **gaucho literature**, which was as prevalent in 19th-century Uruguay as it was in **Argentina** and had a number of practitioners, such as **Antonio Lussich**. The literary texts that gave the country its founding mythologies were products of **romanticism**: the narrative verse of **Juan Zorrilla de San Martín**, especially the frontier story told in *Tabaré* (1888), and the **historical novels** of **Eduardo Acevedo Díaz**.

The aesthetics of **modernismo** produced several poets whose work has become part of the Latin American canon, including **Julio Herrera y Reissig, María Eugenia Vaz Ferreira,** and **Delmira Agustini**. The prose writers contemporary with them, **Javier de Viana, Carlos Reyles,** and, above all, **Horacio Quiroga,** one of Latin America's most influential short story writers, were inclined to evade the theme of the emergence of the modern state taking place in Uruguay during the first decades of the 20th century and to locate their narratives in the interior, continuing trends in **criollismo**. An exception to this group was **José Enrique Rodó**, who not only was fully engaged in the politics of the time, but whose essay *Ariel* (1900) was widely read and contributed to debates on the nature of Latin America and the direction it should follow in Western culture. **Ángel Rama** is another widely read, but later, writer on Latin America and belongs to a group of well-known Uruguayan literary critics that also includes **Alberto Zum Felde** and **Emir Rodríguez Monegal**.

The periods following modernismo, combining elements of the **avant-garde** and nationalism, produced a rich and eclectic group of poets. **Juana de Ibarbourou, Roberto Ibáñez, Sara de Ibáñez,** and **Susana Soca** were among the prominent figures of the first half of the century, and **Idea Vilariña** and **Ida Vitale** made their mark on the second half. In prose these elements were also reflected in **Francisco Espínola, Enrique Amorim,** and **Felisberto Hernández**. The two most important novelists of the 20th century, however, were **Juan Carlos Onetti** and **Mario Benedetti**, who is also known for his verse. Like other prominent writers active in the last decades of the century, both eventually wrote while in exile. By the 1960s, the crisis of the state was already apparent, and the process through which it passed and its consequences are well represented in the fiction of authors such as as **Cristina Peri Rossi, Carlos Martínez Moreno, Teresa Porzecanski,** and **Armonía Somers**. The spirit of the times, projected onto the wider screen of the history of Latin America as a whole, was caught in particular by **Eduardo Galeano**, and the reinterpretation of history, challenging official versions of the past, is presented in **new historical novels** by **Tomás de Mattos** and **Napoleón Baccino Ponce de León**.

In comparison with other Latin American countries, the **theater** appeared late in Uruguay, a reflection of its colonial experience, the relatively late foundation of Montevideo, and the dominant cultural presence of Buenos Aires on the southern shore of the mouth of the River Plate. The first wave of popularity of the theater is indebted to the figure of the gaucho, which had already been popularized by Bartolomé Hidalgo's dialogues before the Uruguayan actor **José Podestá** brought the character of Juan Moreira to the stage from a novel by the Argentinean **Eduardo Gutiérrez**. The success of the flood of gaucho plays that ensued brought a boom to the theater, from which the social realism of the country's first major dramatist, **Florencio Sánchez**, would emerge in due course, although he earned his reputation in Buenos Aires. At the same time, his contemporary, **Ernesto Herrera**, staying closer to home, contributed his plays to the stages of Montevideo.

Between 1920 and the mid-1940s, against competition from the cinema and the dominance of companies from Buenos Aires, Uruguayan theater declined. With the founding of the Comedia Nacional, it experienced a revival between the mid-1940s and mid-1970s, only to suffer further setbacks under the dictatorial regime of 1973–1985. During its revival, Ángel Rama and Mario Benedetti wrote for the stage, as did **Andrés Castillo**, **Carlos Maggi**, and **Mauricio Ronsencof**, Uruguay's most important dramatist since Florencio Sánchez. Although silenced during the dicatorship, he is one of a group of dramatists, which also includes **Mercedes Rein**, who have written for the theater since redemocratization. *See also* ARIELISMO; CASA DE LAS AMÉRICAS; CHILDREN'S LITERATURE; CIVILIZATION AND BARBARISM; DÍAZ DE GUZMÁN, RUY; FANTASTIC LITERATURE; INDIANISMO; MARÍN CAÑAS, JOSÉ; MIGUEL DE CERVANTES PRIZE; NATURALISM; THEATER OF THE ABSURD; WOMEN.

USIGLI, RODOLFO (Mexico, 1905–1979). Dramatist. As a successful playwright, **theater** historian, teacher, critic, and reviewer, Usigli was a tireless activist on behalf of Mexican theater, in which he came to be a dominant figure. His work was influenced by the Greek and Roman theater, the classical theater of England and France, and some of his European contemporaries, especially the Irish dramatist George Bernard Shaw (1856–1950), from whom he derived his critical focus on social issues and whose practice of writing long polemical prologues to the editions of his plays he imitated.

Usigli's more than 40 works written for the theater include historical plays, psychological dramas, and social and political satires. *El gesticulador* (1937; The Imposter), a satire on political corruption in postrevolutionary Mexico, was one of his most notable early works and one of his best works overall. It was filmed in 1956 as *El impostor* by Emilio Fernández (1904–1986). Like some of his other early pieces, in which the staging of taboo themes was a source of problems, the political content of the play prevented it from being performed until 1943. Usigli's *Corona* (crown) trilogy, dramatizations of three significant episodes of Mexican history, also figures among the dramatist's major accomplishments: *Corona de fuego* (1960; Crown of Fire) is concerned with the conflict of cultures occurring at the time of the conquest of Mexico by the Spanish; *Corona de luz* (1963; *Crown of Light*) focuses on the legend of the Virgen de Guadalupe; and *Corona de sombra* (written in 1943; performed in 1947; *Crown of Shadow*) presents a version of the French intervention in Mexico and the reign of Maximilian and Carlota (1864–1867).

Contemporary politics also figured among Usigli's themes, notably in the plays collected under the title *Tres comedias impolíticas* (1933–1935; Three Impolitic Plays): *Noche de estío* (Summer Night), *El Presidente y el ideal* (The President and the Ideal), and *Estado de secreto* (Secret State). Another group of plays, with a predominantly psychological approach, explores family life through situations such as generational conflict or family secrets. These include *El niño y la niebla* (1936; The Boy and the Mist), *La familia cena en casa* (1942; The Family Dines at Home), *La función de despedida* (1949; Farewell Performance), and *Jano es una muchacha* (1952; Janus Is a Girl). Although not at the same level as his theater, Usigli also wrote poetry, and he produced a successful **crime novel**, *Ensayo de un crimen* (1944; Rehearsal for a Crime), that was the basis of a 1955 film by Luis Buñuel (1900–1983). *See also* HERNÁNDEZ, LUISA JOSEFINA; MAGAÑA, SERGIO.

USLAR PIETRI, ARTURO (Venezuela, 1906–2001). Short story writer, novelist, journalist, and essayist. He was one of Venezuela's most prominent intellectuals of the 20th century and was active in literature and politics, having twice been a candidate for president. "Pizarrón" ("Blackboard"), his syndicated **newspaper** column on current events, was widely read and was a feature in the Venezuelan press for several decades. A concern with Venezuela figures very significantly in Uslar Pietri's many volumes of essays, such as *Letras y hombres de Venezuela* (1948; Men and Letters of Venezuela), *En busca del nuevo mundo* (1968; In Search of the New World), and *Raíces venezolanas* (1986; Venezuelan Roots); in volumes such as *Las nubes* (1951; The Clouds) and *Godos, insurgentes y visionarios* (1986; Conservatives, Insurgents and Visionaries), he also sought to describe the uniqueness of Latin America in general.

Uslar Pietri's most significant literary work belongs to the early part of his career. *Barrabás y otros relatos* (1928; Barrabas and Other Tales) reflects the dominant styles of the time, including **modernismo** and elements of the **avant-garde**, and establishes new directions for the short story. *Red* (1936; Net) contains the author's best-known stories. Although it includes texts belonging to the more traditional style of **criollismo**, Uslar Pietri is also credited with having introduced the style that would lead to **magic realism**. In other collections of stories, such as *Treinta hombres y sus sombras* (1949; Thirty Men and Their Shadows), he retained a focus on rural themes, but in *Pasos y pasajeros* (1966; Passages and Passengers) and *Los ganadores* (1980; The Winners), he turned to more urban topics.

The best known of Uslar Pietri's half dozen novels is *Las lanzas coloradas* (1931; *The Red Lances*), a **historical novel** set in the early 1800s that tells a story about the struggles for power during Venezuela's war of independence. This was followed by *El camino de El Dorado* (1947; The Way to El Dorado), about the exploits of Lope de Aguirre, a subject also taken up by **Miguel Otero Silva** and **Abel Posse**; *Un retrato en la geografía* (1962; Portrait in Geography); *Estación de máscaras* (1964; Season of Masks); *Oficio de difuntos* (1976; Office of the Dead), set in the time of the Venezuelan dictator Juan Vicente Gómez (1908–1935); *La isla de Robinson* (1981; Robinson's Island), in which parallel chronologies are used to narrate the main character's story; and *La visita en el tiempo* (1990; The Visit in Time), which features several iconic figures of Western literature such as Hamlet and Don Juan. For the most part, these novels are stylistically conventional, more in the manner of the author's journalism than the dynamic, cinematographic quality he gave to *Las lanzas coloradas*.

– V –

VACAREZZA, ALBERTO (Argentina, 1886–1959). Dramatist. He was a prolific writer of *sainetes* and claimed to have written more than 100, among the most popular of which were *Tu cuna fue un conventillo* (1921; Your Cradle Was a Tenement), one of the longest running plays in its time, and *El conventillo de La Paloma* (1929; The La Paloma Tenement). Puns, wordplay, and use of the popular dialects lunfardo and cocoliche, considered typical of immigrants to Buenos Aires, were the main characteristics of his work. His other plays include *El juzgado* (1904; The Court), *Los villanos* (1912; The Villains), *El comité* (1914; The Committee), *El último gaucho* (1915; The Last Gaucho), *Cuando un pobre se divierte* (1921; When a Poor Man Has Fun), *El cambalache de la buena suerte* (1925; Pawn Shop of Good Luck), and *La vida es un sainete* (1925; Life Is a Sainete). Vacarezza also wrote popular poetry, which he often recited on the radio, and he was the lyricist of a number of popular tangos that were set to music by established composers and recorded by well-known singers. *See also* THEATER.

VALDELOMAR, ABRAHAM (Peru, 1888–1919). Poet, novelist, short story writer, journalist, and essayist. In addition to his career in journalism, both as a writer and editor, he was briefly involved in politics and held a diplomatic appointment in Italy (1913–1914). A practitioner of several literary genres, he believed writers should be public celebrities, and it was while on a lecture tour that he suffered the fall that caused his premature death. Among his first publications were a series of newspaper **chronicles** (1910) about his short-lived army experiences.

Valdelomar's novels *La ciudad muerta* (1910; Dead City) and *La ciudad de los tísicos* (1910; City of Consumptives) were quite experimental and were the first to introduce certain modern techniques to Peru. Both were published in serial form in newspapers. Other novels include *Los ojos de Judas* (The Eyes of Judas); *El hipocampo de oro* (The Golden Sea Horse); and a fictionalized biography, *La mariscala* (1914; The Marshall's Wife), of Francisca Zubiaga (1803–1835), wife of Agustín Gamarra, who was twice president of Peru between 1829 and 1841. His short stories are included in two collections, *El caballero Carmelo* (1918; Carmelo the Gentleman), about daily life in the port of Pisco, and *Los hijos del sol* (1921; Children of the Sun), based on legends of the Inca Empire. He wrote two collections of essays, *Ensayo sobre la psicología del gallinazo* (1917; Essay on the Psychology of the Vulture), a no-holds-barred view of Lima said to have influenced **Julio Ramón Ribeyro**, and *Belmonte el trágico* (1918; The Tragic Belmonte), on bullfighting.

VALDIVIA, PEDRO DE (Chile, ca. 1500–1554). Chronicler. A Spanish conquistador, he led the first successful Spanish expedition into Chile in 1540 and founded Santiago in 1541. Valdivia's letters to Charles V of Spain, *Cartas de relación de la conquista de Chile* (written 1545–1552; published 1846; *Letters*), constitute a **chronicle** of the conquest, early settlement, and conflicts with the indigenous population of Chile and are the foundational texts of Chilean literature. His exploits were also recorded by **Alonso de Ercilla y Zúñiga** and in the **epic poetry** describing the conquest of Chile to which Ercilla's narrative poem gave rise.

VALENCIA, GUILLERMO (Colombia, 1873–1943). Poet. He had a long career in politics as well as an active literary life, much of it devoted to translation, for which his sensitivity and cultural and linguistic knowledge made him particularly adept. His reputation as a poet rests above all on the collection *Ritos* (1899; Rites), which also appeared in an expanded edition in 1914. Valencia's poetry shows the influence of European **parnassianism** and **symbolism** as well as the growing impact of Spanish American **modernismo**, as represented in the work of fellow Colombian **José Asunción Silva**. His themes include the role of the poet, the brevity of life, religion, and Colombia.

VALENZUELA, LUISA (Argentina, 1938–). Short story writer and novelist. She has traveled widely both within and beyond

Argentina, and has lived for extended periods in several countries, spending 10 years (1979–1989) in the United States. Her literary work includes several books of short stories, such as *Los heréticos* (1967; The Heretics), *Aquí pasan raras cosas* (1975; *Strange Things Happen Here: Twenty-Six Short Stories and a Novel*), *Cambio de armas* (1982; *Other Weapons*), and *Simetrías* (1993; Symmetries).

In these collections, as in her novels, Valenzuela takes aim at human conduct and society, sometimes with humor and often with stark realism. She confronts the violence and state torture in Argentina of the 1960s and 1970s, linking them at times to themes of eroticism and sexuality, and she speaks out against all kinds of censorship, including self-censorship. Gender and sexuality are among the common denominators of much of her fiction, and her feminist stance has placed her among Argentina's most prominent contemporary **women** writers. The transgressive dimension of the content of her work is equally evident in styles of writing that contest the writerly conventions of established forms, and events are frequently narrated in a somewhat surreal manner.

Valenzuela's first novel *Hay que sonreír* (1966; *Clara: Thirteen Short Stories and a Novel*) uses the changing fortunes of her protagonist, initially a prostitute, to reflect on the objectification of women and the opposition between mind and body. *El gato eficaz* (1972; The Effective Cat) is a novel that focuses on the opposition between the masculine and the feminine and the cultural origin of notions of gender. It is characterized by shifting voices, a play with masks, and no clear chronology or fixed points from which to develop a plot. In *Cola de lagartija* (1983; *The Lizard's Tale*), the sources of power and state terror are examined through a protagonist modeled on José López Rega (1916–1989), the notorious minister of social welfare during the presidency of Isabel Perón (1974–1976). *Novela negra con argentinos* (1990; *Black Novel with Argentines*) is also concerned with the recent dark periods of Argentinean history; *Realidad nacional desde la cama* (1990; *Bedside Manners*) and *La travesía* (2001; The Crossing) both deal with the themes of exile and return, conditions both arising from Argentina's most recent period of military dictatorship (1976–1983).

VALLE, JOSÉ CECILIO DEL (Honduras, 1780–1834). He was one of the leaders of Central American independence, first president of the United Provinces of Central America, and one of the drafters of its constitution. Along with **José Trinidad Reyes**, he had considerable influence on the cultural formation of Honduras during the early years of its history as an independent country. His collected writings were published as *Obras completas* (1929–1930; Complete Works).

VALLE, RAFAEL HELIODORO (Honduras, 1891–1959). Poet, essayist, journalist, and historian. He was a well-known journalist whose work appeared throughout the Americas in newspapers in Buenos Aires, Lima, Mexico City, Havana, Los Angeles, and New York. His work as a historian (he held a doctorate in history from the National Autonomous University of Mexico) amounts to some 20 books on Mexico and Central America. Among them are *Iturbide, varón de Dios* (1944; Iturbide, Man of God), *Bolívar en México* (1946; Bolívar in Mexico), and *Historia de las ideas contemporáneas en Centro-América* (1960; History of Contemporary Ideas in Central America). He also compiled a number of bibliographies, including one on the Mexican author **Manuel Ignacio Altamirano** and another on **Hernán Cortés**. Valle's first book of poetry, *El rosal del ermitaño* (1911; The Hermit's Rose Garden) was strongly influenced by **modernismo**, a style he also pursued in three other collections, *Como la luz del día* (1913; Like the Light of Day), *El perfume de la tierra natal* (1917; Scent of Home), and *Ánfora sedienta* (1922; Thirsty Amphora). He wrote lyrical verse on romantic love, intended for public recitation, and his poems have frequently been anthologized.

VALLE ARIZPE, ARTEMIO DE (Mexico, 1888–1961). Novelist, short story writer, and historian. He was the most prolific of the writers in Mexico who wrote a form of the **historical novel** known as the **colonial novel**. In total, he published more than 70 books, all concerned with the past and most with the viceregal period of Mexican history (16th-18th centuries).

Valle Arizpe's novels and collections of short stories include *Vidas milagrosas* (1921; Miraculous Lives), *Tres nichos de un retablo* (1936; Three Niches in an Altar), *Lirios de Flandes* (1938; Lilies from Flanders), and *Cuentos del México antiguo* (1939; Tales from Old Mexico). Many of Valle's stories were collected in a long series of "traditions, legends and events from Viceregal Mexico" in the style of **Ricardo Palma**, whom Valle greatly admired. These include *Historias de vivos y muertos* (1936; Stories of the Living and the Dead), *Andanzas de Hernán Cortés y otros excesos* (1940; Exploits of Hernán Cortés and Other Excesses), *Piedras viejas bajo el sol* (1952; Old Stones Under the Sun), and *Inquisición y crímenes* (1952; Inquisition and Crimes).

In addition to these blends of the historical and the fictional, Valle also produced several biographies and works of history, preferring, of course, his favored viceregal period. Among them are *El Palacio Nacional de México* (1932; The National Palace of Mexico), *Historia de la ciudad de México según los relatos de sus cronistas* (1939; History of Mexico City from Tales by Its Chroniclers), *La Güera Rodríguez* (1950; Blondie Rodríguez), and *Fray Servando* (1951; Fray Servando). *Historia de una vocación* (1960; History of a Vocation) was his autobiography.

VALLE Y CAVIEDES, JUAN DEL (Peru, 1645?–1697?). Poet. Although he also wrote a few short pieces for the **theater**, Valle y Caviedes is best remembered for *Diente del Parnaso* (first published in 1873; The Tooth of Parnassus). This is a collection of 47 poems, mainly satirical verses written in the **baroque** style of the Spanish poet Francisco de Quevedo (1580–1645), often using vulgar language and body humor to poke fun at doctors and their foibles.

VALLEJO, CÉSAR (Peru, 1892–1938). Poet. Although his poetic oeuvre is relatively small, amounting to four major collections, two of which were published posthumously, he is established as one of Latin America's most important poets. His first collection, *Los heraldos negros* (1918; The Black Heralds), with its direct language, unusual imagery, and focus on the solitude of the human experience, already presages a break from existing traditions brought about by a crisis in established beliefs. *Trilce* (1922; *Trilce*) confirmed this direction and the innovative dimension of Vallejo's poetry. It is one of the fundamental texts of the Spanish American **avant-garde** and pushed at the frontiers of language at the time.

Shortly after the publication of *Trilce*, Vallejo left Peru for Europe and spent what remained of his life mainly between France and Spain, including several weeks in the Soviet Union in 1928, after which he joined the Spanish Communist Party. The two collections of verse published after his death both reflect his preoccupation with society and the future of the individual. *España, aparta de mí este cáliz* (1939; *Spain, Take This Cup from Me*) is a set of poems written in response to the Spanish Civil War (1936–1939), in praise of those fighting for the Republicans. In *Poemas humanos* (1939; *Human Poems*), perhaps written over a period of time during the 1920s and 1930s and left unfinished, he reflected on the anguish felt by the individual in society. Vallejo also wrote (unsuccessfully) for the **theater** and produced a considerable amount of fiction and journalism. Of all his works in prose, the novel *El tungsteno* (1931; *Tungsten*), about mine workers in Peru, is the one that continues to be read. See also GONZÁLEZ LEÓN, ADRIANO; GONZÁLEZ PRADA, MANUEL; HERRERA Y REISSIG, JULIO.

VALLEJO, FERNANDO (Colombia, 1942–). Novelist. Much of what Vallejo has published may be considered autobiographical fiction, not just in the sense that he writes first person narratives, but that what he writes refers to his own life experiences. His most celebrated work is *La virgen de los sicarios* (1994; *Our Lady of the Assassins*), the story of a writer who returns to Medellín in Colombia after a prolonged absence. There he forms a relationship with a male adolescent employed as a hitman by one of the drug cartels and tries to come to terms with the city of his past and the present. The novel was the basis of a film made in 2000, although not by Vallejo, who is also a filmmaker.

Before his success with this novel, Vallejo had already begun a series of autobiographical novels under the title *El río del tiempo* (River of Time), of which the first to appear was *Los días azules* (1985; Blue Days). Like *La virgen de los sicarios*, it also deals with themes of violence, social marginality, and homosexuality. Other works include *El desbarrancadero* (2001; The Precipice), about his brother's death from AIDS, which received the 2003 **Rómulo Gallegos Prize**, and *La rambla paralela* (2002; The Parallel Riverbed), about his own death. Vallejo has also written a biography (1995) of **José Asunción**

Silva and, reflecting his scientific training, a collection of essays, *La tautología darwinista y otros ensayos de biología* (1998; Darwinian Tautology and Other Essays on Biology).

VALLEJO, JOSÉ JOAQUÍN (Chile, 1811–1858). Journalist. He wrote under the pseudonym "Jotabeche." As an ardent admirer of the Spanish costumbrista Mariano José de Larra (1809–1837), he showed a similar ascerbic wit and satirical sense of humor in **newspaper** and magazine articles noted for their succinct commentary on everyday situations and topics from social and political life. There have been many compilations of his writings, and he is considered one of the most important contributors to **costumbrismo** in Chile.

VARELA, BLANCA (Peru, 1926–2009). Poet. Although she remained out of the limelight and published only a few books of poetry at irregular intervals, she is one of her country's major poetic voices. Among her themes are a strong sense of discontent, the city, identity, and gender, expressed through intense images that have an aura of **surrealism.** Her books include *Ese puerto existe y otros poemas* (1959; That Port Exists and Other Poems), *Luz de día* (1963; Light of Day), *Valses y otras falsas confesiones* (1972; Waltzes and Other False Confessiones), *Canto villano* (1978; Plain Song), *El libro de barro* (1993; Book of Clay), *Ejercicios materiales* (1994; Material Exercises), *Concierto animal* (1999; Animal Concert), and *El falso teclado* (2001; The Fake Keyboard). *See also* WOMEN.

VARGAS LLOSA, MARIO (Peru, 1936–). Novelist. He was one of the core authors of the **boom** and a source of some controversy for incidents such as a very public argument with the Colombian writer **Gabriel García Márquez** and a shift in political stance from a more leftist position to the conservatism he espoused when he ran as an unsuccessful candidate in the Peruvian presidential election of 1990. A memoir of his campaign was published as *El pez en el agua* (1993; *A Fish in the Water: Memoir*). Since his political defeat, he has lived mainly in Europe and became a Spanish citizen in 1993, but has continued to write about Peru and Latin America. In 1994, he received the **Miguel de Cervantes Prize** and in 2010 was awarded the **Nobel Prize for Literature.**

Among Vargas Llosa's earliest literary ventures was a prize-winning collection of short stories, *Los jefes* (1959; The Leaders), but it was his first novel, *La ciudad y los perros* (1963; *The Time of the Hero*), that established his name and affirmed his ability as a gifted storyteller. It narrates the tribulations of a group of students in the Leoncio Prado Military Academy in Callao, Peru, which the author attended between 1950 and 1952. As a story of authoritarianism, institutionalized violence, and cynicism, it may be read as a microcosm of Peru. The same could be said of Vargas Llosa's next novel, the 1967 **Rómulo Gallegos Prize** winner, *La casa verde* (1966; *The Green House*), although it has a larger cast of characters and a longer chronology and is set in a wider range of locations. Its multiple narrative strands reflect the storytelling, technical virtuosity and narrative innovations that had already appeared in *La ciudad y los perros*, in which changes in time, narration, and point of view are all combined. *Conversación en La Catedral* (1969; *Conversation in The Cathedral*) sustains this style through a conversation between two men in a bar called The Cathedral that opens into an exploration of the time of the presidency of Manuel Odría (1948–1956) in Peru.

In his next two novels, *Pantaleón y las visitadoras* (1973; *Captain Pantoja and the Special Service*) and *La Tía Julia y el escribidor* (1977; *Aunt Julia and the Scriptwriter*), Vargas Llosa adopted a lighter, more parodic tone. The first is the story of an army officer entrusted with providing a prostitution service for soldiers stationed in the jungle, and the second combines elements of the author's life (his work at a radio station and marriage to Julia Urquidi) with the rise and fall of a fictional scriptwriter of radio soap operas. Both novels were the basis for somewhat unsuccessful movies. In *La guerra del fin del mundo* (1981; *The War of the End of the World*), Vargas Llosa turned to historical events, to a rebellion in Brazil that had already figured in *Os Sertões* (1902; *Rebellion in the Backlands*) by **Euclides da Cunha**.

The themes of rebellion and revolution also appear in *Historia de Mayta* (1984; *The Real life of Alejandro Mayta*), which was published at a time when Peru was itself affected by violence from the state and the insurgent Sendero Luminoso. The author's preoccupation with these subjects and with the relationship between the real world and narrative continued in *¿Quién mató a Palomino Molero?*

(1986; *Who Killed Palomino Molero?*) and *El hablador* (1989; *The Storyteller*). More recent novels include the **dictator novel** *La fiesta del chivo* (2000; *The Feast of the Goat*), based on the life of the Dominican strongman Rafael Leonidas Trujillo (1930–1961); *El paraíso en la otra esquina* (2003; *The Way to Paradise*), on the stories about the feminist reformer **Flora Tristán** and the painter Paul Gauguin (1848–1903); and *Travesuras de la niña mala* (2006; *The Bad Girl*), a rewriting of *Madame Bovary* (1857) by Gustave Flaubert (1821–1880), an author who has influenced Vargas Llosa since his early days as a writer.

In addition to fiction, Vargas Llosa has written several significant works of criticism, notably *García Márquez: historia de un deicidio* (1971; García Márquez: The Story of a Deicide) and *La orgía perpetua* (1975; *The Perpetual Orgy*), on the French author Gustave Flaubert. His newspaper writing and other journalism has been collected in three volumes, *Contra viento y marea* (1983, 1986, 1990; *Against Wind and Tide*), and he has published several works for the **theater**, including *La huida del inca* (1952; The Flight of the Inca) and *La señorita de Tacna* (1981; The Girl from Tacna). *See also* RIBEYRO, JULIO RAMÓN; SABINO, FERNANDO; SALAZAR BONDY, SEBASTIÁN.

VARGAS TEJADA, LUIS (Colombia, 1802–1829). Dramatist. He wrote a series of tragedies in the classical style on Indian and political themes, most of which have not survived. Among them is *La madre de Pausanias* (Pausanias' Mother), written in reply to the tyranny of **Simón Bolívar**. Vargas Tejada's main claim to fame, however, is his authorship of *Las convulsiones* (1829; The Convulsions), a comedy of manners with which Colombian **theater** is considered to have had its beginning in the postindependence era.

VARGAS VILA, JOSÉ MARÍA (Colombia, 1860–1933). Novelist. He was a best-selling author in his time, churning out a very large number of pulp novels, many exploring the darker sides of life. Some examples are *Aura o las violetas* (1887; Dawn, or the Violets), *Lo irreparable* (1889; Irreparable), *Las rosas de la tarde* (1901; Evening Roses), *El cisne blanco (novela psicologica)* (1917; The White Swan: A Psychological Novel), *Eleonora (novela de la vida* *artística)* (1917; Eleonora: A Novel of Artistic Life), *Los discípulos de Emaús (novela de la vida intelectual)* (1917; The Disciples of Emmaus: A Novel of Intellectual Life), and *María Magdalena (novela lírica)* (1917; Mary Magdalene: A Lyrical Novel).

Although a highly popular author and lionized by some, Vargas Vila was persona non grata for others on account of his controversial opinions and rumored crimes. In his literary style, he followed the exotic aspects of **modernismo**. Philosophically, he was closer to **existentialism**, but his politics brought him within range of anarchism. He was virulently anti-American and anticlerical and expressed his views in a series of hightly polemical writings, among them: *Los providenciales* (1892; The Lucky Ones), *Los divinos y los humanos* (1904; The Divine and the Human), and *Los césares de la decadencia* (1907; Decadent Caesars). One of his most widely circulated books was *La muerte del cóndor* (1913, Death of the Condor), about Eloy Alfaro, president of Peru (1906–1911). Notwithstanding his popularity and financial success as a writer, Vargas Vila lived much of his life in isolation and died, almost forgotten, in Barcelona.

VARNHAGEN, FRANCISCO ADOLFO DE (Brazil, 1816–1878). Historian. Although not technically a literary writer, Varnhagen, the son of a Portuguese mother and a German father, is mentioned in literary histories for his role in the consolidation of national culture under emperor Pedro II (1831–1889) through his research and historical writings, such as *História Geral do Brasil* (1854–1857; General History of Brazil). He also composed a historically oriented novel, *O Descobrimento do Brasil: Crônica do Fim do Século XV* (1840; The Discovery of Brazil: Chronicle of the End of the 15th Century), which appeared in periodical installments, and he edited the important three-volume *Florilégio da Poesia Brasileira* (1850–1853; Anthology of Brazilian Poetry).

VASCONCELOS, JOSÉ (Mexico, 1882–1959). Essayist and autobiographer. As a prominent intellectual in postrevolutionary Mexico, his tenure as minister of education between 1920 and 1924 had a significant impact on the formation of Mexican cultural institutions. He was also a prolific writer whose work continues to attract attention and criticism. His four volumes of memoirs, *Ulises criollo* (1935;

A Mexican Ulysses), La tormenta (1936; The Storm), *El desastre* (1938; The Disaster), and *El proconsulado* (1939; The Proconsul), are notable commentaries on his life and times, and the first two in particular are often read in the context of the **novel of the Mexican Revolution**. Other writings by Vasconcelos, such as *La raza cósmica* (1925; *The Cosmic Race*), *Indología: una interpretación de la cultura ibero-americana* (1926; Indology: An Interpretation of Ibero-American Culture), *Estética* (1933; Aesthetics), and *Bolivarismo y Monroísmo* (1934; Bolivar and the Monroe Doctrine), have figured prominently in discussions about Latin America, its people, its politics, and its culture. *La raza cósmica*, especially, occupies an important place in the history of debates about Mexican identity.

VAZ FERREIRA, MARÍA EUGENIA (Uruguay, 1875–1924). Poet. She belonged to the same generation of Uruguayans as **Enrique Rodó, Horacio Quiroga, Julio Herrera y Reissig**, and **Delmira Agustini**, and was the first in a group of Latin American writers, including **Gabriela Mistral, Alfonsina Storni**, and **Juana de Ibarbourou**, who established a voice for **women** in poetry. She wrote metaphysical, brooding poetry that addressed the unanswerable questions about life, death, love, and hope. She published little, however. *La isla de los cánticos* (1924; Island of Canticles) appeared in the same year as her death and was followed a number of years later *by La otra isla de los cánticos* (1959; The Other Island of Canticles).

VELA, EUSEBIO (Mexico, 1688–1737). Dramatist. Involved in all aspects of production and performance, he was a notable figure of the 18th century, whose emphasis on the mechanics of staging associates him with the **baroque** style of the age. He is reputed to have been the author of a dozen plays, although only three survive: *Apostolado de las Indias y martirio de un cacique* (Apostolate of the Indies and Martyrdom of a Chieftain), *Si el amor excede al arte, ni amor ni arte a la prudencia* (If Love Is Greater Than Art, Neither Love Nor Art Are Wise), and *La pérdida de España* (The Loss of Spain). *See also* THEATER.

VELOSO, CAETANO (Brazil, 1942–). Musician and lyricist. One of the main exponents of the counterculture movement Tropicália in the

1960s and 1970s, Caetano Veloso is one of Brazil's most recognized popular musicians. His connection to literature is mainly through his involvement in this movement, which brought together popular artists and erudite culture, such as **concrete poetry**, some of whose devices are seen in many of the popular lyrics of the period. Veloso published an autobiographical account of Tropicália, *Verdade Tropical* (1997; *Tropical Truth*), and a volume of his song lyrics, *Letra Só* (2003; Only Lyrics). *See also* GULLAR, FERREIRA; SALOMÃO, WALY; TOLENTINO, BRUNO.

VENEZUELA. The territory that constitutes Venezuela today was not occupied by an advanced society in pre-Columbian times and was a culturally marginalized region in the colonial era. It figures in **Juan de Castellanos**'s verse **chronicle**, but the first major history of the conquest and colonization was the 18th-century narrative by **José Agustín Oviedo y Baños**. Yet, although Venezuela produced no outstanding **baroque** writers, it was the birthplace of **Simón Bolívar** and **Andrés Bello**, two of the most prominent figures of the independence period, whose writings include some of Latin America's foundational texts. However, the devastation caused by the war for independence and the civil wars that followed did not leave the country in a favorable position to develop a strong literary tradition.

Costumbrismo, with its focus on local life and customs, was the predominant trend of the last part of the 19th century, but Venezuelan literature came into its own more strongly in the 20th century. **Modernismo** produced several important figures, notably **Manuel Díaz Rodríguez** in prose and **Rufino Blanco Fombona** in poetry, while the prose poems of **José Antonio Ramos Sucre** bridged the shift to later aesthetic trends. In fiction, the most significant development in the first half of the 20th century is marked by **Rómulo Gallegos**'s 1929 classic **novel of the land** *Doña Bárbara*. The foundations of a national tradition were further consolidated in the novel, short story, and essay by writers such as **Arturo Uslar Pietri, Mariano Picón Salas, Ramón Díaz Sánchez**, and **Miguel Otero Silva**. Although the **avant-garde** had yet to exert a strong influence, developments in psychology are present in the novels of **Teresa de la Parra** and **Enrique Bernardo Núñez**, and the **fantastic** figures in the short stories of **Julio Garmendia**.

The European avant-garde is more apparent in poetry since the 1950s in the work of **Juan Liscano, Vicente Gerbasi, Ramón Palomares**, and **Rafael Cadenas**, although, as in the rest of Latin America, poetry since the 1980s, represented in Venezuela by **Rafael Arráiz Lucca**, has inclined to follow the personal style of the individual poet rather than wider aesthetic trends. The same may be said of fiction. Venezuela produced no **boom** author, but fiction flourished in the second half of the 20th century through writers such as **Guillermo Menses, Oswaldo Trejo, Salvador Garmendia**, and **Adriano González León**, and the wider trends in Latin American fiction are also represented, for example, developments in the historical novel in the work of **Francisco Herrera Luque**.

The **theater** in Venezuela is also a predominantly 20th-century phenomenon when measured in terms of its success at obtaining wide recognition. In both the colonial period and the 19th century, there were active theaters and dramatists, even if European drama was often preferred. Cultural development in the first half of the 20th century was affected by the prevailing dictatorships, to the extent that the freedom to stage socially critical works or to pursue new trends in theater was curtailed. Plays in the manner of costumbrismo and **criollismo** predominated often in the form of the *apropósito*, as the Venezuelan version of the *sainete* was called. However, the 1950s brought social and political change to the country and the introduction of trends in the theater that had already become established elsewhere. Among these was the influence of figures such as Bertold Brecht, Antonin Artaud, and Constantin Stanislavski. The leading figure in the renaissance of Venezuelan theater at this time was **César Rengifo**, who had important followers in **Isaac Chocrón, José Ignacio Cabrujas**, and **Román Chalbaud**. A number of theatrical institutions and companies were founded at this time, including the **Nuevo Grupo** (1967) and the Fundación Rajatabla (1971). They not only fostered a high level of activity in Venezuela, but also brought a wider reputation in the 1970s and 1980s, established through participation in international festivals. Since then other dramatists have emerged, such as **Gustavo Ott** and **Mariela Romero**, who represents the growing importance of a number of female playwrights. *See also* CIVILIZATION AND BARBARISM; HISTORICAL NOVEL; JOURNALS; MAGIC REALISM; NEO-CLASSICISM; THEATER OF CRUELTY.

VERA, PEDRO JORGE (Ecuador, 1914–1999). Dramatist, novelist, and short story writer. Although he tried his hand at poetry, he is better known for his contributions to other genres. As a dramatist, he contributed to the social theater in Ecuador with plays such as *El dios de la selva* (1941; God of the Jungle), *Hamlet resuelve su duda* (1952; Hamlet Resolves His Doubt), and *Luto eterno* (1956; Eternal Mourning). His novels include *Los animales puros* (1946; Pure Animals), about intellectuals and revolutionaries in Guayaquil; *Tiempo de muñecos* (1971; Time of the Puppets); *El pueblo soy yo* (1975; I Am the People); and *Por la plata baila el perro* (1987; The Dog Dances for Money). His greatest successes, however, were his short stories, of which there are several collections: *Un ataúd abandonado* (1968; An Abandoned Coffin), *Los mandamientos de la ley de Dios* (1972; The Commandments of God's Law), *Jesús ha vuelto* (1978; Jesus Has Returned), and *¡Ah, los militares!* (1984; Ah, the Military!). *See also* THEATER.

VERBITSKY, BERNARDO (Argentina, 1907–1979). Novelist. After trying out the law and medicine, he eventually entered journalism. His first novel, *Es difícil aprender a vivir* (1941; Learning to Live Is Difficult), generally set the pattern his fiction would follow: realistically told stories of life in Argentina, often set in an urban milieu. His novels include *Una pequeña familia* (1951; A Small Family), *Calles de tango* (1953; Tango Streets), *Un noviazgo* (1957; An Engagement to Marry), *Villa miseria también es América* (1957; Shantytown Is Also America), *Un hombre de papel* (1966; Paper Man), *Hermana y sombra* (1977; Sister and Shadow), and *A pesar de todo* (1978; In Spite of It All). His fiction also includes two volumes of short stories: *Café de los angelitos* (1950; Little Angel Café) and *La tierra es azul* (1961; The Land Is Blue). In addition to one collection of poems, *Megatón* (1942; Megaton), he wrote screenplays and books on literature, including one on the American dramatist Arthur Miller (1915–2005), and another on Shakespeare and Cervantes.

VERDEAMARELISMO. In the context of modernist tendencies in Brazil, **Plínio Salgado**, **Paulo Menotti del Picchia**, and **Cassiano Ricardo** authored the manifesto "O Curupira e o Carão" (1927; "The Curupira Being and the Big-Faced Monster"), in which they criticized the **Week of Modern Art** and founded a new art movement called "Movimento Verde Amerelo" (Green Yellow Movement), also known as "Verdeamarelismo" (Green-Yellowism). The movement had a conservative nationalist focus and militantly promoted antirationalist values. In reaction to **Oswald de Andrade**'s **antropofagia**, these authors and **Raul Bopp** drafted "Manifesto do Verdeamarelismo ou da Escola da Anta" (1929; "Green-Yellow Manifesto or of the School of the Tapir"), starting a polemic. Eventually, Bopp and Ricardo dropped out and the movement degenerated into a fascist trend known as Integralism, led by Salgado.

VERÍSSIMO, ÉRICO (Brazil, 1905–1975). Novelist and short story writer. Born in the southern state of Rio Grande do Sul, Veríssimo worked briefly as a pharmacist before he decided on a literary career. He first was secretary and editor for *Revista do Globo* for the publishing house Globo, and he translated English novels, especially by Aldous Huxley (1894–1963) and Somerset Maugham (1874–1965), which eventually influenced his own writing. His first novel, *Clarissa* (1933; Clarissa), a fictional memoir in the style of **Brazilian modernism**, was the first of a cycle of novels that launched his career. Four more novels in this cycle are *Caminhos Cruzados* (1935; *Crossroads*), *Música ao Longe* (1935; Music from Afar), *Um Lugar ao Sol* (1936; A Place in the Sun), and *Saga* (1940; Saga). The short story collections *Fantoches* (1932; Puppets) and *As Mãos do Meu Filho* (1935; The Hands of My Son), and the novels *Olhai os Lírios do Campo* (1938; *Consider the Lilies of the Field*), *O Resto É Silêncio* (1943; *The Rest Is Silence*), and *Noite* (1954; *Night*), mostly set in the region of Rio Grande do Sul, helped consolidate his reputation as a writer in the vein of **regionalism**. Invited by the government, Veríssimo journeyed to the United States in 1941 and then published a book of travel writing, *Gato Preto em Campo de Neve* (1941, Black Cat in a Snowfield), based on his experiences. Other books describing travel in the United States, Mexico, and Israel include *A Volta do Gato Preto* (1941; The Return of the Black Cat), *México, História de uma Viagem* (1957; *Mexico*), and *Israel em Abril* (1970, Israel in April).

Veríssimo's reputation as a novelist, however, rests on his trilogy *O Tempo e o Vento* (Time and the Wind), the first volume of which, *O*

Continente (1949; The Continent), was a **best seller** and was praised by critics. The other volumes are *O Retrato* (1951; The Portrait) and *O Arquipélago* (Books 1 & 2, 1961; Book 3, 1962; The Archipelago). This epic saga tells of the settlement of southern Brazil and the consolidation of its patriarchal society, a work committed to the social and the local but with universal aspirations and exhibiting a concern with narrative time. Veríssimo later produced more universal and psychological urban fiction inspired by recent international topics, including *O Senhor Embaixador* (1965; The Ambassador), *O Prisoneiro* (1967; The Prisoner), and *Incidente em Antares* (1972; Incident in Antares). He also published many books of **children's literature**, the essay *Brazilian Literature: An Outline* (1945), and a volume of memoirs, *Solo de Clarineta: Memórias* (2 vols., 1973–1976; Clarinet Solo: Memoirs), whose title hints at Veríssimo's lifelong passion for music. See also VERÍSSIMO, LUIS FERNANDO.

VERÍSSIMO, LUÍS FERNANDO (Brazil, 1936–). Novelist, journalist, and short story writer. Son of **Erico Veríssimo**, Luis Fernando Veríssimo first took up writing as a translator and journalist. His own novels and short stories often rely on the creation of specific characters who reappear in several of his works. He is noted as a **best seller**, prolific humorist, and writer of short prose pieces that chronicle aspects of contemporary life in Brazil. Among his main works are *O Analista de Bagé* (1981; The Analyst from Bagé), *Comédias da Vida Privada* (1994; Comedies of Private Life), *O Clube dos Anjos* (1998; *The Club of Angels*), *Borges e os Orangotangos Eternos* (2000; Borges and the Eternal Orangotangos), and *As Mentiras Que os Homens Contam* (2000; Lies Men Tell).

VERÍSSIMO DIAS DE MATOS, JOSÉ (Brazil, 1857–1916). Born in the northern state of Pará, Veríssimo studied in Rio, but went back to his home state, where he worked as a journalist and educator. He traveled to Europe and participated in literary and anthropological congresses, eventually settling in Rio, where he became a full-time educator and critic, a cofounder of the Brazilian Academy of Letters (*see* ACADEMIAS), and editor of the **journal** *Revista Brasileira* (Brazilian Review). Veríssimo is remembered as one of the three most important critics of his time, together with Tristão de

Alencar Araripe Júnior (1848–1911) and **Sílvio Romero**, who were influenced by Hyppolite Taine (1828–1893), Ferdinand Brunetière (1849–1908), **positivism**, and **naturalism**. Veríssimo followed a different path, relying mostly on his own observations along with philosophical and moral judgments, yet attempting unbiased global appreciations. Among his sociological essays are *Cenas da Vida Amazônica* (1888; Scenes of Amazonian Life), *Educação Nacional* (1890; National Education), *A Amazônia: Aspectos Econômicos* (1892; The Amazon: Economic Aspects), *Que é Literatura? E Outros Escritos* (1907; What Is Literature? and Other Writings), *Interesses da Amazônia* (1915; Interests of the Amazon), and *Homens e Coisas Estrangeiros* (3 vols., 1902–1910; Foreign Men and Things). His *História da Literatura Brasileira* (1916; History of Brazilian Literature), *A Literatura Nacional e os Estudos Literários* (1894; National Literature and Literary Studies), and *Estudos brasileiros* (1904; Brazilian Studies) were major landmarks of Brazilian literary history in a crucial moment of national definition.

VIANA, JAVIER DE (Uruguay, 1868–1926). Short story writer. He was an unsuccessful landowner from a family of landowners and made his living as a writer. His first book was a collection of short stories, *Campo* (1896; The Country), which established the rural focus of much of his writing and places him within the prevailing trend of **criollismo**. A novel, *Gaucha* (1899; Gaucha), appeared not long after, but Viana's reputation rests principally on his **gaucho** stories, of which he published more than a dozen collections during the last 15 years of his life. These include *Leña seca* (1911; Dry Wood), *Yuyos* (1912; Weeds), *Cardos* (1919; Thistles), *Abrojos* (1919; Burrs), *Del campo y de la ciudad* (1921; From the Country and the City), *La Biblia gaucha* (1925; The Gaucho Bible), and *Tardes del fogón* (1925; Evenings by the Campfire).

VIEIRA, ANTÔNIO (Brazil, 1608–1697). Orator and prose writer. Born in Portugal, Vieira was educated in Brazil and spent his life between the two countries, with a brief period in Rome. A brilliant student, he soon joined the Jesuit order and became one of the most important defenders of the Indians in Brazil and the Jews in Portugal. He had an eventful life, often running into trouble because of the outspoken political and religious views he expressed as an orator. Three volumes of *Cartas* (1735–1746; Letters) and a 16-volume collection of *Sermões* (1679–1748; Sermons) are considered prime examples of **baroque** rhetoric and argumentation. His works, noted for their elegance and style in the use of the Portuguese language, are required reading for many university students in Brazil and Portugal. His *Obras do Padre Antônio Vieira* (1854–1858; Works of Father Antonio Vieira) span 25 volumes. *See also* RIBEIRO, JOÃO UBALDO.

VIEIRA, JOSÉ GERALDO (Brazil, 1897–1977). Novelist. Born in the Azores, Vieira arrived in Brazil when he was three. Although his first publication was a prose poem based on images of Greece, *O Triste Epigrama* (1919; The Sad Epigram), he is noted mostly for his psychological novels of introspection from the second phase of **Brazilian modernism**. His works include *A Mulher que Fugiu de Sodoma* (1931; The Woman Who Fled Sodom), *Território Humano* (1936; Human Territory), *A Quadragésima Porta* (1943; The Fortieth Door), *A Túnica e os Dados* (1947; The Tunic and the Dice), *A Ladeira da Memória* (1950; The Slope of Memory), *Terreno Baldio* (1961; Waste Land), and *A Mais Que Branca* (1975; The More Than White).

VILALTA, MARUXA (Mexico, 1932–). Dramatist. Although she began her writing career as a novelist and short story writer, it is in **theater** that she has made her name. Her first play, *Los desorientados* (1960; The Confused), about the egocentricity of youth, was adpated from a novel. *Un país feliz* (1963; A Happy Country) deals with the distortion of truth under dictatorships, and *El 9* (1965; No. 9) is about the mechanization of humanity. In two plays of the same period, *La última letra* (1964; The Last Letter) and *Cuestión de narices* (1966; A Matter of Noses), her work took a turn toward the **theater of the absurd** in order to present the contradictions between what people say and what they do. Other titles include *Nada como el piso 16* (1976; Nothing Like Apt. 16); *Historia de él* (1978; Story of Him); and *Una mujer, dos hombres y un balazo* (1981; A Women, Two Men, and a Bullet), a collection of four one-act plays. She has written several plays with religious themes: *Una voz en el desierto: vida de*

San Jerónimo (1991; A Voice in the Wilderness: Life of Saint Je-
rome), *Francisco de Asís* (1992; Francis of Assisi), *Jesucristo entre
nosotros* (1994; Christ Among Us), and *Ignacio y los jesuitas* (1997;
Ignatius and the Jesuits). More recently, she has written a play on the
Mexican Revolution, *1910* (2000), and *Con vista a la bahía* (2007;
With a View of the Bay). *See also* WOMEN.

VILARIÑO, IDEA (Uruguay, 1920–). Poet. She was one of
Uruguay's most important poets of the 1940s and 1950s. Her
first collections, *La suplicante* (1945; The Supplicant) and *Cielo,
cielo* (1947; Heaven, Heaven), were both quite short, but already
showed the individuality of her voice, which appeared more
strongly in the collections that followed: *Por aire sucio* (1951;
Through Dirty Air); *Nocturnos* (1955; Nocturns), in which the
spareness of her writing is very evident; and *Poemas de amor*
(1958; Love Poems), a collection dedicated to her former husband,
Juan Carlos Onetti. Suffering and death, solitude and fear are
among her recurring themes, written in an extraordinarily econo-
mical style. Her later collections are *Pobre Mundo* (1966; Poor
World), *Poesía* (1970; Poetry), *No* (1980; No), *Canciones* (1993;
Songs), *Poesía 1945–1990* (1994; Poetry 1945–1990), and *Poesía
completa* (2002; Complete Poems). Vilariño has written books on
Julio Herrera y Reissig and **Rubén Darío**, and two books on
tango: *Las letras de tango* (1965; Tango Lyrics) and *El tango can-
tado* (1981; The Sung Tango). Her verse translations of Shakespeare have been performed very successfully, and several of her
song lyrics are very popular. *See also* WOMEN.

VILLA, FRANCISCO (Mexico, 1877–1923). Known more popularly
as Pancho Villa, although his real name was José Doroteo Arango.
As a general in the revolutionary army in Mexico, he entered the
capital in triumph in 1913 with **Emiliano Zapata**. Two years later,
he was defeated by a rival revolutionary general, Álvaro Obregón
(1880–1928), and spent much of the last years of his life as a virtual
outlaw. His career as a revolutionary general figures significantly in
the **novel of the Mexican Revolution**, notably in the work of authors
such as **Martín Luis Guzmán, Mariano Azuela**, and **Rafael F. Muñoz**. *See also* CAMPOBELLO, NELLIE.

VILLAURRUTIA, XAVIER (Mexico, 1903–1950). Poet and dramatist. As a member of **Los Contemporáneos**, his work is associated with the **avant-garde**. Known for his epigrammatic wit and linguistic virtuosity, his poetry is contained mainly in three collections: *Reflejos* (1926; Reflections), *Nostalgia de la muerte* (1938; Nostalgia for Death), and *Canto a la primavera y otros poemas* (1948; Song to Spring and Other Poems). Of these, *Nostalgia de la muerte*, and the "Nocturnos" (Nocturns) included in this book, are among his most successful poems. Villaurrutia was a very active figure in experimental **theater** as a director, translator, and author. He published a set of five one-act plays under the title *Autos profanos* (1943; Secular Allegories) and six three-act dramas for commercial production. His theater shows the influence of both classical mythology, William Shakespeare (1564–1616), and Jean Racine (1639–1699), as well as recent European dramatists such as Jean Cocteau (1889–1963), Antonin Artaud (1896–1948), and Luigi Pirandello (1867–1936). His best-known play is *Invitación a la muerte* (1940; Invitation to Death), a modern adaptation of Shakespeare's *Hamlet*, a work that reflected his growing preoccupation with death. He also wrote literary and film criticism and a short novel, *Dama de corazones* (1928; Queen of Hearts). The Xavier Villaurrutia Prize for literature was established in his honor in 1955. *See also* BASURTO, LUIS G.; CHUMACERO, ALÍ; TORRES BODET, JAIME.

VIÑAS, DAVID (Argentia, 1929–). Novelist. Although a contemporary of the **boom** generation, he has not attracted the same level of attention. His novels are often on political subjects and center on real events as representative moments of particular periods in Argentinean history. His first novel, *Cayó sobre su rostro* (1955; He Fell on His Face), conveys the passage of power to the liberal president Hipólito Yrigoyen in 1916. *Los años despiadados* (1956; The Pitiless Years) is set in the presidency of **Juan Domingo Perón**. Among the later novels, *Los dueños de la tierra* (1958; Owners of the Land), deals with conflicts over land tenure in Patagonia in the time of Yrigoyen; *La semana trágica* (1966; The Tragic Week) is concerned with a period of labor conflicts in 1919, also in Yrigoyen's time; and *Los hombres de a caballo* (1967; Men on Horseback) is a family chronicle that covers several generations of Argentinean history. *Cuerpo a cuerpo* (1979; Body to Body) is a darker novel about a journalist exploring the life of a general. It was written in exile in Spain, where Viñas had taken refuge from the dictatorship in Argentina, which had claimed the lives of his two children and close friends. The author's more recent novels include *Prontuario* (1993; File) and *Tarabul, o los últimos argentinos del siglo XX* (2006; Tarabul, or the Last Argentineans of the 20th Century).

In a historical vein similar to that developed in his novels, Viñas has written very successfully for the **theater**: *Sara Goldman, mujer de teatro* (1956; Sara Goldman, Woman of the Theater), *Lisandro* (1972; Lysander), *Túpac Amaru* (1973; Tupac Amaru), and *El fusilamiento de Dorrego* (1973; The Execution of Dorrego). He is also the author of a number of volumes of essays on politics and literature in Argentina, as well as of several well-received books on politics and literature, including *Literatura argentina y realidad política: de Sarmiento a Cortázar* (1970; Argentinean Literature and Political Reality: From Sarmiento to Cortázar) and *Indios, ejército y fronteras* (1982; Indians, Army, and Frontiers).

VITALE, IDA (Uruguay, 1923–). Poet. Having lived much of her life outside Uruguay, she is better known in **Mexico** and the United States than in her own country. In contrast to many poets, she is not inclined to develop the autobiographical in her verse. Her first three books form a group: *La luz de esta memoria* (1949; The Light of This Memory) reflects a nostalgia for the past, *Palabra dada* (1953; Given Word) emphasizes solitude, and *Cada uno en su noche* (1960; Each in His Night) has a somewhat elegiac mood. With *Oidor andante* (1972; Walking Listener), her focus turned to the instability and ineffectiveness of language, and she brought references to Montevideo into her work. This was followed by *Fieles* (1976; Faithful), *Jardín de sílice* (1980; Silicon Garden), *Elegías en otoño* (1982; Elegies in Autumn), *Entrecasa* (1984; Around the House), and *Sueños de la constancia* (1988; Dreams of Constance), all published in Mexico.

Léxico de afinidades (1994; Lexicon of Affinities) and *Donde vuela el camaleón* (1996; Where the Cameleon Flies) are both collections of short pieces of poetic prose, a mix of different kinds of texts, some about everyday life, others about literary and cultural figures, and with a highly playful tone, especially *Donde vuela el camaleón*. A similar variety is found in *Procura de lo imposible* (1998; Acquire the Impossible), 90 poems about places, people, life, the land, and the inability of literature to capture life. By contrast, *Reducción del infinito* (2000; Reduction of the Infinite) is more restrained and is an interaction with the Uruguayan poet **Julio Herrera y Reissig**. Among Vitale's works published since then are *De plantas y animales: acercamientos literarios* (2003; Of Plants and Animals: Literary Approaches) and *El abc de byobu* (2004; Byobu's ABC), the latter a collection of pieces in prose that introduce a character named Byobu. *See also* WOMEN.

– W –

WALSH, MARÍA ELENA (Argentina, 1930–). Poet, short story writer, singer/song writer. At the age of 17 she published *Otoño imperdonable* (1947; Unforgiveable Autumn), a collection of critically acclaimed, neo-romantic poems. This was followed by *Apenas viaje* (1948; Scarce Journey) and *Baladas con Ángel* (1952; Ballads with Ángel), written in collaboration with Ángel Bonomini (1929–1994). Shortly after, Walsh left Argentina for France, where she formed a folklore singing duo with Leda Valladares (1919–). At the same time, she also turned to **children's literature** and produced a series of books for children in the 1960s: *Tutú Marambá* (1960; Tutu Maramba), *El reino del revés* (1963; Topsy-Turvy Land), *Zoo loco* (1964; Crazy Zoo), *Cuentopos de Gulubú* (1966; Storytales of Gulubú), and *Dailán Kifki* (1966; Dailan Kifki). Her stories are highly imaginative and make ample use of nonsense and wordplay.

On her return to Argentina, she revived her singing career and had considerable impact on the music scene. Collections of her song lyrics appeared in *Juguemos en el mundo* (1970; Let's Play in the World) and *Cancionero contra el mal de ojo* (1976; Songbook Against the Evil Eye). Her writing for children continued, acquiring a political edge and serving to combat stereotypes with books such as *El diablo inglés* (1974; The English Devil), a new look at the British invasion of 1806; *Bisa Vuela* (1985), a title meaning "Bisa Flies" that plays on the Spanish word *bisabuela*, meaning "great-grandmother"; and *La nube traicionera* (1989; The Traiterous Cloud).

Walsh has also written for adults. *Hecho a mano* (1965; Hand-made) is a collection of love poems that focus on **women**; *Los poemas* (1984; The Poems) gathers together the poetry Walsh had been writing over a period of time; *Novios de antaño, 1930–1940* (1990; Lovers of a Bygone Age) was a **best seller**, a look at life in a past decade; and *Desventuras en el País-Jardín-de-Infantes* (1993; Misadventures in Kindergarten Land) was a collection of her newspaper articles, including many of those written during the dictatorship of the 1970s and 1980s, when she used both her writing and her music to combat oppression.

WALSH, RODOLFO (Argentina, 1927–1977). Journalist and short story writer. His *Operación masacre* (1957; Operation Massacre), an account of the assassination of members of the political opposition during the presidency of Pedro Eugenio Aramburu (1955–1958), established investigative journalism in Argentina. It was one of the first examples of the nonfiction novel and anticipated later documentary and **testimonio** writing in Latin America. Walsh wrote two other books in the same genre, *¿Quién mató a Rosendo?* (1969; Who Killed Rosendo?) and *El caso Satanowsky* (1973; The Satanowsky Case), but without his earlier success. His first collection of short stories, *Variaciones en rojo* (1953; Variations in Red), consisted of three works of **crime fiction**. Two later volumes, *Los oficios terrestres* (1965; Terrestrial Trades) and *Un kilo de oro* (1967; A Kilo of Gold), contain stories written in the manner of **Julio Cortázar**. Walsh also wrote two plays, *La granada* (1965; The Grenade) and *La batalla* (1981; The Battle), denouncing the military. He was a politically militant member of the Montoneros guerrillas and was shot and disappeared in a police ambush in 1977. *See also* THEATER.

WAST, HUGO (Argentina, 1883–1962). Novelist. Born Gustavo Martínez de Zuviría, he was a commercially successful writer who wrote a large number of popular novels. Among the more enduring of these are *Flor de durazno* (1911; Peach Blossom), *La casa de los cuervos* (1916; House of the Crows), *Valle negro* (1918; Black Valley), *Desierto de piedra* (1925; Stone Desert), *El camino de las llamas* (1930; The Way of the Flames), *Oro* (1935; Gold), and *666* (1942). He was a Catholic Nationalist, openly anti-Semitic and pro-Nazi, whose attitudes were reflected both in his fiction and his many essays. He was director of the national library for 25 years and minister of education during the presidency of General Pedro Pablo Ramírez (1943–1944), succeeding in introducing the teaching of religion into what had hitherto been a secular system of education.

WEEK OF MODERN ART. The "Semana de Arte Moderna" (or Week of Modern Art) was a series of events staged in the Municipal Theater of São Paulo, **Brazil**, on 13, 15, and 17 February 1922, including lectures, poetry readings, concerts, and an art exhibit. Among the literary participants (either directly or through their texts read at the events) were **José Pereira da Graça Aranha, Ronald de Carvalho, Paulo Menotti del Picchia, Mário de Andrade, Manuel Bandeira, Rui Ribeiro Couto, Plínio Salgado**, and **Oswald de Andrade**. The events were widely covered in the papers and caused a fair degree of public scandal among the conservative public of São Paulo, as they evidenced the provocation typical of European artistic **avant-garde** movements. Although many critics agree that modernist works were produced in Brazil previous to the Week, it has served as a benchmark to date the beginning of **Brazilian modernism**. *See also* ALMEIDA, GUILHERME DE; COELHO NETO, HENRIQUE MAXIMIANO; LOBATO, JOSÉ BENTO MONTEIRO; MACHADO, ANTÓNIO DE ALCÂNTARA; MILLIET DA COSTA E SILVA, SÉRGIO; PRADO, PAULO; SCHMIDT, AUGUSTO FREDERICO; SYMBOLISM.

WESTPHALEN, EMILIO ADOLFO (Peru, 1911– 2001). Poet. Of the same generation as **César Moro** and **Martín Adan**, Westphalen published two collections of verse in the 1930s, *Las ínsulas extrañas* (1933; Strange Islands) and *Abolición de la muerte* (1935; Abolition of Death). Both were influenced by **surrealism** and Spanish mysticism. The first, with a title taken from a line of St. John of the Cross (1542–1591), explores the inner music of the mystic; the second represents the pursuit of the beloved. After these two books, although he was engaged in other activities associated with literature, such as editing and teaching, Westphalen did not collect his own verse again for publication until the 1980s.

In *Otra imagen deleznable* (1980; Another Insignificant Image), he republished earlier work with some additional poems and then published a series of more accessible, less complex books of poetry that also included prose poems. These were *Arriba bajo el cielo* (1982; Up Beneath the Sky), *Máximas y mínimas de experiencia pedestre* (1982; Maxima and Minima in Pedestrian Experience), *Ha vuelto la Diosa Ambarina* (1986; The Goddess Ambarina Has Returned), *Belleza de una espada clavada en la lengua* (1988; The Beauty of a Sword Piercing the Tongue), *Bajo zarpas de la quimera: poemas 1930–1988* (1991; Beneath Paws of Illusion: Poems 1930–1991), and *Falsos rituales y otras patrañas* (1999; False Rituals and Other Tall Tales).

WOLFF, EGON (Chile, 1926–). Dramatist. He is the author of about 20 plays and one of Chile's most popular and successful commercial dramatists. Social conflict is customarily at the center of his plays, which focus on characters whose attitudes and behavior are determined by the ideology derived from their social class. *Mansión de lechuzas* (1958; Mansion of Owls) dramatizes the situation of a widow and her family challenged by Italian neighbors in the kind of conflict that is often played out in Wolff's **theater**. In *Parejas de trapo* (1959; Rag Couples), the conflict between self-serving members of the upper and middle classes is set against the social ethics of immigrants. In *Los invasores* (1963; The Invaders), a wealthy industrialist fears the invasion of his home by the homeless, although the audience is left in doubt about whether the invasion is real or imagined. In *Flores de papel* (1970; *Paper Flowers*), an encounter between a middle-class woman and an unemployed man off the street explores their differences and the common ground they find through communication. Some of the political tension in Wolff's drama, such as *Flores de papel*, is marked by the rise and fall of the Popular Unity government in Chile (1970–1973). His other plays include *El signo de Caín* (1969; The Sign of Cain), *Kindergarten* (1977; Kindergarden), *Espejismo* (1978; Illusion), *Álamos en la azotea* (1981; Poplars on the Terrace), *La balsa de la Medusa* (1984; The Raft of the Medusa), and *Tras una puerta cerrada* (2000; Behind a Closed Door).

WOMEN. The presence of women in the contemporary Latin American literary scene is firmly established both as writers and as subjects of a discourse that recognizes their psychological complexity, the diversity of their social roles, the specificity of feminine points of view, the particularities of female bodies and desires, and the nature of women's experiences. Yet this has all come about mainly in the last century. The claiming of the public sphere by women in Latin America, as in many other regions of the world, is a relatively recent phenomenon.

Literature in the colonial period was a territory that left little space for women. Conventual life offered some opportunity, but there were limitations. The environment it provided for reflection led to a body of significant writings, such as the spiritual and biographical works of **Madre Castillo (Colombia)**, but it ultimately denied creativity and intellectual freedom. As discovered by **Sor Juana Inés de la Cruz (Mexico)**, Latin America's most prominent female writer of the colonial era, the convent was no refuge from the constraints of a patriarchal society.

During the colonial period, much of the 19th century, and the early years of the 20th, albeit to a lesser extent, women were publicly absent from literature as writers and present mainly through representation in the work of male authors. This meant that women often figured in relation to the expression of male feelings and desires, or were described stereotypically to convey notions such as beauty, innocence, or maternity. In the **romantic** novel, such as *Clemencia* (1869; *Clemencia*) by **Ignacio Manuel Altamirano** (Mexico) or *Cumandá, o un drama entre salvajes* (1879; Cumandá, or a Drama Among Savages) by **Juan León Mera (Ecuador)**, women were cast in highly symbolic roles in narratives intended to illustrate the nation's struggle toward an ordered society in control of the elements that constitute it, in which the female characters are often representative of the perils facing the nation itself. In **naturalist** fiction, such as *Santa* (1903; Santa) by **Federico Gamboa** (Mexico) or *Historia de arrabal* (1922; Suburban Story) by **Manuel Gálvez (Argentina)**, stories of women forced into prostitution serve to dramatize the corrupting influences of the new urban environments and growing industrialization at the beginning of the 20th century.

Nevertheless, by the late 19th century women were acquiring a more prominent profile in literary circles. In her early fiction, **Mercedes Cabello de Carbonera** (**Peru**) followed the conventions of romanticism, but became more socially critical in later works. **Júlia Lopes de Almeida** (**Brazil**) and **Soledad Acosta de Samper** (Colombia) were more inclined to **realism**, and both narrated the lives of everyday women in their fiction. Whether through literary **journals** or salons, Acosta de Samper and **Juana Manuela Gorriti** (**Argentina**) fostered the literary and intellectual life of both sexes and, in this regard, anticipated the work of **Victoria Ocampo** (Argentina), who was celebrated for such activities in the mid-20th century. The promotion of women writers, in addition to her proto-feminism, also figured in the engagement with literature by **Clorinda Matto de Turner** (Peru), although she is best known for her classic novel *Aves sin nido* (1889; *Torn from the Nest*), one of the founding texts of **indigenismo**.

The first half of the 20th century saw the appearance of a number of significant women poets. Of these, the most celebrated is **Gabriela Mistral** (**Chile**) who, in 1945, became Latin America's first **Nobel** laureate and is the only Latin American woman to have been honored with the award to date. In Brazil, **Gilka Machado** wrote erotic poetry in the styles established by **parnassianism** and **symbolism** and was considered the greatest woman poet of Brazil in her age, before falling into oblivion. In Spanish America, **Delmira Agustini** and **Juana de Ibarborou**, both from **Uruguay**, and **Alfonsina Storni** from Argentina, inherited the style of **modernismo** and fashioned it to their own aesthetic needs and the predominantly lyrical tone employed to convey their feelings and experiences. As a group, they are in some respects pioneers, writers who claimed the legitimacy of women as poets for the generations that followed them in the **avant-garde** and post-avant-garde periods. Among some of their notable successors are **Claribel Alegría** and **Claudia Lars** (**El Salvador**); **Norah Lange** and **Alejandra Pizarnik** (Argentina); **Blanca Varela** (Peru); **Cecília Meireles, Adélia Prado,** and **Ana Cristina César** (Brazil); and **Idea Vilariño** and **Ida Vitale** (Uruguay), whose poetry embodies the perspective of their identity as women and embraces themes that range widely, from the personal to the social, from politics to philosophy.

Though women have distinguished themselves in poetry, the impact of feminism and what is commonly known as the "women's movement" has perhaps been felt more strongly in prose, given its higher circulation in both national and international markets. The Brazilian novelist, journalist, and political activist **Patrícia Galvão**, also known as Pagu, wrote fiction such as *Parque Industrial* (1933; *Industrial Park*), a tale of class oppression in São Paulo influenced by avant-garde vocabularies. Narratives of the female subject were undertaken in a variety of modes in the mid-20th century. The writing of **Marta Brunet** (Chile), in novels such as *Humo hacia el sur* (1946; Smoke in the South), is related to **criollismo**, realism, and **naturalism**, whereas **María Luisa Bombal**, in *La última niebla* (1935; *The Final Mist*), uses the techniques of **surrealism**. Yet, like others of their generation, both authors are equally concerned in their works with verisimilitude in the psychological portrayal of female characters, the conflict between interior worlds and society, female sexuality, and the expectations placed on women by a patriarchal society. These are among the issues explored by **Marta Lynch** (Argentina) in her novels of female desire and politics and best represented in *La señora Ordóñez* (1967; Mrs. Ordóñez), or by the Brazilians **Lygia Fagundes Telles** and **Clarice Lispector** in their respective novels, *Ciranda de Pedra* (1954; *Stone Dance Song*) and *A Paixão Segundo G.H.* (1964; *The Passion According to G.H.*). On a different scale, women writers of the same period also explored wider themes of national interest, such as the rebellions that have punctuated Mexico's often conflicted history, such as **Rosario Castellanos**'s *Oficio de tinieblas* (1962; *The Book of Lamentations*), about a 19th-century indigenous revolt, and **Elena Garro**'s story of the Cristero Wars (1926–1929), *Los recuerdos del porvenir* (1963; *Recollection of Things to Come*). Both were ground-breaking works in their day.

Since the mid-20th century the growing strength of feminism and the evolution of social attitudes toward women have been reflected in Latin America in an explosive increase in the cohort of women writers and the continuing exploration by women of themselves as subjects and social beings. Although there were no women **boom** writers, the **post-boom** generation includes several female authors, whose work has been widely translated and recognized. Among the most prominent are **Isabel Allende** (Chile), who won international recognition with her novel *La casa de los espíritus* (1982; *The House of the Spirits*), and **Laura Esquivel** (Mexico), who owes her celebrity to *Como agua para chocolate* (1989; *Like Water for Chocolate*). Both novels were international **best sellers**, and both tell the history of their author's country from the perspective of recent generations of women, not without significant touches of **magic realism**. In Brazil, **Nélida Piñon** produced a comparable family saga, *A República dos Sonhos* (1984; *The Republic of Dreams*), which also became well known beyond her own country.

Among other women whose writing has had national significance and has become known internationally, **Luisa Valenzuela** (Argentina) has examined her country's recent history of political violence and the problems of exile and return; **Elena Poniatowska** (Mexico), using her skills as a journalist, has written **testimonios** on the Mexican Revolution, the **Tlatelolco massacre**, and the 1985 earthquake that devastated parts of Mexico City; and **Gioconda Belli (Nicaragua)** has written about the role of women in the Sandinista Revolution (1979) in her novel *La mujer habitada* (1988; *The Inhabited Woman*). The world of politics and the social structure were also the themes of the early fiction of **Cristina Peri Rossi** (Uruguay), although her recent work has focused more on eroticism, female sexuality, and **lesbianism**. Others who have also explored such themes successfully while offering a critique of the conventional expectations placed on women by society include the Chilean **Diamela Eltit** and the Brazilians **Hilda Hilst** and **Joyce Cavalcante**.

Examples of nonfiction prose already cited above in connection with works by Elena Poniatowska draw attention to testimonial writing. One of the most celebrated examples of this genre in Latin America, however, is that based on the experiences of the **Nobel Peace Prize** winner **Rigoberta Menchú (Guatemala)**, *Me llamo Rigoberta Menchú y así me nació la conciencia* (1982; *I, Rigoberta Menchú: An Indian Woman in Guatemala*). Another example is the narrative of **Domitila Barrios de Chungara** (Ecuador), *Si me permiten hablar: testimonio de Domitila, una mujer de las minas de Bolivia* (1978; *Let Me Speak! Testimony of Domitila, a Woman of the Bolivian Mines*). Just as they have fought for their own rights and social recognition, women have also stood behind the marginalized and the exploited, whose stories they have told to publicize their plight and seek social vindication. Latin American women are also prominent in the fields of journalism, cultural commentary, and literary criticism, **Beatriz Sarlo** (Argentina) and **Margo Glantz** (Mexico) being among those who have excelled in these areas, while others, such as Clarice Lispector, who are best known for their fiction, have established their reputations as journalists or as writers of **chronicles**.

The 20th century also witnessed the growing presence of women in the theater as writers, directors, and entrepreneurs. In Chile, **Isidora Aguirre** has written on many themes in drama that are a strong indication of her social commitment, and among her best plays are those that, like her historical drama *Lautaro: epopeya del pueblo mapuche* (1982; Lautaro: Epic of the Mapuche), implement the principles of **Brechtian theater**. In Mexico, **Sabina Berman** has also written historical plays, and plays are a significant part of the oeuvre of **Maruxa Vilalta**, who has also developed dramas on religious and social themes. The dramatization of issues concerning women is a particular strength of another Mexican dramatist, **Luisa Josefina Hernández**. In Argentina, the most celebrated woman dramatist is **Griselda Gambaro**, whose plays often employ the techniques of the **theater of the absurd** and the **theater of cruelty** to expose the problem of state violence in her country. Among her best-known pieces is *El campo* (1967; *The Camp*). In Brazil, Hilda Hilst has also written important pieces for the theater, including *Rato no Muro* (Mouse in the Wall) and *A Possessa* (The Possessed Woman), influenced by her poetry and the environment of São Paulo. Thus, as in poetry and prose, Latin American theater has an established cohort of distinguished women playwrights whose work not only embraces a wide range of themes but ensures, as do the women poets and prose writers, that issues of concern to women, and women themselves, remain in the forefront of contemporary literature. *See also* ACOSTA, DELFINA; ACUÑA DE FIGUEROA, FRANCISCO; AGUSTÍN, JOSÉ; AMADO, JORGE; ÁNGEL, ALBALUCÍA; BARROS, PÍA; BOULLOSA, CARMEN; BRITTON, ROSA MARÍA; BUITRAGO, FANNY; BULLRICH, SILVINA; CAMPOBELLO, NELLIE; CAMPOS, JULIETA; COUTINHO, SÔNIA; CUNHA, HELENA PARENTE; EICHELBAUM, SAMUEL; FERNÁNDEZ DE LIZARDI, JOSÉ JOAQUÍN; FUTORANSKY, LUISA; GALLARDO, SARA; GAMERO, LUCIA; GORODISCHER, ANGÉLICA; GUIDO, BEA-

TRIZ; IBÁÑEZ, SARA DE; IPARRAGUIRRE, SYLVIA; LISBOA, HENRIQUETA; LYRA, CARMEN; MASTRETTA, ÁNGELES; MENDOZA, MARÍA LUISA; MERCADER, MARTHA; MERCADO, TUNUNA; NARANJO, CARMEN; OCAMPO, MARÍA LUISA; OCAMPO, SILVINA; ODIO, EUNICE; OLLÉ, CARMEN; OREAMUNO, YOLANDA; OROZCO, OLGA; PARRA, TERESA DE LA; PARRA, VIOLETA; PETIT, MAGDALENA; PLA, JOSEFINA; POESIA MARGINAL; POLETTI, SYRIA; PORTAL, MAGDA; PORZECANSKI, TERESA; POST-BOOM; PUGA, MARÍA LUISA; QUEIRÓS, DINAH SILVEIRA DE; QUEIRÓS, RAQUEL DE; RAZNOVICH, DIANA; REBELO, MARQUES; RÍO, ANA MARÍA DEL; ROFFÉ, REINA; ROMERO, MARIELA; SOCA, SUSANA; SOMERS, ARMONÍA; TRABA, MARTA; TRISTÁN, FLORA; VAZ FERREIRA, MARÍA EUGENIA; YÁÑEZ COSSÍO, ALICIA; ZAMORA, DAISY.

WYLD OSPINA, CARLOS (Guatemala, 1891–1956). Novelist. Although he also wrote poetry and essays, he is best known as an accomplished novelist in the style of **criollismo**. Among his works are *El solar de los Gonzaga: novela de la ciudad pequeña* (1924; Ancestral Home of the Gonzagas: A Novel of the Small City), *La gringa* (1936; The Foreigner), and *Los lares apagados* (1958; Extinguished Hearths).

– X –

XIMÉNEZ, FRANCISCO (Guatemala, 1666–ca. 1721). Historian. He was a Dominican priest who wrote important early histories of Guatemala and several studies of native languages. Among his accomplishements is the transcription and translation from Quiché of the *Popol Vuh*, one of the most significant records of pre-Columbian mythology from Guatemala.

XISTO, PEDRO (Brazil, 1901–1987). Poet. Born in Pernambuco, Xisto joined Brazil's Foreign Service and served in the Far East and Europe. He began producing haikus in 1949 and actively promoted Brazilian **avant-garde** poetry at home and abroad. Joining the

concrete poetry movement in the late 1950s, he published poems in the **journal** *Noigandres 3*. He also translated many haikus.

– Y –

YÁÑEZ, AGUSTÍN (Mexico, 1904–1980). Short story writer and novelist. In addition to his success in literature, he was a prominent political figure, having served as governor of the state of Jalisco (1953–1959) and later as minister of education during the presidency of Gustavo Díaz Ordaz (1964–1970). Much of his early writing focused on Jalisco, his native state. He wrote a number of books on the places and people of the region: *Por tierras de Nueva Galicia* (1928; Through the Lands of New Galicia), *Espejismo de Juchitán* (1940; Illusions of Juchitán), *Genio y figura de Guadalajara* (1942; The Genius and Form of Guadalajara), and *Yahualica* (1946). His first collections of stories also emerged from his Jalisco experiences and include *Flor de juegos antiguos* (1942; Garland of Traditional Games), on childhood, and *Archipiélago de mujeres* (1943; Archipelago of Women), a rewriting of a number of classic love stories from European literature in a Mexican context and from the perspective of adolescence. *Los sentidos al aire* (1964; Feelings in the Air) also brought a group of stories together from the same source. In *La ladera dorada* (1978; The Golden Hillside), however, he developed themes of maturity and old age, drawing on mythology, the Bible, and European literature. Although not published until close to the end of his life, its conception and some of its content belong to the early period.

Yáñez's first novel, *Al filo del agua* (1947; *The Edge of the Storm*), was also his most successful and a landmark in Mexican literature. It is set in a small town in Jalisco at a time immediately before the beginning of the revolution. Not only did he bring some of the techniques of literary modernism into his writing, such as interior monologue and counterpoint, but he transformed the **novel of the Mexican Revolution** by turning it from a novel based on the narration of events into one that focused on the stresses and traditions of social life and the psychology of characters. In subsequent novels, Yáñez described various regions of Mexico, but without achieving the same impact as in *Al filo del agua*. *La creación* (1959; Creation) and *Ojerosa y pintada* (1960; Hollow-eyed and Painted) are both set in Mexico City, the former a continuation of *Al filo del agua* in the story of one of its characters whose musical career reflects the cultural ferment of postrevolutionary Mexico. By contrast, *La tierra pródiga* (1960; The Abundant Land) and *Las tierras flacas* (1962; The Lean Lands) are set in rural Mexico, the west coast and the arid interior, respectively. Both are versions of the **novel of the land** that deal with the themes of tradition versus progress, chaos against order, **civilization and barbarism**. In one of his last novels, *Las vueltas del tiempo* (1973; The Turns of Time), he again sought to retrieve the world of the characters of *Al filo del agua*. *See also* FUENTES, CARLOS.

YÁÑEZ COSSÍO, ALICIA (Ecuador, 1928–). Novelist. One of Ecuador's most prominent **women** writers, her works focus on the socially disenfranchised and introduce strong female characters who resist the traditional, patriarchal structures of social life in rich, humorously satirical views of life in the Andes. *La cofradía del mullo del vestido de la Virgen Pipona* (1985; *The Potbellied Virgin*), for example, is a tale of clan and gender rivalry over the patron virgin of an Andean town. Her other novels include *Bruna, soroche y los tíos* (1973; *Bruna and Her Sisters in the Sleeping City*), *Yo vendo unos ojos negros* (1979; I Sell Black Eyes), *Más allá de las islas* (1980; Beyond the Islands), *La casa del sano placer* (1989; House of Healthy Pleasure), and *El Cristo feo* (1995; The Ugly Christ).

– Z –

ZALAMEA, JORGE (Colombia, 1905–1969). Poet and essayist. A member of several governments in Colombia, he went into exile in 1948, remained faithful to his socialist ideals, and was unable to return to his native Colombia for fear of imprisonment. His literary production covers a wide range of genres and subjects. In his youth, he toured with a **theater** company and wrote a psychoanalytic drama for the stage, *El regreso de Eva* (1927; Eve's Return), as well as a play called *El rapto de las Sabinas* (1935; The Rape of the Sabine

Women). His essays cover subjects such as literature, history, and art. His major work, however, is his poetry. *El gran Burundún-Burundá ha muerto* (1952; The Great Burundun-Burunda Is Dead) and *La metamorfosis de su Excelencia* (1963; His Excellency's Metamorphosis) are both about tyrants and, as such, are related to the **dictator novel**. The former is a satire of the presidency of Gustavo Rojas Pinilla (1953–1957), the latter the story of a dictator who becomes aware of his faults and decides to reform. In *El sueño de las escalinatas* (1964; Dream of the Stairways), poverty confronts colonialism in a courtroom. Zalamea was the official Spanish translator of the work of Saint-John Perse (1887–1975) and published a number of volumes of his translation. His collection of poems, *La poesía ignorada y olvidada* (1965; Unknown, Forgotten Poetry), received a **Casa de las Américas** prize.

ZAMORA, DAISY (Nicaragua, 1950–). Poet. Born into a wealthy liberal family, her poetry was initially personal, but it became more political as she identified with the Sandinista Revolution in Nicaragua against Anastasio Somoza (1974–1979). She served as vice minister of culture under **Ernesto Cardenal** in the postrevolutionary government. Her poetry collections include *La violenta espuma* (1982; *The Violent Foam*), *En limpio se escribe la vida* (1988; *Clean Slate*), *A cada quien la vida* (1994; *Life for Each*), *Fiel al corazón: poemas de amor* (2005; *Faithful to the Heart: Love Poems*), and *Tierra de nadie, tierra de todos* (2007; *No Man's Land, Everybody's Land*). *See also* WOMEN.

ZAPATA, EMILIANO (1879–1919). One of the leaders of the Mexican Revolution, Emiliano Zapata fought for agrarian reform and the improvement of conditions for indigenous people. He has acquired legendary status since his murder by the Mexican army in 1919 and has served as inspiration to more recent guerrilla movements, including the Ejército Zapatista de Liberación Nacional (EZLN; Zapatista National Liberation Army), which emerged in Chiapas in 1994. Zapata's military campaign, like that of **Francisco Villa**, was also taken up in the **novel of the Mexican Revolution** by writers such as **Gregorio López y Fuentes**. *See also* LIST ARZUBIDE, GERMÁN.

ZAPATA OLIVELLA, JUAN (Colombia, 1922–2008). Poet and novelist. In addition to the novels *Pisando el camino de ébano* (1984; Treading the Ebony Trail), *Historia de un joven negro* (1990; Story of a Young Black), and *Una mujer sin raíces* (1991; A Woman without Roots), he also produced several volumes of poetry, including *Bullanguero: poesía popular* (1974; Party Time: Popular Poetry) and *Panacea: poesía liberada* (1976; Panacea: Liberated Poetry), on Afro-Colombian themes. **Manuel Zapata Olivella**, Juan's brother, was also a prominent Afro-Colombian writer.

ZAPATA OLIVELLA, MANUEL (Colombia, 1920–2004). Novelist. He was a doctor by profession who also wrote studies in ethnography, short stories, and plays, as well as the novels for which he is best known. Much of his work focuses on social injustice, especially in relation to Afro-Colombian communities. His early novels are concerned with the social reality of Colombia. *Tierra mojada* (1947; Wet Earth) tells the story of a conflict between landowners and the dispossessed. *La calle 10* (1960; Street 10) is set during the **la violencia** in the aftermath of the assassination of the presidential candidate Jorge Eliécer Gaitán (1948). *En Chimá nace un santo* (1964; *A Saint Is Born in Chimá*), a narrative that achieved some international success, is about religious fanaticism manifested in the conflict between Catholicism and local beliefs. With *Chambacú: corral de negros* (1963; *Chambacú: Black Slum*), a novel that exemplifies the connection between poverty and crime, Zapata Olivella began to write more specifically about Afro-Colombians and would become Colombia's most prominent writer of African descent. His novel *Changó, el gran putas* (1983; Changó the Whoremonger) is a work of epic proportions that traces the history of African Americans from the 16th to the 20th centuries. **Juan Zapata Olivella**, Manuel's brother, was also a prominent Afro-Colombian writer.

ZAPIOLA, JOSÉ (Chile, 1802–1885). Musician. Zapiola's contribution to the world of literature consists of a series of **newspaper** articles published between 1872 and 1876 in *La Estrella de Chile,* which constitute one of Chile's significant examples of **costumbrismo.** In due course they were collected under the title *Recuerdos de treinta* *años* (Memories of Thirty Years); they offer a view of life in Chile in the first half of the 19th century.

ZÁRATE, AGUSTÍN DE (Spain, 1514–1560). Chronicler. He is remembered for his **chronicle** *Historia del descubrimiento y conquista del Perú* (1555; *The Discovery and Conquest of Peru*).

ZORRILLA DE SAN MARTÍN, JUAN (Uruguay, 1857–1931). Poet. A post-romantic writer whose work is closely identified with Uruguayan nationalism. His narrative poems *La leyenda patria* (1879; Legend of the Fatherland) and *Tabaré* (1888; *Tabaré: An Indian Legend of Uruguay*) are both set in the history of Uruguay and exalt the author's perception of national values. *Tabaré* is a frontier tale of captivity, love, and tragedy from the time of the conquest and has obtained the greater recognition of the two. It is a work of 19th-century **indianismo**, endeavoring to re-create the life, customs, and language of the extinguished Charrúa people. Zorrilla de San Martín was also the author of numerous prose works, notably *La epopeya de Artigas* (1910; The Epic of Artigas), on the life and times of José Gervasio Artigas (1764–1850), the *caudillo* or leader considered Uruguay's founding father. In contrast to the **arielismo** of his contemporary and fellow Uruguayan **Enrique Rodó**, Zorrilla saw the spiritual and intellectual future of Latin America in the dissemination of Christian idealism.

ZUM FELDE, ALBERTO (Uruguay, 1889–1976). Essayist and critic. Born in Argentina, he grew up in Uruguay and was director of the National Library for many years. He was influenced by **arielismo** and became one of the country's leading literary critics and cultural commentators. His main publications, most having to do with Uruguay, were *Crítica de la literatura uruguaya* (1921; Criticism of Uruguayan Literature), *Proceso intelectual del Uruguay* (1930; The Intellectual Development of Uruguay), *Reseña de la historia cultural y literaria del Uruguay* (1945; Review of the Cultural and Literary History of Uruguay), *Índices críticos de la literatura hispanoamericana* (2 vols., 1954 and 1959; Critical Indices of Spanish American Literature), and *La narrativa en Hispanoamérica* (1964; Narrative in Spanish America).

ZURITA, RAÚL (Chile, 1950–). Poet. Marked by his experience of the Augusto Pinochet dictatorship (1973–1990), including imprisonment and torture, Zurita has sought radical forms of expression. With others of his generation, like **Diamela Eltit**, this has taken forms such as using the city as a canvas or the body as a medium of expression, skywriting, or writing into the landscape by inscribing texts on it to be read from the air. He has also written **concrete poetry**, but since about 1990 has generally inclined to more conventional forms of expression. His work has shown a continuing affiliation with Dante Alighieri (1265–1321), as is evident from some of his titles: *El sermón de la montaña* (1971; The Sermon on the Mount), *Áreas verdes* (1974; Green Areas), *Purgatorio* (1979; *Purgatory*), *Anteparaíso* (1982; *Anteparadise*), *El paraíso está vacío* (1984; Paradise Is Empty), *Canto a su amor desaparecido* (1985; Song to Disappeared Love), *El amor de Chile* (1987; Love of Chile), *La vida nueva* (1994; The New Life), *Poemas militantes* (2003; Militant Poems), *INRI* (2004; *INRI*), *Los países muertos* (2006; The Dead Countries), *Poemas de amor* (2007; Love Poems), *Cinco fragmentos* (2007; Five Fragments), *Las ciudades de agua* (2008; Water Cities), and *In Memoriam* (2008; In Memoriam).

Bibliography

INTRODUCTION

Like Latin American literature itself, writing about the literature also blossomed in the 20th century, especially in the second half. This is not to say that there were no significant works of literary history or criticism before this time, but it is important to draw attention to an increase in their quantity and the degree of interest Latin American literature has generated during the last 60 years. Much of the growth outside Latin America has come about following the consolidation of Latin American literature internationally as an academic discipline. It has been fueled by several factors, namely the Latin American diaspora; an increasing awareness of the strategic, political, and economic importance of the region, notably since the later stages of the Cold War; and the rise of what came to be known as area studies. In this context, Latin America has also acquired greater relevance in a wide range of academic disciplines, and the field of Latin American studies has become more prominent.

The bibliography that follows reflects that growing interest. Although it includes some titles published earlier, particularly some classics of literary history, it consists mainly of works written during the last 30 years. The number of books and essays in English in the bibliography indicates not only a preference for the inclusion of publications in English, but also just how much about Latin American literature has been published in that language and the importance of English in international literary studies. The volume of writing about it in other languages is also very extensive, although, aside from a few entries, the titles listed have been confined mainly to texts published in English, Spanish, or Portuguese.

Extensive as any bibliography of criticism in English might be, however, it has definite limitations. The publication of Brazilian literature in English translation lags behind that of the literature from Spanish American countries, a reflection of the status of Portuguese as a "less frequently taught" language in North America and elsewhere. For the same reason, criticism of Brazilian literature is not as strongly represented in English as it is for some of the Spanish-speaking countries such as Mexico, Argentina, and Chile. Whether from Brazil or Spanish America, much of what is published about Latin American literature, even in countries such as the United States and Britain, especially in academic journals, is published in Spanish or Portuguese. These are, understandably, the *linguae francae* of Latin American literary criticism, and any consideration of the subject also makes it necessary to broach the vast amount of critical work published in Latin America itself, not only about the major authors, but above all about many whose work is relatively unknown outside their own countries or is known principally in Latin America alone.

The first part of the bibliography is an introductory section concerned with Latin American literature in general. A list of reference works (bibliographies, encyclopedias, and dictionaries) is followed by general works of history and criticism. These are followed in turn by several lists in which writings about the different literary genres are collected, and this part of the bibliography concludes with a selection of anthologies, some of which are of literature in translation. Not unexpectedly, given the comments expressed in the Introduction to this volume, there is some variation in meaning of the term "Latin America" used in the titles of the books collected in the introductory section. In some titles, the term refers to Latin America in the broadest sense possible. In others, its meaning is more restricted and may refer only to a particular region or to the few countries that concern the book's author. Readers who are especially interested in Brazilian literature should also be aware that "Latin America" is often used synonymously with "Spanish America." Many books that from their titles might be expected to have a broad coverage may in fact be concerned only with literature from Spanish-speaking America.

Among the more comprehensive undertakings in English are the three-volume *The Cambridge History of Latin American Literature* (1996), edited by Roberto González Echevarría and Enrique Pupo-Walker, and *Literary Cultures of Latin America: A Comparative History* (2004), edited by Mario Valdés and Djelal Kadir, also in three volumes. Both are the products of teams of experts and both encompass the entire region, including the Spanish Caribbean. Of the two, the former has a more traditional structure and is organized historically by century, literary movement, and genre. Brazilian literature is described separately in the third volume. The comparative history by Valdés and Kadir is also organized chronologically, but is a much more expansive project, with a broader cultural orientation, that encompasses language phenomena in general and has essays on topics such as linguistics, literatures in native languages, oral literatures, newspapers and literary journals, and popular literature, as well as on literature understood in a more conventional sense. By contrast, Stephen Hart's *A Companion to Latin-American Literature* (2007) is less encyclopedic, but is a handy, single-volume discussion of both Brazilian and Spanish American literature by periods and genres that also offers a commentary on some of the major texts and authors and outlines the principal literary movements and trends of the region.

Further useful single-volume works include the *Encyclopedia of Latin American Literature* (1997), edited by Verity Smith, and the *Encyclopedia of Contemporary Latin American and Caribbean Literature, 1900–2003* (2004), edited by Daniel Balderston and others. In comparison with Balderston's work, Smith's encyclopedia includes fewer authors but has longer entries on the national literatures and a variety of literary topics, as well as entries on a number of authors and some key works. For more extended essays on some of Latin America's major authors, the four volumes of *Latin American Writers* (1989, 2002), edited by Carlos A. Solé, are also useful. For Spanish American literature, the standard histories in English include those by Enrique Anderson Imbert and Jean Franco, while José Miguel Oviedo's four-volume *Historia de la literatura hispanoamericana* (1995–2001) provides a more updated history in Spanish.

When consulting histories of the literary genres, movements, and periods, it soon becomes clear how little tendency there is in Latin American criticism to cross the boundary of the Spanish–Portuguese divide and to include writers from both linguistic regions in the same narrative. Readers interested in the history of Brazilian literature beyond the scope of the general studies for Latin America already mentioned above are encouraged to consult the section for Brazil in this bibliography.

The *Encyclopedia of Latin American Theater* (2003), edited by Eladio Cortés and Mirta Barrera-Marlys, covers the national theaters of both Brazil and Spanish America, but Willis Knapp Jones's *Behind Spanish American Footlights* (1966), one of the standards of theater history, is more limited, as its title suggests. For writing in prose, books by Georg Gugelberger on *testimonio*, Sylvia Molloy on autobiography, and Peter Earle and Robert Meade on the essay are excellent studies of those genres. Francisco Esteve Barba provides a comprehensive survey of the history chronicle, and Beatriz Pastor provides a detailed analysis of several chronicles. For fiction, the general studies by John Brushwood, Donald Shaw, and Raymond Williams offer detailed surveys and introductions to the principal authors and their works. Two volumes edited by María Salgado, *Modern Spanish American Poets* (2003 and 2004), include essays on the life and works of a large number of poets, while books by Andrew Bush, Mike Gonzalez and David Treece, and William Rowe cover the movements and trends in Latin American poetry through consideration of the work of some of its principal poets.

After the introductory section on Latin America in general, the remaining, but much longer, part of this bibliography consists of a series of sections, one for each of the national literatures included in the dictionary. Each list has two parts: a selection of reference works, including bibliographies, dictionaries, encyclopedias, histories, and anthologies, covering the national literature in question, followed by select bibliographies for specific writers, organized alphabetically by author. These bibliographies for specific writers include both books and articles from academic journals, some published within Latin America, but many published in countries outside the region, notably in North America and Europe. When selecting articles from academic journals published in Latin America, preference was given to those having an established circulation in North America and Europe. A few of the journals cited publish exclusively online, and the archives of an increasing number of journals are being made available through the same medium.

It is noteworthy that the majority of the titles in the reference sections of the bibliographies on national literatures are in Spanish or Portuguese. Although critics writing in English have produced histories of the national literatures of Latin America for encyclopedias and have been interested in the literary history of Latin America as a whole, they have not generally concerned themselves with either writing or translating national histories. Notable exceptions are David William Foster's edited book on the history of Mexican literature and James Higgins's history of Peruvian literature. There are a number of histories of Brazilian literature in English, either written, edited, or translated (such as the volumes by Manuel Bandeira, Afrânio Coutinho, Isaac Goldberg, and Claude Hulet), which are somewhat dated, but most of the standard and the more recent histories remain those in Portuguese by Alfredo Bosi, Antônio Candido, Massaud Moisés, and Luciana Stegagno Picchio.

As may be concluded from the selection of titles throughout this bibliography, many writers in English and many whose studies have been translated into English have made particular genres, themes, authors, or facets of the world of Latin American literature and its authors the primary focus of their work. Their interest has yielded many studies that offer particular insight into the life, times, and work of Latin American literary figures. Among those cited in the bibliographies for specific authors, the following are both accessible and useful. For Argentina, the studies on Jorge Luis Borges by Beatriz Sarlo and Edwin Williamson, Steven Boldy's book on the novels of Julio Cortázar, and Suzanne Jill Levine's literary biography of Manuel Puig are excellent reading. Brazil's Jorge Amado has been the subject of a recent essay collection edited by Keith Brower and others, and Jason Lund and Malcolm McNee have edited a collection on Gilberto Freyre, while monographs such as those by Roberto Schwarz on Joaquim Machado de Assis and by Marta Peixoto and Earl Fitz on Clarice Lispector cover important ground. Chile's two Nobel Prize–winning poets, Gabriela Mistral and Pablo Neruda, are discussed respectively, with considerable insight, by Elizabeth Horan and Matilde Urrutia. The official biography of another of Latin America's Nobel winners, the Colombian Gabriel García Márquez, has been published by Gerald Martin. Richard Callan's study of Miguel Ángel Asturias, Guatemala's Nobel laureate, provides detailed commentary on the novelist's work. It is also part of the series Twayne's World Authors, which includes volumes on several Latin American authors, the Paraguayan Augusto Roa Bastos (by David William Foster) and the Chilean Isabel Allende (by Linda Gould Levine) among them. For Mexico, there is an important study by the Nobel poet and essayist Octavio Paz on Sor Juan Inés de la Cruz, and Mexico's most important 20th-century novelist, Carlos Fuentes, has been studied in a very approachable work by Wendy Faris. Two of Peru's greatest writers, the poet César Vallejo and the novelist Mario Vargas Llosa, have been discussed by Jean Franco and Sara Castro Klarén, respectively. Finally, the internationally recognized Uruguayan chronicler Eduardo Galeano is the subject of a groundbreaking volume by Daniel Fischlin and Martha Nandorfy.

The books singled out for particular mention in the preceding paragraph, as well as all the other titles included in this bibliography, whether in the general section on Latin America or in the sections on national literatures and their authors, may be consulted in important collections such as The Library of Congress in Washington, D.C., and The British Library in London. They may also be found in some of the world's major university libraries, such as those of the University of Texas at Austin, Yale University, the University of Pittsburgh, or Tulane University in the United States; the University of Toronto in Canada; or the Universities of London or Oxford in Great Britain. The library at Brown University at Providence, Rhode Island, has particularly good holdings on Brazil. Readers seeking further bibliographical recources might consult the *International Bibliography* of the Modern Language Association of America (www.mla.org/bilbiography), the *Hispanic American Periodicals Index (HAPI) Online* (www.hapi.ucla.edu), or the *Handbook of Latin American Studies (HLAS) Online* (*www*.loc.gov/hlas), a publication of the U.S. Library of Congress.

GENERAL LATIN AMERICAN HISTORY AND CRITICISM

Bibliographies, Encyclopedias, and Dictionaries

Agosín, Marjorie, ed. *A Dream of Light & Shadow: Portraits of Latin American Women Writers.* Albuquerque: University of New Mexico Press, 1995.

Aira, César. *Diccionario de autores latinoamericanos.* Buenos Aires: Emecé, 2001.

André, María Claudia, and Eva Paulina Bueno, eds. *Latin American Women Writers: An Encyclopedia.* New York: Routledge, 1980.

Balderston, Daniel. *The Latin American Short Story: An Annotated Guide to Anthologies and Criticism.* New York: Greenwood Press, 1992.

Balderston, Daniel, Mike González, and Ana M. López, eds. *Encyclopedia of Contemporary Latin American and Caribbean Literature, 1900–2003.* London: Routledge, 2004.

Brower, Keith H. *Contemporary Latin American Fiction. An Annotated Bibliography.* Pasadena, Calif.: Salem Press, 1989.

Bryant, Shasta M. *Selective Bibliography of Bibliographies of Hispanic American Literature.* 2nd ed. Austin: University of Texas Press, 1976.

Forster, Merlin H., and K. David Jackson. *Vanguardism in Latin American Literature: An Annotated Bibliographical Guide.* Westport, Conn.: Greenwood Press, 1990.

Foster, David William, ed. *A Dictionary of Contemporary Latin American Authors.* Tempe: Center for Latin American Studies, Arizona State University, 1975.

———. *Handbook of Latin American Literature.* 2nd ed. New York: Garland, 1992.

———. *Latin American Writers on Gay and Lesbian Themes: A Bio-critical Sourcebook.* Westport, Conn.: Greenwood Press, 1994.

Marting, Diane E., ed. *Spanish American Women Writers: A Bio-Bibliographical Source Book.* Westport, Conn.: Greenwood Press, 1990.

Osorio, Nelson, ed. *Diccionario enciclopédico de las letras de América Latina.* 3 vols. Caracas: Monte Avila and Biblioteca Ayacucho, 1995.

Sefamí, Jacobo, ed. *Contemporary Spanish American Poets: A Bibliography of Primary and Secondary Sources.* Westport, Conn.: Greenwood Press, 1992.

Smith, Verity, ed. *Encyclopedia of Latin American Literature.* Chicago: Fitzroy Dearborn, 1997.

Solé, Carlos A., and María Isabel Abreu, eds. *Latin American Writers.* 3 vols. New York: Charles Scribner's Sons, 1989.

Solé, Carlos A., and Klaus Müller-Bergh, eds. *Latin American Writers.* Vol. 4, Supp. 1. New York: Charles Scribner's Sons, 2002.

General History and Criticism

Anderson Imbert, Enrique. *Spanish-American Literature: A History.* Detroit, Mich.: Wayne State University Press, 1963.

Bellini, Giuseppe. *Historia de la literatura hispanoamericana.* Madrid: Castalia, 1985.

Beverley, John, and Marc Zimmerman. *Literature and Politics in Central America.* Austin: University of Texas Press, 1990.

Cevallos-Candau, Francisco J., Jeffrey A. Cole, Nina M. Scott, and Nicómedes Suárez Arauz, eds. *Coded Encounters: Writing, Gender and Ethnicity in Colonial Latin America.* Amherst: University of Massachusetts Press, 1994.

Chang-Rodríguez, Raquel. *Violencia y subversion en la prosa colonial hispanoamericana, siglos XVI y XVII.* Madrid: José Porrúa Turanzas, 1982.

Englekirk, John E., I. A. Leonard, J. T. Reid, and J. A. Crow, eds. *An Outline History of Spanish American Literature.* New York: Appleton Century Crofts, 1965.

Fernández Moreno, César, Julio Ortega, and Ivan Schulman, eds. *Latin America in Its Literature.* México, D.F.: Siglo XXI, 1971.

Foster, David William. *Gay and Lesbian Themes in Latin American Writing.* Austin: University of Texas Press, 1991.

——. *Modern Latin American literature.* New York: Ungar, 1975.

Franco, Jean. *The Decline and Fall of the Lettered City.* Cambridge, Mass.: Harvard University Press, 2002.

——. *An Introduction to Spanish-American Literature.* Cambridge: Cambridge University Press, 1994.

Goic, Cedomil, ed. *Historia y crítica de la literatura hispanoamericana.* 3 vols. Barcelona: Editorial Crítica, 1988.

González Echevarría, Roberto. *The Voice of the Masters: Writing and Authority in Modern Latin American Literature.* Austin: University of Texas Press, 1985.

González Echevarría, Roberto, and Enrique Pupo-Walker, eds. *The Cambridge History of Latin American Literature.* 3 vols. Cambridge: Cambridge University Press, 1996.

Hart, Stephen. *A Companion to Latin-American Literature.* Woodbridge, Suffolk: Tamesis, 2007.

Jackson, Richard L., ed. *The Black Image in Latin American Literature.* Albuquerque: University of New Mexico Press, 1976.

Johnson, Julie Greer. *Women in Colonial Spanish American Literature: Literary Images.* Westport, Conn.: Greenwood Press, 1983.

Johnson, Myriam Yvonne. *Latin American Women Writers: Class, Race and Gender.* Albany: State University of New York Press, 1996.

Jrade, Cathy. *Modernismo, Modernity and the Development of Spanish American Literature.* Austin: University of Texas Press, 1998.

Kadir, Djelal. *Questing Fictions: Latin America's Family Romance.* Minneapolis: University of Minnesota Press, 1986.

Kaminsky, Amy. *Reading the Body Politic: Feminist Criticism and Latin American Writers.* Minneapolis: University of Minnesota Press, 1993.

Kuhnheim, Jill S. *Spanish American Poetry at the End of the Twentieth Century: Textual Disruptions.* Austin: University of Texas Press, 2004.

Lindstrom, Naomi, and Carmelo Virgilio, eds. *Woman as Myth and Metaphor in Latin American Literature.* Columbia: University of Missouri Press, 1985.

Martínez, Elena M. *Lesbian Voices from Latin America: Breaking Ground.* New York: Garland, 1996.

Menton, Seymour. *Historia verdadera del realismo mágico.* México, D.F.: Fondo de Cultura Económica, 1998.

Oviedo, José Miguel. *Historia de la literatura hispanoamericana.* 4 vols. Madrid: Alianza, 1995–2001.

Sifuentes-Jáuregui, Ben. *Transvestism, Masculinity and Latin American Literature.* New York: Palgrave, 2002.

Sommer, Doris. *Foundational Fictions: The National Romances of Latin America.* Berkeley: University of California Press, 1991.

Sosnowski, Saúl, ed. *Lectura crítica de la literatura americana.* 4 vols. Caracas: Biblioteca Ayacucho, 1997.

Unruh, Vicky. *Latin American Vanguards: The Art of Contentious Encounters.* Berkeley: University of California Press, 1994.

Valdés, Mario, and Djelal Kadir, eds. *Literary Cultures of Latin America: A Comparative History.* 3 vols. New York: Oxford University Press, 2004.

Genres: History and Criticism

Autobiography, Essay, Chronicle, and Testimonio

Earle, Peter G., and Robert G. Mead. *Historia del ensayo hispanoamericano.* México, D.F.: Ediciones de Andrea, 1965.

Ellis, Robert Richmond. *They Dream Not of Angels but of Men: Homoeroticism, Gender and Race in Latin American Autobiography.* Gainesville: University Press of Florida, 2002.

Fernández, Teodosio. *Los géneros ensayísticos hispanoamericanos.* Madrid: Taurus, 1990.

Gugelberger, Georg, ed. *The Real Thing: Testimonial Discourse and Latin America.* Durham, N.C.: Duke University Press, 1996.

Meyer, Doris, ed. *Reinterpreting the Spanish American Essay: Women Writers of the 19th and 20th Centuries.* Austin: University of Texas Press, 1995.

Molloy, Sylvia. *At Face Value: Autobiographical Writing in Spanish America.* Cambridge: Cambridge University Press, 1991.

Skirius, John, ed. *El ensayo hispanoamericano del Siglo XX.* México, D.F.: Fondo de Cultura Económica, 1981.

Sklodowska, Elzbieta. *Testimonio hispanoamericano: historia, teoría, poética.* New York: Peter Lang, 1992.

Stabb, Martin. *The Dissenting Voice: The New Essay in Spanish America, 1960–1985.* Austin: University of Texas Press, 1994.

Novel and Short Story

Alonso, Carlos J. *The Spanish American Regional Novel: Modernity and Autochthony.* Cambridge: Cambridge University Press, 1990.

Avelar, Idelber. *The Untimely Present: Post-dictatorial Latin American Fiction and the Task of Mourning.* Durham, N.C.: Duke University Press, 1999.

Bacarisse, Salvador, ed. *Contemporary Latin American Fiction.* Edinburgh: Scottish Academic Press, 1980.

Bloom, Harold, ed. *Modern Latin American Fiction.* New York: Chelsea House, 1990.

Brotherston, Gordon. *The Emergence of the Latin American Novel.* Cambridge: Cambridge University Press, 1979.

Brushwood, John S. *Genteel Barbarism: Experiments in Analysis of Nineteenth-Century Spanish-American Novels.* Lincoln: University of Nebraska Press, 1981.

———. *The Spanish American Novel: A Twentieth-Century Survey.* Austin: University of Texas Press, 1975.

Foster, David William, and Virginia Ramos Foster, eds. *Alternate Voices in the Contemporary Latin American Narrative.* Columbia: University of Missouri Press, 1985.

Gonzalez, Ann, and William Luis, eds. *Modern Latin-American Fiction Writers.* Detroit, Mich.: Gale Research, 1994.

Kerr, Lucille. *Reclaiming the Author: Figures and Fictions from Spanish America.* Durham, N.C.: Duke University Press, 1991.

King, John, ed. *Modern Latin American Fiction: A Survey.* London: Faber & Faber, 1987.

Lindstrom, Naomi. *Early Spanish American Narrative.* Austin: University of Texas Press, 2004.

——. *Twentieth Century Spanish American Fiction.* Austin: University of Texas Press, 1994.

Martin, Gerald. *Journeys through the Labyrinth: Latin American Fiction in the Twentieth Century.* London: Verso, 1989.

Menton, Seymour. *Latin America's New Historical Novel.* Austin: University of Texas Press, 1993.

Shaw, Donald. *The Post-Boom in Spanish American Fiction.* Albany: State University of New York Press, 1998.

Swanson, Philip. *The New Novel in Latin America: Politics and Popular Culture after the Boom.* Manchester: Manchester University Press, 1995.

——, ed. *Landmarks in Modern Latin American Fiction.* London York: Routledge, 1990.

Williams, Raymond L. *The Columbia Guide to the Latin American Novel Since 1945.* New York: Columbia University Press, 2007.

——. *The Postmodern Novel in Latin America: Politics, Culture, and the Crisis of Truth.* New York: St Martin's Press, 1995.

——. *The Twentieth-century Spanish American Novel.* Austin: University of Texas Press, 2003.

Poetry

Bush, Andrew. *The Routes of Modernity: Spanish American Poetry from the Early Eighteenth to the Mid-Nineteenth Century.* Lewisburg, Pa.: Bucknell University Press, 2002.

Gonzalez, Mike, and David Treece. *The Gathering of Voices: The Twentieth-century Poetry of Latin America.* London: Verso, 1992.

Huízar, Angélica Jiménez. *Beyond the Page: Latin American Poetry from the Calligrame to the Virtual.* Bethesda, Md.: Academica Press, 2008.

Kirkpatrick, Gwen. *The Dissident Legacy of Modernismo: Lugones, Herrera y Reissig, and the Voices of Modern Spanish American Poetry.* Berkeley: University of California Press, 1989.

Kuhnheim, Jill S. *Spanish American Poetry at the End of the Twentieth Century: Textual Disruptions.* Austin: University of Texas Press, 2004.

Rowe, William. *Poets of Contemporary Latin America: History and the Inner Life.* Oxford: Oxford University Press, 2000.

Salgado, María A., ed. *Modern Spanish American Poets: First Series*. Detroit, Mich.: Gale 2003.

——, ed. *Modern Spanish American Poets: Second Series*. Detroit, Mich.: Gale, 2004.

Yurkievich, Saúl. *Fundadores de la nueva poesía latinoamericana: Vallejo, Huidobro, Borges, Girondo, Neruda, Paz, Lezama Lima*. Barcelona: Ariel, 1984.

Theater

Albuquerque, Severino J. *Violent Acts: A Study of Contemporary Latin American Theatre*. Detroit, Mich.: Wayne State University Press, 1991.

Cortés, Eladio, and Mirta Barrera-Marlys, eds. *Encyclopedia of Latin American Theater*. Westport, Conn.: Greenwood Press, 2003.

De Costa, Elena. *Collaborative Latin American Popular Theater: From Theory to Form, from Text to Stage*. New York: Peter Lang, 1992.

Flores, Yolanda. *The Drama of Gender: Feminist Theater by Women of the Americas*. New York: Peter Lang, 2000.

Harvell, Tony A. *Latin American Dramatists since 1945: A Bio-Bibliographical Guide*. Westport, Conn.: Praeger, 2003.

Jones, Willis Knapp. *Behind Spanish American Footlights*. Austin: University of Texas Press, 1966.

Larson, Catherine, and Margarita Vargas, eds. *Latin American Women Dramatists*. Bloomington: Indiana University Press, 1998.

Lyday, Leon F., and George Woodyard, eds. *Dramatists in Revolt: The New Latin American Theater*. Austin: University of Texas Press, 1976.

Martin, Randy. *Socialist Ensembles: Theater and State in Cuba and Nicaragua*. Minneapolis: University of Minnesota Press, 1994.

Suárez Radillo, Carlos Miguel. *El teatro barroco hispanoamericano: ensayo de una historia crítico-antológica*. 3 vols. Madrid: Ediciones J. Porrúa Turanzas, 1981.

——. *El teatro neoclásico y costumbrista hispanoamericano: una historia crítico-antológica*. Madrid: Ediciones Cultura Hispánica, Instituto de Cooperación Iberoamericana, 1984.

——. *El teatro romántico hispanoamericano: una historia crítico-antológica*. Madrid: Ediciones Cultura Hispánica, Instituto de Cooperación Iberoamericana, 1993.

Taylor, Diana. *Theatre of Crisis: Drama and Politics in Latin America*. Lexington: University Press of Kentucky, 1991.

Taylor, Diana, and Juan Villegas, eds. *Negotiating Performance: Gender, Sexuality and Theatricality in Latin/o America*. Durham, N.C.: Duke University Press, 1995.

Versenyi, Adam. *Theatre in Latin America: Religion, Politics, and Culture from Cortés to the 1980s*. Cambridge: Cambridge University Press, 1993.
Weiss, Judith A., *et al*. *Latin American Popular Theatre*. Albuquerque: University of New Mexico Press, 1993.

Anthologies

Anderson Imbert, Enrique, and E. Florit, eds. *Literatura hispanoamericana*. 2 vols. New York: Holt, Rinehart & Winston, 1970.
Arciniegas, Germán, ed. *The Green Continent*. New York: Alfred A. Knopf, 1944.
Caracciolo-Trejo, E., ed. *The Penguin Book of Latin American Verse*. Harmondsworth: Penguin Books, 1971.
Castro-Klaren, Sara, Sylvia Molloy, and Beatriz Sarlo, eds. *Women's Writing in Latin America: An Anthology*. Boulder, Colo.: Lynn Rienner, 1991.
Colecchia, Francesca, and Julio Matas, eds. *Selected Latin American One-Act Plays*. Pittsburgh, Pa.: University of Pittsburgh Press, 1973.
Dauster, Frank N., Leon Lyday, and George W. Woodyard, eds. *Nueve dramaturgos hispanomericanos*. 3 vols. Ottawa: Girol Books, 1979.
Englekirk, John E., I. A. Leonard, J. T. Reid, and J. A. Crow, eds. *An Anthology of Spanish American Literature*. 2 vols. Englewood Cliffs, N.J.: Prentice-Hall, 1968.
Fitts, Dudley, ed. *Anthology of Contemporary Latin American Poetry*. Westport, Conn.: Greenwood Press, 1976.
Flores, Ángel, ed. *Narrativa hispanoamericana*. 8 vols. México, D.F.: Siglo XXI, 1981.
Foster, David William. *Twentieth-century Spanish American Literature to 1960*. New York: Garland, 1997.
———, ed. *Twentieth-century Spanish American Literature Since 1960*. New York: Garland, 1997.
Grünfeld, M., ed. *Antología de la poesía latinoamericana de vanguardia*. Madrid: Hiperión, 1995.
Menton, Seymour, ed. *El cuento hispanoamericano: antología crítico-histórica*. México, D.F.: Fondo de Cultura Económica, 1964.
Neglia, Erminio G., and Luis Ordaz, eds. *Repertorio selecto del teatro hispanoamericano contemporáneo*. Tempe: Center for Latin American Studies, Arizona State University, 1981.
Oviedo, José Miguel, ed. *Antología crítica del cuento hispanoamericano (1830–1920)*. Madrid: Alianza, 1989.
———, ed. *Antología crítica del cuento hispanoamericano del siglo XX (1920–1980)*. 2 vols. Madrid: Alianza Editorial, 1992.

Ripoll, Carlos, and Andrés Valespino, eds. *Teatro hispanoamericano: antología crítica.* 2 vols. New York: Anaya, 1972–1973.

Rodríguez Monegal, Emir, ed. *The Borzoi Anthology of Latin American Literature.* 2 vols. New York: Alfred A. Knopf, 1977.

Rotker, Susana, ed. *Ensayistas de nuestra América.* 2 vols. Buenos Aires: Losada, 1994.

Sucre, Guillermo, ed. *Antología de la poesía hispanoamericana moderna.* 2 vols. Caracas: Monte Avila, 1993.

ARGENTINA

Resources: Bibliographies, Histories, Anthologies

Benedetti, Héctor Ángel, ed. *Las mejores letras de tango: antología de doscientas cincuenta letras, cada una con su historia.* Buenos Aires: Seix Barral, 1998.

Berdia, Norberto, ed. *Poesía argentina contemporánea* [anthology]. Buenos Aires: Fundacion Argentina para la Poesia, 1978.

Blanco Amores de Pagella, Ángela, ed. *Iniciadores del teatro argentino* [anthology]. Buenos Aires: Ministerio de Cultura y Educación, 1972.

Chávez, Fermín, ed. *Historia y antología de la poesía gauchesca.* Buenos Aires: Ediciones Margus, 2004.

Fernández, Gerardo, ed. *Teatro argentino contemporáneo: antología.* Madrid: Sociedad Estatal Quinto Centenario, 1992.

Fontanarrosa, Roberto, ed. *Cuentos de fútbol argentino* [anthology]. Buenos Aires: Aguilar, Altea, Taurus, Alfaguara, 1997.

Foster, David William. *Argentine Literature: A Research Guide.* 2nd ed. New York: Garland, 1982.

Gandolfo, Elvio E., and Eduardo Hojman, eds. *El terror argentino: cuentos* [anthology]. Buenos Aires: Alfaguara, 2002.

Jitrik, Noé, ed. *Historia critica de la literatura argentina.* 11 vols. Buenos Aires: Emecé, 1999.

Libertella, Héctor, ed. *Veinticinco cuentos argentinos del siglo XX: una antología definitiva.* Buenos Aires: Perfil, 2002.

Marcó, Susana, ed. *Antología del género chico criollo.* Buenos Aires: Editorial Universitaria de Buenos Aires, 1976.

Montaldo, G., and G. Nouzeilles, eds. *The Argentina Reader.* Durham, N.C.: Duke University Press, 2002.

Ordaz, Luis, ed. *Breve historia del teatro argentino* [anthology]. Buenos Aires: Editorial Universitaria de Buenos Aires, 1962– .

Pellettieri, Osvaldo. *Cien años de teatro argentino (1886–1990): del "Moreira" a Teatro Abierto.* 2nd ed. Buenos Aires: Galerna, 1994.

Prieto, Martín. *Breve historia de la literatura argentina.* Buenos Aires: Aguilar, Altea, Taurus, Alfaguara, 2006.

Rita Gardiol, ed. *The Silver Candelabra & Other Stories: A Century of Jewish Argentine Literature.* Pittsburgh, Pa.: Latin American Literary Review Press, 1997.

Salvador, Nélida, ed. *Lírica argentina posterior a 1950.* Buenos Aires: Instituto de Literatura Argentina "Ricardo Rojas," Facultad de Filosofía y Letras, Universidad de Buenos Aires, 1988.

——, ed. *Novela argentina del siglo XX: estudio crítico y bibliografía.* Buenos Aires: Ediciones Academia del Sur, 2006.

Salvador, Nélida, *et al. Revistas literarias argentinas: 1960–1990: Aporte para una bibliografía.* Buenos Aires: Fundación Inca Seguros, 1996.

Souto, Marcial, ed. *La ciencia ficción en la Argentina: antología crítica.* Buenos Aires: EUDEBA, 1985.

Select Bibliography for Specific Writers

César Aira

Contreras, Sandra. *Las vueltas de César Aira.* Rosario: Viterbo, 2002.

Juan Bautista Alberdi

Goodrich, Diana Sorensen. "The Wiles of Disputation: Alberdi Reads *Facundo.*" In *Sarmiento: Author of a Nation,* edited by Tulio Halperín Donghi, Iván Jaksic, Gwen Kirkpatrick, and Francine Masiello, 294–313. Berkeley: University of California Press, 1994.

O'Connell, Patrick L. "*Peregrinación de luz del día*: la desilusión de Juan Bautista Alberdi." *Acta Literaria* 29 (2004): 93–104.

José Álvarez (Fray Mocho)

Rodríguez Pérsico, Adriana. "Fray Mocho, un cronista de los márgenes." In *Fronteras de la modernidad en América Latina,* edited by Hermann Herlinghaus and Mabel Moraña, 111–20. Pittsburgh, Pa.: Instituto Internacional de Literatura Iberoamericana, University of Pittsburgh, 2003.

Villanueva, Graciela. "Modalidades de la sátira en los cuentos de Fray Mocho." In *La Satire en Amérique Latine: formes et fonctions. La Satire entre deux siècles,* edited by Françoise Aubès and Florence Olivier, I: 75–83. Paris: Sorbonne Nouvelle, 2007.

Enrique Anderson Imbert

Arancibia, Juana Alcira, ed. *Homenaje a Enrique Anderson Imbert.* Westminster, Calif.: Instituto Literario y Cultural Hispánico, 2001.

Hall, Nancy Abraham, and Lanin A. Gyurko, eds. *Studies in Honor of Enrique Anderson Imbert.* Newark, Del.: Cuesta, 2003.

Roberto Arlt

Corral, Rose. *El obsesivo circular de la ficción: asedios a* Los Siete locos *y* Los Lanzallamas *de Roberto Arlt.* México, D.F.: Colegio de México, 1992.

Flint, Jack M. *The Prose Works of Roberto Arlt: A Thematic Approach.* Durham, N.C.: University of Durham, 1985.

Gnutzmann, Rita. "Bibliografía de y sobre Roberto Arlt." *Chasqui: Revista de Literatura Latinoamericana* 25, no. 2 (1996): 44–62.

González, H. *Arlt, política y locura.* Buenos Aires: Colihue, 1996.

Martínez, V. J. *The Semiotics of a Bourgeois Society: An Analysis of the* Aguafuertes porteñas *by Roberto Arlt.* Potomac, Md.: Scripta Hispánica, 1991.

Pellettieri, Osvaldo, ed. *Roberto Arlt: dramaturgia y teatro independiente.* Buenos Aires: Galerna; Fundación Roberto Arlt, 2000.

Zubieta, Ana Maria. *El discurso narrativo arltiano, intertextualidad, grotesco y utopía.* Buenos Aires: Hachette, 1987.

Hilario Ascasubi

Sosa de Newton, Lily. *Genio y figura de Hilario Ascasubi.* Buenos Aires: Eudeba, 1981.

Jorge Asís

Burgos, N. *Jorge Asís: los límites del canon.* Buenos Aires: Catálogos, 2001.

Adolfo Bioy Casares

Gallagher, David. "The Novels and Short Stories of Adolfo Bioy Casares." *Bulletin of Hispanic Studies* 52–53 (1975): 247–66.

García Muñoz, Gerardo. *El sueño creador: Adolfo Bioy Casares, el ABC de la invención*. Chimalistac, México, D.F.: Consejo Nacional para la Cultura y las Artes, 1994.

Levine, Suzanne Jill. *Guia de Adolfo Bioy Casares*. Madrid: Editorial Fundamentos, 1982.

Navascués, Javier de. *El esperpento controlado: la narrativa de Adolfo Bioy Casares*. Pamplona: Navarra University Press, 1995.

Ryden, Wendy. "Bodies in the Age of Mechanical Reproduction: Competing Discourses of Reality and Representation in Bioy Casares's *The Invention of Morel*." *Atenea* 21, nos. 1–2 (2001): 193–207.

Snook, Margaret L. *In Search of Self: Gender and Identity in Bioy Casares' Fantastic Fiction*. New York: Peter Lang, 1998.

Tamargo, Maria Isabel. *La narrativa de Bioy Casares: El texto como escritura lectura*. Madrid: Playor, 1983.

Jorge Luis Borges

Alazraki, Jaime, ed. *Borges and the Kabbalah and Other Essays on His Fiction and Poetry*. New York: Cambridge University Press, 1988.

Balderston, Daniel. *Out of Context: Historical Reference and the Representation of Reality in Borges*. Durham, N.C.: Duke University Press, 1993.

Bell-Vilada, Gene H. *Borges and His Fiction: A Guide to His Mind and Art*. Austin: University of Texas Press, 2000.

Costa, René de. *Humor in Borges*. Detroit, Mich.: Wayne State University Press, 2000.

Di Giovanni, Norman Thomas. *The Lesson of the Master: On Borges and His Work*. New York: Continuum, 2003.

Friedman, Mary Lusky. *The Emperor's Kites; A Morphology of Borges' Tales*. Durham, N.C.: Duke University Press, 1987.

Frisch, Mark. *You Might Be Able to Get There from Here: Reconsidering Borges and the Postmodern*. Madison, N.J.: Fairleigh Dickinson University Press, 2004.

Irwin, John T. *The Mystery to a Solution: Poe, Borges, and the Analytic Detective Story*. Baltimore, Md.: Johns Hopkins University Press, 1994.

Jenckes, Kate. *Reading Borges after Benjamin: Allegory, Afterlife, and the Writing of History*. Albany: State University of New York Press, 2007.

Merrell, Floyd. *Unthinking Thinking: Jorge Luis Borges, Mathematics, and the New Physics*. West Lafayette, Ind.: Purdue University Press, 1991.

Molloy, Sylvia. *Signs of Borges*. Durham, N.C.: Duke University Press, 1994.

Sarlo, Beatriz. *Jorge Luis Borges: A Writer on the Edge*. London: Verso; 1993.

Stabb, Martin S. *Borges Revisited*. Boston: Twayne. 1991.

Waisman, Sergio. *Borges and Translation: The Irreverence of the Periphery.* Lewisburg, Pa.: Bucknell University Press, 2005.

Williamson, Edwin. *Borges: A Life.* New York: Viking, 2004.

Silvina Bullrich

Balderston, Daniel. "Dos literatos del Proceso: H. Bustos Domecq y Silvina Bullrich." *Nuevo Texto Crítico* 3, no. 1 (1990): 85–93.

Stevens, James R. "*Los burgueses* of Silvina Bullrich: A Study of Generational Decadence." *MACLAS: Latin American Essays* 2 (1988): 35–39.

Villanueva-Collado, Alfredo. "(Homo)sexualidad y periferia en la novelística de Marta Brunet y Silvina Bullrich." In *El descubrimiento y los desplazamientos: la literatura hispanoamericana como diálogo entre centros y periferias,* edited by Juana Alcira Arancibia, 79–94. Westminster, Calif.: Instituto Literario y Cultural Hispánico, 1990.

Eugenio Cambaceres

Bazán-Figueras, Patricia. *Eugenio Cambaceres: precursor de la novela argentina contemporánea.* New York: Peter Lang, 1994.

Cymerman, Claude. *Diez estudios cambacerianos acompañados de una biobibliografía.* Rouen: Université de Rouen, 1993.

Spicer-Escalante, Juan Pablo. "A Non-Imperial Eye/I: Europe as Contact Zone in Eugenio Cambaceres's *Música sentimental* (1884)." *Brújula: Revista Interdisciplinaria Sobre Estudios Latinoamericanos* 3, no. 1 (2004): 53–68.

Estanislao del Campo

Castillo, Carolina. "Para una lectura del Fausto criollo." *Espéculo: Revista de Estudios Literarios* 23 (2003): n.p.

Ginger, Andrew. "Cultural Modernity and Atlantic Perspectives: Estanislao del Campo's *Fausto* (1866) and Its French Contemporaries." *Atlantic Studies: Literary, Cultural, and Historical Perspectives* 4, no. 1 (2007): 27–36.

Haroldo Conti

Restivo, N., and C. Sánchez. *Haroldo Conti, con vida.* Buenos Aires: Nueva Imagen, 1986.

Romano, E. *Haroldo Conti: Mascaró.* Buenos Aires: Hachette, 1986.

Julio Cortázar

Alazraki, Jaime, Ivar Ivask, and Joaquín Marco, eds. *Julio Cortázar: The Final Island*. Norman: University of Oklahama Press, 1978.

Boldy, Steven. *The Novels of Julio Cortázar*. Cambridge: Cambridge University Press, 1980.

Burgos, Fernando, ed. *Los ochenta mundos de Cortázar: ensayos*. Madrid: EDI-6, 1987.

Carter, E. Dale, ed. *Otro round: estudios sobre la obra de Julio Cortázar*. Sacramento: California State University, 1988.

Goloboff, Mario. *Julio Cortázar: la biografía*. Buenos Aires: Seix Barral, 1998.

Lastra, Pedro, ed. *Julio Cortázar*. Madrid: Taurus, 1981.

Peavler, Terry J. *Julio Cortázar*. Boston: Twayne, 1990.

Rodríguez-Luis, Julio. *The Contemporary Praxis of the Fantastic: Borges and Cortázar*. New York: Garland; 1991.

Schmidt-Cruz, Cynthia. *Mothers, Lovers, and Others: The Short Stories of Julio Cortázar*. Albany: State University of New York Press, 2003.

Tcherepashenets, Nataly. *Place and Displacement in the Narrative Worlds of Jorge Luis Borges and Julio Cortázar*. New York: Peter Lang, 2008.

Yovanovich, Gordana. *Julio Cortázar's Character Mosaic: Reading the Longer Fiction*. Toronto: University of Toronto Press, 1991.

Roberto Cossa

Bulman, Gail A. "Humor and National Catharsis in Roberto Cossa's *El saludador*." *Latin American Theatre Review* 36, no. 1 (2002): 5–18.

Ciria, Alberto. "Variaciones sobre la historia argentina en el teatro de Roberto Cossa." *Revista Canadiense de Estudios Hispanicos* 18, no. 3 (1994): 445–53.

Woodyard, George. "The Theatre of Roberto Cossa: A World of Broken Dreams." *Bucknell Review: A Scholarly Journal of Letters, Arts and Sciences* 40, no. 2 (1996): 94–108.

Francisco Defilipis Novoa

Pelletieri, Osvaldo. "Francisco Defilippis Novoa: Teoría y práctica de la modernización en los veinte." *Gestos: Teoria y Practica del Teatro Hispanico* 5, no. 10 (1990): 156–60.

Marco Denevi

Brant, Herbert J. "Camilo's Closet: Sexual Camouflage in Denevi's *Rosaura a las diez.*" In *Bodies and Biases: Sexualities in Hispanic Cultures and Literatures,* edited by David William Foster and Roberto Reis, 203–16. Minneapolis: University of Minnesota Press, 1996.

Gotschilich, Guillermo. "*Ceremonia secreta* de Marco Denevi: enigma y ritualización." *Revista Chilena de Literatura* 33 (1989): 87–101.

Lagmanovich, David. "Los microtextos dramáticos de Marco Denevi." In *Teatro, memoria y ficción,* edited by Osvaldo Pellettieri, 219–24. Buenos Aires: Galerna, 2005.

Armando Discépolo

Pelletieri, Osvaldo. *Obra dramática de Armando Discépolo.* Buenos Aires: Galerna, 1990.

Osvaldo Dragún

Gladhart, Amalia. "Narrative Foreground in the Plays of Osvaldo Dragún." *Latin American Theatre Review* 26, no. 2 (1993): 93–109.

Schmidt, D. "The Theatre of Osvaldo Dragun." In *Dramatists in Revolt: The New Latin American Theatre,* edited by L. F. Lyday and G. Woodyard, 37–58. Austin: University of Texas Press, 1976.

Esteban Echeverría

Agresti, Mabel Susana. "Una lectura de 'El matadero' de Esteban Echeverría." *Revista de Literaturas Modernas* 24 (1991): 137–56.

Haberly, David T. "Male Anxiety and Sacrificial Masculinity: The Case of Echeverría." *Hispanic Review* 73, no. 3 (2005): 291–307.

Kreis, Karl-Wilhelm. "Teoría y práctica literaria: el romanticismo progresista de Esteban Echeverría y la presentación de los indios en *La cautiva.*" In *Texto social: estudios pragmáticos sobre literatura y cine. Homenaje a Manfred Engelbert,* edited by Annette Paatz and Burkhard Pohl, 49–62. Berlin: Tranvía, 2003.

Luna Silva, Claudia. "Días de sangre y de furia: 'El matadero' de Esteban Echeverría." *Excavatio: Emile Zola and Naturalism* 21, nos. 1–2 (2006): 84–94.

Operé, Fernando. "*La cautiva* de Echeverría: el trágico señuelo de la frontera." *Bulletin of Spanish Studies* 80, no. 5 (2003): 545–54.

Skinner, Lee. "Carnality in 'El matadero.'" *Revista de Estudios Hispánicos* 33, no. 2 (1999): 205–26.

Samuel Eichelbaum

Cruz, Jorge. *Samuel Eichelbaum*. Buenos Aires: Ediciones Culturales Argentinas, 1962.

José Pablo Feinmann

Grandis, Rita de. *Reciclaje cultural y memoria revolucionaria: la práctica polémica de José Pablo Feinmann*. Buenos Aires: Editorial Biblos, 2006.

Macedonio Fernández

Borinsky, A. *Macedonio Fernández y la teoría crítica*. Buenos Aires: Corregidor, 1987.

Bueno, Mónica. *Macedonio Fernández, un escritor de fin de siglo: genealogía de un vanguardista*. Buenos Aires: Corregidor, 2000.

Obieta, A. de. *Macedonio: Memorias errantes*. Buenos Aires: Manuel Pamplin Editor, 1999.

Piglia, Ricardo, ed. *Diccionario de la novela de Macedonio Fernández*. Buenos Aires: Fondo de Cultura Economía, 2000.

Rodolfo Enrique Fogwill

Drucaroff, Elsa. "Rememoración de alto riesgo: sobre *Pájaros de la cabeza* de Rodolfo Fogwill." *Texto Crítico* 8, no. 14 (2004): 109–33.

Ferroggiaro, Federico G. "La pichiguerra: una lectura de *Los pichiciegos*." *Espéculo: Revista de Estudios Literarios* 37 (2007–2008): n.p.

Rodrigo Fresán

Areco Morales, Macarena Luz. "Rodrigo Fresán." *Hispamérica: Revista de Literatura* 36, no. 106 (2007): 47–59.

Kurlat Ares, Silvia G. "Rupturas y reposicionamientos: la innovación estética de Rodrigo Fresán." *Revista Iberoamericana* 69, no. 202 (2003): 215–27.

Plotnik, Viviana P. "Mitos de la nación y posmodernidad en *Historia argentina* de Rodrigo Fresán." *Hispamérica: Revista de Literatura* 87 (2000): 127–35.

Luisa Futoransky

Beard, L. J. "A Is for Alphabet, K Is for Kabbalah: Luisa Futoransky's Babelic Metatext." *Intertexts* 1, no. 1 (1997): 25–39.

Nofal, Rossana. "Luisa Futoransky: migraciones de la palabra poética." *Inti: Revista de Literatura Hispánica* 61–62 (2005): 159–67.

Schwartz, Marcy E. *Writing Paris: Urban Topographies of Desire in Contemporary Latin American Fiction.* Albany: State University of New York Press; 1999.

Manuel Gálvez

Cánovas, Rodrigo. "Lecturas de la novela argentina *Nacha Régules* (1919): ilusiones de cambio social." *Taller de Letras* 29 (2001): 9–19.

Jiménez, L. A. *Literatura y soledad en la narrativa de Manuel Gálvez.* Buenos Aires: Pena Lillo, 1990.

Szmetan, Ricardo. "Bibliografía seleccionada y comentada sobre Manuel Gálvez (1882–1962)." *Revista inter-americana de bibliografía* 43, no. 4 (1993): 571–610.

Walker, John. "Literature and Theology: Manuel Gálvez, *Cautiverio* and the Catholic Novel." *Studies in Honor of Myron Lichtblau,* edited by Fernando Burgos, 341–58. Newark, Del: Juan de la Cuesta, 2000.

Sara Gallardo

Rey Beckford, Ricardo. "Dos novelas de Sara Gallardo." *Ciberletras* 18 (2007): n.p.

Pérez, Alberto Julián. "*Eisejuaz* y la gran historia americana." In *La mujer en la literatura del mundo hispánico,* edited by Juana Arancibia, 239–49. Westminster, Calif.: Instituto Literario y Cultural Hispánico, 2005.

Griselda Gambaro

Boling, Becky. "Reenacting Politics: The Theater of Griselda Gambaro." In *Latin American Women Dramatists: Theater, Texts, and Theories,* edited by Catherine Larson and Margarita Vargas, 3–22. Bloomington: Indiana University Press, 1998.

Bulman, Gail A. "Moving On: Memory and History in Griselda Gambaro's Recent Theater." *Studies in Twentieth and Twenty-First Century Literature* 28, no. 2 (2004): 379–95.

Jehenson, Myriam Yvonne. "Staging Cultural Violence: Griselda Gambaro and Argentina's 'Dirty War.'" *Mosaic: A Journal for the Interdisciplinary Study of Literature* 32, no. 1 (1999): 85–104.

López-Calvo, Ignacio. "Lesbianism and Caricature in Griselda Gambaro's *Lo impenetrable.*" *Journal of Lesbian Studies* 7, no. 3 (2003): 89–103.

Magnarelli, Sharon. "Staging Shadows/Seeing Ghosts: Ambiguity, Theatre, Gender, and History in Griselda Gambaro's *La señora Macbeth.*" *Theatre Journal* 60, no. 3 (2008): 365–82.

Molinaro, Nina L. "Discipline and Drama: Panoptic Theatre and Griselda Gambaro's *El campo.*" *Latin American Theatre Review* 29, no. 2 (1996): 29–41.

Taylor, Claire Louise. "Bodily Mutilation and the Dismemberment of Discourse in the Novels of Griselda Gambaro." *Forum for Modern Language Studies* 37, no. 3 (2001): 326–36.

Taylor, D. *Theatre of Crisis: Drama and Politics in Latin America.* Lexington: University of Kentucky Press, 1991.

Wannamaker, Annette. "'Memory Also Makes a Chain': The Performance of Absence in Griselda Gambaro's *Antigona Furiosa.*" *Journal of the Midwest Modern Language Association* 33, no. 3 (2000): 73–85.

Zandstra, Dianne Marie. *Embodying Resistance: Griselda Gambaro and the Grotesque.* Lewisburg, Pa.: Bucknell University Press, 2007.

Juan Gelman

Correa Mujica, Miguel. "Juan Gelman y la nueva poesía hispanoamericana." *Espéculo: Revista de Estudios Literarios* 18 (2001): n.p.

Fabry, Geneviève. *Las formas del vacío: la escritura del duelo en la poesía de Juan Gelman.* Amsterdam: Rodopi, 2008.

Friolet, Philippe. *La Poétique de Juan Gelman: Une Écriture à trois visages.* Paris: Harmattan, 2006.

Gomes, M. "Juan Gelman en la historia de la poesía hispanoamericana reciente: neorromanticismo y neoexpressionismo." *Revista iberoamericana* 63, no. 181 (1997): 649–64.

Alberto Gerchunoff

Aizenberg, Edna. *Books and Bombs in Buenos Aires: Borges, Gerchunoff and Argentine Jewish Writing.* Hanover: University Press of New England, 2002.

———. *Parricide on the Pampa? A New Study and Translation of Alberto Gerchunoff's* Los gauchos judíos. Frankfurt: Vervuert: 2000.

Gover de Nasatsky, M. E. *Bibliografía de Alberto Gerchunoff.* Buenos Aires: Fondo Nacional de la Artes, 1976.

Mempo Giardinelli

Bowsher, Kerstin. "Nation and Identity in Crisis and Beyond: Mempo Giardinelli's *Santo oficio de la memoria.*" *Hispanic Review* 75, no. 1 (2007): 61–80.
O'Connell, Patrick L. "Narrating Memory and the Recuperation of Identity by Mempo Giardinelli: 'Una historia sin olvido.'"*Confluencia: Revista Hispánica de Cultura y Literatura* 15, no. 1 (1999): 46–57.
Pellón, Gustavo. "Ideology and Structure in Giardinelli's *Santo Oficio de la memoria.*" *Studies in Twentieth Century Literature* 19, no. 1 (1995): 81–99.
Stone, Kenton V. "Mempo Giardinelli and the Anxiety of Borges's Influence." *Chasqui: Revista de Literatura Latinoamericana* 23, no. 1 (1994): 83–90.

Oliverio Girondo

Montilla, Patricia M. *Parody, the Avant-Garde, and the Poetics of Subversion in Oliverio Girondo.* New York: Peter Lang, 2007.
Nóbile, B. de. *El acto experimental.* Buenos Aires: Losada, 1972.
Pio del Corro, G. *Olivero Girondo: los límites del signo.* Buenos Aires: Fernando García Cambeiro, 1976.

Alberto Girri

Cueto, Sergio. "Girri: un ejercicio de lectura." *Inti: Revista de Literatura Hispánica* 52–53 (2000–2001): 149–68.
Moore, Esteban. "Alberto Girri: la búsqueda de la lengua." *Espéculo: Revista de Estudios Literarios* 29 (2005): n.p.
Villanueva, Alberto. "Alberto Girri, poesía y objetvidad." *Hispamérica: Revista de Literatura* 30, no. 88 (2001): 113–18.

Eduardo González Lanuza

Castillo, Horacio. "Eduardo González Lanuza: perplejidad y transparencia." *Boletín de la Academia Argentina de Letras* 65, nos. 257–258 (2000): 319–26.
Fuente, Ovidio. "La trayectoria poética de Eduardo González Lanuza: la metáfora ultraísta como instrumento de creación lírica." *Cuadernos Americanos* 21, no. 2 (2007): 145–62.

Raúl González Tuñón

Borge, Jason. "Boedo Circense: Leónidas Barletta, Raúl González Tuñón, and the Limits of Tradition." *Hispanic Review* 76, no. 3 (2008): 257–79.
Lindstrom, Naomi. "*La rosa blindada*: A Functional Social Text in Poetry?" *Revista de Estudios Hispanicos* 26, no. 3 (1992): 413–33.
Mirkin, Zulema. *Raúl González Tuñón: cronista, rebelde y mago.* Buenos Aires: Instituto Literario y Cultural Hispánico, 1991.

Angélica Gorodischer

Balboa Echeverría, M., and E. Gimbernat-González. *Boca de dama: la narrativa de Angélica Gorodischer.* Buenos Aires: Feminaria, 1995.
Esplugas, Celia. "Challenging Political Corruption: The Liberated Feminist in 'Juice of Mango.'" *Modern Language Studies* 27, nos. 3–4 (1997): 93–100.
O'Connor, Patrick. "Fabulous Historians: Ursula Le Guin and Angélica Gorodischer." *Journal of the Fantastic in the Arts* 16, no. 2 (2005): 128–41.

Carlos Gorostiza

Larson, Catherine. "The Play's the Thing: Theater and the Ludic in Dramas by Griselda Gambaro, Carlos Gorostiza and Matilda Wilde." *Hecho Teatral: Revista de Teoría y Práctica del Teatro Hispánico* 3 (2003): 37–57.
Misemer, Sarah M. "Bridging the Gaps in Cultural Memory: Carlos Gorostiza's *El puente* and Gabriel Peveroni's *Sarajevo esquina Montevideo.*" *Latin American Theatre Review* 39, no. 1 (2005): 29–47.
Montes Huidobro, M. "Poder o no poder: la argentinidad según Carlos Gorostiza." In *Teatro argentino durante El Proceso (1976–1983)*, edited by Juana A. Arancibia and Zulema Mirkin, 99–111. Buenos Aires: Vinciguerra, 1992.
Pellettieri, Osvaldo. "Peronismo y teatro (1945–1955)." *Cuadernos Hispanoamericanos* 588 (1999): 91–99.

Juana Manuela Gorriti

Grzegorczyk, Marzena. *Private Topographies: Space, Subjectivity, and Political Change in Modern Latin America.* New York: Palgrave Macmillan, 2005.
Martin, Leona S. "Nation Building, International Travel, and the Construction of the Nineteenth-Century Pan-Hispanic Women's Network." *Hispania:*

A Journal Devoted to the Teaching of Spanish and Portuguese 87, no. 3 (2004): 439–46.

Urraca, Beatriz. "Juana Manuela Gorriti and the Persistence of Memory." *Latin American Research Review* 34, no. 1 (1999): 151–73.

Vergara, Magda. "In Defense of Motherhood: Juana Manuela Gorriti's Ambivalent Portrayal of a Slave Woman in *La quena*." *Romance Notes* 36, no. 3 (1996): 277–82.

Beatriz Guido

Clifford, Joan. "The Female Bildungsromane of Beatriz Guido." *Hispanófila* 132 (2001): 125–39.

Osorio, E. *Beatriz Guido*. Buenos Aires: Planeta, 1991.

Polit Dueñas, Gabriela. "Caudillo Politics and the Poetics of Masculinity in Beatriz Guido's Anti-Peronist Novel." *Latin American Literary Review* 33, no. 65 (2005): 73–87.

Ricardo Güiraldes

Alonso, Carlos. *The Spanish American Regional Novel: Modernity and Autochthony*. Cambridge: Cambridge University Press, 1990.

Bach, Caleb. "Poet of Shadows on the Pampa." *Américas* 54, no. 5 (2002): 14–21.

Battistessa, A. J. *Ricardo Güiraldes: en la huella spiritual y expresiva de un argentino (1886–1986)*. Buenos Aires: Corregidor, 1987.

Di Antonio, Robert. "*Don Segundo Sombra*: Sexual Stereotyping and the Voluntary Isolation Syndrome." *Confluencia: Revista Hispánica de Cultura y Literatura* 5, no. 2 (1990): 139–41.

Michelsen, Jytte. *Ricardo Güiraldes: un poeta del viaje*. Madrid: Verbum, 2005.

Spicer-Escalante, J. P. "Ricardo Güiraldes's Américas: Reappropriation and Reacculturation in *Xaimaca* (1923)." *Studies in Travel Writing* 7, no. 1 (2003): 9–28.

Luis Gusmán

Balderston, Daniel. "Latent Meanings in Ricardo Piglia's *Respiración artificial* and Luis Gusman's *En el corazón de junio*." *Revista Canadiense de Estudios Hispánicos* 12, no. 2 (1988): 207–19.

Rosman, Silvia. "The Father, the Law, Desire: Perversions of the Letter in Luis Gusmán's *Villa*." *Romance Studies* 26, no. 1 (2008): 99–108.

Eduardo Gutiérrez

Hart, Stephen. "Public Execution and the Body Politic in the Work of the Argentine Folletinista Eduardo Gutiérrez." *Bulletin of Hispanic Studies* 76, no. 5 (1999): 673–90.

Rodríguez McGill, Carlos. "Los folletines gauchescos de Eduardo Gutiérrez: transculturación modernizante gaucha y la aculturación del inmigrante." *Delaware Review of Latin American Studies* 4, no. 1 (2003): n. p.

José Hernández

Albarracín-Sarmiento, Carlos. *Estructura del Martín Fierro*. Amsterdam: Benjamins, 1981.

Carilla, Emilio. *La creacion del Martín Fierro*. Madrid: Gredos, 1973.

Dellepiane, Ángela B. *Concordancias del poema "Martín Fierro."* 2 vols. Buenos Aires: Academia. Argentina de Letras, 1995.

Ghiano, Juan C., ed. *José Hernández (estudios reunidos en conmemoración del centenario de* El gaucho Martín Fierro*) 1872–1972*. La Plata: Universidad Nacional de La Plata, 1973.

Verdugo, Iber. *Teoría aplicada del estudio literario: análisis del Martín Fierro*. México, D.F.: Universidad Nacional Autónoma de México, 1980.

Weinberg de Magis, Liliana. *Ezequiel Martínez Estrada y la interpretación del Martín Fierro*. México, D.F.: Universidad Nacional Autónoma de México, 1992.

Bartolomé Hidalgo

Carricaburo, Norma. "Literatura y oralidad en la poesía gauchesca de Hidalgo." *Boletín de la Academia Argentina de Letras* 61, nos. 239–240 (1996): 21–51.

Sylvia Iparraguirre

Perkowska, Magdalena. *Historias híbridas: la nueva novela histórica latinoamericana (1985–2000) ante las teorías posmodernas de la historia*. Frankfurt: Vervuert, 2008.

Rhoden, Laura Barbas. "Ecology, Coloniality, Modernity: Argentine Fictions of Tierra del Fuego." *Mosaic: A Journal for the Interdisciplinary Study of Literature* 41, no. 1 (2008): 1–18.

Roberto Juarroz

Campanella, Hebe N. "Una aventura hacia lo absoluto: la creación pura en 'poesía vertical' de Roberto Juarroz." *Letras de Buenos Aires* 20, no. 45 (2000): 52–59.

Margarit, Lucas. "Roberto Juarroz: la palabra en una casa de espejos." *Inti: Revista de Literatura Hispánica* 52–53 (2000): 117–28.

Stern, Emily E. "Roberto Juarroz (1925–31 March 1995)." In *Modern Spanish American Poets: First Series,* edited by María A. Salgado, 166–70. Detroit, Mich.: Gale, 2003.

Osvaldo Lamborghini

Fangmann, Cristina. "Lamborghini avanza." In *Literature and Society: Centers and Margins,* edited by José García, Betina Kaplan, Carlos Lechner, Andrea Parra, and Mario Santana, 49–60. New York: Department of Spanish and Portuguese, Columbia University, 1994.

Giorgi, Gabriel. "Diagnósticos del raro: cuerpo masculino y nación en Osvaldo Lamborghini." In *Heterotropías: narrativas de identidad y alteridad latino-americana,* edited by Carlos A. Jáuregui and Juan Pablo Dabove, 321–42. Pittsburgh, Penn.: Instituto Internacional de Literatura Iberoamericana, University of Pittsburgh, 2003.

Vázquez, Karina Elizabeth. "Turbio fondeadero: política e ideología en la poética neobarrosa de Osvaldo Lamborghini y Néstor Perlongher." *Ciberletras* 17 (2007): n.p.

Norah Lange

López-Luaces, Marta. *That Strange Territory: The Representation of Childhood in Texts of Three Latin American Women Writers.* Newark, Del.: Cuesta, 2004.

Miguel, M. E. de. *Norah Lange.* Buenos Aires: Planeta, 1991.

Unruh, Vicky. *Performing Women and Modern Literary Culture in Latin America: Intervening Acts.* Austin: University of Texas Press. 2006.

Enrique Larreta

Ibieta, G. *Tradition and Renewal in "La gloria de don Ramiro."* Potomac, Md.: Scripta Humanistica, 1986.

Vicente Fidel López

Solares-Larrave, Francisco. "Texts, History and Narrative Discourse in Two 19th-Century Spanish American Historical Novels." *Latin American Literary Review* 31, no. 61 (2003): 58–78.

Leopoldo Lugones

Fraser, Howard M. *In the Presence of Mystery: Modernist Fiction and the Occult.* Chapel Hill: Department of Romance Languages, University of North Carolina at Chapel Hill, 1992.

Jitrik, N. *Leopoldo Lugones: mito nacional.* Buenos Aires: Ediciones Palestra, 1960.

Kirkpatrick, G. *The Dissonant Legacy of Modernism: Lugones, Herrera y Reissig and the Voices of Modern Spanish American Poetry.* Berkeley: University of California Press, 1989.

Martinez Estrada, Ezequiel. *Leopoldo Lugones: retrato sin tocar.* Buenos Aires: Emecé, 1968.

Teobaldi, Daniel Gustavo. *La plenitud de la palabra: el pensamiento poético de Leopoldo Lugones.* Córdoba: Copista, 1998.

———. *Leopoldo Lugones, escritor épico.* Córdoba: Copista, 1999.

Benito Lynch

French, Jennifer L. *Nature, Neo-Colonialism, and Spanish American Regional Writers.* Hanover, N. H.: University Press of New England, for Dartmouth College, 2005.

Marta Lynch

Foster, David William. "Raping Argentina: Marta Lynch's *Informe bajo llave.*" *The Centennial Review* 35, no. 3 (1991): 663–80.

Lambright, Anne. "History, Gender, and Unsuccessful Revolutions in Marta Lynch's *La Señora Ordóñez.*" *Hispanófila* 134 (2002): 105–18.

Paley de Francescato, M. "Marta Lynch." *Hispamérica* 10 (1975): 33–44.

Villanueva-Collado, Alfredo. "Metasexualidad, vasallaje y parasitismo en *Al vencedor* de Marta Lynch." *Hispanófila* 108 (1993): 59–74.

Eduardo Mallea

Lewald, H. E. *Eduardo* Mallea. Boston: Twayne, 1977.

Lichtblau, M. I. *El arte estilístico de Eduardo Mallea.* Buenos Aires: Goynarte Editor, 1967.

——, ed. *Eduardo Mallea ante la crítica*. Miami: Universal, 1985.

Polt, J. H. R. *The Writings of Eduardo Mallea*. Berkeley: University of California Press, 1959.

Lucio V. Mansilla

Brown, J. Andrew. *Test Tube Envy: Science and Power in Argentine Narrative*. Lewisburg, Pa.: Bucknell University Press, 2005.

Jagoe, Eva-Lynn Alicia. *The End of the World as They Knew It: Writing Experiences of the Argentine South*. Lewisburg, Pa.: Bucknell University Press, 2008.

Leopoldo Marechal

Cheadle, Norman. *The Ironic Apocalypse in the Novels of Leopoldo Marechal*. London: Támesis, 2000.

Jofré, Manuel Alcides. *Narrativa argentina contemporanea: representación de lo real en Marechal, Borges y Cortázar*. La Serena, Chile: Facultad de Humanidades, Universidad de la Serena, 1991.

Navascués, Javier de. *Adán Buenosayres: una novela total (estudio narratológico)*. Pamplona: Editorial Universitaria de Navarra, 1992.

José Mármol

Ardavín, Carlos X., ed. *Anatomía de un poeta: aproximaciones críticas a José Mármol*. Santo Domingo: Ediciones Librería La Trinitaria, 2005.

Civantos, Christina. "Exile Inside (And) Out: Woman, Nation, and the Exiled Intellectual in José Mármol's *Amalia*." *Latin American Literary Review* 30, no. 59 (2002): 55–78.

Lindsay, Claire. "The Two Amalias: Irony and Influence in José Mármol's Novel and Rosario Ferré's Short Story." *Tesserae: Journal of Iberian and Latin American Studies* 4, no. 1 (1998): 5–20.

Tomás Eloy Martínez

Davies, Lloyd Hughes. "Sight, Sensibility, Simulation: Tomás Eloy Martínez's *El vuelo de la reina*." *Neophilologus* 92, no. 1 (2008): 63–76.

Díaz, Gwendolyn. "Making the Myth of Evita Perón: Saint, Martyr, Prostitute." *Studies in Latin American Popular Culture* 22 (2003): 181–92.

Fares, G. "Historia y literatura en Argentina: *Santa Evita* de Tomás Eloy Martínez." In *Vision de la narrativa hispánica: ensayos,* edited by J. Cruz Mendizabal and J. Fernández Jiménez, 56–69. Indiana: Indiana University of Pennsylvania, 1999.

Fickelscherer de Mattos, Cristine. "Tomás Eloy Martínez: una bibliografía." *Espéculo: Revista de Estudios Literarios* 23 (2003): n.p.

Perkowska, Magdalena. *Historias híbridas: la nueva novela histórica latinoamericana (1985–2000) ante las teorías posmodernas de la historia.* Frankfurt: Vervuert, 2008.

Ezequiel Martínez Estrada

Earle, Peter G. *Prophet in the Wilderness: The Works of Ezequiel Martínez Estrada.* Austin: University of Texas Press, 1971.

Maharg, J. *A Call to Authenticity: The Essays of Ezequiel Martínez Estrada.* Romance Monographs. Oxford: University of Mississippi, 1977.

Weinberg de Magis, Liliana. *Ezequiel Martínez Estrada y la interpretación del Martín Fierro.* México, D.F.: Universidad Nacional Autónoma de México, 1992.

Martha Mercader

Urraca, Beatriz. "Una vida de novela: Martha Mercader and the Contemporary Argentine Historical Novel." *Ciberletras* 14 (2005): n.p.

Tununa Mercado

Corbatta, Jorgelina. "Formas del exilio y la memoria en dos textos de Tununa Mercado." In *Actas del XIV Congreso de la Asociación Internacional de Hispanistas,* edited by Isaías Lerner, Robert Nival, and Alejandro Alonso, IV: 111–16. Newark, Del: Cuesta, 2004.

Kaplan, Marina. "Reading an Absent Sense: Tununa Mercado's *En estado de memoria.*" *Comparative Literature* 58, no. 3 (2006): 223–40.

Enrique Molina

Juliá, Mercedes. *Las ruinas del pasado: aproximaciones a la novela histórica posmoderna.* Madrid: Logos, 2006.

Zonana, Víctor Gustavo. "El hijo pródigo en la poesía del '40: Enrique Molina." *Revista de Literaturas Modernas* 31 (2001): 193–218.

———. "La elegia funeral en los poetas del 40: Enrique Molina." *Revista de literaturas modernas* 27 (1994): 239–57.

Ricardo Molinari

Pousa, N. *Ricardo E. Molinari.* Buenos Aires: Ediciones Culturales Argentinas, 1961.

Daniel Moyano

Gil Amate, Virginia. *Daniel Moyano: la búsqueda de una explicación.* Oviedo: Departamento de Filología Española, Universidad de Oviedo, 1993.

Gnutzmann, Rita. "Bibliografía de y sobre Daniel Moyano." *Chasqui: Revista de Literatura Latinoamericana* 21, no. 1 (1992): 117–20.

Hollabaugh, Linda L. "Daniel Moyano's *Libro de navíos y borrascas*: The Expression of Territorial Exile." In *The Literature of Emigration and Exile,* edited by James Whitlark and Wendell Aycock, 143–55. Lubbock: Texas Tech University Press, 1992.

Manuel Mujica Láinez

Carasuzán, M. E. *Manuel Mujica Láinez.* Buenos Aires: Ediciones Culturales Argentinas, 1962.

Clemons, Gregory A. "The Use of Humor in Manuel Mujica Láinez's *Crónicas reales*." *Hipertexto* 8 (2008): 3–21.

Cruz, J. *Genio y figura de Manuel Mujica Láinez.* Buenos Aires: EUDEBA, 1978.

Prinkey, Troy J. "Discovery of the Self and Authorial Outing of the Protagonist in Manuel Mujica Láinez's *El retrato amarillo*." *Céfiro* 2 (2002): 49–55.

Tacconi de Gómez, María del Carmen. "Historia, ficción y mito en el discurso narrativo de Manuel Mujica Láinez." *Boletín de la Academia Argentina de Letras* 63, nos. 247–248 (1998): 175–86.

Héctor A. Murena

Frugoni de Fritzsche, T. *Murena: un escritor argentino ante los problemas del país y de su literatura.* Buenos Aires: Taladriz, 1985.

Lagos, M. I. *H. A. Murena en sus ensayos y narraciones: de líder revisionista a marginado.* New York: Maiten, 1976.

Conrado Nalé Roxlo

Reverte Bernal, Concepción. *Teatro y Vanguardia en Hispanoamérica.* Madrid, Frankfurt: Iberoamericana, Vervuert, 2006.

Silvina Ocampo

Klingenberg, P. *Fantasies of the Feminine: The Short Stories of Silvia Ocompo.* Lewisburg, Pa.: Bucknell University Press, 1999.

López-Luaces, Marta. *That Strange Territory: The Representation of Childhood in Texts of Three Latin American Women Writers.* Newark, Del.: Cuesta, 2004.

Tomassini, G. *El espejo de Cornelia: la obra cuentistica de Silvina Ocampo.* Buenos Aires: Editorial Plus Ultra, 1995.

Victoria Ocampo

Kaminsky, Amy K. *Argentina: Stories for a Nation.* Minneapolis: University of Minnesota Press 2008.

Meyer, Doris. *Victoria Ocampo: Against the Wind and the Tide.* Austin: University of Texas Press, 1990.

Steiner, P. O. *Victoria Ocampo: Writer, Feminist, Woman of the World.* Albuquerque: University of New Mexico Press, 1999.

Olga Orozco

Kuhnheim, Jill S. *Gender, Politics, and Poetry in Twentieth Century Argentina.* Gainesville: University Press of Florida, 1996.

Nicholson, Melanie. "From Sibyl to Witch and Beyond: Feminine Archetype in the Poetry of Olga Orozco." *Chasqui: Revista de Literatura Latinoamericana* 27, no. 1 (1998): 11–22.

———. "Olga Orozco and the Poetics of Gnosticism." *Revista de Estudios Hispánicos* 35, no. 1 (2001): 73–90.

Juan L. Ortiz

Freidemberg, Daniel. "Reverberaciones, llamados, misterios: Juan L. Ortiz." *Inti: Revista de Literatura Hispánica* 52–53 (2000): 79–98.

Gramuglio, María Teresa. "Juan L. Ortiz, un maestro secreto de la poesía argentina." *Cuadernos Hispanoamericanos* 644 (2004): 45–57.

Eduardo Pavlovsky

Geirola, Gustavo. "Eduardo Pavlovsky (10 December 1933–)." In *Latin American Dramatists: First Series,* edited by Adam Versényi, 236–52. Detroit, Mich.: Gale, 2005.

Roberto J. Payró

Szmetan, Ricardo. "Roberto J. Payró y el teatro argentino de principios de siglo: bibliografía general puesta al día." *Latin American Theatre Review* 33, no. 2 (2000): 113–32.

Néstor Perlongher

Bollig, Ben. "Néstor Perlongher and Mysticism: Towards a Critical Reappraisal." *Modern Language Review* 99, no. 1 (2004): 77–93.
———. "Néstor Perlongher and the Avant-Garde: Privileged Interlocutors and Inherited Techniques." *Hispanic Review* 73, no. 2 (2005): 157–84.

Manuel Peyrou

Castagnino, R. "Manuel Peyrou: el testimonio novelesco de una época argentina" *Revista de la Biblioteca Nacional* 2, no. 3 (1983): 21–34.
Peyrou, Óscar. "Manuel Peyrou, el hermano secreto de Borges." *Cuadernos hispanoamericos* 562 (1997): 81–86.

Ricardo Piglia

Jagoe, Eva-Lynn Alicia. "The Disembodied Machine: Matter, Femininity and Nation in Piglia's *La ciudad ausente*." *Latin American Literary Review* 23, no. 45 (1995): 5–17.
Kefala, Eleni. "Ricardo Piglia and the Syncretist Machine: 'Moral Stories' in the Postcontemporary Wor(l)d." *Revista Canadiense de Estudios Hispánicos* 29, no. 3 (2005): 585–604.
Levinson, Brett. "Trans(re)lations: Dictatorship, Disaster and the 'Literary Politics' of Piglia's *Respiración artificial*." *Latin American Literary Review* 25, no. 49 (1997): 91–120.
Ortega, Francisco A. "Between Midnight and Dawn: The Disabling of History and the Impoverishment of Utopia in Ricardo Piglia's *Artificial Respiration*." *South Atlantic Quarterly* 106, no. 1 (2007): 153–82.

Page, Joanna. "Crime, Capitalism, and Storytelling in Ricardo Piglia's *Plata quemada*." *Hispanic Research Journal: Iberian and Latin American Studies* 5, no. 1 (2004): 27–42.

——. "Writing as Resistance in Ricardo Piglia's *La ciudad ausente*." *Bulletin of Spanish Studies: Hispanic Studies and Researches on Spain, Portugal, and Latin America* 81, no. 3 (2004): 343–60.

Weiss, Timothy. *Translating Orients: Between Ideology and Utopia.* Toronto: University of Toronto Press, 2004.

Alejandra Pizarnik

Bassnett, Susan. "Blood and Mirrors: Imagery of Violence in the Writings of Alejandra Pizarnik." In *Latin American Women's Writing: Feminist Readings in Theory and Crisis,* edited by Anny Brooksbank Jones and Catherine Davies, 127–47. New York: Oxford University Press, 1996.

Bollig, Ben. "How Many Ways to Leave Your Country? On Exile and Not-Belonging in the Work of Alejandra Pizarnik." *Modern Language Review* 104, no. 2 (2009): 421–37.

Borinsky, Alicia. "Alejandra Pizarnik: The Self and Its Impossible Landscapes." In *A Dream of Light and Shadow: Portraits of Latin American Women Writers,* edited by Marjorie Agosín, 291–302. Albuquerque: University of New Mexico Press, 1995.

Goldberg, F. G. *Alexandra Pizarnik: "Este espacio que somos."* Gaithersburg, Maryland: Hispamerica, 1994.

Pina, C. *Alexandra Pizarnik.* Buenos Aires: Planeta, 1991.

Manuel T. Podestá

Nouzeilles, Gabriela. "Ficciones paranoicas de fin de siglo: naturalismo argentino y policía médica." *MLN* 112, no. 2 (1997): 232–52.

Salto, Graciela Nélida. "El debate científico y literario en torno de *Irresponsable,* de Manuel T. Podestá." *Anclajes: Revista del Instituto de Análisis Semiótico del Discurso* 2, no. 2 (1998): 77–103.

Syria Poletti

Martella, Gianna M. "Pioneers: Spanish American Women Writers of Detective Fiction." *Letras Femeninas* 28, no. 1 (2002): 31–44.

Schiminovich, Flora H. "Two Argentine Female Writers Perfect the Art of Detection: María Angélica Bosco & Syria Poletti." *Review: Latin American Literature and Arts* 42 (1990): 16–20.

Abel Posse

Bowsher, Kerstin. "Chimeras of Progress, Mirages of Modernity: Abel Posse's *El inquietante día de la vida.*" *Modern Language Review* 100, no. 1 (2005): 97–112.
———. "Shipwrecks of Modernity: Abel Posse's *El largo atardecer del caminante.*" *Forum for Modern Languages and Studies* 38, no. 1 (2002): 88–98.
Chanady, Amaryll. "Abel Posse and the Rewriting of the Aguirre Myth." In *Latin American Postmodernisms,* edited by Richard A. Young, 175–87. Amsterdam: Rodopi 1997.
Waldemer, Thomas. "Paradise and Its Discontents: Clothing and Nakedness in *Los Perros del Paraíso.*" *RLA: Romance Languages Annual* 8 (1996): 673–77.

Puig Manuel

Bacarisse, Pamela. *Impossible Choices: The Implications of the Cultural References in the Novels of Manuel Puig.* Calgary and Cardiff: University of Calgary and University of Wales Press, 1993.
———. *The Necessary Dream: A Study of the Novels of Manuel Puig.* Cardiff: University of Wales Press, 1988.
Balderston, Daniel, and Francine Masiello, eds. *Approaches to Teaching Puig's "Kiss of the Spider Woman."* New York: Modern Language Association of America, 2007.
Biron, Rebecca E. *Murder and Masculinity: Violent Fictions of Twentieth-Century Latin America.* Nashville, Tenn.: Vanderbilt University Press, 2000.
Kerr, Lucille. *Suspended Fictions: Reading Novels by Manuel Puig.* Urbana: University of Illinois Press, 1987.
Levine, Suzanne Jill. *Manuel Puig and the Spider Woman: His Life and Fictions.* New York: Farrar, Straus & Giroux, 2000.
Tittler, Jonathan. *Manuel Puig.* New York: Twayne, 1993.

Diana Raznovich

Glickman, Nora. "Parodia y desmitificación del rol femenino en el teatro femenino de Diana Raznovich." *Latin American Theatre Review* 28, no. 1 (1994): 89–100.

Taylor, Diana. "Fighting Fire with Frivolity: Diana Raznovich's Defiant Acts." In *Performance, pathos, política de los sexos: teatro postcolonial de autoras latinoamericanas,* edited by Heidrun Adler and Kati Röttger, 69–81. Frankfurt: Vervuert, 1999.

Andrés Rivera

Cruz Martínez, Patricia. "Rivera y su visión de Rosas." In *Segundas Jornadas Internacionales de Literatura Argentina/Comparatística: Actas,* edited by Daniel Altamiranda, 471–76. Buenos Aires: Universidad de Buenos Aires, 1997.

Garcia Simon, Diana. "Andrés Rivera o la excusa de la novela histórica." *Revista Interamericana de Bibliografía/Inter-American Review of Bibliography* 49, nos. 1–2 (1999): 187–93.

Gnutzmann, Rita. "Historia, utopía y fracaso en *La revolución es un sueño eterno* de Andrés Rivera." In *La novela latinoamericana entre historia y utopía,* edited by Sonja M. Steckbauer, 122–35. Eichstätt: Katholische Universität Eichstätt, 1999.

Reina Roffé

Locklin, Blake Seana. "'Qué triste es ser mujer': The Chinese Microcosm of Reina Roffé's *Monte de Venus.*" *Revista de Estudios Hispánicos* 33, no. 3 (1999): 473–94.

Tierney-Tello, Mary-Beth. "From Silence to Subjectivity: Reading and Writing in Reina Roffé's *La rompiente.*" *Latin American Literary Review* 21, no. 42 (1993): 34–56.

Ricardo Rojas

Becco, H. R. "Bibliografia de Ricardo Rojas." *Revista iberamericana* 23 (1958): 335–50.

Chanady, Amaryll. "Ricardo Rojas's *Eurindia*: The Contradictions of Inclusive Models of Identity." *Revista de Estudios Hispánicos* 34, no. 3 (2000): 585–604.

Paya, C., and E. Cardenas. *El primer nacionalismo argentino: Manuel Gálvez y Ricardo Rojas.* Buenos Aires: Pena Lillo, 1978.

Germán Rozenmacher

Glickman, Nora. "Desarraigo contemporáneo en la narrativa de Germán Rozenmacher." In *Latin American Fiction Today,* edited by Rose S. Minc,

109–17. Takoma Park, Md. and Upper Montclair, N.J.: Hispamerica and Montclair State College, 1980.

Kaiser-Lenoir, Claudia. "*El avión negro*: de la realidad a la caricatura grotesca." *Revista Canadiense de Estudios Hispánicos* 7, no. 1 (1982): 149–58.

Lichtblau, Myron I. "La rememoración y la ironía en 'Blues en la noche' de Germán Rozenmacher." In *Studies in Honor of Donald W. Bleznick,* edited by Delia V. Galván, Anita K. Stoll, and Philippa Brown Yin, 95–100. Newark, Del.: Juan de la Cuesta, 1995.

Ernesto Sábato

Catarina, Carlos. *Sábato: entre la idea y la sangre.* San José, Costa Rica, 1973.

Dellepiane, Ángela B. *Ernesto Sábato: el hombre y su obra.* New York: Las Américas Publishing, 1968.

Oberhelman, Harley Dean. *Ernesto Sábato.* New York: Twayne, 1970.

Roberts, Gemma. *Análisis existencial de* Abaddón, el exterminador *de Ernesto Sábato.* Boulder, Colo.: Society of Spanish & Spanish-American Studies, 1990.

Sauter, Silvia, ed. *Sábato: símbolo de un siglo: visiones y (re)visiones de su narrativa.* Buenos Aires: Corregidor, 2005.

Urbina, Nicasio. *La significación del género: estudio semiótico de las novelas y ensayos de Ernesto Sábato.* Miami: Universal, 1992.

Wainerman, Luis. *Sábato y el misterio de los ciegos.* Buenos Aires: Losada, 1971.

Juan José Saer

Premant, Julio. *La dicha de saturno: escritura y melancolía en la obra de Juan José Saer.* Rosario: Beatriz Viterbo Editora, 2002.

Riera, Gabriel. *Littoral of the Letter: Saer's Art of Narration.* Lewisburg, Pa.: Bucknell University Press; 2006.

Solotorevsky, Myrna. *La relación mundo-escritura en textos de Reinaldo Arenas, Juan José Saer, Juan Carlos Martini.* Gaithersburg, Md.: Hispamérica, 1994.

Domingo Faustino Sarmiento

Fuente, Ariel de la. *Children of Facundo: Caudillo and Gaucho Insurgency during the Argentine State-Formation Process (La Rioja, 1853–1870).* Durham, N.C.: Duke University Press, 2000.

Gonzalez, Nelly S. "Domingo Faustino Sarmiento: A Bibliography of Critical Monographs and Articles." *Bulletin of Bibliography* 49, no. 4 (1992): 269–76.

Goodrich, Diana Sorensen. *Facundo and the Construction of Argentine Culture*. Austin: University of Texas Press, 1996.

Halperín Donghi, Tulio, Iván Jaksic, Gwen Kirkpatrick, and Francine Masiello, eds. *Sarmiento: Author of a Nation*. Berkeley: University of California Press, 1994.

Ramos, Julio. *Divergent Modernities: Culture and Politics in Nineteenth-Century Latin America*. Durham, N.C.: Duke University Press, 2001.

Carlos Somigliana

Basabe, Omar. "*El avión negro*: el discurso político implícito en la parodia a una irrealidad grotesca." *Confluencia: Revista Hispánica de Cultura y Literatura* 11, no. 1 (1995): 163–72.

Osvaldo Soriano

Carbajal, Brent J. "Controlled Chaos: Military Dictatorship in Osvaldo Soriano's *Cuarteles de invierno*." *Hispanic Journal* 27, no. 2 (2006): 85–93.

Díaz-Zambrana, R. "'La carretera es la vida': la ética picaresca en *Una sombra ya pronto serás* de Osvaldo Soriano." *Neophilologus* 89, no. 2 (2005): 249–59.

Soumerou, Raúl. "Crónica de la derrota con honra: tres novelas de Osvaldo Soriano: *Triste, solitario y final*; *No habrá más penas ni olvido*; *Cuarteles de invierno*." *Cahiers d'Etudes Romanes* 16 (1990): 77–98.

Alfonsina Storni

Rodríguez Gutiérrez, Milena. *Lo que en verso he sentido: la poesía feminista de Alfonsina Storni*. Granada: Universidad de Granada, 2007.

Salgado, María. "Alfonsina Storni in Her Self-Portraits: The Woman and the Poet." *Confluencia: Revista Hispánica de Cultura y Literatura* 7, no. 2 (1992): 37–46.

Stiefel Ayala, Marta, ed. *Proceedings of the International Literature Conference: Homage to Agustini, Ibarbourou, Mistral, Storni*. Calexico, Calif.: Institute for Border Studies, San Diego State University, 1991.

Teitler, Nathalie. "Redefining the Female Body: Alfonsina Storni and the Modernista Tradition." *Bulletin of Spanish Studies: Hispanic Studies and*

Researches on Spain, Portugal, and Latin America 79, nos. 2–3 (2002): 171–92.

Titiev, Janice G. "Alfonsina Storni in and out of the Canon." *Monographic Review/Revista Monográfica* 13 (1997): 310–18.

Unruh, Vicky. *Performing Women and Modern Literary Culture in Latin America: Intervening Acts.* Austin: University of Texas Press, 2006.

Mario Szichman

Friedman, Edward. "The Novel as Revisionist History: Art as Process in *A las 20:25, la Señora entró en la inmortalidad* and *Tiempo al tiempo.*" *Yiddish* 9 (1993): 24–33.

Morello Frosch, Marta. "Texts Inscribed on the Margins of Argentinian Literature: *A las 20:25, la Señora entró en la inmortalidad.*" *Yiddish* 9 (1993): 34–43.

Ricardo Talesnik

Basabe, Omar. "*El avión negro*: el discurso político implícito en la parodia a una irrealidad grotesca." *Confluencia: Revista Hispánica de Cultura y Literatura* 11, no. 1 (1995): 163–72.

Corvalán, Graciela. "Ricardo Talesnik." *Hispamérica: Revista de Literatura* 31, no. 92 (2002): 81–89.

Jacobo Timerman

Arrington, Melvin S., Jr. "Dissident Voices in Argentina and Cuba: The Testimonial Writings of Jacobo Timerman and Armando Valladares." *SECOLAS Annals: Journal of the Southeastern Council on Latin American Studies* 21 (1990): 33–40.

Héctor Tizón

Deffis de Calvo, Emilia. "Héctor Tizón." *Hispamérica: Revista de Literatura* 31, no. 93 (2002): 65–73.

Massei, Adrián Pablo. "Las voces de la memoria: escritura y exilio en *La casa y el viento*, de Héctor Tizón." *Hispanic Journal* 20, no. 1 (1999): 141–55.

Marta Traba

Kantaris, Elia Geoffrey. "The Silent Zone: Marta Traba." *The Modern Language Review* 87, no. 1 (1992): 86–101.

Navarro, Emilia. "Women and War: Gendered Destruction." In *ICLA '91 Tokyo: The Force of Vision, II: Visions in History; Visions of the Other,* edited by Earl Miner, 261–67. Tokyo: International Comparative Literature Association, 1995.

Picon Garfield, E. *Women's Voices from Latin America: Interviews with Six Contemporary Authors.* Detroit: Wayne State University Press, 1985.

Schlau, Stacey. "*Conversación al sur:* Dialogue as History." *Modern Language Studies* 22, no. 3 (1992): 98–108.

Nemesio Trejo

Pellarolo, Silvia. *Sainete criollo/democracia/representación: el caso de Nemesio Trejo.* Buenos Aires: Corregidor, 1997.

Alberto Vacarezza

Castro, Donald S. "The *palomas* and *gavilanes:* Gender in the Sainetes of Alberto Vacarezza." *Latin American Theatre Review* 38, no. 1 (2004): 127–43.

———. "Villa Crespo: A Porteño Neighborhood: Alberto Vacarezza's Theatric View and Reality." In *LA CHISPA '99: Selected Proceedings,* edited by Gilbert Paolini and Claire J. Paolini, 79–90. New Orleans: Tulane University, 1999.

Luisa Valenzuela

Cordones-Cook, Juanamaría. *Poética de transgresión en la novelística de Luisa Valenzuela.* New York: Peter Lang, 1991.

Díaz, Gwendolyn, ed. *La palabra en vilo: narrativa de Luisa Valenzuela.* Santiago de Chile: Cuarto Propio, 1996.

———. *Luisa Valenzuela sin máscara.* Buenos Aires: Feminaria, 2002.

Magnarelli, Sharon. *Reflections/Refractions: Reading Luisa Valenzuela.* New York: Peter Lang, 1988.

Medeiros-Lichem, María Teresa. *Reading the Feminine: Voice in Latin American Women's Fiction: From Teresa de la Parra to Elena Poniatowska and Luisa Valenzuela.* New York: Peter Lang, 2002.

Niebylski, Dianna C. *Humoring Resistance: Laughter and the Excessive Body in Latin American Women's Fiction.* Albany: State University of New York Press, 2004.

Tompkins, Cynthia Margarita. *Latin American Postmodernisms: Women Writers and Experimentation.* Gainesville: University Press of Florida, 2006.

Bernardo Verbitsky

Lockhart, Darrell B. "La semiotización del cuerpo judío: 'La culpa' de Bernardo Verbitsky." *Boletín de Humanidades* 4 (2002–2003): 55–64.

David Viñas

Dill, Hans-Otto. "The Riders Get off the Horse: David Viñas and the Demise of the Authoritarian Argentine Military." In *Post-Authoritarian Cultures: Spain and Latin America's Southern Cone,* edited by Luis Martín-Estudillo and Roberto Ampuero, 34–57. Nashville: Vanderbilt University Press, 2008.

Glickman, Nora. "Viñas' *En la semana trágica*: A Novelist's Focus on an Argentine Pogrom." *Yiddish* 5, no. 4 (1984): 64–71.

Valverde, Estela. "Una bibliografía en busca de un autor: David Viñas." *Chasqui: Revista de Literatura Latinoamericana* 17, no. 2 (1988): 110–28.

María Elena Walsh

Domínguez Colavita, Federica. "El paralelismo en la poesía de María Elena Walsh: la paradoja poética: regla y ruptura." *Revista/Review Interamericana* 19, nos. 3–4 (1989).

Foster, David William. "Playful Ekphrasis: María Elena Walsh and Children's Literature in Argentina." *Mester* 13, no. 1 (1984): 40–51.

Sibbald, K. M. "Una autobiografía ex-céntrica: *Novios de antaño* de María Elena Walsh." In *Memorias y olvidos: autos y biografías (reales, ficticias) en la cultura hispánica,* edited by J. Pérez Magallón, R. de la Fuente Ballesteros, and K. M. Sibbald, 349–58. Valladolid: Universitas Castellae, 2003.

Rodolfo Walsh

Aguilar, Gonzalo. "Rodolfo Walsh, beyond Literature." *Review: Literature and Arts of the Americas* 75, no. 40 (2007): 231–37.

Neyret, Juan Pablo. "Volver a las fuentes: periodismo y literatura en 'Esa mujer' de Rodolfo Walsh y *Santa Evita* de Tomás Eloy Martínez." In *Intergéneros culturales: literatura, artes y medios,* by Armando Capalbo, 317–21. Buenos Aires: BM, 2005.

BOLIVIA

Resources: Dictionaries, Histories, Anthologies

Ávila Echazú, Edgar. *Historia y antología de la literatura boliviana.* Tarija: Universidad Boliviana, 1978.

Cáceres Romero, Adolfo. *Nueva historia de la literatura boliviana.* 3 vols. La Paz: Los Amigos del Libro, 1987.

Diaz Machicao, Porfirio. *Antologia del teatro boliviano.* La Paz: Editorial Don Bosco, 1979.

Guzmán, Augusto. *La novela en Bolivia.* La Paz: Editorial Juventud, 1955.

Ortega, José, and Adolfo Cáceres Romero. *Diccionario de la literatura boliviana.* La Paz: Editorial Los Amigos del Libro, 1977.

Reyes, Sandra, ed. *Oblivion and Stone: A Selection of Contemporary Bolivian Poetry and Fiction.* Fayetteville: University of Arkansas Press, 1998.

Santos, Rosario, ed. *The Fat Man from La Paz: Contemporary Fiction from Bolivia.* New York: Seven Stories Press, 2000.

Velásquez Guzmán, Mónica. *Antología de la poesía boliviana: ordenar la danza.* Santiago de Chile: LOM Ediciones, 2004.

Wiethüchter, Blanca, and Alba María Paz-Soldán. *Hacia una historia crítica de la literatura en Bolivia.* 2 vols. La Paz: PIEB, 2003.

Select Bibliography for Specific Writers

Alcides Arguedas

Aronna, Michael. *"Pueblos enfermos": The Discourse of Illness in the Turn-of-the-century Spanish and Latin American Essay.* Chapel Hill: University of North Carolina, 1999.

García, Gustavo V. "*Raza de bronce*: ¿novela de hambrientos?" *Neophilologus* 87, no. 4 (2003): 575–88.

Pastor, Ricardo. "Bibliography of Alcides Arguedas." *Bolivian Studies* 11 (2004): 12–23.

Prada-Oropeza, R. "Presentación critica de Alcides Arguedas." *Texto Critico* 1, no. 1 (1995): 217–37.

Domitila Barrios de Chungara

Canonge, Hector A. "Domitila Chungara: Self and Other." In *Beyond Indigenous Voices,* edited by Mary H. Preuss, 23–29. Lancaster, Calif.: Labyrinthos, 1996.

Sanjinés C., Javier. "Beyond Testimonial Discourse: New Popular Trends in Bolivia." In *The Real Thing: Testimonial Discourse and Latin America,* edited by Georg M. Gugelberger, 254–65. Durham, N.C.: Duke University Press, 1996.

———. "From Domitila to 'los relocalizados': Testimony and Marginality in Bolivia." *Inti: Revista de Literatura Hispánica* 32–33 (1990): 138–47.

Raúl Botelho Gonsálvez

Muñoz, Willy. "*La lanza capitana*: texto y contexto." *Gestos: Teoria y Practica del Teatro Hispanico* 6, no. 11 (1991): 135–45.

Guillermo Francovich

Gómez-Martínez, José Luis. "Homenaje a Guillermo Francovich (1901–1990)." *Cuadernos Americanos* 27 (1991): 69–85.

Ricardo Jaimes Freyre

Carilla, E. *Ricardo Jaimes Freyre*. Buenos Aires: Ediciones Culturales Argentinas. 1967.

García, Gustavo V. "Del mito a la modernidad: unidad y dicotomía en *Castalia bárbara*." *Revista de Estudios Hispánicos* 35, no. 2 (2001): 347–68.

Gutiérrez, José Ismael. "Crítica y modernidad en las revistas literarias: *La Revista de América* de Rubén Darío y Ricardo Jaimes Freyre o el eclecticismo modernista en las publicaciones literarias hispanoamericanas de fin de siglo." *Revista Iberoamericana* 62, no. 175 (1996): 367–83.

Salmón, Josefa. "Ricardo Jaimes Freyre (12 May 1866?-24 April 1933)." In *Modern Spanish American Poets: First Series,* edited by María A. Salgado, 162–65. Detroit, Mich.: Gale, 2003.

Scott, Robert. "The Visual Artistry of Ricardo Jaimes Freyre's 'En las montañas.'" *Studies in Short Fiction* 28, no. 2 (1991): 195–201.

Jesús Lara

García Pabón, Leonardo. *De Incas, Chaskañawis, Yanakunas y Chullas: estudios sobre la novela mestiza en los Andes*. Alicante: Universidad de Alicante, 2007.

Muñoz, Willy O. "La realidad boliviana en la narrativa de Jesús Lara." *Revista Iberoamericana* 52, no. 134: 225–41.

Tarica, Estelle. *The Inner Life of Mestizo Nationalism*. Minneapolis: University of Minnesota Press, 2008.

Jaime Sáenz

Monasterios P., Elizabeth. "Jaime Sáenz (8 October 1921–16 August 1986)." In *Modern Spanish American Poets: First Series,* edited by María A. Salgado, 376. Detroit, Mich.: Gale, 2003.

———. "Poéticas del conflicto andino." *Revista Iberoamericana* 73, no. 220 (2007): 541–61.

Rivera-Rodas, Oscar. "La poesía de Jaime Sáenz." *Inti: Revista de Literatura Hispánica* 18–19 (1983–1984): 59–82.

Sanjinés C., Javier. "Jaime Sáenz (8 October 1921–13 August 1986)." In *Modern Latin-American Fiction Writers: Second Series,* edited by William Luis, 350. Detroit, Mich.: Gale, 1994.

Néstor Taboada Terán

Cummings, Gerardo. "Néstor Taboada Terán: una entrevista." *Arizona Journal of Hispanic Cultural Studies* 6 (2002): 141–49.

Paz Soldán, Alba María. "La irrupción del Quechua en la obra de Taboada Terán y de Dávila Andrade." In *Literatura como intertextualidad: IX Simposio Internacional de Literatura,* edited by Juana Alcira, 570–76. Buenos Aires: Instituto Literario y Cultural Hispánico, 1993.

Richards, Keith. "Internalized Exiles: Three Bolivian Writers." In *Comparing Postcolonial Literatures: Dislocations,* edited by Ashok Bery and Patricia Murray, 134–43. New York: St. Martin's Press, 2000.

Franz Tamayo

Fernández, D. *La poesía lirica de Franz Tamayo.* La Paz: Los Amigos del Libro, 1968.

Salmón, Josefa. "La lucha por la diferencia: mestizaje y etnicidad en Franz Tamayo." *Hispamérica: Revista de Literatura* 31, no. 91 (2002): 29–39.

———. "Naturaleza e historia en la ideología nacionalista de Franz Tamayo y Alcides Arguedas." In *La Chispa '89: Selected Proceedings,* edited by G. Paolini, 277–83. New Orleans: Tulane University, 1989.

Sanjinés C., Javier. "Tamayo, observador: negociando lo 'letrado' con lo visual." In *Convergencia de tiempos: estudios subalternos/contextos latinoamericanos estado, cultura, subalternidad,* edited by Ileana Rodríguez, 405–24. Amsterdam: Rodopi, 2001.

BRAZIL

Resources: Bibliographies, Dictionaries, Histories, Anthologies

Aguiar, Flávio, ed. *Antologia do Teatro Brasileiro: A Aventura Realista e o Teatro Musicado.* São Paulo: Ed. SENAC São Paulo, 1998.

——. *Antologia do Teatro Brasileiro: O Teatro de Inspiração Romântica.* São Paulo: Ed. SENAC São Paulo, 1997.

Bandeira, Manuel. *Brief History of Brazilian Literature, 1886–1958.* Translated by Ralph Edward Ingalls Dimmick. Washington, D.C.: Pan American Union, 1958.

——, ed. *Apresentação da Poesia Brasileira: Seguida de uma Antologia de Versos.* 2nd ed. Rio de Janeiro: Casa do Estudante do Brasil, 1946.

Bishop, Elizabeth, and Emanuel Brasil, eds. *An Anthology of Twentieth-Century Brazilian Poetry.* Middletown, Conn.: Wesleyan University Press, 1972.

Bonvicino, Régis, Michael Palmer, and Nelson Ascher, eds. *Nothing the Sun Could Not Explain: 20 Contemporary Brazilian Poets, Volume 3.* The PIP (Project for Innovative Poetry) Anthology of World Poetry of the 20th Century. Los Angeles: Green Integer, 2003.

Bosi, Alfredo. *História Concisa da Literatura Brasileira.* São Paulo: Editora Cultrix, 1981.

Brasil, Emanuel, and William Jay Smith. *Brazilian Poetry (1950–1980).* Middletown, Conn.: Wesleyan University Press, 1983.

Brito, Mário da Silva. *História do Modernismo Brasileiro.* Rio de Janeiro: Civilização Brasileira, 1971.

Broca, José Brito, and José Galante de Sousa. *Introdução ao Estudo da Literatura Brasileira.* Rio de Janeiro: Instituto Nacional do Livro, Ministério da Educação e Cultura, 1963.

Brookshaw, David. *Race and Color in Brazilian Literature.* Metuchen, N.J.: Scarecrow Press, 1986.

Cafezeiro, Edwaldo, and Carmem Gadelha. *História do Teatro Brasileiro: Um Percurso de Anchieta a Nelson Rodrigues.* Rio de Janeiro: Editora UFRJ, EDUERJ, FUNARTE, 1996.

Candido, Antônio. *Formação da Literatura Brasileira.* São Paulo: Martins, 1971.

Candido, Antônio, and J. Aderaldo Castello. *Presença da Literatura Brasileira: História e Antologia.* Rio de Janeiro: Bertrand Brasil, 2001 [1985].

Chamberlain, Bobby J. *Portuguese Language and Luso-Brazilian Literature: An Annotated Guide to Selected Reference Works.* New York: Modern Language Association of America, 1989.

Coutinho, Afrânio. *An Introduction to Literature in Brazil.* New York: Columbia University Press, 1969.

Ellison, Fred P. *Brazil's New Novel: Four Northeastern Masters, José Lins do Rego, Jorge Amado, Graciliano Ramos, Rachel de Queiroz.* Westport, Conn.: Greenwood Press, 1979.

Fitz, Earl E. *Brazilian Narrative Traditions in a Comparative Context.* New York: Modern Language Association of America, 2005.

Foster, David William, and Walter Rela. *Brazilian Literature: A Research Bibliography.* New York: Garland, 1990.

Goldberg, Isaac. *Brazilian Literature, 1887–1938.* New York: Gordon Press, 1975.

Haberly, David T. *Three Sad Races: Racial Identity and National Consciousness in Brazilian Literature.* Cambridge: Cambridge University Press 1983.

Hulet, Claude L., ed. *Brazilian Literature.* 3 vols. Washington, D.C.: International Institute of Ibero-American Literature/Georgetown University Press, 1974.

Jackson, K. David. *Oxford Anthology of the Brazilian Short Story.* Oxford: Oxford University Press, 2006.

Levine, Robert M., and John J. Crocitti, eds. *The Brazil Reader: History, Culture, Politics.* Durham, N.C.: Duke University Press, 1999.

Magaldi, Sábato. *Panorama do Teatro Brasileiro.* São Paulo: Global Editora, 1997.

Moisés, Massaud, ed. *História da Literatura Brasileira.* 5 vols. São Paulo: Editora Cultrix/Editora da Universidade de São Paulo, 1983–1989.

———. *Pequeno Dicionário de Literatura Brasileira.* 5th ed. São Paulo: Editora Cultrix, 1998.

Pereira, Lúcia Miguel. *Prosa de Ficção: De 1870 a 1920.* Rio de Janeiro: J. Olympio, 1957.

Perrone, Charles. *Seven Faces: Brazilian Poetry Since Modernism.* Durham, N.C.: Duke University Press, 1996.

Prado, Décio de Almeida. *História Concisa do Teatro Brasileiro: 1570–1908.* São Paulo: EDUSP, Imprensa Oficial, 1999.

Ramos, Péricles Eugênio da Silva. *Do Barroco ao Modernismo: Estudos de Poesia Brasileira.* Rio de Janeiro: Livros Técnicos e Científicos, 1979.

Rector, Monica, and Fred. M. Clark. *Brazilian Writers.* Detroit, Mich.: Gale, 2005.

Sousa, Américo Guerreiro de, and Ian Robin Warner. *An Anthology of Modern Portuguese and Brazilian Prose.* London: Harrap, 1978.

Stegagno Picchio, Luciana. *História da Literatura Brasileira.* Rio de Janeiro: Editora Nova Aguilar, 1997.

Vieira, Nelson. *Jewish Voices in Brazilian Literature: The Discourse of Alterity.* Gainesville: University Press of Florida, 1995.

Select Bibliography for Specific Writers

Caio Fernando Abreu

Arenas, Fernando. "Small Epiphanies in the Night of the World: The Writings of Caio Fernando Abreu." In *Lusosex: Gender and Sexuality in the*

Portuguese-Speaking World, edited by Susan Canty Quinlan and Fernando Arenas, 235–57. Minneapolis: University of Minnesota Press, 2002.

Capistrano de Abreu

MacNicoll, Murray G. "Capistrano de Abreu: The First Critic of *Brás Cubas.*" *Romance Notes* 22, no. 2 (1981): 177–81.

Casimiro José Marques de Abreu

Tringali, Dante. "A Retórica Amorosa de Casimiro de Abreu." *Revista de Letras* 21 (1981): 13–23.

Adonias Filho

Albuquerque, M. Fátima M. "The Brazilian Nationalist Myth in Adonias Filho's Corpo Vivo." *Portuguese Studies* 3 (1987): 149–58.

Matias Aires Ramos da Silva de Eça

Simões, Manuel G. "Percursos do Iluminismo em Portugal: Matias Aires e o 'Problema de Arquitectura Civil.'" *Rassegna Iberistica* 56 (1996): 153–61.

Bernardo Ajzenberg

"Bernardo Ajzenberg (São Paulo, 1959) [Interview]." *Nuevo Texto Crítico* 2, nos. 41–42 (2008): 70–71.

José de Alencar

Campos, Haroldo de, and Randal Johnson. "Iracema: A Vanguard Archaeography." In *Tropical Paths: Essays on Modern Brazilian Literature,* edited by Randal Johnson, 11–29. New York: Garland, 1993.
Franco, Jean, et al. *José de Alencar: Iracema.* Oxford: Oxford University Press, 2000.
Newcomb, Robert Patrick. "José de Alencar's Critical Writing: Narrating National History in the Romantic Era." *Luso-Brazilian Review* 44, no. 1 (2007): 1–19.

Valente, Luiz Fernando. "Alencar's Flawed Blueprints." In *Homenagem a Alexandrino Severino: Essays on the Portuguese Speaking World,* edited by Margo Milleret and Marshall C. Eakin, 148–66. Austin, Tex.: Host, 1993.

Wassermann, Renata R. Mautner. "The Red and the White: The 'Indian' Novels of José de Alencar." *PMLA: Publications of the Modern Language Association of America* 98, no. 5 (1983): 815–27.

Guilherme de Almeida

Berrettini, Célia. "Guilherme de Almeida e o Francês." *Revista da Academia Paulista de Letras* 38, no. 99 (1981): 179–98.

Gomes, Danilo. "Poesia, Conto e Crônica." *Jornal de Letras: Mensario de Letras, Artes e Ciencias* 337, no. 2 (1979): 5.

Júlia Lopes de Almeida

Wasserman, Renata R. Mautner. *Central at the Margin: Five Brazilian Women Writers.* Lewisburg, Pa.: Bucknell University Press, 2007.

Manuel Antônio de Almeida

Aiex, Nola Kortner. "*Memórias de um Sargento de Milícias* as Menippean Satire." *Romance Quarterly* 28, no. 2 (1981): 199–208.

Soares, Marcus Vinicius Nogueira, and Ross G. Forman. "*Memoirs of a Militia Sergeant*: A Singular Novel." *Portuguese Literary & Cultural Studies* 4–5 (2000): 113–20.

Manuel Inácio da Silva Alvarenga

Houaiss, Antônio. *Seis Poetas e um Problema.* Rio de Janeiro: Ministério da Educaçao e Cultura, Serviço de Documentação, 1960.

Silva, Domingos Carvalho da. *Gonzaga e Outros Poetas.* Rio de Janeiro: Orfeu, 1970.

Antônio Frederico de Castro Alves

Braga, Thomas. "Castro Alves and the New England Abolitionist Poets." *Hispania: A Journal Devoted to the Teaching of Spanish and Portuguese* 67, no. 4 (1984): 585–93.

——. "France in the Poetry of Castro Alves." *Modern Language Studies* 16, no. 3 (1986): 122–33.

Graden, Dale T. "History and Motive as Seen Through Antônio Frederico de Castro Alves's 'Saudacão a Palmares.'" *Brasil/Brazil: Revista de Literatura Brasileira/A Journal of Brazilian Literature* 9 (1993): 27–44.

Haberly, David T. "Heine and Castro Alves: A Question of Influence." *Romanische Forschungen* 97, nos. 2–3 (1985): 239–48.

Francisco Alvim

Bessa, Antônio Sérgio, and Claudio Brandt. "Francisco Alvim." *BOMB* 102 (2008): 72–77.

Coelho, Joaquim-Francisco. "Sob *O Sol dos Cegos*." *Minas Gerais, Suplemento Literário* 13 (April 1974): 8.

Jorge Amado

Brower, Keith H., Earl E. Fitz, and Enrique Martínez-Vidal, eds. *Jorge Amado: New Critical Essays*. New York: Routledge, 2001.

Miller, Michael. "Jorge Amado's *Dona Flor and Her Two Husbands* and Antônio Flores' *The Land*: Contrasting Portraits of Brazilian Regionalism." *MACLAS: Latin American Essays* 4 (1990): 279–86.

Moser, Robert H. *The Carnivalesque Defunto: Death and the Dead in Modern Brazilian Literature*. Athens: Ohio University Press, 2008.

Moutinho, Isabel. "Jorge Amado's *Tocaia Grande*: A Frontier Novel." *RLA: Romance Languages Annual* 6 (1994): 551–55.

Swarnakar, Sudha. "Jorge Amado: The Brazilian Zola." *Excavatio: Emile Zola and Naturalism* 21, nos. 1–2 (2006): 1–19.

Vieira, Nelson H. "Myth and Identity in Short Stories by Jorge Amado." *Studies in Short Fiction* 23, no. 1 (1986): 25–34.

Moacir Amâncio

Waldman, Berta. "Poesia Nômade." In *Ata,* by Moacir Amâncio, 7–23. Rio de Janeiro: Editora Record, 2007.

José de Anchieta

Alves Filho, Paulo Edson, and John Milton. "Inculturation and Acculturation in the Translation of Religious Texts: The Translations of Jesuit Priest José de

Anchieta into Tupi in 16th-Century Brazil." *Target: International Journal of Translation Studies* 17, no. 2 (2005): 275–96.

Braga-Pinto, César. "José de Anchieta: Performing the History of Christianity in Brazil." *Portuguese Literary & Cultural Studies* 4–5 (2000): 435–43.

Wasserman, Renata. "The Theater of José de Anchieta and the Definition of Brazilian Literature." *Luso-Brazilian Review* 36, no. 1 (1999): 71–85.

Williams, Frederick G. "Faith and Feminism vs. Philandering and Firearms, or Taming the Wilds of Brazil: An Analysis of Father Anchieta's Morality Play *When in Espirito Santo Was Received a Relic of the Eleven Thousand Virgins,* together with an English Translation." *Mediterranean Studies* 10 (2001): 117–42.

Carlos Drummond de Andrade

Campos, Haroldo de, and Manuel Ulacia. "Drummond, maestro de cosas." *Vuelta* 12, no. 136 (1988): 45–47.

Campos, Mario do Carmo. "Poetics and Contemporary Culture in Drummond and Borges." In *Latin America as Its Literature,* edited by Maria Elena Valdés, Mario Valdés, and Richard Young, 89–104. Whitestone, N.Y.: Council on National Literatures, 1995.

Martins, Wilson. "Carlos Drummond de Andrade and the Heritage of Modernismo." In *Twayne Companion to Contemporary World Literature: From the Editors of World Literature Today,* edited by Pamela A. Genova, 880–82. New York: Twayne, 2003.

Santiago, Silviano, and Sonia Frías. "Memorias de Carlos Drummond de Andrade." *Casa de las Américas* 34, no. 192 (1993): 120–25.

Valente, Luiz Fernando. "William Carlos Williams and Carlos Drummond de Andrade: A Poetics of Generosity." *Ellipsis: Journal of the American Portuguese Studies Association* 3 (2005): 7–19.

José Oswald de Sousa Andrade

Bary, Leslie. "The Tropical Modernist as Literary Cannibal: Cultural Identity in Oswald de Andrade." *Chasqui: Revista de Literatura Latinoamericana* 20, no. 2 (1991): 10–19.

Castro-Klarén, Sara. "A Genealogy for the 'Manifesto antropófago,' or the Struggle Between Socrates and the Caraïbe." *Nepantla: Views from the South* 1, no. 2 (2000): 295–322.

Jackson, Kenneth David. "Primitivismo e Vanguarda: O 'Mau Selvagem' do Modernismo Brasileiro." *Arquivos do Centro Cultural Português* 23 (1987): 975–82.

Schwartz, Jorge. *Vanguarda e Cosmopolitismo na Década de 20. Oliverio Girondo e Oswald de Andrade*. São Paulo: Perspectiva, 1983.

Vinkler, Beth Joan. "The Anthropophagic Mother, Other: Appropriated Identities in Oswald de Andrade's 'Manifesto Antropófago.'" *Luso-Brazilian Review* 34, no. 1 (1997): 105–11.

Mário Raul de Morais Andrade

Foster, David William. "Mário de Andrade: On Being São Paulo-wise in *Paulicéia Desvairada*." *Iberoamericana: América Latina-España-Portugal* 5, no. 19 (2005): 27–40.

Lokensgard, Mark. "Inventing the Modern Brazilian Short Story: Mário de Andrade's Literary Lobbying." *Luso-Brazilian Review* 42, no. 1 (2005): 136–54.

López, Kimberle S. "Modernismo and the Ambivalence of the Postcolonial Experience: Cannibalism, Primitivism, and Exoticism in Mário de Andrade's *Macunaíma*." *Luso-Brazilian Review* 35, no. 1 (1998): 25–38.

Madureira, Luís. *Cannibal Modernities: Postcoloniality and the Avant-garde in Caribbean and Brazilian Literature*. Charlottesville: University Press of Virginia, 2005.

Perrone, Charles A. "Presentation and Representation of Self and City in *Paulicéia Desvairada*." *Chasqui: Revista de Literatura Latinoamericana* 31, no. 1 (2002): 18–27.

Rosenberg, Fernando J. "The Geopolitics of Affect in the Poetry of Brazilian Modernism." In *Geomodernisms: Race, Modernism, Modernity,* edited by Laura Doyle and Laura Winkiel, 77–95. Bloomington: Indiana University Press, 2005.

Willis, Bruce Dean. *Aesthetics of Equilibrium: The Vanguard Poetics of Vicente Huidobro and Mário de Andrade*. West Lafayette, Ind.: Purdue University Press, 2006.

Augusto dos Anjos

Bruflat, Alan. "Dramatic Tension in the Poetry of Augusto dos Anjos." *Hispania: A Journal Devoted to the Teaching of Spanish and Portuguese* 72, no. 3 (1989): 780–82.

Vasconcelos, Montgomery José de. "The Carnivalized Poetics of Augusto dos Anjos." In *Semiotics around the World: Synthesis in Diversity, I-II,* edited by Irmengard Rauch and Gerald F. Carr, 497–500. Berlin: Mouton de Gruyter, 1997.

Arnaldo Antunes

Ferraz, Eucanaã, and Claudio Brandt. "Arnaldo Antunes." *BOMB* 102 (2008): 50–55.

Marçal Aquino

Dalcastagnè, Regina. "Cruzando Fronteiras: Três Invasões na Narrativa Brasileira Contemporânea." *Revista Cerrados* 12, no. 15 (2003): 57–66.

José Pereira da Graça Aranha

Eakin, Marshall C. "Race and Ideology in Graça Aranha's *Canaã*." *Ideologies and Literature: Journal of Hispanic and Lusophone Discourse Analysis* 3, no. 14 (1980): 3–15.
Paes, José Paulo. *Canaã e o Ideário Modernista*. São Paulo: Universidade de São Paulo, 1992.

Nelson Ronny Ascher

Ascher, Nelson. "Being a Poet in Brazil." *Boundary 2: An International Journal of Literature and Culture* 26, no. 1 (1999): 39–42.

Joaquim Maria Machado de Assis

Fitz, Earl E. "Machado de Assis' [Assis's] Reception and the Transformation of the Modern European Novel." *Portuguese Literary & Cultural Studies* 13–14 (2004): 43–57.
Graham, Richard, ed. *Machado de Assis: Reflections on a Brazilian Master Writer*. Austin: University of Texas Press, 1999.
Jackson, K. David. "Machado de Assis in English: A Selected Bibliography." *Portuguese Literary & Cultural Studies* 13–14 (2004): 627–46.
Moser, Robert H. *The Carnivalesque Defunto: Death and the Dead in Modern Brazilian Literature*. Athens: Ohio University Press, 2008.
Rocha, João Cezar de Castro. "The Author as Plagiarist: The Case of Machado de Assis." *Portuguese Literary & Cultural Studies* 13–14 (2004): 643–63.
Schwarz, Roberto. *A Master on the Periphery of Capitalism: Machado de Assis*. Translated by John Gledson. Durham, N.C.: Duke University Press, 2001.
Wasserman, Renata R. Mautner. "Race, Nation, Representation: Machado de Assis and Lima Barreto." *Luso-Brazilian Review* 45, no. 2 (2008): 84–106.

Tristão de Ataíde (pseudonym of Alceu Amoroso Lima)

Carpeaux, Otto Maria. *Alceu Amoroso Lima*. Rio de Janeiro: Graal, 1978.
Coutinho, Afrânio. *Tristão de Athayde, o Crítico*. Rio de Janeiro: Agir, 1979.

Affonso Ávila

Cirne, Moacy. "Affonso Ávila: O Discurso do Poeta." *Minas Gerais, Suplemento Literário* 18, no. 898 (1983): 6.
Nunes, Sebastião. "Affonso Ávila: 30 Anos de Poesia." *Minas Gerais, Suplemento Literário* 18, no. 897 (1983): 1.

Aluísio Azevedo

Bletz, May. "Race and Modernity in *O Cortiço* by Aluísio de Azevedo." *LL Journal* 2, no. 1 (2007): 1–10.
Santiago, Silviano. "The Wily Homosexual (First-and Necessarily Hasty-Notes)." In *Queer Globalizations: Citizenship and the Afterlife of Colonialism*, edited by Arnaldo Cruz-Malavé and Martin F. Manalansan, 13–19. New York: New York University Press, 2002.

Artur Azevedo

Montello, Josue, ed. *Artur Azevedo*. Rio de Janeiro: Agir, 1963.
Moser, Gerald M. "Artur Azevedo's Last Dramatic Writings: The 'Teatro a Vapor' Vignettes (1906–1908)." *Latin American Theatre Review* 10, no. 1 (1976): 23–35.

Carlito Azevedo

Franco, Marcia Arruda. "Apresentando Carlito Azevedo: (Um Diálogo com João Cabral)." *Colóquio/Letras* 157–158 (2000): 337–41.

Manuel Antônio Álvares de Azevedo

Albuquerque, Severino João. "A Brazilian Intermediary in the Transmission of European Romantic Ideas: Alvares de Azevedo." *Romance Notes* 23, no. 3 (1983): 220–26.
Marchant, Elizabeth A. "Naturalism, Race, and Nationalism in Aluísio Azevedo's *O Mulato*." *Hispania: A Journal Devoted to the Teaching of Spanish and Portuguese* 83, no. 3 (2000): 445–53.
Warrin, Donald O. "On the Function of the Poetic Sign in Alvares de Azevedo." *Luso-Brazilian Review* 17, no. 1 (1980): 93–105.

Manuel Bandeira

Hernández, Rafael. *Una poética de la despreocupación: modernidad e identidad en cuatro poetas latinoamericanos.* Santiago, Chile: Cuarto Propio, 2003.

Oliver, Elide Valarini. "Mário, the Brazilian and Manuel, the Lusitanian: Notes on the Brazilian Language in the Correspondence between Mário de Andrade and Manuel Bandeira." *Portuguese Studies* 23, no. 2 (2007): 167–90.

Reckert, Stephen. "Beyond the Frontier: 'Liminality' in Three Modern Poets." *Portuguese Studies* 5 (1989): 81–88.

Slater, Candace. *This Earth, That Sky: Poems by Manuel Bandeira.* Berkeley: University Press of California, 1989.

Tobias Barreto de Meneses

Montello, Josué. *A Polêmica de Tobias Barreto com os Padres do Maranhão.* Rio de Janeiro: José Olympio/MEC, 1978.

Olavo Brás Martins dos Guimarães Bilac

Conde, Maite. "Film and the Crônica: Documenting New Urban Experiences in Turn of the Century Rio de Janeiro." *Luso-Brazilian Review* 42, no. 2 (2005): 66–88.

Antônio Bivar

Schoenbach, P. J. "Rio and São Paulo Theatres in 1970: National Dramaturgy." *Latin American Theatre Review* 5, no. 2 (1972): 67–80.

Augusto Boal

Jackson, Adrian. *Games for Actors and Non-Actors.* London: Routledge, 2002.

Smith, Steven K. "Activist Theater: From Brecht through Boal." *Brecht Yearbook/Das Brecht-Jahrbuch* 30 (2005): 278–99.

Fernando Bonassi

Silva, Maurício. "A Narrativa Minimalista de Fernando Bonassi." *Estudos de Literatura Brasileira Contemporânea* 28 (2006): 47–58.

Stanton, William. "Apocalipse 1, 11 in São Paulo: Aesthetic Vertigo or Exploitation?" *TDR: The Drama Review: A Journal of Performance Studies* 46, no. 4 (2002): 86–100.

Régis Bonvicino

Cisneros, Odile. "De Nothing the Sun para Cadenciando-um-ning: Bonvicino e uma Década de Trocas Poéticas Brasil/EUA." *Et Cetera: Revista de Literatura & Arte* 1 (2003): 99–103.

Raul Bopp

Araújo, Ana. "*Macunaíma* de Mário de Andrade e *Cobra Norato* de Raul Bopp na Re-Definição da Identidade Brasileira." *RLA: Romance Languages Annual* 4 (1992): 375–81.

Esteves, António Roberto. "Cobra Norato de Raul Bopp: Leituras Possíveis." *Revista de Letras* 28 (1988): 73–83.

Rubem Braga

Vernon, Richard. "Rubem Braga (12 January 1913–17 December 1990)." *Brazilian Writers,* edited by Monica Rector and Fred M. Clark, 107–11. Detroit, Mich.: Gale, 2005.

Paulo Henriques Britto

Arrojo, Rosemary. "O Tradutor 'Invisível' por Ele Mesmo: Paulo Henriques Britto entre a Humildade e a Onipotência." *Trabalhos em Lingüística Aplicada* 36 (2000): 159–65.

Chico Buarque

Albuquerque, Severino João. "In Praise of Treason: Three Contemporary Versions of *Calabar.*" *Hispania: A Journal Devoted to the Teaching of Spanish and Portuguese* 74, no. 3 (1991): 556–63.

Perrone, Charles. *Masters of Contemporary Brazilian Song: MPB 1965–1985.* Austin: University of Texas Press, 1989.

Wilson Bueno

Pereira Filho, João Antônio. "Autonomias, Bazar dos Dias num Tempo de Wilson Bueno." *Minas Gerais, Suplemento Literário* 23, no. 1132 (1989): 12.

Antônio Callado

Sá, Lúcia. "An Epic of the Brazilian Revolution: Callado's *Quarup*." *Portuguese Studies* 14 (1998): 195–204.

Waldemer, Thomas P. "Revenge of the Cannibal: Surrender and Resistance in Antônio Callado's Nativist Novels." *Luso-Brazilian Review* 34, no. 1 (1997): 113–23.

Adolfo Caminha

Edison, Thomas Wayne. "Sadism, Scopofilia, and Masochism in Adolfo Caminha's *Bom-Crioulo*." *PALARA: Publication of the Afro-Latin/American Research Association* 8 (2004): 73–85.

Foster, David William. "Adolfo Caminha's *Bom-Crioulo*: A Founding Text of Brazilian Gay Literature." *Chasqui: Revista de Literatura Latinoamericana* 17, no. 2 (1988): 13–22.

Ginway, M. Elizabeth. "National Building and Heroic Undoing: Myth and Ideology in *Bom-Crioulo*." *Modern Language Studies* 28, nos. 3–4 (1998): 41–56.

Howes, Robert. "Race and Transgressive Sexuality in Adolfo Caminha's *Bom-Crioulo*." *Luso-Brazilian Review* 38, no. 1 (2001): 41–62.

Villanueva-Collado, Alfredo. "Homoerotic, Heteroracial Relationships in the Latin American Naturalist Novel: *Bom-Crioulo* and *Hombres sin mujer*." *RLA: Romance Languages Annual* 7 (1995): 647–52.

Pero Vaz de Caminha

Gumbrecht, Hans Ulrich. "Who Was Pero Vaz de Caminha?" *Portuguese Literary & Cultural Studies* 4–5 (2000): 423–34.

Janiga-Perkins, Constance G. *Immaterial Transcendences: Colonial Subjectivity as Process in Brazil's Letter of Discovery (1500)*. New York: Peter Lang, 2001.

Augusto de Campos

Bessa, Antônio Sérgio. "The 'Image of Voice' in Augusto de Campos' *Poetamenos*." *Ciberletras* 17 (2007): n.p.

Clüver, Claus. "Augusto de Campos' 'Terremoto': Cosmology as Ideogram." *Contemporary Poetry: A Journal of Criticism* 3, no. 1 (1978): 39–55.

Funkhouser, Chris. "Augusto de Campos, Digital Poetry, and the Anthropophagic Imperative." *Ciberletras* 17 (2007): n.p.

Greene, Roland. "From Dante to the Post-Concrete: An Interview with Augusto de Campos." *Harvard Library Bulletin* 3, no. 2 (1992): 19–35.

Milton, John. "A Translation Model from Latin America: The Translation Theory and Practice of Augusto and Haroldo de Campos." In *Theoretical Issues and Practical Cases in Portuguese-English Translations,* 35–43. Lewiston, N.Y.: Mellen, 1996.

Portela, Manuel. "Untranslations and Transcreations." *Text: An Interdisciplinary Annual of Textual Studies* 15 (2002): 305–20.

Vieira, Else Ribeiro Pires. "New Registers for Translation in Latin America." In *Rimbaud's Rainbow: Literary Translation in Higher Education,* 171–95. Amsterdam, Netherlands: Benjamins, 1998.

———. "A Postmodern Translational Aesthetics in Brazil." In *Translation Studies: An Interdiscipline,* 65–72. Amsterdam: Benjamins, 1994.

Haroldo de Campos

Bessa, Antônio Sérgio, and Odile Cisneros, eds. *Novas: Selected Writings, Haroldo de Campos.* Evanston, Ill.: Northwestern University Press, 2007.

Greene, Roland. "Baroque and Neobaroque: Making Thistory." *PMLA: Publications of the Modern Language Association of America* 124, no. 1 (2009): 150–55.

Jackson, K. David. "Traveling in Haroldo de Campos's *Galáxias*: A Guide and Notes for the Reader." *Ciberletras* 17 (2007): n.p.

Longland, Jean R. "On Translating Haroldo de Campos." *Dispositio: Revista Americana de Estudios Comparados y Culturales/American Journal of Comparative and Cultural Studies* 7, nos. 19–21 (1982): 189–202.

Maciel, Maria Esther. "Points of Convergence: Latin America in Dialogue with the Orient: A Conversation with Haroldo de Campos." *Hispanic Research Journal: Iberian and Latin American Studies* 2, no. 3 (2001): 253–67.

Médici Nóbrega, Thelma, and John Milton. "The Role of Haroldo and Augusto de Campos in Bringing Translation to the Fore of Literary Activity in Brazil." In *Agents of Translation,* edited by John Milton and Paul Bandia, 257–77. Amsterdam: Benjamins, 2009.

Ortega, Julio, Haroldo de Campos, and Alfred J. Mac Adam. "Concrete Poetry and Beyond." *Review: Latin American Literature and Arts* 36 (1986): 36–45.

Perloff, Marjorie. "'Concrete Prose' in the Nineties: Haroldo de Campos's *Galáxias* and After." *Contemporary Literature* 42, no. 2 (2001): 270–93.

Portela, Manuel. "Untranslations and Transcreations." *Text: An Interdisciplinary Annual of Textual Studies* 15 (2002): 305–20.

Vieira, Else Ribeiro Pires. "Liberating Calibans: Readings of Antropofagia and Haroldo de Campos' Poetics of Transcreation." In *Post-Colonial Translation: Theory and Practice*, edited by Susan Bassnett and Harish Trivedi, 95–113. London: Routledge, 1999.

Zurbrugg, Nicholas. "Programming Paradise: Haraldo [Haroldo] de Campos, Concrete Poetry, and the Postmodern Multimedia Avant-Garde." In *Writing Aloud: The Sonics of Language*, edited by Brandon LaBelle and Christof Minego, 7–35. Los Angeles: Errant Bodies, with Ground Fault Recordings, 2001.

Antônio Candido

Antelo, Raúl, ed. *Antônio Candido y los estudios latinoamericanos*. Pittsburgh, Pa.: Instituto Internacional de Literatura Iberoamericana, University of Pittsburgh, 2001.

Lund, Joshua. "Barbarian Theorizing and the Limits of Latin American Exceptionalism." *Cultural Critique* 47 (2001): 54–90.

Schwarz, Roberto, R. Kelly Washbourne, and Neil Larsen. "National Adequation and Critical Originality." *Cultural Critique* 49 (2001): 18–42.

Lúcio Cardoso

Albuquerque, Severino João. "Fictions of the Impossible: Clarice Lispector, Lúcio Cardoso, and 'Impossibilidade.'" In *In Lusosex: Gender and Sexuality in the Portuguese-Speaking World*, edited by Susan Canty Quinlan and Fernando Arenas, 84–103. Minneapolis: University of Minnesota Press, 2002.

Bernardo Carvalho

Beal, Sophia. "Becoming a Character: An Analysis of Bernardo Carvalho's *Nove noites*." *Luso-Brazilian Review* 42, no. 2 (2005): 134–49.

Brizuela, Natalia, and Clélia Donovan. "Bernardo Carvalho." *BOMB* 102 (2008): 14–20.

Ronald de Carvalho

Lopes, Albert R., and Willis D. Jacobs. "Ronald de Carvalho, the 'Balanced Voice.'" *University of Kansas City Review* 19 (1953): 163–68.

Paro, Maria Clara Bonetti. "Ronald de Carvalho e Walt Whitman." *Revista de Letras* 32 (1992): 141–51.

Catulo da Paixão Cearense

Alvarenga, Maria Marta Wagner. *Sobre a Poesia Simples de Catulo da Paixão Cearense, Força das Imagens e Inspiração.* Rio de Janeiro: Ed. Cadernos da Serra, 1978.

Ana Cristina César

Muschietti, Delfina. "Ana Cristina César/Alejandra Pizarnik: Dos formas de utopía." *Travessia* 24 (1992): 105–12.

Mário Chamie

Medina, Cremilda. "Mário Chamie entre a Ação da Poética e a Poética da Ação." *Minas Gerais, Suplemento Literário* 20, no. 962 (1985): 9.

Henrique Maximiano Coelho Neto

Johnson, Lemuel A. "The Romance Bárbaro as an Agent of Disappearance: Henrique Coelho Netto's *Rei Negro* and Its Conventions." In *Voices from Under: Black Narrative in Latin America and the Caribbean,* 223–48. Westport, Conn.: Greenwood, 1984.

Pierson, Colin M. "Coelho Neto: Introduction of African Culture into Brazilian Drama." *Latin American Theatre Review* 9, no. 2 (1976): 57–62.

Paulo Coelho

Hart, Stephen M. "Cultural Hybridity, Magical Realism, and the Language of Magic in Paulo Coelho's *The Alchemist.*" *Romance Quarterly* 51, no. 4 (2004): 304–12.

Monet-Viera, Molly. "Post-Boom Magical Realism: Appropriations and Transformation of a Genre." *Revista de Estudios Hispánicos* 38, no. 1 (2004): 95–117.

Cláudio Manuel da Costa

Muzzi, Eliana Scotti. "A Arcádia e as Douradas Minas na Obra de Cláudio Manuel da Costa." In *Barrocos y modernos: nuevos caminos en la investigación del barroco iberoamericano,* edited by Petra Schumm, 163–73. Frankfurt: Vervuert, 1998.

Horácio Costa

Cisneros, Odile. "Um Olhar Re/Introspectivo: Poemas Recentes de Horácio Costa." *Sebastião: Novos Olhos Sobre a Nova Poesia Brasileira* 2 (2002): 76–79.

Afrânio Coutinho

Leal, Flávio. "Afrânio Coutinho: A Luz de uma Teoria Estética da História da Literatura." *Espéculo: Revista de Estudios Literarios* 41 (2009): n.p.

Sônia Coutinho

Ferreira-Pinto Bailey, Cristina. "Tales of Two Cities: The Space of the Feminine in Sonia Coutinho's Fiction." *Hispanic Issues On Line* 3 (2008): 9–29.

Lobo, Luiza. "Sonia Coutinho Revisits the City." In *Latin American Women's Writing: Feminist Readings in Theory and Crisis,* edited by Annie Brooksbank Jones and Catherine Davies, 163–78. New York: Oxford University Press, 1996.

Rui Ribeiro Couto

P., A. C. "Ruy Ribeiro Couto." *Revista Interamericana de Bibliografia/Inter-American Review of Bibliography* 14 (1964): 238–40.

Euclides da Cunha

Amory, Frederic. "Euclides da Cunha and Brazilian Positivism." *Luso-Brazilian Review* 36, no. 1 (1999): 87–94.

Anderson, Mark D. "From Natural to National Disasters: Drought and the Brazilian Subject in Euclides da Cunha's *Os Sertões.*" *Hispania: A Journal Devoted to the Teaching of Spanish and Portuguese* 91, no. 3 (2008): 547–57.

Valente, Luiz Fernando. "Brazilian Literature and Citizenship: From Euclides da Cunha to Marcos Dias." *Luso-Brazilian Review* 38, no. 2 (2001): 11–27.

Helena Parente Cunha

Beard, Laura J. "The Mirrored Self: Helena Parente Cunha's *Mulher no Espelho.*" *College Literature* 22, no. 1 (1995): 103–18.

Gass, Joanne. "Where Am I? Who Am I? The Problem of Location and Recognition in Helena Parente Cunha's *Woman between Mirrors*." *Studies in Twentieth and Twenty First Century Literature* 29, no. 1 (2005): 63–78.

Godsland, Shelley. *Writing Reflection, Reflecting on Writing Female Identity and Lacan's Mirror in Helena Parente Cunha and Sylvia Molloy*. Valladolid, Spain: Universitas Castellae, 2006.

Lockhart, Melissa Fitch. "Erotic Subversions in Helena Parente Cunha's *Mulher no Espelho*." *Chasqui: Revista de Literatura Latinoamericana* 27, no. 1 (1998): 3–10.

Safi-Eddine, Khadija. "*Woman between Mirrors*: Writing the Self." *Modern Language Studies* 24, no. 2 (1994): 48–56.

Tesser, Carmen Chaves. "Post-Structuralist Theory Mirrored in Helena Parente Cunha's *Woman between Mirrors*." *Hispania: A Journal Devoted to the Teaching of Spanish and Portuguese* 74, no. 3 (1991): 594–97.

Antônio Gonçalves Dias

Jobim, José Luís. "Gonçalves Dias." *Portuguese Literary & Cultural Studies* 4–5 (2000): 103–11.

Wyatt, Loretta Sharon. "The Charm of a Golden Past: Iberia in the Writings of Washington Irving and Antonio Gonçalves Dias." In *The Old and New World Romanticism of Washington Irving,* edited by Stanley Brodwyn, 105–11. Westport, Conn.: Greenwood, 1986.

Valdomiro Autran Dourado

Lucas, Fábio, and Randal Johnson. "Memoirs Told to the Mirror: Autran Dourado and Darcy Ribeiro." In *In Tropical Paths: Essays on Modern Brazilian Literature,* edited by Randal Johnson, 165–82. New York: Garland, 1993.

Moser, Robert H. "Rosalina's Ghostly Seed: The Story of Miscarried Patriarchal Legacies in Autran Dourado's Opera dos Mortos." *Luso-Brazilian Review* 42, no. 1 (2005): 199–213.

José de Santa Rita Durão

Hulet, Claude L. "The Noble Savage in Caramuru." In *Homage to Irving A. Leonard: Essays on Hispanic Art, History and Literature,* edited by Raquel Chang-Rodríguez et al., 123–30. East Lansing: Latin American Studies Center, Michigan State University, 1977.

Mário Faustino

Campos, Augusto de. "Mário Faustino, o Último 'Verse Maker.'" *O Estado de São Paulo, Suplemento Literário* (August 19, 1967): 3, 6.

Coelho, Joaquim-Francisco. "Morte e Resurreição de Mário Faustino." *Luso-Brazilian Review* 3, no. 2 (1966): 89–97.

Nunes, Benedito, introd. *A Poesia de Mário Faustino*. Rio de Janeiro: Civilização Brasileira, 1966.

Silva, Antônio Manoel dos Santos. "A Estrutura Radial num Poema de Mário Faustino." *Luso-Brazilian Review* 20, no. 2 (1983): 258–74.

Millôr Fernandes

Dória, Gustavo A. "Sobre Millôr Fernandes." *Revista de Teatro* 453 (1985): 29–31.

Witte, Ann. "Feminismo e Anti-Feminismo em Leilah Assunção e Millôr Fernandes." *Dactylus* 9 (1988): 15–20.

Rubem Fonseca

Ballantyne, Christopher J. "Between Bandits and Writers: The Rhetoric of Violence in Rubem Fonseca." *Luso-Brazilian Review* 23, no. 2 (1986): 1–20.

Schøllhammer, Karl Erik. "The Case of Rubem Fonseca-The Search for Reality." *Portuguese Literary & Cultural Studies* 4–5 (2000): 223–31.

Schulenburg, Chris T. "*O Cobrador* and the Crisis of Violence: The Brazilian City at a Crossroads." *Latin American Literary Review* 34, no. 68 (2006): 25–39.

Vieira, Nelson H. "'Evil Be Thou My Good': Postmodern Heroics and Ethics in *Billy Bathgate* and *Bufo & Spallanzani*." *Comparative Literature Studies* 28, no. 4 (1991): 356–78.

Armando Freitas Filho

Treece, David. "'O detetive do olhar': An Introduction to the Poetry of Armando Freitas Filho." In *A Primavera Toda para Ti*, edited by Margarida Calafate Ribeiro, 275–81. Lisbon: Presença, 2004.

Gilberto de Melo Freyre

Arroyo, Jossianna. "Brazilian Homoerotics: Cultural Subjectivity and Representation in the Fiction of Gilberto Freyre." In *In Lusosex: Gender and Sexu-*

ality in the Portuguese-Speaking World, edited by Susan Canty Quinlan and Fernando Arenas, 57–83. Minneapolis: University of Minnesota Press, 2002.

Lund, Joshua, and Malcolm McNee. *Gilberto Freyre e os Estudos Latino-americanos.* Pittsburgh, Pa.: Instituto Internacional de Literatura Iberoamericana, University of Pittsburgh, 2006.

Priore, Mary Del, David Shepherd, and Tania Shepherd. *"The Mansions and the Shanties:* 'The Flesh and the Stone' in Nineteenth-Century Brazil." *Portuguese Literary & Cultural Studies* 4–5 (2000): 65–71.

Rocha, João Cezar de Castro, and Shoshanna Lurie. "The Origins and Errors of Brazilian Cordiality." *Portuguese Literary & Cultural Studies* 4–5 (2000): 73–85.

Rodríguez Larreta, Enrique, Nöel de Sousa, and Mark Streeter. "The Road to *Casa-Grande:* Itineraries by Gilberto Freyre." *Portuguese Literary & Cultural Studies* 4–5 (2000): 41–49.

Wood, Marcus. "Slavery, History, and Satire: The Legacy of Gilberto Freyre." In *Recharting the Black Atlantic: Modern Cultures, Local Communities, Global Connections,* edited by Annalisa Oboe, 128–44. New York: Routledge, 2008.

Patrícia Galvão a.k.a. Pagu

Bryan, Catherine M. "Antropofagia and Beyond: Patricia Galvão's *Industrial Park* in the Age of Savage Capitalism." *Ciberletras* 16 (2007): n.p.

Jackson, K. David. "Alienation and Ideology in *A Famosa Revista* (1945)." *Hispania: A Journal Devoted to the Teaching of Spanish and Portuguese* 74, no. 2 (1991): 298–304.

Kanost, Laura M. "Body Politics in Patrícia Galvão's *Parque Industrial."* *Luso-Brazilian Review* 43, no. 2 (2007): 90–102.

Owen, Hilary. "Discardable Discourses in Patrícia Galvão's *Parque Industrial."* In *Brazilian Feminisms,* edited by Solange Ribeiro de and Judith Still, 68–84. Nottingham: University of Nottingham, 1999.

Unruh, Vicky. *Performing Women and Modern Literary Culture in Latin America: Intervening Acts.* Austin: University of Texas Press, 2006.

José Basílio da Gama

Schüler, Donaldo. "O Uraguai: A Epopéia da Conquista do Sul." *Brasil/Brazil: Revista de Literatura Brasileira/A Journal of Brazilian Literature* 10 (1993): 25–46.

Teixeira, Ivan. *Obras Poéticas de Basílio da Gama.* São Paulo: Universidade de São Paulo, 1996.

Pero de Magalhães Gândavo

Janiga-Perkins, Constance G. "Pêro de Magalhães Gândavo's História da Província Santa Cruz: Paradise, Providence, and How Best to Turn a Profit." *South Atlantic Review* 57, no. 2 (1992): 29–44.

Alfredo Dias Gomes

Anderson, Robert N. "Alfredo Dias Gomes (19 October 1922–18 May 1999)." In *Brazilian Writers,* edited by Monica Rector and Fred M. Clark, 152–60. Detroit, Mich.: Gale, 2005.

Tomás Antônio Gonzaga

Nola Kortner. "A Luso-Brazilian Classic: The Formal Satire as 'Cartas Chilenas.'" *Zagadnienia Rodzajow Literackich: Woprosy Literaturnych Zanrov/ Les Problemes des Genres Litteraires* 23, no. 1 [44] (1980): 45–61.

Gianfrancesco Guarnieri

Anderson, Robert N. "Gianfrancesco Guarnieri (6 August 1934–)." In *Brazilian Writers,* edited by Monica Rector and Fred M. Clark, 200–206. Detroit, Mich.: Gale, 2005.

Reis, Roberto. "Escracha! Eu sou batata, entende? Família e Autoritarismo no Moderno Teatro Brasileiro." *Latin American Theatre Review* 28, no. 1 (1994): 49–66.

Alphonsus de Guimaraens

Finetto, Dário. "Alphonsus de Guimaraens e o Simbolismo em Minas." *Minas Gerais, Suplemento Literário* 24, no. 1169 (1991): 12–13.

Bernardo Joaquim da Silva Guimarães

Borim, Dário. "Retrato Social às Avessas: A Inserção Classista e Sexista em *A Escrava Isaura.*" *Revista de Crítica Literaria Latinoamericana* 27, no. 54 (2001): 67–75.

Haberly, David T. "The Mythification of Tiradentes: Two Brazilian Literary Legends." *Romance Quarterly* 52, no. 1 (2005): 64–77.

Ferreira Gullar

Guyer, Leland R. "*Poema Sujo*: Last Will and Testament." *Selecta: Journal of the Pacific Northwest Council on Foreign Languages* 8 (1987): 96–101.
Sternberg, Ricardo da Silveira Lobo. "Memory and History in Ferreira Gullar's *Poema Sujo*." *Revista Canadiense de Estudios Hispánicos* 14, no. 1 (1989): 131–43.

Milton Hatoum

Ingenschay, Dieter. "Between the Boom and the Arabesque. 'Hemispheric Writing' in Juan Goytisolo's *Paisajes después de la batalla* and Milton Hatoum's *Relato de um Certo Oriente*." In *ArabAmericas: Literary Entanglements of the American Hemisphere and the Arab World,* edited by Friederike Pannewick, 165–87. Frankfurt: Vervuert, 2006.

Hilda Hilst

Albuquerque, Gabriel. "*Rútilo Nada*, de Hilda Hilst: Confissão e Deslocamento das Paixões." *Estudos de Literatura Brasileira Contemporânea* 25 (2005): 147–57.
Ferreira, Ermelinda. "Da Poesia Erudita à Narrativa Pornográfica: Sobre a Incursão de Hilda Hilst no Pósmodernismo." *Estudos de Literatura Brasileira Contemporânea* 21 (2003): 113–27.
Quinlan, Susan Canty. "O Exílio Fictício em *A Obscena Senhora D* de Hilda Hilst." *Revista de Crítica Literaria Latinoamericana* 20, no. 40 (1994): 61–68.

Sérgio Buarque de Holanda

Morse, Richard M. "Balancing Myth and Evidence: Freyre and Sérgio Buarque." *Luso-Brazilian Review* 32, no. 2 (1995): 47–57.
Rocha, João Cezar de Castro, and Shoshanna Lurie. "The Origins and Errors of Brazilian Cordiality." *Portuguese Literary & Cultural Studies* 4–5 (2000): 73–85.

Ledo Ivo

Albuquerque, Severino João. "Perdidos em Maceió: Alienação em *Angústia* e *Ninho de Cobras*." *Chasqui: Revista de Literatura Latinoamericana* 16, nos. 2–3 (1987): 11–21.

Pinto, Júlio. "Peircean Semiotic and Narrative Time: Lêdo Ivo's *Ninho de Cobras*." *Romance Notes* 27, no. 1 (1986): 3–12.

Pedro Kilkerry

Campos, Augusto de. *Re/Visão de Kilkerry*. São Paulo: Fundo Estadual de Cultura, 1971.

Sebastião Uchoa Leite

Andrade, Paulo. "O Museu Imaginário: Uma Leitura da Poesia de Sebastião Uchoa Leite." *Estudos de Literatura Brasileira Contemporânea* 22 (2003): 195–208.

Fortuna, Felipe. "O Remorso dos Códigos: Uma Leitura da Poesia de Sebastião Uchoa Leite." *Colóquio/Letras* 157–158 (2000): 331–37.

Silva, Paulo César Andrade da. "O Poeta-Espião: A Representação do Sujeito Lírico na Poesia de Sebastião Uchoa Leite/The Spy-Poet: The Lyric Subject Representation in Sebastião Uchoa Leite's Poetry." *Estudos Lingüísticos* 31 (2002): n.p.

Paulo Leminski

Perrone, Charles. "Perhappiness." *Brasil/Brazil: Revista de Literatura Brasileira/A Journal of Brazilian Literature* 5, no. 7 (1992): 75–82.

Valente, Luiz Fernando. "Paulo Leminski e a Poética do Inútil." *Hispania: A Journal Devoted to the Teaching of Spanish and Portuguese* 76, no. 3 (1993): 419–27.

Afonso Henriques de Lima Barreto

Bollig, Ben. "*Triste Fim de Policarpo Quaresma*, or the Sad End of Party Politics in Belle Epoque Brazil." *Hispanic Research Journal: Iberian and Latin American Studies* 4, no. 1 (2003): 59–71.

Courteau, Joanna. "The Demise of Myth in *Triste Fim de Policarpo Quaresma*." *Brasil/Brazil: Revista de Literatura Brasileira/A Journal of Brazilian Literature* 3, no. 3 (1990): 32–43.

Daniel, Mary L. "Ethnic Love/Hate in the *Inéditos* of Lima Barreto." *Hispania: A Journal Devoted to the Teaching of Spanish and Portuguese* 79, no. 3 (1996): 389–99.

Rabassa, Gregory. "From Lima Barreto to Osman Lins: Reinventing the Novel to Invent Brazil." *Review: Latin American Literature and Arts* 64 (2002): 6–9.

Resende, Beatriz, and Shoshanna Lurie. "*The Patriot*: The Exclusion of the Hero Full of Character." *Portuguese Literary & Cultural Studies* 4–5 (2000): 157–66.

Vernon, Richard. "Policarpo Quaresma: The Candide of Positivism." *Romance Notes* 44, no. 3 (2004): 235–45.

Vital, Selma. "Lima Barreto: From the Margin of the Margin." *Cincinnati Romance Review* 23 (2004): 183–95.

Wasserman, Renata R. Mautner. "Race, Nation, Representation: Machado de Assis and Lima Barreto." *Luso-Brazilian Review* 45, no. 2 (2008): 84–106.

Jorge de Lima

Brayner, Sonia. "Jorge de Lima e a *Invenção de Orfeu*." *Revista Iberoamericana* 50, no. 126 (1984): 175–87.

Costa, Horácio. "Apuntes sobre el poema largo en América Latina (José Gorostiza y Octavio Paz, Jorge de Lima y Haroldo de Campos)." *Cuadernos Americanos* 20, no. 3 (2006): 215–24.

Kasdorf, Hans. "Jorge de Lima: The Medical 'Poet-Priest' of Northeastern Brazil." *College Language Association Journal* 14 (1970): 75–86.

Lobo, Luiza. "O Clássico e o Moderno em *Invenção de Orfeu*, de Jorge de Lima." *Revista Brasileira de Lingua e Literatura* 5, no. 11 (1983): 18–23.

Stegagno Picchio, Luciana, and Mark Ridd. "Jorge de Lima: Universal Poet." *Portuguese Studies* 1 (1985): 151–67.

Osman Lins

Christensen, Peter G. "Erich Fromm's Escape from Freedom: A Reference Point for Osman Lins' *Nove, Novena*." *Chasqui: Revista de Literatura Latinoamericana* 23, no. 2 (1994): 30–38.

Dean, James Seay. "Seas of the Dead: Nautical Strands in Osman Lins' *Avalovara*." *Discurso: Revista de Estudios Iberoamericanos* 10, no. 2 (1993): 73–84.

Moisés, Massaud, and Randal Johnson. "Osman Lins's Avalovara: A Novel of Love?" In *Tropical Paths: Essays on Modern Brazilian Literature*, edited by Randal Johnson, 153–64. New York: Garland, 1993.

Paulo Lins

Barros, Sandro R. "Politicizing Identities: Language, Violence, and Racial Determination in Paulo Lins' *Cidade de Deus*." In *The Image of Violence in Literature, Media, and Society II*, edited by Will Wright and Steven Kaplan, 227–34. Pueblo: Society for the Interdisciplinary Study of Social Imagery, Colorado State University–Pueblo, 2007.

Durão, Fabio Akcelrud. "Towards a Model of Inclusive Exclusion: Marginal Subjectivation in Rio de Janeiro." *Contracorriente: A Journal of Social History and Literature in Latin America* 3, no. 2 (2006): 88–106.

Peixoto, Marta. "Rio's Favelas in Recent Fiction and Film: Commonplaces of Urban Segregation." *PMLA: Publications of the Modern Language Association of America* 122, no. 1 (2007): 170–78.

Henriqueta Lisboa

Lobo Filho, Blanca. "The Poetry of Emily Dickinson and Henriqueta Lisboa." *Proceedings of the Pacific Northwest Conference on Foreign Languages* 20 (1969): 103–12.

Virgillo, Carmelo. "The Image of Woman in Henriqueta Lisboa's 'Frutescência.'" *Luso-Brazilian Review* 23, no. 1 (1986): 89–106.

Clarice Lispector

Barbosa, Maria José Somerlate. *Clarice Lispector: Mutações Faiscantes = Sparkling Mutations*. Belo Horizonte, Minas Gerais: Gam Editora, 1997.

Cixous, Hélène. *Reading with Clarice Lispector*. Minneapolis: University of Minnesota Press, 1990.

Fitz, Earl E. *Clarice Lispector*. Boston: Twayne Publishers, 1985.

———. *Sexuality and Being in the Poststructuralist Universe of Clarice Lispector: The Différance of Desire*. Austin: University of Texas Press, 2001.

Marting, Diane E. *Clarice Lispector: A Bio-Bibliography*. Westport, Conn.: Greenwood Press, 1993.

———. *The Sexual Woman in Latin American Literature: Dangerous Desires*. Gainesville: University Press of Florida, 2001.

Peixoto, Marta. *Passionate Fictions: Gender, Narrative, and Violence in Clarice Lispector*. Minneapolis: University of Minnesota Press, 1994.

Waldman, Berta. *Clarice Lispector: A Paixão Segundo C.L.* São Paulo: Escuta 1993.

José Bento de Monteiro Lobato

Penteado, J., and Whitaker Roberto. "The Children of Lobato: The Imaginary World in Adult Ideology." *Bookbird: A Journal of International Children's Literature* 38, no. 2 (2000): 18–22.

Ignácio de Loyola Brandão

Krabbenhoft, Kenneth. "Ignácio de Loyola Brandão and the Fiction of Cognitive Estrangement." *Luso-Brazilian Review* 24, no. 1 (1987): 35–45.

Joaquim Manuel de Macedo

Cardoso, André. "Children Playing by the Sea: The Dynamics of Appropriation in the Brazilian Romantic Novel." In *Sullen Fires across the Atlantic: Essays in Transatlantic Romanticism,* edited by Newman Lance et al. College Park: University of Maryland, 2006.

António de Alcântara Machado D'Oliveira

DiAntonio, Robert. "Alcântara Machado's *Gaetaninho*: A Passage from Myth to Anti-Myth." *Annali Istituto Universitario Orientale, Napoli, Sezione Romanza* 28, no. 2 (1986): 567–72.

Aníbal Machado

Dean, Maria Angélica Lopes. "Metáfora e Prosopopéia: O Universo Animado de Aníbal Machado." *Luso-Brazilian Review* 19, no. 1 (1982): 93–109.

Souza, Sílvia Lúcia M. M. de. "O Imaginário na Ficção de Aníbal Machado." *Minas Gerais, Suplemento Literário* 22, no. 1129 (1989): 12–13.

Dionélio Machado

Abriata, Vera Lúcia Rodella. "Naziazeno e a Submissão ao Discurso do Outro em *Os Ratos*." *Revista de Letras* 31 (1991): 127–36.

Vescio, Luiz Eugenio. "Porto Alegre: A Instalação do Capitalismo Urbano Mostrado por Intermédio de Naziazeno Barbosa." *História* 19 (2000): 305–26.

Gilka Machado

Sadlier, Darlene J. "The Locus Eroticus in the Poetry of Gilka Machado." *Romance Notes* 45, no. 1 (2004): 99–106.

Domingos José Gonçalves de Magalhães

Barros, Roque Spencer Maciel de. *A Significação Educativa do Romantismo Brasileiro: Gonçalves de Magalhães*. São Paulo: Editora da Universidade de São Paulo, 1973.
Nitschack, Horst. "Entre el poema épico y la novela: La fundación de la literatura brasileña." In *Ficciones y silencios fundacionales: literaturas y culturas poscoloniales en América Latina (siglo XIX)*, edited by Friedhelm Schmidt-Welle, 257–72. Frankfurt: Vervuert, 2003.

Gregório de Mattos e Guerra

Campos, Haroldo. *O Sequestro do Barroco na Formação da Literatura Brasileira: O Caso Gregório de Mattos*. Bahia: Fundação Casa de Jorge Amado, 1989.
Costigan, Lúcia Helena S. "Gregório de Matos: 'The Mouth of Hell.'" *Review: Latin American Literature and Arts* 43 (1990): 53–59.
Dixon, Paul B. "'Intimate Immensity' in a Sonnet by Gregório de Matos." *Romance Notes* 28, no. 3 (1988): 235–39.

Glauco Mattoso

Butterman, Steven F. *Perversions on Parade: Brazilian Literature of Transgression and Postmodern Anti-aesthetics in Glauco Mattoso*. San Diego: San Diego State University Press, 2005.

Cecília Meireles

Bernucci, Leopoldo M. "That Gentle Epic: Writing and Elegy in the Heroic Poetry of Cecília Meireles." *MLN* 112, no. 2 (1997): 201–18.
Peixoto, Marta. "The Absent Body: Female Signature and Poetic Convention in Cecília Meireles." *Bulletin of Hispanic Studies* 65, no. 1 (1988): 87–100.
Peña, Karen. "Italian Effigies in Ethical Light: Synecdoche and Representation in Cecília Meireles's Mature Poems (1945–56)." *Journal of Romance Studies* 7, no. 2 (2007): 53–74.

Sadlier, Darlene J. "Looking into the Mirror in Cecília Meireles' Poetry." *Romance Notes* 23, no. 2 (1982): 119–22.

Stackhouse, Kenneth A. "The Sea in the Poetry of Cecília Meireles." *Luso-Brazilian Review* 18, no. 1 (1981): 183–95.

João Cabral de Melo Neto

Barbosa, João Alexandre, et al. "A Study of João Cabral de Melo Neto." *World Literature Today: A Literary Quarterly of the University of Oklahoma* 66, no. 4 (1992): 622–33.

Campos, Haroldo de, and Djelal Kadir. "The Geometry of Commitment." *World Literature Today: A Literary Quarterly of the University of Oklahoma* 66, no. 4 (1992): 617–21.

Candido, Antônio. "Poesia ao Norte." *Colóquio/Letras* 157–158 (2000): 13–19.

Dixon, Paul B. "The Geography-Anatomy Metaphor in João Cabral de Melo Neto's Morte e Vida Severina." *Chasqui: Revista de Literatura Latinoamericana* 11, no. 1 (1981): 33–40.

Parker, John M. "João Cabral de Melo Neto: 'Literalist of the Imagination.'" In *Twayne Companion to Contemporary World Literature: From the Editors of World Literature Today*, 891–98. New York: Twayne, 2003.

Peixoto, Marta. *Poesia com Coisas. Uma Leitura de João Cabral de Melo Neto*. São Paulo: Perspectiva, 1884.

Read, Justin. "Alternative Functions: João Cabral de Melo Neto and the Architectonics of Modernity." *Luso-Brazilian Review* 43, no. 1 (2006): 65–93.

Reckert, Stephen. "João Cabral: From Pedra to Pedra." *Portuguese Studies* 2 (1986): 166–84.

Zenith, Richard. "João Cabral de Melo Neto: An Engineer of Poetry." *Latin American Literary Review* 15, no. 30 (1987): 26–42.

Murilo Mendes

Antelo, Raúl. "Murilo, o Surrealismo e a Religião." *Luso-Brazilian Review* 41, no. 1 (2004): 107–20.

Picchio, Luciana Stegagno. "'ULALUME': Um Jogo entre o Som e o Sentido de Murilo Mendes." *Remate de Males: Revista do Departamento de Teoria Literária* 21 (2001): 9–14.

Williams, Bruce. "I Am the Eye That Penetrates: Cinema and the Nostalgic Gaze of Murilo Mendes's *Poemas*." *Chasqui: Revista de Literatura Latinoamericana* 30, no. 2 (2001): 35–45.

Augusto Meyer

Carvalhal, Tania Franco. "Autobiographical Writing in Brazil: The 'Proustians' Jorge de Lima, Augusto Meyer, and Pedro Nava." In *The I of the Beholder: A Prolegomenon to the Intercultural Study of Self,* edited by Steven Sondrup and Kenneth J. Miller, 95–108. Provo, Utah: International Comparative Literature Association, 2002.

Sérgio Milliet da Costa e Silva

Atik, Maria Luiza Guarnieri. "Sérgio Milliet: Um Mediador Cultural." *Todas as Letras: Revista de Língua e Literatura* 1 (1999): 43–52.

Camarani, Ana Luiza Silva. "Sérgio Milliet, Gide e Montaigne: A Função Intelectual e o Diário Íntimo." *Revista de Letras* 34 (1994): 247–56.

Vinícius de Moraes

Banks, Jared. "Cinematic Adaptation: Orfeu Negro da Conceição." *Canadian Review of Comparative Literature/Revue Canadienne de Littérature Comparée* 23, no. 3 (1996): 791–801.

Brown, Ashley. "Vinícius de Moraes (1913–1980): A Tribute." *World Literature Today: A Literary Quarterly of the University of Oklahoma* 56, no. 3 (1982): 472–73.

Oliveira, Celso de. "Orfeu da Conceição: Variation on a Classical Myth." *Hispania: A Journal Devoted to the Teaching of Spanish and Portuguese* 85, no. 3 (2002): 449–54.

Perrone, Charles A. "Don't Look Back: Myths, Conceptions, and Receptions of Black Orpheus." *Studies in Latin American Popular Culture* 17 (1998): 155–77.

Joaquim Nabuco

Almino, João. "The Earthenware and the Iron Pot: Nabuco's Utopia for the Two Americas." *Luso-Brazilian Review* 45, no. 2 (2008): 1–18.

Araújo, Valdei Lopes, Marcelo Amorim, and Mark Streeter. "Politics as History and Literature." *Portuguese Literary & Cultural Studies* 4–5 (2000): 303–11.

Graham, Richard. "Joaquim Nabuco, Conservative Historian." *Luso-Brazilian Review* 17, no. 1 (1980): 1–16.

Isfahani-Hammond, Alexandra Aryana. "Joaquim Nabuco's 'Black Mandate.'" *Hispania: A Journal Devoted to the Teaching of Spanish and Portuguese* 85, no. 3 (2002): 466–75.

Abdias do Nascimento

Martins, Leda. "A Ritual Choreography: The Orishas' Steps in *Sortilégio*." *Callaloo* 18, no. 4 (1995): 863–70.

Richards, Sandra L. "Constructions of Afro-Brazilian Identity in the Theatre of the 1950s: The Case of Zora Seljan and Abdias do Nascimento." In *Atlantic Cross-Currents: Transatlantiques*, 129–46. Trenton, N.J.: Africa World, 2001.

Turner, Doris J. "Black Theater in a 'Racial Democracy': The Case of the Brazilian Black Experimental Theater." *College Language Association Journal* 30, no. 1 (1986): 30–45.

Zwerling, Philip. "The Political Agenda for Theatricalizing Religion in Shango de Ima and Sortilege II: Zumbi Returns." *Journal of Religion and Theatre* 3, no. 2 (2004): 303–16.

Raduan Nassar

Buescu, Helena Carvalhão. "How Far Is Modernity from Here? Brazil, Portugal: Two Novels in Portuguese." In *How Far Is America from Here?*, edited by Theo D'haen et al., 263–69. Amsterdam: Rodopi, 2005.

Sotelino, Karen Catherine Sherwood. "Notes on the Translation of *Lavoura Arcaica* by Raduan Nassar." *Hispania: A Journal Devoted to the Teaching of Spanish and Portuguese* 85, no. 3 (2002): 524–33.

Manuel da Nóbrega

Sturm, Fred Gillette. "'Estes Têm Alma como Nós?' Manuel da Nóbrega's View of the Brazilian Indians." In *Empire in Transition: The Portuguese World in the Time of Camões*, edited by Richard A. Preto-Rodas, 72–82. Gainesville: University of Florida Press, Center for Latin American Studies, 1985.

Villalta, Luis Carlos. "Eve, Mary and Magdalene: Stereotypes of Women in Sixteenth-Century Brazil." In *Brazilian Feminisms*, edited by Solange Ribeiro de and Judith Still, 15–33. Nottingham: University of Nottingham, 1999.

Alberto de Oliveira

Azevedo Filho, Leodegário A. de. "A Estética Parnasiana em Alberto de Oliveira." *Revista Brasileira de Língua e Literatura* 4, no. 10 (1982): 31–35.

Pereira, Teresinka. "Alberto de Oliveira: Um Parnasiano Romântico." *Minas Gerais, Suplemento Literário* (July 16, 1977): 5.

Manuel Botelho de Oliveira

Bernucci, Leopoldo M. "Disfraces gongorinos en Manuel Botelho de Oliveira." *Cuadernos Hispanoamericanos* 570 (1997): 73–92.

Costigan, Lúcia Helena. "La cultura barroca y el nacimiento de la conciencia criolla en el Brasil." In *Relecturas del Barroco de Indias*, 303–30. Hanover, N.H.: Ediciones del Norte, 1994.

Ribeiro, João Roberto Inácio. "O Gongorismo na Poesia Latina de Manuel Botelho de Oliveira." *Revista de Letras* 32 (1992): 199–206.

Rodrigues-Moura, Enrique. "Manoel Botelho de Oliveira, autor del impreso *Hay amigo para amigo. Comedia famosa y nueva*, Coimbra, Oficina de Tomé Carvalho, 1663." *Revista Iberoamericana* 71, no. 211 (2005): 555–73.

Fernando Paixão

Paixão, Fernando. "Diálogo Poético Brasil-Portugal: O Outro Eu-Própio." In *A Palavra Poética na América Latina: Avaliação de uma Geração*, edited by Horácio Costa, 89–95. São Paulo: Memorial, 1992.

Afrânio Peixoto

Cilley, Melissa A. "Brazilian Literature and Culture Interpreted by Afrânio Peixoto." *Hispania: A Journal Devoted to the Teaching of Spanish and Portuguese* 31, no. 4 (1948): 446–48.

Vianna Filho, Luiz, ed. *Afrânio Peixoto*. Rio de Janeiro: Agir, 1963.

Inácio José de Alvarenga Peixoto

Lapa, Manuel Rodrigues. *Vida e obra de Alvarenga Peixoto*. Rio de Janeiro: Instituto Nacional do Livro, 1961.

Luís Carlos Martins Pena

Aiex, Nola Kortner. "Martins Pena: Parodist." *Luso-Brazilian Review* 18, no. 1 (1981): 155–60.

Lyday, Leon F. "Satire in the Comedies of Martins Pena." *Luso-Brazilian Review* 5, no. 2 (1968): 63–70.

Pierson, Colin M. "Martins Pena: A View of Character Types." *Latin American Theatre Review* 11, no. 2 (1978): 41–48.

Paulo Menotti del Picchia

Lopez, Albert R., and Willis D. Jacobs. "Menotti del Picchia and the Spirit of Brazil." *Books Abroad* 26 (1952): 240–43.

Décio Pignatari

Pignatari, Décio. "The Concrete Poets of Brazil." *Times Literary Supplement* (1964): 791.
Pignatari, Décio, and Kevin Marc Benson Mundy. "Montage, Collage, Bricolage, or: Mixture Is the Spirit." *Dispositio: Revista Americana de Estudios Comparados y Culturales/American Journal of Comparative and Cultural Studies* 6, nos. 17–18 (1981): 41–44.
Pignatari, Décio, and Jon M. Tolman. "Concrete Poetry: A Brief Structural-Historical Guideline." *Poetics Today* 3, no. 3 (1982): 189–95.

Nélida Piñon

Beard, Laura J. "Consuming Passions in *A Doce Canção de Caetana*." *Monographic Review/Revista Monográfica* 21 (2005): 104–16.
Clark, David Draper. "Nélida Piñon." *World Literature Today: A Literary Quarterly of the University of Oklahoma* 79, no. 1 (2005): 7–28.
Marting, Diane. "Female Sexuality in *A Casa da Paixão* by Nélida Piñón: A Ritual Wedding Song in Narrative." In *Love, Sex and Eroticism in Contemporary Latin American Literature,* edited by Alun Kenwood, 143–52. Melbourne: Voz Hispánica, 1992.

Raul d'Ávila Pompéia

Castello, José Aderaldo. "Memória e Ficção: De Raul Pompéia a José Lins do Rego." *Remate de Males: Revista do Departamento de Teoria Literária* 15 (1995): 33–44.
David, Sérgio Nazar. "Raul Pompéia (Raul d'Avila Pompéia)." In *Brazilian Writers,* edited by Monica Rector and Fred M. Clark, 281–85. Detroit: Gale, 2005.
Silva, Marciano Lopes. "A Pandora de Raul Pompéia." *Acta Scientiarum* 24, no. 1 (2002): 29–38.

Adélia Prado

Bolton, Betsy. "Adélia Prado: Romanticism Revisited." *Luso-Brazilian Review* 29, no. 2 (1992): 45–58.
Watson, Ellen Doré, et al. "Adélia Prado." *BOMB* 70 (2000): 62–67.

Paulo Prado

Almeida, Tereza Virgínia de. "'A Portrait of Brazil' in the Postmodern Context." *Portuguese Literary & Cultural Studies* 4–5 (2000): 343–49.

Qorpo-Santo

Maggi, Armando. "The 'Natural Relationship': Qorpo-Santo's Plays and the Liminal Performance of Morality." *Luso-Brazilian Review* 36, no. 2 (1999): 1–12.

Dinah Silveira de Queirós

Leal de Martínez, María Teresa. "Dinah Silveira de Queiroz: An Innovator in Brazilian Literature." *Rice University Studies* 64, no. 1 (1978): 81–88.

Raquel de Queirós

Courteau, Joanna. "*O Galo de Ouro*: Deconstruction of the Male Hero." In *O Amor das Letras e das Gentes: In Honor of Maria de Lourdes Belchior Pontes,* edited by João Camilo dos Santos, 363–69. Santa Barbara: Center for Portuguese Studies, University of California, Santa Barbara, 1995.
Wasserman, Renata R. Mautner. *Central at the Margin: Five Brazilian Women Writers.* Lewisburg, Pa.: Bucknell University Press, 2007.

Mário Quintana

Domingos, Adenil Alfeu. "A Linguagem Semi Simbólica do Poema/The Poem's Semi-Simbolical [Semi-Symbolical] Languages." *Estudos Lingüísticos* 32 (2003): n.p.
Oliveira, Rejane Pivetta de. "Lili no Espelho de Alice: A Linguagem e o Sonho da Infância em Mário Quintana." *Revista Língua & Literatura* 10, no. 14 (2008): 103–15.

Graciliano Ramos

Jentsch-Grooms, Lynda. "Myth and Feminine Symbology in *Vidas Secas*." *Cincinnati Romance Review* 8 (1989): 59–66.

Karpa-Wilson, Sabrina. "The Ethical Self in Graciliano Ramos's *Infância*." *Luso-Brazilian Review* 42, no. 1 (2005): 154–79.

Mazzara, Richard A. "The City in the Works of Graciliano Ramos." In *The City in the Latin American Novel*, edited by Bobby J. Chamberlain, 57–68. East Lansing: Latin American Studies Center & Department of Romance & Classical Languages, Michigan State University, 1980.

Oliveira, Celso Lemos de. *Understanding Graciliano Ramos*. Columbia: University of South Carolina Press, 1988.

Williams, Geraint. "Silence and Domination in the Relationship between Strong and Weak Characters in *Angústia*: A Sociological Reading of the Novel." *Bulletin of Hispanic Studies* 84, no. 2 (2007): 227–44.

Marques Rebelo

Chagas, Carlos, Filho. *Elogio de Marques Rebelo (Eddy Dias da Cruz)*. Rio de Janeiro: São José, 1974.

Jozef, Bella. "Dez Anos da Morte de Marques Rebelo." *Colóquio/Letras* 76 (1983): 61.

José Lins do Rego Cavalcanti

Fitz, Earl E. "The Brazilian Novel as Sociology: *O Moleque Ricardo*." *Studies in Afro-Hispanic Lit* 2–3 (1978): 106–17.

Gomes, Heloisa Toller, David Shepherd, and Tania Shepherd. "Plantation Boy: The Memory of Loss." *Portuguese Literary & Cultural Studies* 4–5 (2000): 167–76.

Jordan, David M. "Regionalism, Nationalism, and Modernism: José Lins do Rêgo's *Fogo Morto*." In *Imagination, Emblems and Expressions: Essays on Latin American, Caribbean, and Continental Culture and Identity*, edited by Helen Ryan-Ransom, 65–72. Bowling Green, Ohio: Popular, 1993.

Kelly, John R. "Jose Lins do Rego and the Ideological Origins of Brazilian Northeastern Realism (1922–1932)." *Revista de Estudios Hispánicos* 13 (1979): 201–7.

Preto-Rodas, Richard A. "The Black Presence and Two Brazilian Modernists: Jorge de Lima and Jose Lins do Rego." In *Tradition and Renewal: Essays on Twentieth-Century Latin American Literature and Culture*, 81–101. Urbana: University of Illinois Press, 1975.

Darcy Ribeiro

Columbus, Claudette Kemper. "Mother Earth in Amazonia and in the Andes: Darcy Ribeiro and José María Arguedas." In *Literature and Anthropology*, edited by Philip Dennis and Wendell Aycock, 165–80. Lubbock: Texas Tech University Press, 1989.

DiAntonio, Robert E. "Darcy Ribeiro's *Maíra*: Fictional Transfiguration and the Failure of Cultural Pluralism." *Chasqui: Revista de Literatura Latinoamericana* 15, no. 1 (1985): 11–18.

Ventura, Roberto. "Literature, Anthropology, and Popular Culture in Brazil: From José de Alencar to Darcy Ribeiro." *Komparatistische Hefte* 11 (1985): 35–47.

João Ubaldo Ribeiro

DiAntonio, Robert. "Chthonian Visions and Mythic Redemption in João Ubaldo Ribeiro's *Sergeant Getúlio*." *MFS: Modern Fiction Studies* 32, no. 3 (1986): 449–58.

Dodman, Maria João. "'Diz-me o que comes e eu te direi quem és': Food, Cannibalism and Identity in João Ubaldo Ribeiro's *Viva o Povo Brasileiro*." In *Defiant Deviance: The Irreality of Reality in the Cultural Imaginary*, 65–78. New York: Peter Lang, 2006.

Myers, Robert. "Translating History and Self-Translation: João Ubaldo Ribeiro's *Viva o Povo Brasileiro*." *Brasil/Brazil: Revista de Literatura Brasileira/A Journal of Brazilian Literature* 12 (1994): 29–38.

Tolman, Elizabeth Ely. "Biblical Beginnings and Endings in Ubaldo Ribeiro's *O Sorriso do Lagarto*." In *Essays on Hispanic and Luso-Brazilian Literature and Film in Memory of Dr. Howard M. Fraser*, 12–21. Mobile: University of South Alabama, 2000.

Valente, Luiz Fernando. "Fiction as History: The Case of João Ubaldo Ribeiro." *Latin American Research Review* 28, no. 1 (1993): 41–60.

Cassiano Ricardo Leite

Moreira, Luiza Franco. "'All Silent . . . Only One Singing': Contradictions in the Brazil of Cassiano Ricardo's *Martim Cererê*." *Cultural Critique* 38 (1997): 107–35.

Nöth, Winfried. "Symmetry in Signs and in Semiotic Systems." *Interdisciplinary Journal for Germanic Linguistics and Semiotic Analysis* 3, no. 1 (1998): 47–62.

João do Rio (pseudonym of Paulo Barreto)

Conde, Maite. "Film and the Crônica: Documenting New Urban Experiences in Turn of the Century Rio de Janeiro." *Luso-Brazilian Review* 42, no. 2 (2005): 66–88.

Jones, Julie. "Paulo Barreto's 'O Bebê de Tarlatana Rosa': A Carnival Adventure." *Luso-Brazilian Review* 24, no. 1 (1987): 27–33.

Sloan, Steve. "Fragments, Patterns, and the Modernization of the City through the Crônicas of João do Rio." *Mester* 34 (2005): 35–54.

Nelson Rodrigues

Clark, Fred M. *Impermanent Structures: Semiotic Readings of Nelson Rodrigues' Vestido de Noiva, Album de Família, and Anjo Negro.* Chapel Hill: Department of Romance Languages, University of North Carolina at Chapel Hill, 1991.

Dennison, Stephanie. "Nelson Rodrigues in the 1990s: Two Recent Screen Adaptations." In *The New Brazilian Cinema,* edited by Lúcia Nagib, 175–91. London: Tauris, 2003.

———. "Nelson Rodrigues into Film: Two Adaptations of *O Beijo no Asfalto.*" In *Latin American Cinema: Essays on Modernity, Gender, and National Identity,* edited by Lisa Shaw, 125–33. Jefferson, N.C.: McFarland, 2005.

George, David. "Encenador Gerald Thomas's Flash and Crash Days: Nelson Rodrigues without Words." *Latin American Theatre Review* 30, no. 1 (1996): 75–88.

———. "Nelson 2 Rodrigues." *Latin American Theatre Review* 21, no. 2 (1988): 79–93.

Johnson, Randal. "Nelson Rodrigues as Filmed by Arnaldo Jabor." *Latin American Theatre Review* 16, no. 1 (1982): 15–28.

Xavier, Ismail. "The Humiliation of the Father: Melodrama and Cinema Novo's Critique of Conservative Modernization." *Screen* 38, no. 4 (1997): 329–44.

———. "Nelson and Nelson: Mirror Images and Social Drama in *Boca de Ouro.*" In *Latin American Cinema: Essays on Modernity, Gender, and National Identity,* edited by Lisa Shaw, 93–109. Jefferson, N.C.: McFarland, 2005.

Sílvio Romero

MacNicoll, Murray Graeme. "Sílvio Romero and Machado de Assis: A One-Sided Rivalry (1870–1914)." *Revista Interamericana de Bibliografia/Inter-American Review of Bibliography* 31 (1981): 366–77.

Zilberman, Regina, David Shepherd, and Tania Shepherd. "Between Two Histories: From Sílvio Romero to José Veríssimo." *Portuguese Literary & Cultural Studies* 4–5 (2000): 549–57.

João Guimarães Rosa

Avelar, Idelber. "The Logic of Paradox in Guimarães Rosa's *Tutaméia*." *Latin American Literary Review* 22, no. 43 (1994): 67–80.

Coutinho, Eduardo de Faria. *The "Synthesis" Novel in Latin America: A Study of João Guimarães Rosa's Grande Sertão: Veredas*. Chapel Hill: Department of Romance Languages, University of North Carolina, 1991.

Dixon, Paul B. *Reversible Readings: Ambiguity in Four Modern Latin American Novels*. Tuscaloosa: University of Alabama Press, 1985.

Galvão, Walnice Nogueira, and Charles A. Perrone. "Heteronymy in Guimarães Rosa." In *Tropical Paths: Essays on Modern Brazilian Literature*, edited by Randal Johnson, 123–131. New York: Garland, 1993.

Merrim, Stephanie. "The Art of the Preface in Guimarães Rosa's Tutaméia." *Review: Latin American Literature and Arts* 29 (1981): 10–11.

———. "Grande Sertão: Veredas: 'A Mighty Maze but Not without a Plan.'" *Chasqui: Revista de Literatura Latinoamericana* 13, no. 1 (1983): 32–67.

———. "Sagarana: A Story System." *Hispania: A Journal Devoted to the Teaching of Spanish and Portuguese* 66, no. 4 (1983): 502–10.

Perrone, Charles A. "Guimarães Rosa Through the Prism of Magic Realism." In *Tropical Paths: Essays on Modern Brazilian Literature*, edited by Randal Johnson, 101–22. New York: Garland, 1993.

Rosenfield, Kathrin H. "Devil to Pay in the Backlands and João Guimarães Rosa's Quest for Universality." *Portuguese Literary & Cultural Studies* 4–5 (2000): 197–205.

Valente, Luiz Fernando. "Affective Response in *Grande Sertão: Veredas*." *Luso-Brazilian Review* 23, no. 1 (1986): 77–88.

———. "Fiction and the Reader: The Prefaces of Tutaméia." *Hispanic Review* 56, no. 3 (1988): 349–62.

Murilo Rubião

DiAntonio, Robert E. "Biblical Correspondences and Eschatological Questioning in the Metafiction of Murilo Rubião." In *Twayne Companion to Contemporary World Literature: From the Editors of World Literature Today, I*, 869–74. New York: Twayne, 2003.

Ginway, M. Elizabeth. "The Metaphor of Engineering in J. J. Veiga and Murilo Rubião." *Brasil/Brazil: Revista de Literatura Brasileira/A Journal of Brazilian Literature* 9 (1993): 45–56.

Nance, Kimberly A. "Quotidian Magic: Rubião's 'O Ex-Mágico da Taberna Minhota' and Todorov's 'New Fantastic.'" *Romance Notes* 43, no. 1 (2002): 3–11.

Oliveira, Marly Amarilha. "The Harlequin of Murilo Rubião: The Silent Experience." *Portuguese Studies* 4 (1988): 196–203.

Fernando Sabino

Fleury, Odilon Helou. "A Produção de Sentido em uma Narrativa de Fernando Sabino." *Alfa: Revista de Lingüística* 39 (1995): 71–85.

Lopes, Maria Angélica. "Fernando Sabino (Fernando Tavares Sabino)." In *Brazilian Writers,* edited by Monica Rector and Fred M. Clark, 346–51. Detroit, Mich.: Gale, 2005.

Mann, Celeste Dolores. "O Geraldo Viramundo de *O Grande Mentecapto*: Um Carnavalizador Carnavalizado." *Torre de Papel* 3, no. 2 (1993): 37–44.

Plínio Salgado

Dorea, Augusta Garcia. *O Romance Modernista de Plínio Salgado.* São Paulo: IBRASA/INL, 1978.

Waly Salomão

Arêas, Vilma. "TRES VEZES UM-Apontamento-." *Remate de Males: Revista do Departamento de Teoria Literária* 21 (2001): 153–73.

Ornellas, Sandro. "Nomadismo Poético nos Anos 50–70: Apontamentos de Pesquisa sobre Três Poetas da Desterritorialização em Língua Portuguesa." *Estudos de Literatura Brasileira Contemporânea* 25 (2005): 95–120.

Frei Vicente do Salvador

Freitas, Divaldo. "Uma Pequena Achega à Biografia de Frei Vicente do Salvador." *Occidente* 58 (1960): 120–22.

Willeke, Venâncio, O.F.M. "A Missiologia de Frei Vicente de Salvador." *Revista do Instituto Histórico e Geográfico de São Paulo* 62 (1966): 181–91.

Silviano Santiago

Avelar, Idelber. *The Untimely Present: Postdictatorial Latin American Fiction and the Task of Mourning.* Durham, N.C.: Duke University Press,1999.

Franconi, Rodolfo A. "Being Brazilian in the States: Between Fiction and Reality." *Hispania: A Journal Devoted to the Teaching of Spanish and Portuguese* 88, no. 4 (2005): 726–32.

Jackson, K. David. "The Prison-House of Memoirs: Silviano Santiago's *Em Liberdade.*" In *Tropical Paths: Essays on Modern Brazilian Literature,* edited by Randal Johnson, 199–219. New York: Garland, 1993.

Posso, Karl. *Artful Seduction: Homosexuality and the Problematics of Exile.* Oxford: European Humanities Research Centre, University of Oxford, 2003.

Quinlan, Susan Canty. "Cross-dressing: Silviano Santiago's Fictional Performances." In *Lusosex: Gender and Sexuality in the Portuguese-Speaking World,* edited by Susan Canty Quinlan and Fernando Arenas, 208–32. Minneapolis, Minn.: University of Minnesota Press, 2002.

Augusto Frederico Schmidt

Givens, Terryl L. "Augusto Frederico Schmidt: Reconsiderations on His Romanticism." *Luso-Brazilian Review* 28, no. 2 (1991): 27–35.

Tolman, Jon M. "A.F. Schmidt and C. Peguy: A Comparative Stylistic Analysis." *Comparative Literature Studies* 11 (1974): 277–305.

Moacyr Scliar

Balbuena, Monique R. "Sepharad in Brazil: Between the Metaphorical and the Literal in *Entre Moisés e Macunaíma.*" *Yiddish/Modern Jewish Studies* 15, nos. 1–2 (2007): 31–44.

Barr, Lois Baer. "The Jonah Experience: The Jews of Brazil According to Scliar." In *The Jewish Diaspora in Latin America: New Studies on History and Literature,* edited by David Sheinein and Lois Baer Barr, 33–52. New York: Garland, 1996.

Glickman, Nora. "Os Voluntários: A Jewish-Brazilian Pilgrimage." *Yiddish* 4, no. 4 (1982): 58–64.

Lindstrom, Naomi. "Oracular Jewish Tradition in Two Works by Moacyr Scliar." *Luso-Brazilian Review* 21, no. 2 (1984): 23–33.

Vieira, Nelson H. "Judaic Fiction in Brazil: To Be and Not to Be Jewish." *Latin American Literary Review* 14, no. 28 (1986): 31–45.

———. "Post-Holocaust Literature in Brazil: Jewish Resistance and Resurgence as Literary Metaphors for Brazilian Society and Politics." *Modern Language Studies* 16, no. 1 (1986): 62–70.

Gabriel Soares de Sousa

Lima, Francisco Ferreira de. "Os Padecimentos do Império: Gabriel Soares de Sousa e Sua Pequena Trágico-Marítima." *Scripta: Revista do Programa de Pós-Graduação em Letras e do CESPUC-PUC Minas* 10, no. 19 (2006): 180–88.

Martins, Wilson. "O Brasil em 1587 e o *Tratado Descritivo De* Gabriel Soares de Souza." *O Estado de São Paulo, Suplemento Literário* (December 31, 1972): 6.

João da Cruz e Sousa

Sayers, Raymond. "The Black Poet in Brazil: The Case of João Cruz e Sousa." *Luso-Brazilian Review* 15, supp. (1978): 75–100.

Whitmore, Don. "Cruz e Souza's Musical References." *Luso-Brazilian Review* 15, no. 1 (1978): 63–68.

Joaquim de Sousândrade

Avelar, Idelber. "A Arquitextura de Sousândrade: Política e Poética." In. *3o Congresso ABRALIC, Niterói, 10 a 12 de agosto de 1992,* 685–90. São Paulo: Editora da Universidade de São Paulo, 1995.

Campos, Haroldo de, et al. *Re/visão de Sousândrade.* 3rd ed. São Paulo: Perspectiva, 2002.

Williams, Frederick G. "The Wall Street Inferno: A Poetic Rendering of the Gilded Age." *Chasqui: Revista de Literatura Latinoamericana* 5, no. 2 (1976): 15–32.

Ariano Vilar Suassuna

Barker, Dan, and Penny Newman. "Redemption and Damnation in the Auto da Compadecida." In *Leeds Papers on Hispanic Drama,* edited by Margaret Rees, 153–66. Leeds: Trinity & All Saints College, 1991.

Lyday, Leon F. "The *Barcas* and the *Compadecida*: Autos Past and Present." *Luso-Brazilian Review* 11, no. 1 (1974): 84–88.

Resende, Aimara da Cunha. "Text, Context, and Audience: Two Versions of Romeo and Juliet in Brazilian Popular Culture." In *Latin American Shakespeares,* edited by Bernice Kliman and Rick J. Santos, 270–89. West Madison, N.J.: Fairleigh Dickinson University Press, 2005.

Alfredo D'Escragnolle Visconde de Taunay

Campos, Haroldo de. "Ierecê e Iracema: Do Verismo Etnográfico à Magia Verbal." In *Ierecê a Guaná Seguido de Os Indios do Distrito de Miranda, Vocabulário da Língua Guaná ou Chané*, 145–72. São Paulo: Iluminuras, 2000.

Candido, Antônio. "A Sensibilidade e o Bom Senso do Visconde de Taunay." In *Ierecê a Guaná Seguido de Os Indios do Distrito de Miranda, Vocabulário da Língua Guaná ou Chané*, 95–108. São Paulo: Iluminuras, 2000.

Jones, Maro Beath. "Character Sources of Taunay's Innocencia." *Hispania: A Journal Devoted to the Teaching of Spanish and Portuguese* 7, no. 5 (1924): 310–16.

Wasserman, Renata R. Mautner. "Financial Fictions: Emile Zola's *L'Argent*, Frank Norris' *The Pit*, and Alfredo de Taunay's *O Encilhamento*." *Comparative Literature Studies* 38, no. 3 (2001): 193–214.

Lygia Fagundes Telles

Almeida, Sandra Regina Goulart. "Castration and Melancholia in Lygia Fagundes Telles's *As Horas Nuas*." *RLA: Romance Languages Annual* 3 (1991): 339–43.

Berry (Luschei) Horton, Glenna. "Supernatural Ants in Lygia Fagundes Telles." *Monographic Review/Revista Monográfica* 20 (2004): 260–69.

Brown, Richard L. "Lygia Fagundes Telles: Equalizer of the Sexes." *Romance Notes* 32, no. 2 (1991): 157–61.

Ferreira-Pinto, Cristina. "Feminist Consciousness in the Novel of Lygia Fagundes Telles." *Modern Language Studies* 23, no. 4 (1993): 4–17.

Lisboa, Maria Manuel. "Darkness Visible: Alternative Theology in Lygia Fagundes Telles." *Brazilian Feminisms*, edited by Solange Ribeiro de and Judith Still, 133–54. Nottingham: University of Nottingham, 1999.

Sharpe, Peggy. "Fragmented Identities and the Progress of Metamorphosis in Works by Lygia Fagundes Telles." In *International Women's Writing: New Landscapes of Identity*, edited by Anne E. Brown and Marjanne E. Goozé, 78–85. Westport, Conn.: Greenwood, 1995.

Wasserman, Renata R. Mautner. *Central at the Margin: Five Brazilian Women Writers*. Lewisburg, Pa.: Bucknell University Press, 2007.

Dalton Trevisan

Burrell, Karen. "Social Prejudice Examined in Dalton Trevisan's 'O Ciclista.'" *Rocky Mountain Review of Language and Literature* 36, no. 2 (1982): 111–18.

Gordus, Andrew M. "The Vampiric and the Urban Space in Dalton Trevisan's *O Vampiro de Curitiba.*" *Rocky Mountain Review of Language and Literature* 52, no. 1 (1998): 13–26.

Ledford-Miller, Linda. "The Perverse Passions of Dalton Trevisan." In *Literature and the Bible,* 61–77. Amsterdam: Rodopi, 1993.

———. "Shoes for Little Peter: Narrative Technique in Trevisan's Not-At-All Exemplary Novella, *Pedrinho.*" *Brasil/Brazil: Revista de Literatura Brasileira/A Journal of Brazilian Literature* 3, no. 4 (1990): 37–50.

Vieira, Nelson H. "Bruxaria [Witchcraft] and Espiritismo [Spiritism]: Popular Culture and Popular Religion in Contemporary Brazilian Fiction." *Studies in Latin American Popular Culture* 15 (1996): 175–88.

———. "João e Maria: Dalton Trevisan's Eponymous Heroes." *Hispania: A Journal Devoted to the Teaching of Spanish and Portuguese* 69, no. 1 (1986): 45–52.

———. "Narrative in Dalton Trevisan." *Modern Language Studies* 14, no. 1 (1984): 11–21.

Francisco Adolfo de Varnhagen

Moreira, Thiers Martins. *Visão em Vários Tempos: I.* Rio de Janeiro: São José, 1970.

Vianna, Hélio. "Singularidade de um Historiador: A Propósito da 7a Edição Integral da *História Geral do Brasil* e da 5a Edição da *História da Independencia* de Francisco Adolfo Varnhagen, Visconde de Porto Seguro." *Revista do Instituto Histórico e Geográfico do Brasil* 264 (1964): 354–72.

Caetano Veloso

Borim, Dário, Jr. "Light and Obscurity in *Tropical Truth.*" *Portuguese Literary & Cultural Studies* 8 (2002): 463–70.

Braga-Pinto, César. "How to Organize a Movement: Caetano Veloso's Tropical Path." *Studies in Latin American Popular Culture* 19 (2000): 103–12.

Dunn, Christopher. *Brutality Garden: Tropicália and the Emergence of a Brazilian Counterculture.* Chapel Hill: University of North Carolina Press, 2001.

Leu, Lorraine. "Language and Memory in Popular Song: Brazil's Caetano Veloso." *Journal of Romance Studies* 3, no. 1 (2003): 87–103.

Perrone, Charles. *Masters of Contemporary Brazilian Song.* Austin: University of Texas Press, 1989.

Perrone, Charles, and Christopher Dunn. *Brazilian Popular Music & Globalization.* New York: Routledge, 2002.

Saul, Scott. "The Seductions of Caetano Veloso." *Raritan: A Quarterly Review* 24, no. 4 (2005): 45–69.

Érico Veríssimo

García, Frederick C. H. "Érico Veríssimo's Nameless Soldiers in a Nameless War." *Los Ensayistas: Georgia Series on Hispanic Thought* 10–11 (1981): 65–77.

Mazzara, Richard A. "Parallels between the Theater of Jorge Andrade and the Modern 'Cycle' Novel of Brazil." *Hispania: A Journal Devoted to the Teaching of Spanish and Portuguese* 66, no. 2 (1983): 192–201.

McGovern, Timothy. "Totemism and Neurosis in Two Brazilian Novels." *Mester* 24, no. 1 (1995): 143–55.

McGuire, Harriet C. "Parallels." *Brasil/Brazil: Revista de Literatura Brasileira/A Journal of Brazilian Literature* 18 (1997): 69–81.

Vessels, Gary M. "Literary Lies and the Modern Novel: Érico Veríssimo's Characters Theorize the Novel-Writing Process." *Brasil/Brazil: Revista de Literatura Brasileira/A Journal of Brazilian Literature* 13 (1995): 71–85.

Luís Fernando Veríssimo

Golin, Cida. "Luís Fernando Veríssimo: A Crônica como um Jazz-Improviso." *Brasil/Brazil: Revista de Literatura Brasileira/A Journal of Brazilian Literature* 10 (1993): 101–12.

Pöppel, Hubert. "Juegos narrativos en las novelas policíacas de Hugo Chaparro Valderrama y Luís Fernando Veríssimo." *Estudios de Literatura Colombiana* 3 (1998): 57–72.

Vieira, Nelson H. "The Gigolo of Words." *Brasil/Brazil: Revista de Literatura Brasileira/A Journal of Brazilian Literature* 11 (1994): 93–97.

Antônio Vieira

Castillo, Moisés, and Brad Nelson. "The Theologico-Political Program of Antônio Vieira in the Context of Baroque Guided Culture." *RLA: Romance Languages Annual* 9 (1997): 429–37.

Costigan, Lúcia Helena. "Bartolomé de Las Casas and His Counterparts in the Luso-Brazilian World." In *Approaches to Teaching the Writings of Bartolomé de Las Casas,* 235–42. New York: Modern Language Association of America, 2008.

Domingues, Beatriz Helena. "Tradition and Modernity in Sixteenth-and Seventeenth-Century Iberia and the Iberian American Colonies." *Mediterranean Studies* 8 (1999): 193–218.

Gomez, Fernando. "Jesuit Proposals for a Regulated Society in a Colonial World: The Cases of Antonio Ruiz de Montoya and Antônio Vieira." *Mester* 27 (1998): 93–127.

Hansen, João Adolfo, et al. "Guidelines for Reading Vieira." *Portuguese Literary & Cultural Studies* 4–5 (2000): 445–52.

Rabassa, Gregory. "Padre Antônio Vieira: Brazil's Medieval Modern." *Review: Latin American Literature and Arts* 43 (1990): 13–16.

———. "Vieira in the Maranhão: Out of Pragmatism, Prophecy." *Colonial Latin American Review* 1, nos. 1–2 (1992): 175–84.

Williams, Frederick G. "Putting God on Trial: Father Antônio Vieira's *Sermon for the Success of Portuguese Arms Against Those of Holland*." *Tinta* (1998): 17–36.

José Geraldo Vieira

Coelho, Nelly Novaes. "José Geraldo Vieira: 40 Anos de Romance." *Colóquio/Letras* 5 (1972): 71–73.

Dantas, Paulo. "Relembrando José Geraldo Vieira." *Minas Gerais, Suplemento Literário* 14, no. 747 (1981): 8.

Perez, Renard. "José Geraldo Vieira, Escritor Injustamente Esquecido." *Minas Gerais, Suplemento Literário* 22, no. 1066 (1987): 4–5.

Pedro Xisto

Grass, Roland. "Concrete Treatment of Space." *Visual Literature Criticism: A New Collection*, 135–40. Carbondale: Southern Illinois University Press, 1979.

CHILE

Resources: Bibliographies, Dictionaries, Histories, Anthologies

Alegría, Fernando. *Poesía chilena en el siglo XX*. Concepción: Ediciones Literatura Americana Reunida, 2007.

Cánepa Guzmán, Mario. *Historia del teatro chileno*. Santiago: Editorial Universidad Técnica del Estado, 1974.

Concha, Jaime. *Poesía chilena*. Santiago de Chile: Editorial Quimantú, 1973.

Enrique Lafourcade. *Antología del cuento chileno.* 3 vols. Barcelona: Ediciones Acervo, 1981.

Fein, John M. *Modernismo in Chilean Literature: The Second Period.* Durham, N.C.: Duke University Press, 1965.

Foster, David William. *Chilean Literature: A Working Bibliography of Secondary Sources.* Boston: G.K. Hall, 1978.

Goic, Cedomil. *Bibliografía de la novela chilena del siglo* XX. Santiago de Chile: Editorial Universitaria, 1962.

———. *La novela chilena: los mitos degradados.* 5th ed. Santiago de Chile: Editorial Universitaria, 1991.

Muñoz González, Luis. *Diccionario de movimientos y grupos literarios chilenos.* Concepción: Universidad de Concepción, 1993.

Nómez, Naín. *Antología crítica de la poesía chilena.* 4 vols. Santiago: LOM Ediciones, 1996.

Piña, Juan Andrés. *Teatro chileno contemporáneo: antología.* Madrid: Quinto Centenario, Fondo de Cultura Económica, Centro de Documentación Teatral, 1992.

Román-Lagunas, Jorge. *The Chilean Novel: A Critical Study of Secondary Sources and a Bibliography.* Lanham, Md.: Scarecrow Press, 1995.

Select Bibliography for Specific Writers

Isidora Aguirre

Campo, Alicia del. "Isidora Aguirre (22 March 1919–)." In *Latin American Dramatists: First Series,* edited by Adam Versényi, 3–17. Detroit, Mich.: Gale, 2005.

Dölz Blackburn, Inés. "La historia en dos obras de teatro chileno contemporáneo." *Confluencia: Revista Hispánica de Cultura y Literatura* 6, no. 2 (1991): 17–24.

Flores, Arturo C. "Teatro testimonial: *Retablo de Yumbel* de Isidora Aguirre." *Hispanic Journal* 12, no. 1 (1991): 123–32.

Versényi, Adam. "Social Critique and Theatrical Power in the Plays of Isidora Aguirre." In *Latin American Women Dramatists: Theater, Texts, and Theories,* edited by Catherine Larson and Margarita Vargas, 159–77. Bloomington: Indiana University Press, 1998.

Fernando Alegría

Donahue, Moraima de Semprun. *Figuras y contrafiguras en la poesía de Fernando Alegria.* Pittsburgh, Pa.: Latin American Literary Review Press, 1981.

Guerra Cunningham, Lucía. "Historia y memoria en la narrativa de Fernando Alegría." *Revista Chilena de Literatura* 48 (1996): 23–38.

Isabel Allende

Castillo de Berchenko, Adriana, and Pablo Berchenko. *La narrativa de Isabel Allende: claves de una marginalidad.* Perpignan: Centre de Recherches Ibériques et Latin-Américaines, Université de Perpignan, 1990.

Cox, Karen Castellucci. *Isabel Allende: A Critical Companion.* Westport, Conn.: Greenwood, 2003.

Davies, Lloyd. *Isabel Allende:* La casa de los espíritus. London: Grant & Cutler, 2000.

Feal, Rosemary G., ed. *Isabel Allende Today: An Anthology of Essays.* Pittsburgh, Pa.: Latin American Literary Review, 2002.

Hart, P. *Narrative Magic in the Fiction of Isabel Allende.* Cranbury, N.J.: Associated University Presses, 1989.

Levine, Linda Gould. *Isabel Allende.* New York: Twayne, 2002.

Riquelme Rojas, Sonia, ed. *Critical Approaches to Isabel Allende's Novels.* New York: Peter Lang, 1991.

Rodden, John, ed. *Conversations with Isabel Allende.* Austin: University of Texas Press, 2004.

Eduardo Barrios

Davison, Ned J. *Eduardo Barrios.* New York: Twayne, 1970.

Walker, John. *Metaphysics and Aesthetics in the Works of Eduardo Barrios.* London: Tamesis, 1983.

Pía Barros

Bell, Andrea L. "Creating Space in the Margins: Power and Identity in the *Cuentos breves* of Pía Barros and Cristina Peri Rossi." *Studies in Short Fiction* 33, no. 3 (1996): 345–53.

Pelage, Catherine. "Pia Barros y Diamela Eltit: transgresión y literatura femenina en Chile." *La palabra y el hombre* 114 (2000): 59–77.

Trevizán, Liliana. "Pía Barros (1956)." In *Escritoras chilenas: novela y cuento,* edited by Patricia Rubio, 579–93. Santiago: Cuarto Propio, 1999.

Alberto Blest Gana

Contreras, Alvaro. "*Martín Rivas* o la política del amor." *Texto Crítico* 7, no. 7 (1998): 83–96.

Gotschlich R., Guillermo. "Alberto Blest Gana y su novela histórica." *Revista Chilena de Literatura* 38 (1991): 29–58.

——. "Cien años de *Durante la reconquista*." *Revista Chilena de Literatura* 52 (1998): 5–15.

Roberto Bolaño

Bel, Jacqueline, ed. *Mémoire et désenchantement chez Juan Gelman et Roberto Bolaño/Memoria y desencanto en Juan Gelman y Roberto Bolaño*. Boulogne sur Mer: Centre d'Études et de Recherche sur les Civilisations et les Littératures Européennes, 2007.

Corral, Will H. "Roberto Bolaño: Portrait of the Writer as Noble Savage." *World Literature Today: A Literary Quarterly of the University of Oklahoma* 80, no. 6 (2006): 47–50.

Trelles, Diego. "El lector como detective en *Los detectives salvajes* de Roberto Bolaño." *Hispamérica: Revista de Literatura* 34, no. 100 (2005): 141–51.

María Luisa Bombal

Agosin, M. S. *Las desterradas del paraíso: protagonistas en María Luisa Bombal*. New York: Senda Nueva de Ediciones, 1983.

Guerra-Cunningham, L. *La narrativa de María Luisa Bombal: una visión de la existencia femenina*. Madrid: Playor, 1980.

Kostopoulos-Cooperman, C. *The Lyrical Vision of Maria Luisa Bombal*. London: Tamesis Books, 1988.

Marta Brunet

Balart Carmona, Carmen. *Narrativa chilena femenina: Marta Brunet*. Santiago de Chile: Santillana, 1999.

Augusto D'Halmar

Molloy, Sylvia. "Of Queens and Castanets: Hispanidad, Orientalism, and Sexual Difference." In *Queer Diasporas,* edited by Cindy Patton and Benigno Sánchez-Eppler, 105–21. Durham, N.C.: Duke University Press; 2000.

Sternbach, Nancy Saporta. "Augusto D'Halmar's *Juana Lucero*: Woman in a Trance." In *Women and Violence in Literature: An Essay Collection,* edited by Katherine Anne Ackley, 51–87. New York: Garland, 1990.

Villanueva-Collado, Alfredo. "El puer virginal y el doble: configuraciones arquetípicas en *La pasión y muerte del cura Deusto*, por Augusto D'Halmar." *Chasqui: Revista de Literatura Latinoamericana* 25, no. 1 (1996): 3–11.

Jorge Diaz

Boling, Becky. "Crest or Pepsodent: Jorge Díaz's *El cepillo de dientes*." *Latin American Theatre Review* 24, no. 1 (1990): 93–103.
Monleon, Jorge, ed. *Jorge Diaz*. Madrid: Taurus, 1967.
Woodyard, G. "Jorge Diaz and the Liturgy of Violence." In *Dramatists in Revolt: The New Latin American Theatre,* edited by L. F. Lyday and G. Woodyard, 59–76. Austin: University of Texas Press, 1976.

José Donoso

Adelstein, M., ed. *Studies on the Works of José Donoso: An Anthology of Critical Essays.* Lewiston, N.Y.: Edwin Mellen, 1990.
Finnegan, Pamela May. *The Tension of Paradox: José Donoso's The Obscene Bird of Night as Spiritual Exercises.* Athens: Center for International Studies, Ohio University, 1992.
Magnarelli, Sharon. *Understanding José Donoso.* Columbia: University of South Carolina Press, 1993.
Mandri, F. *José Donoso's "House of Fiction": A Dramatic Construction of Time and Place.* Detroit: Wayne State University Press, 1995.
McMurray, G. *José Donoso.* Boston: Twayne, 1979.
Morell, Hortensia R. *José Donoso y el surrealismo: "Tres novelitas burguesas."* Madrid: Pliegos, 1990.
Murphy, Marie. *Authorizing Fictions: José Donoso: "Casa de campo."* London: Tamesis, 1992.
Swanson, Philip. *José Donoso: The "Boom" and Beyond.* Liverpool: Francis Cairns, 1988.

Ariel Dorfman

McClennen, Sophia A. "The Diasporic Subject in Ariel Dorfman's Heading South, Looking North." *MELUS: The Journal of the Society for the Study of the Multi-Ethnic Literature of the United States* 30, no. 1 (2005): 169–88.
Morace, Robert A. "The Life and Times of *Death and the Maiden*." *Texas Studies in Literature and Language* 42, no. 2 (2000): 135–53.
Oropesa, S. *La obra de Ariel Dorfman*. Madrid: Pliegos, 1992.

Droguett Carlos

Teobaldo A. Noriega. *La novelística de Carlos Droguett: aventura y compromiso.* Madrid: Editorial Pliegos, 1983.

Joaquín Edwards Bello

Jones, Julie. "The Hero as Flâneur: Edwards Bello's *Criollos en París*." *Inti: Revista de Literatura Hispánica* 34–35 (1991–1992): 141–48.

Silva Castro, Raúl. "Joaquín Edwards Bello y Daniel de la Vega, prosistas chilenos." *Revista hispánica moderna* 34 (1968): 791–98.

Jorge Edwards

Otero, J. "Subjectividad y mito como modos narratives en *Persona non grata*." *Confluencia* 5, no. 2 (1990): 47–53.

Rojas Pina, B. "*El antifitrion* de Jorge Edwards: reescritura de mitos en el contexto de la dictadura y el exilio chilenos." *Chasqui* 21, no. 1 (1992): 77–91.

——. "El narrador en *El museo de cera* de Jorge Edwards." *Acta literaria* 19 (1994): 69–85.

Schopf, Federico. "Jorge Edwards y la nueva novela histórica en Hispanoamérica." *Atenea: Revista de Ciencia, Arte y Literatura de la Universidad de Concepción* 490 (2004): 87–98.

Schulz-Cruz, Bernard. "Bibliografía sobre Jorge Edwards." *Chasqui: Revista de Literatura Latinoamericana* 24, no. 1 (1995): 60–75.

Vila, María Pilar. "Ficciones autobiográficas: a propósito de *Adiós, poeta . . .* de Jorge Edwards." *Taller de Letras* 29 (2001): 147–62.

Diamela Eltit

Bartow, Joanna R. *Subject to Change: The Lessons of Latin American Women's Testimonio for Truth, Fiction, and Theory.* Chapel Hill: University of North Carolina Press, 2005.

Brito, E. *Campos Minados: Literatura post golpe en Chile.* Santiago: Cuarto Propio, 1990.

Gómez, Antonio, ed. *Provisoria-mente: textos para Diamela Eltit.* Rosario: Viterbo, 2007.

Holmes, Amanda. *City Fictions: Language, Body, and Spanish American Urban Space.* Lewisburg, Pa.: Bucknell University Press; 2007.

Lagos, María Inés, ed. *Creación y resistencia: la narrativa de Diamela Eltit, 1983–1998.* Santiago: Centro de Estudios de Género y Cultura en América Latina, Facultad de Filosofía y Humanidades, Universidad de Chile, 2000.

Lértora, Juan Carlos, ed. *Una poética de literatura menor.* Santiago: Cuarto Propio, 1993.

Norat, Gisela. *Marginalities: Diamela Eltit and the Subversion of Mainstream Literature in Chile.* Newark: University of Delaware Press, 2002.

Tompkins, Cynthia Margarita. *Latin American Postmodernisms: Women Writers and Experimentation.* Gainesville: University Press of Florida, 2006.

Alonso de Ercilla y Zúñiga

Aquila, August J. *Alonso de Ercilla y Zúñiga: A Basic Bibliography.* London: Grant & Cutler, 1975.

Cordero, María de Jesús. *The Transformations of Araucania from Valdivia's Letters to Vivar's Chronicle.* New York: Peter Lang, 2001.

Davis, Elizabeth B. *Myth and Identity in the Epic of Imperial Spain.* Columbia: University of Missouri Press, 2000.

Nicolopulos, James. *The Poetics of Empire in the Indies: Prophecy and Imitation in "La Araucana" and "Os Lusíadas."* University Park: Pennsylvania State University Press, 2000.

Pierce, Frank. *Alonso de Ercilla y Zúñiga.* Amsterdam: Rodopi, 1984.

Ramón Griffero

Bravo-Elizondo, Pedro. "Ramón Griffero: nuevos espacios, nuevo teatro." *Latin American Theatre Review* 20, no. 1 (1986): 95–101.

Luis Alberto Heiremans

Peden, Margaret Sayers. "The Theater of Luis Alberto Heiremans: 1928–1964." In *Dramatists in Revolt: The New Latin American Theater,* edited by Leon F. Lyday and George W. Woodyard, 120–32. Austin: University of Texas Press, 1976.

Vicente Huidobro

Concha, Jaime. *Vincente Huidobro.* Madrid: Júcar, 1980.

De Costa, René. *Vincente Huidobro: The Careers of a Poet.* Oxford: Clarendon Press, 1984.

Perdigó, Luisa Marina. *The Origins of Vicente Huidobro's "Creacionismo" (1911–1916) and Its Evolution (1917–1947)*. Lewiston, N.Y.: Mellen, 1994.

Sarabia, Rosa. *La poética visual de Vicente Huidobro*. Frankfurt: Vervuert, 2007.

Willis, Bruce Dean. *Aesthetics of Equilibrium: The Vanguard Poetics of Vicente Huidobro and Mário de Andrade*. West Lafayette, Ind.: Purdue University Press, 2006.

Enrique Lafourcade

Litchblau, Myron. "Narrative Perspectives in Enrique Lafourcade's *La fiesta del rey Acab.*" In *El cono sur: dinámica y dimensiones de su literatura*, edited by Rose S. Minc, 175–81. Upper Montclair, N.J.: Montclair State College, 1985.

José Victorino Lastarria

Subercaseaux, Bernardo. "Filosofia de la historia: novela y sistema expresivo en la obra de J. V. Lastarria (1840–1848)." *Ideologies and Literature: A Journal of Hispanic and Luso-Brazilian Studies* 3, no. 11 (1979): 56–84.

———. "Romanticismo y liberalismo en el primer Lastarria." *Revista Iberoamericana* 47, nos. 114–15 (1981): 301–12.

Pedro Lemebel

Del Pino, A. M. "Chile: Una loca geografía o las crónicas de Pedro Lemebel." *Hispamerica* 27, nos. 80–81 (1998): 17–28.

Palaversich, Diana. "The Wounded Body of Proletarian Homosexuality in Pedro Lemebel's *Loco afán.*" *Latin American Perspectives* 292 (2002): 99–118.

Parys, Jodie. "Forging (Comm)unity through Hybridity, HIV, and Marginalization: Pedro Lemebel's *Loco afán: crónicas del sidario.*" *Dissidences: Hispanic Journal of Theory and Criticism* 4–5 (2008): n.p.

Enrique Lihn

Correa-Díaz, Luis. *Lengua muerta: poesía, post-literatura y erotismo en Enrique Lihn*. Providence, R.I.: Inti, 1996.

Lastra, Pedro. *Conversaciones con Enrique Lihn*. Santiago: Atelier, 1990.

Travis, Christopher M. *Resisting Alienation: The Literary Work of Enrique Lihn.* Lewisburg, Pa.: Bucknell University Press, 2007.

Baldomero Lillo

Román-Lagunas, Jorge. "Bibliografía de y sobre Baldomero Lillo." *Revista Chilena de Literatura* 37 (1991): 141–56.

Germán Luco Cruchaga

Gilmore, Elsa M. "Germán Luco Cruchaga (7 May 1894–2 June 1936)." In *Latin American Dramatists: First Series,* edited by Adam Versényi, 199–205. Detroit, Mich.: Gale, 2005.

Gabriela Mistral

Agosín, Marjorie, ed. *Gabriela Mistral: The Audacious Traveler.* Athens: Ohio University Press, 2003.

Arrigoita, L. de. *Pensamiento y forma en la prosa de Gabriala Mistral.* San Juan: Editorial de la Universidad de Puerto Rico, 1989.

Fiol-Matta, Licia. *A Queer Mother for the Nation: The State and Gabriela Mistral.* Minneapolis: University of Minnesota Press, 2002.

Horan, Elizabeth. *Gabriela Mistral: An Artist and Her People.* Washington, D.C.: Organization of American States, 1994.

Rubio, Patricia. *Gabriela Mistral ante la crítica: bibliografía anotada.* Santiago: Dirección de Bibliotecas, Archivos y Museos, 1995.

Stiefel Ayala, Marta, ed. *Proceedings of the International Literature Conference: Homage to Agustini, Ibarbourou, Mistral, Storni.* Calexico, Calif.: Institute for Border Studies, San Diego State University, 1991.

Tamura, Satoko. *Los sonetos de la muerte de Gabriela Mistral.* Madrid: Gredos, 1998.

Pablo Neruda

Dawes, Greg. *Verses against the Darkness: Pablo Neruda's Poetry and Politics.* Lewisburg, Pa.: Bucknell University Press, 2006.

Feinstein, Adam. *Pablo Neruda: A Passion for Life.* New York: Bloomsbury, 2004.

Felstiner, J. *Translating Neruda: The Way to Macchu Picchu.* Stanford, Calif.: Stanford University Press, 1980.

Méndez-Ramírez, Hugo. *Neruda's Ekphrastic Experience: Mural Art and Canto General.* Lewisburg, Pa.: Bucknell University Press, 1999.
Poirot, Luis. *Pablo Neruda: Absence and Presence.* New York: Norton, 1990.
Rodríguez Monegal, Emir. *El viajero inmóvil.* Buenos Aires: Losada, 1966.
Santi, E. M. *Pablo Neruda: The Poetics of Prophecy.* Ithaca, N.Y.: Cornel University Press, 1982.
Urrutia, Matilde. *My Life with Pablo Neruda.* Stanford, Calif.: Stanford University Press, 2004.

Marco Antonio de la Parra

Thomas, Charles Philip, ed. *The Theatre of Marco Antonio de la Parra: Translations and Commentary.* New York: Peter Lang, 1995.

Nicanor Parra

Gottlieb, Marlene, ed. *Nicanor Parra: antes y después de Jesucristo: antología de artículos críticos.* Princeton, N.J.: Linden Lane, 1993.
Grossman, E. *The Antipoetry of Nicanor Parra.* New York: New York University Press, 1975.
Olivera, Sonia Mereles. *Cumbres poéticas latinoamericanas: Nicanor Parra y Ernesto Cardenal.* New York: Peter Lang, 2003.

Violeta Parra

Dölz-Blackburn, Inés. "Violeta Parra: Singer of Life." In *A Dream of Light and Shadow: Portraits of Latin American Women Writers,* edited by Marjorie Agosín, 143–57. Albuquerque: University of New Mexico Press, 1995.

Petit Magdalena

Araya G., Juan Gabriel. "Magdalena Petit Marfan (1903–1968)." In *Escritoras chilenas: novela y cuento,* edited by Patricia Rubio, 159–68. Santiago: Cuarto Propio, 1999.

Pedro Prado

Colburn, Heather L. "Pedro Prado (8 October 1886–31 January 1952)." In *Modern Spanish American Poets: First Series,* edited by María A. Salgado, 305–11. Detroit, Mich.: Gale, 2003.

Juan Radrigán

Roark, Carolyn D. "Juan Radrigán (23 January 1937–)." In *Latin American Dramatists: First Series,* edited by Adam Versényi, 261–70. Detroit, Mich.: Gale, 2005.

Ana María del Río

Galarce, Carmen. "Ana María del Río (1948)." In *Escritoras chilenas: novela y cuento,* edited by Patricia Rubio, 501–20. Santiago: Cuarto Propio, 1999.

Gonzalo Rojas

Coddou, Marcelo. *Nuevos estudios sobre la poesía de Gonzalo Rojas.* Santiago: Sinfronteras, 1986.

Giordano, Enrique, ed. *Poesía y poética de Gonzalo Rojas.* Santiago: Ediciones del Maitén, 1987.

Rojas, N. *Estudios sobre la poesía de Gonzalo Rojas.* Madrid: Playor, 1984.

Manuel Rojas

Cortés, Darío A. *La narrativa anarquista de Manuel Rojas.* Madrid: Pliegos, 1986.

Rodríguez Reeves, R. "Bibliografía de y sobre Manuel Rojas." *Revista iberoamericana* 95 (1986): 285–313.

Pablo de Rokha

Ferrero, M. *Pablo de Rokha, guerrillero de la poesía.* Santiago: Editorial Universitaria, 1967.

Lamberg, F. *Vida y obra de Pablo de Rokha.* Santiago: Zigzag, 1965.

Nómez, Naín. *Pablo de Rokha y Pablo Neruda: la escritura total.* Santiago and Ottawa: Documentas and Cordillera, 1992.

Marcela Serrano

Gálvez-Carlisle, Gloria. "Marcela Serrano (1951)." In *Escritoras chilenas: novela y cuento,* edited by Patricia Rubio, 553–77. Santiago: Cuarto Propio, 1999.

O'Connell, Patrick L. "The Voice of Silence in Marcela Serrano's *Para que no me olvides*." *Monographic Review/Revista Monográfica* 16 (2000): 336–44.
Quinn, Kate. "Private Detectives, Private Lives: The Detective Fiction of Sergio Gómez and Marcela Serrano." In *Hispanic and Luso-Brazilian Detective Fiction: Essays on the* Género Negro *Tradition,* edited by Renée W. Craig-Odders, Jacky Collins, and Glen S. Close, 162–79. Jefferson, N.C.: McFarland, 2006.

Antonio Skármeta

Lemaître, Monique. *Skármeta, una narrativa de la liberación.* Santiago: Pehuén, 1991.
Lira, C. *Skarmeta: La inteligencia de los sentidos.* Santiago de Chile: Dante, 1985.
Shaw, Donald L. *Antonio Skármeta and the Post-Boom.* Hanover, N.H.: Ediciones del Norte, 1994.
Yovanovich, Gordana. *Play and the Picaresque: "Lazarillo de Tormes," "Libro de Manuel," and "Match Ball."* Toronto: University of Toronto Press, 1999.

Benjamín Subercaseaux

Tienkem, Arturo. "Chile en la obra de Benjamín Subercaseaux." *Literatura Chilena: Creacion y Critica* 11 (1987): 6–10.

Pedro de Valdivia

Cordero, María de Jesús. *The Transformations of Araucania from Valdivia's Letters to Vivar's Chronicle.* New York: Peter Lang, 2001.

Egon Wolff

Boyd, Jennifer. "*Flores de papel* as Criticism: The Artist and the Tradition." *Latin American Theatre Review* 23, no. 2 (1990): 7–12.
Helsper, Norma. "The Ideology of Happy Endings: Wolff's *Mansión de Lechuzas*." *Latin American Theatre Review* 26, no. 2 (1993): 123–30.
Swanson, Philip. "Novel Theatre: Egon Wolff's *Los invasores* and the Idea of the New in Latin-American Drama." *Bulletin of Spanish Studies: Hispanic Studies and Researches on Spain, Portugal, and Latin America* 82, nos. 3–4 (2005): 387–402.

Raúl Zurita

Rowe, William. "Raúl Zurita and American Space." *Indiana Journal of Hispanic Literatures* 1, no. 2 (1993): 25–39.

Vela Córdova, Roberto. "Taking On the Chicago Boys: Raúl Zurita's Poetry as a Response to Privatization." In *Into the Mainstream: Essays on Spanish American and Latino Literature and Culture,* edited by Jorge Febles, 76–90. Newcastle upon Tyne: Cambridge Scholars, 2006.

Weintraub, Scott. "Messianism, Teleology, and Futural Justice in Raúl Zurita's *Anteparaíso.*" *CR: The New Centennial Review* 7, no. 3 (2007): 213–38.

COLOMBIA

Resources: Bibliographies, Histories, Anthologies

Echeverría, Rogelio. *Antologia de la poesía colombiana.* Bogotá: Editorial Carlos Valencia Editores, 1992.

España Arenas, Gonzalo, et al. *Narrativa de las guerras civiles colombianas* [anthology and criticism]. 5 vols. Bucaramanga: Colombia, Ediciones Universidad Industrial de Santander, 2003.

Giraldo, Luz Mary. *Cuentos caníbales: antología de nuevos narradores colombianos.* Bogotá: Alfaguara, 2002.

Gómez Restrepo, Antonio. *Historia de la literatura colombiana.* 3 vols. Bogotá: Litografía Villegas, 1956–1957.

González Cajiao, Fernando. *Teatro colombiano contemporáneo: antología.* Madrid: Fondo de Cultura Económica, Centro de Documentación Teatral, 1992.

Jiménez, David. *Antología de la poesía colombiana.* Bogotá: Grupo Editorial Norma, 2005.

———. *Historia de la crítica literaria en Colombia.* Bogotá: Centro Editorial Universidad Nacional de Colombia, 1992.

Orjuela, Héctor H. *Bibliografía del teatro colombiano.* Bogotá: Instituto Caro y Cuervo, 1974.

Porras Collantes, Ernesto. *Bibliografía de la novela en Colombia.* Bogotá: Instituto Caro y Cuervo, 1976.

Rodríguez-Arenas, Flor María. *Bibliografía de la literatura colombiana del siglo XIX.* 2 vols. Buenos Aires: Stockcero, 2006.

Weiss, Judith A., ed. *Colombian Theatre in the Vortex: Seven Plays.* Lewisburg: Bucknell University Press, 2004.

Williams, Raymond L. *The Colombian Novel 1844–1987.* Austin: University of Texas Press, 1991.

Select Bibliography for Specific Writers

Soledad Acosta de Samper

Alzate, Carolina, and Montserrat Ordóñez, eds. *Soledad Acosta de Samper: escritura, género y nación en el siglo XIX.* Frankfurt: Vervuert, 2005.

Ordóñez, Montserrat, ed. *Soledad Acosta de Samper: una nueva lectura.* Bogotá: Fondo Cultural Cafetero, 1988.

Albalucía Ángel

Betancur, Adriana. "La mujer represora: análisis de los mecanismos femeninos de represión en *Misiá Señora* y *Estaba la pájara pinta sentada en el verde limón* de Albalucía Ángel." *Divergencias: Revista de Estudios Lingüísticos y Literarios* 5, no. 1 (2007): 61–69.

Osorio de Negret, Betty. "La narrativa de Albalucía Ángel, o la creación de una identidad femenina." In *Literatura y diferencia: escritoras colombianas del siglo XX,* 2 vols., edited by María Mercedes Jaramillo, Betty Osorio de Negret, and Ángela Inés Robledo, I: 372–98. Santafé de Bogotá: Uniandes, 1995.

Uribe, Graciela. "El devenir mujer en la propuesta estética de Albalucía Ángel." In *Literatura y cultura: narrativa colombiana del siglo XX,* 3 vols., edited by María Mercedes Jaramillo, Betty Osorio, and Ángela I. Robledo, III: 204–24. Bogotá: Ministerio de Cultura, 2000.

Gustavo Álvarez Gardeazábal

Williams, Raymond L., ed. *Aproximaciones a Gustavo Álvarez Gardeazábal.* Bogotá: Plaza y Janés, 1977.

Zambrano, Jaime, ed. *La violencia en Colombia: la ficción de Álvarez Gardeazábal y el discurso histórico.* New York: Peter Lang, 1997.

Germán Arciniegas

Cobo-Borda, Juan Gustavo. *Germán Arciniegas: 90 años escribiendo: un intento de bibliografía.* Bogotá: Universidad Central/Instituto Colombiano de Estudios Latinoamericanos y del Caribe, 1990.

Enrique Buenaventura

Kronik, John W. "Enrique Buenaventura in the Context of Spanish American Theater." In *Studies in Honor of Myron Lichtblau,* edited by Fernando Burgos, 185–94. Newark, Del.: Juan de la Cuesta, 2000.

Sosa-Ramírez, Manuel. *El Nuevo Teatro español y latinoamericano: un estudio transatlántico: 1960–1980.* Boulder, Colo.: Society of Spanish and Spanish-American Studies, 2004.

Watson, M. "Enrique Buenaventura's Theory of Committed Theatre." *Latin American Theatre Review* 9, no. 2 (1976): 43–48.

Fanny Buitrago

Lutes, Leasa Y. *Allende, Buitrago, Luiselli: Aproximaciones teóricas al concepto del "Bildungsroman" femenino.* New York: Peter Lang, 2000.

Montes Garcés, Elizabeth, ed. *El cuestionamiento de los mecanismos de representación en la novelística de Fanny Buitrago.* New York: Peter Lang, 1997.

Utley, Gregory. "The Development of Subjectivity in Fanny Buitrago's *Señora de la miel.*" *Hispanic Journal* 25, nos. 1–2 (2004): 131–43.

Eduardo Caballero Calderón

Carrillo S., German D. "*El buen salvaje* de Caballero Calderon." *Thesaurus: Boletin del Instituto Caro y Cuervo* 28 (1973): 195–223.

Iriarte Núñez, Helena. "Eduardo Caballero Calderón y la historia de los años cincuenta." In *Literatura y cultura: narrativa colombiana del siglo XX,* 3 vols., edited by María Mercedes Jaramillo, Betty Osorio, and Ángela I. Robledo, I: 280–95. Bogotá: Ministerio de Cultura, 2000.

Levy, Kurt L. "Caballero Calderón: autor en busca de personaje." In *Violencia y literatura en Colombia,* edited by Jonathan Tittler, 129–37. Madrid: Orígenes 1989.

Tomás Carrasquilla

Levy, Kurt L. *Tomás Carrasquilla.* Boston: Twayne, 1980.

Mejía Duque, Jaime. *Tomás Carrasquilla.* Bogotá: Procultura, 1990.

Rodríguez-Arenas, Flor María, ed. *Tomás Carrasquilla: nuevas aproximaciones críticas.* Medellín: Universidad de Antioquia, 2000.

Juan de Castellanos

Restrepo, Luis Fernando. *Un nuevo reino imaginado: "Las elegías de varones ilustres de Indias" de Juan de Castellanos.* Bogotá: Instituto Colombiano de Cultura Hispánica, 1999.

———, ed. *Antología crítica de Juan de Castellanos: "Elegías de varones ilustres de Indias."* Bogotá: Pontifica Universidad Javeriana, 2004.

Madre Castillo

McKnight, Kathryn Joy. *The Mystic of Tunja: The Writings of Madre Castillo, 1671–1742.* Amherst: University of Massachusetts Press, 1997.

Germán Castro Caycedo

Aristizábal, Luis H. "Germán Castro Caycedo, del periodismo a la literatura." *Boletin Cultural y Bibliografico* 27, nos. 24–25 (1990): 12–33.

Oscar Collazos

Gómez, Blanca Inés. "Oscar Collazos: novela y autobiografía." In *Literatura y cultura: narrativa colombiana del siglo XX,* 3 vols., edited by María Mercedes Jaramillo, Betty Osorio, and Ángela I. Robledo, I: 641–60. Bogotá: Ministerio de Cultura, 2000.

Santiago García

Garavito, Lucía. "Santiago García (20 December 1928–)." In *Latin American Dramatists: First Series,* edited by Adam Versényi, 167–83. Detroit, Mich.: Gale, 2005.

Gabriel García Márquez

Bell, Michael. *Gabriel García Márquez: Solitude and Solidarity.* London: Macmillan, 1993.
Bell-Villada, Gene H. *Gabriel García Márquez: The Man and His Work.* Chapel Hill: University of North Carolina Press, 1990.
———, ed. *Conversations with Gabriel García Márquez.* Jackson: University Press of Mississippi, 2006.
———. *Gabriel García Márquez's "One Hundred Years of Solitude": A Casebook.* New York: Oxford University Press, 2002.
Fahy, Thomas. *Gabriel García Márquez's "Love in the Time of Cholera": A Reader's Guide.* New York: Continuum, 2003.
González, Nelly S. *Bibliographic Guide to Gabriel García Márquez, 1992–2002.* Westport, Conn.: Praeger, 2003.
Hart, Stephen M. *Gabriel García Márquez: "Crónica de una muerte anunciada."* London: Grant and Cutler, 1994.
Martin, Gerald. *Gabriel García Márquez: A life.* New York: Alfred A. Knopf, 2009.

Oberhelman, Harley D. *Gabriel García Márquez: A Study of the Short Fiction.* Boston: Twayne, 1991.

Pelayo, Rubén, ed. *Gabriel García Márquez: A Critical Companion.* Westport, Conn.: Greenwood, 2001.

Penuel, Arnold M. *Intertextuality in García Márquez.* New York: Spanish Literature Publications, 1994.

Sims, Robert L. *The First García Márquez: A Study of His Journalistic Writing from 1948 to 1955.* Lanham, Md.: University Press of America, 1992.

Valdés, María Elena de, ed. *Approaches to Teaching García Márquez's "One Hundred Years of Solitude."* New York: Modern Language Association of America, 1990.

León de Greiff

Pino del Rosario, Mari. "León de Greiff (22 July 1895–11 July 1976)." In *Modern Spanish American Poets: First Series,* edited by María A. Salgado, 125–32. Detroit, Mich.: Gale, 2003.

Jorge Isaacs

Fabre-Maldonado, Niza. *Americanismos, indigenismos, neologismos y creación literaria en la obra de Jorge Icaza.* Ecuador: Abrapalabra, 1993.

Magnarelli, Sharon. *The Lost Rib: Female Characters in the Spanish American Novel.* Lewisburg, Pa.: Bucknell University Press, 1985.

McGrady, Donald. *Jorge Isaacs.* New York: Twayne, 1972.

Sommer, Doris, *Foundational Fictions: The National Romances of Latin America.* Berkeley: University of California Press, 1991.

Luis Carlos López

Zubiría, Ramón de. "Aproximación a Luis Carlos López." *Thesaurus: Boletín del Instituto Caro y Cuervo* 47, no. 2 (1992): 368–82.

Rafael Maya

Mejía Velilla, D. "Recordando la poesía de Rafael Maya." *Boletín de la Academia Colombiana* 47, nos. 29–32 (1997): 29–32.

Manuel Mejía Vallejo

Corbatta, Jorgelina. "Recordando a Manuel Mejía Vallejo: el hombre y su obra." In *Literatura y cultura: narrativa colombiana del siglo XX,* 3 vols., edited by María Mercedes Jaramillo, Betty Osorio, and Ángela I. Robledo, I: 367–83. Bogotá: Ministerio de Cultura, 2000.

Williams, Raymond L. "Manuel Mejía Vallejo (23 April 1923–)." In *Modern Latin-American Fiction Writers: First Series,* edited by William Luis, 214–20. Detroit, Mich.: Gale, 1992.

Álvaro Mutis

García Aguilar, Eduardo. *Celebraciones y otros fantasmas: una biografía intelectual de Álvaro Mutis.* Bogotá: T-M Editores, 1993.

Hernández, Consuelo. *Alvaro Mutis: una estética del deterioro.* Caracas: Monte Avila, 1996.

Mutis Durán, Santiago, ed. *Álvaro Mutis: de lecturas y algo del mundo (1943– 1997).* Barcelona: Seix Barral, 2000.

Quiroz, Fernando. *El reino que estaba para mí: conversaciones con Álvaro Mutis.* Barcelona: Grupo Editorial Norma, 1993.

Rafael Núñez

Miramón, Alberto. *La angustia creadora en Núñez y Pombo.* Bogotá: Caro y Cuervo, 1975.

William Ospina

Araújo Fontalvo, Orlando. "Ursúa: ficción e historia de una nueva crónica de Indias." *Espéculo: Revista de Estudios Literarios* 35 (2007): n.p.

Barreras del Rio, C. "William Ospina o el placer de la lectura." *Revista del ateneo puertorriqueño* 6, nos. 16–18 (1996): 296–313.

José Eustasio Rivera

Núñez-Faraco, Humberto. "Magical-realist Elements in José Eustasio Rivera's *The Vortex.*" In *A Companion to Magical Realism,* edited by Stephen M. Hart and Wen-Chin Ouyang, 114–22. Woodbridge: Tamesis, 2005.

Ordóñez, M., ed. *La vorágine: textos críticos.* Bogotá: Alianza Editorial, 1987.

Peña Gutiérrez, I. *Breve historia de José Eustasio Rivera.* Bogotá: Ed. Magisterio, 1988.

Perus, Françoise. *De selvas y selváticos: ficción autobiográfica y poética narrativa en Jorge Isaacs y José Eustasio Rivera.* Bogotá: Plaza & Janés, 1998.

Juan Rodríguez Freyle

Folger, Robert. "Cien años de burocracia: *El carnero* de Juan Rodríguez Freyle." *Iberoromania* 58 (2003): 49–61.

Hermosilla, Luis. "Los contratos narrativos en *El carnero* de Juan Rodríguez Freyle." *Symposium: A Quarterly Journal in Modern Literatures* 52, no. 3 (1998): 131–41.

Rodríguez-Arenas, Flor María. "Los 'casos' de *El carnero*, o la retórica en la escritura de la historia colonial santafereña." *Revista Iberoamericana* 65, no. 186 (1999): 149–69.

José Asunción Silva

Cobo Borda, Juan Gustavo, ed. *Leyendo a Silva*. Bogotá: Instituto Caro y Cuervo, 1997.

LoDato, Rosemary C. *Beyond the Glitter: The Language of Gems in Modernista Writers Rubén Darío, Ramón del Valle-Inclán, and José Asunción Silva*. Lewisburg, Pa.: Bucknell University Press, 1999.

Guillermo Valencia

Espinosa, G. *Guillermo Valencia*. Bogotá: Procultura, 1989.

Karsen, S. *Guillermo Valencia, Colombian Poet*. New York: Hispanic Institute, 1951.

Fernando Vallejo

DuPouy, Steven M. "Fernando Vallejo." In *Latin American Writers on Gay and Lesbian Themes,* edited by David William Foster, 439–43. Westport, Conn: Greenwood Press, 1994.

Fernández L'Hoeste, Héctor D. "*La virgen de los sicarios* o las visiones dantescas de Fernando Vallejo." *Hispania* 83, no. 4 (2000): 757–67.

Jaramillo, María Mercedes. "Fernando Vallejo: desacralización y memoria." In *Literatura y cultura: narrativa colombiana del siglo XX*, 3 vols., edited by María Mercedes Jaramillo, Betty Osorio, and Ángela I. Robledo, I: 407–39. Bogotá: Ministerio de Cultura, 2000.

José María Vargas Vila

Escobar Uribe, A. *El divino Vargas Vila*. Bogotá: Ediciones Tercer Mundo, 1968.

Guerrieri, Kevin G. *Palabra, poder y nación: la novela moderna en Colombia de 1896 a 1927.* Ciudad Juárez: Universidad Autónoma de Ciudad Juárez; 2004.

Triviño Anzola, C. *El sentido trágico de la vida en la obra de Vargas Vila.* Madrid: Ediciones de la Universidad Complutense, 1988.

Jorge Zalamea

Chehade Durán, Nayla. "Jorge Zalamea en el panorama literario colombiano." In *Literatura y cultura: narrativa colombiana del siglo XX,* 3 vols., edited by María Mercedes Jaramillo, Betty Osorio, and Ángela I. Robledo, I: 257–79. Bogotá: Ministerio de Cultura, 2000.

Juan Zapata Olivella

Rodríguez-Martínez, Patricia. "Juan Zapata Olivella, el 'guerrero de lo imaginario' colombiano." In *"Chambacú, la historia la escribes tú": ensayos sobre cultura afrocolombiana,* edited by Lucía Ortiz, 103–32. Frankfurt: Vervuert, 2007.

Manuel Zapata Olivella

Captain-Hidalgo, Y. *The Culture of Fiction in the Works of Manuel Zapata Olivella.* Columbia: University of Missouri Press, 1993.

Lewis, M. A. *Treading the Ebony Path: Ideology and Violence in Contemporary Afro-Colombian Prose Fiction.* Columbia: University of Missouri Press, 1987.

Tillis, Antonio D. *Manuel Zapata Olivella and the "Darkening of Latin American Literature."* Columbia: University of Missouri Press, 2005.

COSTA RICA

Resources: Histories, Anthologies

Alfonso Chase, ed. *El amor en la poesía costarricense* [anthology]. San José: Editorial Costa Rica, 2000.

Baeza Flores, Alberto. *Evolución de la poesía costarricense, 1954–1977.* San José: Editorial Costa Rica, 1978.

Bell, Carolyn, and Patricia Fumero, eds. *Drama contemporáneo costarricense, 1980–2000* [anthology]. San José: Editorial de la Universidad de Costa Rica, 2000.

Bonilla, Abelardo. *Historia y antología de la literatura costarricense.* 2 vols. San José: Editorial Universitaria, 1957–1961.

Duncan, Quince, *et al. Historia crítica de la narrativa costarricense.* San José: Editorial Costa Rica, 1995.

Garnier, Leonor, ed. *Antología femenina del ensayo costarricense.* San José: Ministerio de Cultura, Juventud y Deportes, 1976.

González, Jézer, ed. *Antología del relato costarricense, 1930–1970.* San José: Editorial de la Universidad de Costa Rica, 2000.

Menton, Seymour. *El cuento costarricense.* México, D.F.: Andrea, 1964.

Quesada Soto, Alvaro. *La formación de la narrativa nacional costarricense.* San José: Editorial de la Universidad de Costa Rica, 1986.

Sandoval de Fonseca, Virginia. *Resumen de literatura costarricense.* San José: Editorial Costa Rica, 1978.

Sotelo, Rogelio. *Literatura costarricense: antología y biografías.* San José: Librería e Imprenta Lehmann, 1927.

Valdeperas, Jorge. *Para una nueva interpretación de la literatura costarricense.* San José: Editorial Costa Rica, 1979.

Zúñiga Díaz, Francisco. *El soneto en la poesía costarricense* [anthology]. San José: Editorial de la Universidad de Costa Rica, 1979.

Select Bibliography for Specific Writers

Quince Duncan

Martin-Ogunsola, Dellita. *The Eve/Hagar Paradigm in the Fiction of Quince Duncan.* Columbia: University of Missouri Press, 2004.

Mosby, Dorothy E. *Place, Language, and Identity in Afro-Costa Rican Literature.* Columbia: University of Missouri Press, 2003.

Carlos Luis Fallas

Rojas Pérez, Walter. *Costa Rica violada: el caso de "Mamita Yunai."* San José: Editorial Porvenir; 2006.

Manuel González Zeledón

Amoretti Hurtado, María. *Magón . . . : la irresistible seducción del discurso.* San José: Perro Azul, 2002.

Carmen Lyra

Horan, Elizabeth Rosa, ed. *The Subversive Voice of Carmen Lyra: Selected Works.* Gainesville: University Press of Florida, 2000.

José Marín Cañas

Quesada Soto, Alvaro. "Experimentación discursiva e hibridación genérica en *El infierno verde.*" *Revista de Filología y Lingüística de la Universidad de Costa Rica* 24, no. 1 (1998): 7–22.

Carmen Naranjo

Martínez, Luz Ivette. *Carmen Naranjo y la narrativa femenina en Costa Rica.* San José: EDUCA, 1987.

Nelson, Ardis L. "Carmen Naranjo and Costa Rican Culture." In *Reinterpreting the Spanish American Essay: Women Writers of the 19th and 20th Centuries,* edited by Doris Meyer, 177–87. Austin: University of Texas Press, 1995.

Eunice Odio

Chen Sham, Jorge, ed. *La palabra innumerable: Eunice Odio ante la crítica.* San José: Universidad de Costa Rica, Instituto Literario y Cultural Hispánico, 2001.

Yolanda Oreamuno

Gold, Janet. "Feminine Space and the Discourse of Silence: Yolanda Oreamuno, Elena Poniatowska, and Luisa Valenzuela." In *In the Feminine Mode: Essays on Hispanic Women Writers,* edited by Noël Valis and Carol Maier, 195–203. Lewisburg, Pa.: Bucknell University Press, 1990.

Gold, Janet N. "Yolanda Oreamuno: The Art of Passionate Engagement." In *Reinterpreting the Spanish American Essay: Women Writers of the 19th and 20th Centuries,* edited by Doris Meyer, 157–66. Austin: University of Texas Press, 1995.

Russotto, Márgara. "Propuestas de cultura: visiones de Costa Rica en las escritoras de la modernidad centroamericana (Yolanda Oreamuno, Eunice Odio, Carmen Naranjo)." *Revista Iberoamericana* 71, no. 210 (2005): 177–88.

ECUADOR

Resources: Bibliographies, Dictionaries, Histories, Anthologies

Ansaldo Briones, C., ed. *Antología del cuento ecuatoriano.* Guayaquil: Universidad Católica Santiago de Guayaquil/Universidad Andina Simón Bolívar, 1993.

Barrera, Isaac J. *Historia de la literatura ecuatoriana.* Quito: Libresa, 1979.

Donoso Pareja, Miguel, ed. *Antología de narradoras ecuatorianas.* Quito: Libresa, 1997.

Jaramillo, G. *Indice de la narrativa ecuatoriana.* Quito: Editora Nacional, 1992.

López de Martínez, Adelaida, and Gloria da Cunha-Giabbai, eds. *Narradoras ecuatorianas de hoy.* San Juan: Universidad de Puerto Rico, 2000.

Luzuriaga, Gerardo. *Bibliografía del teatro ecuatoriano 1900–1982.* Quito: Casa de la Cultura Ecuatoriana, 1984.

Ribadeneira, Edmundo. *La moderna novela ecuatoriana.* Quito: Editorial Universitaria, 1981.

Rodríguez Castelo, Hernán, ed. *Lírica ecuatoriana contemporánea.* 2 vols. Quito, Ecuador: Círculo de Lectores, 1979.

Sacoto, Antonio. *La novela ecuatoriana, 1970–2000.* Quito: Minsterio de Educación y Cultura, 2000.

Vallejo, Raúl. *Cuento ecuatoriano de finales del siglo XX.* Quito: Libresa, 1999.

Vera, Pedro Jorge. *Antología de autores ecuatorianos: cuentos.* Quito: Ediciones Indoamericanas, 1980.

Select Bibliography for Specific Writers

Jorge Enrique Adoum

Martínez, Pablo. "Strategies of (Re)presentation in the New Ecuadorian Novel: *Between Marx and a Naked Woman* and the Aesthetics of Violence." *New Novel Review: Nueva Novela/Nouveau Roman Review* 3, no. 1 (1995): 83–106.

Martínez Arévalo, Pablo. *Jorge Enrique Adoum: ideología, estética e historia (1944–1990).* Lexington: University of Kentucky, 1990.

O'Bryan-Knight, Jean. "Love, Death, and Other Complications in Jorge Enrique Adoum's *Ciudad sin ángel*." *Hispanic Journal* 20, no. 2 (1999): 291–309.

Demetrio Aguilera Malta

Fama, Anthony. *Realismo mágico en la narrativa de Aguilera Malta.* Madrid: Playor, 1978.

Heise, Karl H. *El grupo de Guayaquil: arte y técnica de sus novelas sociales.* Madrid: Playor, 1975.

Luzuriaga, Gerardo A. *Del realismo al expresionismo: el teatro de Aguilera Malta.* Madrid: Ediciones Plaza Mayor, 1971.

Jorge Carrera Andrade

Córdova, H. *Itinerario poético de Jorge Carrera Andrade.* Quito: Casa de la Cultura Ecuatoriana, 1986.

Gleaves, Robert M. "The Reaffirmation of Analogy: An Introduction to Jorge Carrera Andrade's Metaphoric System." *Confluencia: Revista Hispánica de Cultura y Literatura* 10, no. 1 (1994): 33–41.

Muñoz, Gabriel Trujillo. "Aurosia, the Utopian Planet: Jorge Carrera Andrade's Latin American Vision." *New York Review of Science Fiction* 17 (2004): 4–6.

Ojeda, E. *Jorge Carrera Andrade: introducción al estudio de su vida y su obra.* New York: Eliseo Torres, 1971.

José de la Cuadra

Carrión de Fierro, F. *José de la Cuadra, precursor del realismo mágico.* Quito: Ediciones de la Pontificia Universidad Católica del Ecuador, 1993.

Robles, Humberto E. *Testimonio y tendencia mítica en la obra de José de la Cuadra.* Quito: Casa de la Cultura Ecuatoriana, 1976.

Ween, Lori. "Family Sagas of the Americas: *Los sangurimas* and *A Thousand Acres.*" *The Comparatist: Journal of the Southern Comparative Literature Association* 20 (1996): 111–25.

Wishnia, Kenneth. "Ideology, Orality and Colonization: The Translation of José de la Cuadra's *Los sangurimas* (1934)." *Meta: Journal des Traducteurs/Translators' Journal* 40, no. 1 (1995): 24–30.

Nelson Estupiñán Bass

Richards, Henry J. "Mimesis of Product and Process in Nelson Estupiñán Bass's *Senderos brillantes.*" *Discurso: Revista de Estudios Iberoamericanos* 10, no. 1 (1992): 119–35.

———. "Nelson Estupiñán Bass and the Historico-Political Novel: From Theory to Praxis." *Afro-Hispanic Review* 21, nos. 1–2 (2002): 144–53.

Joaquín Gallegos Lara

Pérez, G. R. "Tres narradores de la costa del Ecuador." *Revista Interamericana de Bibliografía* 20 (1970): 169–90.

Enrique Gil Gilbert

Pérez, G. R. "Tres narradores de la costa del Ecuador." *Revista Interamericana de Bibliografía* 20 (1970): 169–90.

Jorge Icaza

Chalupa, Federico. "The Ecuadorian City and Modernity: Jorge Icaza's Quito." In *The Image of the City in Literature, Media, and Society,* edited by Will Wright and Steven Kaplan, 149–53. Pueblo: Society for the Interdisciplinary Study of Social Imagery, University of Southern Colorado, 2003.

Cueva, Agustín. *Jorge Icaza.* Buenos Aires: Centro Editor de America Latina, 1968.

Fabre-Maldonado, Niza. *Americanismos, indigenismos, neologismos y creación literaria en la obra de Jorge Icaza.* Ecuador: Abrapalabra, 1993.

Foote, Deborah C. "Survival of the Fittest: Animal Imagery in Jorge Icaza's *Huasipungo* and the Reader's Perception of the Indian." In *Beyond Indigenous Voices,* edited by Mary H. Preuss, 139–42. Lancaster, Calif.: Labyrinthos, 1996.

Lorente Medina, Antonio, *La narrativa menor de Jorge Icaza.* Valladolid, Spain: Universidad de Valladolid, 1980.

Mafla-Bustamante, Cecilia. "A Study of the English Translation of Jorge Icaza's *Huasipungo.*" In *The Knowledges of the Translator: From Literary Interpretation to Machine Classification,* edited by Malcolm Coulthard and Patricia Anne Odber de Baubeta, 259–78. Lewiston, N.Y.: Mellen, 1996.

Juan León Mera

Guevara, Darío O. *Juan León Mera o el hombre de cimas.* Quito: Ministerio de Educación Pública, 1944.

Padrón, Ricardo. "Cumandá and the Cartographers: Nationalism and Form in Juan Leon Mera." *Annals of Scholarship: An International Quarterly in the Humanities and Social Sciences* 12, nos. 3–4 (1998): 217–34.

Sacoto, Anthony. *The Indian in the Ecuadorian Novel*. New York: Las Américas, 1967.

Sommer, Doris. *Foundational Fictions: The National Romances of Latin America*. Berkeley: University of California Press, 1991.

Juan Montalvo

Lander, María Fernanda. "Héroes y corruptos en *Las Catilinarias* de Juan Montalvo." *Colorado Review of Hispanic Studies* 4 (2006): 205–20.

Ochoa Penroz, Marcela. "Juan Montalvo: una reescritura del *Quijote* en América." *Inti: Revista de Literatura Hispánica* 46–47 (1997–1998): 57–70.

José Joaquín Olmedo

Conway, Christopher. "Gender, Empire and Revolution in *La victoria de Junín*." *Hispanic Review* 69, no. 3 (2001): 299–317.

Adalberto Ortiz

Cyrus, Stanley A. "Ethnic Ambivalence and Afro-Hispanic Novelists." *Afro-Hispanic Review* 21, nos. 1–2 (2002): 185–89.

Handelsman, Michael. "Las contradicciones ineludibles del 'no-racismo' ecuatoriano: a propósito de *Juyungo* como artefacto de la diáspora afroamericana." *Chasqui: Revista de Literatura Latinoamericana* 27, no. 1 (1998): 79–91.

Pablo Palacio

Donoso Pareja, M., ed. *Pablo Palacio: Valoración múltiple*. Havana: Centro de Investigaciones Literarias, Casa de las Américas, 1987.

Manzoni, C. *El mordisco imaginario: crítica de la crítica en Pablo Palacio*. Buenos Aires: Editorial Biblos, 1994.

Martinez, E. *Before the Boom: Latin American Revolutionary Novels of the 1920s*. Lanham, Md.: University Press of America, 2001.

Alfredo Pareja Diezcanseco

Handelsman, Michael. "'Baldomera' y la tra(d)ición del órden patriarcal." *Inti: Revista de Literatura Hispánica* 40–41 (1994–1995): 195–205.

Ribadeneira, E. "La obra narrativa de Alfredo Pareja Diezcanseco." *Revista Iberoamericana* 54, nos. 144–145 (1988): 763–69.

Ángel Felicísimo Rojas

Calderón Chico, C. *Tres maestros: Ángel F. Rojas, Adalberto Ortiz y Leopoldo Benites Vinueza se cuentan a sí mismos.* Guayaquil: Casa de la Cultura, 1991.

Pedro Jorge Vera

Martul Tobio, Luis. "La construcción del dictador populista en *El pueblo soy yo.*" *Revista Iberoamericana* 58, no. 159 (1992): 489–500.

Robles, Isabel. "Entre la politica y la literatura: las novelas de Pedro Jorge Vera." *Cuadernos Hispanoamericanos: Revista Mensual de Cultura Hispánica* 328 (1977): 130–43.

Alicia Yáñez Cossío

Angulo, María-Elena. "Ideologeme of 'mestizaje' and Search for Cultural Identity in *Bruna, soroche y los tíos* by Alicia Yáñez Cossío." *Translation Perspectives* 6 (1991): 205–13.

Gladhart, Amalia. "Padding the Virgin's Belly: Articulations of Gender and Memory in Alicia Yáñez Cossío's *La cofradía del mullo del vestido de la Virgen Pipona.*" *Bulletin of Hispanic Studies* 74, no. 2 (1997): 235–44.

Handelsman, Michael. "En busca de una mujer nueva: rebelión y resistencia en *Yo vendo unos ojos negros* de Alicia Yáñez Cossío." *Revista Iberoamericana* 144–45 (1988): 893–901.

Saine, Ute Margaret. "Female Representation and Feminine Mystique in Alicia Yáñez Cossío's 'La mujer es un mito.'" *Letras Femeninas* 26, nos. 1–2 (2000): 63–79.

EL SALVADOR

Resources: Encyclopedias, Dictionaries, Histories, Anthologies

Argueta, Manlio, ed. *Poesia de El Salvador* [anthology]. San José: Editorial Universitaria Centroamericana, 1983.

Escobar Galindo, David. *Indice de la poesía salvadoreña.* 2nd ed. San Salvador: UCA Editores, 1987.

Guillén, Orlando, ed. *Hombres como madrugadas: la poesía de El Salvador* [anthology]. Barcelona: Antropos, 1985.

Jaramillo Levi, Enrique, and Leland H. Chambers. *Contemporary Short Stories from Central America*. Austin: University of Texas Press, 1994.
Rodríguez Díaz, Rafael. *Temas salvadoreños*. San Salvador: UCA Editores, 1992.
Yanes, Gabriela, ed. *Mirrors of War: Literature and Revolution in El Salvador*. London: Zed Books, 1985.

Select Bibliography for Specific Authors

Claribel Alegría

Aparicio, Yvette. "Reading Social Consciousness in Claribel Alegría's Early Poetry." *Cincinnati Romance Review* 18 (1999): 1–6.
Boschetto-Sandoval, Sandra M., ed. *Claribel Alegría and Central American Literature: Critical Essays*. Athens: Ohio University Center for European Studies, 1994.
Coronel Utrecho, José. *Líneas para un boceto de Claribel Alegría*. Managua: Nueva Nicaragua, 1989.
Craft, Linda J. *Novels of Testimony and Resistance from Central America*. Gainesville: University Press of Florida, 1997.
McGowan, Marcia Phillips. "The Poetry of Claribel Alegría: A Testament of Hope." *Latin American Literary Review* 32, no. 64 (2004): 5–28.
Treacy, Mary Jane. "A Politics of the Word: Claribel Alegría's *Album familiar* and *Despierta, mi bien, despierta*." *Intertexts* 1, no. 1 (1997): 62–77.
Velásquez, Antonio. *Las novelas de Claribel Alegría: historia, sociedad, y (re) visión de la estética literaria centroamericana*. New York: Peter Lang, 2002.

Arturo Ambrogi

Burns, E. Bradford. "Una visita al pasado con Arturo Ambrogi." *Américas* 35, no. 5 (1983): 12–13.
Tinajero, Araceli. "Viajeros modernistas en Asia." *Ciberletras* 4 (2001): n.p.

Manlio Argueta

Anderson, Robert K. "Manlio Argueta: A 'Committed' Third World Author." *South Eastern Latin Americanist* 43, nos. 1–2 (1999): 38–49.
Bencastro, Mario. "El Salvador's Poet of Recovery." *Américas* 53, no. 2 (2001): 48–51.
Chanady, Amaryll. "Excentric Positionalities: Mimicry and Changing Constructions of the Centre in the Americas." In *How Far Is America from*

Here?, edited by Theo D'haen, Paul Giles, Djelal Kadir, and Lois Parkinson Zamora, 233–46. Amsterdam: Rodopi, 2005.

Craft, Linda J. *Novels of Testimony and Resistance from Central America.* Gainesville: University Press of Florida, 1997.

Ibsen, Kristine. "Biblical Rhetoric and Social Justice in *Un día en la vida.*" *Hispanic Journal* 22, no. 2 (2001): 447–53.

Roque Dalton

Aparicio, Yvette. "Literary Convention and Revolution in Roque Dalton's *Taberna y otros lugares.*" *Revista de Estudios Hispánicos* 32, nos. 1–2 (2005): 169–81.

Harlow, Barbara. "Testimonio and Survival: Roque Dalton's *Miguel Mármol.*" In *The Real Thing: Testimonial Discourse and Latin America,* edited by Georg M. Gugelberger, 70–83. Durham: Duke University Press, 1996.

Lindo-Fuentes, Héctor. *Remembering a Massacre in El Salvador: The Insurrection of 1932, Roque Dalton, and the Politics of Historical Memory.* Albuquerque: University of New Mexico Press, 2007.

Seager, Dennis L. "Heteroglossia and Voice in the Poetry of Roque Dalton." *Readerly/Writerly Texts: Essays on Literature, Literary/Textual Criticism, and Pedagogy* 3, no. 1 (1995): 179–91.

Francisco Gavidia

Brenner, Michael Gardner. "Francisco Gavidia: Foundation Stone of Salvadorean Culture." In *Studies in Language and Literature,* edited by Charles Nelson, 87–89. Richmond: Department of Foreign Languages, Eastern Kentucky University, 1976.

Guevara, Rigoberto. "Inconformismo y reforma en la poesía de Francisco Gavidia." *Crítica Hispánica* 29, nos. 1–2 (2007): 151–63.

Claudia Lars

Gómez Lance, Betty Rita. "Dualidad de mundos en la poesía de Claudia Lars." *Káñina: Revista de Artes y Letras de la Universidad de Costa Rica* 5, no. 1 (1981): 77–82.

Perricone, Catherine R. "The Poetic Character of Claudia Lars." *Circulo: Revista de Cultura* 9 (1980): 47–55.

Umanzor, Marta A. "El modernismo en El Salvador: la poética de Claudia Lars." In *Delmira Agustini y el Modernismo: nuevas propuestas de género,* edited by Tina Escaja, 165–74. Rosario, Argentina: Viterbo, 2000.

Hugo Lindo

Alcides Paredes, Jorge "Una lectura bajtiniana de *¡Justicia, Señor Gobernador!* de Hugo Lindo." *Ixquic: Revista Hispánica Internacional de Análisis y Creación* 6 (2005): 32–46.

Miller, Elizabeth Gamble. "Retracing the Translation Process: Hugo Lindo's 'Only the Voice.'" *Translation Review* 7 (1981): 32–40.

Salarrué (pseudonym of Salvador Salazar Arrué)

Acevedo, Ramón Luis. *La novela centroamericana.* Río Piedras, Puerto Rico: Editorial Universitaria, 1982.

Boland, Roy C. "Un poema de Salarrué inspirado por García Lorca." *Cultura: Revista del Ministerio de Educación de El Salvador* 68–69 (1980): 188–91.

López Vallecillos, Italo. "El realismo mágico en *Cuentos de barro.*" *Cultura: Revista del Ministerio de Educación de El Salvador* 68–69 (1980): 183–87.

Navascués, Javier de. "Sobre conejos sandiyeros y otras zarandajas: el microcuento en Salarrué." *RILCE: Revista de Filología Hispánica* 16, no. 3 (2000): 625–37.

GUATEMALA

Resources: Encyclopedias, Dictionaries, Histories, Anthologies

Albizúrez Palma, Francisco. *Grandes momentos de la literatura guatemalteca.* Guatemala: Editorial José de Pineda Ibarra, 1983.

——, and Catalina Barrios. *Historia de la literatura guatemalteca.* 3 vols. Guatemala: Editorial Universitaria, 1981–1987.

Liano, Dante. *Ensayos de literatura guatemalteca.* Rome: Bulzoni, 1992.

López, Carlos. *Diccionario bio-bibliográfico de literatos guatemaltecos.* México: Editorial Praxis, 1993.

Lorand de Olazagasti, Adelaida. *El indio en la narrativa guatemalteca.* San Juan: Editorial Universitaria, 1968.

Méndez de la Vega, Luz. *Flor de varia poesía: poetas humanistas.* Guatemala: Editorial José de Pineda Ibarra, 1978.

Menton, Seymour. *Historia crítica de la novela guatemalteca.* Guatemala: Editorial Universitaria, 1960.

Zimmerman, Marc. *Literature and Resistance in Guatemala: Textual Modes and Cultural Politics from "El señor Presidente" to Rigoberta Menchú.* 2 vols. Athens: Ohio University Press, 1995.

————, and Raúl Rojas, eds. *Voices from the Silence: Guatemalan Literature of Resistance* [anthology]. Athens: Ohio University Center for International Studies, 1998.

Select Bibliography for Specific Writers

Rafael Arevalo Martínez

Callan, Richard J. "Archetypes in Stories by Rafael Arévalo Martínez." *Crítica Hispánica* 17, no. 2 (1995): 293–301.

Klein, Dennis A. "The Supernatural Elements in Selected Stories of Rafael Arévalo Martínez." *Monographic Review/Revista Monografica* 4 (1988): 60–68.

Liano, Dante. *Rafael Arévalo Martínez, fuentes europeas, lengua y estilo.* Rome: Bulzoni, 1992.

Rosser, Harry L. "Reflections in an Equine Eye: Arévalo Martínez' 'Psycho-Zoology.'" *Latin American Literary Review* 14, no. 28 (1986): 21–30.

Salgádo, María A. *Rafael Arévalo Martínez.* Boston: Twayne, 1979.

Miguel Ángel Asturias

Callan, Richard J. *Miguel Ángel Asturias.* New York: Twayne, 1970.

Giacoman, Helmy F., ed. *Homenaje a Miguel Ángel Asturias: variaciones interpretativas en torno a su obra.* New York: Las Américas, 1971.

Leal, Luis. *Myth and Social Realism in Miguel Ángel Asturias.* Urbana: University of Illinois Press, 1968.

Moore, Richard E. *Miguel Ángel Asturias: A Checklist of Works and Criticism.* New York: American Institute for Marxist Studies, 1979.

Preble-Niemi, Oralia, ed. *Cien años de magia: ensayos críticos sobre la obra de Miguel Ángel Asturias.* Guatemala: F & G, 2006.

Prieto, René. *Miguel Ángel Asturias's Archaeology of Return.* Cambridge: Cambridge University Press, 1990.

Rodríguez, Teresita. *La problemática de la identidad en* El Señor Presidente *de Miguel Ángel Asturias.* Amsterdam: Rodopi, 1989.

Royano Gutiérrez, Lourdes. *Las novelas de Miguel Ángel Asturias desde la teoría de la recepción.* Valladolid: Universidad de Valladolid, 1993.

Luis Cardoza y Aragón

Arias, Arturo. "Consideraciones en torno al género y la génesis de *Guatemala, las líneas de su mano.*" *Tragaluz* 2, no. 15 (1987): 24–28.

Mejía, José. "Los últimos poemas de Luis Cardoza y Aragón." *Cuadernos Americanos* 193 (1974): 185–203.

Rodríguez, Francisco. "La poética en Luis Cardoza y Aragón." *Káñina: Revista de Artes y Letras de la Universidad de Costa Rica* 23, no. 2 (1999): 37–46.

Serrata Córdova, José Eduardo. "El ensayo de Luis Cardoza y Aragón: una escritura heterodoxa." *Remate de Males* 16 (1996): 77–79.

Hugo Carrillo

Durán-Cogan, Mercedes F. "Instancias de poder en *El corazón del espantapá-jaros* de Hugo Carrillo." *Gestos: Teoría y Práctica del Teatro Hispánico* 11, no. 22 (1996): 87–104.

———. "La puesta en escena como subversión en una obra de Hugo Carillo." *Revista Canadiense de Estudios Hispánicos* 25, no. 1 (2000): 151–68.

Otto René Castillo

Hernandez Novas, Raul. "Otto René Castillo: la patria peregrina." *Casa de las Americas* 108 (1978): 4–10.

Iffland, James. "Ideologías de la muerte en la poesía de Otto René Castillo." *Ideologies and Literature: Journal of Hispanic and Lusophone Discourse Analysis* 4, no. 1 (1989): 95–148.

Manuel Galich

Márceles Daconte, Eduardo. "Manuel Galich: la identidad del teatro latino-americano." *Latin American Theatre Review* 17, no. 2 (1984): 55–63.

Peña Gutiérrez, Isaísa. "Manuel Galich: entre la historia y el teatro latinoameri-canos." *Conjunto: Revista de Teatro Latinoamericano* 114–115 (1999): 3–11.

Westlake, E. J. "Performing the Nation in Manuel Galich's *El tren amarillo.*" *Latin American Theatre Review* 31, no. 2 (1998): 107–17.

Enrique Gómez Carrillo

Bauzá Echeverría, Nellie. *Las novelas decadentistas de Enrique Gómez Carrillo.* Madrid, Spain: Pliegos, 1999.

Bujaldón de Estevez, Lila. "El modernismo, el Japón y Enrique Gómez Carrillo." *Revista de Literaturas Modernas* 31 (2001): 53–72.

González, Aníbal. *La crónica modernista hispanoamericana.* Madrid: Porrúa Turanzas, 1983.

Flavio Herrera

Felker, William. "Flavio Herrera: A Bibliography." *Revista Interamericana de Bibliografía* 28 (1978): 291–304.

Rigoberta Menchú

Beverley, John. *Testimonio: On the Politics of Truth.* Minneapolis: University of Minnesota Press, 2004.

Carey-Webb, Allen, ed. *Teaching and Testimony: Rigoberta Menchú and the North American Classroom.* Albany: State University of New York Press, 1996.

Stoll, David. *Rigoberta Menchú and the Story of All Poor Guatemalans.* Boulder, Colo: Westview, 1999.

José Milla y Vidaurre

Skinner, Lee. "Colonial (Dis)Order: Inheritance and Succession in José Milla's Historical Novels." *Latin American Literary Review* 27, no. 54 (1999): 80–95.

Solares-Larrave, Francisco. "Crónicas, retratos y documentos: trampas a la historia en *Los nazarenos* (1867) de José Milla y Vidaurre." In *Ilustres autores guatemaltecos del Siglo XIX y XX,* edited by Oralia Preble-Niemi and Luis A. Jiménez, 33–49. Guatemala: Artemis Edinter, 2004.

Mario Monteforte Toledo

Rogachevsky, Jorge R. "Mario Monteforte Toledo y la problemática de identidad cultural en Guatemala." In *Ilustres autores guatemaltecos del Siglo XIX y XX,* edited by Oralia Preble-Niemi and Luis A. Jiménez, 125–44. Guatemala: Artemis Edinter, 2004.

Rokas, Nicholas W. "Bibliografía crítica selecta de Mario Monteforte Toledo." *Revista Interamericana de Bibliografía/Inter-American Review of Bibliography* 36 (1986): 29–38.

———. "El individuo y la sociedad en los cuentos de Mario Monteforte Toledo." *Abside: Revista de Cultura Mejicana* 41 (1977): 242–62.

Augusto Monterroso

Campos, Marco Antonio, ed. *La literatura de Augusto Monterroso*. México, D.F.: Universidad Nacional Autónoma de México, 1988.

Corral, Wilfrido H. *Lector, sociedad y género en Monterroso*. Xalapa: Centro de Investigaciones Lingüístico-Literarias de la Universidad Veracruzana, 1985.

Roux de Caicedo, Lina de. *Augusto Monterroso: la fábula en Monterroso, lugar de encuentro con la verdad*. Bogotá: Serie de Escritores de las Américas, 1991.

Ruffinelli, Jorge, ed. *Monterroso*. Xalapa: Centro de Investigaciones Lingüístico-Literarias de la Universidad Veracruzana, 1976.

Carlos Solórzano

Andrea, P. F. de. *Carlos Solorzano, bibliografia*. México, D.F.: CLE, 1970.

Feliciano, Wilma. "Myth and Theatricality in Three Plays by Carlos Solórzano." *Latin American Theatre Review* 25, no. 1 (1991): 123–33.

Richards, Katharine C. "The Mexican Existentialism of Solórzano's *Los fantoches*." *Latin American Literary Review* 9 (1976): 63–69.

Rivas, Esteban. *Carlos Solórzano y el teatro hispanoamericano*. México, D.F.: Impresos Anahuac, 1970.

Rosenberg, John R. "The Ritual of Solórzano's *Las manos de Dios*." *Latin American Theatre Review* 17, no. 2 (1984): 39–48.

HONDURAS

Resources: Encyclopedias, Dictionaries, Histories, Anthologies

Argueta, Mario R. *Diccionario crítico de obras literarias hondureñas*. Tegucigalpa: Guaymuras, 1993.

Cárdenas Amador, Galel, ed. *Primer simposio de literatura hondureña*. Tegucigalpa: Universidad Nacional Autónoma de Honduras, 1991.

Durón, Rómulo E. *Honduras literaria*. 2 vols. Tegucigalpa: Ministerio de Educación, 1996–1999.

López Lazo, José D., ed. *Voces de la literatura hondureña actual*. Tegucigalpa: Universidad Nacional Autónoma de Honduras, 1994.

Martínez, José Francisco. *Literatura hondureña y su proceso generacional.* Tegucigalpa: Universidad Nacional Autónoma de Honduras, 1987.

Select Bibliography for Specific Writers

Juan Ramón Molina

Alvarado, Leonel. "Sirenas, bananos y Sandino: modernismo y modernización en Centroamérica." *Cuadernos Americanos* 18 (2004): 77–96.

Roberto Sosa

Bardini, Roberto. "Roberto Sosa: poesía y política en Honduras." *Plural: Revista Cultural de Excelsior* 11 (1982): 13–15.
White, Steven F. "Roberto Sosa: Fabulador y creador de un nuevo bestiario." In *La literatura centroamericana: visiones y revisiones,* edited by Jorge Román-Lagunas, 327–32. Lewiston, N.Y.: Mellen.

José Cecilio del Valle

McCallister, Rick. "The Dawn of Modernity in Central America: José Cecilio del Valle." *Journal of Hispanic Philology* 18, nos. 1–3 (1993): 127–40.

Rafael Heliodoro Valle

Dorn, G.M. "Rafael Heliodoro Valle." In *Latin American Writers,* edited by C. A. Solé and M. I. Abreu, II, 721–25. New York: Scribners, 1989.

MEXICO

Resources: Encyclopedias, Dictionaries, Histories, Anthologies

Argudín, Yolanda. *Historia del teatro en México: desde los rituales prehispánicos hasta el arte dramático de nuestros días.* México, D.F.: Panorama Editorial, 1985.
Argüelles, Juan Domingo, ed. *Dos siglos de poesía mexicana: del XIX al fin del milenio: una antología.* México: Océano, 2001.
Brushwood, John S. *Mexico in Its Novel: A Nation's Search for Identity.* Austin: University of Texas Press, 1966.

Carballo, Emmanuel. *Protagonistas de la literatura mexicana México*. México, D.F.: Alfaguara, 2005.

Cortés, Eladio, ed. *Dictionary of Mexican Literature*. Westport, Conn.: Greenwood Press, 1992.

Díaz Ruiz, Ignacio. *El cuento mexicano en el modernismo: antología*. México, D.F.: Universidad Nacional Autónoma de México, 2006.

Domínguez Michael, Christopher. *Diccionario crítico de la literatura mexicana: 1955–2005*. México, D.F.: Fondo de Cultura Económica, 2007.

——, ed. *Antología de la narrativa mexicana del siglo XX*. 2 vols. México, D.F.: Fondo de Cultura Económica, 1989–1991.

Foster, David William. *Mexican Literature: A Bibliography of Secondary Sources*. Metuchen: Scarecrow Press, 1992.

——, ed. *Mexican Literature: A History*. Austin: University of Texas Press, 1994.

Frischmann, Donald H. *El nuevo teatro popular en México*. México, D.F.: Instituto Nacional de Bellas Artes, 1990.

Garza Cuarón, Beatriz., et al. *Historia de la literatura mexicana: desde sus orígenes hasta nuestros días*. 2 vols México, D.F.: Siglo Veintiuno Editores, 1996.

González Peña, Carlos. *History of Mexican Literature*. Dallas: Southern Methodist University Press, 1968.

Herbert H. Hoffman. *Cuento mexicano index*. Newport Beach: Headway Publications, 1978.

Ita, Fernando de. *Teatro Mexicano contemporáneo: antología*. Madrid: Sociedad Estatal Quinto Centenario, Fondo de Cultura Económica, and Sociedad General de Escritores de México, 1991.

Kuri-Aldana, Mario, and Vicente Mendoza Martínez. *Cancionero popular mexicano*. México: Consejo Nacional para la Cultura y las Artes, 2001.

Lamb, Ruth Stanton. *Mexican Theatre of the Twentieth Century: Bibliography & Study*. Claremont: Ocelot Press, 1975.

Langford, Walter M. *The Mexican Novel Comes of Age*. Notre Dame, Ind.: University of Notre Dame Press, 1971.

Martínez, José Luis. *The Modern Mexican Essay* [anthology]. Toronto: University of Toronto Press, 1965.

Ocampo, Aurora M., ed. *Diccionario de escritores mexicanos, siglo XX: desde las generaciones del Ateneo y novelistas de la Revolución hasta nuestros días*. 7 vols. Mexico: Universidad Nacional Autónoma de México, 1988.

Rey, Mario. *Historia y muestra de la literatura infantil mexicana*. México: SM de Ediciones and Consejo Nacional para la Cultura y las Artes, 2000.

Rutherford, John. *An Annotated Bibliography of the Novels of the Mexican Revolution of 1910–1917. In English and Spanish*. Troy, N.Y.: Whitston Publishing Co., 1972.

Saz, Agustin del, ed. *Antologia general de la poesia mexicana: siglos XVI–XX.* Barcelona: Bruguera, 1972.

Teatro mexicano del siglo XX. 5 vols. México, D.F.: Fondo de Cultura Económica, 1956.

Víctor Manuel Mendiola, Miguel Ángel Zapata and Miguel Gomes, eds. *Tigre la sed: antología de poesía mexicana contemporánea, 1950–2005.* Madrid: Hiperión, 2006.

Williams, Raymond L., and Blanca Rodríguez. *La narrativa posmoderna en México.* Xalapa: Universidad Veracruzana, 2002.

Select Bibliographies for Specific Writers

José Agustín

Carter, June C. D., and Donald L. Schmidt, eds. *José Agustín: Onda and Beyond.* Columbia: University of Missouri Press, 1986.

Duncan, J.Ann, *Voices, Visions, and a New Reality: Mexican Fiction since 1970.* Pittsburgh, Pa.: University of Pittsburgh Press, 1986.

Schelonka, Gregory. "Youth, Government, and the Fear of Globalization in José Agustín's *De perfil.*" In *Proceedings of the 23rd Louisiana Conference on Hispanic Languages and Literatures,* edited by Alejandro Cortázar and Christian Fernández, 181–93. Baton Rouge: Department of Foreign Languages and Literatures, Louisiana State University, 2003.

Steele, Cynthia. "Patriarchy and Apocalypse in *Cerca del fuego,* by José Agustín." *Studies in Twentieth Century Literature* 14, no. 1 (1990): 61–80.

Ignacio Manual Altamirano

Alba-Koch, Beatriz de. "Writing the Nation in Nineteenth-Century México, D.F.: Liberalism, Cosmopolitanism, and Indigenismo in Altamirano." *Hispanófila* 142 (2004): 101–16.

Brushwood, John S. *The Romantic Novel in Mexico.* Columbia: University of Missouri Press, 1954.

Conway, Christopher. "Ignacio Altamirano and the Contradictions of Autobiographical Indianism." *Latin American Literary Review* 34, no. 67 (2006): 34–49.

Melgarejo Acosta, María del Pilar. "Altamirano's Demons." *Colorado Review of Hispanic Studies* 4 (2006): 49–63.

Segre, Erica. "An Italicised Ethnicity: Memory and Renascence in the Literary Writings of Ignacio Manuel Altamirano." *Forum for Modern Language Studies* 36, no. 3 (2000): 266–78.

Hernando Alvarado Tezozomoc

Cortés, Rocío. "(De)mystifying Sacred Geographical Spaces in Hernando de Alvarado Tezozomoc's *Crónica mexicana.*" In *Mapping Colonial Spanish America: Places and Commonplaces of Identity, Culture, and Experience,* edited by Santa Arias and Mariselle Meléndez, 68–83. Lewisburg, Pa.: Bucknell University Press, 2002.

Eligio Ancona

Gerassi-Navarro, Nina. *Pirate Novels: Fictions of Nation Building in Spanish America.* Durham, N.C.: Duke University Press, 1999.

Nevárez, Lisa "'My Reputación Precedes Me': La Malinche and Palimpsests of Sacrifice, Scapegoating, and Mestizaje in *Xicoténcatl* and *Los mártires del Anáhuac.*" *Decimonónica: Journal of Nineteenth Century Hispanic Cultural Production* 1, no. 1 (2004): 67–85.

Skinner, Lee. "Martyrs of Miscegenation: Racial and National Identities in Nineteenth-Century Mexico." *Hispanófila* 132 (2001): 25–42.

Homero Aridjis

Perkowska, Magdalena. *Historias híbridas: la nueva novela histórica latino-americana (1985–2000) ante las teorías posmodernas de la historia.* Madrid and Frankfurt: Iberoamericana and Vervuert; 2008.

Stauder, Thomas, ed. *'La luz queda en el aire': estudios internacionales en torno a Homero Aridjis.* Frankfurt: Vervuert, 2005.

Juan José Arreola

Acker, Bertie. *El cuento mexicano contemporáneo, Rulfo, Arreola y Fuentes, temas y cosmovisión.* Madrid: Playor, 1984.

Burt, John R., "This Is No Way to Run a Railroad: Arreola's Allegorical Railroad and a Possible Source." *Hispania: A Journal Devoted to the Teaching of Spanish and Portuguese* 71, no. 4 (1988): 806–11.

D'Lugo, Carol Clark. "Arreola's *La feria:* The Author and the Reader in the Text." *Hispanófila* 33, no. 1 (1989): 57–68.

Gilgen, Read G. "Absurdist Techniques in the Short Stories of Juan José Arreola." *Journal of Spanish Studies: 20th Century* 8 (1980): 67–77.

Herz, Theda Mary. "Continuity in Evolution: Juan José Arreola as Dramatist." *Latin American Theatre Review* 8, no. 2 (1975): 15–26.

Poot Herrera, Sara. *Un giro en espiral: el proyecto literario de Juan José Arreola.* Guadalajara: Universidad de Guadalajara, 1992.
Washburn, Yulan M. *Juan José Arreola.* Boston: Twayne, 1983.

Mariano Azuela

Herbst, Gerhard R. *Mexican Society as Seen by Mariano Azuela.* New York: Abra, 1977.
Langford, Walter M. *The Mexican Novel Comes of Age.* Notre Dame, Ind.: Notre Dame University Press, 1971.
Leal, Luis. *Mariano Azuela.* New York: Twayne, 1971.
Parra, Max. *Writing Pancho Villa's Revolution: Rebels in the Literary Imagination of Mexico.* Austin: University of Texas Press, 2005.
Robe, Stanley L. *Azuela and the Mexican Underdogs.* Berkeley: University of California Press, 1979.
Ruffinelli, Jorge. *Literatura e ideología: el primer Mariano Azuela (1896–1918).* México, D.F.: Premiá Editor, 1982.
Sommers, Joseph. *After the Storm: Landmarks of the Modern Mexican Novel.* Albuquerque: University of New Mexico Press, 1968.

Bernardo de Balbuena

Perelmuter, Rosa. "¿Merece la pena leer *El Bernardo*? Lectura y lectores del poema épico de Bernardo de Balbuena." *Revista Iberoamericana* 61, nos. 172–73 (1995): 461–66.

Toribio de Benavente (Motolinía)

Baudot, Georges. "Amerindian Image and Utopian Project: Motolinía and Millenarian Discourse." In *Amerindian Images and the Legacy of Columbus,* edited by René Jara and Nicholas Spadaccini, 375–400. Minneapolis: University of Minnesota Press, 1992.
Díaz Balsera, Viviana. "Erasing the Pyramid under the Cross: Motolinía's History of the Indians of New Spain and the Construction of the Nahua Christian Subject." *Journal of Spanish Cultural Studies* 4, no. 1 (2003): 111–23.

Sabina Berman

Bixler, Jacqueline E. "Power Plays and the Mexican Crisis: The Recent Theatre of Sabina Berman." In *Performance, pathos, política de los sexos: teatro postcolonial de autoras latinoamericanas,* edited by Heidrun Adler and Kati Röttger, 83–99. Frankfurt: Vervuert, 1999.

———, ed. *Sediciosas seducciones: sexo, poder y palabras en el teatro de Sabina Berman.* Iztapalapa: Escenología, 2004.

Larson, Catherine. *Games and Play in the Theater of Spanish American Women.* Lewisburg, Pa.: Bucknell University Press, 2004.

Niebylski, Dianna C. "Caught in the Middle: Ambiguous Gender and Social Politics in Sabina Berman's Play *Entre Villa y una mujer desnuda.*" *Revista de Estudios Hispánicos* 39, no. 1 (2005): 153–77.

Carmen Boullosa

Dröscher, Barbara, ed. *Acercamientos a Carmen Boullosa: actas del simposio "Conjugarse en infinitivo—la escritora Carmen Boullosa."* Berlin: Frey, 1999.

Gundermann, Eva. *Desafiando lo abyecto: una lectura feminista de "Mejor desaparece" de Carmen Boullosa.* Frankfurt: Peter Lang, 2002.

Santos, Cristina. *Bending the Rules in the Quest for an Authentic Female Identity: Clarice Lispector and Carmen Boullosa.* New York: Peter Lang, 2004.

Ángel de Campo

Márquez, Celina. "La estética realista en *La rumba* de Ángel de Campo, Micrós." *Palabra y el Hombre: Revista de la Universidad Veracruzana* 99 (1996): 163–73.

Olea Franco, Rafael. "Sentimentalismo e ironía en Ángel de Campo." *Literatura Mexicana* 16, no. 2 (2005): 29–50.

Nellie Campobello

Linhard, Tabea Alexa. *Fearless Women in the Mexican Revolution and the Spanish Civil War.* Columbia: University of Missouri Press, 2005.

Meyer, Doris. "The Dialogics of Testimony: Autobiography as Shared Experience in Nellie Campobello's *Cartucho.*" In *Latin American Women's Writing: Feminist Readings in Theory and Crisis,* edited by Anny Brooksbank Jones and Catherine Davies, 46–65. New York: Oxford University Press, 1996.

———. "Divided Against Herself: The Early Poetry of Nellie Campobello." *Revista de Estudios Hispánicos* 20, no. 2 (1986): 51–63.

Robles, Martha. *La sombra fugitiva: escritoras en la cultura nacional.* 2 vols. México, D.F.: Universidad Nacional Autónoma de México, 1985.

Unruh, Vicky. *Performing Women and Modern Literary Culture in Latin America: Intervening Acts.* Austin: University of Texas Press, 2006.

Julieta Campos

Feracho, Lesley. *Linking the Americas: Race, Hybrid Discourse, and the Reformulation of Feminine Identity.* Albany: State University of New York Press, 2005.

Lagos-Pope, María-Inés. "Cat/Logos: The Narrator's Confession in Julieta Campos' *Celina o los gatos* (Celina or the Cats)." In *Splintering Darkness: Latin American Women Writers in Search of Themselves,* edited by Lucía Guerra Cunningham, 31–42. Pittsburgh, Pa.: Latin American Literary Review Press, 1990.

Tompkins, Cynthia M. "Intertextuality as Différance in Julieta Campos' *El miedo de perder a Eurídice*: A Symptomatic Case of Latin American Postmodernism." In *The Postmodern in Latin and Latino American Cultural Narratives,* edited by Claudia Ferman, 153–80. New York: Garland, 1996.

Emilio Carballido

Bisset, Judith Ishmael. "Visualizing Carballido's *Orinoco*: The Play in Two Imagined Performances." *Gestos: Teoria y Practica del Teatro Hispánico* 5, no. 9 (1990): 65–74.

Bixler, Jacqueline Eyring. "A Theatre of Contradictions: The Recent Works of Emilio Carballido." *Latin American Theatre Review* 18, no. 2 (1985): 57–65.

Cypess, Sandra Messinger. "I, Too, Speak: 'Female' Discourse in Carballido's Plays." *Latin American Theatre Review* 18, no. 1 (1984): 45–52.

Peterson, Karen. "Existential Irony in Three Carballido Plays." *Latin American Theatre Review* 10, no. 2 (1977): 29–35.

Taylor, Diana. "Mad World, Mad Hope: Carballido's *El día que soltaron los leones*." *Latin American Theatre Review* 20, no. 2 (1987): 67–76.

Rosario Castellanos

Ahern, Maureen, and Mary Seale Vásquez, eds. *Homenaje a Rosario Castellanos.* Valencia: Albatros, 1980.

Bigas Torres, Sylvia. *La narrativa indigenista mexicana del Siglo XX.* Guadalajara: Editorial Universidad de Guadalajara, 1990.

Gil Iriarte, María Luisa. *Testamento de Hécuba: mujeres e indígenas en la obra de Rosario Castellanos.* Seville: Universidad de Sevilla, 1999.

Lavou Zoungbo, Victorien, ed. *El indio Malanga: écrire la domination en Amérique Latine: Rosario Castellanos, "Balún Canán," 1957; José María Arguedas, "Los ríos profundos," 1958; Jorge Icaza, "El Chulla Romero y Flores," 1958*. Perpignan: Presse Universitaire de Perpignan, 2006.

O'Connell, Joanna. *Prospero's Daughter: The Prose of Rosario Castellanos*. Austin: University of Texas Press, 1995.

Tarica, Estelle. *The Inner Life of Mestizo Nationalism*. Minneapolis: University of Minnesota Press, 2008.

Alí Chumacero

Mejía Valera, Manuel. "La poesía de Alí Chumacero." *Cuadernos Americanos* 27 (1991): 86–95.

Hernán Cortés

Boruchoff, David A. "Beyond Utopia and Paradise: Cortés, Bernal Díaz and the Rhetoric of Consecration." *MLN* 106, no. 2 (1991): 330–69.

Jorge Cuesta

Ramírez, Israel. "Jorge Cuesta: persona real y persona figurada. Algunas consideraciones biográficas." *Literatura Mexicana* 14, no. 2 (2003): 115–46.

Rafael Delgado

Ramos Escandón, Carmen. "The Novel of Porfirian Mexico: A Historian's Source: Problems and Methods." *Ideologies and Literature: Journal of Hispanic and Lusophone Discourse Analysis* 3, no. 14 (1981): 118–33.

Bernal Díaz del Castillo

Beckjord, Sarah H. *Territories of History: Humanism, Rhetoric, and the Historical Imagination in the Early Chronicles of Spanish America*. University Park: Pennsylvania State University Press, 2007.

Cortínez, Verónica. *Memoria original de Bernal Díaz del Castillo*. Huixquilucan: Oak, 2000.

Serés, Guillermo. "Vida y escritura de Bernal Díaz del Castillo." *Literatura: Teoría, Historia, Crítica* 6 (2004): 15–62.

Salvador Díaz Mirón

Sotelo, Abigaíl. "Del romanticismo al modernismo; la búsqueda de la forma en Salvador Díaz Mirón." *Divergencias: Revista de Estudios Lingüísticos y Literarios* 3, no. 2 (2005): 75–84.

Salvador Elizondo

Bell, Steven M. "Postmodern Fiction in Spanish America: The Examples of Salvador Elizondo and Nestor Sánchez." *Arizona Quarterly: A Journal of American Literature, Culture, and Theory* 42, no. 1 (1986): 5–16.
Curley, Dermot. *En la isla desierta: una lectura de la obra de Salvador Elizondo.* México, D.F.: Fondo de Cultura Económica, 1989.
Jara, René. *Farabeuf: estrategias de la inscripción narrativa.* Xalapa: Universidad Veracruzana, 1982.
Marth, Hildegard. "Space-Time in Salvador Elizondo's *Farabeuf.*" *Acta Litteraria Academiae Scientiarum Hungaricae* 31, nos. 1–2 (1989): 103–14.

Laura Esquivel

Glenn, Kathleen Mary. "Postmodern Parody and Culinary Narrative Art in Laura Esquivel's *Como agua para chocolate.*" *Chasqui: Revista de Literatura Latinoamericana* 23, no. 2 (1994): 39–47.
Marquet, Antonio. "¿Cómo escribir un best-seller? La receta de Laura Esquivel." *Plural: Revista Cultural de Excelsior* 237 (1991): 58–67.
Niebylski, Dianna C. *Humoring Resistance: Laughter and the Excessive Body in Latin American Women's Fiction.* Albany: State University of New York Press, 2004.
Saltz, Joanne. "Laura Esquivel's *Como agua para chocolate*: The Questioning of Literary and Social Limits." *Chasqui: Revista de Literatura Latinoamericana* 24, no. 1 (1995): 30–37.
Taylor, Claire Louise. "Body-Swapping and Genre-Crossing: Laura Esquivel's *La ley del amor.*" *Modern Language Review* 92, no. 2 (2002): 324–35.
Zubiaurre, Maite. "Culinary Eros in Contemporary Hispanic Female Fiction: From Kitchen Tales to Table Narratives." *College Literature* 33, no. 3 (2006): 29–51.

José Joaquín Fernández de Lizardi

Alba-Koch, Beatriz de. "'Enlightened Absolutism' and Utopian Thought: Fernández de Lizardi and Reform in New Spain." *Revista Canadiense de Estudios Hispánicos* 24, no. 2 (2000): 295–306.

Raffi-Beroud, Catherine, ed. *En torno al teatro de Fernández Lizardi.* Amsterdam: Rodopi, 1998.
Spell, Jefferson Rea. *The Life and Works of José Joaquín Fernández de Lizardi.* Philadelphia: University of Pennsylvania Press, 1931.
Vogeley, Nancy. *Lizardi and the Birth of the Novel in Spanish America.* Gainesville: University Press of Florida, 2001.

Heriberto Frías

Chávez, Daniel. "*Tomochic*: Nationalist Narrative, Homogenizing Late Nineteenth-Century Discourse and Society in Mexico." *Chasqui: Revista de Literatura Latinoamericana* 35, no. 2 (2006): 72–88.

Carlos Fuentes

Abeyta, Michael. *Fuentes, "Terra Nostra," and the Reconfiguration of Latin American Culture.* Columbia: University of Missouri Press, 2006.
Brody, Robert, and Charles Rossman, eds. *Carlos Fuentes: A Critical View.* Austin: University of Texas Press, 1982.
Durán, Gloria. *The Archetypes of Carlos Fuentes: from Witch to Androgyne.* Hamden, CT: Shoestring Press, 1980.
Faris, Wendy. *Carlos Fuentes.* New York: Ungar, 1983.
Feijoo, Gladys. *Lo fantástico en los relatos de Carlos Fuentes.* New York: Senda Nueva de Ediciones, 1985.
Giacoman, Helmy F., ed. *Homenaje a Carlos Fuentes: variaciones interpretativas en torno a su obra.* New York: Las Américas, 1971.
Ibsen, Kristine. *Author, Text and Reader in the Novels of Carlos Fuentes.* New York: Peter Lang, 1993.
Ordiz, Francisco Javier. *El mito en la obra narrativa de Carlos Fuentes.* León: Universidad de León, 1987.
van Delden, Maarten. *Carlos Fuentes, Mexico, and Modernity.* Nashville: Vanderbilt University Press; 1998.

Sergio Galindo

Carballido, Emilio. "El teatro de Sergio Galindo." *La Palabra y el Hombre: Revista de la Universidad Veracruzana* 85 (1993): 21–23.
Espinaza, José María. "Sergio Galindo ante la crítica." *La Palabra y el Hombre: Revista de la Universidad Veracruzana* 85 (1993): 17–20.
Hernández Palacios, Esther. "La felicidad perdida: una lectura de dos novelas de Sergio Galindo." *Texto Crítico* 2, no. 2 (1996): 125–41.

Federico Gamboa

Brushwood, John S. "Message and Meaning in Federico Gamboa's *Suprema ley.*" In *Homenaje a Luis Leal: estudios sobre literatura hispanoamericana,* edited by Donald W. Bleznick and Juan O. Valencia, 27–41. Madrid: Insula, 1978.

Castillo, Debra A. "Meat Shop Memories: Federico Gamboa's *Santa.*" *Inti: Revista de Literatura Hispánica* 40–14 (1994–1995): 175–92.

Juan García Ponce

Bruce-Novoa, Juan. "Eroticism, Counterculture, and Juan García Ponce." *CR: The New Centennial Review* 5, no. 3 (2005): 1–33.

Good, Carl. "The Reading of Community in the Early Novels of Juan García Ponce." *CR: The New Centennial Review* 5, no. 3 (2005): 105–41.

Loustaunau, Esteban. "The Creation of Imaginative Reality in García Ponce's *Pasado presente.*" *CR: The New Centennial Review* 5, no. 3 (2005): 83–104.

Rodríguez-Hernández, Raúl. "All Streetcars Are Named Desire: The Lost Cities of Juan García Ponce's *Personas, lugares y anexas.*" *CR: The New Centennial Review* 5, no. 3 (2005): 35–64.

———. *Mexico's Ruins: Juan García Ponce and the Writing of Modernity.* Albany: State University of New York Press, 2007.

Elena Garro

García, Mara L., ed. *Baúl de recuerdos: homenaje a Elena Garro.* Tlaxcala: Universidad Autónoma de Tlaxcala, 1999.

Melgar, Lucía, ed. *Elena Garro: lectura múltiple de una personalidad compleja.* Puebla: Benemérita Universidad Autónoma de Puebla, 2002.

Melgar-Palacios, Lucía. *Writing Dark Times: Elena Garro, Writing and Politics.* Princeton, N.J.: Princeton University Press, 2000.

Stoll, Anita, ed. *A Different Reality: Essays on the World of Elena Garro.* Lewisburg, Pa.: Bucknell University Press, 1990.

Winkler, Julie A. *Light into Shadow: Marginality and Alienation in the Work of Elena Garro.* New York: Peter Lang, 2001.

Margo Glantz

Jörgensen, Beth E. "Margo Glantz: Tongue in Hand." In *Reinterpreting the Spanish American Essay: Women Writers of the 19th and 20th Centuries,* edited by Doris Meyer, 188–96. Austin: University of Texas Press, 1995.

Lindstrom, Naomi. "The Heterogeneous Jewish Wit of Margo Glantz." In *Memory, Oblivion, and Jewish Culture in Latin America,* edited by Marjorie Agosín, 115–30. Austin: University of Texas Press, 2005.

Fernán González de Eslava

Fernández, Teodosio. "Sobre el teatro de Fernán González de Eslava." *Anales de Literatura Española* 13 (1999): 41–50.
Frenk, Margit. "La poesía de González de Eslava: entre la vieja España y la nueva." *Calíope: Journal of the Society for Renaissance and Baroque Hispanic Poetry* 4, nos. 1–2 (1998): 72–85.
Paz, Yanira. "Sobre los coloquios de Fernán González de Eslava." *Cincinnati Romance Review* 17 (1998): 99–104.

Enrique González Martínez

Cobo Borda, Juan Gustavo. "El fin del modernismo o la poesía como perenne plagio de sí misma: Enrique González Martínez (México, 1871–1952)." *Hora de Poesía* 59–60 (1988): 49–54.
Rosser, Harry L. "Enrique González Martinez: 'matacisnes' y concepción estética." *Cuadernos Americanos* 243, no. 4 (1982): 181–88.

Gorostiza Celestino

Quinteros, Isis. "La consagración del mito en la epopeya mexicana: *La Malinche* de Celestino Gorostiza." *Latin American Theatre Review* 19, no. 1 (1985): 33–42.
Silva, Juan Francisco. "El color del teatro mexicano: Celestino Gorostiza." *Dramateatro Revista Digital* 4 (2001): n.p.

José Gorostiza

Gelpí, Juan G. *Enunciación y dependencia en José Gorostiza: estudio de una máscara poética,* México, D.F.: Universidad Nacional Autónoma de México, 1984.
Marrero Henríquez, José M. "La creación del poema en *Muerte sin fin* de José Gorostiza." *Syntaxis* 23–24 (1990): 121–28.
Silva, Maria Aparecida da. "Vida y muerte de las vanguardias poéticas: José Gorostiza." *Espéculo: Revista de Estudios Literarios* 15 (2000): n.p.

Xirau, Ramón. *Tres poetas de la soledad: Villaurrutia, Gorostiza, Paz.* México, D.F.: Robredo, 1955.

Manuel Gutiérrez Nájera

Gómez del Prado, Carlos. *Manuel Gutiérrez Nájera: vida y obra.* México, D.F.: Andrea, 1964.

González, Anibal. *La crónica modernista hispanoamericana.* Madrid: Porrúa Turanzas, 1983.

Gutiérrez, José Ismael. *Manuel Gutiérrez Nájera y sus cuentos: de la crónica periodística al relato de ficción.* New York: Peter Lang, 1999.

Schulman, Ivan. *Genesis del modernismo: Martí, Nájera, Silva, Casal.* México, D.F.: El Colegio de México, 1966.

Martín Luis Guzmán

Abreu Gómez, Emilio. *Martín Luis Guzmán.* México, D.F.: Empresas Editoriales, 1968.

Bruce-Novoa, Juan. "Martín Luis Guzmán's Necessary Overtures." *Discurso Literario: Revista de Temas Hispánicos* 4, no. 1 (1986): 63–83.

Megenney, William W., ed. *Five Essays on Martín Luis Guzmán.* Riverside: Latin American Studies Program, Univiversity of California, 1978.

Luisa Josefina Hernández

Cohen, Deb. "Defining and Defying 'Woman' in Four Plays by Luisa Josefina Hernández." *Latin American Theatre Review* 30, no. 2 (1997): 89–102.

Magnarelli, Sharon. "Sub/In/Di-Verting the Oedipus Syndrome in Luisa Josefina Hernández's *Los huéspedes reales.*" *Inti: Revista de Literatura Hispánica* 40–41 (1994): 93–112.

Efraín Huerta

Aguilar-Melantzón, Ricardo. "Efraín Huerta en la poesía mexicana." *Revista Iberoamericana* 151 (1990): 419–30.

Jorge Ibargüengoitia

Arias, Ángel. "Ibargüengoitia y la nueva novela histórica: *Los relámpagos de agosto.*" *RILCE: Revista de Filología Hispánica* 17, no. 1 (2001): 17–32.

González, Alfonso, *Euphoria and Crisis: Essays on the Contemporary Mexican Novel.* Fredericton, New Brunswick: York Press, 1990.

Herz, Theda M. "Jorge Ibargüengoitia's Carnival Pageantry: The Mexican Theatre of Power and the Power of Theatre." *Latin American Theatre Review* 28, no. 1 (1994): 31–47.

Rehder, Ernest. "Ibargüengoitia's *Estas ruinas que ves* as a Neo-costumbrista Novel: In the Spanish Tradition." *Hispanic Journal* 11, no. 1 (1990): 61–76.

Sor Juana Inés de la Cruz

Daniel, Lee A. *The Loa of Sor Juana Inés de la Cruz.* Fredricton, New Brunswick: York Press, 1994.

Kirk, Pamela. *Sor Juana Inés de la Cruz: Religion, Art, and Feminism.* New York: Continuum, 1998.

Luciani, Frederick. *Literary Self-Fashioning in Sor Juana Inés de la Cruz.* Lewisburg, Pa.: Bucknell University Press, 2004.

Merrim, Stephanie. *Early Modern Women's Writing and Sor Juana Inés de la Cruz.* Nashville, Tenn.: Vanderbilt University Press, 1999.

———, ed. *Feminist Perspectives on Sor Juana Inés de la Cruz.* Detroit: Wayne State University Press, 1991.

Paz, Octavio. *Sor Juana or the Traps of Faith.* Cambridge, Mass.: Bel Knap Press, 1988.

Tavard, George H. *Juana Inés de la Cruz and the Theology of Beauty.* Notre Dame, Ind.: Notre Dame University Press, 1991.

Diego de Landa

Castro-Vázquez, Isabel. "*Relación de las cosas de Yucatán* y el surgimiento de la identidad proto-criolla en la colonia." *Romance Review* 13 (2003): 9–21.

Restall, Matthew. "A Reevaluation of the Authenticity of Fray Diego de Landa's *Relación de las cosas de Yucatán.*" *Ethnohistory* 49, no. 3 (2002): 651–69.

Vicente Leñero

Anderson, Danny J. *Vicente Leñero: The Novelist as Critic.* New York: Peter Lang, 1989.

Bissett, Judith I. "Constructing the Alternative Version: Vicente Leñero's Documentary and Historical Drama." *Latin American Theatre Review* 18, no. 1 (1985): 71–78.

Grossman, Lois S. "*Los albañiles*, Novel and Play: A Two-Time Winner." *Latin American Theatre Review* 9, no. 2 (1976): 5–12.

McCracken, Ellen. "Vicente Lenero's Critical Contribution to the Boom: From *Telenovela* to *Novela-testimonio.*" In *In Requiem for the "Boom"—Premature? A Symposium,* edited by Rose S. Minc and Marilyn R. Frankenthaler, 174–85. Montclair, N.J.: Montclair State College, 1980.

Olivares, Jorge. "Scribbling the Canon: Vicente Leñero's *El garabato.*" *Symposium: A Quarterly Journal in Modern Literatures* 48, no. 2 (1994): 135–54.

Germán List Arzubide

Benedet, Sandra María. "Modernidades estridentistas: el movimiento estridentista de Germán List Arzubide." *Palabra y el Hombre: Revista de la Universidad Veracruzana* 112 (1999): 69–72.

Francisco López de Gómara

Carman, Glen. *Rhetorical Conquests: Cortés, Gómara, and Renaissance Imperialism.* West Lafayette, Ind.: Purdue University Press, 2006.

Roa-de-la-Carrera, Cristián A. *Histories of Infamy: Francisco López de Gómara and the Ethics of Spanish Imperialism.* Boulder: University Press of Colorado, 2005.

José López Portillo y Rojas

Grass, Roland L. *José Lopez-Portillo y Rojas: A Novelist of Social Reform in Mexico Before the Revolution of 1910.* Macomb: Western Illinois University, 1970.

Ramón López Velarde

De la Fuente, Carmen. *López Velarde: su mundo intelectual y afectivo.* México, D.F.: Federación Editorial Mexicana, 1971.

Murray, Frederic W. *La imagen arquetípica en la poesía de Ramón López Velarde.* Chapel Hill: University of North Carolina Press, 1972.

Gregorio López y Fuentes

Torriente, Lolo de la. "*El indio* y *Huasteca* en su tiempo." In *Recopilacion de textos sobre la novela de la Revolucion Mexicana,* edited by Rogelio Rodriguez Coronel, 278–82. Havana: Casa de las Americas, 1975.

Sergio Magaña

Boling, Becky. "Language and Performance: Representation and Invention in Magaña's *Los enemigos.*" *Gestos: Teoría y Práctica del Teatro Hispánico* 10, no. 19 (1995): 119–30.

Cypess, Sandra Messinger. "Myth and Metatheatre: Magaña's *Malinche* and *Medea.*" *Bucknell Review: A Scholarly Journal of Letters, Arts and Sciences* 40, no. 2 (1996): 37–52.

Quackenbush, Howard. "The Anti-Theatre in *El suplicante* by Sergio Magana." *Latin American Theatre Review* 13 (1980): 87–93.

Manuel Maples Arce

Flores, Tatiana. "Clamoring for Attention in Mexico City: Manuel Maples Arce's Avant-Garde *Manifesto Actual No 1.*" *Review: Literature and Arts of the Americas* 69 (2004): 208–20.

Gallo, Rubén. "Maples Arce, Marinetti and Khlebnikov: The Mexican Estridentistas in Dialogue with Italian and Russian Futurisms." *Revista Canadiense de Estudios Hispánicos* 31, no. 2 (2007): 309–24.

Ángeles Mastretta

Knights, Vanessa. "(De)Constructing Gender: The Bolero in Ángeles Mastretta's *Arráncame la vida.*" *Journal of Romance Studies* 1, no. 1 (2001): 69–84.

Laffey, Lee-Ann. "Pulling the Fulcrum and Propelling Higher: Acts of Female Empowerment in Ángeles Mastretta's *Mujeres de ojos grandes.*" *RLA: Romance Languages Annual* 11 (1999): 524–29.

Lavery, Jane Elizabeth. *Ángeles Mastretta: Textual Multiplicity.* Woodbridge: Tamesis, 2005.

Thornton, Niamh. *Women and the War Story in Mexico: La novela de la Revolución.* Lewiston, N.Y.: Mellen, 2006.

María Luisa Mendoza

Locklin, Blake Seana. "Reconstructing Fertility: Reproducing the Family in María Luisa Mendoza's *El perro de la escribana.*" *Ciberletras* 12 (2005): n.p.

Long, Ryan F. *Fictions of Totality: The Mexican Novel, 1968, and the National-Popular State.* West Lafayette, Ind.: Purdue University Press, 2008.

Servando Teresa de Mier

Jara, René. "The Inscription of Creole Consciousness: Fray Servando de Mier." In *1492–1992: Re/Discovering Colonial Writing*, edited by René Jara and Nicholas Spadaccini, 349–79. Minneapolis: University of Minnesota Press, 1989.

Pérez Mejía, Ángela. "'Into the Lion's Mouth': Parody as a Possibility for Displacement Writing in Servando Teresa de Mier." *Studies in Travel Writing* 7, no. 1 (2003): 63–81.

Ross, Kathleen. "A Natural History of the Old World: The *Memorias* of Fray Servando Teresa de Mier." *Revista de Estudios Hispánicos* 23, no. 3 (1989): 87–99.

Carlos Monsiváis

Egan, Linda. *Carlos Monsiváis: Culture and Chronicle in Contemporary Mexico*. Tucson: University of Arizona Press, 2001.

———. "Emblematic Revelations of a Just World to Come in Carlos Monsiváis's *Nuevo catecismo para indios remisos*." *Revista Canadiense de Estudios Hispánicos* 32, no. 2 (2008): 333–61.

Gelpí, Juan G. "Walking in the Modern City: Subjectivity and Cultural Contacts in the Urban *Crónicas* of Salvador Novo and Carlos Monsiváis." In *The Contemporary Mexican Chronicle: Theoretical Perspectives on the Liminal Genre*, edited by Ignacio Corona and Beth E. Jörgensen, 201–20. Albany: State University of New York Press, 2002.

Moraña, Mabel, ed. *El arte de la ironía: Carlos Monsiváis ante la crítica*. México D.F.: Universidad Nacional Autónoma de México, 2007.

Rafael F. Muñoz

Parra, Max. *Writing Pancho Villa's Revolution: Rebels in the Literary Imagination of Mexico*. Austin: University of Texas Press, 2005.

Amado Nervo

Chaves, José Ricardo. "La literatura fantástica de Amado Nervo." *Texto Crítico* 4, no. 8 (2001): 229–35.

Peters, Kate. "Fin de siglo Mysticism: Body, Mind, and Transcendence in the Poetry of Amado Nervo and Delmira Agustini." *Indiana Journal of Hispanic Literatures* 8 (1996): 159–76.

Southworth, Susan L. "Sounding the Great Vacío: The Abyss in the Poetry of Rubén Darío and Amado Nervo." *Neophilologus* 85, no. 3 (2001): 397–409.

Salvador Novo

Dávila, Roxanne. "Mexico City as Urban Palimpsest in Salvador Novo's *Nueva Grandeza Mexicana.*" *Studies in the Literary Imagination* 33, no. 3 (2000): 107–23.

Gollnick, Brian. "Silent Idylls, Double Lives: Sex and the City in Salvador Novo's *Estatua de sal.*" *Mexican Studies/Estudios Mexicanos* 21, no. 1 (2005): 231–50.

Long, Mary K. "Writing the City: The Chronicles of Salvador Novo." In *The Contemporary Mexican Chronicle: Theoretical Perspectives on the Liminal Genre,* edited by Ignacio Corona and Beth E. Jörgensen, 181–200. Albany: State University of New York Press, 2002.

Bernardo Ortiz de Montellano

Forster, Merlin H. "Los relatos breves de Ortiz de Montellano: incursión en la prosa vanguardista mexicana." In *El cuento mexicano: homenaje a Luis Leal,* edited by Sara Poot Herrera, 219–35. México, D.F.: Universidad Nacional Autónoma de México, 1996.

Manuel José Othón

Castro Leal, Antonio. "La poesía de Manuel José Othón (1858–1906)." *Cuadernos Americanos* 171 (1970): 161–84.

Gilberto Owen

Boldridge, Effie. "The Refabrication of Literary Personae in the Poetry of Gilberto Owen." *Revista de Estudios Hispánicos* 22 (1995): 109–19.

Boldridge, Effie J. "The Poetic Process in Gilberto Owen." *Romance Notes* 14 (1973): 476–83.

José Emilio Pacheco

Docter, Mary. "José Emilio Pacheco: A Poetics of Reciprocity." *Hispanic Review* 70, no. 3 (2002): 373–92.

D'Lugo, Carol Clark. "Narrative and Historical Commitment in Pacheco's *Morirás lejos.*" *Chasqui: Revista de Literatura Latinoamericana* 19, no. 2 (1990): 33–42.

———. "Towards a Transatlantic Reading of Good and Evil in José Emilio Pacheco's *Morirás lejos.*" *Torre: Revista de la Universidad de Puerto Rico* 33 (2004): 401–10.

Friis, Ronald J. "A Comala of the Mind: José Emilio Pacheco's Early Theory of Influence." *MIFLC Review* 7 (1997–1998): 127–36.

Jiménez de Báez, Yvette, Diana Morán, and Edith Negrín. *Ficción e historia: la narrativa de José Emilio Pacheco.* México, D.F.: El Colegio de México, 1979.

Malamud, Randy. "The Culture of Using Animals in Literature and the Case of José Emilio Pacheco." *CLCWeb: Comparative Literature and Culture* 2, no. 2 (2000): n.p.

Verani, Hugo J., ed. *La hoguera y el viento: José Emilio Pacheco ante la crítica.* México, D.F.: Era, 1993.

Fernando del Paso

Fiddian, Robin W. *The Novels of Fernando del Paso.* Gainesville: University Press of Florida, 2000.

Guerrero, Elisabeth. "Burying the Emperor: Mourning in Fernando del Paso's *Noticias del Imperio.*" *Latin American Literary Review* 34, no. 67 (2006): 94–110.

Long, Ryan F. *Fictions of Totality: The Mexican Novel, 1968, and the National-Popular State.* West Lafayette: Purdue University Press, 2008.

Sánchez-Prado, Ignacio M. "Dying Mirrors, Medieval Moralists and Tristram Shandies: The Literary Traditions of Fernando del Paso's *Palinuro of Mexico.*" *Comparative Literature* 60, no. 2 (2008): 142–63.

Thomas, Peter N. "Historiographic Metafiction and the Neobaroque in Fernando del Paso's *Noticias del imperio.*" *Indiana Journal of Hispanic Literatures* 6–7 (1995): 169–84.

Manuel Payno

García de la Sierra, Rodrigo. "El cronotopo del autor en *Los bandidos de Río Frío.*" *Literatura Mexicana* 14, no. 1 (2003): 63–86.

Palti, Elías. "Narrar lo inenarrable: literatura, nación y muerte en *El fistol del diablo* de Manuel Payno." *Iberoamericana* 19 (2005): 7–26.

Sandoval, Adriana. "Madres, viudas y vírgenes en *Los bandidos de Río Frío.*" *Literatura Mexicana* 13, no. 1 (2002): 55–88.

Octavio Paz

Fein, John M. *Octavio Paz: A Reading of His Major Poems, 1957–1976.* Lexington: University Press of Kentucky, 1986.
Guberman, Mariluci da Cunha. *Octavio Paz y la estética de transfiguración de la presencia.* Valladolid: Universitas Castellae, 1998.
Hozven, Roberto. *Octavio Paz: viajero del presente.* México, D.F.: Colegio de México, 1994.
Pastén B., and J. Agustín. *Octavio Paz: crítico practicante en busca de una poética.* Madrid: Pliegos, 1999.
Phillips, Rachel. *The Poetic Modes of Octavio Paz.* London: Oxford University Press, 1972.
Quiroga, José. *Understanding Octavio Paz.* Columbia: University of South Carolina Press, 1999.
Underwood, Leticia Iliana. *Octavio Paz and the Language of Poetry: A Psycholinguistic Approach.* New York: Peter Lang, 1992.
Williamson, Rodney. *The Writing in the Stars: A Jungian Reading of the Poetry of Octavio Paz.* Toronto: University of Toronto Press, 2007.
Wilson, Jason. *Octavio Paz.* Boston: Twayne, 1986.

Carlos Pellicer

Moretta, Eugene. "Carlos Pellicer y la poesía de compromiso social." In *Essays in Honor of Frank Dauster,* edited by Kirsten F. Nigro and Sandra M. Cypess, 87–103. Newark, Del.: Juan de la Cuesta, 1995.

Sergio Pitol

Choi, You-Jeong. "Artes en conjunción en la obra de Sergio Pitol." *Espéculo: Revista de Estudios Literarios* 37 (2007–2008): n.p.
Costa, Olga. *Sergio Pitol.* Guanajuato: Gobierno del Estado de Guanajuato, 1983.
García Díaz, Teresa. "Un viaje laberíntico por los mundos de Sergio Pitol." *Texto Crítico* 5, no. 9 (2001): 259–79.
Martínez Morales, José Luis. "La frontera de lo fantástico en la cuentística de Sergio Pitol." *Palabra y el Hombre: Revista de la Universidad Veracruzana* 131 (2004): 55–71.
Montelongo, Alfonso. *Vientres troqueles: la narrativa de Sergio Pitol.* Xalapa: Universidad Veracruzana, 1998.

Elena Poniatowska

Jörgensen, Beth E. *The Writing of Elena Poniatowska: Engaging Dialogues.* Austin: University of Texas Press, 1994.

Medeiros-Lichem, María Teresa. *Reading the Feminine: Voice in Latin American Women's Fiction: From Teresa de la Parra to Elena Poniatowska and Luisa Valenzuela.* New York: Peter Lang, 2002.

Perkowska, Magdalena. *Historias híbridas: la nueva novela histórica latinoamericana (1985–2000) ante las teorías posmodernas de la historia.* Frankfurt: Vervuert, 2008.

Roberts-Camps, Traci. *Gendered Self-Consciousness in Mexican and Chicana Women Writers: The Female Body as an Instrument of Political Resistance.* Lewiston, N.Y.: Mellen, 2008.

Schaefer, Claudia. *Textured Lives: Women, Art, and Representation in Modern Mexico.* Tucson: University of Arizona Press, 1992.

Schuessler, Michael K. *Elena Poniatowska: An Intimate Biography.* Tucson: University of Arizona Press, 2007.

Sklodowska, Elzbieta. *Testimonio hispanoamericano: historia, teoría, poética.* New York: Peter Lang, 1992.

Thornton, Niamh. *Women and the War Story in Mexico: La novela de la Revolución.* Lewiston, N.Y.: Mellen, 2006.

María Luisa Puga

López, Irma M. *Historia, escritura e identidad: la novelística de María Luisa Puga.* New York: Peter Lang, 1996.

Unruh, Vicky. "Puga's Fictions of Equivalence: The Tasks of the Novelist As Translator." In *Voice-Overs: Translation and Latin American Literature,* edited by Daniel Balderston and Marcy Schwartz, 194–203. Albany: State University of New York Press, 2002.

Urrutia, Carlos. "María Luisa Puga: Heroine of Writing." *Voices of Mexico* 73 (2005): 65–72.

Emilio Rabasa

Ramos Escandón, Carmen. "The Novel of Porfirian Mexico: A Historian's Source: Problems and Methods." *Ideologies and Literature: Journal of Hispanic and Lusophone Discourse Analysis* 3, no. 14 (1981): 118–33.

José Revueltas

Murad, Timothy. "Before the Storm: José Revueltas and Beginnings of the New Narrative in Mexico." *Modern Language Studies* 8, no. 1 (1977–1978): 57–64.

Ramírez Santacruz, Francisco, ed. *El terreno de los días: homenaje a José Revueltas.* México, D.F.: Benemérita Universidad Autónoma de Puebla, 2007.

Ruffinelli, Jorge. *Jose Revueltas.* México, D.F.: Universidad Veracruzana, 1977.

Slick, Sam L. *José Revueltas.* Boston: Twayne, 1983.

Alfonso Reyes

Cuspinera, Margarita Vera, ed. *Alfonso Reyes: homenaje de la Facultad de Filosofía y Letras.* México, D.F.: Fondo de Cultura Económica, 1981.

Patout, Paulette. *Alfonso Reyes y Francia.* México, D.F.: Colegio de México, 1990.

Pineda Franco, Adela, and Ignacio M. Sánchez Prado, eds. *Alfonso Reyes y los estudios latinoamericanos.* Pittsburgh, Pa.: Instituto Internacional de Literatura Iberoamericana, University of Pittsburgh, 2004.

Reyes, Alicia. *Genio y figura de Alfonso Reyes.* Buenos Aires: Eudeba, 1976.

Robb, James Willis. "Alfonso Reyes: una bibliografía selecta (1907–1990)." *Revista Iberoamericana* 57, nos. 155–156 (1991): 691–736.

———. *Por los caminos de Alfonso Reyes.* México, D.F.: INBA, 1981.

José Rubén Romero

López, Kimberle S. "Discourse and 'Desire to Be Other' in Picaresque and Testimonial: The Revolution in José Rubén Romero's *La vida inútil de Pito Pérez.*" *Chasqui: Revista de Literatura Latinoamericana* 26, no. 1 (1997): 75–92.

Stone, Robert S. "Pito Pérez: Mexican Middleman." *Mexican Studies/Estudios Mexicanos* 21, no. 2 (2005): 369–402.

Juan Ruiz de Alarcón

Foley, Augusta E. *Occult Arts and Doctrine in the Theater of Juan Ruiz de Alarcón.* Geneva: Droz, 1972.

Parr, James A. *After Its Kind: Approaches to the comedia.* Kassel: Reichenberger, 1991.

Poesse, Walter. *Juan Ruiz de Alarcón.* New York: Twayne, 1972.
Vargas de Luna, Javier. *Las dos ciudades de Juan Ruiz de Alarcón.* Puebla: Universidad de las Américas Puebla, 2006.

Juan Rulfo

Fares, Gustavo C. *Juan Rulfo: la lengua, el tiempo y el espacio.* Buenos Aires: Almagesto, 1994.
Giacoman, Helmy F., ed. *Homenaje a Juan Rulfo: variaciones interpretativas en torno a su obra.* Long Island City: Anaya-Las Americas, 1974.
González Boixo, José Carlos. *Claves narrativas de Juan Rulfo.* León: Universidad de León, 1984.
Jiménez de Baez, Yvette. *Juan Rulfo, del páramo a la esperanza.* Mexico City: Fondo de Cultura Económica, 1990.
Leal, Luis. *Juan Rulfo.* Boston: Twayne, 1983.
López Mena, Sergio. *Los caminos de la creación en Juan Rulfo.* Mexico City: Universidad Nacional Autónoma de México, 1993.
Lorente-Murphy, Silvia. *Juan Rulfo: realidad y mito de la revolución mexicana.* Madrid: Pliegos, 1988.
Portal, Magda. *Rulfo: dinámica de la violencia.* Madrid: Ediciones Cultura Hispánica, 1984.
Ruffinelli, Jorge. *El lugar de Rulfo y otros ensayos.* Xalapa: Universidad Veracruzana, 1980.

Jaime Sabines

Argüelles, Juan Domingo. "Jaime Sabines and Poetic Emotion." *Voices of Mexico* 48 (1999): 102–04.
Barrera Parrilla, Beatriz . "Cyborgs inmortales y trogloditas enamoradas: antropología de Jaime Sabines." *Revista de Crítica Literaria Latinoamericana* 31, no. 61 (2005): 131–50.
Guedea, Rogelio. "Jaime Sabines: la palabra en el tiempo." *Hispamérica: Revista de Literatura* 34, no. 101 (2005): 15–24.
Plasencia Saavedra, Mónica. "Jaime Sabines y la Biblia." *Literatura Mexicana* 16, no. 1 (2005): 89–103.

Bernardino de Sahagún

Quiñones Keber, Eloise, ed. *Representing Aztec Ritual: Performance, Text, and Images in the Work of Sahagún.* Boulder: University Press of Colorado, 2002.

Schwaller, John Frederick, ed. *Sahagún at 500: Essays on the Quincentenary of the Birth of Fr. Bernardino de Sahagún*. Berkeley, Calif.: Academy of American Franciscan History, 2003.

Gustavo Sainz

Fernández, Salvador C. *Gustavo Sainz: Postmodernism in the Mexican Novel*. New York: Peter Lang, 1999.

Hancock, Joel. "Re-Defining Autobiography: Gustavo Sainz's *A la salud de la serpiente*." *Revista de Estudios Hispánicos* 29, no. 1 (1995): 139–52.

Oram, Lydia Miranda. "Constructing the Hybrid/Transcultural Subject: Interpellating Tradition through Translation in Gustavo Sáinz's *Gazapo*." *Metamorphoses: Journal of the Five-College Seminar on Literary Translation* 16, no. 1 (2008): 54–72.

Swanson, Philip. "Only Joking? Gustavo Sainz and *La princesa del palacio de hierro*: Funniness, Identity and the Post-Boom." *Studies in Twentieth Century Literature* 19, no. 1 (1995): 101–15.

Guillermo Schmidhuber de la Mora

Martínez, Christine D. "El valor de la libertad en el teatro de Guillermo Schmidhuber de la Mora." *Latin American Theatre Review* 24, no. 1 (1990): 29–39.

Montañez, Carmen. "Guillermo Schmidhuber: el dramaturgo y su obra." *Ariel* 8 (1992): 56–62.

Justo Sierra O'Reilly

Gerassi-Navarro, Nina. *Pirate Novels: Fictions of Nation Building in Spanish America*. Durham, N.C.: Duke University Press, 1999.

Solares-Larrave, Francisco. "Texts, History and Narrative Discourse in Two 19th-Century Spanish American Historical Novels." *Latin American Literary Review* 31, no. 61 (2003): 58–78.

Carlos de Sigüenza y Góngora

Graniela-Rodríguez, Magda. "Of Listeners, Narrative Voices, Readers and Narratees: The Structural Interlock of *Infortunios de Alonso Ramírez* by Carlos de Sigüenza y Góngora." *Readerly/Writerly Texts: Essays on Literature, Literary/Textual Criticism, and Pedagogy* 1, no. 2 (1994): 127–38.

López, Kimberle S. "Identity and Alterity in the Emergence of a Creole Discourse: Sigüenza y Góngora's *Infortunios de Alonso Ramírez.*" *Colonial Latin American Review* 5, no. 2 (1996): 253–76.

Ross, Kathleen. "Carlos de Sigüenza y Góngora y la cultura del Barroco hispanoamericano." In *Relecturas del Barroco de Indias,* edited by Mabel Moraña, 223–43. Hanover, N.H.: Ediciones del Norte, 1994.

Luis Spota

Manzo-Robledo, Francisco. "Reading the Other Side of the Story: Ominous Voice and the Sociocultural and Political Implications of Luis Spota's *Murieron a mitad del río.*" *Studies in Twentieth Century Literature* 25, no. 1 (2001): 173–95.

Pouwels, Joel B. "Luis Spota Revisited: An Overview of His Narrative Art." *Revista Hispánica Moderna* 47, no. 2 (1994): 421–35.

José Juan Tablada

Bohn, Willard. "The Visual Trajectory of José Juan Tablada." *Hispanic Review* 69, no. 2 (2001): 191–208.

Hernández Palacios, Esther. "José Juan Tablada: tradición y modernidad." *Texto Crítico* 5, no. 9 (2001): 103–17.

Lara Velázquez, Esperanza. *La iniciación poética de José Juan Tablada.* México, D.F.: Universidad Nacional Autónoma de México, 1988.

Mendieta Alatorre, Ángeles. *Tablada y la gran época de la transformación cultural.* México, D.F.: Secretaría de Educación Pública, 1966.

Tanabe, Atsuko. *El japonismo de José Juan Tablada.* México, D.F.: Universidad Nacional Autónoma de México, 1981.

Paco Ignacio Taibo II

Hernández Martín, Jorge. "Paco Ignacio Taibo II: Post-Colonialism and the Detective Story in Mexico." In *The Post-Colonial Detective,* edited by Ed Christian, 159–75. Basingstoke: Palgrave, 2001.

Hunt, Daniel P. "Allegories of Power in Two Historical Novels of Paco Ignacio Taibo II." *Selecta: Journal of the Pacific Northwest Council on Foreign Languages* 16 (1995): 13–18.

Lake, Darlene M. "Of Borders and Bad Guys: Transculturalism and National Identity in Two Novels of Detection by Paco Ignacio Taibo II." *Nueva Literatura Hispánica* 5–7 (2001–2003): 77–92.

Jaime Torres Bodet

Karsen, Sonja P. *Jaime Torres Bodet*. New York: Twayne, 1971.

Rodolfo Usigli

Beardsell, Peter R. *A Theatre for Cannibals: Rodolfo Usigli and the Mexican Stage*. Rutherford, N.J.: Fairleigh Dickinson University Press, 1992.

Cohen, Deb. "Usigli's *Medio tono* and the Transition to Modern Mexican Theatre." *Latin American Theatre Review* 35, no. 1 (2001): 63–74.

Foster, David William. *Estudios sobre teatro méxicano contemporáneo: semiología de la competencia teatral*. New York: Peter Lang, 1984.

Gann, Myra S. "*El gesticulador*: Tragedy or Didactic Play?" *Inti: Revista de Literatura Hispánica* 32–33 (1990–1991): 148–57.

Artemio de Valle Arizpe

Olea Franco, Rafael. "Estéticas narrativas de la década de 1920: Azuela y Valle-Arizpe." *Literatura Mexicana* 12, no. 2 (2001): 67–96.

José Vasconcelos

De Beer, Gabriella. *José Vasconcelos and His World*. New York: Las Américas, 1966.

Fell, Claude. *José Vasconcelos: los años del águila, 1920–1925*. México, D.F.: Universidad Nacional Autónoma de México, 1989.

Haddox, John H. *Vasconcelos of Mexico, Philosopher and Prophet*. Austin: University of Texas Press, 1967.

Miller, Marilyn Grace. *Rise and Fall of the Cosmic Race: The Cult of Mestizaje in Latin America*. Austin: University of Texas Press, 2004.

Ochoa, John A. *The Uses of Failure in Mexican Literature and Identity*. Austin: University of Texas Press, 2004.

Robles, Martha. *Entre el poder y las letras: Vasconcelos en sus memorias*. México, D.F.: Fondo de Cultura Económica, 1989.

Maruxa Vilalta

Bearse, Grace. "Maruxa Vilalta: Social Dramatist." *Revista de Estudios Hispánicos* 18, no. 3 (1984): 399–406.

Holzapfel, Tamara. "The Theatre of Maruxa Vilalta: A Triumph of Versatility." *Latin American Theatre Review* 14, no. 2 (1981): 11–18.

Magnarelli, Sharon. "Maruxa Vilalta: una voz en el desierto." In *Latin American Women Dramatists: Theater, Texts, and Theories,* edited by Catherine Larson and Margarita Vargas, 23–40. Bloomington: Indiana University Press, 1998.

——. "Women and Revolution: Maruxa Vilalta's *1910.*" *Latin American Theatre Review* 37, no. 1 (2003): 5–23.

Solórzano, Carlos. "El teatro de Maruxa Vilalta." *Latin American Theatre Review* 18, no. 2 (1985): 83–87.

Xavier Villaurrutia

Dauster, Frank N. *Xavier Villaurrutia.* New York: Twayne, 1971.

Forster, Merlin H. *Fire and Ice: The Poetry of Xavier Villaurrutia.* Chapel Hill: University of North Carolina Press, 1976.

Irwin, Robert McKee. "As Invisible as He Is: The Queer Enigma of Xavier Villaurrutia." In *Reading and Writing the Ambiente: Queer Sexualities in Latino, Latin American, and Spanish Culture,* edited by Susana Chávez-Silverman and Librada Hernández, 114–46. Madison: University of Wisconsin Press, 2000.

Moretta, Eugene. *La poesía de Xavier Villaurrutia.* México, D.F.: Fondo de Cultura Económica, 1976.

Paz, Octavio. *Xavier Villaurrutia en persona y en obra.* México, D.F.: Fondo de Cultura Económica, 1978.

Weinberger, Eliot, ed. *Nostalgia for Death: Poetry by Xavier Villaurrutia and Hieroglyphs of Desire: A Critical Study of Villaurrutia by Octavio Paz.* Port Townsend, Wash.: Copper Canyon, 1992.

Agustín Yáñez

Detjens, Wilma Else. *Home as Creation: The Influence of Early Childhood Experience in the Literary Creation of Gabriel García Márquez, Agustín Yáñez and Juan Rulfo.* New York: Peter Lang, 1993.

Giacoman, Helmy F., ed. *Homenaje a Agustín Yáñez: variaciones interpretativas en torno a su obra.* New York: Las Américas, 1973.

Harris, Christopher. *The Novels of Agustín Yáñez: A Critical Portrait of Mexico in the Twentieth Century.* Lewiston, N.Y.: The Edwin Mellen Press, 2000.

Jiménez de Báez, Yvette, and Rafael Olea Franco, eds. *Memoria e interpretación de "Al filo del agua."* México, D.F.: El Colegio de México, 2000.

Marquet, Antonio. *Archipiélago dorado: el despegue creador en la obra narrativa de Agustín Yáñez.* Azcapotzalco: Universidad Autónoma Metropolitana, Azcapotzalco, 1997.

Olea Franco, Rafael, ed. *Agustín Yáñez: una vida literaria.* Mexico: El Colegio de México, 2007.
Young, Richard A. *Agustín Yáñez y sus cuentos.* London: Támesis, 1978.

NICARAGUA

Resources: Anthologies

Aldaraca, Bridget, *et al,* eds. *Nicaragua in Revolution: the poets speak / Nicaragua en revolución: los poetas hablan.* Minneapolis, Minn.: Marxist Educational Press, 1980.
Antologia del cuento nicaragüense Managua. Managua: Club del Libro Nicaragüense, 1957.
Arellano, Jorge Eduardo. *Literatura nicaragüense.* Managua: Ediciones Distribuidora Cultural, 1997.
Obando Sancho, Víctor, *et al,* eds. *Antología poética de la Costa Caribe de Nicaragua.* Managua: URACCAN, 1998.
Ramírez, Sergio, ed. *Cuento nicaraguense* [anthology]. Buenos Aires: Editorial Nueva America, 1985.
White, Steven F., ed. *Poets of Nicaragua: a Bilingual Anthology 1918–1979.* Greensboro, N.C.: Unicorn Press, 1982.

Select Bibliography for Specific Writers

Gioconda Belli

Barbas-Rhoden, Laura. *Writing Women in Central America: Gender and the Fictionalization of History.* Athens: Ohio University Press, 2003.
Craft, Linda J. *Novels of Testimony and Resistance from Central America.* Gainesville: University Press of Florida, 1997.
Dawes, Greg. *Aesthetics and Revolution: Nicaraguan Poetry, 1979–1990.* Minneapolis: University of Minnesota Press, 1993.
González, Ana. "Transgressing Limits: Belli's *El taller de las mariposas.*" *Ciberletras* 17 (2007): n.p.
March, Kathleen. "Engendering the Political Novel: Gioconda Belli's *La mujer habitada.*" In *Women Writers in Twentieth-Century Spain and Spanish America,* edited by Catherine Davies. Lewiston, N.Y.: Mellen, 1993.
Moyano, Pilar. "The Transformation of Nation and Womanhood: Revisionist Mythmaking in the Poetry of Nicaragua's Gioconda Belli." In *Interventions: Feminist Dialogues on Third World Women's Literature and Film,* edited by Bishnupriya Ghosh and Brinda Bose, 79–95. New York: Garland, 1997.

Richards, Timothy A. B. "Resistance and Liberation: The Mythic Voice and Textual Authority in Belli's *La mujer habitada*." In *Critical Essays on the Literatures of Spain and Spanish America,* edited by Luis T. González-del-Valle and Julio Baena, 209–14. Boulder, Colo.: Society of Spanish and Spanish-American Studies, 1991.

Rodríguez, Ileana. *House/Garden/Nation: Space, Gender, and Ethnicity in Post-Colonial Latin American Literatures by Women.* Durham, N.C.: Duke University Press, 1994.

Omar Cabezas

Ross, Peter. "Between Fiction and History: Omar Cabezas's *La montaña es algo más que una inmensa estepa verde.*" In *War and Revolution in Hispanic Literature,* edited by Roy Boland and Alun Kenwood, 97–108. Melbourne: Voz Hispánica, 1990.

Ernesto Cardenal

Barrow, Geoffrey R. "Divine Praises in Ernesto Cardenal." *Neophilologus* 83, no. 4 (1999): 559–75.

Borgeson, Jr, Paul W. *Hacia el hombre nuevo: poesía y pensamiento de Ernesto Cardenal.* London: Támesis, 1984.

Calabrese, Elisa, ed. *Ernesto Cardenal: poeta de la liberación latinoamericana.* Buenos Aires: García Cambeiro, 1975.

DeHay, Terry. "The Kingdom of God on Earth: Ernesto Cardenal's *Salmos.*" In *Postcolonial Literature and the Biblical Call for Justice,* edited by Susan VanZanten Gallagher, 48–59. Jackson: University Press of Mississippi, 1994.

Jiménez, Luis A. "Bibliography of Criticism: Ernesto Cardenal: 1980–1992." *Ometeca* 2, no. 2 (1991): 135–39.

Kauffmann, Ruth A. "Ernesto Cardenal's *Cántico cósmico*: A Vision for the Future." *Confluencia: Revista Hispánica de Cultura y Literatura* 11, no. 2 (1996): 3–18.

Olivera, Sonia Mereles. *Cumbres poéticas latinoamericanas: Nicanor Parra y Ernesto Cardenal.* New York: Peter Lang, 2003.

Pring-Mill, Robert. "Cardenal's Treatment of Amerindian Cultures in *Homenaje a los indios americanos.*" *Renaissance & Modern Studies* 35 (1992): 52–74.

Urdanivia Bertarelli, Eduardo. *La poesía de Ernesto Cardenal: cristianismo y revolución.* Lima: Latinoamericana Editores, 1984.

José Coronel Urtecho

Arellano, Jorge Eduardo. "Bibliografía básica de José Coronel Urtecho." *Encuentro: Revista de la Universidad Centroamericana* 9 (1976): 129–32.

Arellano, Jorge E. "La poesía de José Coronel Urtecho." *Cuadernos Hispanoamericanos: Revista Mensual de Cultura Hispánica* 277–278 (1973): 307–17.

Oviedo, José Miguel. "Nicaragua: Voices in Conflict." *Review: Latin American Literature and Arts* 31 (1982): 19–25.

White, Steven F. "Translation in Nicaraguan Poetry as a Literary Weapon against Imperialism." *Translation Perspectives* 6 (1991): 165–71.

Pablo Antonio Cuadra

Chen Sham, Jorge, ed. *Volver . . . a la fuente del canto: Actas del I Simposio Internacional de Poesía Nicaragüense del Siglo XX (Homenaje a Pablo Antonio Cuadra)*. Managua: Asociación Pablo Antonio Cuadra, 2005.

Fuentes Aburto, Moisés Elías. "Pablo Antonio Cuadra y Ernesto Cardenal: mito y épica de la nicaraguanidad." *Cuadernos Americanos* 20, no. 1 (2006): 169–79.

Guardia, Gloria. "Pablo Antonio Cuadra: poeta y pensador cristiano." *Cuadernos Americanos* 16, no. 6 (2002): 146–64.

Layera, Ramón "De la vanguardia al teatro nicaragüense actual: valoración de Pablo Antonio Cuadra." *Revista Iberoamericana* 57, no. 157 (1991): 1033–41.

Oviedo, José Miguel. "Nicaragua: Voices in Conflict." *Review: Latin American Literature and Arts* 31 (1982): 19–25.

White, Steven F. *El mundo más que humano en la poesía de Pablo Antonio Cuadra: un estudio ecocrítico*. Managua: Asociación Pablo Antonio Cuadra, 2002.

Rubén Darío

Acereda, Alberto. *Ruben Darío, poeta trágico: una nueva visión*. Barcelona: Teide, 1992.

Bourne, Louis. *Fuerza invisible: lo divino en la poesía de Rubén Darío*. Málaga: Universidad de Málaga, 1999.

Ellis, Keith. *Critical Approaches to Rubén Darío*. Toronto: University of Toronto Press, 1974.

Fraser, Howard M. *In the Presence of Mystery: Modernist Fiction and the Occult*. Chapel Hill: Department of Romance Languagess, University of North Carolina, 1992.

Ingwersen, Sonya A. *Light and Longing: Silva and Darío: Modernism and Religious Heterodoxy.* New York: Peter Lang, 1986.

Martínez Domingo, José María. *Los espacios poéticos de Rubén Darío.* New York: Peter Lang, 1995.

Pérez, Alberto Julián. *La poética de Rubén Darío: crisis post-romantica y modelos literarios modernistas.* Madrid: Orígenes, 1992.

Rama, Ángel. *Rubén Darío y el Modernismo (circunstancia socioeconómica de un arte americano).* Caracas: Biblioteca de la Universidad Central de Venezuela, 1970.

Schulman, Iván A., ed. *Recreaciones: ensayos sobre la obra de Rubén Darío.* Hanover, N.H.: Ediciones del Norte, 1992.

Skryme, Raymond. *Rubén Darío and the Pythagorean Tradition.* Gainesville: University Presses of Florida, 1975.

Urbina, Nicasio, ed. *Miradas críticas sobre Rubén Darío.* Managua: Fundación Internacional Rubén Darío, 2005.

Watland, Charles D. *Poet-Errant: A Biography of Rubén Darío.* New York: Philosophical Library, 1965.

Zavala, Iris M., ed. *Rubén Darío: el modernismo.* Madrid: Alianza, 1989.

Joaquín Pasos

Unruh, Vicky. "The *Chinfonía burguesa*: A Linguistic Manifesto of Nicaragua's Avant-Garde." *Latin American Theatre Review* 20, no. 2 (1987): 37–48.

White, Steven. "Breve retrato de Joaquín Pasos." *Inti: Revista de Literatura Hispánica* 21 (1985): 67–73.

Yúdice, George. "Poemas de un joven que quiso ser otro." *Inti: Revista de Literatura Hispánica* 18–19 (1983–1984): 1–25.

Sergio Ramírez

Cabrera, Enriqueta. "Sergio Ramírez: Between Reality and Fiction." *Américas* 58, no. 5 (2006): 10–15.

Henighan, Stephen. "History after History's End: Cultural Reconstruction in *Margarita, está linda la mar.* In *Latin American Narratives and Cultural Identity: Selected Readings,* edited by Irene Maria F. Blayer and Mark Cronlund Anderson, 62–74. New York: Peter Lang, 2004.

Polit-Dueñas, Gabriela. "When Politicans Construct Father-Wor(l)ds. Sergio Ramírez's *Adiós Muchachos.*" *Romance Notes* 44, no. 2 (2003): 163–72.

Ross, Peter. "The Politician as Novelist: Sergio Ramírez's *Castigo divino*." *Antípodas: Journal of Hispanic Studies of the University of Auckland and La Trobe University* 3 (1991): 165–75.

Salomón de la Selva

Rosenstein, Roy. "Nicaraguan Poet as Wandering Jew: Salomón de la Selva and 'Mi primer judío.'" *Latin American Literary Review* 18, no. 35 (1990): 59–70.
White, Steven F. "Salomón de la Selva: poeta comprometido de la 'otra' vanguardia." *Revista Iberoamericana* 57, no. 157 (1991): 915–21.

Daisy Zamora

Jiménez, Luis A. "Una mirada al cuerpo en los textos poéticos de Daisy Zamora." In *Afrodita en el trópico: erotismo y construcción del sujeto femenino en obras de autoras centroamericanas*, edited by Oralia Preble-Niemi, 123–32. Potomac, Md.: Scripta Humanistica, 1999.
Ogden, Estrella. "La cuestión femenina en la poesía de Daisy Zamora." In *Volver . . . a la fuente del canto: Actas del I Simposio Internacional de Poesía Nicaragüense del Siglo XX (Homenaje a Pablo Antonio Cuadra)*, edited by Jorge Chen Sham, 355–63. Managua: Asociación Pablo Antonio Cuadra, 2005.

PANAMA

Resources: Enclyclopedias, Dictionaries, Histories, Anthologies

Garcia, S. Ismael. *Historia de la literatura panameña*. México, D.F.: Universidad Nacional Autónoma de México, 1972.
Jaramillo Levi, Enrique, ed. *Poesía panameña contemporánea (1929–1979)*. México, D.F.: Liberta-Sumaria, 1980.
Miró, Rodrigo. *Itinerario de la poesía en Panamá (1502–1974)*. Panama City: Editorial Universitaria, 1974.
———. *La literatura panameña (origen y proceso)*. San José, Costa Rica: Imprenta Trejos Hermanos, 1972.

Select Bibliography for Specific Writers

Rosa María Britton

López Cruz, Humberto, ed. *Rosa María Britton ante la crítica*. Madrid: Verbum, 2007.

Darío Herrera

Jiménez, Luis A. "Darío Herrera, poeta panameño modernista." In *Encuentro con la literatura panameña*, edited by Humberto López Cruz, 93–108. Panama: Círculo de Lectura de la Universidad Católica Santa María La Antigua, 2003.
———. "Remapping 'modernista' Aesthetics in Darío Herrera's 'Intangible.'" *Diáspora: Journal of the Annual Afro-Hispanic Literature and Culture Conference* 13 (2003): 62–67.

Enrique Jaramillo Levi

Aguilar, Alfredo, ed. *Puertas y ventanas: acercamientos a la obra literaria de Enrique Jaramillo Levi*. San José: Editorial Universitaria Centroamericana, 1990.
Birmingham-Pokorny, Elba D., ed. *Critical Perspectives in Enrique Jaramillo-Levi's Work: A Collection of Critical Essays*. Miami, Fla.: Universal, 1996.
Hoeg, Jerry. "Enrique Jaramillo Levi Looks at Writing and Being Written in *Caracol y otros cuentos*." *Diáspora: Journal of the Annual Afro-Hispanic Literature and Culture Conference* 13 (2003): 22–32.
Santiago-Stommes, Ivelisse. "Reflections of Metafiction in *Duplications and Other Stories* by Enrique Jaramillo-Levi." *Diáspora: Journal of the Annual Afro-Hispanic Literature and Culture Conference* 13 (2003): 16–21.

Ricardo Miró

Espino Barahona, Erasto Antonio. "'Patria', de Ricardo Miró o el país como memoria afectiva." *Espéculo: Revista de Estudios Literarios* 31 (2005–2006): n.p.
Gewecke, Frauke. "La heterogeneidad como rasgo fundamental de la modernidad y del Modernismo hispanoamericanos: *Las noches de Babel* de Ricardo Miró." In *La modernidad revis(it)ada: literatura y cultura latinoamericanas de los siglos XIX y XX*, edited by Inke Gunia, Katharina Niemeyer, Sabine Schlickers, and Hans Paschen, 168–82. Berlin: Tranvía, 2000.

Rogelio Sinán

Chen Sham, Jorge. "La vivencia de la culpa y la mostración de lo neofantástico en 'La boina roja' de Rogelio Sinán." *Diáspora: Journal of the Annual Afro-Hispanic Literature and Culture Conference* 13 (2003): 45–53.
Espener, Maida Watson. "Notes on the Theme of the Black in the Literary Creation of Rogelio Sinán." In *Homenaje a Lydia Cabrera*, edited by Reinaldo Sánchez, José Antonio Madrigal, and José Sánchez-Boudy, 259–63. Miami, Fla.: Ediciones Universal, 1978.
Jaramillo Levi, Enrique. "El Rogelio Sinán que recordará la historia." *Confluencia: Revista Hispánica de Cultura y Literatura* 8–9, nos. 2–1 (1993): 7–11.

PARAGUAY

Resources: Dictionaries, Histories, Anthologies

Amaral, Raúl. *El modernismo poético en el Paraguay (1901–1916)*. Asuncion: Alcándara, 1982.
———. *El romanticismo paraguayo 1860–1910*. Asuncion: Alcándara, 1985.
Bareiro Saguier, Rubén, *et al. Literatura guaraní del Paraguay*. Asunción: Servilibro, 2004.
Delgado, Susy, ed. *25 nombres capitales de la literatura paraguaya*. Asunción: Servilibro, 2005.
Díaz Pérez, Viriato. *Literatura del Paraguay*. Palma de Mallorca: Luis Ripoll, 1980.
Luis María Martínez. *El trino soterrado: Paraguay, aproximación al itinerario de su poesía social* [anthology]. Asunción: Ediciones Intento, 1985–1986.
Pecci, Antonio. *Teatro breve del Paraguay* [anthology]. Asunción: Ediciones NAPA, 1981.
Peiró, José Vicente. *La narrativa paraguaya actual: 1980–1995*. Asunción: Uninorte, 2006.
Pérez-Maricevich, Francisco. *Diccionario de la literatura paraguaya*. Asunción: Instituto Colorado de Cultura, 1984.
Rodríguez-Alcalá, Hugo. *Historia de la literatura paraguaya*. Asunción: Editorial El Lector, 1999.
Suárez, Victorio V. *Literatura paraguaya, 1900–2000: expresiones de los representantes contemporáneos*. Asunción: Servilibro, 2001.
———. *Proceso de la literatura paraguaya: perfil histórico, bibliografía y entrevistas a los más destacados escritores paraguayos*. Asunción: Criterio Ediciones, 2006.

Teresa Méndez-Faith, ed. *Antología de la literatura paraguaya*. Asunción: El Lector, 2004.

———. *Teatro paraguayo de ayer y de hoy*. 2 vols. Asunción: Intercontinental Editora, 2001.

Select Bibliography for Specific Writers

Rubén Bareiro Saguier

Basson, Helene C. "The Legacy of Guaraní in the Fiction of Gabriel Casaccia, Rubén Bareiro Saguier and Augusto Roa Bastos." *Mester* 24, no. 2 (1995): 65–80.

Navarro, Felipe. "El ave de vuelo mestizo: aproximación a la poesía de Rubén Bareiro Saguier." *Hispamérica: Revista de Literatura* 17, no. 49 (1988): 101–6.

Weldt, Helene. "Cases of Ambiguity in Rubén Bareiro Saguier's *Ojo por diente*." *Hispanófila* 36, no. 1 (1992): 41–57.

Hérib Campos Cervera

Reyes, Juan José. "Campos Cervera: escritor militante." *Discurso Literario: Revista de Temas Hispánicos* 1, no. 2 (1984): 289–93.

Gabriel Casaccia

Collmer, Robert G. "The Displaced Person in the Novels of Gabriel Casaccia." *RE: Artes Liberales* 3, no. 2 (1970): 37–46.

Feito, Francisco E. *El Paraguay en la obra de Gabriel Casaccia*. Buenos Aires: Garcia Cambeiro, 1977.

Méndez-Faith, Teresa. "Exilio y estructuración espacio-temporal en la novelística de Gabriel Casaccia." *Escritura: Revista de Teoría y Crítica Literarias* 8, no. 16 (1983): 179–90.

Rodríguez-Alcalá, Hugo. "Introducción al estudio de la novelística de Gabriel Casaccia." *Nueva Narrativa Hispanoamericana* 4 (1974): 91–103.

Julio Correa

Bogado, Víctor. "Julio Correa (1890–1953), dramaturgo paraguayo comprometido con su realidad social." *Dramateatro Revista Digital* 11 (2004): n.p.

Ruy Díaz de Guzmán

Guérin, Miguel Alberto. "Discurso histórico y discurso ficcional en *La Argentina*, de Ruy Díaz de Guzman." *Río de la Plata: Culturas* 11–12 (1991): 67–76.
Marcos, Juan Manuel. "Ruy Díaz de Guzmán in the Context of Paraguayan Colonial Literature." *MLN* 102, no. 2 (1987): 387–92.

Josefina Plá

Larson, Catherine. *Games and Play in the Theater of Spanish American Women*. Lewisburg, Pa.: Bucknell University Press, 2004.
Mateo del Pino, Ángeles. "En la piel de la mujer: un recorrido por la cuentística de Josefina Plá." *Philologica Canariensia: Revista de Filología de la Universidad de las Palmas de Gran Canaria* (1994): 281–97.
Rodríguez-Alcalá, Hugo. "Josefina Plá y la poesía." *Papeles de Son Armadans* 58 (1970): 19–64.
Steckbauer, Sonja M. "La 'paraguayidad' en la cuentística de Josefina Plá." In *Dos orillas y un encuentro: la literatura paraguaya actual*, edited by Mar Langa Pizarro, 235–47. Alicante: Centro de Estudios Iberoamericanos Mario Benedetti, Universidad de Alicante, 2005.

Augusto Roa Bastos

Battiliana, Carlos. *Reflexiones sobre "Hijo de hombre" de Augusto Roa Bastos*. Frankfurt: Lang, 1979.
Bergero, Adriana J. *El debate político: modernidad, poder y disidencia en Yo el Supremo de Augusto Roa Bastos*. New York: Peter Lang, 1994.
Burgos, Fernando, ed. *Las voces del karaí: estudios sobre Augusto Roa Bastos*. Madrid: Edelsa-Edi 6, 1988.
Foster, David William. *Augusto Roa Bastos*. Boston: Twayne; 1978.
Giacoman, Helmy F. *Homenaje a Augusto Roa Bastos: variaciones interpretativas en torno a su obra*. Long Island City: Anaya-Las Americas, 1973.
Marcos, Juan Manuel. *Roa Bastos, precursor del post-boom*. Mexico City: Katún, 1983.
Sosnowski, Saúl, ed. *Augusto Roa Bastos y la producción cultural americana*. Buenos Aires: Ediciones de la Flor, 1986.
Weldt-Basson, Helene Carol. *Augusto Roa Bastos's "I The Supreme": A Dialogic Perspective*. Columbia: University of Missouri Press, 1993.

Elvio Romero

Peiró Barco, José Vicente. "Elvio Romero, Rubén Bareiro Saguier, Renée Ferrer, Jacobo Rauskin: calas de la poesía paraguaya." In *Dos orillas y un encuentro: la literatura paraguaya actual*, edited by Mar Langa Pizarro, 193–210. Alicante: Centro de Estudios Iberoamericanos Mario Benedetti, Universidad de Alicante, 2005.

Szanto, Endre Fulei. "Realidad e ilusión en los poemas de Elvio Romero." In *Actas del simposio internacional de estudios hispánicos: Budapest, 18–19 de agosto de 1976*, edited by Matyas Horanyi, 277–83. Budapest: Akademia Kiado, 1978.

PERU

Resources: Bibliographies, Dictionaries, Histories, Anthologies

Aldrich, Earl M., Jr. *The Modern Short Story in Perú*. Madison: University of Wisconsin Press, 1966.

Bendezú, Edmundo. *La novela peruana: de Olavide a Bryce*. Lima: Editorial Lumen, 1992.

Castro Urioste, José, and Roberto Ángeles. *Dramaturgia Peruana* [anthology]. Lima: Latinoamericana Editores, 1999.

Chang-Rodríguez, Raquel, ed. *Cancionero peruano del siglo XVII*. Lima: La Católica, 1983.

Foster, David William. *Peruvian Literature: A Bibliography of Secondary Sources*. Westport, Conn.: Greenwood Press, 1981.

García-Bedoya Maguiña, Carlos. *Para una periodizacíon de la literatura peruana*. Lima: Latinoamericana Editores, 1990.

González Vigil, Ricardo, ed. *Poesía peruana siglo XX*. 2 vols. Lima: Petroperú, Ediciones COPÉ, 1999.

Hesse Murga, José, ed. *Teatro peruano contemporáneo* [anthology]. Madrid: Aguilar 1963.

Higgins, James. *A History of Peruvian Literature*. Liverpool: Cairns, 1987.

———. *Hitos de la poesía peruana: siglo XX*. Lima: Milla Batres, 1993.

Ruiz-Ortega, Gabriel. *Disidentes: muestra de la nueva narrativa peruana* [anthology]. Lima: Revuelta Editores, 2007.

Sánchez, Luis Alberto. *La literatura peruana: derrotero para una historia cultural del Perú*. 5 vols. Lima: Editorial de Ediventas, 1965.

Sologuren, Javier, ed. *Antología general de la literatura peruana*. México, D.F.: Fondo de Cultura Económica, 1981.

——. *Poesía del Perú: de la época precolombina al modernismo.* Buenos Aires: Editorial Universitaria de Buenos Aires, 1977.

Toro Montalvo, César. *Manual de literatura peruana.* Lima: A.F.A. Editores, 1990.

Watson, María Isabel. *El cuadro de costumbres en el Perú decimonónico.* Lima: La Católica, 1979.

Yáñez, Luis, *Cuentos peruanos.* 2 vols. Lima: Editorial Universo, 1972.

Select Bibliography for Specific Writers

Martín Adán

Bendezú, Edmundo. *La poética de Martín Adán.* Lima, 1969.

Kinsella, John M. *Tradición, modernidad y silencio: el mundo creativo de Martín Adán.* Oxford: University of Mississippi, Department of Modern Languages, 2001.

Sobrevilla, David. "De lo barroco en el Perú de Martín Adán." *Lienzo: Revista de la Universidad de Lima* 19 (1998): 305–56.

Verani, Hugo J. "*La casa de cartón* de Martín Adán y el relato vanguardista hispanoamericano." In *Actas del X Congreso de la Asociación de Hispanistas.* 4 vols, edited by Antonio Vilanova, IV: 1077–84. Barcelona: Promociones y Publicaciones Universitarias, 1992.

Weller, Hubert P. "The Poetry of Martín Adán." In *Romance Literary Studies: Homage to Harvey L. Johnson,* edited by Marie A. Wellington and Martha O'Nan, 151–60. Potomac, Md.: Porrúa Turanzas, 1979.

Alonso Alegría

Luchting, Wolfgang A. "Optimism as Rite de passage? Alonso Alegría's *El cruce sobre el Niagara.*" *Research Studies* 47 (1979): 253–61.

Morris, Robert J. "Alonso Alegría: Dramatist and Theatrical Activist." *Latin American Theatre Review* 9, no. 2 (1976): 49–55.

Ciro Alegría

Marcone, Jorge. "Del retorno a lo natural: *La serpiente de oro,* la 'novela de la selva' y la crítica ecológica." *Hispania: A Journal Devoted to the Teaching of Spanish and Portuguese* 81, no. 2 (1998): 299–308.

Rodriguez-Florido, Jorge J. "Bibliografía de y sobre Ciro Alegría." *Chasqui: Revista de Literatura Latinoamericana* 4, no. 3 (1975): 23–54.

——. "Ciro Alegría y el tema negra." *Afro-Hispanic Review* 6, no. 1 (1987): 3–8.

Rodriguez-Peralta, Phyllis. "Ciro Alegria: Culmination of Indigenist-Regionalism in Peru." *Journal of Spanish Studies: Twentieth Century* 7 (1979): 337–52.

Vilariño de Olivieri, Matilde. *La novelística de Ciro Alegría. San Juan,* Puerto Rico: Editorial Universitaria, 1980.

Zubizarreta, Armando. "Realidad y ficción en *Los perros hambrientos* de Ciro Alegría." *Revista de Crítica Literaria Latinoamericana* 24, no. 48 (1998): 159–72.

José María Arguedas

Columbus, Charlotte Kemper. *Mythological Consciousness and the Future: José María Arguedas.* New York: Peter Lang, 1986.

Forgues, Roland, ed. *Arguedas y "Los ríos profundos."* Toulouse: Presse Universitaire du Mirail, 2004.

Franco, Sergio R., ed. *José María Arguedas: hacia una poética migrante.* Pittsburgh, Pa.: Instituto Internacional de Literatura Iberoamericana, University of Pittsburgh, 2006.

Lambright, Anne. *Creating the Hybrid Intellectual: Subject, Space, and the Feminine in the Narrative of José María Arguedas.* Lewisburg, Pa.: Bucknell University Press, 2007.

Larco, Juan, ed. *Recopilacion de textos sobre Jose Maria Arguedas.* Havana: Casa de las Americas, 1976.

Muñoz, Silverio. *José María Arguedas y el mito de la salvación por la cultura.* Lima: Horizonte, 1987.

Ortega, Julio, ed. *The Fox from Up Above and the Fox from Down Below.* Pittsburgh, Pa.: University of Pittsburgh Press, 2000.

Rowe, William. *Mito e ideología en la obra de José María Arguedas.* Lima: Instituto Nacional de Cultura, 1979.

Varona-Lacey, Gladys M. *José María Arguedas: más allá del indigenismo.* Miami: Universal, 2000.

Jaime Bayly

Ruz, Robert. *Contemporary Peruvian Narrative and Popular Culture: Jaime Bayly, Iván Thays and Jorge Eduardo Benavides.* Woodbridge: Tamesis, 2005.

Belli Carlos Germán

Higgins, James. "The Poetry of Carlos Germán Belli." *Bulletin of Hispanic Studies* 47 (1970): 327–39.

Lasarte, F. "Pastoral and Counter-Pastoral: The Dynamics of Belli's Poetic Despair." *MLN* 94, no. 2 (1979): 301–20.

Zapata, Miguel Ángel, ed. *El pesapalabras: Carlos Germán Belli ante la crítica.* Lima: Tabla de Poesía Actual, 1994.

Alfredo Bryce Echenique

Duncan, Jennifer Ann. "Language as Protagonist: Tradition and Innovation in Bryce Echenique's *Un mundo para Julius*." *Forum for Modern Language Studies* 16 (1980): 120–35.

Ferreira, César. "Bryce Echenique y la novela del posboom: lectura de *La última mudanza de Felipe Carrillo*." *Chasqui: Revista de Literatura Latinoamericana* 22, no. 2 (1993): 34–48.

Ortega, Julio. "Alfredo Bryce Echenique y la estética de la exageración." *Cuadernos Hispanoamericanos: Revista Mensual de Cultura Hispánica* 512 (1993): 71–86.

Rodríguez-Peralta, Phyllis. "The Subjective Narration of Bryce Echenique's *La vida exagerada de Martín Romaña*." *Hispanic Journal* 10, no. 2 (1989): 139–51.

Scholz, Lásló. "Realidad e irrealidad en *Tantas veces Pedro* de Alfredo Bryce Echenique." *Acta Litteraria Academiae Scientiarum Hungaricae* 33, nos. 1–4 (1991): 175–85.

Wood, David. "Bibliografía de Alfredo Bryce Echenique." *Revista Interamericana de Bibliografía/Inter-American Review of Bibliography* 44, no. 1 (1994): 81–108.

Zúñiga, Maximiliano E. "Las estrategias narrativas de Alfredo Bryce Echenique en *La vida exagerada de Martín Romaña* y *El hombre que hablaba de Octavia de Cádiz*." *Hispanic Journal* 22, no. 1 (2001): 309–28.

Mercedes Cabello de Carbonera

Guiñazú, Cris. "La mujer en/de la vida pública en el siglo XIX: un estudio de *Blanca Sol*." *Cuadernos de Aldeeu* 21 (2005): 35–50.

Mathews, Cristina. "The Masquerade as Experiment: Gender and Representation in Mercedes Cabello de Carbonera's *El conspirador: autobiografía de un hombre público*." *Hispanic Review* 73, no. 4 (2005): 467–89.

Peluffo, Ana. "Las trampas del naturalismo en *Blanca Sol*: prostitutas y costureras en el paisaje urbano de Mercedes Cabello de Carbonera." *Revista de Crítica Literaria Latinoamericana* 28, no. 55 (2002): 37–52.

Voysest, Oswaldo. "Clorinda Matto and Mercedes Cabello: Reading Emile Zola's Naturalism in a Dissonant Voice." *Excavatio: Emile Zola and Naturalism* 11 (1998): 195–201.

———. "Fashion and Characterization in Mercedes Cabello's *Blanca Sol* and Emile Zola's *La Curée*: Tailored Differences." *Excavatio: Emile Zola and Naturalism* 10 (1997): 112–29.

José Santos Chocano

Rodriguez-Peralta, Phyllis W. *José Santos Chocano*. New York: Twayne, 1970.

Grégor Díaz

Morris, Robert J. "The Theater of Grégor Díaz." *Latin American Theatre Review* 23, no. 1 (1989): 79–87.

Pedro de Cieza de León

León, Pedro R. *Algunas observaciones sobre Pedro de Cieza de León y la Crónica del Perú*. Madrid: Gredos, 1973.

MacCormack, Sabine. "Demons, Imagination, and the Incas." *Representations* 33 (1991): 121–46.

Zaro, Juan J. "Translation and Historical Stereotypes: The Case of Pedro Cieza de León's *Crónica del Perú*." *TTR: Traduction, Terminologie, Rédaction: Etudes sur le Texte et Ses Transformations* 13, no. 1 (2000): 113–35.

José Diez Canseco

Cabanillas Cárdenas, Carlos F. "Ciudad y modernidad: tres versiones de Lima en la narrativa de José Díez Canseco." In *La ciudad imaginaria*, edited by Javier de Navascués, 105–33. Frankfurt: Vervuert, 2007.

Sanchez, Luis Alberto. "Jose Diez Canseco, novelista peruano (1904–1949)." In *Homage to Irving A. Leonard: Essays on Hispanic Art, History and Literature*, edited by Raquel Chang-Rodriguez, Donald A. Yates, and Robert G. Mead, 209–17. East Lansing: Latin American Studies Center, Michigan State University, 1977.

José María Egurén

Areta Marigó, Gema. *La poética de José María Eguren.* Seville: Alfar, 1993.
Higgins, James. "The Rupture Between Poet and Society in the Work of José María Eguren." *Kentucky Romance Quarterly* 20 (1973): 59–74.
Rodríguez-Peralta, Phyllis. "The Modernism of José María Eguren." *Hispania: A Journal Devoted to the Teaching of Spanish and Portuguese* 56 (1973): 222–29.

Juan de Espinosa Medrano (El Lunarejo)

Chang-Rodríguez, Raquel. *Hidden Messages: Representation and Resistance in Andean Colonial Drama.* Lewisburg, Pa.: Bucknell University Press, 1999.
Tamayo Rodriguez, J. Agustín. *Estudios sobre Juan de Espinosa Medrano (El Lunarejo).* Lima: Ediciones Librería "Studium," 1971.

El Inca Garcilaso de la Vega

Amador, Raysa. *Aproximación histórica a los Comentarios reales.* Madrid: Pliegos, 1984.
Chang-Rodríguez, Raquel, ed. *Beyond Books and Borders: Garcilaso de la Vega and "La Florida del Inca".* Lewisburg, Pa.: Bucknell University Press, 2006.
Crowley, Frances G. *Garcilaso de la Vega, el Inca and His Sources in "Comentarios Reales de los Incas."* The Hague: Mouton, 1971.
Fernández, Christian. *Inca Garcilaso: imaginación, memoria e identidad.* Lima: Fondo Editorial de la Universidad Nacional Mayor de San Marcos, 2004.
Steigman, Jonathan D. *"La Florida del Inca" and the Struggle for Social Equality in Colonial Spanish America.* Tuscaloosa: University of Alabama Press, 2005.
Zamora, Margarita. *Language, Authority, and Indigenous History in the "Comentarios reales de los Incas."* Cambridge: Cambridge University Press, 1988.

Isaac Goldemberg

Rosser, Harry L. "Being and Time in *La vida a plazos de don Jacobo Lerner.*" *Chasqui: Revista de Literatura Latinoamericana* 17, no. 1 (1988): 43–49.

Schneider, Judith Morganroth. "Cultural Meanings in Isaac Goldemberg's Fiction." *Folio: Essays on Foreign Languages and Literatures* 17 (1987): 128–40.

Manuel González Prada

Tauzin, Isabelle. *Manuel González Prada: escritor de dos mundos.* Lima: Instituto Francés de Estudios Andinos, 2006.

Felipe Guaman Poma de Ayala

Adorno, Rolena. *New Studies of the Autograph Manuscript of Felipe Guaman Poma de Ayala's "Nueva corónica y buen gobierno."* Copenhagen: Museum Tusculanum, 2003.
Bauer, Ralph. "'EnCountering' Colonial Latin American Indian Chronicles: Felipe Guaman Poma de Ayala's Hisory of the 'New' World." *American Indian Quarterly* 25, no. 2 (2001): 274–312.
Clavero, Dolores. "The Discourse of the Newly-Converted Christian in the Work of the Andean Chronicler Guaman Poma de Ayala." In *Christian Encounters with the Other,* edited by John C. Hawley, 44–55. New York: New York University Press, 1998.
García Castellón, Manuel G. *Guaman Poma de Ayala, pionero de la teología de la liberación.* Madrid: Pliegos, 1992.

Alberto Hidalgo

Armand, Octavio. "Poemas conmigo: posible ámbito del yo en la poesía de Alberto Hidalgo." *Cuadernos Hispanoamericanos: Revista Mensual de Cultura Hispánica* 371 (1981): 301–12.
O'Hara, Edgar. "Alberto Hidalgo, hijo del arrebato." *Revista de Crítica Literaria Latinoamericana* 13, no. 26 (1987): 97–113.

Diego Hojeda

Davis, Elizabeth B. "The Politics of Effacement: Diego de Hojeda's Humble Poetics." *Bulletin of Hispanic Studies* 71, no. 3 (1994): 339–57.
Pierce, Frank. "Diego de Hojeda, Religious Poet." In *Homenaje a William L. Fichter: estudios sobre el teatro antiguo hispánico y otros ensayos,* edited by David A. Kossoff and José Amor y Vásquez, 585–99. Madrid: Castalia, 1971.

Yorba-Gray, Galen B. "*La Christiada* in Its Colonial Context." *Hispania: A Journal Devoted to the Teaching of Spanish and Portuguese* 85, no. 1 (2002): 1–11.

Enrique López Albújar

Beane, Carol. "Black Character: Toward a Dialectical Presentation in Three South American Novels." In *Voices From Under: Black Narrative in Latin America and the Caribbean*, edited by William Luis, 181–98. Westport, Conn: Greenwood, 1984.

———. "Mestizaje: 'civilización' or 'barbarie': Prospects for Cultural Continuity in *Matalaché, Pobre negro* and *Cumboto.*" *Studies in Afro-Hispanic Literature* 2–3 (1978–1979): 199–212.

Harrison, Elizabeth. "Two Reactions to the Marginal Situation: The Mulatto in *Matalaché* and *Las lanzas coloradas.*" *Afro-Hispanic Review* 3, no. 2 (1984): 20–24.

José Carlos Mariátegui

Berger, Víctor, ed. *Ensayos sobre Mariátegui.* Lima: Biblioteca Amauta, 1987.

Castro, Juan E. de "José Carlos Mariátegui and Cultural Studies." *Ciberletras* 6 (2002): n.p.

Fernández, Roberta. "José Carlos Mariátegui: A Biography in Social Context." In *A Ricardo Gullón: sus discípulos*, edited by Adelaida López de Martínez, 89–102. Erie, Pa.: Publicación de la Asociación de Licenciados y Doctores Españoles en Estados Unidos, 1995.

Foster, David W. "A Checklist of Criticism on José Carlos Mariátegui." *Los Ensayistas: Georgia Series on Hispanic Thought* 10–11 (1981): 213–57.

Stein, William W. *Dance in the Cemetery: José Carlos Mariátegui and the Lima Scandal of 1917.* Lanham, Md.: University Press of America, 1997.

Unruh, Vicky. "Mariátegui's Aesthetic Thought: A Critical Reading of the Avant-Gardes." *Latin American Research Review* 24, no. 3 (1989): 45–69.

Wise, David. "A Peruvian Indigenista Forum of the 1920s: José Carlos Mariátegui's *Amauta.*" *Ideologies and Literature: Journal of Hispanic and Lusophone Discourse Analysis* 3, no. 13 (1980): 70–104.

Clorinda Matto de Turner

Berg, Mary G. "Role Models and Andean Identities in Clorinda Matto de Turner's *Hima-Sumac.*" In *Studies in Honor of Denah Lida*, edited by Mary

G. Berg and Lanin A. Gyurko, 297–305. Potomac, Md.: Scripta Humanistica, 2005.

———. "Writing for Her Life: The Essays of Clorinda Matto de Turner." In *Reinterpreting the Spanish American Essay: Women Writers of the 19th and 20th Centuries*, edited by Doris Meyer, 80–89. Austin: University of Texas Press, 1995.

Bryan, Catherine M. "Making National Citizens: Gender, Race, and Class in Two Works by Clorinda Matto de Turner." *Cincinnati Romance Review* 15 (1996): 113–18.

Peluffo, Ana. "Why Can't an Indian Be More Like a Man? Sentimental Bonds in Manuel González Prada and Clorinda Matto de Turner." *Revista de Estudios Hispánicos* 38, no. 1 (2004): 3–21.

César Moro

Altuna, Elena. "César Moro: escritura y exilio." *Revista de Crítica Literaria Latinoamericana* 20, no. 39 (1994): 109–25.

Martos, Marco. "La poesía de César Moro." In *Encuentro Internacional de Peruanistas: Estado de los estudios histórico-sociales sobre el Perú a fines del siglo XX,* 2 vols., II: 389–93. Lima: Universidad de Lima, 1998.

Oviedo, Jose Miguel. "Sobre la poesía de César Moro." *Lexis: Revista de Linguistica y Literatura* 1 (1977): 101–5.

Carmen Ollé

Hart, Stephen M. "Three Tropes of Postmodernism in Contemporary Peruvian Poetry." *Neophilologus* 89, no. 4 (2005): 575–85.

Minardi, Giovanna. "Carmen Ollé." *Hispamérica: Revista de Literatura* 28, no. 83 (1999): 55–59.

Zapata, Miguel-Ángel. "Carmen Ollé y la fisiología de la pasión." *Confluencia: Revista Hispánica de Cultura y Literatura* 12, no. 2 (1997): 181–85.

Carlos Oquendo de Amat

Monguio, Luis. "Un vanguardista peruano: Carlos Oquendo de Amat." In *Homenaje a Luis Leal: estudios sobre literatura hispanoamericana*, edited by Donald W. Bleznick and Juan O. Valencia, 203–14. Madrid: Insula, 1978.

Montauban, Jannine. "La parodia en 5 metros de poemas de Carlos Oquendo de Amat." *Cifra Nueva: Revista de Cultura* 9–10 (1999): 101–11.

Julio Ortega

Adler, Heidrun. "Julio Ortega's Peruvian Inferno." *Latin American Theatre Review* 15, no. 1 (1981): 53–58.

Morris, Robert J. "The Docudrama of Julio Ortega." In *Selected Proceedings of the Thirty-Fifth Annual Mountain Interstate Foreign Language Conference,* edited by Ramón Fernández-Rubio, 255–62. Greenville, S.C.: Furman University, 1987.

———. "The Theatre of Julio Ortega since His 'Peruvian Hell.'" *Latin American Theatre Review* 19, no. 2 (1986): 31–37.

Clemente Palma

Castillo-Feliú, Guillermo I. "Clemente Palma's Creative Deception." *West Virginia University Philological Papers* 30 (1984): 41–46.

Kason, Nancy M. *Breaking Traditions: The Fiction of Clemente Palma.* Lewisburg, Pa.: Bucknell University Press, 1988.

———. "The Dystopian Vision in *XYZ* by Clemente Palma." *Monographic Review/Revista Monografica* 3, nos. 1–2 (1987): 33–42.

———. "Elements of the Fantastic in 'La granja blanca' by Clemente Palma." In *The Fantastic in World Literature and the Arts,* edited by Donald E. Morse, 115–21. Westport, Conn: Greenwood, 1987.

Ricardo Palma

Cabañas, Miguel A. "Subjectivity and Empire: Representations of Historiography in Ricardo Palma's *Tradiciones peruanas.*" *Ciberletras* 12 (2005): n.p.

Compton, Merlin D. "Palma's Lima: A Record of Dark Delights." *Américas* 34, no. 6 (1982): 27–31.

Flores, Ángel, and Jose Miguel Oviedo, eds. *Orígenes del cuento hispanoamericano: Ricardo Palma y sus tradiciones: estudios, textos y análisis.* México, D.F.: Premia, 1979.

Morris, Robert J. "Ricardo Palma and the Contemporary Peruvian Theatre." *Romance Notes* 14 (1973): 465–68.

Ortega, Julio, ed. *Tradiciones peruanas.* Madrid: Unesco, 1996.

Rodríguez-Peralta, Phyllis. "Liberal Undercurrents in Palma's *Tradiciones peruanas.*" *Revista de Estudios Hispánicos* 15, no. 2 (1981): 283–97.

Tudela, Elisa Sampson Vera. "Hearing Voices: Ricardo Palma's Contextualization of Colonial Peru." In *Debating World Literature,* edited by Christopher Prendergast, 214–32. London: Verso, 2004.

Felipe Pardo y Aliaga

Cornejo Polar, Jorge. "*El espejo de mi tierra* y el costumbrismo en el Perú." In *Homenaje a don Luis Monguío*, edited by Jordi Aladro-Font and David Dabaco, 145–88. Newark, Del.: Cuesta, 1997.

———. "Felipe Pardo y Aliaga: una mirada diferente." In *Encuentro Internacional de Peruanistas: Estado de los estudios histórico-sociales sobre el Perú a fines del siglo XX*, 2 vols., II: 273–83. Lima: Universidad de Lima, 1998.

Pedro Peralta y Barnuevo

Hill, Ruth. "Between Reason and Piety: Inventio and Verisimilitude in Pedro de Peralta's Prologue to *Lima fundada* (1732)." *Dieciocho: Hispanic Enlightenment* 17, no. 2 (1994): 129–41.

Williams, Jerry M. "Anonymous Satire in Peralta Barnuevo's *Diálogo de los muertos*: la causa académica." *Hispanófila* 108 (1993): 1–14.

———. "Creole Identity in Eighteenth-century Peru: Race and Ethnicity." In *How Far Is America from Here?*, edited by Theo D'haen, Paul Giles, Djelal Kadir, and Lois Parkinson, 369–81. Amsterdam: Rodopi, 2005.

———. "Peralta Barnuevo's *Loa para la comedia*: The Tragic Reign of Luis I." *Dieciocho: Hispanic Enlightenment* 23, no. 1 (2000): 7–25.

Magda Portal

Arrington, Melvin S. "Madga Portal: Vanguard Critic." In *Reinterpreting the Spanish American Essay: Women Writers of the 19th and 20th Centuries*, edited by Doris Meyer, 148–56. Austin: University of Texas Press, 1995.

Unruh, Vicky. *Performing Women and Modern Literary Culture in Latin America: Intervening Acts*. Austin: University of Texas Press, 2006.

Julio Ramón Ribeyro

Bialowas Pobutsky, Aldona. "Cultural Alienation and Colonial Desire in 'Alienación' by Julio Ramón Ribeyro." *Romance Notes* 47, no. 2 (2007): 163–70.

Luchting, Wolfgang A. "El teatro de Julio Ramón Ribeyro." *Hispamérica: Revista de Literatura* 31, no. 11 (1982): 93–100.

Patiño, Ana Mercedes. "The Versatility of the Short Story in Julio Ramón Ribeyro: Analyses of Three Stories: 'While the Candle Burns,' 'Explanations to a Local Policeman' and 'The Carousel.'" *Readerly/Writerly Texts: Essays on Literature, Literary/Textual Criticism, and Pedagogy* 8, nos. 1–2 (2000): 131–51.

Rodriguez-Peralta, Phyllis. "Counterpart and Contrast in Julio Ramón Ribeyro's Two Novels." *Hispania: A Journal Devoted to the Teaching of Spanish and Portuguese* 62, no. 4 (1979): 619–25.

Vogely-Cuadros, Anita. "The Cultural Hero and the Martyr: Didactic Tools of Julio Ramón Ribeyro." *Dactylus* 8 (1987): 92–95.

Sebastián Salazar Bondy

Luchting, Wolfgang A. "Sebastián Salazar Bondy's Last Novel." *Journal of Spanish Studies: Twentieth Century* 1 (1973): 45–63.

Morris, R. J. "The Theatre of Sebastián Salazar Bondy." *Latin American Theatre Review* 4, no. 1 (1970): 59–71.

Spitta, Silvia. "Lima the Horrible: The Cultural Politics of Theft." *PMLA: Publications of the Modern Language Association of America* 122, no. 1 (2007): 294–300.

Luis Alberto Sánchez

Mead, Robert G., Jr. *Homenaje a Luis Alberto Sánchez.* Madrid: Insula; 1983.

Manuel Scorza

Aldaz, Anna-Marie. *The Past of the Future: The Novelistic Cycle of Manuel Scorza.* New York: Peter Lang, 1990.

Estrada, Oswaldo. "Bakhtinian Approaches to the Indigenous World of Manuel Scorza." *Romance Notes* 47, no. 2 (2007): 153–61.

Rodríguez Ortiz, Oscar. *Sobre narradores y héroes: a propósito de Arenas, Scorza y Adoum.* Caracas: Monte Avila, 1980.

Schmidt, Friedhelm. "Bibliografía de y sobre Manuel Scorza: nuevas aportaciones." *Revista de Critica Literaria Latinoamericana* 19, no. 37 (1993): 355–59.

Shaw, Bradley A. "The Indigenista Novel in Peru after Arguedas: The Case of Manuel Scorza." *Selecta: Journal of the Pacific Northwest Council on Foreign Languages* 3 (1982): 141–47.

Manuel Ascensio Segura

Albónico, Aldo. "Costumbrismo satírico peruano: la comedia *Ña Catita* de Manuel Ascensio Segura." In *Romanticismo, VI: El costumbrismo romántico*, edited by Joaquín Alvarez Barrientos et al., 11–19. Rome: Bulzoni, 1996.

Cornejo Polar, Jorge. *Estudios de literatura peruana*. Lima: Universidad de Lima, 1998.

Enrique Solari Swayne

Natella, A.A. "Enrique Solari Swayne and *Collacocha*." *Latin American Theatre Review* 4, no. 2 (1971): 39–44.

Vidal, Hernán. "Desarrollismo, teatro y cultura nacional peruana: *No hay isla feliz* de Sebastián Salazar Bondy y *Collacocha* de Enrique Solari Swayne." *Gestos: Teoría y Práctica del Teatro Hispánico* 3, no. 5 (1988): 53–84.

Javier Sologuren

Cabrera, Miguel. "Milenaria luz: la metáfora polisémica en la poesía de Javier Sologuren." *Cuadernos Americanos* 259, no. 2 (1985): 189–204.

Granados, Pedro. "Estancias, síntesis de imágenes aéreas en la poesía de Javier Sologuren." In *Encuentro Internacional de Peruanistas: Estado de los estudios histórico-sociales sobre el Perú a fines del siglo XX*, 2 vols., II: 339–51. Lima: Universidad de Lima, 1998.

Zapata, Miguel Ángel. "Continuidad de la voz en Javier Sologuren." *Inti: Revista de Literatura Hispánica* 26–27 (1987–1988): 337–54.

Flora Tristán

Busse, Erika. "Flora Tristán and Peruvian Feminists in the Twentieth Century." *Journal of Women's History* 15, no. 3 (2003): 124–28.

Dijkstra, Sandra. "The City as Catalyst for Flora Tristán's Vision of Social Change." In *Women Writers and the City: Essays in Feminist Literary Criticism*, edited by Susan Merrill Squier. Knoxville: University of Tennessee Press, 1984.

Sivert, Eileen Boyd. "Flora Tristán: The Joining of Essay, Journal, Autobiography." In *The Politics of the Essay: Feminist Perspectives*, edited by Ruth-Ellen Boetcher Joeres, and Elizabeth Mittman, 57–72. Bloomington: Indiana University Press, 1993.

Abraham Valdelomar

Arroyo Reyes, Carlos. "Luces y sombras del incaísmo modernista peruano: el caso de los cuentos incaicos de Abraham Valdelomar." *Cuadernos His-*

panoamericanos: Revista Mensual de Cultura Hispánica 539–540 (1995): 213–24.

Goldman, Myrna. "Color Imagery in Abraham Valdelomar's Prose Fiction." *Romance Quarterly* 29, no. 2 (1982): 143–53.

Núñez, Estuardo. "Valdelomar y los orígenes de la vanguardia." *Hispamérica: Revista de Literatura* 20, no. 60 (1991): 133–40.

Juan del Valle y Caviedes

Costigan, Lúcia Helena S. "Colonial Literature and Social Reality in Brazil and the Viceroyalty of Peru: The Satirical Poetry of Gregório de Matos and Juan del Valle y Caviedes." In *Coded Encounters: Writing, Gender, and Ethnicity in Colonial Latin America*, edited by Francisco Javier Cevallos-Candau, Jeffrey A. Cole, Nina M. Scott, and Nicomedes Suárez-Araúz, 87–100. Amherst: University of Massachusetts Press, 1994.

Lasarte, Pedro. "En torno al sujeto americano en la poesía de Juan del Valle y Caviedes." In *La Chispa '97: Selected Proceedings*, edited by Claire J. Paolini, 233–44. New Orleans: Tulane University, 1997.

Reedy, Daniel. "Juan del Valle y Caviedes a los tres siglos: olvidado y renombrado." In *Encuentro Internacional de Peruanistas: Estado de los estudios histórico-sociales sobre el Perú a fines del siglo XX*, 2 vols., II: 503–12. Lima: Universidad de Lima, 1998.

César Vallejo

Beutler, Gisela, ed. *César Vallejo: Actas del Coloquio Internacional, Freie Universität Berlin 7–9 junio 1979*. Tübingen: Niemeyer, 1981.

Flores, Ángel, ed. *Aproximaciones a César Vallejo*. Long Island City: Las Americas, 1971.

Franco, Jean. *César Vallejo: The Dialectics of Poetry and Silence*. Cambridge: Cambridge University Press, 1976.

García, Mara L., ed. *Poeta de los Andes: homenaje a César Vallejo*. Lima: Marsol Ediciones; 2008.

Hart, Stephen. *Religión, política y ciencia en la obra de César Vallejo*. London: Támesis, 1987.

Higgins, James. *Vision del hombre y de la vida en las ultimas obras de César Vallejo*. México, D.F.: Siglo XXI, 1970.

Larrea, Juan. *César Vallejo y el surrealismo*. Madrid: Visor, 1976.

Neale-Silva, Eduardo. *César Vallejo en su fase trílcica*. Madison: University of Wisconsin Press, 1975.

Sharman, Adam, ed. *The Poetry and Poetics of César Vallejo: The Four Angles of the Circle*. Lewiston, N.Y.: Mellen, 1997.

Blanca Varela

Barrientos Silva, Violeta. "Física y metafísica de la poesía de Blanca Varela." *Revista de Literatura Ajos & Zafiros* 3–4 (2002): 45–57.

Bermúdez, Silvia. "Extrañamiento y escritura: Blanca Varela y sus *Ejercicios materiales*." *Tesserae: Journal of Iberian and Latin American Studies* 7, no. 2 (2001): 117–27.

Muñoz Carrasco, Olga. "Voz y desvelo en la poesía de Blanca Varela." *Cuadernos Hispanoamericanos* 668 (2006): 53–59.

Valdivia Baselli, Alberto. "Blanca Varela: panorámica de una conciencia que despierta." *Revista de Literatura Ajos & Zafiros* 3–4 (2002): 15–26.

Mario Vargas Llosa

Boland, Roy Charles. *Mario Vargas Llosa: Oedipus and the 'Papa' State: A Study of Individual and Social Psychology in Mario Vargas Llosas Novels of Peruvian Reality: From "La ciudad y los perros" to "Historia de Mayta."* Madrid: Voz, 1988.

Booker, M. Keith. *Vargas Llosa among the Postmodernists*. Gainesville: University Press of Florida, 1994.

Castro-Klarén, Sara. *Understanding Mario Vargas Llosa*. Columbia: University of South Carolina Press, 1990.

Fenwick, M. J. *Dependency Theory and Literary Analysis: Reflections on Vargas Llosa's "The Green House."* Minneapolis, Minn.: Institute for the Study of Ideologies & Literatures, 1981.

Giacoman, Helmy F., ed. *Homenaje a Mario Vargas Llosa: variaciones interpretativas en torno a su obra*. Long Island City, N.Y.: Anaya-Las Americas, 1972.

Köllmann, Sabine. *Vargas Llosa's Fiction and the Demons of Politics*. Bern: Peter Lang, 2002.

Kristal, Efraín. *Temptation of the Word: The Novels of Mario Vargas Llosa*. Nashville, Tenn.: Vanderbilt University Press, 1998.

O'Bryan-Knight, Jean. *The Story of the Storyteller: "La tía Julia y el escribidor," "Historia de Mayta," and "El hablador" by Mario Vargas Llosa*. Amsterdam: Rodopi; 1995.

Vargas de Luna, Javier, ed. *Perú en el espejo de Vargas Llosa*. Puebla: Universidad de las Américas Puebla, 2008.

Zapata, Miguel Ángel, ed. *Mario Vargas Llosa and the Persistence of Memory.* Lima: Universidad Nacional Mayor de San Marcos, 2006.

Emilio Adolfo Westphalen

Bary, Leslie. "El surrealismo en Hispanoamérica y el 'yo' de Westphalen." *Revista de Crítica Literaria Latinoamericana* 14, no. 27 (1988): 97–110.
Llera, José Antonio. "La poesía de Emilio Adolfo Westphalen." *Cuadernos Hispanoamericanos* 623 (2002): 63–75.
Rodríguez, Néstor E. "La (po)ética negativa de Emilio Adolfo Westphalen." *Bulletin of Hispanic Studies* 83, no. 3 (2006): 193–202.

Agustín de Zárate

Hampe Martínez, Teodoro. "Agustín de Zárate: precisiones en torno a la vida y obra de un cronista indiano." *Cahiers du Monde Hispanique et Luso-Bresilien/Caravelle* 45 (1985): 21–36.

URUGUAY

Resources: Bibliographies, Dictionaries, Histories, Anthologies

Achugar, Hugo, ed. *El descontento y la promesa: nueva/joven narrativa uruguaya* [anthology]. Montevideo: Ediciones Trilce, 2008.
Benedetti, Mario. *Literatura uruguaya siglo XX.* Montevideo: Alfa, 1969.
Bollo, Sarah. *El modernismo en el Uruguay: ensayo estilístico.* Montevideo: Universidad de la República, 1976.
Englekirk, John E., and Margaret M. Ramos. *La narrativa uruguaya; estudio crítico-bibliográfico.* Berkeley: University of California Press, 1967.
Mariño, Roberto, ed. *Compendio de literatura gauchesca del Uruguay.* Montevideo: Ediciones Polifemo, 2006.
Mirza, Roger, ed. *Teatro uruguayo contemporáneo: antología.* Madrid: Fondo de Cultura Económica, 1992.
Moreira, Rubinstein, ed. *Poesía compartida, veinte poetas uruguayos contemporáneos.* Montevideo: Ediciones La Urpila, 1982.
Morón, Jorge, ed. *El cuento uruguayo: narradores uruguayos de hoy* [anthology]. Montevideo: Ediciones La Gotera, 2002.
Oreggioni, Alberto, ed. *Diccionario de literatura uruguaya.* 3 vols. Montevideo: Arca, 1987–1991.

Real de Azúa, Carlos, ed. *Antología del ensayo uruguayo contemporáneo.* 2 vols. Montevideo: Universidad de la República, 1964.

Rela, Walter. *Diccionario de escritores uruguayos.* Montevideo: Editorial. de la Plaza, 1986.

———. *Historia del teatro uruguayo 1808–1968.* Montevideo: Ediciones Banda Oriental, 1969.

———. *Repertorio bibliográfico del teatro uruguayo, 1816–1964.* Montevideo: Síntesis, 1965.

Rodríguez Monegal, E. *Literatura uruguaya del medio siglo.* Montevideo: Alfa, 1966.

Scott, Renée, ed. *Escritoras uruguayas: una antología crítica.* Montevideo: Ediciones Trilce, 2002.

Trigo, Abril. *Caudillo, estado, nación: literatura, historia e ideología en el Uruguay.* Gaithersburg, Md.: Hispamérica, 1990.

Visca, Arturo Sergio, ed. *Antología del cuento uruguayo.* 6 vols. Montevideo: Ediciones de la Banda Oriental, 1968.

Zum Felde, Alberto. *Proceso intelectual del Uruguay.* 3 vols. Montevideo: Ediciones del Nuevo Mundo, 1967.

Select Bibliography for Specific Writers

Eduardo Acevedo Díaz

Ainsa, Fernando. "De la novela de la historia a la novela histórica: el ejemplo de Eduardo Acevedo Díaz." *Río de la Plata: Culturas* 11–12 (1991): 135–46.

Crelis Secco, Susana. "La nación uruguaya en la literatura: Eduardo Acevedo Díaz y la creación de una nación." *Alba de América: Revista Literaria* 20, nos. 37–38 (2001): 415–24.

Delmira Agustini

Escaja, Tina, ed. *Delmira Agustini y el Modernismo: nuevas propuestas de género.* Rosario: Viterbo, 2000.

James, William. *Dependence, Independence, and Death: Toward a Psychobiography of Delmira Agustini.* New York: Peter Lang, 2009.

Stephens, Doris T. *Delmira Agustini and the Quest for Transcendence.* Montevideo: Geminis, 1975.

Stiefel Ayala, Marta, ed. *Proceedings of the International Literature Conference: Homage to Agustini, Ibarbourou, Mistral, Storni.* Calexico, Calif.: Institute for Border Studies, San Diego State University, 1991.

Enrique Amorim

Mose, Kendrick E. A. *Enrique Amorim: The Passion of a Uruguayan.* New York: Plaza Mayor, 1972.

Rojas, Santiago. "El gaucho en Amorim: progreso y folklore vistos desde un ángulo social." *Romance Quarterly* 38, no. 1 (1991): 85–93.

Villamil, Ana María. "Realismo y fantástico en el universo de Enrique Amorim." *Rio de la Plata: Culturas* 4–6 (1987): 319–26.

Napoleón Baccino Ponce de León

Perkowska-Alvarez, Magdalena. "A Fool's Point of View: Parody, Laughter, and the History of the Discovery in *Maluco: la novela de los descubridores* by Napoleón Baccino Ponce de León." In *A Twice-Told Tale: Reinventing the Encounter in Iberian/Iberian American Literature and Film,* edited by Santiago Juan-Navarro and Theodore Robert Young, 253–74. Newark: University of Delaware Press, 2001.

Quintana Millamoto, María Esther. "Crónicas del bufón: aproximación crítica a *Maluco, la novela de los descubridores.*" Montevideo: Linardi y Risso, 2008.

Mario Benedetti

Alemany, Carmen, ed. *Mario Benedetti: inventario cómplice.* Alicante: Universidad de Alicante, 1998.

Fornet, Ambrosio, ed. *Recopilación de textos sobre Mario Benedetti.* Havana: Casa de las Americas, 1976.

Geldrich-Leffman, Hanna. "Body and Voice: The Dialogue of Marriage in the Short Stories of Mario Benedetti." *Chasqui: Revista de Literatura Latinoamericana* 25, no. 1 (1996): 39–51.

Gregory, Stephen W. G. *Humanist Ethics or Realist Aesthetics? Torture, Interrogation and Psychotherapy in Mario Benedetti.* Victoria: La Trobe University, 1991.

Jordan, Paul R. "From Bureaucratic Alienation to Political Exile: Evolving Views of Uruguayan Identity in the Work of Mario Benedetti." *Modern Language Review* 100, no. 2 (2005): 383–95.

Tisnado, Carmen. "Performing the Unspeakable: Defeating Censorship in Two Stories by Mario Benedetti." In *Censorship and Cultural Regulation in the Modern Age,* edited by Beate Müller, 169–87. Amsterdam: Rodopi, 2004.

Andrés Castillo

Cordones-Cook, Juanamaría. "El teatro negro uruguayo de Andrés Castillo." *Latin American Theatre Review* 29, no. 2 (1996): 85–94.

Francisco Espínola

Martinez Moreno, Carlos. "Imagen múltiple de Francisco Espínola." *Texto Crítico* 2 (1975): 123–30.
Visca, Arturo Sergio. "Francisco Espínola, narrador." *Revista Iberoamericana* 58, nos. 160–161 (1992): 975–99.

Eduardo Galeano

Bell, Virginia E. "Counter-Chronicling and Alternative Mapping in *Memoria del fuego* and *Almanac of the Dead.*" *MELUS* 25, nos. 3–4 (2000): 5–30.
Fischlin, Daniel, and Martha Nandorfy. *Eduardo Galeano: Through the Looking Glass.* Montreal: Black Rose, 2002.
Lovell, W. George. "Re-Membering America: The Historical Vision of Eduardo Galeano." *Queen's Quarterly* 99, no. 3 (1992): 609–17.
Palaversich, Diana. "Eduardo Galeano's *Memoria del fuego* as Alternative History." *Antipodas: Journal of Hispanic Studies of the University of Auckland and La Trobe University* 3 (1991): 135–50.
Saz, Sara M. "Breath, Liberty, and the Word: Eduardo Galeano's Interpretation of History." *SECOLAS Annals: Journal of the Southeastern Council on Latin American Studies* 21 (1990): 59–70.
Wilson, S. R. "Eduardo Galeano: Exile and a Silenced Montevideo." *Chasqui: Revista de Literatura Latinoamericana* 9, nos. 2–3 (1980): 30–38.

Felisberto Hernández

Camarillo, Glenis. "Lo grotesco en el cuento 'Ursula' de Felisberto Hernández." *Revista de Literatura Hispanoamericana* 48 (2004): 82–92.
Chichester, Ana Garcia. "Metamorphosis in Two Short Stories of the Fantastic by Virgilio Piñera and Felisberto Hernández." *Studies in Short Fiction* 31, no. 3 (1994): 385–95.
Graziano, Frank. "An Introduction to Felisberto Hernández's Poetics." *Indiana Journal of Hispanic Literatures* 2, no. 2 (1994): 185–201.
Hernández, Ana María. "Los objetos en tres cuentos de Felisberto Hernández." In *Rumbos de lo fantástico: actualidad e historia*, edited by Ana María Morales and José Miguel Sardiñas, 31–45. Palencia: Cálamo, 2007.

Merrim, Stephanie. "Felisberto Hernández's Aesthetic of 'lo otro': The Writing of Indeterminacy." *Revista Canadiense de Estudios Hispánicos* 11, no. 3 (1987): 521–540.

Rey Beckford, Ricardo. "Felisberto Hernández o la máscara de lo cotidiano." *Ciberletras* 13 (2005): n.p.

Sicard, Alain, ed. *Felisberto Hernandez ante la critica actual*. Caracas: Monte Avila, 1977.

Sucre, Natalia. "Distracting Art: Reading Shock in Felisberto Hernández's 'Las Hortensias.'" *Hispania: A Journal Devoted to the Teaching of Spanish and Portuguese* 86, no. 3 (2003): 482–92.

Julio Herrera y Reissig

Burt, John R. "The Presence and Meaning of Dogs in Julio Herrera y Reissig's *Los éxtasis de la montaña (eglogánimas)*." *Hispanic Journal* 9, no. 2 (1988): 143–47.

Ferrari, Americo. "La poesía de Julio Herrera y Reissig." *Inti: Revista de Literatura Hispánica* 5–6 (1977): 62–71.

Kirkpatrick, Gwen. *The Dissonant Legacy of Modernismo: Lugones, Herrera y Reissig, and the Voices of Modern Spanish American Poetry*. Berkeley: University of California Press, 1989.

———. "The Limits of modernismo: Delmira Agustini and Julio Herrera y Reissig." *Romance Quarterly* 36, no. 3 (1989): 307–14.

Sara de Ibáñez

Sternheim, Marci. "Sara de Ibáñez: The Battle to Create." In *In the Feminine Mode: Essays on Hispanic Women Writers*, edited by Noël Valis and Carol Maier, 54–65. Lewisburg, Pa.: Bucknell University Press, 1990.

Zapata, Celia de. "Two Poets of America: Juana de Asbaje and Sara de Ibáñez." In *Latin American Women Writers: Yesterday and Today*, edited by Yvette E. Miller and Charles M. Tatum, 115–26. Pittsburgh, Pa.: Latin American Literary Review, 1977.

Juana de Ibarbourou

Arbeleche, Jorge. *Juana de Ibarbourou*. Montevideo: Arca, 1980.

Contreras Romo, María del Rocío. "El placer de la palabra o la palabra del placer, la poesía de Juana de Ibarbourou." *Espéculo: Revista de Estudios Literarios* 22 (2002–2003): n.p.

San Román, Gustavo. "Expression and Silence in the Poetry of Juana de Ibarbourou and Idea Vilariño." In *Women Writers in Twentieth-Century Spain and Spanish America*, edited by Catherine Davies. Lewiston, N.Y.: Mellen, 1993.

Stiefel Ayala, Marta, ed. *Proceedings of the International Literature Conference: Homage to Agustini, Ibarbourou, Mistral, Storni*. Calexico, Calif.: Institute for Border Studies, San Diego State University, 1991.

Antonio Lussich

Bynum, B. Brant. "The Evolution of *Los tres gauchos orientales*." *Hispanófila* 31, no. 2 (1988): 68–75.

Carlos Maggi

Gregory, Stephen. "Maids, Ruminants and Pincushions: Carlos Maggi's Essays on the State of Uruguay." *AUMLA: Journal of the Australasian Universities Language and Literature Association* 87 (1997): 75–92.

Quackenbush, Louis Howard. "Theatre of the Absurd, Reality, and Carlos Maggi." *Journal of Spanish Studies: Twentieth Century* 3 (1975): 61–72.

Carlos Martínez Moreno

Harrison, Brady "'The Gringos Perfected It in Vietnam': Torture and the American Adviser in Claribel Alegría's *Family Album* and Carlos Martínez Moreno's *El Infierno*." *Atenea* 26, no. 2 (2006): 9–19.

Young, Richard. "War Is Hell: Dante in Uruguay." In *Literature and War*, edited by David Bevan, 179–92. Amsterdam: Rodopi, 1990.

Tomás de Mattos

González Alvarez, José Manuel. "Metaficción y espejos de la escritura en *La fragata de las máscaras* de Tomás de Mattos: una mirada rioplatense." *Río de la Plata: Culturas* 29–30 (2004): 569–77.

Stewart, Iain A. D. "Forgetting Amnesia: Tomás de Mattos's *¡Bernabé, Bernabé!* and Uruguayan Identity." *Revista Canadiense de Estudios Hispánicos* 24, no. 2 (2000): 383–96.

Juan Carlos Onetti

Ainsa, Fernando. *Las trampas de Onetti*. Montevideo: Editorial Alfa, 1970.

Chao, Ramón. *Un posible Onetti*. Barcelona: Ronsel, 1994.

Giacoman, Helmy F., ed. *Homenaje a Juan Carlos Onetti: variaciones interpretativas en torno a su obra.* Long Island City, N.Y.: Anaya-Las Americas, 1974.

Jones, Yvonne P. *The Formal Expression of Meaning in Juan Carlos Onetti's Narrative Art.* Cuernavaca: Centro Intercultural de Documentacion, 1971.

Kadir, Djelal. *Juan Carlos Onetti.* Boston: Twayne, 1977.

Maloof, Judy. *Over Her Dead Body: The Construction of Male Subjectivity in Onetti.* New York: Peter Lang, 1995.

Milián-Silveira, María C. *El primer Onetti y sus contextos.* Madrid: Pliegos, 1986.

Millington, Mark. *Reading Onetti: Language, Narrative and the Subject.* Liverpool: Cairns, 1985.

Verani, Hugo J., ed. *Juan Carlos Onetti.* Madrid: Taurus, 1987.

Cristina Peri Rossi

Cochrane, Helena Antolin. "Androgynous Voices in the Novels of Cristina Peri Rossi." *Mosaic: A Journal for the Interdisciplinary Study of Literature* 30, no. 3 (1997): 97–114.

Cosse, Rómulo, ed. *Cristina Peri Rossi, papeles críticos.* Montevideo: Librería Linardi y Risso, 1995.

Damlé, Amaleena. "Gender Performance in the Work of Judith Butler and Cristina Peri Rossi's *La nave de los locos.*" *Dissidences: Hispanic Journal of Theory and Criticism* 4–5 (2008): n.p.

Feal, Rosemary Geisdorfer. "Queer Theory, Sexuality, and Women's Writing from Latin America: The Example of Cristina Peri Rossi." *Intertexts* 1, no. 1 (1997): 51–61.

Gilmour, Nicola. "Mothers, Muses and Male Narrators: Narrative Transvestism and Metafiction in Cristina Peri Rossi's *Solitario de amor.*" *Confluencia: Revista Hispánica de Cultura y Literatura* 15, no. 2 (2000): 122–36.

Ibáñez Quintana, Nuria. "Returning to Eros: Body and Language in Cristina Peri Rossi's Erotic Poetry." In *Into the Mainstream: Essays on Spanish American and Latino Literature and Culture*, edited by Jorge Febles, 91–104. Newcastle upon Tyne: Cambridge Scholars, 2006.

Potvin, Claudine. "Gender, Photograph, and Desire: Visual Practices in *El amor es una droga dura* by Cristina Peri Rossi." *Mosaic: A Journal for the Interdisciplinary Study of Literature* 38, no. 1 (2005): 169–85.

San Román, Gustavo. "Fantastic Political Allegory in the Early Work of Cristina Peri Rossi." *Bulletin of Hispanic Studies* 67, no. 2 (1990): 151–64.

José J. Podestá

Navarrete, José Francisco. "Aventuras de Juan Moreira en tierras huarpes." In *Indagaciones sobre el fin de siglo (teatro iberoamericano y argentino)*, edited by Osvaldo Pellettieri, 235–40. Buenos Aires: Galerna, Fundación Roberto Arlt, 2000.

Podestá, Guido A. "La reescritura de Juan Moreira: la política del decorum en el teatro argentino." *Latin American Theatre Review* 25, no. 1 (1991): 7–19.

Teresa Porzecanski

Flori, Mónica. "De almíbares, perfumes y sedas: la recuperación histórico-biográfica en *Perfumes de Cartago* de Teresa Porzecanski." *Alba de América: Revista Literaria* 17, no. 32 (1999): 235–43.

Flori, Mónica R. "Teresa Porzecanski." *Hispamérica: Revista de Literatura* 30, no. 89 (2001): 51–61.

Sum Scott, Renée. "Desarraigo e identidad: el inmigrante judío uruguayo en *La piel del alma*, de Teresa Porzecanski." In *Memoria histórica, género e interdisciplinariedad: los estudios culturales hispánicos en el siglo XXI*, edited by Santiago Juan-Navarro and Joan Torres-Pou, 55–63. Madrid: Biblioteca Nueva, 2008.

Horacio Quiroga

Berg, Mary G. "Horacio Quiroga." In *Poe Abroad: Influence, Reputation, Affinities*, edited by Lois Davis Vines, 239–43. Iowa City: University of Iowa Press, 1999.

Bratosevich, Nicolas A. S. *El estilo de Horacio Quiroga en sus cuentos*. Madrid: Gredos, 1973.

Flores, Ángel, ed. *Aproximaciones a Horacio Quiroga*. Caracas: Monte Avila, 1976.

French, Jennifer L. "'A Geographical Inquiry into Historical Experience': The Misiones Stories of Horacio Quiroga." *Latin American Literary Review* 30, no. 59 (2002): 79–99.

———. *Nature, Neo-Colonialism, and the Spanish American Regional Writers*. Hanover, N.H.: University Press of New England, for Dartmouth College, 2005.

Garth, Todd S. "Horacio Quiroga's Heroic Paradigm." *Revista Canadiense de Estudios Hispánicos* 29, no. 3 (2005): 453–68.

Gunnels, Bridgette W. "An Ecocritical Approach to Horacio Quiroga's 'Anaconda' and 'Regreso de Anaconda.'" *Mosaic: A Journal for the Interdisciplinary Study of Literature* 39, no. 4 (2006): 93–110.

Orgambide, Pedro. *Horacio Quiroga: una historia de vida.* Buenos Aires: Planeta, 1994.

Ángel Rama

Barros-Lémez, Alvaro, ed. *Bibliografía sumaria: Ángel Rama: 1926–1983.* College Park: Department of Spanish and Portuguese, University of Maryland, 1984.

D'Allemand, Patricia. *Hacia una crítica cultural latinoamericana.* Berkeley, Calif.: Latinoamericana, 2003.

González, José Eduardo. "Dialectics of Archaism and Modernity: Technique and Primitivism in Ángel Rama's *Transculturación narrativa en América Latina.*" In *Primitivism and Identity in Latin America: Essays on Art, Literature, and Culture,* edited by Erik Camayd-Freixas and José Eduardo González, 89–107. Tucson: University of Arizona Press, 2000.

Larre Borges, Ana Inés. "Ángel Rama: la aventura de *Marcha* en su destino intelectual." *Exégesis: Revista de la Universidad de Puerto Rico en Humacao* 19, nos. 54–56 (2006): 27–33.

Moraña, Mabel, ed. *Ángel Rama y los estudios latinoamericanos.* Pittsburgh, Pa.: Instituto Internacional de Literatura Iberoamericana, 1997.

Perus, Françoise. "¿Qué nos dice hoy *La ciudad letrada* de Ángel Rama?" *Revista Iberoamericana* 71, no. 211 (2005): 363–72.

Carlos Reyles

Ghiano, Juan Carlos. "Carlos Reyles en su centenario." *Cuadernos del Idioma: Revista de Cultura y Pensamento* 3 (1970): 133–49.

Grass, Roland. "Carlos Reyles and the Impact of the Symbolist-Decadent Novel in Spanish America." *American Hispanist* 2, no. 15 (1977): 11–13.

Llambias de Azevedo, Alfonso. "Cronología de Carlos Reyles." *Cuadernos del Idioma: Revista de Cultura y Pensamento* 3 (1970): 150–54.

José Enrique Rodó

Brotherston, Gordon. "The Literary World of José Enrique Rodó (1871–1917)." In *Homenaje a Luis Alberto Sánchez,* edited by Robert G. Mead Jr., 95–103. Madrid: Insula, 1983.

Costable de Amorín, Helena. *Rodó: pensador y estilista.* Montevideo: Academia Nacional de Letras, 1973.

Ette, Ottmar, ed. *José Enrique Rodó y su tiempo: cien años de Ariel.* Frankfurt: Vervuert, 2000.

Montero, Oscar. "Modernismo and Homophobia: Darío and Rodó." In *Sex and Sexuality in Latin America*, edited by Daniel Balderston and Donna J. Guy, 101–17. New York: New York University Press, 1997.

Rama, Ángel. *Ariel. Motivos de Proteo.* Caracas: Ayacucho, 1979.

Rodríguez Monegal, Emir. "Darío and Rodó: Two Versions of the Symbolist Dream in Spanish American Letters." In *The Symbolist Movement in the Literature of European Languages*, edited by Anna Balakian, 669–77. Budapest: Akadémiai Kiadó, 1982.

San Román, Gustavo. "Political Tact in José Enrique Rodó's *Ariel*." *Forum for Modern Language Studies* 36, no. 3 (2000): 279–95.

van Delden, Maarten. "The Survival of the Prettiest: Transmutations of Darwin in José Enrique Rodó's Ariel." In *Constellation Caliban: Figurations of a Character*, edited by Nadia Lie and Theo D'haen, 145–61. Amsterdam: Rodopi, 1997.

Emir Rodríguez Monegal

Roggiano, Alfredo A. "Emir Rodríguez Monegal o el crítico necesario." *Revista Iberoamericana* 52, nos. 135–136 (1986): 623–30.

Mauricio Rosencof

Forné, Anna. "El desdoblamiento de identidades en *El bataraz* de Mauricio Rosencof." *Hipertexto* 9 (2009): 95–105.

Wasem, Marcos. "Regímenes ficcionales de *Las cartas que no llegaron* de Mauricio Rosencof." *LL Journal* 1, no. 2 (2006): n.p.

Carlos Sabat Ercasty

Moran, Dominic. "Veinte poemas de amor 1: Turning Point or Synthesis?" *Bulletin of Spanish Studies: Hispanic Studies and Researches on Spain, Portugal, and Latin America* 84, no. 6 (2007): 759–76.

Rama, Carlos M. "Raíces españolas del poeta uruguayo Carlos Sabat Ercasty." *Cuadernos Hispanoamericanos: Revista Mensual de Cultura Hispánica* 333 (1978): 480–90.

Florencio Sánchez

Foster, David William. "Ideological Shift in the Rural Images in Florencio Sánchez's Theater." *Hispanic Journal* 11, no. 1 (1990): 97–106.

Gabriele, John P. "The Art of the Unexpressed: Silence as Rhetorical Device in *Barranca abajo*." *Monographic Review/Revista Monográfica* 16 (2000): 216–27.

Giordano, Enrique. *La teatralización de la obra dramática: de Florencio Sánchez a Roberto Arlt.* México, D.F.: Premià (Red de Jonás), 1982.

Taler, Fiona. "The Role of the Victim in the Plays of Florencio Sánchez." *FULGOR: Flinders University Languages Group Online Review* 1, no. 2 (2003): 14–22.

Armonía Somers

Biron, Rebecca E. "Armonía Somers 'El despojo': Masculine Subjectivity and Fantasies of Domination." *Latin American Literary Review* 21, no. 42 (1993): 7–20.

Clark, Maria B. "Desirous Fiction or 'El hombre del túnel' by Armonía Somers." *RLA: Romance Languages Annual* 4 (1992): 404–10.

Dalmagro, María Cristina. "The Reversal of Innocence: Somers, Dickens, and a 'Shared Oliver.'" *Dickens Studies Annual: Essays on Victorian Fiction* 36 (2005): 319–30.

Niebylski, Dianna C. *Humoring Resistance: Laughter and the Excessive Body in Latin American Womens Fiction.* Albany: State University of New York Press, 2004.

Potvin, Claudine. "De-Scribing Postmodern Feminism." In *Latin American Postmodernisms*, edited by Richard A.Young, 221–37. Amsterdam: Rodopi, 1997.

Snook, Margaret L. "Who's Pulling the St(r)ing? Gender and Class in Armonía Somers's 'Muerte por alacrán.'" *Ciberletras* 13 (2005): n.p.

Sullivan, Mary-Lee. "The Imaginary Real in Three Short Stories by Armonía Somers." *Cincinnati Romance Review* 23 (2004): 165–82.

María Eugenia Vaz Ferreira

Fernandez Alonso, Maria del Rosario. "Angustia existencial en la poesía de María Eugenia Vaz Ferreira: breve homenaje en el centenario de su nacimiento: 1875–1924." *Cuadernos Hispanoamericanos: Revista Mensual de Cultura Hispánica* 303 (1975): 634–52.

Perricone, Catherine R. "Un acercamiento revisionista al modernismo: el caso de María Eugenia Vaz Ferreira." In *Studies in Honor of Gilberto Paolini*, edited by Mercedes Vidal Tibbits, 423–39. Newark, Del.: Juan de la Cuesta, 1996.

Trueba Mira, Virginia. "La identidad poética de María Eugenia Vaz Ferreira." In *Delmira Agustini y el Modernismo: nuevas propuestas de género*, edited by Tina Escaja, 155–64. Rosario, Argentina: Viterbo, 2000.

Javier de Viana

Garganigo, John F. *Javier de Viana.* New York: Twayne, 1972.

Idea Vilariño

Berry-Bravo, Judy. "Idea Vilariño's Negation of Poetry." *Monographic Review/Revista Monografica* 6 (1990): 282–92.
———. "Poemas de amor de Idea Vilariño: experimento con el discurso amoroso." *La Torre: Revista de la Universidad de Puerto Rico* 9, no. 34 (1995): 175–89.
San Román, Gustavo. "Expression and Silence in the Poetry of Juana de Ibarbourou and Idea Vilariño." In *Women Writers in Twentieth-Century Spain and Spanish America,* edited by Catherine Davies, 157–75. Lewiston, N.Y.: Mellen, 1993.

Ida Vitale

Ramond, Michèle. "La noche alquímica de Ida Vitale." *Nuevo Texto Crítico* 3, no. 1 (1990): 132–52.
Villanueva, Alberto. "Notas sobre Reducción del infinito de Ida Vitale." *Hipertexto* 4 (2006): 148–54.
———. "Soltar el mirlo: noticia de lo imposible alcanzado por Ida Vitale." *Hispamérica: Revista de Literatura* 31, no. 91 (2002): 111–17.
Zapata, Miguel Ángel. "Ida Vitale: entre lo claro y lo conciso del poema." *Inti: Revista de Literatura Hispánica* 26–27 (1987–1988): 355–61.

Juan Zorilla de San Martín

Bente, Thomas O. "*Cumandá* y *Tabaré*: dos cumbres del indianismo romántico hispanoamericano." *Revista Interamericana de Bibliografia/Inter-American Review of Bibliography* 41, no. 1 (1991): 15–23.
Esquer Torres, Ramón. "Juan Zorrilla de San Martín y Gustavo Adolfo Bécquer." *Revista de Filología Española* 52 (1971): 537–61.
Frederick, Bonnie "Reading the Warning: The Reader and the Image of the Captive Woman." *Chasqui: Revista de Literatura Latinoamericana* 18, no. 2 (1989): 3–11.
San Román, Gustavo. "Negotiating Nationhood: The Repressed Desire of the Native in *Tabaré*." *Forum for Modern Language Studies* 29, no. 4 (1993): 300–10.

Alberto Zum Felde

Cortazzo, Uruguay. "Crítica literaria, colonialismo e identidad en Alberto Zum Felde." *Revue Romane* 18, no. 2 (1983): 228–39.
———. "Tradición y renovación en la crítica literaria del Uruguay." *Cuadernos Americanos* 2, no. 3 (1988): 137–51.

VENEZUELA

Resources: Encyclopedias, Dictionaries, Histories, Anthologies

Aray, Edmundo. *Aquí Venezuela cuenta* [anthology]. Montevideo: ARCA, 1968.
———, ed. *Poesía venezolana: antología esencial*. Madrid: Visor Libros, 2005.
Belrose, M. *La época del modernismo en Venezuela: 1988–1925*. Caracas: Monte Avila, 1996.
Bibliografía de la novela venezolana. Caracas: Universidad Central de Venezuela, 1963.
Diccionario general de la literatura venezolana. Mérida: Editorial Venezolana, 1987.
Hidalgo de Jesús, Amarilis. *La novela moderna en Venezuela*. New York: Peter Lang, 1995.
Kohut, Karl, ed. *Literatura venezolana hoy: historia nacional y presente urbano*. Caracas: Universidad Central de Venezuela, 2004.
———. *10 novelas venezolanas*. Caracas: Monte Avila Editores, 1972.
Larrazábal Henríquez, Osvaldo, et al. *Bibliografía del cuento venezolano*. Caracas: Universidad Central de Venezuela, 1975.
Liscano, Juan. *Panorama de la literatura venezolana actual*. Caracas: Alfadil, 1995.
Medina, José Ramón. *Noventa años de literatura venezolana (1900–1990)*. Caracas: Monte Avila Editores, 1993.
Meneses, Guillermo. *Antología del cuento venezolano*. Caracas: Monte Ávila Editores, 1994.
Monasterios, Rubén. *Un enfoque crítico del teatro venezolano*. Caracas: Monte Ávila Editores, 1975.
Pantin, Yolanda, and Ana Teresa Torres, eds. *El hilo de la voz: antología crítica de escritoras venezolanas del siglo XX*. Caracas: Fundación Polar and Angria Ediciones, 2003.
Picón-Salas, Mariano. *Formación y proceso de la literatura venezolana*. Caracas: Monte Ávila, 1984.
Ramos Guédez, José Marcial. *El negro en la novela venezolana*. Caracas: Universidad Central de Venezuela, 1980.

Rodríguez B., Orlando, ed. *Teatro venezolano contemporáneo: antología*. Madrid: Sociedad Estatal Quinto Centenario and Fondo de Cultura Económica, 1991.

Salas, Alejandro, ed. *Antología comentada de la poesía venezolana*. Caracas: Alfadil Ediciones, 1989.

Sambrano Urdaneta, Oscar. *Contribución a una bibliografía general de la poesía venezolana en el siglo XX*. Caracas: Universidad Central de Venezuela, 1979.

Suárez Radillo, Carlos Miguel, ed. *13 autores del nuevo teatro venezolano* Larrazábal Henríquez, Osvaldo. Caracas: Monte Ávila, 1971.

Select Bibliography for Specific Writers

Rafael Arráiz Lucca

Flores, María Antonieta. "La inevitable visión sombría." *Inti: Revista de Literatura Hispánica* 37–38 (1993): 253–55.

Andrés Bello

Avila Martel, Alamiro de, ed. *Estudios sobre la vida y obra de Andrés Bello*. Santiago: Editoral de la Universidad de Chile, 1973.

Jaksic, Iván. *Andrés Bello: Scholarship and Nation-Building in Nineteenth-Century Latin America*. Cambridge: Cambridge University Press, 2001.

Millares Carlo, Agustín. *Bibliografía de Andrés Bello*. Madrid: Fundación Universitaria. Española, 1978.

Murillo, Fernando. *Andrés Bello: historia de una vida y de una obra*. Caracas: Casa de Bello, 1986.

Schmitt, Christian, ed. *La Gramática de Andrés Bello (1847–1997)*. Bonn: Romanistischer, 2000.

Torrejón, Alfredo. *Andrés Bello y la lengua culta: la estandarización del castellano en América en el siglo XIX*. Boulder, Colo.: Society of Spanish & Spanish-American Studies, 1993.

Rufino Blanco Fombona

Gil López, Ernesto J. "La máscara de Rufino Blanco Fombona: una aportación a la novela de dictadura." In *Actas del X Congreso de la Asociación de Hispanistas*, 4 vols., III: 637–41. Barcelona: Promociones y Publicaciones Universitarias, 1992.

Karsen, Sonja. "La corrupción del gobierno de Venezuela según Blanco-Fombona en *El hombre de oro*." In *La literatura iberoamericana del siglo*

XIX: Memoria del XV Congreso Internacional de Literatura Iberoameri-cana, edited by Renato Rosaldo and Robert Anderson, 61–66. Tucson: University of Arizona, 1974.

Rivas Dugarte, Rafael Ángel. *Fuentes para el estudio de Rufino Blanco Fom-bona (1874–1944)*. Caracas: Centro de Estudios Latinoamericanos. Rómulo Gallegos, 1979.

Silva Beauregard, Paulette. "La feminización del héroe moderno y la novela en *Lucía Jerez* y *El hombre de hierro.*" *Revista de Crítica Literaria Latino-americana* 26, no. 52 (2000): 135–51.

Simón Bolívar

Albada Jelgersma, Jill E. "Simón Bolívar en *El general en su laberinto*, de Gabriel García Márquez." *Tesserae: Journal of Iberian and Latin American Studies* 7, no. 1 (2001): 55–62.

Brown, Matthew. *Adventuring through Spanish Colonies: Simón Bolívar, Foreign Mercenaries and the Birth of New Nations*. Liverpool: Liverpool University Press, 2006.

Conway, Christopher B. *The Cult of Bolívar in Latin American Literature*. Gainesville: University Press of Florida, 2003.

Méndez-Ramírez, Hugo. "Simón Bolívar y la imaginación literaria americana: Gabriel García Márquez, Jorge Luis Borges y Pablo Neruda." *Bulletin of Hispanic Studies* 74, no. 2 (1997): 197–212.

José Ignacio Cabrujas

Nigro, Kirsten. "History Grand and History Small in Recent Venezuelan The-atre: Rial's *Bolívar* and Cabrujas' *Acto cultural.*" *Theatre Annual: A Journal of Performance Studies* 44 (1989–1990): 37–46.

———. "Pop Culture and Image-Making in Two Latin American Plays." *Latin American Literary Review* 17, no. 33 (1989): 42–49.

Versényl, Adam. "'¿Como se llena un vacío?': Cabrujas' *El día que me quieras* and Filling the Void in Colombian Theater." *Gestos: Teoría y Práctica del Teatro Hispánico* 7, no. 13 (1992): 158–62.

Rafael Cadenas

Guerrero, Gustavo. "Rafael Cadenas: en busca de una espiritualidad terrenal." *Cuadernos Hispanoamericanos: Revista Mensual de Cultura Hispánica* 558 (1996): 71–81.

Isava, Luis Miguel. "Amante: summa poética de Rafael Cadenas." *Revista Iberoamericana* 60, nos. 166–167 (1994): 267–87.

Mondragón, Amelia. "Poesía post-vanguardista y Rafael Cadenas." *MACLAS: Latin American Essays* 19 (2006): 130–48.

Román Chalbaud

Azparren Giménez, Leonardo. "Román Chalbaud: el realismo crítico en el teatro venezolano de los sesenta." *Latin American Theatre Review* 33, no. 2 (2000): 21–41.

Isaac Chocrón

Friedman, Edward. "The Beast Within: The Rhetoric of Signification in Isaac Chocrón's *Animales feroces*." *Folio: Essays on Foreign Languages and Literatures* 17 (1987): 167–83.

———. "Girl Trouble: Gender Gaps in Isaac Chocrón's *Toda una Dama*." *Cincinnati Romance Review* 18 (1999): 61–69.

Nigro, Kirsten F. "A Triple Insurgence: Isaac Chocrón's *La revolución*." *Rocky Mountain Review of Language and Literature* 35, no. 1 (1981): 47–53.

Younoszai, Barbara. "Not Establishing Limits: The Writing of Isaac Chocrón." *Inti: Revista de Literatura Hispánica* 37–38 (1993): 155–61.

Manuel Díaz Rodríguez

Di Prisco, Rafael. "Díaz Rodríguez: modernismo y criollismo." In *Literatura y política en América Latina*, edited by Rafael Di Prisco and Antonio Scocozza, 239–49. Caracas: Casa de Bello, 1995.

Larubia-Prado, Francisco. "*Sangre patricia*: la aventura del héroe mítico en la novela modernista." *Revista Canadiense de Estudios Hispánicos* 13, no. 2 (1989): 255–60.

Matteson, Marianna Merritt. *Manuel Díaz Rodríguez: Evolution and Dynamics of the Stylist*. Potomac: Scripta Humanistica, 1993.

Mora, Gabriela. "Modernismo decadentista: confidencias de psiquis de Manuel Díaz Rodríguez." *Revista Iberoamericana* 63, nos. 178–179 (1997): 263–74.

Prendes Guardiola, Manuel. "La vida ante el arte en *Sangre patricia*." In *La literatura hispanoamericana con los cinco sentidos: Actas del V Congreso Internacional de la AEELH*, edited by Eva Valcárcel, 595–600. La Coruña: Universidade da Coruña, 2002.

Russi, David P. "Metaphor and Aesthetic Response in Díaz Rodríguez's *Idolos rotos*." *Revista de Estudios Hispánicos* 17–18 (1990–1991): 167–83.

Ramón Díaz Sánchez

Geisdorfer Feal, Rosemary. "Patriarchism and Racism: The Case of *Cumboto*." *Afro-Hispanic Review* 2, no. 1 (1983): 25–28.

Johnson, Harvey L. "Perspectives on the Soul of Venezuela: The Novels of Ramón Díaz Sánchez." In *In Retrospect: Essays on Latin American Literature*, edited by Elizabeth S. Rogers and Timothy J. Rogers, 149–60. York, S.C.: Spanish Literature Publications Co., 1987.

Persico, Alan. "Identity and the Struggle for Significance in *Mene* and *Cuentos del negro cubano*." *Journal of Caribbean Studies* 10, no. 3 (1995): 235–51.

———. "Ramón Díaz Sánchez: The Poetics of Duality and Passion." *Afro-Hispanic Review* 14, no. 1 (1995): 40–47.

Rómulo Gallegos

Alonso, Carlos J. *The Spanish American Regional Novel: Modernity and Autochthony*. Cambridge: Cambridge University Press, 1990.

Díaz Seijas, Pedro, ed. *Rómulo Gallegos ante la crítica*. Caracas: Monte Avila, 1980.

Dunham, Lowell. *Romulo Gallegos: An Oklahoma Encounter and the Writing of the Last Novel*. Norman: University of Oklahoma Press, 1974.

Liscano, Juan. *Rómulo Gallegos y su tiempo*. Caracas: Monte Ávila, 1979.

Marban, Hilda. *Rómulo Gallegos: el hombre y su obra*. Madrid: Playor, 1973.

Paley, Nicholas M. *Dos novelas de la tierra*. Monterrey: Editorial Universitaria Interamericana de Monterrey, 1972.

Ramos Calles, Raúl. *Los personajes de Gallegos: a través del psicoanálisis*. Caracas: Monte Ávila, 1984.

Rodriguez-Alcala, Hugo, ed. *Nine Essays on Rómulo Gallegos*. Riverside: Latin American Studies Program, University of California, 1979.

Shaw, D. L. *Gallegos: Doña Bárbara*. London: Grant & Cutler, 1972.

Julio Garmendia

Barrera Linares, Luis. "Julio Garmendia: mito y realidad/ambigüedad e ironía." *Escritura: Revista de Teoría y Crítica Literarias* 17, nos. 33–34 (1992): 21–46.

Moraña, Mabel. "A propósito de la recepción de la narrativa de Julio Garmendia." *Actualidades: Centro de Estudios Latinoamericanos "Rómulo Gallegos"* 3–4 (1977–1978): 63–91.

Sambrano Urdaneta, Oscar. "En busca del reino perdido: para una poética del cuento en Julio Garmendia." *Revista Iberoamericana* 60 (166–167): 427–34.

Vega, Marta de la. "Cultura popular y populismo en la narrativa de Julio Garmendia." *Escritura: Revista de Teoría y Crítica Literarias* 13, nos. 25–26 (1988): 141–88.

Salvador Garmendia

Bravo, Victor. "Salvador Garmendia: la expresión de lo fantástico." *Revista Iberoamericana* 60, nos. 166–167 (1994): 495–501.

Brushwood, John S. "Cinco novelas de Salvador Garmendia: el impacto sobre los hábitos perceptivos." *Hispania: A Journal Devoted to the Teaching of Spanish and Portuguese* 60, no. 4 (1977): 884–90.

Delgado D., María Elena *"Memorias de altagracia*: la infancia y la búsqueda de lo absoluto." *Cifra Nueva: Revista de Cultura* 2 (1994): 59–77.

Delprat, François. "Los espacios imaginarios en las novelas de Salvador Garmendia, de *Los pequeños seres* a *El único lugar posible.*" In *Literatura venezolana hoy: historia nacional y presente urbano*, edited by Karl Kohut, 243–52. Frankfurt: Vervuert, 1999.

Perozo Naveda, Blas. "Historia, novela urbana, migración: mecanismos de significación para explorar la obra de Salvador Garmendia." *Revista de Literatura Hispanoamericana* 42 (2001): 7–17.

Rama, Ángel. "Salvador Garmendia: culminacion de una narrativa." *La Palabra y el Hombre: Revista de la Universidad Veracruzana* 10 (1974): 17–22.

Adriano González León

Gnutzmann, Rita. "Adriano González León, *País portátil*: entre el documento y la ficción." *Hispanófila* 63 (1978): 89–102.

Páramo, Ma Luisa. "La emoción de las imágenes y la anécdota de las palabras: Adriano González León." *Espéculo: Revista de Estudios Literarios* 8 (1998): n.p.

Pulizzi de Arévalo, Giovanna. "La narrativa de Adriano González León: voces y recuerdos del ente ficcional." *Revista de Literatura Hispanoamericana* 39 (1999): 153–62.

Francisco Herrera Luque

Chibán, Alicia. "De genealogías y revelaciones: la novela como indagación histórica en Francisco Herrera Luque." In *Murales, figuras, fronteras: narrativa e historia en el Caribe y Centroamérica*, edited by Patrick Collard and Rita de Maeseneer, 111–22. Frankfurt: Vervuert, 2003.

Pineda, Hugo. "Francisco Herrera Luque: siquiatra novelista." *Afro-Hispanic Review* 1, no. 3 (1982): 13–16.

Villanueva-Collado, Alfredo. "Metasexualidad y mestizaje en *Los amos del valle* de Francisco Herrera Luque." *Inti: Revista de Literatura Hispánica* 32–33 (1990): 95–105.

Juan Liscano

Doudoroff, Michael. "*Nuevo mundo Orinoco* de Juan Liscano: reflexiones sobre sus contextos." *Inti: Revista de Literatura Hispánica* 37–38 (1993): 81–87.

Zapata, Miguel Ángel. "La poesía de Juan Liscano: materia prima de la gran obra." *Inti: Revista de Literatura Hispánica* 26–27 (1987–1988): 225–34.

Guillermo Meneses

Balza, José. "Meneses: el 'Yo' imposible." In *Literatura venezolana hoy: historia nacional y presente urbano*, edited by Karl Kohut, 227–33. Frankfurt Vervuert, 1999.

Kulin, Katalin. "Guillermo Meneses: *La mano junto al muro*." In *El espacio en la narrativa moderna en lengua española*, edited by Gabriella Menczel and László Scholz, 227–32. Budapest: Eötvös József Könyvkiadó, 2003.

Lasarte Valcárcel, Javier. "Nacionalismo populista y desencanto: poéticas de modernidad en la narrativa de Guillermo Meneses." *Revista Iberoamericana* 60, nos. 166–67 (1994): 77–96.

Sifontes Greco, Lourdes C. "Guillermo Meneses: del cuento al cuaderno metaficcional: una lectura de las proyecciones de la especularidad en la cuentística meneseana hacia la escritura de *El falso cuaderno de Narciso Espejo*." *Revista Iberoamericana* 60, nos. 166–67 (1994): 169–84.

Zacklin, Lyda. *La narrativa de Guillermo Meneses*. Caracas: Dirección de Cultura, Universidad Central de Venezuela, 1985.

Enrique Bernardo Núñez

Bohórquez, Douglas. "*Después de Ayacucho*, de Enrique Bernardo Núñez." *Cifra Nueva: Revista de Cultura* 1 (1992): 11–15.

Carrera, Gustavo Luis. "Cubagua y la fundación de la novela venezolana estéticamente contemporánea." *Revista Iberoamericana* 60, nos. 166–167 (1994): 451–56.

Hirshbein, Cesia. "El ensayo literario en Venezuela: Enrique Bernardo Núñez, ensayista, historiador y cronista de la ciudad de Caracas." In *Actas del XIV Congreso de la Asociación Internacional de Hispanistas, IV: Literatura hispanoamericana*, edited by Isaías Lerner, Robert Nival, and Alejandro Alonso, 245–51. Newark, Del: Cuesta, 2004.

———. "Prosa caribeña de Enrique Bernardo Núñez: su novela *Cubagua* y su ensayo *Orinoco*." *Cuadernos Americanos* 16, no. 6 (2002): 59–73.

Pacheco, Carlos. "El secreto de la isla: *Cubagua* como crítica de la historia y la novela." *Iberoamericana: Lateinamerika Spanien Portugal* 24, nos. 2–3 (2000): 187–205.

Miguel Otero Silva

Delgado, Luisa Elena. "Miguel Otero Silva y la nueva novela venezolana." *Anales de Literatura Hispanoamericana* 13 (1984): 203–97.

Galster, Ingrid. "El conquistador Lope de Aguirre en la nueva novela histórica." In *La invención del pasado: la novela histórica en el marco de la posmodernidad*, edited by Karl Kohut, 196–204. Frankfurt: Vervuert, 1997.

Lefère, Robin. "Historia y ficción: la figura de Lope de Aguirre." In *1898–1998: fines de siglos: historia y literatura hispanoamericanas*, edited by Jacques Joset and Philippe Raxhon, 129–46. Geneva: Droz, 2000.

Muñoz Bravo, Meridalba. "Vistas de la ciudad moderna en la literatura venezolana: presencias en dos novelas de Miguel Otero Silva." In *La ciudad imaginaria*, edited by Javier de Navascués, 233–49. Frankfurt: Vervuert, 2007.

Osorio, Nelson. "La historia y las clases en la narrativa de Miguel Otero Silva." *Casa de las Américas* 33, no. 190 (1993): 34–41.

Ramón Palomares

Alfonzo, Rafael José. "Ramón Palomares: nueva visión de lo telúrico." *Cifra Nueva: Revista de Cultura* 5–6 (1997): 9–18.

Arellano, Américo. "Oralidad y transculturación en la poesía de Ramón Palomares." *Revista Iberoamericana* 60, nos. 166–67 (1994): 233–48.

Pineda de Sansone, Beatriz. "Cosmogonía en la obra de Ramón Palomares." *Revista de Literatura Hispanoamericana* 36 (1998): 25–42.

Teresa de la Parra

Bohórquez, Douglas. *Teresa de la Parra: del diálogo de géneros y la melancolía.* Caracas: Monte Ávila and Consejo de Desarrollo Científico, Humanístico y Tecnológico (CDCHT), Universidad de Los Andes, 1997.

Byron, Kristine. "'Books and Bad Company': Reading the Female Plot in Teresa de la Parra's *Ifigenia.*" *Modern Language Quarterly: A Journal of Literary History* 64, no. 3 (2003): 349–76.

Garrels, Elizabeth. *Las grietas de la ternura: nueva lectura de Teresa de la Parra.* Caracas: Monte Ávila, 1986.

Kimberly Ann Nance. "Pied Beauty: Juxtaposition and Irony in Teresa de la Parra's *Las memorias de Mamá Blanca.*" *Letras Femeninas* 16, nos. 1–2 (1990): 45–49.

Lemaître, Louis Antonine. *Mujer ingeniosa: vida de Teresa de la Parra.* Madrid: La Muralla, 1987.

Lindstrom, Naomi. "Woman between Paris and Caracas: *Iphigenia* by Teresa de la Parra." In *Unfolding the City: Women Write the City in Latin America,* edited by Anne Lambright and Elisabeth Guerrero, 233–50. Minneapolis: University of Minnesota Press, 2007.

Molloy, Sylvia. "Disappearing Acts: Reading Lesbian in Teresa de la Parra." In *¿Entiendes? Queer Readings, Hispanic Writings,* edited by Emilie L. Bergmann and Paul Julian Smith, 230–56. Durham, N.C.: Duke University Press, 1995.

Russ, Elizabeth. "Disordering History, Denying Politics: Performative Strategies in Teresa de la Parra's *Influencia de la mujer en la formación del alma americana.*" *Latin American Literary Review* 34, no. 67 (2006): 161–69.

Mariano Picón Salas

Jaimes, Héctor. "La historia y la autobiografía en los ensayos de Mariano Picón-Salas." *Hispanófila* 125 (1999): 23–36.

Márquez Rodríguez, Alexis. "Mariano Picón Salas: el arte y la costumbre de pensar." *Revista Iberoamericana* 60, nos. 166–67 (1994): 31–45.

Mead, Robert G., Jr. "Mariano Picón Salas y otras voces de protesta en el moderno ensayo hispanoamericano." *Cuadernos Americanos* 202 (1975): 97–108.

Morin, Thomas D. *Mariano Picón Salas.* Boston: Twayne, 1979.

Osorio Tejeda, Nelson. "Reflexión sobre las obras de Mariano Picón Salas." *Cuadernos Americanos* 15, no. 4 (2001): 72–81.

Zambrano, Gregory. "Mariano Picón Salas: el narrador, el ensayista y los caminos de la historia." *Cuadernos Americanos* 15, no. 4 (2001): 96–110.

José Antonio Ramos Sucre

Castañón, Adolfo. "José Antonio Ramos Sucre: historia verdadera de dos ciudades." *Vuelta* 21, no. 255 (1998): 52–56.

Guzmán Toro, Fernando. "José Antonio Ramos Sucre: poeta de la soledad y la melancolía." *Revista de Literatura Hispanoamericana* 47 (2003): 60–68.

Rodríguez Silva, Aníbal. "Hermenéutica y conocimiento en la poesía de Ramos Sucre." *Cifra Nueva: Revista de Cultura* 7 (1998): 105–12.

Ruiz Barrionuevo, Carmen. "Juegos del espacio y estrategias del personaje en José Antonio Ramos Sucre." *Revista Iberoamericana* 58, no. 159 (1992): 597–609.

Tenreiro, Salvador. "Para una poética del sujeto en la obra de J. A. Ramos Sucre." *Escritura: Revista de Teoría y Crítica Literarias* 11, no. 21 (1986): 25–48.

César Rengifo

Osorio T., Nelson. "La alucinación del petróleo en una obra de César Rengifo." *Hispamerica: Revista de Literatura* 21, no. 63 (1992): 81–87.

Paternina Ríos, Zoila. "César Rengifo y el teatro venezolano." *Latin American Theatre Review* 32, no. 2 (1999): 117–36.

Suarez Radillo, Carlos M. "Vigencia de la realidad venezolana en el teatro de César Rengifo." *Latin American Theatre Review* 5, no. 2 (1972): 51–61.

Osvaldo Trejo

Barrera Linares, Luis. "La narrativa breve de Oswaldo Trejo: más allá del textualismo." *Inti: Revista de Literatura Hispánica* 37–38 (1993): 97–106.

———. "Oswaldo Trejo: los cuentos de un disidente." *Revista de Literatura y Artes Venezolanas* 2, no. 1 (1996): 45–55.

———. "Oswaldo Trejo: pautas para una propuesta de la (in)comunicación literaria." *Revista Iberoamericana* 60, nos. 166–67 (1994): 199–218.

Arturo Uslar Pietri

Aínsa, Fernando. "Entre la decepción y la esperanza: *La isla de Robinsón* de Arturo Uslar Pietri: de la historia a la utopía." *Hispamerica: Revista de Literatura* 24, no. 72 (1995): 101–10.

Cruz-Cámara, Nuria. "*Las lanzas coloradas*: el anti-buen salvaje de Rousseau." *PALARA: Publication of the Afro-Latin/American Research Association* 3 (1999): 83–93.

Gnutzmann, Rita. "La historia de Lope de Aguirre según Uslar Pietri: *El camino de El Dorado.*" *Revista de Crítica Literaria Latinoamericana* 17, no. 34 (1991): 135–45.

González, Beatriz. "*Barrabás* de Arturo Uslar Pietri en la Venezuela de 1928." *Revista de Critica Literaria Latinoamericana* 11, no. 6 (1980): 47–63.

Hamilton, Carlos D. "Arturo Uslar Pietri, novelista contemporáneo." *Cuadernos Americanos* 242, no. 3 (1982): 209–27.

López Marroquín, Rubén. "Arturo Uslar Pietri: una biografía intelectual." *Cuadernos Americanos* 7, no. 40 (1993): 146–63.

About the Authors

Richard Young (B.A., University of London; Ph.D., University of Alberta) is professor emeritus of Spanish and Latin American studies at the University of Alberta, Canada, where he taught for almost 40 years. He is the author of books on the Spanish dramatist Lope de Vega and on the Latin American novelists Alejo Carpentier, Julio Cortázar, and Agustín Yáñez. His publications include numerous articles on many other Latin American authors and on aspects of Latin American culture, as well as books in translation and bibliography. His edited volumes include *Latin American Postmodernisms* (Amsterdam, 1997); *Music, Popular Culture, Identities* (Amsterdam, 2002); and, in collaboration with Stephen Hart, *Contemporary Latin American Cultural Studies* (London, 2003). He was editor of *Revista Canadiense de Estudios Hispánicos* from 1996 until 2003. His most recent book is *Cultures of the City* (Pittsburgh, 2010), edited in collaboration with Amanda Holmes.

Odile Cisneros (B.A., Wellesley College; Ph.D., New York University) is associate professor in the Department of Modern Languages and Cultural Studies and the Program in Comparative Literature at the University of Alberta. She is the author of reviews and articles on Latin American literature, particularly Mexican and Brazilian, in international journals. She coedited *Novas: Selected Writings of Haroldo de Campos* (Northwestern University Press, 2007). Prof. Cisneros is also an active literary translator and has published book-length translations of work by Régis Bonvicino, Rodrigo Rey Rosa, and Jaroslav Seifert.

Breinigsville, PA USA
14 December 2010
250965BV00001BC/1/P